The Community of the Resurre...

A Centenar~ ~

The Community of the Resurrection

A Centenary History

Alan Wilkinson

SCM Press Ltd

To
FENELLA

ISBN 0 334 02526 5 (pbk)
ISBN 0 334 02531 1 (hbk)

First published 1992
by SCM Press Ltd
26–30 Tottenham Road, London N1 4BZ

Typeset at The Spartan Press Ltd,
Lymington, Hants
and printed in Great Britain by
Mackays of Chatham, Kent

Contents

List of Illustrations

Between pages 178 and 179

Preface

'What is the subject of your new book?' people have asked. My reply – 'The history of the Community of the Resurrection' has conveyed a great deal to some, little or nothing to others. To some of my questioners in England the Community – 'CR' – was already well-known: they had visited Mirfield (its Mother House in Yorkshire) for Commemoration Day, for conferences or retreats; or they had met CR brethren through parish missions; or they knew priests trained at Mirfield Theological College; or they had stayed at other CR houses. When I visited Zimbabwe in 1983 the security man who frisked me at the airport and the waiters at the hotel all knew of CR – they regarded its secondary school for blacks at Penhalonga as the best in the country. Visiting Johannesburg in 1983 and 1991, I discovered that CR was well known to black and white Anglicans there because for seventy years it had trained most of the black Anglican clergy (including Archbishop Tutu), because of its work in the townships, because of its schools and because of its witness against apartheid. But to some English people CR was unfamiliar until I mentioned Trevor Huddleston (its best-known member) or the depiction of its work in the novel *Cry, the Beloved Country* or such names as Charles Gore (CR's founder), Walter Frere, Keble Talbot, Raymond Raynes, Lionel Thornton and Harry Williams.

What then is the Community? What have been its main spheres of work?

The Community of the Resurrection is a Religious Order for men within the Anglican Communion. For much of the last hundred years it has been the most influential and the best known of the Anglican Religious Communities. It was founded in 1892 by Charles Gore and five other priests at Pusey House, Oxford. CR's original Rule stated:

> The Community of the Resurrection shall consist of celibate priests who desire to combine together to reproduce the life of the first Christians of whom it is recorded in the Acts of the Apostles that they were continuing steadfastly in the Apostles' doctrine and fellowship, the breaking of bread and prayers and the multitude of them that believed were of one heart and life and no one called any of the things that belonged to him his own but they had all things common.

(Later the Rule was changed to allow laymen to join the Community.)

Gore, a Whig aristocrat with a sensitive social conscience, had become a national figure in 1889. That year he took a leading part in the founding of the Christian Social Union which became the most notable Anglican society for the promotion of social concern and action. In the same year Gore edited *Lux Mundi*, a theological symposium which inaugurated 'Liberal Catholicism', a creatively new mutation of Anglo-Catholicism. Liberal Catholicism in its various phases became the predominant theological tradition not only of CR, but also of Anglicanism, the norm with which other traditions interact and to which they tend to approximate.

In 1893 Gore and the brethren moved from Pusey House to Radley, near Oxford, where Gore became vicar. However, Gore was wretched there and in 1895 became a Canon of Westminster Abbey where he resided with a few brethren until he became Bishop of Worcester in 1902. The brethren had always hoped to work in the North, so in 1898 the bulk of the Community moved to Mirfield in the industrial West Riding. This move was a consequence of the predominantly Christian socialist convictions of the brethren which made them deeply concerned about the gulf between the church and the industrial working classes.

In 1903 the Community inaugurated in England and South Africa its two most important works. Through its Theological College at Mirfield and its university Hostel in Leeds it offered a five year course of training, free of charge, for ordinands from poor homes. It also opened a house in Johannesburg and developed work among Africans – ordination training, a network of schools and missions and later its famous ministry in the townships. It also transformed St John's College into one of the leading public schools for whites in southern Africa. However, in later years apartheid legislation forced its withdrawal from most of its key institutions and areas of work.

Until 1983 CR worked in Zimbabwe at St Augustine's Penhalonga from which it established a chain of missions and schools. At Penhalonga, as in Johannesburg, it pioneered secondary education for blacks. For twenty-one years (until 1976) it also worked in the West Indies – notably for several years at Codrington Theological College, Barbados. Those trained at its three theological colleges have not only enriched the parish ministry but also (particularly in southern Africa) the episcopate. In addition, CR became known through its output of scholarly and popular theological literature, through its retreats and parish missions in Britain and several other countries and through its ecumenical work, particularly with Roman Catholic and Eastern Orthodox Christians.

By 1958 the Community had ten houses and eighty-five brethren, including eleven lay brethren; in addition two of the brethren were bishops. At the time of writing, the Community comprises forty-four brethren, including seven lay brothers, plus three episcopal brethren. The Mother House and College continue at Mirfield. C R also has houses in London, Sunderland and Johannesburg and retreat houses at Mirfield and Hemingford Grey.

The first time I heard anything about the Community of the Resurrection was at Sunday Mattins on 21 March 1954 in Manchester Cathedral. The preacher (the Rt Rev. Frank Woods, Bishop of Middleton) told us it was St Benedict's Day and then proceeded to elucidate monasticism with special reference to the Community. He knew C R well, for he had been vicar of Huddersfield. (Later he became Archbishop of Melbourne.) He roused my interest, so when the secretary of the Fraternity of the Resurrection at my parish church offered me a copy of the *CR Quarterly* I gladly read it and a year or so later joined the parish trip to Commemoration Day for my first visit to Mirfield. The weather was murky. The rain dripped off the trees into our cups of weak tea. But the worship was splendid. I remember thinking that if I ever trained for ordination I would want to come to Mirfield. When I arrived at the College in 1957, the sanity and sturdiness of C R's Catholicism, its radical social tradition and (after six years at Cambridge) its northern setting was just what I wanted. Ever since I have felt deep gratitude and affection for C R. I feel more at home in a C R house than anywhere else in the church.

The photograph on the cover of this book is of a small painting in the Community Church at Mirfield by an artist of the school of Quentin Massys (1466–1530). The Risen Christ seems teasingly to be looking in another direction, but if you look closely you discover that his orb contains representations of ordinary life. It is therefore a fitting symbol of C R's humour and of its belief that the common, the everyday, is the material for transfiguration and resurrection.

This is the first history of the Community, though a popular seventy-page account of its first sixty years was produced in 1952. I am very conscious of the privilege and responsibility which the brethren have given me by commissioning this centenary history. With characteristic liberality and openness they have provided every facility; there have been no closed doors. I am enormously grateful to those brethren who have read and checked the typescript. But I alone am responsible for the selection and interpretation of the material.

I have tried to set the richly varied life of C R within the religious, social and political context with which it has interacted. I have also tried to make this history something of a bran-tub – it is not only for those who know C R in one or more of its manifestations, but for others who are interested in (for example) Theological Education, Religious Orders, Christian Socialism, Anglo-Catholicism, the relationship of church to society, C R's work in Africa or in C R's great number of fascinating personalities beginning with Gore and Frere. I have devoted a good deal of space to exploring C R's origins. A centenary is a time for reappropriating and reassessing the past in order to know how to move into the future.

> And the end of all our exploring
> Will be to arrive where we started
> And know the place for the first time.
> (T.S. Eliot 'Little Gidding')

The main sources of this history are: the *CR Quarterly* (published four times a year since 1903), the Chronicle (a record of CR's life in each house produced by one of its members), minute books, scrap books, letters and other manuscript and printed material in the archives at Mirfield, the Borthwick Institute (York), the Priory in Johannesburg and the National Archives in Harare. I have been much helped by many interviews with brethren and with a wide range of people who have been involved in the work and life of the Community. I have also drawn upon printed sources, most of which are indicated in the notes. In 1980 someone calculated that there were 604 publications by various brethren in the library at Mirfield. I cannot claim to have read them all, but the main ones are indicated in the text or notes.

A good deal of CR's history is oral and passed on in the form of stories and customs. Their transmission incorporates the newcomer into the family life and memory of the Community. Many are amusing. So (for example) the places in choir occupied by the older brethren are known as 'Cemetery Row'. 'I see you've been moved up to Cemetery Row' one brother comments to another. I have re-told some of these stories, because though they may have the character of 'myth', they express the history and ethos of CR as understood and transmitted by its members. Yet it is also the job of the historian to challenge communal memory and evaluations by producing new stories, new interpretations.

There are two terms which are inevitably tricky in such a history as this. The first is the term 'Religious Life' which describes those who live under the three vows. Nowadays few like it. It sounds both pietistic and condescending. But there is no agreed alternative. So it has to stand. But I use it as rarely and as neutrally as possible. The other tricky term is 'Anglo-Catholic'. One could use the term to describe (say) John Keble, E. B. Pusey, Bishop Charles Gore, Fr Dolling, Fr Kelly SSM, Bishop E. S. Talbot, Bishop Walter Frere CR, Canon Peter Green, Fr Keble Talbot CR, Austin Farrer, Michael Scott, Fr John Groser, Bishop Ambrose Reeves, Fr Raymond Raynes CR, Archbishop Ramsey and Archbishop Tutu. But simply to produce that list is to become aware that 'Anglo-Catholicism' has always been a moving target, a multifarious phenomenon. So to a Methodist (for example) CR is 'Anglo-Catholic'. The Methodist then gets very confused when he reads in a recent *CR Quarterly* that one of the brethren reviewing a book specifically denies that he is an 'Anglo-Catholic'. The confusion deepens when he hears a Mirfield Father describing another as 'one of our more Protestant brethren'. Thus all generalizations about Anglo-Catholics have many exceptions. My central contention about Anglo-Catholicism in this book is that it was liberating for Anglo-Catholics to break with Puseyism and then to realize the limitations of the Englishness and academicism of the Gore-Frere-Dearmer tradition. But many Anglo-Catholics, particularly in the Religious Orders, then made a fatal mistake. Instead of using their freedom to interact creatively with Eastern Orthodoxy and Protestantism, as well as Roman Catholicism, they lost the proper confidence that Gore and Frere had in the Anglican right to be different, and locked themselves up in a quasi-Roman prison of their own devising, and then threw away the key. The result was particularly stultifying, not least because these Anglo-Catholics chose to copy a type of Roman Catholicism that by the 1930s was already on its way out. It took all the authority of the Second Vatican Council and all the cheek of the 1960s, radicals to prize open the jammed prison door.

I am conscious that I have said all too little about members of other Religious Communities and many other clergy and lay people who worked with or for CR. I think also of those who have served CR for many years like (to choose someone from whom I received such excellent meals) Miss Doris Horsfall who was on the domestic staff of the College from 1935 to 1971 and cook from 1947.

It would have been quite impossible to produce a history of a Community which has worked in so many different places and guises without a lot of help from a great number of people. I am immensely grateful to brethren who have given me warm hospitality at Mirfield, at Emmaus (Sunderland), at St Katharine's Foundation, Stepney, at St Augustine's Penhalonga (Zimbabwe), at St Peter's Rosettenville and St Peter's Turffontein (Johannesburg). In addition I have received much from the Community of the Epiphany in Truro; the Priory of Our Lady in Burford; the Order of the Holy Paraclete in Harare, Johannesburg, Whitby and York; the Society of the Precious Blood at Burnham Abbey.

I want also to express my appreciation to librarians and archivists at the Borthwick Institute, the British Library, the Cambridge University Library, the libraries of Chichester Theological College, Dewsbury, Huddersfield, Lambeth Palace, Mirfield, the RIBA London, St Catharine's College Cambridge, the National Archives in Harare, the Church of the Province Archives at Witwatersrand University, the Wimbledon Reference Library and the Wimbledon Society.

Many individuals have generously provided various kinds of assistance, among them, Mr W. E. Arnold, the Rt Rev. John Austin Baker (Bishop of Salisbury), Dr Richard Baty, the Rt Rev. Timothy Bavin (Bishop of Portsmouth), The Rev. Robert Beaken, Mr Patrick Bickersteth, the late Fr Hugh Bishop, Canon H. Miles Brown, Fr Richard Duffield (Birmingham Oratory), the Rev. David (Bernard) Chamberlain, Mr Graham Davies, Miss Margaret Dewey (Archivist of SSM), the Rev. Richard Dickson, the Rev.

Barry Fenton, Mrs Joy Ferguson, Miss Betty Gawthorpe, Miss Dorothy Halsall, the Headmaster and Archivist of Harrow School, the Headmaster and Archivist of St John's College Johannesburg, the Rev. Alan Heslop, Canon Eric James, the late Dr R. C. D. Jasper, Canon Peter Keightley, Dr Lorna Kendall, Mr James Khuele, the Rev. Keith Kinnaird, the Rev. David Lane, the Librarian and the Keeper of the Muniments, Westminster Abbey, Canon J. D. Llewellyn Jones, the Rev. Arthur Longworth, the Rev. Justus Markus, the Rev. Christian Molefe, Professor Es'kia Mphahlele, the Ven. Wilmot Ngobese, Canon Robin Osborne, the late Mr Alan Paton, Mr John Peart-Binns, Mrs Marion Pobjoy, the Rev. Dan Pope, the late Archbishop Michael Ramsey, the Rev. Hugh (Keble) Prosser, the Ven. Raymond Ravenscroft, Canon J. C. Read, Canon T. Rockley, Mr Gilbert Rondozai, the Rev. Dr Geoffrey Rowell, the Rev. Theodore Simpson, the Rt Rev. Kenneth Skelton, Mr N. D. Southey, the staff and students of St Augustine's Penhalonga, Dr Robert Towler, Canon John Tsebe, Mr Nimrod Tubane, the Rev. William Wheeldon, Mr and Mrs Deane Yates, Mrs Militza Zernov.

Edward Holland, who like my wife is a distant relative of Henry Scott Holland, Gore's closest friend, has kindly advised me about matters architectural. I dedicate this book to my wife, Fenella, not only because she has taken such a keen and supportive interest in it, joined me in several of the visits in connection with it and typed the final script, but because she has been for me a source of resurrection.

Portsmouth
August 1991

Alan Wilkinson

Abbreviations

ANC	African National Congress
CBS	Confraternity of the Blessed Sacrament
CR	Community of the Resurrection
CRQ	*CR Quarterly*: published for Lady Day (LD) St John the Baptist Day (JB) Michaelmas (MD) Christmas (CD)
CSI	Church of South India
CSL	Church Socialist League
CSU	Christian Social Union
CSMV	Community of St Mary the Virgin
CZR	Chita che Zita Rinoyera (Community of the Holy Name)
DRC	Dutch Reformed Church
ECU	English Church Union
FR	Fraternity of the Resurrection
GSM	Guild of St Matthew
ILP	Independent Labour Party
OHP	Order of the Holy Paraclete
OMC	Oxford Mission to Calcutta
OTC	Officers' Training Corps
SDC	Society of the Divine Compassion
SPB	Society of the Precious Blood
SPCK	Society for Promoting Christian Knowledge
SPG	Society for the Propagation of the Gospel
SR	Society of the Resurrection

SSJE   Society of St John the Evangelist

SSM   Society of the Sacred Mission

UMCA   Universities' Mission to Central Africa

WCC   World Council of Churches

Acknowledgments

Photographs 12 and 15 are reproduced by permission of Fr Aelred Stubbs CR and Mrs Militza Zernov respectively. The other photographs are reproduced by permission of the Community of the Resurrection from its archives at Mirfield. I am grateful for permission to make quotations in the text from the following: T. S. Eliot, 'Little Gidding' and 'Ash Wednesday' from *Collected Poems 1909–1962*, Faber & Faber; Edwin Muir, 'The Journey Back' from *Collected Poems*, Faber & Faber; R. S. Thomas, 'The Priest' from *Not That He Brought Flowers*, Rupert Hart-Davis.

I

Seek the Beginnings

Seek the beginnings, learn from whence you came,
And know the various earth of which you are made.
(Edwin Muir 'The Journey Back')

In 1892 Charles Gore founded the Community of the Resurrection. What a fascinating, enigmatic and complex personality he was! Though Gore left the Community after nine years (when he became Bishop of Worcester) and during nearly all those years was semi-detached from it, he has continued to influence and at times to vex it. For the gifts which CR received from Gore were rich and variegated but also uncomfortable. After a hundred years, CR will want to explore those gifts again. In order to understand the history and ethos of CR it is therefore essential to begin with Gore's background and life.

In the wider world too Gore's magnetism persists – hence the continuing flow of books and articles about him. Michael Ramsey remarked:

> I remember myself in the years between the wars, feeling that Gore had become old-fashioned and that William Temple had more to say to our times. Today when I read and recall these two great men it is Temple who now seems rather dated in thought and idiom while Gore speaks with the mysteriousness of a timeless authority.

Certainly Gore's own contemporaries were clear about his stature. Hensley Henson as an undergraduate was lastingly helped by Gore. Yet when nominated to the see of Hereford he received through Gore a wound that never healed. Nevertheless just after Gore died he wrote:

> I judge him to have been the most considerable English Churchman of his time, not the most learned, nor the most eloquent, but so learned, so eloquent, so versatile, and so energetic that he touched the life of his generation at more points, and more effectively, than any of his contemporaries.[1]

The early life of Charles Gore

Charles Gore was born on 22 January 1853 in a large two-storied house of three bays on Wimbledon Common, the third son of the Hon. Charles Alexander Gore and his wife the Countess of Kerry. Part of the house dates back to 1705. At the beginning of the nineteenth century it was lived in by the second Viscount Melville, First Lord of the Admiralty, then until 1846 (when the Gores took it over) by Lord Lyndhurst, three times Lord Chancellor. It was later called Westside House, but was then known as 'Mr Gore's House' or 'Lady Kerry's on the West Side'. Later on Charles would simply address letters to his mother 'The Countess of Kerry, Wimbledon, London SW'. Behind it stretched forty acres of grounds. The huge garden ended in a ha-ha, beyond which was a boating pond, summer houses, a dense wood with pigeons and pheasants, and a farm with cows, pigs and poultry. Beyond that were half a dozen hayfields, usually let off. Though only seven miles from Hyde Park Corner, the estate might have been in Sussex or Wiltshire. From the back of the house there were views of open country. Wimbledon itself was still a rustic village.

In the eighteenth and nineteenth centuries the presence in Wimbledon of wealthy and distinguished people made it an important centre of Georgian and Victorian society. Among the Gores' friends were their neighbours John Murray (whose firm later published many of Charles Gore's books); Sir Bartle Frere (a distinguished proconsul in India and South Africa, related to Walter Frere, second Superior of CR); and Jenny Lind, the famous Swedish soprano. In 1861 the Holland family moved to Gayton Lodge (just over the border in Putney) an Italianate Victorian villa with a dragon for a weathervane.[2] Henry Scott Holland (1847–1918), their second child, was fourteen when the family moved to Wimbledon. He was to become Charles Gore's closest friend. Holland's father was an independent gentleman, wealthy enough not to have to do anything in particular. His wife was daughter of the first Lord Gifford. Henry went off to Eton and Balliol.

Next door to the Gore residence was Cannizaro House set in fifty acres and employing twelve indoor and nine outdoor servants. The Schusters who moved there in 1879 threw huge garden parties with sometimes over a thousand guests who included British and foreign royalty, artists, poets, and politicians. Cannizaro House is now a smart hotel, but Westside House, now flats, when visited in 1990, was sadly dilapidated: paint peeled in the hall; outside, shutters hung askew. The remains of the garden (the estate was sold off) was overgrown. John Gore, Charles' nephew, remembered the drawing room as particularly grand, though very chilly in winter, heated by a single coal fire; its windows opened on to the garden; Sèvres and Chelsea porcelain graced the chimney-piece.

No room that I have ever lived in since gave the same sense of permanence, dignity and peace. Here Whig aristocracy continued to guard inviolate the surviving treasures and traditions of a glorious past, rigid still in its patience, its endurance of discomfort, its prejudices, its superbly narrow exclusiveness, its belief in the virtue of practising religion and morality and of building character by discipline.

Upstairs only a meagre section of the regularly scrubbed floorboards was carpeted. There was no bathroom. Even the drawing room chairs were deliberately not too comfortable. It was a serious house with an atmosphere of self discipline, hard work and devout religion, wealthy but in no sense luxurious. When in 1893 Lady Kerry was seriously ill, she was angry with her husband for increasing the heating.

Gore's father, nephew of the third Earl of Arran, grew up near Dublin. There was no money to send him to school or university, and he became a page at the Viceregal Lodge. But moving to London in 1829 he rapidly rose in the civil service helped by his connections. One of his aunts was married to a royal duke. In 1839 he was appointed Commissioner of Woods and Forests at the age of twenty-eight. In 1845 he married Lady Augusta Ponsonby, daughter of the fourth Earl of Bessborough and widow of the Earl of Kerry, the eldest son of the third Marquis of Lansdowne. Thus Charles Gore was bred into the very heart of aristocratic Whigdom. Throughout his life he was fascinated by his family history. When he was a Canon at Westminster Abbey he enjoyed showing visitors the tomb of his relation an Earl of Kerry, the inscription on which concludes (in double quotation marks) "Hang all the Law and the Prophets". On closer inspection this remarkable statement is preceded by ' . . . ever studious to fulfil those two great commandments on which he had been taught by his divine Master'. Gore reacted with pained surprise when C. A. Alington (later Dean of Durham) was unable to identify the houses where the great Whig families had lived. Tubby Clayton, founder of Toc H, described Gore as a 'great saint', but added that those who observed him closely 'could never forget the aristocrat in him. If he should suffer fools, it was not gladly.' To the end of his life Gore retained the Whig pronunciation of certain words.

Gore had an elder half-sister, two elder brothers and two sisters. Two boisterous brothers of his mother, founders of I Zingari, brought laughter and much talk of cricket and theatricals into the house. It was natural that Charles should be invited to Buckingham Palace for a Children's Fancy Dress Ball. It was natural that the family took a house in London during the season and that they spent the autumn in the Highlands. Thus he was born into a large house with a distinguished history, on a large estate, into a large family with many influential connections. It was a setting which gave him space. He was to need space for the rest of his life.

The family worshipped every Sunday at Christ Church. His mother was deeply religious but insisted on occupying the front pew and receiving communion before the rest of the congregation. Charles was to develop a very different view of the eucharist as mutual and interdependent fellowship in the body of Christ, in which individualism had no place. In his preface to *Belief in God* (1921) Gore described the impact upon his imagination as a boy of eight or nine of a novel of protestant propaganda *Father Clement* (1823, by Grace Kennedy):

> I had been brought up in ordinary old-fashioned English Church ways. I had only
> attended very Low Church services. I had never heard of the Oxford Movement. I
> knew nothing about Catholicism, except as a strange superstition, called Popery.
> But the book described confession and absolution, fasting, the Real Presence, the
> devotion of the Three Hours, the use of incense, etc., and I felt instinctively and at
> once that this sort of sacramental religion was the religion for me.

However much in later days he used all the resources of his formidable
intellect to defend and explain Catholicism and deeply distrusted the appeal to
religious experience, Catholicism also powerfully appealed to his imagination.
Charles was sent to a fashionable preparatory school at Malvern. His letters
home show his love of life, his independence of mind and his resistance to
emotional appeals. '*The Old Curiosity Shop* makes me roar with laughing' he
wrote. Throughout his life he used humour to protect himself against
anything which seemed to threaten to take him over. He dismissed the books
distributed by the headmaster for Sunday reading as 'stupid'. A regular supply
of port wine built up his uncertain health.

In 1866 Charles followed his brothers to Harrow, where by the sixth form
he developed into a brilliant scholar. His brother, Spencer, went on to
represent England at cricket and become the first Lawn Tennis Champion of
England. Charles, however, was not a natural sportsman. The school's
religious atmosphere was evangelical. But Gore and some friends formed a
group which was High Church and politically radical. As there was then no
weekly eucharist at school, they went to the local parish church. A sermon on
'Disciplined Life' preached in the school chapel in 1868 by B. F. Westcott, an
assistant master (later Bishop of Durham) had a profound effect on Gore,
then fifteen. Afterwards, Westcott had the sermon printed and circulated to
the boys and in his preface expressed the earnest hope that one of them would
take up his challenge. Westcott contended that St Benedict, St Francis and St
Ignatius Loyola had each expressed the disciplined life in a different form
appropriate to his period.

> History thus teaches us that social evils must be met by social organization. A life of
> absolute and calculated sacrifice is a spring of immeasurable power. In the past it has
> worked marvels, and there is nothing to prove that its virtue is exhausted.

The Saxon race was now called to promote an asceticism appropriate to its
world-wide mission.

> . . . nothing from old times will meet our exigencies. We want a rule which shall
> answer to the complexity of our own age. We want a discipline which shall combine
> the sovereignty of soul of Antony, the social devotion of Benedict, the humble love of
> Francis, the matchless energy of the Jesuits . . .

In conclusion he drew attention to the fact that when Antony, Benedict and Francis responded to their call they were not much older than some of his hearers.[3]

It is not clear how far Westcott influenced Gore in other ways.[4] Did Gore derive his Platonism and his veneration of the Greek Fathers from Westcott? When in 1892 Gore commended the Moravian practice of families living in community, had he been influenced by Westcott's exploration of this idea while at Harrow? Did Westcott's socialism influence Gore? Yet at Harrow Westcott lived the life of a scholarly recluse and took little interest in political affairs until the 1880s. Though both Westcott and Gore contrasted individualism and socialism as two opposed views of human life, Westcott's socialism was nebulous and a-political, whereas Gore's socialism expressed itself in political particularities. Westcott was an ardent advocate of imperialism, Gore its stern critic. However, Westcott's teaching that because of the incarnation, the gospel has a relevance to every part of life and his belief in the solidarity of humanity were central to Gore's life.

The sole Anglo-Catholic member of staff at Harrow, the Rev. William Done Bushell, arrived the same year as Gore. In 1897 he bought Caldey Island, off South Wales. In 1900 he invited Abbot Aelred Carlyle and his Anglican Benedictines to move there. In 1906 he sold the island to them. It is therefore clear that Bushell was deeply interested in the monastic life, but whether this interest had developed when Gore was at Harrow is not known. In any case Bushell's commitment to this romantic revival of mediaeval monasticism shows that he was thinking along very different lines than either Westcott or Gore.

In 1870 Gore sat for a Balliol scholarship. In the evenings he greatly enjoyed deluding the University 'bulldogs' into thinking that he was an undergraduate, trying to escape from their clutches, then when he was caught explaining that he was not a member of the university. It was an early example of his ambivalence towards authority which was to characterize him as Superior and Bishop. During the Christmas vacation with the congratulations ringing in his ears for having won a scholarship he made his first confession. It was an act of self-oblation. But it was also a declaration of independence from the religion of both his school and home.

When Gore went up to Balliol in October 1871 his fellow undergraduates included H. H. Asquith, the future Prime Minister, and Alfred Milner, the future Higher Commissioner for South Africa. Under Benjamin Jowett (Master from 1870) Balliol became a nursery for public men. Though Gore's parents were wealthy, they did not believe in ostentatious living and gave him only the minimum allowance. During this time he attended his first retreat, probably at the Cowley house of the Society of St John the Evangelist (SSJE) for whose founder, Fr R. M. Benson, he formed a deep respect. At Balliol he was permanently affected by the teaching of T. H. Green, a fellow from

1860.[5] Later, Gore and his associates were deeply influenced by Green's *Lay Sermons* with their rejection of hedonism and their appeal for self-sacrifice. However, Gore never allowed Green's Hegelianism to deflect him from his primary appeal to biblical categories. Green taught that only in community did the individual find true significance, that the church, if it is to be a bearer of the gospel, must promote social welfare and political justice and that the divine mind touched the mind of human beings through all aspects of human life. Green's influence is to be traced therefore not only in *Lux Mundi* but also in the creation of both the Christian Social Union and the Community of the Resurrection. Holland, a devoted pupil of Green's, wrote in his preface to a collection of sermons by various preachers on social themes, *Lombard Street in Lent* (1911):

> He broke for us the sway of individualistic Sensationalism. He released us from the fear of agnostic Mechanism. He taught us the reality of the co-operative life and the inspiration of the community. He gave us back the language of self-sacrifice, and taught us how we belonged to one another in the one life of organic humanity.

In Union debates Gore supported radical causes and defended the trade unions. The efforts of Joseph Arch, the Primitive Methodist, to organize agricultural labourers made a deep impression on Gore. Shortly before his death Gore said that a tour of Oxford villages with Arch had been a turning point in his life, but that F. D. Maurice had only been a minor influence upon his social attitudes. Nevertheless Gore pasted into his first cuttings book (begun in 1873) an obituary of Maurice, who had died the previous year, which paid tribute to his unceasing work for the welfare of the working classes, though he never flattered them.

In 1875 Gore became a fellow of Trinity. As a young don he followed the pattern of Harrow and Balliol: he was respected by all, but known intimately to only a few. He insisted that undergraduates drank wine with him. 'You must have some; it may be necessary to cut off the right hand, but this *is* a right hand and meant to be used.' The savage humour characteristically combined catholic affirmation and catholic asceticism. He enjoyed making conversation stoppers, the kind of remark which amused people, and afterwards was much quoted, yet kept people at a distance. It was the typical strategy of the shy, vulnerable person who desires attention but fears closeness. So when he was offered tea by a fanatically teetotal bishop's wife, he is said to have replied, 'Thank you, but I never drink anything but alcoholic beverages.' Anglo-Catholics showed that Christians could be serious without being evangelically earnest. Did Gore's remnant theology of the church derive as much from his personal difficulty in coping with large heterogeneous groups as from his passion for disciplined holiness?

As a small boy Gore had felt called to ordination. In December 1876 he was made deacon. Beforehand he had written to his mother about his joys and trepidations. He affirmed that he was a High Churchman, but though sympathetic to the ritualists, found them 'very injudicious & even offensive & arrogant'. He was ordained priest two years later. From the first he felt called to celibacy. In order to get parochial experience, he went to Christ Church, Bootle for three months in the summer of 1879 as a curate, and in 1880 began an attachment to St Margaret's Toxteth Park where he spent several vacations in the next few years. It was his first experience of working among ordinary people. He missed the companionship of Oxford.

When he became a don in 1875 he was drawn into a circle of rather older men who, Gore wrote, 'were already at work at the urgent task of seeking to conciliate the claims of reason and revelation, and so to interpret the ancient, catholic faith as not to lay an intolerable strain upon the free action of the intellect'.[6] It included Holland (now at Christ Church), E. S. Talbot (appointed first Warden of Keble College in 1869) and J. R. Illingworth, fellow of Jesus and tutor at Keble from 1872. In 1883 Illingworth became rector of Longworth, a tiny village near Oxford. He remained there until he died in 1915. His precarious health and his writing compelled such retirement, but he compared his vocation to the monks and hermits of old and to the seventeenth-century Anglican community at Little Gidding. Before marriage his wife had considered entering the Wantage sisterhood; he had thought of Cowley, and worn a hair shirt. Gore and Holland as young men had adopted certain unstated but severe ascetic practices, but later took the view that ordinary life and the church's injunctions provided enough opportunities for self-mortification. By contrast, E. B. Pusey, despite the disapproval of his confessor John Keble, scourged himself nightly while reciting Psalm 51 and wore a hair shirt. He recommended both practices to his penitents.

In 1872 Illingworth joined a reading party at St David's which included Wilfrid Richmond (later to be associated with the formation of the Christian Social Union). It was repeated in 1873. Richmond wrote:

> It was during this year that there grew in our minds the idea, the dream, of a brotherhood life, a fellowship of those who were devoted to the Truth. It was inspired to some extent of what we knew of the Oratorians.

Among the books they read was a biography of the French Oratorian Henri Perreyve. The first meeting of what Holland called 'the Holy Party' (the name mocked evangelical earnestness) was held in 1875 at Brighstone in the Isle of Wight. It was influenced by a retreat which some of them had attended in 1874 conducted by A. P. Forbes (Bishop of Brechin) the 'Scottish Pusey', in which he exhorted his hearers to develop a Christian philosophy: 'Exoriare aliquis' ('Arise somebody'). The Holy Party would take over a parish for a month while the vicar was on holiday. The daily programme began with 7 a.m. Holy

Communion or meditation. After breakfast there was silence and study until the mid-day office and lunch. In the afternoon, after a walk, a selected book was discussed. After Evensong and supper there was more discussion. Gore was not at Brighstone but joined many subsequent meetings. Illingworth liked to trace a continuity stretching from the reading party at St David's to the Holy Party through to the *Lux Mundi* group and the annual meetings at Longworth (1890–1914). Holland wrote about the Holy Party: 'We would work, and play, and talk over the possibilities of an Anglican Oratorian community: and be exceedingly happy.'

In Victorian public schools and universities, ideals of friendship, often expressed in passionate language, fed by Plato and St John's Gospel, flourished in an atmosphere of pre-Freudian innocence. Gore when a Fellow at Trinity would walk in the garden with his arm round an undergraduate's neck in what was later called 'the Cuddesdon cuddle'. Even at that period some found it embarrassing. Holland wrote from a reading party to his brother: 'Have I not myself lived by friendship all my life? Have I not fed on it as my daily bread?' In the same letter he described the dangers of passionate friendships, but in language so erotic he must have been unaware of its implications:

> I have known the inevitable melancholy: each soul stands over against another – each yearns to unite itself with each: but each has veils light as gauze, yet rigid as steel, which close each round to itself: in vain they reach out embracing arms to each other; in vain they cling to each other; the unity cannot attain its fullness, its satisfaction: the two stand apart, confused: delicious sympathies may cross and re-cross, from one to another, touching, entwining, binding, but not dissolving the barriers . . . We fall back exhausted: disappointed: barren: we feel as if friendship broke down under us, and we had no outlet but despair.

But on another occasion Holland's over-ripe celebration of reading parties flowed on unchecked:

> . . . we spent the days that hold in them the promise and the fragrance of some earthly paradise . . . There were no invading cares. There were no duties. There were no conventions . . . we were a band of friends who were sufficient for each other . . . Round us the loveliness of some selected fairy spot ringed us in. The hills waited upon us: the rivers ran for us: the great sea laughed as we plunged into its green Cornish waters. Nature was on our side: and we were one with it. These were the magic hours, that fed our lips with honey-dew.

David Newsome comments 'these were not the times, and this was not the world, of a theology of the Cross . . . The theology of the *Lux Mundi* group . . . could hardly fail to be a demonstration of the way in which man had been elevated and ennobled by the supreme event of the Incarnation'.[7] The east window in Longworth church given by the group at Holland's suggestion to commemorate its tenth meeting in 1900 depicts not a suffering, but a glorified Christ, with a reassuring text below: 'I am come a light into the world. I came not to judge the world, but to save the world' (John 12.46–7). But unlike Holland, Gore sensed that the world was tragically flawed. His ambivalence towards human relationships sprang from a deep inner reserve. Yet Gore created both the Society and the Community of the Resurrection. Holland for all his talk of friendship and community joined neither. Holland remembered the Longworth meetings not only for the jokes and the strawberries but also for the severity of Gore's chairmanship. The ethos of the Holy Party with its mixture of prayer, study, silence and friendship fed Gore's desire to create a perpetuation of something like it in some form of permanent association.

In 1879 the Oxford Mission to Calcutta (OMC) was inaugurated with Gore's support as a brotherhood without life long obligations, but with two main principles:

1. It should be free to develop its work as experience and circumstances might direct.
2. Members should form a religious brotherhood under a rule definite enough to give real strength and support to the spiritual life, and yet sufficiently elastic to enable the community to undertake work of very various kinds.[8]

In 1880 Gore was appointed Vice-Principal of Cuddesdon Theological College, near Oxford. Founded by Samuel Wilberforce, Bishop of Oxford, and opened in 1854, it had numbered Edward King among its Principals and H. P. Liddon among its Vice-Principals. It expected its students to conform to a discipline of prayer and study. Gore had experienced community life at Harrow, Balliol and Trinity, religious foundations in which all prayed, worked, lived and shared meals together. But Cuddesdon offered a more concentrated experience of community life in which all shared one vocation, one faith and one discipline. He kept a picture of King on one wall of his study, an exemplum of Tractarian holiness, and a picture of Jowett on another: 'when I feel I am stressing an argument too far, I look at Jowett and he pulls me up'. The two portraits represented that interaction between Liberalism and Catholicism in Gore which was becoming evident in his teaching about biblical criticism. For Gore, OMC provided an attractive model for, and Cuddesdon a happy experience of, communal living.

Pusey House

In September 1882 E. B. Pusey died aged 82.[9] He had held the Oxford Movement together after Newman's secession in 1845. It was the end of an era. As long as Pusey was alive the younger Anglo-Catholics felt themselves

under his restraint. The liberal symposium *Essays and Reviews* (1860), to which
Jowett had contributed, revolted him. He stood firmly against the developing
biblical criticism. Pusey's ascetic teaching turned his wife from being a
sceptical, high-spirited young woman into a religious neurotic willing to accept
for herself and their children his rigid austerities, despite her developing
tuberculosis and their children's frail health. He and his wife (taught by him)
subjected their children to brutal beatings and spiritual torture. After his wife's
death in 1839 he withdrew from society, convinced that her death was God's
punishment for his sins. The new church of St Saviour's, Leeds (begun 1842)
for which Pusey paid anonymously, showed his concern for the urban poor. His
decision to be referred to as 'Penitent' on the foundation stone makes clear its
equally deep personal significance. Its original dedication to the Holy Cross, the
quotations on the foundation stone from the Litany appealing for deliverance
through the cross and passion of Christ, Pusey's decision that violet was the
colour for the altar cloth in the present state of the church: all exemplified a very
different spirituality from that of *Lux Mundi*, the incarnationalism of which so
influenced the ethos of CR. When John Keble became his confessor in 1846 he
was horrified that Pusey lived by such rules as 'Never, if I can, to look at the
beauty of nature, without inward confession of unworthiness'; 'Not to smile, if I
can help it, except with children'; 'To drink cold water at dinner, as only fit to be
where there is not a drop "to cool this flame"'; 'To make the fire to me from time
to time the type of hell'. By contrast Keble often used the sitting room
mantelpiece for writing, ready to break off to play with the family. When he went
to Edinburgh to attend the hearing of a doctrinal case, he spent the first day not
at the trial, but playing trains with his host's children on the floor. Though Keble
was highly conservative theologically and politically, and would have been
horrified by Gore's political and theological views, some of the poems from his
Christian Year (1827) which became popular hymns, were nearer to the outlook
of *Lux Mundi* than to that of Pusey:

> The works of God above, below,
>   Within us and around,
> Are pages in that book, to show
>   How God Himself is found.   ('Septuagesima Sunday')

> We need not bid, for cloister'd cell,
> Our neighbour and our work farewell,
> Nor strive to wind ourselves too high
> For sinful man beneath the sky:

> The trivial round, the common task,
> Would furnish all we ought to ask;
> Room to deny ourselves; a road
> To bring us, daily, nearer God.   ('Morning')

Baron Friedrich von Hügel (the lay Roman Catholic theologian and friend of E. S. Talbot and his son Keble, fourth Superior of CR) thought that Pusey and many of his followers were 'really not Catholic'. Pusey had made himself incapable 'of taking any interest in anything that was not directly, technically religious . . . quite uncatholic, quite unlike the greatest of the Catholic saints, quite unlike the Jesus of the Synoptists, with all of whom God is the God of Nature as of Grace – a God deeply interested . . . in not directly religious things . . .'[10] 'Nobody living could recall the time when he had not been there' wrote Holland about Pusey; his mind had been formed before the ideas of Evolution and Development had become the accepted categories of thought, therefore he was incapable of being a guide into the new world. 'So we buried him: and, with him, we buried a whole generation, which could never quite recur.'[11]

Pusey's followers were determined to create a worthy memorial. Henry Parry Liddon (Canon of St Paul's and until 1882 Professor of Exegesis, the devoted disciple and biographer of Pusey) proposed that a 'home of sacred learning and a rallying-point for Christian faith' should be created in Oxford, which would provide pastoral care for undergraduates. 'Objections to Revealed Truth, both as a whole and in detail, multiply year by year, and these objections require careful replies. It is not too much to say, that if the needs of modern thought are to be satisfactorily met, certain portions of the Christian Evidences require to be restated.' This could have been understood as an invitation to theological adventure only by those ignorant of Pusey and Liddon. The Committee purchased a house in St Giles for Pusey's Library. The librarians were required to be unmarried.[12]

Liddon asked Gore to be Principal Librarian. Gore wrote in May 1883 with a long list of hesitations: he was happy in the pastoral work at Cuddesdon; if he moved he wanted to go into a parish; he did not wish to return to Oxford as a pure academic; he could not accept Pusey's attitude to biblical criticism; he rejected the ideal of Oxford as a purely Anglican institution; he was politically radical; he did not want to return to the 'luxurious' life of a don. If he were to accept, he would order the house on the basis of 'a sort of dinner-at-midday standard of rather rigorous simplicity' and live apart from the Oxford social round. Holland held out the inducement of a parish district of poor people to whom Gore would minister. This did not materialize. However, Gore agreed and was appointed in November 1883 to begin work the following October. He told Liddon how he hoped that the Religious Life might develop at Pusey House. Liddon thought him entirely worthy to represent 'the great name of Pusey'. But E. S. Talbot (like Holland on the executive committee of the Pusey Memorial Fund) alarmed Liddon by supporting a proposal to admit women to certain examinations. Liddon had earlier lamented Talbot's leading role in the foundation of Lady Margaret Hall for women. 'It seems madness to Christian common-sense. Dr Pusey deplores it every day, but his influence has had no weight in checking the enterprise.' Then Gore, soon after his appointment was announced, worried Liddon by welcoming (in a University sermon) the growing acceptance of evolution by Christians. In 1879 Pusey had deplored the theory as a threatening cloud which would wreck the faith of many, and trusted that God would raise up naturalists to refute it. Was the memory of Pusey going to be safe in the hands of Gore and his friends?

Meanwhile the health of two OMC brethren had broken down. Gore sailed to India in December 1883 to help out. He was passionately committed to the world-wide church. He also loved travel. His sailing companions were agreeable except for two flirtatious young women. Overt sexuality made Gore uneasy. He asked his mother to send out a copy of the life of F. D. Maurice, just published. By Easter he was so enthralled by India he was tempted to stay. But by the end of September 1884 he was back in Oxford.

Pusey House was opened on 9 October 1884. At first there was just one house opposite St John's College. The second, next door, was not opened until 1889. (The present building, designed by Temple Moore, was begun in 1912.) The Bishop of Oxford dedicated the house. Liddon read a lesson from Wisdom. Gore was now thirty-one. As colleagues he appointed Frank Edward Brightman, a reclusive liturgist ('bound in vellum' an American visitor described him) and Vincent Stuckey Coles who preferred people to books.[13] Like Holland, Coles had a capacity for friendship, which he had to struggle to sanctify. He believed that celibacy was the natural vocation for the priest. A wealthy man, he gave much of his money away, especially to poor ordinands. The Librarians had a common rule of prayer and lived simply. Gore believed that they should aim at a standard of life which they would wish an artisan to enjoy.

Gore began to exercise a remarkable influence upon undergraduates. In 1885 Hensley Henson, aged twenty-two, fellow of All Souls, (Bishop of Durham 1920–39) went to see Gore, deeply troubled as to what he should do with his life. Gore knelt with him in the chapel for two and a quarter hours. In 1887 Henson was ordained and became Head of Oxford House, Bethnal Green, surrounded by some of the worst housing in London. Gore opened men's eyes to the glory of God and the needs of the poor. In his first term he created controversy by inviting Stewart Headlam, the Christian socialist priest, founder of the Guild of St Matthew, to address a meeting of its Oxford branch in Pusey House. Someone wrote:

> Sing a song of thousands,
>   Thirty, say, or more,
> Spent in subsidizing
>   Brightman, Stuckey, Gore.
> When the House was opened,
>   Straightway Headlam came –
> Was not that a pretty thing
>   To do in Pusey's name?

Rapidly Gore became the most powerful religious force in Oxford. Arthur Shearly Cripps, later a prophetic priest and champion of African rights in Rhodesia, recalled a sermon by Gore at St Barnabas' church:

> What went we forth – we boys of old – to hear?
> One with wan face, rough brows, and hermit's beard,
> A brooding preacher. How o'ercast and blear'd
> Were his encavern'd eyes, how slow to clear! . . .
> Then that light blaz'd at last, that Whirlwind blew:
> He bow'd himself before the o'rruling might
> Of driving gusts with furious lightnings bright:
> To a prophet's stature, while we gaz'd, he grew . . .

Not good poetry perhaps, but it conveys Gore's fascination. Yet Gore was subject to his characteristic moods of self-depreciation and restlessness: 'I wish I didn't hate Oxford.'

The Society of the Resurrection

On 4 October 1887 a number of clergy attended a retreat at Keble College conducted by Gore, after which the Society of the Resurrection was formed. Gore was elected Superior on 7 October in Pusey House and on 8 October twenty-one members were professed. Gore's original name 'The Society of the Christian Hope' had been challenged by Liddon: 'make it objective; call it the Society of the Resurrection'. Liddon's felicitous suggestion is easy to understand. But why did Gore focus on 'Christian Hope'? Did Gore believe that it was something distinctive, different from secular hope – as say derived from evolutionary theory? At times Gore expressed his faith in evolutionary language, and spoke optimistically about features of the modern world, but fundamentally his view of history was sombre: ' . . . human nature, as we have had experience of it in history, presents in great measure a scene of moral ruin, so that Christ enters not merely to consummate an order but to restore it, not to accomplish only but to redeem.'[14] Beneath all Gore's wit and laughter there was sometimes a deep despondency. The first page of his cuttings book, begun when he was twenty, included a poem 'The Suicide' which described how a young man went through every vice and then took his own life. Perhaps it was not just the world and the church which needed hope, but also Gore himself? Gore stood more often at the foot of the cross than Holland. This explains why he did not choose as its name 'The Society of the Incarnation' as might have been expected from the editor-to-be of *Lux Mundi* with its subtitle 'A Series of Studies in the Religion of the Incarnation'. Nor did he call it (say) 'The Society of the Atonement' (there was already a 'Society of the Holy Cross'). Gore welcomed the shift towards the incarnation, but warned that it must not be at the cost of abandoning the preaching of the atonement. Gore accepted the title 'The Society of the Resurrection' not because the resurrection by itself was the source of hope, but because he believed that the resurrection enabled the work of the atonement to be realized in human beings through the Spirit in the church.[15]

The Society of the Resurrection (SR) originated in the desire of the clergy of Pusey House to be linked by a common rule, by prayer and a commitment to celibacy with the brethren of the OMC who had been encouraged to look upon the House as their English base. So from the outset SR was committed to the world-wide church. Gore also hoped that out of SR a community would emerge. This is clear from a letter Gore wrote in October 1887 to G. H. Tremenheere who had known Gore since 1879 and who had just joined SR. Gore asked him to join the staff at the House:

> I think it is likely Community life wd help you & that it wd be of great profit to the Church that you shd give yourself to prayer & study & such work as naturally grows out of it (preaching etc etc). We greatly and increasingly need non-parochial Priests . . . If you come here we shd offer Board & Lodging etc (all told) & whatever more was necessary up to £100, all to arrangement. We haven't come to a common purse yet.

Gore explained in another letter the purpose of SR: 'This is, we hope, a step – not more – in the direction of an Oratorian sort of community.' Tremenheere did not accept Gore's suggestion, though he spent three months at the House in 1889.[16]

The care of the members of SR gave Gore a new outlet for pastoral work, though he lamented that he was not doing anything for the poor. The 24 members of SR in 1887 included 3 members of OMC, Coles and Brightman of the House, Darwell Stone (Principal 1909–34) and George Longridge, one of the founding members of CR. There were also 6 associates. The 1901 list included 74 members and 39 associates, the 16 CR brethren and 5 members of OMC, a total of 134 – a remarkable increase. The growth of SR showed both how valuable it was and the magnetism of Gore himself. Four bishops (Madagascar, Madras, St Johns and Zululand) were listed, and five who later joined CR: Henry Alston and Alfred Drury (members), Bernard Horner, Eustace Hill and Timothy Rees (associates). Others listed included Frank Weston (later a famous Bishop of Zanzibar), a member, and Charles Brent (then in Boston USA, later a leading ecumenist), an associate. Of the total, 35 were working outside Britain: in Japan, Rhodesia, Turkey, India, Canada, USA, Korea, Africa and China.

The revival of Religious Orders

Why were Religious Orders, and associations like SR, revived in the Church of England in the nineteenth century?[17]

Though the Oxford Movement began as an agitation for church defence and appealed to the teaching of the early church and the Anglican Fathers, it was the Romantic movement which put wind into the sails of Catholicism (both Anglican and Roman). Wordsworth, like Keble, taught that there was a hidden glory in the material world, in ordinary life and people – a belief which was conducive to the development of incarnationalism and sacramentalism. However, another type of Romanticism encouraged the flight from ordinary life into dreams and fantasies. Newman in his *Apologia* (1864) outlined the influences which delivered people from the rationalism of the eighteenth century, among which he mentioned particularly that of Walter Scott who turned minds towards the middle ages. The interaction between mediaevalist Romanticism and Catholicism was clear in A. W. Pugin's *Contrasts* (1836), the Young England movement, the novels of Disraeli, the whole Gothic revival and in the revulsion against urban and industrial life which inspired the eccentric Anglican Benedictine communities created by Joseph Leicester Lyne (Fr Ignatius) and Aelred Carlyle. This mediaevalist Romanticism was also expressed by Burne-Jones, the Pre-Raphaelite painter, once a High Church ordinand, who declared: 'The more materialistic Science becomes, the more angels shall I paint.' Again he remarked: 'I love Christmas Carol Christianity, I couldn't do without Mediaeval Christianity. The central idea of it and all that it has gathered to itself made the Europe that I exist in'. The Pre-Raphaelites described themselves as a Brotherhood. William Morris and G. E. Street (the architect) at one time talked of creating monasteries. Gore pointed out to the Royal Commission on Ecclesiastical Discipline (1906) the interaction between the aesthetic movement and the revival of Catholic worship.

But there was another type of appeal to the past. Some keen to revive community life demonstrated that it had a respectable pedigree in the post-Reformation period. In particular, interest in the community founded at Little Gidding in 1625 was re-awakened by a series of books culminating in the popular novel *John Inglesant* (1881) by J. H. Shorthouse. Among those who eagerly read the novel were E. S. Talbot, J. R. Illingworth, Hugh Benson and Scott Holland. Shorthouse came to Keble to talk to what Holland called 'our gang' after his novel was published.

The yearning to escape from modern life into a dream-world made no appeal to Gore or his associates. Indeed some churchpeople, including Pusey, advocated religious communities not as an escape from industrialism, but as the only way in which the urban masses could be cared for and evangelized. In 1855 Fr Charles Lowder created the Society of the Holy Cross influenced by St Vincent de Paul. Lowder believed that the needs of urban parishes could only be met by groups of clergy living, praying and working together.[18] When religious communities were justified largely for their pastoral value, it is not surprising that women's communities pre-dated those for men. The first community for women was founded in 1845. The first stable men's community (SSJE) began in 1866. For women at that period, there were few opportunities for communal life or pastoral work. For men, the opportunities for both were manifold. Public schools and Oxbridge colleges offered a quasi-Benedictine pattern of community life and worship, providing the crucial formation for many clergy. The new theological colleges continued or began priestly formation through community. Some clergy and laymen were attracted to teach in the Tractarian Woodard schools because of their quasi-monastic life.[19]

At the Church Congress of 1885 Fr R. M. Benson, founder of SSJE, rejected the utilitarian argument and struck a supernatural note:

> Religious houses are a witness to the truth. They tell the joy of poverty . . . I will not speak of religious communities as a means of getting work done very cheaply! Such an idea I can only regard as a sacrilege, an insult to God . . . I cannot contemplate religious communities as a means of extricating us from the embarrassments which are simply occasioned by a sinful habit of greed . . . A religious community speaks by its mere existence. In the calm joy of a religious house we seem to hear the daughter of Zion laughing the world to scorn. This nineteenth century needs to be called back from the accumulation of material enjoyments.[20]

Gore, Holland and the others had discussed the possibility of an Oratorian community. The one they were likely to have known best was that founded by Newman and based in Birmingham from 1849. Gore's own contacts with Newman seem to have been, however, occasional and inconsequential. But several books about the Oratorians were published in the latter half of the nineteenth century. Holland paid a visit to Newman's Oratory in 1877 'all agog with the Oratorian Ideal' but returned home with his 'ardour rather damped'.

Newman had become a Roman Catholic in October 1845. He was able to create a new foundation in 1848 so soon after his conversion because as an Anglican he had already known St Philip Neri's concept of the Oratory, and because he could draw upon his own experience of an Oxford College. It was to Oxford that Newman looked rather than to the austere regime at Littlemore, as is made clear in an address of 1848:

> Now I will say in a word what is the nearest approximation in fact to an Oratorian Congregation that I know, and that is, one of the Colleges in the Anglican Universities. Take such a College, destroy the Head's House, annihilate wife and children and restore him to the body of fellows, change the religion from Protestant to Catholic, and give the Head and Fellows missionary and pastoral work, and you have a Congregation of St Philip before your eyes. And in matter of fact the Congregation is in the Annals sometimes called a College . . . An Oratorian has his own rooms, and his own furniture . . . He is to have his things about him, his books

and little possessions. In a word, he is to have what an Englishman expresses by the distinctive word *comfort* . . . Meanness, poverty, austerity, forlornness, sternness, are words unknown in an Oratorian House.

As the Oratory imposed no vows and few rules, the charity and the tact which ought to exist between educated gentlemen should be the common bonds. Because the work and worship of its members were individual, daily communal meals and regular residence were crucial to foster fellowship. Newman believed that his model was particularly suitable for Oxbridge converts engaged in intellectual work and preaching. He had rejected Dominican, Jesuit, Redemptorist and Benedictine forms. It was to be a home, a 'nest', not a monastery or like the house of a modern congregation, and therefore must be small enough for all to know one another. Its members would be superior in rank and education to the parochial clergy, with sufficient means to maintain themselves. The laws of the community should be written on their hearts rather than imposed from without:

> Thus to shift for oneself, to depend upon one's own resources, consideration, fellow feeling, knowledge of character, tact, good judgement are the characteristics of an Oratorian whereas the Jesuit does not know what tact is, cannot enter into the minds of others, and is apt to blunder in most important matters from this habit of mechanical obedience to a Superior and a system.[21]

Gore's understanding of s r, and later of c r, was in some ways similar to Newman's concept. Gore and the majority of s r and early c r brethren came from the same Oxbridge ethos as Newman. Like Newman, Gore believed that charity rather than elaborate rules should bind a community together. Like Newman, Gore wanted a home not a monastery and small enough for all its members to know one another. Neither Gore nor Newman had a monastic vocation, but felt drawn to community life, and to simplicity but not to Franciscan poverty. Like the Oratory, Pusey House and c r employed servants. Both Newman and Gore emphasized the importance of intellectual work and preaching, and believed that brethren should exercise initiative. Neither wanted to be an authoritarian Superior. There were also differences: for the members of s r and c r, brought up on the *Book of Common Prayer*, worship was corporate not individual; c r decided upon a common purse and community of goods; s r and c r were committed to overseas missionary work and c r to social action, neither of which figured in Newman's Oratory. Newman declared 'It is the saying of holy men that, if we wish to be perfect, we have nothing more to do than to perform the ordinary duties of the day well.' The c r Rule contained exactly the same advice from Dr Pusey.

All over the country rapid industrialization and urbanization were fragmenting community life. In response, many new forms of community were created, ranging from Robert Owen's model community at New Lanark (1800) to

Letchworth garden city (1903). Tractarianism and the religious associations which it produced were partly responses to social and religious fragmentation. In 1800 the Church of England could claim to be coextensive with the English nation in law, if not in fact. By the end of the century, with Roman Catholics, Nonconformists, Jews and agnostics admitted to Parliament, with the disestablishment of the Church of Ireland (1871) and the Church in Wales facing the same fate, the Church of England was still a national institution but was painfully conscious of the large numbers who denied its claims to be the national church. Pluralism had impelled the search for a separate and more distinct identity adumbrated by Newman in Tract 1 (1833) and expressed by the term 'Anglican'. So clergy in urban parishes looked for support from clerical colleagues which their brethren in villages received from the local community. The Tractarian and Evangelical teaching about the sacred nature of the ministry was reinforced by the new theological colleges which gave clergy a more separate professional identity. Whereas in Kilvert's diary we read of a squire looking like an old-fashioned clergyman, by the end of the century clergy increasingly wore a distinctive uniform. Clergy began to meet in clerical chapters and diocesan synods and the Convocations were revived. Church Congresses which gave a voice to both clergy and laity were inaugurated in 1861. The wide variety of activities recorded in the clerical diaries of Francis Kilvert and B. J. Armstrong were contracting to more directly liturgical, sacramental and evangelistic functions.[22] Previously one could virtually belong to the Church of England simply by being English. Now it wanted to define its 'membership'. Hence the creation in 1919 of the Church Assembly, Diocesan Conferences and Parochial Church Councils (with their attendant electoral rolls). Over the years Gore had passionately urged that the Church of England must become a more disciplined, defined and holy church, more worthy to be called the salt of the earth. Of this SR and CR were for Gore affirmations and instruments.

'We know two things of the Angels – that they cry Holy, Holy, Holy, and that they do God's bidding' – so asserted the Tractarian Newman. The remedy for sin according to the Tractarians was a holy, disciplined and obedient life. 'Pusey, Newman and Keble were not unaware that almost every writer they admired, both in the early church and in the Middle Ages, was a monk. All the Christian writings they proposed to their fellow Christians came from the milieu of monasticism.'[23] For Gore holiness meant apartness from, but not abandonment of, the world. The church had to be distinct in order to minister to people. Its primary functions were to witness to the righteousness of God by its life and worship and to draw human beings into fellowship with one another through their fellowship with God. He distrusted mysticism because it tended to divorce religion from morality and he was unsympathetic to contemplative communities which did no parochial work. For Gore, St John's Gospel was like a foreign country which it was a delight to visit, but when he returned to St Paul it was like coming home. 'St Paul . . . teaches us that the right way to understand the action of God in the Incarnation is to contemplate it morally.'[24]

In 1910 Gore, then Bishop of Birmingham, summarized succinctly that concept of the church which he formed in his early days and from which he never wavered:

> He found his ideal in the early Christian Church . . . Their great success was due to the fact that they were serious about their creed and about their worship; that they laid an immense amount of stress upon personal conduct and character; and they recognized in the broadest and fullest way the obligation of brotherhood and sisterhood binding them all together . . . The Christian Church became a middle class in respect to wealth in the Roman Empire – a middle class equally removed from poverty and from wealth because they were bound by that law of brotherhood . . . They preferred sincerity and thoroughness to popularity and numbers . . . The fashion at the present time was to have a good old national Church. Let everybody be inside . . . The result was what? That they hardly knew whether a man belonged or did not. (*Birmingham Daily Post* 17 March 1910)

So it was entirely congruent that Gore should try to reproduce within this lax church a society which could reproduce the character of the early Christians. However, many who supported the creation of such societies with stricter rules of membership, criticized Gore for trying to reshape the whole Church of England on what they regarded as a sectarian model.

These then were the main factors which created the revival of religious communities in the Church of England in the nineteenth century: romantic mediaevalism; the revival of interest in Little Gidding; the needs of urban parishes; the quasi-Benedictine character of Anglican institutions; an awareness of the crucial role that Religious Orders were playing in the burgeoning of English Roman Catholicism; the need for the Church of England to develop a more sharply defined identity over against an increasingly pluralist society; a new quest for holiness which largely resorted to clerical and monastic models. All of these, to varying degrees, influenced the creation of SR and CR.

It was not until 1889 that Gore became a national figure with the formation of the Christian Social Union (CSU) and the publication of *Lux Mundi*. The creation of OMC (1879) to which Gore committed himself deeply and his foundation of SR (1887) had been accomplished with the minimum of publicity. After 1889 Gore became a controversial figure in the life of church and nation. At first this shy, private and angular priest suffered deeply in this new role. Later he came to enjoy being combative. By 1889 Gore was committed to embodiments of the four imperatives which were to call CR into being in 1892: a group living a disciplined life of devotion and mission (SR including the embryonic cr); Liberal Catholicism (*Lux Mundi*); a fleshing out of the gospel in social concern and action (csu); a pledge of support to the world-wide church with the catholic richness of its different cultures and races (sr).

The Christian Social Union

It was not until the Christian Socialist movement of 1848–54 that a prophetic critique of the social *status quo* emerged within the Church of England, led by J. M. Ludlow, Charles Kingsley and F. D. Maurice.[25] Though not really socialists in the modern sense, and retaining many conservative attitudes, nevertheless they rejected naked economic individualism in favour of co-operation for the common good, and exercised an enormous influence on subsequent generations. Maurice offered an alternative theology to traditional orthodoxy, both catholic and evangelical, by starting, not with human sinfulness, but with the assertion that everyone is already in Christ. Stewart Headlam founded the Guild of St Matthew in 1877. At its peak it never had more than 400 members, but included a number who subsequently proclaimed their socialism on a wider platform – Conrad Noel, Percy Dearmer, J. G. Adderley, P. E. T. Widdrington, F. L. Donaldson and C. W. Stubbs. Headlam had too many quarrels with authority and his socialism was too revolutionary for him to be able to shift attitudes in the Church of England as a whole. Nor was the remarkable sermon of 1886 by Thomas Hancock (a member of gsm) on Mary as the Mother of revolutionary socialism calculated to win over the nervous. Hancock was virtually unemployed for ten years. Headlam held no clerical post after 1878. The hero of Shaw's *Candida* (1895), a member of gsm and csu, was partly modelled on Headlam.

By the 1880s socialism was in the air. 'We are all socialists now' was attributed to both the Liberal leader Sir William Harcourt and (astonishingly) to Edward VII. The Queen's Private Secretary (Sir Henry Ponsonby, related to Gore) wrote from Balmoral in 1883 that most recent political speeches discussed socialism. 'I don't exactly know what it means. It don't [sic] mean the Socialism of the German Revolutionists but means I suppose Associationalism as opposed to Individualism . . . '[26] Ponsonby was right. Collectivism and Individualism were commonly contrasted at that period. 'Socialism' usually signified something akin to the municipal policies of Joseph Chamberlain in Birmingham, the 'new Liberalism' as it was called. As Ponsonby said in his letter: 'Statesmen can direct the current of the advancing tide and use it beneficially instead of allowing it to overflow and destroy everything.'

Why, asked Beatrice Webb, the Fabian, did a demand for state intervention arise from men of intellect and property? She answered: 'The origin of the ferment is to be discovered in a new consciousness of sin' – by this she did not mean 'personal sin': 'The consciousness of sin was a collective or class consciousness; a growing uneasiness amounting to conviction, that the industrial organization, which had yielded rent, interest and profits on a stupendous scale, had failed to provide a decent livelihood and tolerable conditions for a majority of the inhabitants of Great Britain.' This consciousness of sin usually expressed itself (she continued) by dedicated personal service, sometimes by open confession of failure and by a dedication to reorganize society on a more equalitarian basis. She quoted Arnold Toynbee, an economics tutor at Balliol and a disciple of T. H. Green, who declared in 1883:

> We – the middle classes, I mean, not merely the very rich – we have neglected you; instead of justice we have offered you charity, and instead of sympathy we have offered you hard and unreal advice; but I think we are changing . . . we have sinned against you grievously . . . but if you will forgive us – nay, whether you will forgive us or not – we will serve you, we will devote our lives to your service . . . We are willing to give up the life we care for, the life with books and with those we love.

He asked one thing in return: that if he and his fellows succeeded in improving social conditions, the people would really lead 'a better life', and remember that 'material civilization' was not an end in itself, but a means to 'grow upwards towards the heavens . . . but if you do not, then our reparation will be in vain'.[27] Note the religious cast of thought; penitential language derived from the Prayer Book; the pledge of self-emptying; the reference to reparation. But Toynbee's attitude was extraordinarily (if innocently) *de haut en bas*; he and his fellows believed they had everything to give, but it never crossed their minds that they might have something to receive.

The large number of public school missions and university settlements, founded in the poor areas of large cities, particularly London, during the last quarter of the century, embodied this type of social commitment. The sacrificial and flamboyant ministry of Father Dolling at the Winchester College Mission in the Portsmouth slums (1885–95) created widespread public admiration of such ventures. Dolling (Harrow and Cambridge), a supporter of Headlam (Eton and Cambridge), was a socialist in the tradition of *noblesse oblige*. He was admired by Gore and Holland and had a decisive influence on Keble Talbot when he was a boy at Winchester. Toynbee Hall, Whitechapel (1884) the memorial to Arnold Toynbee, and Oxford House, Bethnal Green (1885) expressed the new concern of Oxbridge for the poor. Holland hoped that Oxford House (and St Stephen's House Theological College Oxford, for whose foundation he was chiefly responsible) would embody Oratorian principles. Through such missions and settlements, many found vocations to various types of ministry. C. R. Attlee (Haileybury and Oxford) as the result of his visits to his school mission in Limehouse became a socialist and leaving his comfortable home, went to work there and later at Toynbee Hall. When A. F. Winnington Ingram (Marlborough and Oxford) became Head of Oxford House in 1888 he was totally ignorant of how the poor lived. But Toynbee Hall, for example, with its quad and dining room decorated with college shields, was an attempt to transplant Oxbridge into Whitechapel. The assumption was that the visitors were civilized and the locals were not. Missionaries overseas usually took a similar attitude to other cultures and faiths.[28]

Holland believed that *The Bitter Cry of Outcast London* (1883) by Andrew Mearns, Secretary of the London Congregational Union, had stirred the conscience of Oxford. In 1891 Randall Davidson, preparing for his work as Bishop of Rochester, read the writings of Charles Booth in which he concluded that the vast majority of the poor were outside all religious bodies except the Roman Catholic church. *In Darkest England and the Way Out* (1890) by William Booth, the Salvation Army leader, provided graphic accounts of urban destitution. R. Mudie-Smith in *The Religious Life of London* (1904) advocated street preaching, the social gospel and ministers with large hearts and small stipends as the proper response to the alienation of the workers from the churches.

It is in this context that we should evaluate the expressions of social concern and interest in socialism within the Church of England. Holland and Wilfrid Richmond created a group called 'Pesek' (Politics, Economics, Ethics and Christianity) in Oxford in 1879. In 1887 the Church Congress discussed socialism. In 1888 it was on the agenda of the Lambeth Conference of bishops of the Anglican Communion and Holland addressed them on the subject. A Conference committee chaired by Bishop Moorhouse of Manchester concluded that if by socialism was meant the union of labour with land and capital, and a general concern for the material and moral welfare of the poor, then there was no contradiction between socialism and Christianity. It set its face against state ownership of land and capital, but supported the purchase of land by labourers and co-operative societies. The government should do more to protect the workers from 'the evil effects of unchecked competition'. But much 'the best help is self-help'. Clergy should be trained in economics, 'enter into friendly relations with Socialists' and demonstrate 'how much of what is good and true in Socialism is to be found in the precepts of Christ'. The bishops' encyclical pointed out the 'excessive inequality' in the distribution of goods, urged the study of 'what is popularly called Socialism' and the support of any schemes for 'redressing the social balance'.

The launching of the Christian Social Union at a meeting presided over by Holland in June 1889 was thus more a response to a general concern, inside and outside the churches, than a prophetic initiative. Westcott became its first President in November. Holland became Chairman of the Committee. Gore succeeded Westcott as President in 1901. The aims of the CSU were:

1. To claim for the Christian Law the ultimate authority to rule social practice.

2. To study in common how to apply the moral truths and principles of Christianity to the social and economic difficulties of the present time.

3. To present Christ in practical life as the Living Master and King, the enemy of wrong and selfishness, the power of righteousness and love.

Its Anglican and eucharistic basis was demonstrated by the rubric requesting its members to pray for it at Holy Communion, and particularly on or about the feasts of the Epiphany, Ascension and Michaelmas. CSU told its critics that its type of social witness had been commended by the Lambeth Conference of 1888.

CSU grew directly out of the work of the Guild of St Matthew and gained some of its first adherents from the ranks of GSM. In Oxford, for example, the GSM branch run by John Carter (a founding member of CR) was dissolved and reconstituted as a CSU branch. Naturally Headlam felt resentful and asked what the CSU leaders had been doing while GSM was bearing the burden and heat of the day on its own.

One of the initial two CSU secretaries was Cyril Bickersteth (another founding member of CR). One of his earliest tasks in September 1889 was to rush off to Wales at the request of some CSU leaders to implore Frederick Temple, Bishop of London, to return from his holiday to resume his mediation in the London Dock Strike. In confusion Bickersteth left without money, and had to return and wait while his friends emptied their pockets. Reaching Shrewsbury he telegraphed 'What am I to say to him? What is he to do?' After this feeble beginning, Bickersteth was, however, successful in persuading Temple to return.

CSU aimed to study and publicize social and economic problems, but also engaged in social action. In 1893 the Oxford branch (under John Carter) compiled a list of 20 local firms which paid trade union wages and encouraged its members to buy only from them. By 1900 the list had grown to 146 firms. Other branches followed suit. In 1898–9 a CSU deputation of bishops, college heads and other notables lobbied the Commons to demand a revision of the factory acts. Gore was a keen supporter of the Co-operative movement. 'I am arrayed' (he once remarked) 'from head to foot in garments of Co- operative production. These boots I have sent back three times. The wicked shops are best.'

The leadership of CSU was sufficiently respectable and its programme sufficiently generalized to embrace a wide variety of views and people. Though in 1892 its manifesto for the London County Council included a call for women councillors, in February 1890 at the inauguration of the Oxford branch, Percy Dearmer had to threaten to resign before women were allowed to become members. In 1900 CSU had 35 branches and over 4,000 members with roughly equal proportions of laypeople and clergy. By 1902 Battyeford (to which CR moved in 1898) had a branch with sixteen members, not including

members of CR. CSU was particularly successful in penetrating the episcopate. Between 1889 and 1913, 16 out of the 53 episcopal appointments went
to members of CSU, whereas only one member of GSM (C. W. Stubbs) became an English bishop (Truro). Christians in other churches followed suit
and formed Social Unions. One result of the papal encyclical *Rerum Novarum*
(1891) the so-called 'Workers' Charter', was the creation of the Catholic
Social Guild in 1909. After the demise of CSU (it merged to form the
Industrial Christian Fellowship in 1920) its influence can be traced in the
left-wards shift of the episcopate epitomized by William Temple, and more
recently in *Faith in the City* (1985).

Gore wrote a chapter on CSU in Stephen Paget's life of Holland. CSU was
'a tardy act of repentance'. Those who formed it were very various – some
academics, some fired by Maurice, Kingsley or *Ecce Homo*, some from the
Settlement movement. CSU was in a general sense 'socialist' because it was
opposed to laissez-faire, but not in the sense that it had a political programme,
for example of state ownership. It was limited to churchpeople: only those who
shared the same sacramental system could awaken others to 'the real social
meaning of their baptism, their confirmation and their holy communion'. The
doctrines of the incarnation and Trinity, the Pauline doctrine of the church as
a social organism promoting brotherhood, the doctrine of redemption through
sacrifice and the sacraments supplied the motives for social action. Looking
back from 1920 Gore believed that CSU had been largely responsible for the
changed attitude of the church towards society. But he candidly lamented
that it had not stirred the average priest or congregation and had failed to
create a body of church trade unionists who could have influenced the Labour
movement.

In his Bampton Lectures of 1891 Gore made clear his profoundly moral
attraction to the doctrine of kenosis. 'It is an act of moral self-denial such as
can be an example to us men in our efforts at sympathy and self-sacrifice.' The
incarnation brings with it 'a Christian socialism, by the very fact that the law of
brotherhood is the law of Christ'. Yet then, and on many subsequent
occasions, he also made clear his belief that, however much we may and
should do to better social conditions, the 'obstacles to progress in every class
are within rather than without; they lie in jealousy, in suspicion, in self-
assertion, in lust, in dishonesty, in carelessness – in a word in sin'. Christ alone
is 'the true emancipator' because he 'bases the regeneration of society on the
conversion and renewal of men'.[29]

The CSU's 'socialism' was heavily qualified. Gore indignantly rejected a
newspaper report that it was a 'Christian *Socialist* Union'. But the readiness of
CSU to campaign for social justice and to justify this theologically, was wholly
foreign to the tradition represented by Newman, Keble and Benson, though
Pusey had vehemently drawn attention to the sufferings of the poor and asked
why such poverty should exist.[30] However, if the leaders of the Oxford

Movement, apart from Pusey, had little to offer society except an anxious message about the dangers it posed to the church, the sacramentalism it inculcated was fundamental to CSU, GSM and later groups.

In November 1889 Ben Tillett stayed at Pusey House and he and John Burns addressed a meeting at which Gore took the chair. This visit by leaders of the recent Dock Strike received some bad publicity. That Gore should entertain Tillett and take the chair at the meeting was to Liddon 'a very serious indiscretion', but he comforted himself that Gore had acted thus 'in the hope of doing Mr Tillett some religious good'. Despite such occasional contacts with Labour leaders, working class participation in CSU was virtually non-existent.

Lux Mundi

That November *Lux Mundi* was published.[31] Edited by Gore and written by members of the Holy Party, it attempted a dynamic fusion between aspects of Tractarianism, Greek patristic thought, Broad Church liberalism and biblical criticism. Gore wrote in the Preface:

> We have written then in this volume not as 'guessers at truth', but as servants of the Catholic Creed and Church, aiming only at interpreting the faith we have received. On the other hand, we have written with the conviction that the epoch in which we live is one of profound transformation, intellectual and social, abounding in new needs, new points of view, new questions . . . That is to say theology must take a new development.

Several of the contributors appeared to be directly in the Tractarian succession. Gore was Principal of Pusey House and Talbot was Warden of Keble. But whereas the Tractarians had regarded secular thought as an enemy, *Lux Mundi* claimed that it could be an ally. The Logos was at work in the whole process of creation, in evolution, art, science, other religions and socialism. It was Gore's essay (or rather a section of it) which created the furore. Yet whereas *Essays and Reviews* (1860) had been condemned by the bishops, and half the clergy had signed a declaration agreeing with the condemnation, and two of its authors were charged with heresy, *Lux Mundi* was not proceeded against. That it was not can be explained only partly by the differences between the two books; it was also a sign of the increasing acceptance of theological pluriformity within the Church of England and of the growing appeal of 'progressive' thought.

Gore's essay is undergirded with patristic references, indicating Gore's belief that it is to scripture and the early church that we must return. Human history to Gore was not a story of progress but of sin and redemption: 'the record of lawlessness, the record of the Spirit striving with man, but resisted, rejected, ignored, quenched' – the weighty words convey Gore's sense of the terrible power of evil. The doctrine of the Spirit is not esoteric or mystical but realized in the common life and in the individuality which the Spirit nourishes within it. (This passage has relevance to his creation of s R and c R.) The Spirit is patient and works slowly. The church is to be mother not magistrate. Then comes the passage which caused the storm. The validity of Christ's use of the stories of the flood and Jonah does not depend upon whether they are historical. Jesus in Matthew 24.37–9 shared the assumption that Psalm 110 was written by David. (Gore shared the view of the biblical critics that it was not Davidic.) In these and in other ways, Christ demonstrated that the incarnation was 'a self-emptying of God' and involved a 'limitation of knowledge'.

Why was this such a bombshell? Conservatives had responded to challenges about the historicity of certain parts of the Bible by adopting an either-or defence. In 1863 Bishop Prince Lee of Manchester declared: 'the very foundation of our faith, the very basis of our hopes, the very nearest and dearest of our consolations are taken from us when one line in that Sacred Volume on which we base everything is declared to be unfaithful or untrustworthy.' And to explain Christ's apparently literal acceptance of the Old Testament as being the result of self-emptying had a dire pedigree. That explanation had been used by Bishop Colenso of Natal, whose books were condemned by the English bishops and who was deposed for heresy by Bishop Gray of Capetown in 1863. Pusey and Liddon had fiercely campaigned against Colenso.[32] The *Christian Commonwealth* bitterly complained on 3 December 1896: 'Canons Driver and Gore and Dean Farrar are now promulgating . . . exactly the views for which Bishop Colenso was prosecuted and excommunicated.' Moreover, Gore dealt with some of the difficulties of the Old Testament by treating it as a record of gradual divine education. But this argument was tainted for conservatives because it had been used in *Essays and Reviews*. On the other hand Gore's determination to erect an electrified fence round the New Testament and Creeds alienated some liberals.[33]

Because Gore had been teaching the substance of his essay for over ten years he did not anticipate the storm it created. The publication of *Lux Mundi* caused a serious breach in relationships between Liddon and Gore. As early as 1884 Liddon had written to Holland, deeply concerned about the younger Churchmen of Oxford:

> . . . there is a difference between the new and the old Churchmanship. The new cares less for authority, and relies more on subjective considerations, and expects more from fallen humanity, and attaches less importance to the Divine organization and function of the Church . . . to yield to such influences means sooner or later some essentially Pantheistic substitute for the Ancient Faith.[34]

Lux Mundi exemplified and deepened the split between what Liddon called 'the new and the old Churchmanship'. Liddon felt a deep sense of obligation to preserve and transmit Pusey's teachings. Pusey believed the death of his wife was God's punishment for his sins which included his early flirtation with liberal theology. It was Liddon who had pressed for Gore to be the first Principal of Pusey House. In October 1889 Gore sent Liddon an advance copy. Liddon might not like the last few pages, but this approach had been helpful to many. 'If you seriously disapprove, it would be a great misery.' Liddon replied that the good will of 'the barbarians' could not be won by concessions. We must think of what was due to Dr Pusey's name and what would sustain confidence in the House. Gore said he thought Liddon knew what he taught about the Old Testament. Liddon agonized at length, appealed to the Fathers and to Pusey and advised Gore to submit the pages to episcopal authority. Liddon noted '*Miserable* about Gore's Essay. It takes the heart out of all one's hopes for Pusey House.' He offered to refund a £500 donation because he felt he had misled the donor by asserting his trust in Gore as Principal. 'It is practically a capitulation at the feet of the young Rationalistic Professors' he lamented to another, 'Not only could Dr Pusey never have written these pages, it would have been difficult to have written anything more opposed to his convictions.' In anguish he wrote in the *Spectator* (12 April 1890): if Christ was mistaken about the authorship of Psalm 110 'why have we taken him at his word as a guide in life and an anchor of the soul in death?' Gore tried to reassure him: 'I wish you knew how very deep the pain is of having given so much pain to you.'

When in April 1890 Liddon was offered the see of St Albans he declined it partly from the reasons of age and health, partly because *Lux Mundi* revealed that he could not depend upon the support of younger High Churchmen. '"Lux Mundi" is a proclamation of revolt against the spirit and principles of Dr Pusey and Mr Keble.' During his final illness that summer Gore (who was one of his executors) visited him regularly but there could be no theological reconciliation.[35] When Liddon died in September Gore was wretched and brooded all day. Some said that *Lux Mundi* had caused Liddon's death.

Many of the cuttings about *Lux Mundi* in the Mirfield archives show alarm and hostility. Historians, anxious to celebrate the book as a great step forward, have sometimes played down the depth and length of the controversy it caused. Fr Benson was profoundly shocked and dubbed it 'Lux Mundana' (worldly light). He liked Gore, but so disapproved of his opinions and those of his friends that he now refused to meet them. Lord Halifax, President of the (Anglo-Catholic) English Church Union, a disciple of Liddon and Pusey, who early on had contemplated joining SSJE, never forgave Gore for making Liddon's last year of life so wretched. 'The longer I live, the more right I think Liddon was about *Lux Mundi*', Halifax wrote in 1922. He also regarded Gore's social radicalism as both cranky and worldly. Halifax remained permanently suspicious of CR. He regarded it as infected with Gore's

religious and political heresies.³⁶ Archdeacon Denison, the veteran Tractarian campaigner against Colenso and *Essays and Reviews*, now agitated
against *Lux Mundi*. We should receive 'humbly and thankfully the Bible which
has been sent . . . from above', he wrote in an Open Letter. When in 1892 he
could not persuade the English Church Union (of which he and Gore were
members) to repudiate the book, he and the vicar of All Saints' Margaret
Street resigned. Denison's friends continued to harry Gore inside the ECU
and in the press. Correspondence raged in July and August 1894 in the *Church
Times*, after a special and sometimes disorderly ECU meeting at which 'the
name of Mr Gore was mentioned more than once in a manner very far from
respectful'. Coles venerated Liddon and regarded *Lux Mundi* as a 'tragedy'
which taught Gore 'where to stop'. Darwell Stone, a member of SR,
considered that parts of it were inconsistent with the church's beliefs. The
Bishop of Lichfield (W. D. Maclagan, later Archbishop of York) told his
diocesan synod: 'One could almost wish that all such treatises might be written
and discussed in the Latin tongue'. Gore was also pursued by the bizarre Fr
Ignatius. When Gore was told what he had said at a meeting in Oxford he
responded 'Funny old thing'. Gore was billed to speak at the 1893 Church
Congress. Ignatius, who had been told in a dream to go, held a prior protest
meeting: 'If Gore is right, Jesus Christ is wrong; if Gore is right, the Bible
must be put out of our houses as a bad Book – a forgery and a deliberate fraud.'
As Gore rose to speak at the Congress, Ignatius shouted repeatedly: 'In the
name of Jesus he has no right to speak.' What is significant about the whole
episode is that such an outburst could gain the support of a proportion of an
educated audience four years after the publication of the book.

Of course Gore had his supporters. Best of all reassurances came from
Bishop King of Lincoln, a conservative Tractarian and disciple of Pusey, who
urged the church to approach the book with sympathy and invited Gore to
conduct the Lincoln clergy retreat in the autumn of 1891. Holland was
astonished at the book's reception. They had been saying these things for
years and assumed everyone was also saying them. 'Now suddenly we find it all
spoken of as a bomb . . . '

At the height of the crisis Gore concluded that he could only continue as
Principal if he had the explicit confidence of the Governors, and so in March
1890 he offered to resign. Liddon still hoped that Gore would withdraw parts
of his essay. Eventually it was decided that a resignation would do even more
harm to Pusey House. Meanwhile Gore was preparing corrections and
additions to a new edition. He was anxious to avoid a permanent split between
the two generations of High Churchmen. He also wanted to reassure the
general public. So he rewrote one passage to make clearer Christ's attitude to
the Old Testament. For the tenth edition (July 1890) he expanded the
Preface from three to twenty-one pages. He vigorously defended his position
but apologized for misunderstandings. His critics were not mollified. When

Gore delivered his Bampton Lectures on the incarnation in 1891 in the University Church, its vicar tried to persuade the University to arraign him for heresy. (Gore continued his exposition of kenosis in *Dissertations* (1895).) William Stubbs, Bishop of Oxford and President of Pusey House, in his visitation charge to the diocese of 1893 implicitly repudiated Gore's position. 'I cannot bear to anticipate a day when the Church shall cry out to Jesus of Nazareth "Thou hast deceived me" . . . '

Lux Mundi represented as well as encouraged a general theological mutation. With Evangelicalism weakened, the focus shifted from the doctrine of the atonement (versions of which had caused increasing moral revulsion) to the incarnation and Christ the teacher. Moral revulsion against hell encouraged universalism. F. D. Maurice taught that human kind was already 'in Christ'. With eternal destiny now assured, attention shifted from preparation for another world to the betterment of this. A slum priest, accused of being concerned with secular issues, replied: 'I speak out and fight about the drains because I believe in the incarnation'. In *Lux Mundi* there was no separate chapter on sin. It did however include an essay on 'Christianity and Politics' – a theme which found no place in *Essays and Reviews*. The new sensitivity towards the poor and weak was also fostered by the development of devotion to the vulnerable Virgin and Child popularized by the Service of Nine Lessons and Carols first held at Truro Cathedral in 1880.

Gore was accused of treachery to the church, the Bible, the Catholic faith, to Liddon, Pusey House and the Tractarian tradition, and above all to Jesus himself. Fortunately Gore received comfort and encouragement from C. W. Furse of Westminster Abbey who had been Principal of Cuddesdon when Gore was Vice-Principal. He realized the depths of Gore's agony: 'Liddon will kill Gore' he remarked when the crisis was at its worst. The label of heretic stuck. Bickersteth once met a churchwoman who was very alarmed that he was a member of Gore's community: 'What, that awful Canon Gore who does not believe in the Bible?'.

How was it (asked S. C. Carpenter) that the *Lux Mundi* pioneer became the defender? Despite all his wide-ranging reading 'he never told us how to meet the new things for the old purpose in a new way':

Was it . . . that Liddon's distress in 1889 was so painful a shock to him that he developed a sort of Never Again complex, and that his transparently honest answers to his own question 'Can we still believe?' were at least partially determined by causes which were unknown to himself?

Conway Davies who knew Gore in his latter years commented:

It was as if the intense conflict of those early days in Oxford had left its mark on a sensitive and highly strung nature so that his mind latterly tended to run into fixed gladiatorial attitudes suitable, let us say, to a battle with a Traditionalist, an encounter with a Darwinian, a deadly grappling with a Papist, and so on. He had been fighting so intensely and on so many different fronts that the alignments almost became established frontiers.[37]

As Paul Avis points out, Gore in his essay boldly ventured forth, but also clearly marked out boundaries to his exploration. After *Lux Mundi* Gore increasingly turned the boundaries into a stockade and as a bishop tried to force the Church of England to live within it. Perhaps his persecution of Henson and the modernists was so unrelenting because he was conscious of having himself started the avalanche which was carrying parts of the stockade away. Likewise, having explored and expressed to the full the Catholicism of the Prayer Book, he was often in bitter dispute with the advanced Anglo-Catholics, who were as little disposed to observe the limits Gore laid down for liturgical practice, as were the Modernists willing to observe the theological limits Gore laid down in *Lux Mundi*. In any case, Gore was ultimately a loner, and the only group with whom he ever fully identified himself was the Holy Party (and that met usually only once a year for a month). Even in that group, with the exception of Holland and Talbot, he held himself apart. This was to have good as well as bad consequences in the history of CR.

The gestation of a community

The year 1889 was momentous for Gore not only because of the formation of the CSU in June and the publication of *Lux Mundi* in November, but because that summer at Pusey House he began the first stages of the creation of a religious community related to, but distinct from, SR.

James Nash (1862–1943), who became a founding member of CR, marked the day he first met Gore as the turning point of his life. After King William's College, Isle of Man he went up to Hertford College, Oxford. On 21 July 1885, up for his final viva, he lunched with Aubrey Moore (a contributor to *Lux Mundi*) and was captivated by Gore who was also there. Gore's 'merry talk' encouraged the shy young Nash to call on him at Pusey to discuss his religious difficulties. He already admired Gore for his courage in inviting Headlam of GSM (of which Nash was a member) to speak at Pusey. Nash was very surprised when next year Gore dropped in on him in.Paris where he was learning French preparatory to a teaching career. They walked in the Bois de Boulogne and Gore invited him to stay at Pusey. A few months later, Nash stood at the door full of misgivings not least because he had had an evangelical upbringing. To his relief he was welcomed by Coles with a hearty laugh. Gore was known as theologian, preacher, social reformer and church leader. But he was also 'an ardent Gospel fisherman, most skilful with rod and line', which cost him much in prayer, nervous effort and intellectual conflict. He told Nash that nothing took more out of him than 'earnest wrestling with some able youth, knowing that on it might depend a life fruitful or barren'. He made 'the casual, careless, indifferent, conscious that he, at all events, thought them worthwhile . . . He had a wonderful capacity for affectionate friendship.' So Nash's faith was strengthened and in 1886 he was ordained to a curacy which Gore had arranged at St Andrew's Bethnal Green. Early in 1889 Nash went to Pusey to be professed in SR. Gore told him that he intended to found a community for those to whom SSJE did not appeal, and invited Nash to help him. 'Many rules, however stringent, without friendship, he was sure did not work; friendship with a few wise rules well kept, makes the machine function.' When Nash returned to Pusey in July he found that William Carter from the Eton Mission, Hackney (nephew of T. T. Carter, founder of the Clewer Sisterhood), J. P. Maud (later Bishop of Kensington), G. A. Cooke (still a layman, later Professor of Hebrew) and Alfred Kettle had just arrived. Richard Rackham, then a layman, arrived the next day. John Carter arrived in August. Some were deterred from joining the enterprise (and later CR) by Gore's heretical reputation, though Gore made it clear that associating themselves with SR or this community did not involve acceptance of his opinions. Darwell Stone, a member of SR, for example, wrote highly critical articles about Gore's theological works without any breach of fellowship.[38]

The seven lived in the house next door which had been recently purchased. They recited the full round of offices in Latin – there was nothing High Church about Latin, it was still common in University worship. But its use indicated that Gore assumed he could take a classical education for granted in would-be members. Silence was kept from Compline to Sext. They cleaned their own rooms. In turn each gave a weekly meditation. They shared their meals and the Chapel with the Librarians. A picture which had belonged to Pusey hung over the altar. At Compline a passage from one of Pusey's sermons was read. The House was then simple and homely, with a garden behind, complete with fruitful damson tree. Each was given the task of studying one of the monastic rules – those of St Basil, St Benedict, the Brothers of the Common Life, the Italian and French Oratorians, the Celtic communities, Cluny, Citeaux, Bec, St Francis, St Dominic, St Ignatius Loyola and Rosmini. In the evenings they met with the Librarians to discuss each in turn. Gore had a particular attraction to the Eastern Rule because he was averse to unnecessary regulations. At the end of August 1889 they drew up a provisional rule on Oratorian lines, aiming as far as possible to reproduce the pattern of life in Acts 2.42–4. Four – Gore, William Carter, John Carter and Nash – accepted the rule for one year.

Gore wanted no publicity. When the earnest Bishop Thorold of Rochester called and asked what they were about, Gore gravely responded that they were learning to ride the bicycle. The four therefore called themselves in private 'The Brothers of the Common Wheel'. Others were told that they were only some clergymen trying to be good. But the embryonic community was only one of several enterprises which claimed Gore's attention – Pusey House; SR; OMC; CSU (created that June); *Lux Mundi* (published that November). Gore appears to have had a deep fear of being trapped. By having several concurrent responsibilities, he was relieved of the necessity to commit himself totally to any one of them. Gore was deeply saddened when the Superior of OMC became a Roman Catholic. So in December Gore set sail for India. It seems casual to create a community in August, and in December to leave the other three to fend for themselves for three months. But a pattern of strategic withdrawal characterized Gore's relationship with CR for the rest of his life. Meanwhile William Carter and James Nash stayed as guests at SSJE to experience the monastic life. Nash's health broke down and he had to leave. William Carter decided he had no vocation and in 1891 became Bishop of Zululand but continued in SR until his marriage in 1904.

The SSJE had such an influence on the early CR that it is important to describe something of its history and ethos.[39] SSJE was founded by R. M. Benson in 1866. It was the first stable community for men in the Church of England. Benson became incumbent of St James' Cowley in 1850. For several years Benson had been in touch with Fr Lowder and the Society of the Holy Cross and so was familiar with the idea of a group of mission priests working together under rule. The full title of SSJE is 'The Mission Priests of St John the Evangelist'. Benson, a respected parish priest, had the confidence of his bishop, Samuel Wilberforce of Oxford, who wrote in August 1865: 'I like the idea of your *College* very much indeed.' Thus the first enduring Religious Order for men sprang not from the romantic periphery, but from the heart of the parochial life. Wilberforce stipulated that no distinctive dress should be worn, nor any vows taken. But Benson through skilful diplomacy obtained from Wilberforce his general approval without any undue interference.

By the time Gore began forming the community, SSJE had houses in the United States, India and South Africa. But it was not until 1884 that the Society had a proper constitution. Until then Benson had controlled decisions autocratically. He had refused to give self-government to the American house and two of the brethren left SSJE. The novitiate could be quite short or last eight years or longer. It was only after twenty-five years as Superior that in 1890 he reluctantly resigned. Numbers joining had diminished and Benson said that no institution should continue to a second generation, for then it would lose its original purpose. Though he considered the Religious Life was entirely compatible with parish work, he followed his mentor Pusey and taught deadness to the world. In the mid-1870s he told his brethren that in the city streets they should be 'like Jonah walking through the streets of Ninevah, a witness to a perishing world, or like moving corpses in the world, living with a life of heaven'. In 1875 he wrote: 'This world can never be to us anything but a hovel and a battlefield.'[40]

Benson's autocracy and his teaching about deadness repelled Gore's brethren. 'We don't want to be like Cowley' runs like a refrain through their early letters. William Carter wrote from Cowley to Nash (who had had to leave because of eye trouble) that if s s j e was the only form of the Religious Life he doubted whether he had a vocation. He believed in the value of a community of priests living a common life to supplement the work of the parish clergy in areas like the East End. But Benson had told him that this was not the Religious Life. He had attended a retreat in which Benson kept quoting 'dead unto the world, but alive unto God'. Carter considered this a misquotation of St Paul who had written not 'dead unto the world', but 'dead unto sin', which was very different. Benson, he thought, was 'Calvinistically inclined'. He had been in touch with his uncle T. T. Carter (an authority on the Religious Life) and he hoped that they might both consult him. When Nash was ill, Benson wrote grimly: 'Pestilences devastate Satan's empire but they hasten the Kingdom of Christ.' Holland walked out of a retreat when Benson expounded the traditional hell.

On 11 October 1891 Walter Frere wrote to Gore from his Stepney curacy about a visit he had paid to Cowley at Coles' suggestion and about his vocation to be a friar. (When James Adderley, former Head of Oxford House, advertised in the *Church Times* for someone to join him to create a community of friars in the East End, Frere's was the only reply. In 1894 Adderley joined two others in creating the Society of the Divine Compassion, a Franciscan community with a special concern for the poor.[41]) Frere said of Cowley:

> I think I saw enough to shew that their ideal and the one I humbly pursue are very different: they seem to be so much *monks* and even monks of the Carthusian type, *hermits*; while the idea before me is rather that of friars – men detached by Vows from three at least of the bonds of the world but living in the world and actively ministering to its masses of untouched men and women. This surely is something quite different to the Cowley ideal but something for which there is a crying need.

He suggested, though he realized it might seem to be 'presumptuous' (Frere was still a curate, had only been ordained four years and had only recently joined s r) that s r should open a house in the East End with stricter rules than s r, with 'regular vows' and a common purse. He considered this to be a more suitable place than Oxford, 'where I know the seed is gradually maturing'. He had already talked with Nash who might join him. Frere's proposal that he should create another community within s r, different in style from that being created at Pusey and which might include Nash was a bold challenge to Gore's judgment and leadership. Obviously he (and Nash too?) thought Gore was being dilatory. By contrast Frere was impatient to begin at once: 'I feel sure it will come and am so strongly drawn towards it that I could not be content to wait unless it was quite certain that the opportunity was not yet to be had.'

John Carter wrote to Rackham the same month: 'The ideal of the s R is truer than that of Cowley because it is both primitive and more modern – Cowley is only mediaeval.' In 1894 Frere recalled that he had been discouraged by what seemed 'mediaeval' at Cowley and had looked for 'something as binding but less monkish: more in the world'. He had started in favour of vows, but had come round to the idea of permanent intention, even though in the last resort this could not be enforced. This seemed right in view of the haze about what powers of dispensation existed and 'the troubles Cowley has experienced'. 'We thus throw St Benet to the winds and return to Apostolic freedom and community ideals . . . '

Walter Carey was ordained the year that *Lux Mundi* was published. He wrote in *Goodbye to my Generation* (1951) of the liberation brought to him by Gore, Dolling and Holland (and later by Dick Sheppard and Basil Jellicoe). He wanted a faith which would transform the whole of life and tackle slums and unemployment. Carey revolted against the Tractarianism of his first vicar who, though a faithful shepherd of souls, had no interest in social problems. After a time, Carey refused to wear the regulation frock coat and top hat and sometimes would dress as a tramp to find out what doss-houses were like. He made friends equally with Roman Catholics and Salvationists.

Though Gore and *Lux Mundi* demonstrated to many like Carey that it was possible to be Catholic without being Puseyite (and much more fun), and though it is clear that Benson belonged to the age of Pusey and Liddon, and Gore did not, yet Gore continued to revere Benson. Benson appealed to the Tractarian side of Gore. Like Benson, Gore rejected the lax church of Christendom. Like Benson, he was deeply sensitive to the ravages of sin. In his sermon for the centenary of Benson's birth in 1924 he recommended his congregation to read Benson's commentary on the Psalms. Benson was an 'old Tory', but he upheld a principle socialists were liable to forget: that no economic or political change, however necessary, can redeem human life. It can only be redeemed from within. Gore also commended Benson for his dread of abstract, intellectualized theology and for preferring primitive standards of faith and worship rather than those of Rome – a lesson modern Anglo-Catholics needed to learn. He, like others, had felt in Benson's presence, 'that is the real thing'.[42] Yet if Gore was more sympathetic to Benson than his associates, he and Benson were very different. G. A. Hollis, later Bishop of Taunton, lived at Pusey House before ordination. He remembered how Gore after preaching on Sunday evenings, often could not sleep. He came to Hollis' room, and the conversation always began 'Got any baccy? Bring some down and I'll read to you'. He produced an old pipe tied with string and sealing wax, and then read poetry, Burke's speeches and told funny stories. As he told story after story, Gore would gradually wriggle out of the chair on to the rug.

Criticism of what Benson and Cowley were thought to stand for has been a regular feature of c R's history. In 1904 Rackham went with members of s s j e to

Iona and lamented their custom of calling one another 'Father'. He hoped that CR would keep its practice of addressing one another by Christian names. In 1905 Cyril Bickersteth gave 'A Retrospect' to the brethren which included critical remarks about Cowley. Most of this passage was omitted because Gore was present. This particular omission, indicated by brackets in the manuscript and below, confirms the impression that some of the early brethren were more critical than Gore of SSJE.

Though Cowley commanded then as now our affection and respect and though we encouraged members of the S.R. to try their vocation with the S.S.J.E. yet we all felt that God was calling us to something at least a little different. [Amongst ourselves and in strict privacy it is fair to say that the future of Cowley was then very uncertain. Fr Benson the founder and first Superior apparently believed that their work was done; he was unwilling to profess any new members; and we knew of certain matters connected with the recall of Father Hall, now Bp of Vermont from America which made us shrink from a view of religious obedience which seemed inconsistent with the wholesome liberty of the individual conscience. The election of Fr Page as Superior and the subsequent changes of the SSJE as well as our own natural development have so far reduced the difference between us that we can scarcely realize how a certain dread of being like Cowley influenced our own early days.]

Despite Bickersteth's claim that a 'dread of being like Cowley' was now well past, it continued. Hubert Northcott, who represented the most austere strain within the Community, and who initially had wanted to go to SSJE, reviewed Benson's *The Religious Vocation* (*CRQ* JB 1939) and considered it very Tractarian. It conveyed, he wrote, an 'almost oppressive sense' that the eye of God was always upon us, and a belief that we had to be dead to the world which Benson regarded as a prison house. He traced Benson back to the Desert Fathers rather than to Thomas Aquinas, St Francis or St Teresa. Geoffrey Curtis was deeply devoted to Benson, but he included just about everyone in his eirenic embrace. An anecdote in the CR mythology relates how some CR brethren visited Cowley. Walking through part of the building which had frosted glass, a CR brother remarked 'What a pity you can't see into the garden, Father.' The Cowley Father retorted 'We haven't come here Father, just to look at the garden.' That this was still being retold at Mirfield in the 1950s indicates the continuing need of CR to define itself over against Cowley with expressions of world-affirmation. Underlying the story is perhaps also an uneasy conviction that there is truth in the charge that there is not much of the desert in the CR tradition.

When Gore returned from India for Easter 1890 after three months' absence, the gestation of the community could be resumed. However, Gore was, as always, busy with many other enterprises, including the preparation of new editions of *Lux Mundi*. Then he went off to Florence for part of the winter of 1890 to prepare his Bampton Lectures for Lent 1891 by which time William Carter was leaving and only Nash and John Carter remained. In August 1891 George Longridge and Cyril Bickersteth arrived to join them, only to find Gore had gone to Cromer. Once again Gore's absence at such a crucial moment suggests a less than whole-hearted commitment.

Cromer 30 August 1891

My dear Longridge and Bickersteth,
I cannot say how great a disappointment it is not to be in Oxford to welcome you. As it is, I have no doubt that the others will have told you all there is to tell. Our aim is simply 'Oratorian' not religious, at least at present. Besides the Resurrection Rule, we aim at saying the whole of the 119th Psalm (if we can), and making a daily half-hour meditation. Also, we do our own bedrooms, before Terce if possible. We do not talk before Terce and after Compline – nor before Sext for mere conversations' sake. We do not go out without leave except in the afternoon. This can always be asked, and is not needed for fixed engagements e.g. to preach or lecture. We aim at devoting our life to prayer, study, work. Thus you will arrange your lives so that what is not occupied by prayer or work or wholesome recreation, should be given to systematic study of Holy Scripture, Theology or studies conducing thereto. This is what we have attained hitherto. Whether in the future we are to go beyond this to vows of religion is a quite open question on which we may hope our minds may be formed by prayer. I will try to be with you at least in this.

Always, yours affectionately in the Lord,
Charles Gore

The wry joke in the last sentence suggests a prick of conscience. Frere's hopes of forming his own community in the East End had not materialized. In February 1892 he arrived at Pusey to test his vocation there.

On 29 March Gore delivered a lecture 'The Social Doctrine of the Sermon on the Mount' in St Paul's Chapter House, London. That Gore should offer the most substantial justification of religious communities he ever made in the context of an exposition of the vocation of CSU, and at one of its meetings, is highly significant. Gore said that in order that society should learn the principle of 'co-operation' rather than 'competition', Christian influence must be concentrated in 'definite Christian centres of moral opinion, where Christ's principles are simply acted upon'. He made three definite proposals: first that CSU should develop a new Christian casuistry for social problems, secondly that it should support those who lose their jobs because of adherence to Christian principles, and

> 3. We should do again what was done in the early monastic movement, as it is represented in St Basil's rule. We should draw together to centres, both in town and country, where men can frankly start afresh and live openly the common life of the first Christians . . . I desire to see formed . . . a community of celibate men, living simply, without other life-vows than those of their baptism or (if priests) of

their priesthood, the life of the first Christians: a life of combined labour, according to different gifts, on a strongly developed background of prayer and meditation, and with real community of goods . . . I have some experience such as warrants a belief that such an ideal might become real . . . such a community would surely be calculated to make men see how holy and happy a thing is Christian life when it can free itself from entanglements . . .

He also commended the Moravian pattern of companies of married people living by common rule. At present (Gore concluded) we are paying too much attention to the development of the outward side of worship. We try too much to 'get people to come to church'. The time has come for the church 'to put social morality, Christian living, in the forefront of its effort'. Thus Gore set the creation of CR in the context of social morality; a religious community should be a paradigm for the right ordering of society.

2

The First Decade

The Community at Pusey House

On St James' Day (25 July) 1892, Gore, Carter, Nash, Longridge, Bickersteth and Frere made their professions in Pusey House Chapel and so formed the Community of the Resurrection. Nash's personal history has already been told. But who were the other four founding members?

John Carter (1861–1944) was a dynamic Canadian who had attended Canada's oldest public school, Upper Canada College, Toronto. After taking a degree at Trinity College, Toronto, he came over to Exeter College Oxford, rowed for his College and graduated in 1887. He became a curate in Limehouse, then returned as assistant chaplain to Exeter 1890–5. Though he was the only one of the six to have come from outside the English social and educational system, he had been fully incorporated into it. A former treasurer and then Vice-President of the Oxford branch of GSM, from 1889–1910 he was Secretary of CSU, then Vice-President. Throughout the life of the CSU journal *The Economic Review* (1891–1914) he was its editor. Through his efforts a branch of CSU was established in the States in 1891. At the inception of CR Carter became its Bursar. He was Bursar of Pusey House until 1921.

In July 1897 Carter preached at Christ Church Cathedral on Acts 4.32, a text dear to CR, for the annual Sunday parade of the Oxford Benefit, Friendly and Trade Societies. He said that there had been many experiments like that described in Acts, but only those with strong religious roots had endured. Though only a few were called to practise the text literally, all Christians should realize that property must be used for 'the common welfare of all'. The newly enriched should learn the old tradition about the duty of giving from the landowners. The societies gathered there encouraged thrift and supported their members. Though the newspaper report of the sermon was headed 'Christian Communism' the message was derived from the *noblesse oblige* of Christian Toryism leavened with the voluntaryist self-help tradition of the older Liberalism. When in 1893 CR moved to Radley, Carter remained at Pusey. In 1894 he declined the offer of the bishopric of Central Africa but without consulting chapter. He continued as a member of CR until 1902 paying visits to Radley, then Mirfield, during vacations.

That Walter Howard Frere (1863–1938) came from an ancient family was obvious from his patrician mien.[1] Seven of his relations appear in the *Dictionary of National Biography*. His grandfather was the first Master, and his father was a fellow of Downing College, Cambridge. Walter Frere was left an orphan as a young boy. This experience reinforced his self-reliance, but also gave him a permanent sense of isolation. 'I sometimes think that being an orphan is liable to make you a bit impersonal' he once said. After preparatory school he went to Charterhouse. Bitter disputes between his guardians made the holidays unhappy and deepened his intense reticence. By contrast he enjoyed Charterhouse, a fact which probably quickened his attraction to community life. At Trinity College, Cambridge he blossomed, became secretary of the University Musical Society, sang, composed songs, learned German and French and went on to take a first in classics, followed by theology. He also developed a social conscience. Wells Theological College attracted him because it was not identified with ritualism. There began his disciplined life of prayer. He was ordained to a title at St Dunstan's Stepney in 1887 under Edwyn Hoskyns later Bishop of Southwell (father of E. C. Hoskyns), whose wife was a socialist in the William Morris tradition and a suffragist. In his district Frere began a ministry to the poor and pioneered a 9.30 a.m. Parish Communion, perhaps the first in England. Leisure hours were spent in the British Museum, and soon he made himself a master of the history of plainsong. Like his father he said the psalms in Hebrew.

Frere, having failed to create his own community, arrived at Pusey on 4 February 1892: 'I go to Oxford . . . to see what they are up to with their brotherhood.' The cool independence of this remark, like his letter to Gore of the previous October, showed he was not going to be daunted or dazzled by Gore. Frere's detachment from Gore was to be of crucial importance when Gore left CR in 1901 and Frere became Superior. He said he wanted to supply a Cambridge element to the undertaking (Frere had a realistic sense of his own independent worth) and that the parochial system needed to be supplemented. His Christian socialism drew him to a simple life: he said it was 'intolerable' for him to possess money, and gave almost all his patrimony to CR. As a historian he understood the immense contribution of Religious Orders to the life of the church. He wanted a disciplined life of worship and prayer, and as a liturgist knew how this should be shaped. He realized his imperious will needed mortification.

George Longridge (1857–1936) was the son of a civil engineer. His sixty years of friendship with Cyril Bickersteth began when they were at Eton together. After Oxford he was ordained in 1881 and went to Wantage as a curate to W. J. Butler, founder of the Community of St Mary the Virgin

(1848), later Dean of Lincoln. The Wantage clergy visited in cassocks and top hats. From 1886 Longridge was in charge of the parish of Grove, Berkshire until he went to Pusey in 1891. His elder brother, W. H. Longridge, joined SSJE and revived Ignatian spirituality in the Church of England. Longridge was a conservative influence in CR: 'so little disposed to hear and practise every new thing' Nash approvingly remarked. He seems to have been the only one of the six who was not a member of CSU.

Cyril Bickersteth (1858–1936) came from the church's leading evangelical clerical family.[2] Seventeen Bickersteths have been ordained since the eighteenth century. Four have become bishops. Cyril's father, Robert, began a life-long commitment to the evangelization of the working classes when rector of the squalid parish of St Giles in the Fields London, 1851–7. As second Bishop of Ripon (1857–84) he consecrated 157 new or rebuilt churches, including the one at Mirfield. Bickersteth, a convinced Evangelical did not believe that working people would be won by ceremonial, nor by liberal theology but by open-air preaching and simple services. Though he was committed to the urban poor he saw nothing incongruous in living in a rural Victorian palace with over twenty bedrooms in eighty-four acres of parkland. This is where Cyril grew up. After Eton and New College Cyril went, not to an Oxbridge theological college, but to Leeds Clergy School. After a curacy in All Saints Bradford 1882–4, he spent a year at All Hallows by the Tower, London, then went back north to be vicar of St Paul's, Pudsey 1885–8, then returned to All Hallows for a further three years. In 1882 Archbishop Benson had asked his old friend A. J. Mason to establish a college of preachers at All Hallows to work among the educated classes. There Bickersteth combined an experience of mission preaching with that of a clerical community. It was through CSU that Bickersteth got to know Gore, who (in his words) 'more than any other man helped us to connect liberal theology and social justice with the Creeds of the Church and the ethics of the Gospel'. When Cyril included in his *Who's Who* entry 'constantly engaged since 1889 in preaching missions' he showed that he was the true son of one whose biography he wrote with such filial devotion.

Thus all six foundation members of CR were bred in leading public schools and the Oxbridge tradition which confirmed their status as members of the governing class. Hensley Henson, brought up at the opposite end of the social scale, when he was an ordinand discussed with the rich aristocrat James Adderley how they should become Franciscans in the East End. But Henson had five poverty-stricken dependents: 'I am not rich enough to be poor' he commented caustically.[3] Longridge and Bickersteth had much more parochial experience than other members of the group, and both had been incumbents. Of the six only Bickersteth had real experience of the industrial north which was to be the setting for much of CR's future life.

The foundation of the Community as distinct from the Society might seem to mark a decisive change. But it is important not to make too much of the change from 'Society' to 'Community'. There was already the Society of St John the Evangelist. Soon there was to be the Society of the Sacred Mission. The term 'Community' was needed to distinguish it from SR of which it was still part. That Gore wanted a communal base for SR is not in doubt. But Gore had no intention of creating a traditional monastic community.

Richard Rackham lived as a layman at Pusey 1888–9 and acted as a research assistant to Gore. He took three firsts and was ordained in 1889 to serve a curacy under Robert Moberly (a contributor to *Lux Mundi*) at Great Budworth, Cheshire. Rackham was accepted as a probationer in April 1893 but did not join the brethren until October. Gore wrote to him encouraging him to come but declined to give him any orders: 'We are not monks . . . I cannot, as before God, who bids us not be called Rabbi, say to people *come & go*, as if I had authority to control their lives more or less absolutely.' Nor was there a common purse, he assured him: 'We at present do not aspire beyond practical community of such property as we can give to the Society from year to year – like the early Christians.' Gore refused the title 'Superior' given in the Rule, and was known as 'Senior'. The brethren called each other by their Christian names, a very unusual practice in male society at that time. But no one called, or referred to, Gore as 'Charles'. This seems to have been more a sign of their reverence for him than deference to his office. Was both his refusal of 'Superior' *and* his failure to encourage the brethren to use his Christian name another sign of his ambivalance? As a young man, his need to develop his own religious and political views had drawn him apart from most of his family. Avis has pointed out that he also seems to have isolated himself from direct theological influences except that of Newman, who, like Gore, ploughed 'a solitary furrow'. For Gore, CR was one of several enterprises. Frere, Bickersteth, Longridge and Nash had taken a decisive step and left their parishes. Gore, who had been at Pusey for eight years, largely continued his previous pattern of life. Carter had his job at Exeter College and was much preoccupied with promoting CSU. Gore made one new venture. In 1892 he took a teaching week at Walsall and clearly had the makings of a great missioner. But his self-depreciation and his fear of adulation overcame his desire to be in touch with ordinary people. He decided mission preaching lay outside his calling.

The Rule stated that CR consisted of celibate priests who 'combine together to reproduce the life of the first Christians' in Acts 2.42,44. They would be occupied in various works 'pastoral, evangelistic, literary, educational' in such ways as would develop the faculties of each member. The 'immediate worship and service of God' took first place. Community life involved 'some sacrifice of individual proclivities' and required 'unselfishness'. Each member 'must learn to merge himself in the Community. The work he is doing must be in his eyes the work of the Community done through him.' They recognized 'the Catholic and Apostolic Rule of Faith and discipline' as normative. After a probation of not less than twelve months, brethren joined the Community with life-long intention, but without 'positive obligation'. Each year they renewed their promise for thirteen months. Brethren were to attend the daily offices and eucharist, to use sacramental confession and to spend not less than two hours a week in meditation. Each brother 'shall seek to have the fewest and simplest wants that are consistent with health and the needs of his work'. He would retain control of his capital, but pay all income into a common fund. His personal needs would be provided by the Community. 'Nothing shall be finally required of any of the brethren which violates his conscience. None of the brethren shall be allowed to abrogate his liberty of leaving the community at the end of the period covered by his annual pledge.' They were to be resident in a Community house except when away on work or on holiday.

The Rule thus struck a careful balance between what was needed to nourish communal life and the needs and rights of its individual members. Brethren wore no habit. They wore cassocks in the house, suits outside. Nor did Gore want them to be known as 'Father'. Matthew 23.1–12 guided Gore's thinking about CR. Bickersteth in his 1905 'Retrospect' said that their experience of attempts at community life in clergy houses had made them realize that something more cohesive than an Oratorian system was needed. The adoption of a common purse was a decisive step. 'To this we were led not only by the wish to make real the vow of poverty but by the strong leaven of Christian Socialism which made us long to reproduce the life of the early Christians described in Acts 4.32.' Some stressed the Religious Life as a vocation. Others felt drawn to it because it was 'the ideal background' for their work. Both were provided for in the Rule.

Frere's diary for 1892–5 reveals how loosely knit CR was in its early days, his dissatisfaction with this and his growing criticism of Gore's lack of total commitment. But he poured out his gratitude to God: 'Things looked dark enough when I was torn away from Stepney . . . But now Thou hast set my feet in a large Room: this is all beyond my best hopes.' However, he firmly believed they should not remain in Oxford. A week after the foundation they all dispersed for holidays until the beginning of September. Frere went with his sister Lucy and another lady to Germany where at Bayreuth they enjoyed 'Parsifal' and 'Tristan', and he worked on manuscripts in various libraries. In October, Longridge, whom Frere more and more appreciated, sailed to Calcutta to help OMC for two years. 'It seems a pity just as we start but I suppose is right.' Frere noted about the Community retreat at Malvern: 'CG not very good to my mind. Beautiful but not practical nor to me helpful.' Though Frere was now seriously beginning his edition of the Sarum Gradual, he was mainly engaged in parish missions. At the Charterhouse Mission he wrote: 'Happy at the real work in the very bosom of poverty.' W. L. Vyvyan, the priest there (later Bishop of Zululand) was 'a real Evangelical Catholic', a combination Frere always commended. Visiting St Peter's London Docks (where the well-known Fr Wainwright was vicar) he noted 'Papistical and pauperizing and no discipline as to Baptisms etc. Clergy Ho. very much anyhow and little or no common life.'

It became clear that Pusey House was not a suitable setting for CR to develop its life. Nor was it beneficial to the House to have two distinct groups of people in the same institution presided over by a Principal who was also a Superior. Gore had now been based in Oxford for over twenty years, so his ties were strong. But the furore over *Lux Mundi* had shaken him. The vicar of the University Church still banned him from preaching there. Sometimes he also felt suffocated by the devotion of his disciples. He felt he had little energy to write, read or think as he was continuously in demand. As early as 1891 he told E. S. Talbot that the brethren were not finding Oxford conducive. Gore and most of the brethren had then thought that they ought to move to a northern working class parish – perhaps Bradford which Bickersteth knew well. At the beginning of 1893 Gore decided he should resign. Gore considered a rural parish, though Talbot (now vicar of Leeds) and Coles (who had been a country priest for twelve years) doubted the wisdom of this. Perhaps Gore was influenced by Illingworth's life at Longworth? Frere wrote in his diary with asperity: 'All depended on CG's position at PH and suddenly he who had felt the difficulty of going to a town came out with a clear decision that he must leave and go into the country and get peace to read.' Gore received several suggestions of parishes – East London, Bradford, Lincolnshire, Goldthorpe (near Doncaster). Gore's mother described his decision to leave Pusey as 'a very pleasant startle' and was in favour of his going to a parish, but she was justifiably worried at the thought of his being hidden away and dependent only on the society of five other men. His father was glad he was leaving Pusey but was deeply concerned that a four year withdrawal would cause his enemies to 'crow' at his 'sudden eclipse'; afterwards he would find it difficult to return to the public scene again. Neither parent mentioned the needs of the Community and regarded the decision solely in the light of Gore's personal needs. Perhaps that is how he presented it to them. At last in May, with the agreement of the brethren, Gore accepted the living of Radley, five miles south of Oxford. The patron was Radley College, a Tractarian foundation. Bickersteth wrote to Rackham that Gore was looking forward to leisure for reading and needed his help. They hoped to move north in two or three years time. Frere noted rather mordantly that the arrangements for the move had devolved on him, but at least Radley would be a better centre for CR in most ways, and was near Oxford which was essential for Gore. The July Quiet Time which was supposed to cement community life was disrupted by Carter being called away on family business to Canada and Gore's external engagements.

Gore did not leave Oxford quietly. Tom Mann, a leader of the Dock Strike and a founding member of the Social Democratic Federation had been invited to Oxford to explain trade unionism. Gore believed that undergraduates should have the opportunity to hear 'the other side' and chaired the meeting which was held in Exeter College where Carter ministered. Stubbs, Bishop of Oxford, expressed his disapproval, adding that he did not think that Gore was aware of 'the terrible effect' his teaching about biblical criticism was having. Nevertheless he ended 'With best love, yours ever'. Alarmed, Gore asked the bishop whether they would still be welcome at Radley. Stubbs replied that they would, but reiterated his strong criticisms. The new Principal, R. L. Ottley, a contributor to *Lux Mundi*, was shocked by the meeting, and at first wanted Carter to move from the House. But he became reconciled to his continuing residence despite his propaganda work for c s u.

After only a year's existence there were obvious tensions within c r. The majority had wanted to move to a northern industrial town, but Gore decided he needed a rural parish; he and Carter wanted to be near Oxford. Indeed Carter urged that after two or three years, c r should move back to Oxford again. Was it right that Gore's personal needs should so determine the life of the Community? Allowing Carter to remain at Pusey for much of the year weakened communal life, but helped c s u. How far should c r's life be determined by the needs of c s u? In addition, Longridge was going to Calcutta. Should brethren be allowed to go on detached service when there had been so much talk of the need for community? Or was c r to be simply a base camp to which brethren returned between external assignments? Carter's strong commitment to a political expression of Christianity was to be the main factor in his leaving c r in 1902. How far was c r committed to a political Christianity?[4] Frere's doubts about Gore's leadership were already evident. And how would Gore cope deprived of the stimulating life of Oxford after twenty-two years? How would he deal with a rural parish? Would the move enable him to commit himself totally to the Community?

Gore gave a farewell gift to Trinity College Chapel: a new altar cloth of orange-red stamped velvet, a more cheerful colour than the sombre violet which Pusey had proposed for the one at St Saviour's Leeds.

Radley

In prospect Radley seemed admirably suited to Gore's personal needs. However the vicarage could only just accommodate the existing brethren and the couple who looked after them, and there was no space for new recruits. Estimates were obtained for building on a library to free more living space. However, they all thought of Radley as only a temporary resting place. The vicarage consisted of two parts 'connected by a very imperfect join' (in Gore's words): the original timber-framed vicarage, parts of which dated from the thirteenth century, and a new section built 1868/9 in russet coloured brick. (The combined parts served until 1988 when the two were separated and the mediaeval section became the new vicarage.) There were eight bedrooms; five rooms served as dining room, studies, library and living room. It was set in just over an acre of garden. Next door is the parish church of St James (parts of which date from the fourteenth century). The population of the parish was 500. Since the net annual income was only £50, this allowed Gore to retain his Trinity fellowship. Radley station was nearby. In the 1890s the roads south out of Oxford (its population then only 45,000) led quickly into open country, so Radley felt quite isolated. Today the population of Radley is over 6,500 and ring roads and dual carriage-ways bisect the whole area.

The Community moved to Radley during the first week of August, and then brethren dispersed for a month's holiday. Gore was inducted on 21 September 1893. For the previous twenty-five years the Wardens of Radley College had also been vicars of Radley. The Archdeacon of Berkshire told the congregation that small parishes were often very difficult because the people looked on the priest as little more than 'a kindly gentleman', forgetting that he was concerned for their eternal souls. The people no doubt recalled John Radcliffe (incumbent 1807–52) who had lived latterly in Oxford, travelled to Radley on foot, but paused on the way for a pipe of tobacco, so the congregation never knew when he would arrive.

The *Manchester Guardian* reported the move, and hoped that under Gore's leadership, the group, which combined great intellectual distinction and the experience of the hard realities of the East End, would be able to provide help in tackling the difficult social and other problems of the day. Longridge left for Calcutta in October. To Gore's particular delight, Rackham was admitted as a probationer (as novices were then called) that month. Carter came from Oxford for Friday evening discussions and for part of the vacations. The original intention was that Gore and Rackham would look after the parish while the others continued their external work. But Radley was (as Nash noted) 'a damp spot' and Rackham had to leave Radley for two periods because of asthma, but it improved when he slept in the attic bedroom.

Gore was now forty, a few years older than the other brethren. He took his new duties with intense seriousness. He had never even served a normal curacy let alone been an incumbent before. Three weeks after the induction he wrote to his friend Tremenheere 'Pray for a country parson who feels "good intentions" but is terribly at sea.' He trained the choir, visited assiduously, inaugurated a Rogationtide procession round the village, preached on the village green, formed a village band, and made friends with Radley College. He found it hard to adapt his sermons to a village congregation. If a labourer got drunk he felt personally responsible. He poured out his bewilderment to the Bishop of Oxford in a letter of several pages only to receive a terse reply on a postcard 'My dear Gore, don't be a bore.' The bishop's response was a painful exposure of his own naivety and inexperience. He often retold the incident as a funny story, but his humour was frequently a cover for an inner desperation. Walter Carey said of Gore:

'his standards were so high, his moral innocence and rectitude so lofty, that we ordinary, stupid and faulty persons felt almost scared'.

Twenty years ago there were still a few parishioners who remembered Gore: 'he were a funny one, Mr Gore' was the general impression. Gore's extraordinarily savage humour expressed his intense frustration. He dandled a child on his knee and asked 'What would you say if I cut off your head?' Gore visiting another house asked if the father used his razor strop on the boy. He told the squire's daughter-in-law that Radley was the most immoral place he had ever known. Adam Fox, Canon of Westminster Abbey and from 1918–24 Warden of Radley College, regularly revisited Radley and always ended his stories about Gore 'strange man, strange man!'

Gore believed that the church should be a totally committed remnant, 'salt' rather than 'leaven' he said in the discussion after his lecture 'The Social Doctrine of the Sermon on the Mount'. He seemed unaware that many laypeople have an understanding of Christianity quite different from that of the clergy and a capacity to survive clerical enthusiasms and eccentricities with detached amusement. After only three months at Radley, Gore broke down. He left on 23 December and was ordered abroad for two or three months. He went home to Wimbledon before setting off for Spain and Tangier. He wrote to Talbot that it was probably 'a dire mistake coming to a country parish . . . The responsibilities of a country parish are to me at present crushing and its refreshments not great.' Yet he had only 500 people to look after and plenty of clerical support and help. Rackham's absence through illness depressed him and hampered his studies. He felt drained and empty, intellectually and spiritually. He returned to Radley on 7 March 1894, but Frere noted that his health was still 'disappointingly precarious'. On Good Friday Gore preached at a sparsely attended Three Hours' Service. He quoted from Frederick Myers' *St Paul*:

> Desperate tides of the whole great world's anguish
> Forced thro' the channels of a single heart.

Probably the lines expressed his own anguish. Soon after, the churchwardens came to supper. Gore anxiously discussed with them the irregularity of church attendance, but expressed his pleasure at the number of farm workers in church on Good Friday. Of course they came then, they replied, we paid them to. Gore was obviously unaware that it was a common custom for churchgoing farmers to pay wages for Good Friday to those who attended church that day. What to the farmers was a generous gesture for the good of the church, to Gore was a bribe which secured an externally motivated observance, a betrayal of all that Gore believed about the church. Without any real knowledge of either ordinary people or parishes, Gore was now enmeshed in the parochial tangle of religious and moral compromises, formed over centuries, against which his high principles and hypersensitive nature revolted. Not surprisingly the people of Radley were totally unwilling to become the kind of Third Order Gore expected Christian laypeople to be, and certainly not after a few months experience of an extremely uncomfortable incumbent.[5]

At the beginning of May Gore broke down again. This time he was ordered abroad for six months. While he was away Nash looked after the parish. 'Senior worse and worse' Frere wrote in his diary; 'decide he must give up the parish . . . we accept the position as best we can. It is a great blow.' He then quoted in Greek from the opening chorus of the *Agamemnon*: 'Cry woe, woe, but let the good prevail.' The use of this refrain by Frere, the least histrionic of characters, reveals how large and deep he felt Gore's unfolding tragedy to be. Meticulously sensitive as Frere was to the nuances of texts, it seems probable that he was making a shorthand comparison between Gore and Agamemnon, who though every inch a king, resented compromises and suffered from a lack of confidence in his own authority.

When the Community gathered for July Chapter, Frere noted Gore's absence as 'disappointing in one way', but that it had enabled them 'to have very free discussions, talk out many points of difference and do really a good deal at revising and adding to our ways and rule'. Paul Bull and Thomas Barnes were admitted as probationers. Abroad Gore's health improved but it was not until September that he was able to study again. In October he was able to attend the s R Retreat at St Aidan's Birkenhead, but Frere commented 'Senior seems better . . . but overdone again there alas, alas!' Gore did not return into residence until the end of November. Earlier that month he had declined the suggestion of the Deanery of Winchester. He was now greatly attracted by the offer of a canonry at Westminster. He could do useful work (he contended) and it would be a good centre for C R. A special Chapter was called for 29 November to consider this proposal which seemed so natural to Gore, but to the brethren was startling in its implications. After fifteen months at Radley, to which they had gone to meet Gore's special needs, those needs were now to take him away and to split into two the tiny Community of six (one of whom resided at Oxford) and three probationers. Already there were few occasions when all the brethren were together, apart from a total of about six weeks when everyone had to be resident.

On 24 November Frere, in the middle of a mission, wrote to Rackham that he grieved deeply that he differed so much from the others:

I *gravely doubt* its being the best thing for the Senior: he would soon be in the middle of another whirl worse than the Pusey House whirl without either health or leisure for reading, and the Church at large would be all the poorer. It is also because I regard the Radley life as at present so very unsatisfactory: the parish without a head and the centre of the Community without its Senior. Our past year has I trust done us good in making us see our shortcomings and also in making us move a little on our own initiative in the Senior's absence: but what we want above all I think for this next year is to have the Senior at home quietly reading and pulling all our life together a good deal more than it is at present, identifying himself much more with the Community than he has been able to do so far, while meantime the parish work is reorganized under a permanent Vicar. It is of course an immense gain to the Community to have a commanding figure at its head but it may pay too dearly for the privilege. Your comparison ('like Mason at Barking') makes me shudder: that is exactly what I dread above everything. If we are to be a Community we must be something very different to 'a number of young priests living with a distinguished Canon'. That is *ruin* to all that I at least have ever hoped for from the Community.

He wrote again to Rackham on 27 November. Frere assured him that he was not suggesting that Gore should be 'shut up all the year at Radley', but that it was better for him and the Community that he should emerge from time to time from 'rustic seclusion' than be located in London. 'I cannot think a mere *3 months' residence* satisfactory either from the Abbey's or his point of view.' It would be more satisfactory for him to free-lance from 'a quiet centre'. Radley was not an ideal centre, particularly as regards climate, but it was an admirable out-of-the-way place, near to Oxford and London, (Gore's 'main spheres of usefulness') until the Community moved north. Gore needed both 'activity and retirement' which he would get in Radley if someone took over the parish, whereas Westminster would 'annihilate' retirement. He wrote in another letter (to Gore?) that the canonry might break up the Community. 'We aren't strong enough to survive such prelatical splendour: poverty and obscurity are what we want: and really Westminster Abbey is enough to stifle any one's religion.' In deep gloom Frere described the Chapter meeting of 29 November in his diary:

Rather painful as I felt bound to make a protest (alone though not without some sympathy) against accepting Westminster as (i) unsuitable action for a community especially a nascent one therefore more perilous (ii) retrograde for us who desire the development of a stricter and poorer house than Radley and an opening for real parish work among the poor. However everyone agreed and the Senior was absolutely clear as to its being his duty. 'Cry woe, woe, but let the good prevail.' [trans.] Decided to nominate James for the Vicarage . . . I feel very keenly that the acceptance of Westminster is the victory of the laxer view of the Community and the postponement of all realization of what some feel called to. Again shall we stand the publicity and position? At present it seems the Senior's vocation v. the Community's. God grant that events do not prove us to have made a great mistake.

Frere's judgment that after only two years there was a fundamental clash between the Community's vocation and that of its Founder and Superior was as true as it was devastating.

When Longridge returned from Calcutta after two years' absence, Frere felt he had an ally in Chapter: 'quite a rallying up on behalf of the stricter side'. He also noted: 'Senior a lot better and looking eagerly forward to Westminster'. Frere had lost his first battle for a stricter and more communal life. He had stood up courageously against Gore and dared to tell him (and the brethren) what he thought Gore needed and what CR needed from Gore. Paradoxically, when Gore became sidelined and preoccupied at Westminster, space was created for Frere's leadership to emerge. Meanwhile during the post-Christmas residence the brethren enjoyed skating together during a great frost.

What caused Gore's prolonged breakdown, with its dramatic consequences both for himself and CR, and which moved Frere to employ the language of Greek tragedy? Prestige ascribes it almost entirely to the pressures of being a country incumbent, but does not probe very deeply. Frere's diary, of course, was not available to him. John Gore pointed out how often Gore was ill and commented 'His constitution was at no time strong, and I doubt whether from his undergraduate days onwards he ever enjoyed for two consecutive days that state which a robust man calls "feeling fit".' Friends noted 'the extraordinary improvement in his health after his first few years as a bishop, the increased ease, the returned serenity'. On the other hand, when Rackham died in 1912 Gore (by then Bishop of Oxford) wrote that he was himself so worn out that he envied him.

Certainly Gore felt trapped by Radley. He seems to have had a deep dread of becoming a trapped victim throughout his life. 'I feel like a fish out of water with a weight on him' he wrote to Talbot; it was 'really humiliating'. Parishioners' accounts of Gore's sadistic fantasies (reminiscent of Hoffmann's *Cautionary Tales* which so terrified Victorian children) suggest someone not simply out of his depth, but at the end of his tether. Recourse to sadistic humour or doleful savaging ('I hate the Church of England') was usually a sign that he was under pressure. Prestige recounts how as a bishop he terrified some vicarage children by acting as an ogre. On another occasion walking in the street he stopped a totally unknown girl of five or six hand-in-hand with her tiny brother. Gore, taking hold of the boy's ears, asked 'Now shall I twist his head round till it comes off?' One morning he woke with this gruesome stanza in his head:

> We are all minced into a mince,
>   From lesser unto lesser grow;
> And pass into a finer sense
>   Of that which we are minced into.

There was a dark, angry, vindictive side to Gore which always forced itself to the surface when under strain.[6]

However much he hated adulation, for over twenty years he had been supported by friends and work in Oxford. This was now removed. In Wimbledon and Oxford (and again at Westminster) he enjoyed freedom, style, space, stimulus. But in Radley his study was dark and claustrophobic. The vicarage was crowded with people. There was no longer a college or bookshop nearby to which he could escape, or the freedom of vacations to which he could look forward. Gore related best to small groups and individuals of intellectual calibre. He was always happiest when in a minority. At Radley he had to minister to an unintellectual generality. He shyed away from close emotional ties. He did not know how to respond to Holland's uninhibited expressions of affection. He was deeply attached to his brother and sister-in-law, Sir Francis and Lady Gore. But Lady Gore used to tease him that if he arrived and the butler told him that she had died, he would walk away unmoved. In CR photographs everyone looks at the camera except Gore who almost always presents a profile staring into the distance; maybe it was because of his weak eyes, but it suggests detachment. Radley parish registers show that he never baptized anyone and took only one funeral.

In Radley for the first time he was confronted by Anglican lay religion which is largely implicit and unarticulated and for which the church (as Gore understood it) is tangential, even dispensable for much of the time. During his breakdown he wrote to Rackham that he was very bad at discovering what people meant unless they were prepared to articulate it plainly. But the average parishioner, especially in rural areas and with a new incumbent, likes to keep a distance, to keep the priest guessing.

> Priests have a long way to go.
> The people wait for them to come
> To them over the broken glass
> Of their vows, making them pay
> With their sweat's coinage for their correction.

So wrote R. S. Thomas out of his experience as a priest in rural Wales. Gore had longed that he and the church should be in vital contact with ordinary people. But when he made an act of kenosis and left Oxford and took on the form of a servant, kenosis broke him. Twenty-five years later he still spoke of his time at Radley as the unhappiest year of his life.

Did he also feel trapped by the Community he had called into being? Those with Gore's temperament often start a venture with enthusiasm, then draw back fearing to be taken over by it; needing yet dreading relationships, they are chronic withdrawers and non-joiners. Antony Grant, the present Prior of Mirfield, has written of 'that strong attraction to community life that too often draws people who are self-isolating, lonely and passionate' (*CRQ* MD 1986). That might be a description of Gore. CR was asking leadership from him.

When he said that it would be 'quite unendurable' to be called 'Superior', and was diffident about giving direction, were these really signs of humility and of a belief in democratic government? When he became a bishop he had no difficulty exercising leadership in an authoritative, even authoritarian, manner. But by then he was on his own, no longer an uneasy first among equals. No Superior could exercise a decisive role in the development of CR from a branch house, on the side-lines, where Gore had (frankly) more interesting things to do than to look after a Community, most of which was elsewhere and which increasingly shaped its life without him. Whether he realized it or not, going to Westminster was an honourable way of finding a seat near the exit – and the door was much more likely to open to set him free in Westminster than at Radley. We should remember that in his nine years of membership, he lived with the whole Community continuously for only about fourteen months (eleven months at Pusey and three months at Radley).

It was becoming clear that CR was not going to continue as a loosely-knit group. Nor was it going to be like a prolonged Holy Party. Several of the brethren – Nash, Bickersteth, Bull, and others who joined in Gore's time – were essentially parish priests and missioners. Frere certainly was an academic – but Gore was uninterested in Frere's world of liturgical scholarship. Gore was emotional, prophetic, often deeply troubled by the paradoxes of experience and the evil of humanity. At Radley, Frere and Rackham used to tease him about his pessimistic moods. Frere did not agonize but dispassionately planned the next step. Frere wanted a disciplined *community* committed to the poor. Through his round of missions Frere was in touch with those ordinary people whom Gore found so problematic. Frere was a Community man. Gore had discovered painfully that he was not. Frere returned happily to Mirfield after being Bishop of Truro. Gore lived on his own in London after his Oxford episcopate; his position as a prelate brother gave him both the degree of attachment to, and the degree of distance from, CR that he required. Gore knew how to charm, amuse and fascinate. But Frere shrank from anything which might draw people to himself.

We now have access to two exceedingly frank estimates of Gore by Frere (we can only guess what Gore would have written about Frere). In 1931 when Albert Mansbridge was preparing a book about Gore he asked for Frere's help. Frere suggested he should contact Bickersteth instead, and wrote of Gore:

> . . . much as I love him I have never yet been able to understand him. I do not think I have ever been quite at ease with him or he with me, though our relations have always been exceedingly cordial and affectionate. He has always been a good deal of a puzzle to me and to tell the honest truth continually also a disappointment. I expect the bottom of it is that his special gift is to a large extent that of a personal fascination, wholly consecrated to God and with immense power and value to those who come under it. But I've not been one of those; you see my difficulty.

When Prestige asked for Frere's help in writing his biography, Frere's reply (13 March 1934) was too devastating for Prestige to print. Gore's capacity to arouse turbulent emotions in Frere, even thirty or more years after they had ceased to be colleagues, is clear from Frere's asperity of tone and awkwardness of style:

> I am afraid you must not look to me as a source of the Gore tradition, it is an awkward thing to write about but here it is. For though circumstances brought us very close together we were never at all intimate or even rarely sympathetic. There was of course a Gore tradition and cult, but I was never inside it; he was very reticent I think to everybody, though probably less so to people who were more naturally in sympathy than we were. I was unattracted and bored with the sermon and so on; but generally wishing that it [blank] rather than what it was, to say the least. As time went on I don't think we got any nearer, but rather less so . . . I don't know anything about his young days . . . George Russell was I suppose at school with him and therefore the story might have whatever authority attaches to that quarter. And so on with other questions which you might ask, I am really not supposed to answer them. Though we were the best of friends our outlooks were quite different, and neither one I think understood the other. I am sorry to be so negative, but there it is. Sometimes I think it is a very Oxfordy business, and I am deeply engrained the other way, and all the Oxford cult and mutual admiration always have repelled me. Sometimes I try and discover another reason, all is chasm in one or other more personal or blameworthy kind; but I never get a real answer. I suppose I come back to merely thinking that its one of the natural unaffinities of life. In that sense it may have been a good thing, but I am afraid its no help to you as a biographer. I am glad Cyril Bickersteth has been to see you, he is much more in the line of the real cult, than I ever have been or could be.

What did Frere mean by 'sometimes I think it is a very Oxfordy business, and I am deeply engrained the other way . . . '?

Gore's appointment to the Abbey was announced on 7 December 1894, and was widely welcomed, though conservatives recalled *Lux Mundi* and were discomforted. He was installed on 16 January 1895 but extensive repairs were needed on the house at 4 Little Cloister so accommodation initially was limited. Frere and Bickersteth lodged there on and off from February. But it was not until December that it was officially opened as a Community house. On the eve of the first Sunday in Advent Gore blessed and censed the altar and the vestments in the Oratory which had been created in the house. The eucharist was celebrated there for the first time next day, 1 December. The Dean allowed weekday eucharists there when there was no early celebration in the Abbey. Those chosen to reside were Rackham, Gore's literary assistant (Westminster was also better for his health) and, ironically, Frere himself. No doubt Westminster was convenient for Frere's researches. Did Gore also think it was prudent to have the Superior-in-waiting at Westminster with him rather than at Radley? Other brethren seem to have resided for short periods, but only Gore and Rackham appear to have been resident throughout the seven years of the House's existence.

When the Community gathered for Chapter it was to Radley they all came. As numbers grew, some had to sleep at a neighbouring farm house. In addition there were usually two or three young men preparing for ordination who came for a year or so and joined in the life of the Community. They lodged with Dr E. G. Monk, formerly organist at York Minster and before that precentor at Radley College. Thus began what was to develop into one of CR's major works – the training of ordinands. To the village they were known as 'The Young Gentlemen', to CR as 'YGs'. One of the first two who arrived from New College in June 1895 was J. M. C. Crum, later Canon of Canterbury, a savage and public opponent of 'The Red Dean' and the author of the haunting Easter hymn 'Now the green blade riseth'. He wrote an account (now at Mirfield) of life at Radley for the memoir of Walter Frere. To Crum, Gore seemed a latter-day Anselm. And though the other brethren were younger, to Crum just down from Oxford, they seemed weather-beaten by parochial experience. They were bound together in a unity yet each was entirely unlike the others; each seemed something of a specialist. Radley was a peaceful place after strenuous parish missions. It gave particular pleasure to one brother that part of the vicarage was pre-Reformation.

> A Vicarage with a garden from which a former vicar had issued, it was asserted, with a rose in his button-hole every day of the year. There was the garden and lawns and birds and great old elm trees and walks, one towards the River with wide water meadows looking across the Thames to Nuneham woods, and the other way lay Radley College and the cricket grounds and oaktrees . . . And Abingdon lay down stream and Oxford upstream and the country was then unspoiled: not a bungalow between Radley and Oxford. So it was a place of farmyard sounds, in early morning, cockcrows and turkey gobbles and a milk separator machine . . . and Berkshire accents everywhere.

Frere made a deep impression on Crum: his conversational style of preaching; his unconventional churchmanship which led him to praise the papacy one minute and the next challenge some accepted custom as not really Catholic; his immense liturgical scholarship; his readiness to sit down at the piano and sing English ballads or German Lieder. Sometimes Gore lectured to the YGs, or would read to them from the English poets or from 'The Little Flowers of St Francis' translating from the Italian as he went along. At Christmas, lads from the village came as Mummers to present the Berkshire version of St George and the Dragon, and clad in wallpaper, fought spirited battles with wooden swords.

A very different perspective on Radley was provided by a Frenchman, Charles Hermeline, whom Frere and Nash had met by chance in Chartres in June 1894 (*CRQ* JB 1980). Frere had spent a fortnight working in libraries in Le

Havre, Rouen and Paris, and meeting French clergy, including Louis Duchesne, the church historian. Frere then met Nash at Chartres and cycled round the Loire visiting Solesmes and other places of interest. In 1897 Hermeline, invited by Frere and Nash, spent a day at Radley. The following year he published an account of his travels to several European countries. Radley must have made a great impression for he devoted nine pages to it. He was puzzled why this group of 'ministres protestants' who were so catholic did not convert. They were attempting to revive the monastic life, were celibate, observed the offices and ate in the refectory under a statue of the Virgin. The newly erected crosses in the graveyard, the Community's use of Gregorian chant and familiarity with continental theology, the Lent and parish missions all created the atmosphere of a Catholic country.

The Community offered its daily worship in the church from finely carved seventeenth-century German choir stalls with miserichords: 6.45 Mattins, 7.15 Eucharist, 8.45 Terce, 1.10 Sext, 4.15 None, 7 Evensong, 9.45 Compline. That Chapter had to prohibit the wearing of greatcoats over surplices indicates that the church was often perishingly cold and damp. Lights were extinguished after Compline, but a brother was permitted to bring his candle down to the library or parlour for reading. Silence was kept in the house until after Sext. Brethren were expected to make their own beds. In July 1895 the Tuesday eucharist became a commemoration of the resurrection, a custom which continued until recently. A special collect was drawn up and used daily from August 1895. It reached its final form in May 1896:

> Almighty and everlasting God who didst form thy Church to be of one heart and soul in the power of the Resurrection and the fellowship of the Holy Ghost, renew her evermore in her first love; and grant such a measure thereof to the Brethren of the Resurrection, that their life may be hallowed, their way directed and their work made fruitful to the good of thy Church and the glory of thy Holy Name . . .

In May 1896 a censer and set of linen vestments were purchased and in September a High Mass was celebrated on Tuesdays during Quiet Time. Nothing was to be said audibly at the eucharist which was not in the Prayer Book. From November 1894 the prayers for the Royal Family were omitted at evensong – an Anglo-Catholic gesture against erastianism. The recently published Revised Version of the Bible was adopted for weekday lessons from October 1893. There were some divisions of opinion: for example a few were in favour of the invocation of saints, but the majority was against it.

Steps were taken to consolidate community life. A form of training for probationers was established. They were to be instructed in the spiritual aims and methods of CR as expressed in the Rule, in theology and for their own particular type of work. They were to pay over whatever income they had into the common fund. If one left, the amount would be returned to him, less a deduction for the cost of his stay. Except in the case of previously agreed personal obligations, the allocation of the income of each brother rested with Chapter. It was decided to give one quarter of Community income to charity. So up to £2 was given to the postman for the purchase of a tricycle, donations were made to locked out quarry-men and to victims of a famine in India. An ordination candidates' fund was created. The church at that time made no systematic provision to meet costs of training either at national or diocesan level. It was a struggle to maintain community fellowship with so many away on missions and other work. In 1896 it was decided that each brother should be resident for at least sixteen weeks annually. Two annual periods of communal residence were devoted to discussion of Community business and the study of theological, social and political issues.

The Radley parish magazine, which first appeared in January 1895, provides vignettes of parochial and CR life. The first issue included Gore's farewell letter:

> Nothing would have surprised me more than if anyone had told me in the autumn of last year that before this Christmas I should have resigned the benefice of Radley. But I found out that, however strong I may hope to be, I could not really manage to work the parish and attend also to the other work which I have and which I cannot get rid of . . . It is a great comfort to me to feel that I shall be living with the community at the Vicarage a great part of the year.

He warmly commended Nash, his successor, to the people. (As it turned out, Gore did not spend much time at Radley apart from the statutory periods.) Parishioners were also told that there had been seventy Christmas communicants. A flood had made many of the houses very damp, so the village children had suffered from chills. Mrs Dockar Drysdale (the 'squiress' Nash called her privately) had donated coals to dry out the cottages. A Radley master had given a lantern lecture on the 'Struggle for Existence' and the 'Origin of Species'. Sermons and lantern lectures had publicized the Zululand mission (whose Bishop, William Carter, was a member of SR). John Carter had accompanied the college servants' concert on the piano. In the next issue, Nash delivered what was to be his constant message: the importance of regular Communion and the need for earnest preparation for it through Confirmation (which he advocated at the then early age of twelve). A paragraph detailing various CR activities referred to the brethren as 'Mr Gore', 'Mr Longridge', 'Mr Bickersteth', etc. At the New Year's Day Social, when the band got tired, Frere and Carter took over and accompanied the dancing. To judge from the magazine, there was nothing 'advanced' about Nash's churchmanship. No doubt the villagers kept clear of CR services when vestments were worn and incense used, though on Maundy Thursday the parish was invited to Stations of the Cross and Nash encouraged the marking of graves with wooden crosses.

He hoped that in years to come Communion would become the main service of the day though he did not abandon Mattins. In July he announced prayers for rain and (contrary to the High Church tradition) encouraged girls to join the choir. He urged people to repent but never mentioned the sacrament of confession or commended fasting attendance at Communion. There were none of those Anglo-Catholic question and answer columns explaining ritual practices. He lamented the failure of men and boys to come to Communion in rural areas. There had been ninety-four Easter communicants in 1896 including college servants 'but not a single lad or young man from the village – none of those confirmed last year'. 'We *must* break this bad custom . . . Why do men not come?' It is significant that even in a parish staffed by skilled mission priests, young men still regarded Confirmation as a leaving ceremony.[7] In April 1897 CR organized a gathering of rural clergy at Radley College for worship, study and discussion. Nash was also concerned about drunkenness at the Radley Feast and he and Bickersteth preached total abstinence on Temperance Sunday.

If there was no Anglo-Catholic teaching in the magazine, neither were there any signs of Christian socialism. Religion appears as a blessing for the *status quo*, yet Nash had been a member of GSM. Mrs Dockar Drysdale is regularly thanked for gifts of blankets and tobacco for cottagers, equipment for the school and for presiding at various social functions. A branch of the National Agricultural Union was formed in Abingdon and Mr Dockar Drysdale presided at meetings. (Far from being a trade union it was created by the Earl of Winchelsea and was supported by farmers who hoped it would pacify the labourers.) It was commended in the magazine because it aimed at 'uniting all classes on the land for a common end'. The Queen's Jubilee was celebrated fulsomely: 'Probably England is the happiest land on earth.' A commemorative bell was added to the peal and Mrs Dockar Drysdale invited the whole village to the Hall for supper and entertainments. All these events showed the Church of England in its traditional role as the provider of social glue and supporter of class deference. But one might have expected some note, even mild, of dissent from the *status quo* from a Community so intimately connected with the CSU and from priests so lately from inner city parishes, though groups of boys from poor parishes in the East End did come to stay from time to time.

Thirty years later, Nash recalled the years at Radley as 'a peaceful happy time which served the purpose of gradually consolidating us and clearing our vision'. Certainly Nash thoroughly enjoyed looking after the people and daily instructing the seventy children in the church school. Crum wrote: 'James loved these speakers of the Berkshire dialect, men and lads and children: he could be anxious as a hen over her chickens: yet it is his laugh that I best remember about him: when children made astonishing use of pronouns "Us never touched he" when a child was crying and he came in as peace-maker . . .'

Many CR missions were in urban areas, but Mrs Illingworth recalled a mission at Longworth in 1894, conducted by Bickersteth and a Wantage sister. Although there were no startling conversions, twenty to thirty people made their confessions, the church was full for nearly every service and there were many communicants and solemn resolutions. From it resulted a weekly cottage meeting and later a boys' Bible class. Frere in his diary also assessed missions in terms of numbers of communions, confessions and resolutions.

Nash was fulfilled at Radley, but Frere was increasingly distressed. In April 1895 he wrote to Bickersteth about the suggestion that Bickersteth should work in Rochdale:

> It is a very serious thing to branch out anew. We shall be in great danger of finding ourselves hermits instead of coenobites – Senior alone at Westminster, John ditto at Oxford, you ditto at Rochdale. If our probationers were to be members this year I think one could certainly risk it, but I suppose neither Paul nor Thomas will be: so 'We are seven'. And seven is very few. On the other hand I think we are quite likely to be in great danger if we merely go on at Radley and Westminster: both are much too respectable to attract the sort of person whom we want and if we don't take care we shall become a little body of middle aged clergymen of unimpeachable respectability, polite manners and various sorts and degrees of individual useful-ness: but no community – much, no poverty – much, no obedience – much, everything in fact that Archdeacon Farrar would like to see.[8] Absit omen. We want a place much more pronounced than either Radley or Westminster can be if we are to do parochial work at all and lay ourselves out to catch parish priests. The quiet repose of Radley – excellent as a training ground – won't attract people; nor the smug respectability of Westminster Abbey.

There were two dangers, he believed. He did not know which was the greater. If we 'enlarge our borders' we run the risk of 'sudden death'. If we do not, then we run the risk of slow extinction, unless we become just a group of mission clergy, and that would require a different method of life.

> If we go to Rochdale we must sacrifice a good deal to make it a *really strong* Community centre and have no half measures or temporizings such as have spoilt our other moves. No women servants: household work a reality: the plainest of comfort . . . House rules very strict . . . e.g. *mornings inviolable* but afternoons and evenings up to Compline very free and evening meal very much open to everyone, parochial and otherwise. I protest strongly in favour of cassocks all about the parish . . . I suppose the Senior would never stand the *parochial brethren* being called Father but some such distinction would be wanted . . . I confess I am less sanguine about the *present* possibility of the scheme than I was: but I am hideously afraid of the Archdeacon Farrar prospect.

Frere's letter written four months after Gore's move to Westminster reveals not only how deeply dissatisfied he was with CR, but also that he had in readiness a plan for a radically different style of community – one which was more strict, more communal, simpler in life-style, but also much more open, offering hospitality to all-comers.

Gore's resistance to any radical departure from his concept of CR led to disagreements. In September 1896 they were still divided as to whether to adopt formally the title 'Senior', as Gore wanted, rather than 'Superior'. In 1897 Gore reminded them that they were not to claim the title of 'Father' and successfully argued against the appointment of a Novice Master. In July 1896 Chapter agreed that Gore could visit North America in 1897, but urged him to spend at least three months in residence at Radley. In August 1897, just before Gore departed for America, Chapter discussed how to strengthen community life. Gore's reaction was characteristic: 'The sabbath was made for man and not man for the sabbath' he quoted.

The call of the North

In the autumn of 1891, Gore had told Talbot that he and most of the brethren had 'a great desire to see whether we could help to consolidate the body of Churchmanship among the working classes'. This could not be realized from Pusey House. They had in mind a working class parish with an institute attached which would give opportunity for preaching, lecturing and writing. 'The heart of several of us is set on the North.' Yet they had moved to rural Radley. The North also beckoned because there was still no Anglican male Religious Order there. But now Gore was happily settled in Westminster. A move north had become impossible unless the rest of CR was prepared to move without him. By January 1897, Frere and his supporters could wait no longer, and a move north was formally proposed, and won almost unanimous approval. Visits were made to possible places, including Prestwich, Manchester. CR thought that it had a friend in the Bishop of Manchester (James Moorhouse) who approved of biblical criticism (provided it was propounded in lectures and not in sermons) and had chaired the Lambeth Conference committee of 1888 which had given socialism a real, if qualified, blessing. But in the event the Bishop quite definitely did not want to have CR in his diocese. In later years Bickersteth claimed that this adverse response was because he had denounced the Girls' Friendly Society. What Bickersteth had said is not recorded, and the story may be the product of his egocentric imagination, but in 1897 he had resigned as examining chaplain to the Bishop of Bath and Wells because of a disagreement about confession. They now looked at an Elizabethan house near Wakefield, reputed to be haunted, and at the Old Hall, Upper Hopton, on the hill across the valley from Mirfield proper, an ancient and charming stone house with timbered wings, next to the church. Both were considered unsuitable.

In July 1897 Gore met Walsham How, Bishop of Wakefield, to discuss the possibility of CR settling in his diocese. How had become the first Bishop of Wakefield in 1888. He claimed that there was not a garden in his diocese where he could pick a flower without blackening his fingers. Now remembered as the author of 'For all the Saints', he had learned much about the problems of the urban church during an impressive ministry as a suffragan bishop in the East End, and had written a sonnet in praise of Fr Dolling. Hall Croft, Mirfield had been How's original choice for his residence. It was conveniently near Mirfield Junction. But the Wakefield people wanted him in the Cathedral town. A moderate High Churchman in the John Keble tradition, How disliked ritualism, and was uneasy about having a free-lance group of clergy in his diocese. Nevertheless he wrote to his son, the Rev. H. W. How, vicar of Mirfield, on 17 July 1897:

> I received the enclosed from Canon Gore just as I was coming up to London, and today I have had a good long talk with him. It turns out that they want to plant their head-quarters, and not a branch house, in the North. I see no reason to refuse them a welcome (as Manchester has done), and it struck me that Mirfield would not be a bad centre, if a suitable house could be had. What do *you* think of the idea? They seem to want to get among our more energetic Northerners. Gore says he has men of different views among his small society of nine, two or three being very moderate men. They do not want to be diocesan, but to work all over England, only to make their home in the North, and they hope to have the Archbishop of Canterbury as visitor; they have no life vows. Would Hall Croft suit them?[9]

After a Chapter discussion in early August, Gore seems to have handed over the negotiations to the brethren led by Frere. Frere was clear what they required: either a smaller house with surrounding land on which to build, or a larger house or disused institution, in 'country surroundings' but 'near a good station'. The idea of taking on a working class parish had obviously evaporated.

On 23 August Frere and Bickersteth went up to Mirfield. Bickersteth wrote in his diary: 'Met Walter at Mirfield at 1.57. Went first to Hall Croft which belongs to Mrs Hague Cook who now lives at Tunbridge Wells. The House is exceedingly good and suitable, the garden, stables and adjacent land does not put it beyond our needs.' But on 10 August Walsham How died. In early September, Gore, just before he left for America for two months, approached How's successor, G. R. Eden, who fortunately reaffirmed How's invitation. In September CR agreed to rent Hall Croft for £200 a year (with the option to purchase for £10,000) from Christmas Day. Gore was far away in America when this crucial decision was made. It was decided to call it the 'House of the Resurrection'. That summer CR had declined an invitation to open a house in Cambridge on the lines of Pusey House. If CR had remained at Radley or moved to Cambridge or Westminster or back to Oxford, its history and ethos would have been quite different. Mirfield with its smoking mill chimneys and Pennine weather, and the sturdiness of northern Anglicanism (influenced both by the northern temperament and the moral uprightness of Nonconformity) provided a totally different matrix than somewhere in the South where Anglo-Catholicism tended to become effete. Interacting with its environment, the Community took on something of the character of the millstone grit with which so many of the surrounding houses, including Hall Croft, were built. On 20 January 1898 George Longridge and Gerard Sampson moved into the new house. They had to sleep on the floor as the furniture had not yet arrived.

Rackham, the writer of the CR Chronicle (a record of Community life maintained since 1892) commented that they left Radley 'with the greatest regret and affectionate recollection of the last four years – on the part of most, if not all'. In 1931 Longridge looked back 'rather longingly' to the days at Radley when the original nucleus was still together in its gentle rural peace, so different from the scarred industrial landscape around Mirfield. For many years the ministry of Nash was remembered by Radley people with affectionate warmth.

The Westminster House

In January 1895 Gore began seven of the happiest years of his life. He now was part of a very different type of community from Radley or that which later developed at Mirfield. His health began to improve immediately he resigned Radley and accepted Westminster, though he had a bad spell in 1896 when he temporarily lost the sight in one eye. Even though he had to sever his twenty-year relationship with Trinity (his salary of £1,000 a year no longer allowed him to retain his fellowship) he was now at the centre of ecclesiastical and political life, and among influential and stimulating people. The liberal tradition at the Abbey now found room for Liberal Catholicism. Dean Bradley was a liberal scholar and old-fashioned churchman. The sub-Dean, Robinson Duckworth, long associated with the Court, enjoyed wearing his various decorations. Albert Wilberforce, fourth son of Bishop Wilberforce, a popular modernist preacher, described himself as 'an honorary member of all the religions'. C. W. Furse, who had pressed the Prime Minister to appoint Gore, had loved him as a son since Cuddesdon days. In 1899 Joseph Armitage Robinson arrived, a New Testament and patristic scholar, another admirer of Gore. The following year Hensley Henson was installed. Once he had knelt in Pusey Chapel with Gore. Now his increasingly liberal theology and his distaste for socialism (especially when preached by an aristocrat), coupled with his very different social background and singularly prickly temperament, created conflicts with Gore which were to mark their relationship until Gore's death.

Gore's house was one of a number of gracious residences opening off Little Cloister. Number 4 (now divided) was a large seventeenth-century house with an imposing staircase, a large drawing room, regarded as one of the finest in central London, with elaborate plaster-work, and eight or more bedrooms. The back, which included Gore's study, looked over the wide expanse of the College garden. Gore once more enjoyed the grace, space, stimulus and freedom in which he flourished. He had to be in residence for only two and a half months of the year – usually March and April and half of August – when his duties involved being present at daily mattins and evensong and preaching on Sunday. He was Canon Treasurer 1896–1900 but the real work was done by lay staff. So he had plenty of spare time to pursue his many interests and concerns.

The furnishing of Number 4 was simple and bare. The drawing room was divided up by bookcases into alcoves in which brethren could study. But when his nieces and nephews came to London, Gore enjoyed giving them tea from a silver teapot and bringing out the silver spoons after a visit to the waxworks or some other jolly excursion. A housekeeper and maid were employed and their wages included beer money. Their male followers created a few problems. But at least the brethren carried up their own coals. They had to keep four months residence between November and June. Mattins and evensong were sometimes said in Latin.

At the end of 1895 Talbot became Bishop of Rochester and lived in Kennington just over the river. Holland had been at St Paul's since 1884. So Gore had his two closest friends nearby, a miniature Holy Party, long-standing relationships closer than any he had formed within C R. The longer Gore was at the Abbey the more he was involved in the affairs of church and state. When he was appointed as Honorary Chaplain to the Queen in 1898 he did not refer the matter to the brethren – it was equivalent to a command. But he was meticulous about keeping the Rule. When on holiday abroad in 1899 he sent a list of rules broken – late for mattins one day, late up two days and only one fast a week observed. In October 1898 he sent the following postcard from Mirfield to Rackham at Westminster:

I hope to turn up at Midday on Monday and to leave for France at 2.45. Of the £5 you gave me I have spent:

visit	to Oxford	12.0 (with cab, tea, tip etc.)
	to Mirfield	14.0
	to Leeds	2.0
		£1.8.0

Remainder £3.12.0. I shall need £4 more to go abroad with (for I have to go to Wakefield and Westminster). Hope to see you with renewed head, but augmented affection. Yours affectionately C.G.

Gore in 1899 at last agreed to the appointment of a brother in charge of probationers and nominated Frere, so Frere went to Mirfield. Characteristically Gore explained that this development was not intended to restrict the personal relationships, liberty or opinions of probationers.

Gore's contribution to the life of the Abbey was immense and varied. The Chapel of St Faith was created and set aside for private prayer. The number of weekday eucharists was increased: after Advent 1901 there was a daily celebration, except for August and September. The choir was revested. When Gore was due to preach, queues formed outside. In 1896 when he gave the first Lent Lectures ever to be held in the Abbey (on the church in Acts) the best seats were taken two hours before. That Good Friday he inaugurated the Three Hours devotion. The Abbey was crowded, particularly with men. Some had remained from the previous service, so spent five hours in church. Yet contemporaries judged that the spell he cast was not due to any naturally attractive presence, voice or manner; his bodily movements in the pulpit were often restless, distracting and abrupt. His power came from the force of an inner conviction, not from rhetorical skills. The *Daily Mail* weekly magazine for 16 April 1899 printed a romantically phrased article headed 'The Canon Eschews all Worldly Possessions to Live a Life as Nearly Like That of the Apostles as is Possible at the Close of this Century' (*CRQ* LD 1982).

Gore also drew many visitors to the house. He held a weekly At Home; church reform and social problems were favourite topics. Numerous individuals sought his counsel. Albert Mansbridge (later the founder of the Workers' Educational Association) as a young man of eighteen met Gore at Westminster and was readily admitted to his friendship and that of the brethren; it was an 'entry into a new and wider life'. On Sunday evenings senior boys from Westminster School would come round and discovered the connection between Catholicism and Trade Unions, and heard him read everything from Milton to Mark Twain. In 1896 he took the choirboys to 'Charley's Aunt'. His delight in the life at the Abbey did not blunt his criticisms. In an Advent sermon in 1896 he criticized many of its monuments. How unreal were the laudatory epitaphs and how unsuitable for a Christian place of worship. He lectured, took retreats and dictated a vast correspondence to a male secretary but wrote his terse, amusing postcards himself. In 1896 Gore, Talbot, A. J. Balfour and Wilfred Ward created the Synthetic Society to discuss the philosophy of religion. During its life its members included J. B. Haldane (later Lord Chancellor), James (later Lord) Bryce, William Temple, Henry Sidgwick, Sir Oliver Lodge, Baron von Hügel, Father Tyrrell and G. K. Chesterton.

The prestige of the Abbey and its close connections with political life gave added publicity and weight to Gore's political and social views. In 1895 he spoke at a meeting in a Baptist Chapel to protest against the Turkish massacre of the Armenians, despite the protests of the local vicar that he was giving support to Nonconformity. But two years earlier he had publicly censured his friend Percy Dearmer, London CSU secretary, for lecturing on Christian socialism in a Methodist chapel (when refused use of the church school) against the wishes of the vicar. Dearmer thought the right of the people to hear him more important than 'professional etiquette'. If Gore had 'been brought up as an agricultural labourer . . . he would agree with me'.[10] Throughout his life Gore never decided whether he was a gamekeeper or a poacher; he was equally attracted to authority and liberty. He preached for the Co-operative Congress and participated in conferences with businessmen. He donated all his school medals to be melted down to help finance the CSU campaign against lead poisoning in factories. He regularly conferred with politicians about industrial legislation and became a shareholder in a London store to protest against its treatment of its employees. He said that paying the market price for clothes and ordering them in good time was on the same level as saying one's prayers, reading the Bible and receiving communion. If private property was essential for the preservation of individuality, its use must be restrained for the common good. Preaching at the 1896 Church Congress he urged the propertied classes to replace their clamour for rights with a sense of stewardship and service. Because society enabled the acquiring of wealth, it had the right to control it if its use damaged the whole body. Yet there was also an evil form of socialism which represented 'nothing more than . . . the unregenerate, uncleansed instinct of a class that is discontented'.[11] In a CSU lecture on the Municipality he contrasted the so-called freedom which the anonymity of London offered (which Aristotle would have regarded as barbarism) with Yorkshire mill-towns where everyone knew one another and felt a mutual responsibility, as in I Corinthians 12. In 1909 he defended Lloyd George's 'People's Budget' in the Lords because it proposed a more equal sharing of burdens between the classes. At Westminster Gore's social concerns became more urgent and specific. It was as though, realizing that he was unable to commit himself to the intimate communal life of CR, he turned instead to promote community within society and between the nations.

Gore became increasingly interested in the women's movement.[12] *The Churchwoman* (6 March 1896) reported Gore's advocacy of women's suffrage in both church and state. The church could no longer maintain the low view of women common in mediaeval society or today among oriental races. Women should be regarded as partners with men. In a lecture given at the Abbey in 1897 he said that in the early church women had a ministry of compassionate works and private teaching. To some extent St Paul's teaching was temporary – for example his advice to widows not to remarry, his refusal to allow women to give public instruction or share in the government of the church. Gore believed that husbands should rule, but that men often treated women as mere conveniences.

In Chapter 1 we noted that the increasing pluralism in Britain was forcing the Church of England to distinguish itself from surrounding society and to revive or create organs of self-determination. After a series of decisions by the Judicial Committee of the Privy Council which reversed decisions by church courts, and the failure of the Public Worship Regulation Act of 1874, it was a significant moment when in 1888 Archbishop Benson, not a secular court, heard the charges of ritual illegalities against Bishop King of Lincoln.[13] Certainly the Church of England was wisely moving towards a greater degree of self-government. But unless the state had held the ring during the bitter controversies of the nineteenth century, the growing (if at times reluctant) acceptance by the church of a degree of internal pluralism would have been retarded. The nomination of Frederick Temple and Charles Gore to bishoprics, and the lack of any desire to proceed against *Lux Mundi* were signs of this. However, many of Gore's proposals for church reform were designed to set strict limits to diversity. In an address to the 1896 Church Congress and in his chapter in *Essays in aid of the Reform of the Church* (1898) he argued that only a considerable degree of self-government (in which laypeople, including women, should share) would bring the Church of England closer to the New Testament, restore its doctrinal and pastoral discipline and reflect the movement in society away from a monarchical and aristocratic, and towards a democratic, concept of society. Though (he told the Congress) a revived discipline should be moderately exercised allowing 'large differences both in teaching and practice', only baptized, confirmed communicants should be allowed to share in the church's government, church courts should be effective, clergy should have to adhere strictly to the two creeds and no liturgical changes should be made by clergy without permission. But subscription to the Articles should be probably abolished and there should be reasonable freedom about ritual. Yet nothing could happen until church membership was clearly defined.[14] Thus Gore's proposals, for which he campaigned and which later formed the basis of his episcopal policy, in certain aspects echoed his concept of CR.

Gore was at this time involved in controversy with three other Harrovians: Hastings Rashdall (Dean of Carlisle 1917–24), Randall Davidson (then Bishop of Winchester) and Fr Dolling. In 1897 Rashdall declared that clergy should give to the Creeds the same generalized assent that they now gave to the Articles. Gore considered this deficient in moral truthfulness. Rashdall could not understand why the liberty which Gore had claimed in *Lux Mundi* should now be denied to others. In the autumn of 1895 Gore mediated unsuccessfully in the controversy between Davidson and Dolling about ritualism at St Agatha's Portsmouth. Gore's natural sympathies were with Dolling because he loved the poor. But Gore believed in obedience to lawful authority, which Dolling did not. After Dolling's impetuous resignation Gore arranged that Bull should oversee the interregnum. A characteristically brisk telegram arrived 'I will be with you at 7.30 p.m. Bull.' Dolling was grateful but thought it 'a little cool'. Gore enjoyed his visit to St Agatha's in January 1896. 'Their parochial balls are the jolliest things I ever saw.'

In 1901 Gore and Rackham produced two notable books. Gore in *The Body of Christ* insisted, contrary to advanced Anglo-Catholicism, that a eucharist without communicants was defective. He (like Holland) opposed devotions to the reserved sacrament; they obscured the truth that the 'sacrament was instituted in order to be eaten'. The *Church Review* (11 April) was profoundly grieved that Gore was drifting away from Catholicism. Rackham's magisterial commentary on Acts remained a standard work for many years. Rackham also gave invaluable help to Gore in preparing his publications for the press, and to Brightman with his edition of Lancelot Andrewes' *Devotions*, to Frere and Moberly with their writings and later to Armitage Robinson (Dean from 1902) in his work on the Abbey records. He had a genius for making indexes – the one for Frere's *Visitation Articles and Injunctions* ran to 185 pages. When CR left Westminster in 1902 Rackham remained. Robinson took in YGs after the Radley pattern, who included C. F. G. Masterman, R. H. Malden and Tubby Clayton, the founder of Toc H. It was Rackham who cured Clayton's doubts, set him firmly on the path to ordination, prepared him for his first confession and introduced him to the spiritual resources of Mirfield.

The Anglo-Boer War

Gore's criticisms of aspects of the conduct of the Anglo-Boer War (1899–1902) brought him notoriety. The CSU was divided. Westcott, its President, believed that imperialism was an expression of Christian brotherhood and service. An empire incorporated many organs into one body and therefore could be an image, however faint, of the Kingdom of God. To Paul Bull also, imperialism, like socialism, extended our vision beyond nationality. He wrote in a Mirfield booklet, *Urgent Church Reform*: 'The distinguishing mark of our age is the revival of a corporate spirit. Imperialism in one direction, Socialism in another, is directing attention to the large visions which exceed the bounds of nationality.' The earlier Christian socialists F. D. Maurice and Charles Kingsley were enthusiastic militarists and J.M. Ludlow encouraged emigration as a means of creating a string of civilizing colonies throughout the world.[15]

Paul Bull (1864–1942) who in his time was one of the best known members of CR, the son of a House of Commons' official, was educated at Hurstpierpoint (a Woodard school) and Worcester College, Oxford. When he arrived at Radley in 1894 he had been a schoolmaster, served a curacy and worked as a missioner in two dioceses. He was professed two years later, though Frere had thought him 'unbalanced'. Richard Barnes (*CRQ* JB 1942) wrote feelingly: 'A strong personality, a strident affection and a fighting spirit avail for driving the devil out of a man or calling to heroism, but they become oppressive in quieter or more ordinary occasions.' The public schools of the time, influenced by Thomas Hughes and Charles Kingsley taught patriotism, spartan habits, sexual purity, hearty masculinity and the duty to serve one's 'inferiors' whether in the slums or in the empire.[16] So did Bull. He, like the public schools and many working class people, was an enthusiastic supporter of the Anglo-Boer war. But he criticized the public schools for separating boys from feminine influences; this caused such emotional suppression that they became rationalists. He told the story of six agnostic officers who fell in love and as a result became communicants. His Catholicism was leavened by Evangelicalism: he believed that the splendid eucharists in the Woodard schools must be accompanied by efforts to win the boys to a personal faith in Jesus as Saviour. Bull had been the obvious person to look after St Agatha's when Dolling resigned. Dolling was another public school imperialist and socialist who combined elaborate ritual with Evangelical hymns sung to popular tunes like 'Home, Sweet Home'.[17]

In 1897 Bull travelled to India as chaplain to the Manchester Regiment for the duration of the voyage. On his return he proposed that a branch of CR should be created to work in the Army. To explore the possiblity, in 1898 he went as chaplain to Aldershot and later to Chelsea. Bull spent nine months as a chaplain in South Africa, returning in January 1901. In 'God and our Soldiers' (*Goodwill* July 1901) Bull wrote romantically about his work. A drunken, foul-mouthed, godless soldier arose from kneeling by his bedside in the barrack room a changed man and put aside beer and tobacco. On Sundays Bull celebrated the eucharist. On weekdays he held evangelistic services. During his Bible classes the men prayed as the Spirit moved them. In the line he held evening prayers round a roaring fire: 'a very Free church'. The men were so brave, self-sacrificial and kind to the enemy: 'all these, I believe, must have pleased God very much in those who were carrying out His terrible Judgments'. Bull knelt in pools of blood by a wounded soldier and showed him a crucifix: 'Ah sir!' (said the soldier) 'His wounds were worse than mine.' Though the Boers often behaved treacherously, Boer families were treated with gentle courtesy, he wrote. Elsewhere Bull defended the burning of Boer farms. We must get rid of 'sickly sentiment'; they were being used as arsenals.

Bull was naive and sentimental, but he was also brave, riding unarmed into battle with the cavalry to cheer on his men. Under fire, when a gun was stuck, he put himself into the shafts and pulled it out with the help of others. He was awarded a medal with five bars. In January 1903 he wrote to Nash, then in Johannesburg, that he still lived much of the time with his memories of the war and that he longed to visit the graves of 'my poor boys'. In *God and our Soldiers* (1904), told in the style of a boys' adventure story, he claimed 'for our army that respect which is due to it, and to show to others what God has shown to me, the strong virtues which burn so brightly in our soldiers' lives'. (It was reprinted in September 1914 with a preface from the Chief of the Imperial General Staff who wrote that it would teach appreciation of the character of the British soldier 'chivalry . . . determination . . . cheerfulness . . . loyal obedience'.)

There was a huge temperamental gulf between Gore and Bull – Bull, often mawkishly sentimental, enjoying the drama and limelight of the missioner's role, difficult to live with, author of many pamphlets 'For Men and Lads Only' on sexual temptation. Yet surprisingly they had a warm regard for one another and Gore sought Bull's help in the preparation of his manual of belief *The Religion of the Church* (1916). But their attitudes to South Africa were utterly different. Gore deplored the Jameson Raid of 1895. Preaching in the Abbey in August 1899 he denounced the cries for vengeance on the Boers for the massacre at Majuba Hill (1881). In December he described the three humiliating British defeats that month as God's warning to the nation for its arrogance. On New Year's Eve 1900 he preached about the hollowness of the belief in progress; morally, imperialism was poverty stricken. Thus Gore courageously stood against the stridently jingoistic national mood and was given the contemptuous label 'pro-Boer'. Gore and Talbot both had members of their families serving in South Africa. Gore's relation the Earl of Airlie was killed in 1900 at the head of his troops. Talbot's son, Neville, and his brother-in-law, General Sir Neville Lyttelton, were both in the thick of it. Sir Neville became Commander-in-Chief in 1902. In 1901 Gore and Talbot wrote to the Secretary for War deploring the conditions in the concentration camps. (Of the 231,000 whites and blacks interned, 42,000 died through inadequate diet and sanitation, of whom the vast majority were women and children. The mother of President P. W. Botha was among those interned; his father was a 'bitter-ender'.) In a letter in the *Times* for 28 October 1901 Gore demanded immediate action to prevent the terrible death rate. 'Otherwise I believe the honour of our country will contract a stain which we shall not be able to obliterate and the whole Christian conscience of the country will be outraged and alienated.' On 31 October W. J. Knox Little, sub-Dean of Worcester, a friend of Cecil Rhodes and a member of the English Church Union, dismissed Gore's letter as 'deplorable' and 'mischievous'. Gore, probably writing under pressure from his radical friends, was 'talking nonsense'. The whole matter was 'better dealt with by the good and brave men in whose hands they are . . . than they can be by bookworms and arm-chair theorists like Mr Gore, in the seclusion of Westminster'.

After the war ended in May 1902, rowdies attacked the palace of the Bishop of Hereford (John Percival) another 'pro-Boer'. Holland had loathed the war. On Peace Night he was sickened because the revellers seemed to have neither remembrance of the dead nor any awareness of the need for reconciliation. He went home and wrote 'Judge eternal, throned in splendour' (included in the *English Hymnal* in 1906):

> Purge this realm of bitter things . . .
> Cleanse the body of this empire
> Through the glory of the Lord.

When CR brethren went to work in South Africa in 1903 they experienced at first hand the war's bitter legacy.

The Bishop of Worcester

On 28 October 1901, the day on which Gore's letter about the concentration camps appeared, he received a letter from the Prime Minister, offering him the see of Worcester. Lord Salisbury believed that it was essential for the new generation of High Churchmen to be represented on the bench. Gore was now very well-known in church and state. He was also very well connected. To Talbot and Holland Gore advanced three reasons against acceptance: it would mean leaving the Community; it would mean an end to all study; it could result in desperate failure. The Community decided to leave the decision to Gore, but each brother was free to express his opinion. Frere, as was to be expected, was against acceptance. On 2 November Gore agreed; on 8 November the news was made public. He announced that he had resigned from membership of the English Church Union and of the Confraternity of the Blessed Sacrament to which he had belonged for nearly thirty years. A bishop (he said) should not be a member of societies which could be involved in controversies which might require his adjudication. On 16 November the Community dispensed him 'from all the obligations carried by his pledge'. Nash voted against this, believing that they had no power to dispense. Gore also resigned from SR. He asked CR to undertake to inform him if it ever was short of funds. This offer was declined with deep appreciation. But Gore did persuade CR to accept the royalties on those books written during his membership. The 'Lux Mundites' gave him a cross and candlesticks. (They are now used in the Abbey.) CR expressed the hope that 'so far as is consistent with his new position' they might continue to be able to look to him 'for the help and counsel which has been of such immense value in all the past history of the Community'. 'The most interesting appointment of recent years' commented the *Morning Leader*, 'we are sure that in this Canon Knox Little will agree with us'. Nonconformists in Birmingham (then part of the diocese) recalled gratefully Gore's close friendship with the Congregationalist R. W. Dale of Carrs Lane Church. The Free Church *British Weekly* commended him as a scholar, preacher and political prophet with particular concern for the urban masses and with friendly contacts with Trade Union leaders. *The Review of Reviews* pointed out the irony that Gore, who had been so critical of the conduct of the war, for which Joseph Chamberlain as Colonial Secretary was responsible and whose power base was Birmingham, should now have Birmingham as part of his diocese. 'Imagine John the Baptist appointed by Pontius Pilate to be Bishop over Galilee when Herod was in his glory . . . ' Henson paid a heartfelt tribute from the Abbey pulpit: 'It is just seventeen years since, as a young graduate, I made the acquaintance of Charles Gore, and every year since has deepened the affection and increased the respect with which he then inspired me.' But a protestant newspaper prayed: 'O Lord, open the blind eyes of this perjured priest before he becomes a Bishop.'

Gore caused consternation among the aristocracy of Worcestershire by refusing to live at Hartlebury Castle, though bishops had lived on the site since the ninth century. Gore gleefully reported to his sister Caroline that they thought he was determined to live over a butcher's shop in Birmingham. In the end he decided to live in a house in Worcester.

But the Church Association and other protestant societies tried to prevent the consecration. A 'Petition of Right' was presented to the King: his essay in *Lux Mundi* had shaken the faith of many; he had been a member of the ECU and CBS; he had founded 'a monastic celibate society known as the Community of the Resurrection'; he had warmly commended the work of the Society of the Sacred Mission and thus 'thinks it wise to found and support monastic establishments of the Romish type'. John Kensit, secretary of the Protestant Truth Society, led a demonstration at the confirmation of the election on 21 January 1902. An appeal to the King's Bench was granted on 24 January, the day before the consecration was due to take place. Gore in his proposals for church reform had urged that confirmations should allow the hearing of objections and therefore argued that his consecration should be postponed. He was now under intense strain: persecuted by protestants who revived all the old painful controversies about *Lux Mundi* and bludgeoned by the Archbishop (Frederick Temple) who wanted the consecration to go ahead as planned. When the case was heard in early February it was dismissed. On 23 February he was consecrated at Lambeth Palace. The Archbishop, now eighty, frail and half blind, leaned upon Gore's arm as the procession left the chapel. (He died that December.) Did Gore, devastated by the renewed accusations against him, remember what the Archbishop had suffered when nominated as Bishop of Exeter in 1869? Because Temple had contributed to the notorious *Essays and Reviews*, Pusey had denounced the nomination as an 'enormity'; the Sub-Dean of Exeter and five of the Chapter had voted against Temple; there had been protests at the confirmation; his service of consecration had been delayed while four bishops entered protests.

On 25 February Gore was enthroned. In the first week he joined the local Co-operative Society and incurred the wrath of local traders by speaking at a Co-operative meeting. Hundreds of people from the great to the humble had helped him with his expenses with their shillings and half crowns enclosed with grateful letters. He insisted on the cheapest possible pastoral staff. The diocese had to get used to his mordant humour. He adorned the walls of his guest bedroom with engravings of Foxe's Protestant Martyrs. He once reduced a Birmingham hostess to despair. She asked distinguished people to meet him, but he had instructed the boy of the house to go round repeating 'A bishop is a useless creature'. He could be scathing about his fellow bishops: 'The whole atmosphere of the episcopate is manipulation of details and avoidance of big principles.' At times overwhelmed by administration, he felt he had given up all chance of doing what he was most fitted for. But he told Talbot 'I think it has been good for the Community my going: and that is a comfort.' Three years later the diocese was divided. He was translated to Birmingham and at last got into his stride. He had resigned £800 from his old see and gave the £10,000 which his mother had left him to endow the new bishopric. He was glad to have a manageably sized diocese and to be freed from landed aristocrats who reminded him of aspects of his background from which he had tried to escape. He rejoiced that there was no palace. He lived instead in what he proudly described as the ugliest villa in Western Europe.

By going to Worcester he had abandoned his early ideal of working out his theology of the church in the intimate and demanding relationships of a religious community. However much the CR Rule stressed the freedom of the individual it also insisted: 'The individual must learn to merge himself in the community.' That Gore had been unable to do. Returning to Mirfield after he had withdrawn from CR, Gore despondently flung himself into the arms of Paul Bull. 'Paul, why am I such a wet blanket on men's enthusiasm? All I have to do to make any institution prosper is – to leave it.'

The Westminster House closed on 4 January 1902. Its only purpose had been to serve Gore's needs. In one sense the division of the small Community into two houses was deleterious. In another sense it was providential. It had enabled Gore to discover an honourable way out of CR. It had enabled the Community to discover its own vocation without the daily presence of Gore's dominant and magnetic personality but also without the aggravation his ambivalence about community life created. If Gore had continued at Westminster as Superior, would Frere have been able to remain in CR?

Because of his health, Rackham stayed on at Westminster, living with Armitage Robinson and lecturing at King's College London. In February 1902 tuberculosis in throat and lungs was diagnosed and he spent most of that year in a sanatorium. In 1911 he moved to Wells when Robinson became Dean. But the next year his tuberculosis flared up again and he died in August. He was buried under the shadow of the Cathedral. 'He was very merry and outspoken' (wrote Robinson) 'utterly uncomplaining, and always ready to help any one. He exercised far more influence than he knew, or seemed to know; for he was exceedingly modest and unobtrusive, and he was quite satisfied with adding to the usefulness of others.'

3

Mirfield

In January 1898 CR moved from Radley to Hall Croft, Battyeford, an area of Mirfield, an industrial town of 15,500 in the West Riding of Yorkshire. Huddersfield, Wakefield, Dewsbury, Leeds and Bradford are all within easy reach. Mirfield, a flourishing woollen town since the fourteenth century, was connected to the canal system in the mid-eighteenth century. When CR arrived at Mirfield, an average of forty barges still passed along the canal each day drawn by plodding horses, or by bargees' wives in harness if the loads were light. Mirfield was now the junction of the London North Western and Lancashire and Yorkshire Railways. Its station, built in 1866, was draughty and gloomy. More trains passed through it daily than almost any other station in the country. At night the whole valley was studded with continually changing red and green signal lights. Night and day the clanging of buffers resounded as goods trains were assembled in its busy marshalling yards. Woollen and corn mills, quarries, a brickworks and barge building also provided employment. Some coal was mined through horizontal shafts, some through pits. Yet on the surrounding hills farming also flourished. Today, the Community is surrounded by modern housing estates. The M62 is only a couple of miles away, yet across the valley is open country with sheep and moorland farmhouses.

'Over the whole landscape, save when rains have washed it, a film of soot has settled', reported an early visitor to the House. 'In rain itself, it is dismal beyond words.' Today, looking along the valley on a day when the steam of the cooling towers pours into the dark lowering Pennine clouds pierced by apocalyptic shafts of grey light and the landscape is drained of all colour, it can look like Sodom and Gomorrah preparing sullenly for the Day of Judgment. Recently some of the houses in the area have been sandblasted and done up with white shutters, making the other still begrimed houses, the derelict mills and the walls of millstone grit look even more sombre. But in spring fresh green leaves emerge from blackened trees and daffodils shine brightly against the dark stone. In autumn and winter perhaps only Turner could do justice to the subtleties of the light. You may love or hate the area, but its tang, which has given CR something of its particular flavour, is unmistakable and unforgettable.

Before the dissolution, there were two monasteries nearby. Bradley Grange was an outpost of Fountains. When Kirklees Cistercian nunnery was dissolved in 1539, five nuns continued their life in a house near Mirfield parish church for over twenty years, perhaps England's last surviving mediaeval religious community. Three others gave up the life; the name of the 'Three Nuns' public house may commemorate them.[1] Up to the First World War old customs lingered. Early on Palm Sunday crowds gathered at a local well to fill bottles with water, believed to have healing properties.

Until recent years, rivalry between church and chapel was keen, sharpened by the usual class differences. Mirfield had a long Nonconformist tradition: Congregationalists (1692), Moravians (1751), Methodists (1780), Baptists (1816). 'A wilder people I never saw in England', John Wesley wrote after one of his five visits. The mixed chapel choirs nourished the musical life of the whole area. In 1900 Mirfield had two choral societies, glee and madrigal groups, male voice quartets, an orchestra and seven bands, including the Mirfield Baptist Military Band. The nineteenth-century Anglican revival strengthened church life in Mirfield. In 1871 a large, assertive, opulent church, costing £30,500, designed by Gilbert Scott in thirteenth-century Gothic, replaced a humbler structure. Consecrated by Bishop Bickersteth, its vicar from 1889 to 1902 was Henry Walsham How, whose father had suggested Hall Croft for CR. Christ Church, Battyeford (1840) became a parish church in 1841; its mission church was built in 1874. Benjamin Wilson (vicar 1870–1916) had a flourishing Sunday School of 502 with 79 teachers, a Cocoa House (to promote temperance), night schools and charitable clubs. He arranged the first open air service in the quarry at Hall Croft in 1883, fifteen years before CR arrived.

Over the centuries the leading families and manufacturers built fine residences especially on the hills where the air was cleaner, like Field Head, opposite Hall Croft, and Roe Head where the three Bronte sisters went to school, and Charlotte taught. Sir Gilbert Scott wrote in *Secular and Domestic Architecture* (1857): 'Providence has ordained the different orders and gradations into which the human family is divided . . . The position of a landed proprietor . . . is one of dignity . . . He is the natural head of his parish or district . . . ' Everyone should look to him for 'a dignified, honourable and Christian example . . . He has been blessed with wealth, and he need not shrink from using it in its proper degree.' Scott might have been describing Thomas Hague Cook, of Hall Croft, the son of Thomas Cook of Dewsbury Mills, which manufactured rugs and blankets.[2] Thomas Cook had given most of the money to build Thornhill Lees church (near Dewsbury), its vicarage and school. When he died in 1861, his son succeeded to his father's interests and in 1867 became proprietor of the Dewsbury Mills Estate. Initially he lived at Field Head. But in 1872 he bought the twenty-one acres opposite, part densely wooded, part market gardens, part quarries. The house, designed by

Kirk and Sons of Huddersfield, architects of Mirfield Town Hall, was completed in 1875. The immediate area round it was laid out as formal gardens but the estate also included greenhouses, conservatories, a kitchen garden, vineries and pasture lands sloping down to a rocky escarpment. The house, which cost £30,000 (as much as Mirfield parish church) consisted of: five reception rooms, billiard and smoking rooms, servants' hall, kitchens, ten principal bedrooms, three dressing rooms, bathroom, linen room, two housemaids' rooms, six bedrooms for servants and cellars. In addition there were two entrance lodges, stables, and a coach house. Yet despite this huge outlay, Cook was still wealthy enough to build a new weaving shed at the mills in 1871 and thirty-six cottages nearby in 1874.

However, on 14 July 1877, after only two years at Hall Croft, Cook died of a heart attack at the age of forty-six. He had been a churchwarden at Battyeford parish church, President of the Mirfield Conservative Club, JP and director of the West Riding Union Bank. He was said to have been the richest man in the neighbourhood, generous to many charities and to his workers. The costly reredos in Mirfield parish church with its alabaster figures and angels in glistening mosaics at either side had been given by him. His widow continued to live at Hall Croft for ten years after her husband's death until, having failed to find a buyer, she moved south. So when the pioneer party of Longridge and Sampson on 20 January 1898 slept on mats in what is now the Upper Library, the house had been empty for over ten years.

Approached from the drive, the left part of the house is earnestly Gothic in a rather tired High Victorian style owing something to Gilbert Scott. But the porch, guarded above by griffins (and originally surmounted by a blind Gothic arch), is Renaissance in inspiration with pink granite shafts on either side with Gothic carving. The bow windows on the south and west ensure the best of the sun and the views. But the right side of the frontage abandoned Gothic pretensions in favour of four-square simplicity. There is a very curious and inexplicable contrast between the two linked sections and no attempt was made to integrate them stylistically. The porch opens into a large square hall with Gothic panelled doors leading off. Gilded ceiling roses and cornices, lincrusta dadoes and marble fireplaces create an atmosphere of High Victorian opulence. From the entrance hall winds a massive Gothic staircase with heavy carving, almost like something by William Burges.

The eucharist was first celebrated in what was now the House of the Resurrection on 27 January 1898. By the end of the month the house was furnished and brethren arrived. Six were resident: Longridge, Nash, Bull, Sampson, Alston and Thomson (all called 'Mr' in Gore's statement about the move). But Nash was to go to Westminster after Easter with Gore, Rackham, Bickersteth and Frere. Carter would be at Mirfield when not at Pusey House. Gore announced that the Archbishop of Canterbury (Temple) had approved the statutes and agreed to become Visitor to the Community – an indication that CR was in the mainstream of life of the church and of its connections with top table.

At Chapter at Radley earlier that month Gore had said that the Community should not give itself into the hands of those who would welcome them, but rather seek out those who at first would fight shy of contact. The main aim should be to help the clergy, spiritually and intellectually. In the North there was a great demand for good preaching, and a great need to promote religion and the Religious Life among women. Frere however insisted that they had not come simply to help the parochial clergy; they should seek out the best forms of non-parochial work.

Local people reacted with a mixture of pride that such a distinguished group should settle in the neighbourhood, and curiosity as to what their purpose was. 'All the brethren are celebrates [sic], but no monastic vows are taken' announced the *Wakefield Express*. On 6 November 1897 the *Dewsbury Reporter*, writing about the forthcoming arrival, made a comment which revealed the gap between the Community and those to whom it was to minister. Its name was 'gruesome' and ambiguous: did the brothers preach a new faith or seek to resuscitate an old one? The aim of the Community was however admirable:

> ... in contradistinction to the revolutionary tendency of the times, and the pampering and hankering after the frivolities of life, even among our cultured and professional people, it seems hardly credible there should be found a small band of earnest men, mostly in the prime and vigour of their day, who have renounced the casual pleasures of life, and consecrated themselves wholly to a class of spiritual work which, while aggressive in its larger purpose, impels them to an exercise of self-sacrifice which is rarely heard of, even in religious circles ...

They were 'mostly gentlemen of means' who had given their income into a common fund, so 'money is a nonentity'. They lived simply, wore no distinctive dress, took missions and retreats and devoted themselves to literary work, for all were 'highly cultured men' of 'advanced thought and learning'. Unfortunately they were forbidden to give help where it was most needed – in vacant parishes or where clergy had broken down. Nevertheless, the clergy of Lancashire and Yorkshire would benefit from their presence because they were moving north 'to get more in touch with the industrial classes' and were concerned about social problems. The Community was 'fervent but un-demonstrative'.

Gore came up from Westminster briefly to superintend what was locally called the 'flitting'. A Mirfield reporter interviewed him though the questions were curtailed as Gore had to get back to London. Gore defined the work of CR as: 'To promote religion amongst the people. To go into populous districts and assist the clergy who are frequently over-worked ... to conduct missions, send out literature, and generally to serve the people.' 'Is the Community a body of Christian socialists?' Gore dodged: 'I cannot answer that directly . . . we may entertain different views.' Was it true that some were 'sons of wealthy and titled persons' who had given their money to the Community? Gore again temporized. It was self-supporting and derived its income from his Canonry and other sources. Was it a 'monastery'? 'Some people may call it a monastery, but we have no life-long monastic vows.'

The House was not formally opened until 4 May when it was blessed by the Bishop of Wakefield with a eucharist celebrated by him in the chapel which had been created in the former billiard room. It had an altar of 'a mediaeval type' above which was a reredos carved by London workmen. In deference to the Bishop's wishes, there was no incense. The Bishop hoped that the Community would pray for the diocese, help the clergy spiritually and intellectually and perhaps provide a home for fallen clergy.

The daily pattern of worship was very similar to that at Radley. Until 1921 there was no Sunday evensong in the chapel. Brethren attended the three parish churches in the area instead – this continued the Radley pattern when the parish was also the CR chapel; it was also an expression of solidarity with the local church and community. It was decided that brethren were 'at liberty' to clean their own boots and were expected to clean their own rooms. However, the domestic staff of gardener, housekeeper and maids did most of the work. The house and grounds were too large to be looked after by half a dozen brethren in their spare time. The servants were expected to attend Terce and Compline daily. The ready acceptance of domestic staff also reflected the homes and colleges from which they came, where servants were taken for granted. J. W. C. Wand (later Bishop of London) as a married curate on £200 a year in 1911, could afford a living-in maid. William Morris would gather fellow socialists for Sunday evening dinner parties to discuss a new order of society while the servants would be washing up below until 11 p.m. and then have to be up at 5 a.m. the next morning, as one of them who joined the staff in 1891 resentfully recalled. It was all very different in Vassall Road, Kennington where Fr Herbert Kelly and another priest in January 1891 began to train ordinands for work overseas. (From this evolved the Society of the Sacred Mission in 1894.) A cook was the only domestic. Everything else was done by priests and students. 'Saturday was scrubbing day' Kelly said in defiance of the genteel respectability of the Church of England he hated.

The cottages, lodges, grass field, greenhouses and lower garden were let out so CR had only to find £120 of the £200 rent. In July CR gave an At Home and about thirty clergy and laity came for conversation and tea. A share was taken out at the Mirfield Co-operative Society and preference given to tradesmen who observed CSU standards. During the July Quiet Time Rackham noted: 'The air was very bracing: it was fine but very windy, and cool in the mornings and evenings.'

Local newspapers described the brethren as 'mostly rich men' and the Community as 'wealthy'; they were 'highly cultured', 'titled', 'intellectual'. How did such a group think that it was going to make contact with the people of the industrial North? Only Bickersteth had any experience of it. When Morris moved into Kelmscott Manor in 1871 the local working people were highly suspicious of those who had come to lift them up. When he tried to preach Arts and Crafts socialism in Stepney, he was met with incomprehension. 'I don't seem to have got at them yet' (he wrote) 'you see this great class gulf lies between us.' CR did not, of course, conceive of the House as a Toynbee Hall for the West Riding, an open house which would provide religion, education and recreation. Indeed working men were not allowed on the premises, except as retreatants or servants, for an occasional meeting, social event, or for evangelistic services in the quarry. CR had decided to live, not in a group of working-class terraced houses, but in an opulent mansion built by the wealthiest employer of the district. What message did this choice of house convey to working people?

Joseph Hird provides a bitter account of what CR looked like to a working-class lad at the beginning of this century.[3] Probably many working people reacted similarly. Today, mixed with the affection with which CR is regarded in the area, and pride at having a nationally known institution associated with Mirfield, there is also a vein of scepticism encapsulated in the derisive name 'the gentlemen's club'. Hird was born in 1898 and brought up in Kitson Hill Road, a few minutes from the House. His father was a blacksmith at the Three Nuns pit nearby, his mother worked at a mill in Huddersfield. Both rose at 5 a.m. so he had to board with friends during the week until he was eight. The only sanitation was a midden in the garden, plagued by flies in the hot weather. He did not see a bathroom until he joined the army. Battyeford Co-operative Society was a true working class institution which cultivated the mind with a lending library as well as sold goods. Working people enjoyed breeding and racing pigeons, coursing rabbits and drinking. The 'Three Nuns' had two distinct rooms: one for gentry, one for working men, with spittoons on either side of the hearth.

To Hird, the parish church was part of a wealthy national organization which did not need to appeal for funds like the chapels. Yet he became attached to Battyeford parish church. He took part in the annual Whit Walk round the parish, singing hymns led by the Military Band. The first stop was Field Head: 'we were showing appreciation of the connection of the gentry with the Established Church'. They also sang at the House. He was highly critical of the clergy; they did not visit the people; the vicar went on holiday to Switzerland from Easter to Whit and spent a month in Ilkley in the summer. The advent of 'T'Resurrection Men' caused 'puzzled incomprehension amongst the workers in the vicinity', not least because they were celibates. But the Community and its neighbours soon settled down to a 'permanent mutual indifference' to one another. The brethren were 'intruders'. They prayed for the workers clattering past in nailed boots to mills and pits, but they had no contact with them. Even Paul Bull preferred preaching socialist sermons to getting in touch with local workers. Yet Hird was then a keen insider: he had been confirmed, was a server, sang in the church choir for ten years and once attended a twenty-four hour retreat at the House. His final verdict is savage: 'Remote interest, without contact, by those gentlemen who knew nothing about the crudities and squalor in which workers were living, almost within a stone's throw, shows how it was possible for the Community to be *in* Mirfield but not *of* it.'

The new Superior

The election of Walter Frere as Superior at the age of thirty-eight in January 1902 was such a momentous change that some have described it as 'The Second Foundation'. 'Who is that man with a face like St Bruno, singing passionate Breton love songs?' asked a visitor to the house of Bishop E. S. Talbot. It was Frere, one of the examining chaplains who, after ordinations, would play anything that was asked for, from the greater part of a Wagner opera to songs by Schubert or Somervell. It was Frere's influence which drew Keble Talbot to Mirfield in 1906.

Mrs Marion Pobjoy (whose husband trained at the College and later wrote the history of Mirfield) grew up in Mirfield at the beginning of the century. In conversation she recalled that her memories of Frere began with music. She, like the brethren, was at home in the culture of the big houses and so viewed Mirfield and C R from a quite different perspective from Hird. As a young girl she played the piano for Mrs Walker Brooke, the daughter of the Hague Cooks of Hall Croft, a grand lady who lived in Warren House below Field Head. She was very musical and had visited the musical centres of Europe, so had much in common with Frere. She and her daughter at Field Head kept open house for the brethren. Marion Pobjoy first met Frere at Warren House. 'He laughed a lot, had a charming grin, lovely, not austere.' In 1920 Frere and Longridge and other brethren encouraged the formation of the Mirfield Civic Society. Frere was its first President. Frere once lectured on Musical Form; while Marion Pobjoy illustrated the lecture on the piano, Frere danced about the platform. 'He had ordinary people lapping it up.' The Civic Society lasted until the late 1920s. By then everything in England was becoming less local as people became more mobile. Another incident corrects the impression that Frere was grimly austere. In 1920 he and Frederick King went by boat to Canada to conduct missions and retreats. In the middle of a storm when Canadian magnates were fortifying themselves with champagne and elderly ladies were being propelled violently across the deck from their chairs, Frere arose and lightly walked to the piano, having on the way restored a truant glass to its owner. He then proceeded to play and sing songs for one and a half hours in most of the languages of Europe. Neville Figgis once remarked of Frere's lilting walk, 'it makes it easier to believe in the Ascension'. When Frere lectured to the Leeds Arts Club in 1910 on mediaeval music his imitation of a popular warbling song created gales of laughter. The Club was one of the most remarkable centres of experimental art and radical thought (including Guild Socialism) outside London. Michael Sadler, Vice-Chancellor of Leeds, a good friend to C R and the Leeds Hostel, became a leading light in the Club.[4]

Brethren preached regularly in local churches. Because of the Nonconformist ethos of the area people expected sermons to be dramatic. After Frere preached at the mission church, an old lady remarked: 'I mak nowt t'Frere; he donna sweeat enough' – 'I don't make anything of Frere, he doesn't sweat enough'. Frere's cool detachment, rationality, orderly mind, discipline and capacity for focussed attention enabled him to do an immense amount of academic work alongside all his duties as Superior – his three volume edition of the *Hereford Breviary* (1904–1915) concluded with 200 pages of indices and tables. For seventeen years he was Superior (1902–13, 1916–22) during this burgeoning period of C R's life. A holiday abroad with Frere was strenuous – there was always work to be done in libraries and each new place had to be trudged round in search of a *pension* disreputable enough to satisfy his severe idea of the simple life.

Frere came to the office of Superior with a clear conception of what C R should be – he had already worked this out in the early days at Radley and even before that. His concept of C R was set out in his *Commentary on the Rule* (1907). Though it had no binding authority it exercised a deep and continuing influence on C R because of the character and status of its author and because it remained the only Commentary until Hubert Northcott's *Commentary* of 1955. Frere's *Commentary* was shrewd and unpietistic, striking a skilful balance between compassion and demand. He presents the Religious Life not as superior to, but as a distinctive expansion of, the general Christian vocation. The Community had learned from all good precedents of the Religious Life without being bound to any particular form of them. 'The ideals are pitched high, but the positive requirements are pitched low; much is left to the spiritual ambition of individuals, and to the uncovenanted claims of community life.' Permanent vows are valuable but 'It has always been the rule of our Community that steadfastness should be supported by other means than vows . . . it is far better that a brother should be free to go, than that he should be bound to a false position.' The basis of the Community is 'an ideal of life', not simply the sharing of a common task. There must be a balance between the duty of the Community to respect individuality and a brother's trust of the Community to achieve this, but 'fidelity to God must be for him of greater moment than either loyalty or obedience to the Community'. Yet a brother should feel an obligation to 'self-repression' as well as to 'self-assertion'. Worship is to be corporate, expressed in the primitive ideal of a common eucharist rather than by the mediaeval practice of private masses. History shows that absolute poverty is unattainable. So the Community practises community of goods and simplicity of life.

Celibacy is good only when, as an act of renunciation in response to God, it leads to 'detachment, to concentration, to efficiency in work, to the forcible taking possession of the kingdom of heaven'. He draws analogies from marriage and family life. Brethren should have 'the mutual society, help and comfort' of one another. Because women's influence is absent, brethren need to pay particular attention to courtesy. Self-centredness is a danger for those deprived of the self-sacrifice which marriage demands. 'In little points of domestic etiquette and manners we follow the model of the well-ordered family.' Yet the Community demands a far greater merging of individuals than a family. He acknowledged the influence of other current social attitudes: in early monasticism the government was parental; in the Cluniac reform it was feudal; among the Jesuits it is military. 'A modern community such as ours very naturally has much that is democratic in its system of government.' A passage about recreation shows him to be in the *Lux Mundi* tradition not that of Pusey or Benson:

> A right use of the world is as important as a right detachment from it, and perhaps as difficult. In the common life of the primitive Church at Jerusalem no trace is discernible of that element so prominent in much monastic asceticism, which, under oriental and pantheistic influences, tends to look upon God's world as evil. As 'sons of the Resurrection' we shall see in the Incarnation that which sanctifies afresh the world of God's making, and leaves only the world that refuses God, 'lying in the Evil One' . . . Our Community therefore lays down no ascetic prohibitions. It recognises that there are many innocent things that a brother will forgo, not because there is evil in them, but because the evil in him or in others is still too strong to allow him as yet to use them rightly.

Bull expounded the Religious Life as an 'emphatic form' of the Christian vocation, a call to special intimacy with Christ and an expression of that 'differentiation of function' appropriate to every developed society. Just as family doctors need the help of specialists, so parish priests need 'the more mobile cavalry of the Religious Orders'. Celibacy also delivered clergy from the class system.[5] A collect, which was widely used by Anglican Communities (including CR) until recently, prayed: 'O Lord, who didst admit to special intimacy with thyself the chosen three among thy twelve apostles, call many even now, both of men and women, to share the like privilege in the Religious Life . . . ' Thus Anglo-Catholics who often campaigned against class barriers in church and state, replaced them by a spiritual caste system which they, just like the upholders of the old social hierarchy, defended as divinely ordained.

The combination of Gore's personal magnetism and vocational uncertainty had almost paralysed the development of CR. But his departure and the closure of the Westminster House in January 1902 freed CR to strengthen its stakes and lengthen its cords (in Talbot's phrase, *CRQ* JB 1942). At last in Frere they had a Superior who lived with the brethren at the Mother House and who was wholly committed to the life and development of the Community. Things began to happen. In 1902, Frere's first year as Superior, the House was purchased on 1 September, the foundation of the Theological College at Mirfield was laid on 28 October and on 13 December the first three brethren left to establish a house in Johannesburg. Thus within a few months CR had decided to inaugurate what were to become its two most important works. Yet it was still quite small with only fourteen professed brethren. Frere's daring was a consequence of his detachment. He appeared to govern CR with a light hand, but his clear mind was always two moves ahead and he often advanced obliquely, like a knight in chess evading capture by partisans (as Talbot put it in Phillips' biography of Frere), a 'strange mixture of saintliness and foxiness'. Because he felt no emotional obligation to the Gore tradition, he was free to select or reject from it whatever he believed CR needed.

That first year there were other significant changes. Frere was to be known as 'Superior'. But a majority wished to be able to call the Superior by his Christian name in ordinary conversation, something no one had ever done with Gore. (It was characteristic of CR that also in January 1902, Chapter heard a paper on the crisis in British industry.) The domestic establishment was reduced to a gardener, housekeeper and two maids. Domestic work to be done by the brethren increased and became compulsory. 'Brethren shall clean their own Boots, do their own coal duty, stamp their own letters and look after their own guests. Brothers in residence shall do Community Guests' Boots and Rooms, wait at Table and clear after meals, except at Breakfast.' Each brother, except the Superior, was expected to do not less than four hours' manual work a week. The use of the term 'Father', which Gore had rejected, now became common, though brethren were free to decide what they wished to be called. The resolution about this began characteristically 'In order to safeguard the liberty of individual brethren . . . ' A deficit was reported – hardly surprising as CR no longer had Gore's salary to draw upon – but smaller than expected because of Gore's donation of his book royalties. The deficit was covered by economies on clothes, cancellation of most charitable subscriptions (£150 had been given away in 1899) and a reduction of the annual individual peculium from £6 to £3. Finances improved somewhat in 1903 when Frere became a Proprietor of *Hymns Ancient and Modern*.

The fact that Hall Croft had been empty for ten years shows that it and the estate were regarded as too expensive to take on at a time of economic depression. In 1897 CR was told it could probably purchase it at less than the asking price of £10,000, so early in 1902 CR offered £5,000. The offer was declined. The brethren now considered purchasing Bank House, a large house (since demolished) on Stocks Bank, on the way into Mirfield. However in April CR's offer for Hall Croft was accepted and the house, with nineteen acres, was transferred to Trustees on 1 September. Frere contributed £2,000, Bickersteth £1,000, Benson, Rackham and Nash each £500, a total of £4,500 in return for 3½% interest till death. The house could now be altered and other building work could be planned. A bell turret was erected on the roof. A Della Robbia plaque of St Dominic and St Francis embracing was placed over the door. (Gore on a visit to Florence in 1890 had greatly admired this.) No doubt the scholarly work of the community was thought of as represented by St Dominic and its concern for the poor by St Francis. 'Domus Resurrectionis MDCCCVIII' was inscribed over the porch. The walls of three bedrooms were demolished to make a more spacious chapel (now the Upper Library). A. H. Skipworth, a London architect, who was to produce notable plans for the church in 1906, designed the altar and a Gothic screen to enclose the brethren's stalls (which faced the altar not each other). The altar (with riddel posts) stood in front of a boarded-up bay window. A plaque of the Virgin and child (now in the Nativity chapel) was placed on the wall at the side of the altar.

In July 1902, John Carter did not renew his pledge. He seems to have withdrawn because of the departure of Gore, the election of Frere and his belief that CR was becoming more monastic. Neither in *Crockford's* nor in *Who's Who* did he include his membership of CR. Carter in a letter of 18 October 1891 to Rackham had taken an instrumental view of the Religious Life. Vows (he wrote), even permanent vows were acceptable if they helped individuals to do their work more effectively.

> But to make vows *per se* something so extraordinary in self-sacrifice that they exalt those who undertake them into a class *absolutely* nearer to God and separate from and on a higher plane than the rest of the body of the faithful, seems to me unChristian . . . the celibate is not *ipso facto* nearer to God than a married person.

He added significantly: 'So long as we have C.G. all goes well and marvellous as he is in the sweep of his sympathies and the breadth of his mind.' In another letter to Rackham of 12 March 1893 he wrote that after a short breathing space for Gore at Radley, CR should move its headquarters back to Pusey House. Carter joined CR as a disciple of Gore's and because it seemed pledged to promote CSU to which Carter was devoting all his dynamism. But Gore had now gone. The purchase of the House made it clear that CR was to be permanently based at Mirfield, not Oxford. He probably suspected that Frere's election would turn CR away from political commitment – though in fact the period when brethren were most publicly and controversially involved in political affairs was after he had left, between 1906 and 1910. But by continuing to live mostly at Pusey, Carter had inevitably become isolated from CR. Carter's election as an Oxford City councillor in 1901 showed his commitment both to politics and to Oxford. He continued to be resident at Pusey until 1921. Until 1933 he was a University member of the City Council, Alderman 1913–32 and Mayor 1925–6. In 1941, aged eighty, he became vicar of Tollesbury, Essex where he died three years later. He seems never to have married.

However much Gore and Frere differed, they were basically agreed about the nature of worship and the need for liturgical discipline. This was fortunate as most of the brethren were keen to 'enrich' the services of the Church of England, and to record every 'advance'. Though the chapel was not a parish church, altar services were placed under the jurisdiction of the Bishop of Wakefield who warmly acknowledged CR's liturgical loyalty and obedience. Because Gore and Frere believed in a restrained English (not Roman) liturgy and believed that lawful authority should be obeyed (even if disagreeable) the CR 'advance' was slow. In 1898 CR agreed to abide by the Lincoln Judgment (that the chalice should not be mixed during the service, the manual acts should be visible and the sign of the cross should not be used) and continued its obedience until 1920. After the Lambeth Opinion of 1899 CR stopped using incense. When its use was resumed in 1902, it was confined to the introit, which was, strictly speaking, not part of the service. In 1898 CR began to use whole sheets of wafers, to symbolize the 'one bread'. In 1902 the *English Liturgy* (of which Frere was one of the editors) was adopted. It provided extra propers for lesser feasts, but in other respects was loyal to the *Prayer Book*. That year the chapel bell began to be rung after the prayer of consecration. Ashes were first used on Ash Wednesday 1903 and pictures and crosses veiled during Lent. In 1904 a Paschal Candle was introduced. The first Christmas crib was set up in 1911. In 1916 when Frere asked for permission to re-arrange the Prayer Book Canon ('the interim rite' as it became known), the bishop regretfully refused. At the opening of the Leeds Hostel in 1910 the building was blessed with prayer and incense, but Gore (by then Visitor) would not use holy water. But he gave permission for holy water stoups in the chapel at Mirfield in 1916 and for the use of holy water at funerals and for the blessing of crosses for the belts of the newly professed. By 1920 the use of the Ten Commandments at the eucharist had gradually withered away.

Hugh Benson

On 1 October 1898 two potential probationers arrived at Mirfield who, in totally different ways, brought painful notoriety to CR: Samuel Healy who (as we shall see in the next chapter) created damaging public controversy by his militant socialism, and Hugh Benson,[6] the youngest son of E. W. Benson, Archbishop of Canterbury 1883–96. Hugh became a contentious figure by his conversion to Roman Catholicism in 1903; his subsequent descriptions of life at Mirfield were seized upon and widely publicized by protestant campaigners. Though the fiery Healy and the dreamy Benson were so very different in background and politics, they became close friends. Benson admired Healy as a missioner, and was deeply grieved when his polemics against the Church of England after his conversion created an irreparable breach.

It is worth spending some time on Benson, partly because writings by and about him provide detailed accounts of life at Mirfield, partly because his life is a sad study in religious and monastic pathology. The two most enduring legacies from the Bensons are the Service of Nine Lessons and Carols, which E. W. Benson promoted when he was Bishop of Truro, and 'Land of Hope and Glory', written by his son Arthur. They were a bizarre and tragic family. E. W. Benson at the age of twenty-four proposed to his future wife when she was twelve. He suffered all his life from deep depressions. After Hugh's birth in 1871 his mother suffered a breakdown during which her latent lesbianism surfaced. After her husband's death she shared the marital bed with Lucy Tait, daughter of the former Archbishop. Hugh, his sisters Maggie and Nellie, his brothers Arthur and Fred, were all, to varying degrees, homosexual and all suffered from mental illnesses. In 1906 Maggie attacked her mother and/or Lucy Tait with a carving knife and thereafter was confined to an asylum. No wonder that Fred and Arthur believed that it was merciful that none of them had married so the line would become extinct. All five found a refuge from life in writing; Fred published 93 books, Arthur 60 and Hugh 40.

After Eton, Trinity College Cambridge and ordination training under Dean Vaughan, Hugh was ordained by his father in 1894. Whereas his older brothers had rejected faith and ecclesiasticism, Hugh from childhood had been fascinated by both. As a boy he had enjoyed being server to his father, dressed in a little scarlet cassock and cap with surplice (now preserved in Truro Cathedral). He was sent to Eton College Mission in Hackney, a tough assignment wholly unsuitable for a delicate and mystical curate. His next curacy – at Kemsing where the wealthy vicar visited in a shining landau – was more to his taste. To Hugh, life was a romantic game punctuated (when he was happy) by cries of 'Isn't it fun?' He was fascinated by satanism, hyponotism, the occult, and ghost stories and relished Pater, Huysmans, Zola, Maeterlinck and Wagner. Young ladies and marriage repelled him. He wished to be sexless. He began a retreat address on 'Purity': 'Contemplate an angel. Feet . . . are unstained. White robe – unsoiled . . . purity shines in his face . . . Never known . . . an impure thought . . . '

At Eton he read Shorthouse's *John Inglesant*. Soon he knew much of it by heart. Its descriptions of community life at Little Gidding and its fusion of Platonism and nostalgic Catholicism created a great longing in him to recreate and share that kind of experience. Up to ordination he had lived either within the closed corporation of his family or in educational institutions. The various palaces in which the family lived (and his mother's mansion where she lived as a widow) were communal establishments with large staffs. As his father was now dead and the family was growing up and dispersing, Hugh was looking for an alternative family: 'to me . . . the community life seems normal.' But Cowley was too severe and not quite human or English enough. So he sought an interview with Gore at Westminster. He thought CR had 'more family spirit' and was greatly taken by Gore and the house. Gore, however, was hesitant and wished Hugh had had more parochial and general experience, but thought he would benefit from disciplined study and an ordered life. Hugh attended the SR retreat in September 1898 before proceeding to Mirfield.

His admission as probationer filled him with excitement and satisfaction. The attraction of Rome faded. His first year was almost wholly spent in prayer and study. He readily slipped into the routine. But he found Lesser Silence intolerable, and was always bursting into his neighbour to report excitedly on what he had just read. True, the ritual was too moderate and he was scornful that there was a sanctuary lamp but no reservation. So he did what he could to push things on a bit. He designed two altar cloths and secured vestments in liturgical colours to replace the plain linen ones. When Frere was elected Superior he rejoiced: 'a lean man, a theologian, liturgiologist, hymnologist, scholar, musician, preacher, athlete and a saint!' He approved of the changes: more silence, manual and domestic work, the use of 'Superior' and 'Father' and an approximation to a habit.

'It is impossible to describe the happiness which I enjoyed at Mirfield', he wrote in his autobiography. He delighted in the fellowship and produced humorous, affectionate sketches of the brethren to send as Christmas cards. In one, some were depicted playing shuttlecock over a clothes line with newspapers as nets. He worked off some of his energy weeding and making a path and steps up from the Quarry. In 1900 his theatrical talents were employed in a New Year's production of 'The Beauty and the Beast' in a local schoolroom. Hugh particularly enjoyed making up the child actors. But then (as Fred observed) to Hugh all human beings were playmates. The Benson children also delighted in the companionship of animals. When Maggie went up to Lady Margaret Hall in 1883 she took her pet goldfinch. In May 1902 CR was given an Irish terrier. Hugh was ecstatic though he would have liked a parrot as well. It slept under his bed. But in September to Hugh's grief it had to be returned to its owner for it had developed a taste for poaching.

But Mirfield was not all fun and games. His spirituality deepened with frequent quiet days and retreats. The corporate character of the eucharist was emphasized by having only one celebration each day. The Mirfield teaching about intercession stayed with him the rest of his life. Daily he recited the rosary – not a practice then encouraged by CR. (Ronald Knox would rattle his rosary during family prayers conducted by his formidable father, the very protestant Bishop of Manchester.) For Hugh, Mirfield was a refuge from problems, personal and ecclesiastical. Even so he was distressed by differences in churchmanship between the local churches which brethren attended for Sunday evensong, and in the world beyond they were even greater. His tensions erupted in Anglo-Catholic sneers. At a mission in Birmingham in 1902 he announced the hymn 'Faith of our Fathers' and added the petulant comment: 'By those fathers I do not mean Cranmer, Ridley, Latimer and that kind of person.' (Ronald and Wilfred Knox defiantly cycled to the Manchester churches of which their father most disapproved. The Knox brothers took a leading part in the Society of SS Peter and Paul, formed in 1911 to promote baroque catholicism and oppose the English Use advocated by Dearmer and Frere. With typical Anglo-Catholic naughtiness it marketed 'Lambeth Frankincense' and 'Ridley and Latimer Votive Candle Stands'.)[7] Anglo-Catholics of this type demanded an authoritative church but, like adolescents, mocked any Anglican authority which declined to allow them to do whatever they wanted.

Benson's work as a missioner and preacher won admiration even from Bull, who said the brethren were enchanted by his eloquence. One sermon was headed by the nineteen places in which he had preached it, from Guisborough to Cambridge, from Bradford to Worthing. When he was at Kemsing he had told his brother Arthur that his vocation lay in preaching not pastoral work. His brother responded by asking pertinently whether he might not find the discipline he needed in doing the pastoral work which did not interest him, rather than in following his own preferences. After his first year of quiet his mission work was constant and hectic. 'We came from our quiet life red-hot with zeal.' At Market Harborough he exulted in the street processions which were saved from the wrath of protestants by God, the Virgin Mary and St Hugh, helped by the police. In one London parish he and another missioner gave interviews and heard confessions for four days, eleven hours a day. One Lent he preached seventy sermons. At other times (as when he realized that he had engagements for two years ahead) he felt on a treadmill. It was a strain to have to arrive always 'at full steam' and to maintain the momentum. Before preaching he would often have to lie prostrate in the vestry overcome with nerves. But after a fortnight's relief at being quiet back at Mirfield, he longed for the thrill of more engagements.

But there were problems. He could not make up his mind to make his profession and spent the unusually long time of three years as a probationer. There were recurring bouts of Roman fever. The socialist sympathies of Gore and some brethren worried him. He was an aesthetic pietist, a romantic imperialist, totally uninterested in social reform. He wondered whether he was really called to community life. Then during Quiet Time in July 1901 just when he was ready to make his profession, he had a profound shock. Gore began a series of lectures on the synoptic problem. Hugh had never heard anything like it before. The Community refused to allow him to absent himself. His naive view of the Bible can be gauged from a sermon which he once preached on a characteristic text: 'Except ye become as little children'. He attacked 'sterile' criticism which questioned the authority of the church: we must bring the Bible to 'Mother'; 'her authority is final, even when she appears to contradict herself'. Gore drew up a memorandum which was accepted by the brethren and conveyed to Hugh. Membership of the Community involved not only acceptance of the Rule but also of its fellowship. While no inquisition was made into individual opinions, acceptance of the Rule necessitated adherence to 'the Catholic faith and practice'; brethren held different views on many subjects, including biblical criticism, but the Community's tradition was one of free discussion in which all sought to learn from one another. It was a decisive moment both for C R and for Hugh. Gore was astonished that Hugh had never read any of the standard New Testament commentaries. When he urged Hugh to do so, he responded that they would turn him into a complete sceptic. (He also confided to a friend that he thought Gore's *The Body of Christ* 'terrible'.)

After four days absence, he recovered his nerve and reiterated his readiness to be professed. But again Gore shook him by asking him if he might go to Rome. He replied 'No'. So he was elected. His mother came up for his delayed profession on 1 August. That afternoon he drove out with his mother, ecstatically content. But he was still searching for an authoritative voice. The brotherhood tried to sustain him in his turmoil. But as he came down the pulpit steps on Easter Day 1903 he knew it was all over. Yet his immensely popular stories *The Light Invisible*, published that year, written in feverish excitement, show that fundamentally he located authority in subjective religious experience and romantic supernaturalism. 'The child lives in a world of romance' was a sub-heading in one of his sermons. It might have been a self-description.

C R prohibited him from any public ministry after Easter. He was granted leave for a while. When he did not renew his pledge on 25 July his membership lapsed. C R paid him the interest on the loan for the purchase of the house and offered him up to £25 to tide him over. It allowed him the royalties on his book of mediaeval prayers but retained the rights to *The Light Invisible* (which proved lucrative). In September he was received into the Roman Church and the next year was ordained. After an unhappy time in Cambridge, he moved in 1908 to the property at Hare Street, Hertfordshire, which he bought with the proceeds of his writings. He had fortified his fragile ego by submitting to Rome, but otherwise now followed his own inclinations, for ever writing successful meretricious novels, for ever on the move, preaching and lecturing. At Hare Street he was surrounded by still unopened boxes of his father's books – the father which none of his children could ever escape or confront.

In September 1914, Hugh visited the Abbot of Caldey, a boyhood friend, who, with most of his monks, had submitted to Rome the previous year. Gore's challenges had shattered the Abbot's make-believe world as earlier they had shattered Benson's. Should Hugh have gone to romantic Caldey rather than unromantic Mirfield? But he would never have stood the enclosed life and Mirfield, like Benson, belonged to the establishment, whereas uncultured Caldey did not. As Ronald Knox observed: 'When you were with the Cowley Fathers, or with the Community of the Resurrection at Mirfield, a sort of Common-room atmosphere prevailed; you had the same background of College traditions, College loyalties, anecdotes about the dons; beyond the grille of the cloister lay a familiar world . . . all *that* you missed at Caldey.'[8] Hugh arrived in a state of mental collapse. But on the last evening he enthralled the monks with his ghost stories – it was a shared interest in the paranormal which sustained his friendship with Lord Halifax after his conversion. The Abbot was also interested in psychic phenomena; his favourite novel was *Dracula*.

Hugh Benson died on 19 October in the Bishop of Salford's house. Blackened by the Salford murk, fronted by soot-stained shrubs, it was a grim setting for the death of a Peter Pan. He was forty-two. Yet he had never lost his love for Mirfield. 'It will be impossible for me ever to acknowledge adequately the debt of gratitude which I owe to the Community of the Resurrection, or the admiration which I always felt, and still feel, toward their method and spirit.' Sometimes he dreamed of being back at Mirfield 'though never, thank God, as an Anglican!' He kept up relationships with some brethren, but could not understand why he was not allowed to visit. Leaving was 'about the most severe external trial I have ever undergone – I kissed, in Greek fashion, the doorposts of my room as I left it for the last time'. Such a public display of warm affection for an Anglican institution was astonishing from a convert of that time. In 1914 sending some royalties from *The Light Invisible* to Mirfield he wrote: it would be 'a joyful day if Mirfield followed Caldey!! I should certainly come again as a Novice'. For its part CR was remarkably forbearing to someone who had given it damaging publicity. The *Quarterly* for Christmas 1914 carried an affectionate obituary (by Bickersteth) – a gesture towards a brother who had both withdrawn and converted, unparalleled in the history of CR.

Reaching out

Further developments were evidence of the new sense of direction which the move to Mirfield and the election of Frere had brought. The Community now confidently reached out, despite the fact that in 1903, after Benson's departure, it had only thirteen professed brethren of whom eight were at Mirfield, four in South Africa and one in Westminster.

As early as 1896, Bull had proposed the creation of some type of Third Order. In January 1903 the Fraternity of the Resurrection (FR) was created for clerical and male lay companions. Clergy were required to keep part of the

SR Rule, laymen to observe a rule about regular Communion, Bible reading, retreat, prayer, fasting, alms giving and confession. A group of Associates was also created for women as well as men. A year later women were admitted to FR membership. FR had its own badge. The first issue of the *Quarterly* appeared for Lady Day 1903. It provided a means of mustering support for the newly founded College and the new work in South Africa, and an essential link between the Community and Fraternity. The cover design (not replaced until 1935) was art nouveau, hardly a tradition one associates with either CR or the West Riding. Creating and sustaining the various new ventures put great pressures on the Community. In March 1903 Frere reported to the South African House that the brethren were ill and overstrained. Rackham was worried because CR was so preoccupied with committees. In October 1904 Frere's health broke down and he went abroad to recover. Perhaps the last straw for Frere had been the campaign against the 1904 edition of *Hymns Ancient and Modern* (of which he had been the chief architect): its sales were poor and a great deal of money was lost. Later Frere was able to turn some of his work to good effect in the 1000 page historical edition (1909) for which he was awarded a Cambridge DD.

By the turn of the century, the 'Mirfield Fathers', as they began to be known, were familiar figures in the neighbourhood, easily identifiable, as increasingly they wore cassocks outside as well as inside the precincts. The locals saw them walking or cycling to and from the station. Some heard them preaching in local churches, or met them at Sunday evensong. CR owned four bicycles. As happens with communally owned property, one of the bicycles was allowed to get into a bad condition, so a committee had to be formed (in true CR fashion) to oversee their use and maintenance. The locals called them 'the petticoit [petticoat] men' or 'T' Resurrection men'. The House was referred to as 'T' Resurrection', 'The House of Correction' or 'The House of Recreation'. So Yorkshire humour mocked the gentlemen of the South who had come to do them good. Later on, when buses began to run, a visitor who asked for the House would hear the conductor shout 'T' Resurrection next stop' and as it began to slow down, 'Any more for t' Resurrection?'. Bull, fresh from a chaplaincy in the Anglo-Boer War, broke down some local barriers. Despite what Hird wrote, Bull's mixture of imperialism and socialism was attractive to working people. CR's various building projects which employed local labour were welcomed by local people at a time of unemployment. Accepting current social distinctions, CR held two garden parties, one for the 'classes' and the other for the 'masses', in 1903, but attendance was disappointing. Various groups such as the Church Union, Diocesan Union of Men's Bible Classes and church teachers used the grounds for meetings. In 1908 tea was given to one of the Clarion Cyclists' Clubs, created by Robert Blatchford, the atheist socialist. Two hundred servers attended the first Corpus Christi Festival in the grounds in 1913.

The various garden parties and At Homes developed into an annual College Commemoration which in turn developed into the annual Commemoration Day. The College then created its own Festival. An experimental College Commemoration was held in July 1908 but the first proper Commemoration was held a year later when 600–700 came. This included a procession to the College for a Te Deum and prayers in the College quadrangle. Two short plays were performed in a tent at the back of the College. In 1910 for the first time the play was performed in the Quarry – 'The Return of Ulysses' by Robert Bridges. It was produced by Frere. Songs and other music by him were performed by students. Several hundred came but catering arrangements underestimated Yorkshire appetites. In 1911 music by Elgar, Grieg, Stanford and Parry was offered in the Quarry and in 1912 sixteenth-century music in the chapel. The 1913 Festival included the York Pageant. By Commemoration 1914, numbers had reached 2,000; a Russian choir sang – probably a fruit of Frere's four visits to Russia between 1909 and 1914. The high cultural tone of these occasions reflected Frere's influence. No attempt was made to relate to, or use working class culture. But at that time churches and chapels unapologetically sought to educate and elevate. If Anglo-Catholicism stood against the social norms by advocating monasticism and confession, because of its incarnationalism and love of tradition, it was able to establish an easy alliance with the arts. This made it attractive to cultured people. But Dolling in the Portsmouth slums rejected what he regarded as the cultural elitism of the Church of England, in favour of the type of music and social events with which working-class people were at home.

CR began also to be well-known in the area and beyond, through the use of the Quarry for Sunday afternoon evangelistic services. The first service arranged by CR was held there in July 1900. It was careful to obtain the consent of local clergy. In 1901 the experiment was repeated and there were good attendances on all four Sundays. Gore, up from London for Chapter, preached and the singing was accompanied by a brass and string band. In 1903 during excavations for stone to complete the College quadrangle, a stone pulpit was built and other improvements made. By 1907 there was seating for 600, but many more stood. That year attendances ranged from 900 to 1,700. In June 1909 the Archbishop of York (Lang) preached to 2,000 men from the diocesan Bible classes. A marvellously evocative picture shows Lang in frock coat, apron and gaiters, like a statue with left arm raised, and many of the men in straw or bowler hats. The Quarry sermons were meaty. The four subjects in 1909 were: 'Have you received the Holy Ghost?'; 'Are your sins forgiven?'; 'How do you keep Sunday?'; 'What happens after Death?'. CR set an example by refusing to sell books at Sunday services. The Quarry was also used for other purposes. A correspondence class from Ruskin Hall (the Oxford working men's college) met there in 1906. It was also used (as we shall see in the next chapter) for highly controversial conferences with Labour leaders in 1906 and 1907.

To West Riding people, the Quarry services were not wholly novel. At the woollen town of Heckmondwike, three miles from Mirfield, a similar annual event (called 'The Heckmondwike Lecture') had been drawing crowds to hear Nonconformist sermons since the mid-eighteenth century. Heckmondwike was a strong centre of Nonconformity, with (in the latter part of the nineteenth century) eight chapels, as well as the parish and the Roman Catholic churches, to serve a population of 10,000. Over 2,600 children attended the many Sunday schools. The astonishing triumphalism of the Upper Independent chapel, built eight years before CR moved to Mirfield, with its gigantic portico, baroque tower and graveyard with huge and elaborate monuments, demonstrated the wealth and pretensions of the local Congregationalist families. A century later, the chapel which symbolized the remarkable ascent of Nonconformity was derelict, its graveyard overgrown. But when it was first opened, the factories closed for the day of the sermons and the town took a holiday. Five very substantial sermons were preached in the three Congregationalist chapels. The fact that in two chapels, a couple of sermons followed one another without a break, and that all five sermons were reported *in extenso* in the local paper, reveals a great deal about the appetite for preaching. The sermons continued until the mid-1970s, exactly when CR concluded that there was no longer any demand for Quarry services and part of the amphitheatre was allowed to fall into disuse. The people of Heckmondwike who (according to Mrs Gaskell's *Life of Charlotte Bronte*) used to worry a good deal about doctrine probably do so no longer, and the ones who are religious today no doubt follow the general trend and prefer affirmative religious celebrations to anything which requires mental effort. No longer are religious events important social occasions gathering local communities together. In any case there are plenty of other ways of spending leisure time.

CR's message to this staunchly Nonconformist area was conveyed by the erection in 1913 of a crucifix, fifteen feet high, on the edge of the escarpment, where it could be seen by passing railway passengers and workers. At the turn of the century there was renewed anxiety that despite all the efforts of the Church of England and the Free Churches to reach and convert working class people, these had largely failed. E. S. Talbot told the 1902 Church Congress: ' . . .there is among us a sense of discouragement. We doubt whether we are making way. There is a sense that we are not on the flow of the tide, and perhaps feel its ebb.' This remark attracted widespread comment for its truth was all too evident. A friend of Gore's, C. F. G Masterman, who married a niece of Mrs Talbot's, and who lived for a time in a tenement in Camberwell and later became a Liberal MP, wrote in 1904:

> We come *from outside* with our gospel, aliens with alien ideas . . . The Anglican church represents the ideas of the upper classes, of the universities . . . The large

Nonconformist bodies represent the ideas of the middle classes . . . Each totally
fails to apprehend a vision of life as reared in a mean street, and now confronting
existence on a hazardous weekly wage, from a block dwelling . . . Our movements and inexplicable energies are received with a mixture of tolerance and
perplexity.[9]

Gore told the 1906 Church Congress that the primitive church was 'ranked
among, and spoke for, the poor'. In the Church of England there was now
freedom for biblical criticism and Catholic ceremonial; spiritually there had
been great revivals; the ideal of a self-governing church was gaining ground;
'we have laboured very hard for the poor, and amongst them'. Yet it 'all hangs
fire'. The church was powerless, 'in spite of even splendid exceptions in this or
that parish, to produce any broad, corporate effect, to make any effective
spiritual appeal by its own proper influence, in the great democracy of
England today. We are not in touch with the mass of the labouring people.'
The church worked among the poor from above, not alongside, for the bishops'
incomes ranked them with the wealthy and the clergy were most at home with
gentry and professional people. Episcopal incomes should be reduced. More
ordinands should be drawn from working-class people and be helped to retain
the outlook of those with whom they had grown up. Working-class people
should be represented at all church meetings.[10]

Talbot, Masterman and Gore were right. But Gore himself illustrated the
problem he addressed. He had found himself incapable of transcending the
background in which he was reared when he was among the working people of
Radley. He frankly confessed to the Congress: 'This sermon is only the cry of
a permanently troubled conscience which cannot see its way.' The brethren
were also products of their own establishment backgrounds. Once working-
class ordinands had been through Leeds University and theological education
at Mirfield and had then been subjected to being moulded by the whole
apparatus and ethos of the Church of England, they were effectively re-
classed. By contrast, the English Roman Catholic Church started with a solid
working-class base, heavily reinforced by Irish immigration. Its clergy were
not trained in universities but in seminaries, where though they were
separated from their peers and became a priestly caste, they retained very
largely the working-class culture from which most of them came. Celibacy
detached them from the pressure to be or become middle class which clerical
marriage exerts. One reason why some Anglo-Catholic priests adopted
ultramontane styles of priesthood and worship was that they saw these being
effective among working-class people in Roman Catholic parishes. The
brethren who arranged the Quarry Services, ran parish missions and
organized the meetings with Labour leaders in 1906 and 1907 had, like Gore,
'a permanently troubled conscience'. What they could not accept was that
English working-class people had their own version of Christianity, which

though dependent upon the churches and chapels being there, did not include regular public worship amongst its essential tenets.

From its earliest days CR had conducted parish missions. This was one of its chief activities and also one of the main ways in which it recruited members of FR and generally became known to the public. CR also conducted many missions overseas – in the United States, Canada, Australia, New Zealand and elsewhere. It also published cheap books of instruction and tracts. By 1906 it had sold 240,000 of the 'Mirfield Manuals', 90,000 of 'Papers for the People' and 375,000 of 'Seeds of Truth'. Bull was the general editor of these series and author of many of the individual tracts. By the 1920s, over 2¼ million of them had been sold.

In English Roman Catholicism, parish missions, often conducted by Religious Orders, had become common. They promoted ultramontane devotion and employed street preaching, processions and dramatic ceremonies. Sermons emphasized the proximity of death and the horrors of hell. People were called to repentance, confession and absolution. Anglo-Catholics learned a good deal from English and French Roman Catholic methods. In 1862 Fr Benson SSJE conducted what was probably the first new type of parish mission. Anglo-Catholics used the term 'parish mission' to distinguish it from Evangelical revivalism which was outside the parochial structures and which was often inter- or non-denominational. People were urged to make a personal commitment to Christ and to express this sacramentally. The mission therefore aimed to persuade many to renew their baptismal vows, make their confessions and to promise regular attendance at the eucharist: a very different programme from Evangelical revivalism. When the mission was conducted by Religious, they followed Roman practice and urged parishioners to join their Third Order.

John Kent's study of Victorian revivalism (to which I am indebted) dismissed claims that a new evangelical Catholicism was emerging, and asserted that the *Lux Mundi* tradition had no interest in evangelism.[11] Yet Frere, lecturing in Russia in 1914, explained that all that was best in the Church of England was a blend between Catholicism and Evangelicalism, and that this was true of CR too.[12] Hugh Benson was happy when a curate accused him of preaching 'a mixture of Romanism and Wesleyanism'. Before preaching, to stoke himself up, he deliberately read the writings of Thomas De Witt Talmage, a sensationalist American Dutch Reformed preacher. Bull wrote (*CRQ* JB 1903) that renewal arose from being in love with Jesus – like Mary, St Francis, John Wesley, Simeon, Pusey, St Teresa and Mrs Booth (an eclectic list indeed). As a militarist and imperialist he was at ease with military metaphors for evangelism common among Evangelicals and Salvationists. 'Until every soul in a parish is rescued from Satan's power, parochial life ought only to be a "rest camp" to prepare for further conflict, and the mission must be a forward movement against the hosts of Satan – a real battle. We must never be content to garrison a half-conquered country.' (He had just returned from the Anglo-Boer War.) Like Dolling, and unlike the Tractarians, he was a great publicist. 'Thou Art the Man' ('800th Thousand'), one of his leaflets for distribution before a parish mission, could be mistaken for an evangelical tract.

> God is sending His Prophets, the Missioners, to help you to see your sins so that they may be **blotted out in the Blood of Christ** . . . **See this sick-bed**. Look at the patient. Hear the frequent cough, the whispered words. The doctor leaves. The clergyman comes. Hear the last prayer . . . A faint struggle – a groan – and it is all over. **Whose death bed** is it? Yours! '**Thou art the man.**' . . . Beyond the Veil two souls are standing, stripped bare and naked, before the Throne of God. Jesus is looking at them. He speaks to one, '**Depart from Me**', and the soul goes shivering away to Hell. Art thou the man?

This was inserted into the *Quarterly* in 1920 when the belief in hell, already weakened by the moral revulsion against it in the nineteenth century, had been banished by the First World War when the bereaved were reassured that those who died for their country were guaranteed a place in heaven.[13] Hugh Benson had also preached traditional hell-fire sermons. 'Listen to the wails of souls in torment' he said. Yet in 1927 when Chapter discussed the question 'What should we teach about hell?' there was a 'general vagueness' about the answer. Bull in *The Missioner's Handbook* (1904) was not a bit vague: 'the fear of Hell and hope of Heaven' is 'the motive of conversion'. Though there is little in it about a social gospel, in *Lectures on Preaching* (1922) Bull firmly rejected a religion which is only concerned about the individual soul and 'substitutes an atomic pietism for the glorious Gospel of the Kingdom of God'. But despite the efforts of old-style missioners like Bull to keep the fear of hell alive, a benign universalism prevailed. Thus one of the chief motives for evangelism and conversion disappeared.

By 1906 ten brethren were more or less continuously engaged in missions. Between August 1910 and January 1911 brethren conducted twenty missions and eight retreats. Brethren took part in the annual mission to hop-pickers. Talbot wrote in 1908: 'I have rarely been more wretched, so far as physical comfort is concerned: under dripping canvas, on muddy sodden grass, in continuous rain; cold, fireless, bathless; our only warmth the poisonous fug of a crowded hoppers' tent . . .' During Lent and Holy Week – the observance of which Anglo-Catholics had done so much to promote – brethren were in great demand: in 1911 they preached in eighteen places from Quebec to Bradford, from Brooklyn to Dundee. Courses were run for missioners. At the one in 1913 Keble Talbot, Timothy Rees and Alfred Drury argued that the need for social reform was an essential theme in any mission. This caused controversy among some of the ninety-five priests attending.

The *Mirfield Mission Hymnbook* (1907), a collection of popular Catholic and Evangelical hymns, was prepared by Bickersteth, Healy and Sampson, all popular missioners. *Ancient and Modern* (first published 1861) was too sober and too moderate in churchmanship for Mirfield missions and the Anglo-Catholic *English Hymnal* (1906) too high-brow. The Moody and Sankey missions had relied heavily on sentimental hymns set to popular tunes. The rise of the hymn in all traditions expressed the shift from a more doctrinal to a more subjective and emotional faith, which E. S. Talbot termed 'diffusive Christianity'. By 1922 the *Mirfield Mission Hymnbook* had sold 700,000 copies. That year a new edition was produced with fifty new hymns which were either more definitely Anglo-Catholic or taught the social gospel. The Preface explained: 'it is the happy experience of our mission fathers that the fullest expression of devotion to our Blessed Lord, and the evangelical assertion of the power of His Precious Blood, leads on to the fullness of Catholic worship and the application of our religion to the social service of mankind'. Seven of the new hymns were by Timothy Rees. Some old catchy tunes were retained because they appealed to ordinary people. It continued to sell until the 1970s.

Building

As numbers grew so various additions to the House became necessary. In 1906 the first major extension was completed – a dining room to seat seventy, designed by Graham and Jessop of Huddersfield in Jacobethan style with projecting bays reminiscent of an Oxbridge college. It also provided extra rooms above. That year, a second extension was finished, designed by Caleb Ritson, the Warden and architect of the College. Plain as a factory, it continued the frontage to the north providing twelve extra rooms, including six for servants. Electric light was installed in 1905 in public rooms and extended to the whole house in 1909, though Frere worried that this was a descent into luxury.

The growth of the Community and College also meant that the house chapel was no longer adequate. There was nowhere large enough for the students to worship with the Community. An article by Frank Biggart (*CRQ* MD 1911) went beyond such pragmatic considerations. Even if the work in South Africa and the College were to cease (he wrote) 'the Community would still go on fulfilling its primary purpose, which is the worship and service of Almighty God'. He added that the beginning of a renewal of 'the dedicated life' was in part a consequent of 'the marked failures of mere philanthropy' (an almost exact quotation from Frere's *Commentary*). By then, CR was less sanguine about, and less committed to, political and social action. Some brethren wanted a large and impressive church because it would make the Community more like a traditional monastery. The belief that a place of worship is an offering to God is biblical; less often remembered is the biblical vein of scepticism about temples, summarized in Acts 7.

In 1905, A. H. Skipworth, the London architect who had designed the altar and screen for the house chapel in 1902, was invited to submit plans for a new chapel and dining room.[14] Skipworth, whose uncle the Bishop of Bristol was friendly with Gore and Frere, was a pupil of Bodley's and a member of the Art Workers' Guild (1884). Influenced by Morris and Ruskin, the Guild aimed to replace industrial methods with craftsmanship. Rooted in Victorian socialism the Guild must have appealed to CR. Like CR, it sought to restore a lost simplicity. The interest of some brethren in Guild Socialism with its nostalgia for mediaeval society dates from this period. Skipworth's submission for the highly contentious competition for a new cathedral for Liverpool (1903) was in the Arts and Crafts tradition. To his deep disappointment it only received an honourable mention. He worked quickly on the designs for Mirfield and these were exhibited in May 1906. His proposed Edwardian Gothic church echoed features of his rejected Liverpool designs. The eye responds to its verticality, rising to a central lantern tower topped by a spire, with the roof supported by flying buttresses. Despite the Gothic windows, the interior was more Byzantine with pillars surmounted by polychromatic arches. The columns supporting the tower formed a type of ciborium over the high altar. Below was a spacious crypt. The Arts and Crafts screen was in marble and metal. Gothic cloisters ran to House and College. Skipworth explained that the windows were high and not too large in order to avoid the glare from which most modern buildings suffered. He wanted to provide 'dim religious light'. The Community had not formally accepted the designs, therefore their public exhibition was embarrassing. At the Greater Chapter in October 1906, strong opposition was expressed to embarking upon such a large scheme. But in April 1907 Skipworth died aged forty-five after years of ill-health. However original his designs (and he skilfully used the dramatic possibilities of the steep slope) the building would have quickly dated and the Community would have been permanently saddled with a very churchy expression of its life and worship, which would have jarred with the plainness of most of the other buildings.

In July other architects were invited to submit designs. At that Chapter, Temple Moore's designs for the Hostel at Leeds were approved. Nearby in Harrogate Temple Moore's finest church, St Wilfrid's, was being built. He 'spoke Gothic with a strong Yorkshire accent' said H. S. Goodhart-Rendel. For Mirfield, Temple Moore designed a characteristically vigorous church in what he called a 'severe type of Early English Gothic'. CR had asked for an 'early simple style'. It was to have a massive central tower surmounted by a squat spire with huge buttresses awkwardly shoring up the west end. Of the four designs submitted, only those by Temple Moore and Walter Tapper were thought to merit further consideration. Both were exhibited at the Garden Party in the summer of 1908. Tapper's very different design was formally accepted by Chapter in July. A document prepared for the Assessor stated bluntly: 'Obviously *not* "Gothic" but probably Byzantine in feeling.'

Why 'obviously *not* Gothic'? There had clearly been a complete change of mind. Having seen Skipworth's designs, CR presumably realized that if it aspired to be genuinely modern as well as primitive, Gothic would not do. Cowley was criticized by some of the early brethren as mediaeval – their new church by Bodley (1896) was Gothic. Perhaps the choice of Byzantine was influenced by Frere's interest in Eastern Orthodoxy? Gore and Bull knew, and Keble Talbot greatly admired, Dolling's Romanesque church in Portsmouth (1893–5). Brethren would know St Aidan's Leeds (1891–4), also Romanesque. Perhaps brethren saw *The Builder* (20 April 1907) in which Skipworth's death was reported and which also included drawings and a photograph of Westminster Cathedral opened in 1903 and designed by J. F. Bentley, another member of the Art Workers' Guild. Interest in the Byzantine style had been growing, but it was Bentley's great and moving building which drew attention to its potentialities. Cardinal Vaughan chose Byzantine because he thought it early Christian, would facilitate congregational participation, was cheaper and was as unlike Westminster Abbey as possible. Tapper's original designs were clearly influenced by both Westminster Cathedral and French Romanesque. The Assessor's notes asked for a nave to seat 100 and choir stalls for 50. Side altars were required 'since all the Fathers wish to officiate at Mass daily' (who authorized that statement?). Since the Community had adopted 'great simplicity of life' the 'austerity and simple dignity of the early Monasteries should be borne in mind'. As finances did not permit immediate completion so operations could be spread over a century. It says much about the self-confidence of the Community, with still only twenty brethren, that it could project itself so far into the future.

Walter Tapper (1861–1935) came from humble stock.[15] He was apprenticed first to Champneys, then worked with Bodley for eighteen years. Before the war he mostly designed churches, including The Ascension Malvern Link, St Erkenwald's Southend-on-Sea, St Mary's Harrogate and The Annunciation Marble Arch: all are Gothic, influenced by Bodley. But the Church of Our Lady and St Thomas, Gorton (1925), built with money donated to CR has a Byzantine flavour. *The Builder* thought that Tapper's Gothic design for Liverpool Cathedral should have won the competition. Later he was disappointed again not to be chosen as the architect of Guildford Cathedral. Perhaps Tapper first became known to CR through his first church, The Ascension at Malvern Link, dedicated by Gore in October 1903 and inspired by thirteenth-century Cistercian churches like Abbey Dore, Herefordshire.

Tapper's first designs for Mirfield re-worked his Liverpool proposals using Byzantine style outside, Romanesque style within. So his west end for Mirfield was derived from the west end of Liverpool; both echoed the west front of Tewksbury Abbey. The east end was to be square like that at Liverpool. Tapper described the style as 'Early Cistercian simplicity – but a modern not Mediaeval building'. He proposed four great bays with a gallery all round. The building would impress by 'stately and impressive proportions' rather than by 'elaboration of detail'. But he suggested that it would need colour, with decorated vaults, stained glass, a high altar of marble with wooden ciborium and screens of marble and metal forming the choir. Overall it should have a 'strong masculine character'.

The drawings of 1909 showed a recessed west front with rose window, topped by cupolas derived from Westminster Cathedral and huge staircases on either side with banded stone. There were also echoes of Albi Cathedral (as at The Annunciation, Marble Arch). The nave was to rise to 72 feet, 30 feet above the Chapel of the Resurrection, the east end of the nave being topped by two further cupolas, with some russet and white banding. Internally it looked French Romanesque. A dense decorative iron screen separated nave and choir. By 1911 the proposed length of the building had grown to 275 feet, and the Chapel of the Resurrection had become apsidal. Cloisters would run to House and College. It is amazing that the Community could contemplate a church so immense and triumphalist. It may have been intended to display Cistercian simplicity. In fact it spoke loudly of both Edwardian opulence and a desire to build an Abbey church on the scale of Rievaulx or Fountains.

The building of the church was delayed by a financial crisis caused by the public controversies to be detailed in the next chapter. In January 1907 a Chapel Fund had been created from accumulated monies. It was a CR principle not to appeal for its own needs. But at last in January 1911 Chapter resolved to build the church without delay. The foundation stone of the Chapel of the Resurrection was laid on 22 July 1911 by Gore during the Commemoration Festival and his Visitation. About 1,500 attended. Gore had explained to Frere that he was 'all for incense' at the ceremony but refused to use holy water or oil. 'I do not take kindly to the anointing of *things* and I am not desirous to introduce holy water. I have declined it here [i.e. in his diocese]. And I think I should still less introduce it in someone else's diocese, even in a religious house.' The *Veni Creator* was sung in Latin. The workmen and their wives had been given tickets for the stonelaying. From the beginning of the work, daily prayers had been said with them and a temperance drink provided. After Christmas they were invited to an entertainment. The screen from the House chapel was given to Battyeford parish church. The first evensong was held in the Chapel of the Resurrection on 13 September 1912. The first bay was provided with a temporary roof. The Chapel of the Ascension was completed with the help of money from American friends; the eucharist was celebrated there for the first time in April 1914. However, Tapper's estimates proved wildly wrong. The first stage cost not £5,000 but £12,000.

From early days CR offered retreats at Mirfield for priests and laymen. Retreats for women were conducted elsewhere. Individuals also came. J. A. Kempthorne, a priest with a social conscience, came to prepare for his consecration as Bishop of Hull in 1910. In 1913 it was decided to build an extra wing for guests and retreatants and separate servants' accommodation, both designed by Chorley of Leeds in Jacobethan style. The appeal for £5,000 was reinforced by a reminder of the great number of lay Roman Catholics who went on retreats. The completion was delayed by a strike, despite the Community's mediation. CR urged that the men's demands should be met and the builder compensated for the extra cost. At last in 1915 the Retreat House could be blessed. A crucifix was placed in each of the eighteen rooms. A manufacturer gave the beds. Stone from the Quarry had again been used. In the *Quarterly* for Christmas 1914 readers were told how much strength the courageous Belgians drew from retreats. The Retreat House was completed in 1926, with accommodation for forty-two. Lay retreats were held at weekends – retreats were not just for the leisured classes. In 1931 'Moreton', St Leonard's, was endowed and given to CR by Mrs Helen Reckitt, the wealthy mother of Maurice Reckitt, the leading light in the Christendom Group. There CR held retreats for women as well as men. In 1931 five retreats for priests and eight for laymen were held at Mirfield and sixteen at 'Moreton' and thirteen at other retreat houses. In 1936 184 priests and 108 laymen came on retreat to Mirfield. 'Moreton' was sold in 1948 and St Francis' House, Hemingford Grey was given that year and opened in 1950 as a replacement.

Laymen

St Benedict, the consolidator of western monasticism in the sixth century, was a layman as were all his monks. But by the tenth century it was becoming usual for monks in the west to be ordained. A division grew up between ordained monks whose life centred on the liturgy and lay brothers, often illiterate, who were labourers and servants who were excused the offices and were not members of Chapter. In recent years this sharp division has diminished greatly. Thomas Merton was ordained but in his latter period his monastic vocation became more important than his priesthood. 'I am practically laicized' (he wrote in 1967) 'My hermit life is expressly a *lay* life.' A member of CR said in conversation: 'My priesthood is not important to me. What is important to me is my membership of the Community'. But the Oxford Movement was essentially clerical. Newman urged the clergy in Tract 1 (1833): 'magnify your office', and they did so. Anglo-Catholic priests who, in righteous anger swept away box pews because they divided the Body of Christ by social class, then erected screens to separate themselves and their semi-clericalized servers from laypeople in the nave. Many women's communities were divided into Choir and Lay Sisters. The All Saints' Community, for example, continued this distinction until 1932.[16] By contrast SDC, influenced by Christian socialism, admitted laymen as well as priests; there was nothing in its Rule preventing a layman becoming Superior. However CR was by its foundation a community for priests, and though eventually and grudgingly it admitted laymen it has remained a predominantly clerical community, and has been lopsided as a result.

In the early years of CR there were six main ways in which laymen were or could have been associated with it, apart of course from joining FR.

In 1906 a lay brotherhood was proposed at Mirfield. The next year two laymen arrived and became probationers and two others later joined them. They were in charge of a 'provost' and had a separate common room and table at meals. The Rule was altered to allow this development. They were partly occupied in printing work in the College cellar. But tensions began to surface. Conditions in the cellar were grim. Brethren had to be reminded not to use the laymen as a 'convenience'. Eventually the laymen seem to have revolted because they were being treated as inferiors and extra servants. Class and educational divisions had been reinforced by sacerdotal self-aggrandisement. In April 1909, despite protests from Figgis, Fitzgerald, Murray and Pearse, the experiment was suspended, the remaining two laymen departed and the printing press and carpenter's bench were sold off. That brethren had no more use for a carpenter's bench was profoundly symbolic.

The South African house in Johannesburg in 1906 proposed that laymen should be associated with the work of the Community there as carpenters, book-keepers, farmers and by taking some share in missionary work, with the hope that they might become lay brothers. A rule was drawn up, but the experiment soon disappeared from the records.

There was an attempt to create a teaching order in association with CR to work at St John's College, Johannesburg, the public school for whites which it took over in 1906. The South African brethren proposed a teaching brotherhood, self-governing and distinct from CR but under its authority. Some brethren would form its nucleus but most of its members would be lay. All would live a modified rule to take account of teaching duties. 'The Teaching Brothers of St John' with Nash (its chief protagonist), Alston and Thomson as members was eventually launched in 1911. Nash argued that the employment of more Religious would keep fees low and prevent the school from becoming a preserve of the rich. But the experiment failed, again it seems because CR and the church were so clericalized.

In 1898 Bull proposed the creation of an Army Brotherhood of soldiers for pastoral and evangelistic work in the army. But were the long periods of absence from the Community which Bull's proposals involved compatible with membership? Bull's ultimate aim was to provide a priest and four lay evangelists for every thousand men, living at a sergeant's level of pay and food. The priests would come to Mirfield as probationers, be professed, normally live in the ranks 'on the principle of the incarnation', then in one of the 'Military Houses of the Resurrection'. Soldiers would be tested for a year in the army, then brought for a year's training to Mirfield, then sent to one of the houses and expected to attend prayer meetings rather than offices. Bull was allowed various opportunities to test out his idea including a year as a chaplain when he was largely exempted from residence. But nothing materialized. In any case Bull went to South Africa as a chaplain in 1900. After that he worked extensively in the army and navy until the First World War conducting evangelistic campaigns and giving purity lectures for the White Cross League.

By 1907 there were six maids. In 1913 it was decided to change to male servants. Though Frere in 1895 had urged 'no women servants', he now feared that male servants would 'institutionalize' the Community and lead to a decline in cleanliness and standards of food. At first his fears were realized. 'Hungry and hollow-eyed, brethren wandered along the corridors, ankle deep in dirt, and with the air of very early Christian martyrs', wrote the Chronicler, but when a more competent and honest steward was appointed, the change worked well. The half dozen or so 'houseboys' aged fourteen to eighteen had their own recreation room, their own row of chairs in chapel and served at the eucharist. This pattern continued until 1939.

Finally, there is the story of how eventually the Community was willing to profess its first lay brother. In July 1918 'Major Sydenham Hoare RFA was accepted as an aspirant'. He came from the right background and was the cousin of Cuthbert Hallward, professed in 1917. He had been at Eton and New College and had an estate. After New College he had worked at Oxford House and in poor parishes in Portsmouth where he met Tubby Clayton. During the war he commanded a battery and was badly wounded. Afterwards he worked for Toc H. At Mirfield the fact that he was a possible ordinand strengthened his eligibility. But in January 1919 he had a mental breakdown and had to leave. That year it was decided that laymen could be received if their character, education and calling fitted them to be priests. No decision was made as to whether they should be members of Chapter. Hoare was allowed to return in September 1922. Then CR dithered. The Community was clear it did not want 'chore-men', but did not know what to do with an educated layman who was not a definite ordinand. So Hoare was kept waiting on the sidelines. He became a 'resident lay companion' with a seat in choir. Then in 1924 it was resolved that Hoare should serve a two year novitiate, observe the Rule except for those parts which applied to priests and do systematic theological study. If professed he would have a seat and vote in Chapter. The Chapter Minutes of the General Chapter of Easter 1924 read bleakly:

Sydenham Hoare has been repeatedly discouraged from any hope of becoming a novice . . . Despite this he has gladly accepted such a place in our life as we could give him, and in it has shown marked signs of vocation and of suitability for our way of life. Thus our reluctance to admit him to the novitiate has had to yield to indications which we do not feel justified in resisting. This should be borne in mind in considering Hoare as a precedent . . . but it will be precedent not just for the admission of a lay Novice, but for an admission after a very special probation unhelped by the prospect of admission. We are of the opinion that for the present no other layman should be considered for the novitiate who has not, in some way similar to that of Sydenham, from within conditions of life in a house of the Community, furnished similar grounds for consideration.

Clayton visited him at Mirfield and found him contentedly happy whether pushing a wheelbarrow, serving in a coarse apron in the refectory, praying hard in the chapel or working out precisely how far he could go by bus on a day off with only threepence in his pocket. In 1926 his novitiate was prolonged for a further year because of the 'experimental character' of the venture. At last in July 1926 he was encouraged to apply for election the following January. But he died on 28 November. It was resolved that he should be regarded posthumously among the professed brethren. Requiems were said every three quarters of an hour from midnight until the Solemn Requiem. Was there not something frenetic about all those masses when the Community had been so grudging towards him in life? Talbot recalled his tenacity of purpose, modesty, interest in healing and the Bullingdon Club blazer he sported at the annual cricket match between Community and College.

C R by (in effect) electing its first lay brother had made a significant step forward. Yet the constant discouragement Hoare received cannot simply be accounted for by doubts about his health. The brethren were extremely reluctant to admit that there could be a lay vocation to the Religious Life as understood by C R. Then, and later, the type of layman who was considered to be most suitable was one who was willing to become, or could be pressurized into becoming, a priest. All the adaptation had to come from the layman. Many brethren could not conceive of living with laymen as equals. It did not occur to them that they had much to receive from laity. One of the greatest failures of Anglo-Catholicism has been its unwillingness and inability to create a genuinely lay spirituality related to the world of work and strong enough to withstand the pressures from priests to clericalize it. C R had to face the question of lay membership again when a very different type of layman, Roger Castle, became a novice in April 1929. But his story belongs to another chapter.

From Oratory to Monastery?

The changes in Community life after Frere became Superior can be traced in the adoption of a more Catholic and monastic terminology, though a letter of 1905 from Frere to Timothy Rees, who was preparing to come to Mirfield, suggests that even in Frere's mind the Community was still quite loosely knit. Frere explained that he would have to be elected as a probationer, followed by a period of a year or two, the first part of which would be spent in quiet study and prayer:

> . . .profession . . . we take to be in *intention* a permanent tie; but it is not so *formally* . . .
> But if any of us finds that his expectations alter and his intention is modified or
> changed (for example, Gore, by being offered a bishopric) he is free when his annual
> pledge expires, or can be freed by the Community earlier, if desirable, and if the
> Community consents and agrees with his change. It freed Gore, but would not free
> Benson, who therefore went on his own responsibility, by letting his annual pledge run
> out unrenewed.

It is odd that Frere spent so much space in telling a potential new brother how easy it was to leave. Frere also remarked that it had not been necessary to refuse a probationer for lack of a private income.[17]

Novices were first called 'probationers'. It was not until 1905 that the brother in charge of them was called 'Guardian'. The term 'novice' was adopted in 1919 but against some opposition. Keble Talbot who that year became the first 'Novice Guardian' was not wholly happy with the term 'novice': it implied a hierarchy, a departure from 'a democratic common life'. In the earliest days Gore's dislike of the term 'Father' and of a habit and the adoption of yearly 'pledges' instead of vows, emphasized the continuity between life outside and within the Community. But 'novice' suggested a greenhorn with everything to learn who had to begin again. In 1907 it was agreed that brethren entering CR could adopt a new Christian name. In 1911 it was resolved that if a probationer to be professed shared the same name as another brother, his name must be changed. To allow or require a change of name reinforced the sense of discontinuity with all that had preceded profession. In 1906 'Quiet Time' became 'Greater Chapter' which in 1915 became 'General Chapter'. From 1916 the head of a house was called 'Prior'. That year 'Father' appeared before the names of the brethren preaching in the Quarry. Probationers were told to call brethren 'Father' followed by the Christian name. In 1912 the South African brethren resolved that outsiders were not to call them by their Christian names. A Community cross to hang on the cassock belt was devised and worn from 1914. From 1904 a short form of Prime was said daily after Mattins in addition to the other offices. The maintenance of the seven-fold office became a mark of Catholic monasticism. In the *Quarterly* and in CR records 'Mass' generally replaced 'Eucharist' by about 1914.

Bickersteth in his 'Retrospect' in July 1905, voiced his thankfulness 'that God's hand has been over us from the first and that the Community has gradually grown into a deeper and fuller life than the most sanguine dared to hope.' How different it was from the early days when publicity was shunned:

> When a conspicuous tower attracts the attention of every passenger from York to
> Manchester, when Mirfield Manuals circulate by the 100,000 and the Reverend

Fathers of the Community are advertised as such throughout the length and breadth of the land, it is no longer possible to be hid, though I venture to submit that for a religious community as for an individual, Christian notoriety and success is full of peril.

He remarked that CR 'has inevitably derived a certain tone and reputation from the fact that its founder was a liberal in theology and a radical in politics' and celebrated its tradition of liberty of opinion and freedom of discussion. 'In the early days our limited numbers, our close and constant personal intercourse and our own common work in discussing and formulating the Rule clause by clause enabled us to understand one another in a way which becomes increasingly difficult as we grow in numbers and as the elder among us are losing the natural readiness of youth to discuss first principles.'

Bickersteth's reminders of the early traditions, his consciousness of change (not all of it welcome), his veneration of the contribution of Gore were set within an atmosphere of calm confidence. It was written before crises and controversies shook CR to its foundations.

4

Crises and Controversies

Between 1907 and 1910 controversy swirled around and within the Community. Without Frere's wise leadership it might not have survived such turbulence intact. In 1907 the Archbishop of Canterbury, its Visitor, arraigned it in public; some supporters withdrew when leading brethren identified themselves with socialism; protestant groups mounted bitter campaigns against it for 'popery'. Also during this period two brethren withdrew in controversial circumstances and another was expelled.

In June 1897 CR decided to invite Frederick Temple ('granite on fire') to become its first Visitor.[1] He seems to have been chosen primarily for his office, though he was known to be sympathetic to religious communities. Gore wrote to him that as the Community seemed now firmly established, it was time to have a Visitor. That August the Lambeth Conference under Temple's presidency, was the first to discuss religious communities. They rendered 'great services to the Church' (the bishops asserted) but needed 'more regulation'. Its Committee on communities advised: 'Right relations to the episcopate involve some well-defined powers of Visitation.' The need of that had been illustrated two years previously. When Archbishop Benson proposed an inquiry into allegations against the Sisters of the Church, he and other patrons were promptly dismissed by the Superior. Benson dubbed her 'the most comically audacious Mother in the Universe'. Priests in religious communities were easier to regulate since they were bound by oaths of canonical obedience and required episcopal licences to officiate.

Temple asked CR for a definition of his role as Visitor. So a section was added to the Rule. 'The Visitor shall be either the Archbishop of Canterbury, or else some bishop in England having jurisdiction in the Province in which a house of the Community is situated.' Besides hearing appeals, he should hold a Visitation every five years or at his discretion, authorize all services, other than those at the altar (which were under the diocesan bishop) and approve alterations of the Rule. Gore explained to Temple that 'the Catholic and Apostolic Rule of Faith and Discipline' in the Rule referred to what was required by the Prayer Book or Anglican formularies. In January 1898 Temple agreed to become Visitor but left the Community to get on with its life. He never held a Visitation. But he was seventy-six when appointed and died four years later. When CR discussed possible successors in 1903 there seemed no obvious candidate.

Archbishop Davidson as Visitor

In January 1904 CR asked Randall Davidson (who had become Archbishop of Canterbury the previous year) to be its Visitor.[2] The decision was disastrous. A number of brethren had serious reservations and two ballots were necessary before his name was agreed. Brethren knew how legalistically Davidson had handled Dolling in 1895. Davidson was not known to have any particular sympathy for the Religious Life (though he had been a member of the 1897 Lambeth Committee) or for theological exploration, or for Christian socialism. Moreover, in his Charge to the Winchester Diocese of 1899 he had claimed that the 'sturdy common-sense of most English Churchmen' disliked 'recondite esoteric symbolism in our Eucharistic Rite. Superstition does not fit in well with the national characteristics God has given us.'[3] At this period protestant agitation, inside and outside Parliament, was exerting intense pressure on the bishops, particularly on the new Archbishop, to bring the clergy to heel. John Kensit, secretary of the Protestant Truth Society publicly protested at the confirmation of Mandell Creighton in 1897 and of Gore in 1902 and regularly disrupted services in ritualist churches. Protestant campaigns were fuelled by Walter Walsh's scandal-mongering book *The Secret History of the Oxford Movement* (1897) and by Lord Halifax's conversations in Rome in 1894–6. In 1900 Kensitites destroyed a memorial cross which Halifax had erected to his sons in Hickleton churchyard. In March 1904 Davidson only prevented an investigation of ritualism by a Parliamentary Select Committee (which to many clergy would have been outrageous secular interference) by proposing a Royal Commission on Ecclesiastical Discipline. This reported in 1906.

However, the prestige which the Archbishop would bring to CR as Visitor in the end won over enough brethren for an invitation to be sent. Two other factors probably played a part. Bickersteth counted Davidson as a personal friend. Davidson's brother-in-law, Crauford Tait, had been engaged to Cyril Bickersteth's sister Florence, but he had died before the marriage. Florence remained close to the Davidsons. Bickersteth would write in chatty letters to Davidson 'Florence may have told you . . . ' The second connection with CR was more bizarre. When Benson was at Mirfield, his mother was sharing a bed with Davidson's sister-in-law. When Benson was contemplating becoming a Roman Catholic in 1903 he opened his heart to Davidson. From Benson (who always spoke warmly of Mirfield) Davidson heard much about the Community.

So on 8 January 1904 Frere wrote to the Archbishop asking him to be Visitor, though he felt diffident as the Community had only thirteen brethren and two probationers. 'I hope I can promise you we shall not be a troublesome body to deal with . . .' Davidson did not reply until May. He had read the Rule carefully but there was one problem. The stipulation that brethren must make their confessions to a priest was a departure (he said) from that loyalty to the Church of England so clear in the rest of the Rule. Frere replied that such a society had the right to impose extra obligations: 'the presence of such a stipulation . . . need not any more suggest that confession is held to be a necessary duty of other members of the Church of England than the presence of provisions about common property suggests that communism is so'. Davidson was anxious to distinguish between those communities which were loyal to the Church of England ('like your own') and those which were not. How could he be Visitor when the Church of England taught that confession was voluntary? In July CR made a concession. The words 'under obedience to conscience' would be added to the injunction about confession. Davidson now agreed to be Visitor and Frere asked him to hold a visitation. After further correspondence, Davidson's relations with CR sailed into clearer waters.

On 3 March 1907 Bickersteth wrote to Davidson to ask him to take part in a London meeting to appeal for funds for a permanent hostel in Leeds. Presumably it was because of his friendship with Davidson that he, not Frere, approached him. (Since 1904 two houses had provided temporary accommodation for ordinands taking degrees at the University before their theological course at Mirfield. CR also needed funds so that it could continue to supply the five years' education free.) Davidson in his reply of 4 March, marked 'Private', wrote more frankly about CR than he had done to Frere:

Florence had already spoken to me . . . and told me that you were going to write. My position is not an altogether easy one in this matter. It is true that I am Visitor of Mirfield . . . But, although Visitor, it would be affectation were I to pretend that I am in real sympathy with the theological and ecclesiastical attitude which is popularly supposed to belong to the Community and its work . . . I think it is certain that my attendance at a meeting gathered to advocate your training of theological students would be thus misleading. But, if I do not misunderstand you, this particular meeting will be held simply to advocate the provision of a Hostel at Leeds for ensuring that your theological students shall have a training in Arts and Philosophy and the like; and this gives to the matter a different complexion if people will take the trouble to discriminate. I wonder if you would feel as Balak felt towards Balaam if I were to attend the meeting and to say frankly that I do not profess to be in full sympathy with the ecclesiastical colour characteristic of your work any more than I am in full sympathy with . . . Highbury or Islington Colleges; but that I believe in the comprehensiveness of the Church of England and am convinced that we want at this time to have experiments of different sorts in dealing with the crying necessity for the training of more clergy . . . and that I support this Leeds plan of yours because it secures a wider range of knowledge outside ecclesiastical wheel-tracks. Perhaps you may think that a speech of that sort would do you more harm than good, and if so, I shall perfectly understand your thinking it better that I should not take part in the meeting. I rather think that in your position that would be my opinion.

Bickersteth disregarded the warning (perhaps he did not want to lose the kudos of having secured the Archbishop) and in a chatty letter of 5 March pressed on. Most of the brethren (he assured the Archbishop) were loyal to the Anglican tradition. 'Florence may have told you that I was accused by the High Church ladies at Cowley of "aggressive protestantism" because I very strongly deprecated . . . compulsory confession, and told them plainly how much the average Englishman dislikes exceptionally elaborate ceremonial . . . ' So Davidson agreed. But he began to get cold feet and sent a telegram on 23 April to Frere to say that he had accepted without sufficient enquiry. He wanted an urgent meeting. The cold feet were partly caused by an Open Letter to the Archbishop dated 22 April issued by the Church Association (founded in 1865 to campaign against ritualism). It quoted writings by Gore, Frere, Sampson and Healy to show that they were teaching 'Romish ritual' and beliefs overthrown at the Reformation. It was horrified that the Archbishop was to preside at a meeting to promote the work of such a society.

Davidson had also been receiving a series of letters from the Bishop of Ripon (William Boyd Carpenter) protesting that, without any consultation with him, the Archbishop was about to give public support to the Hostel which Carpenter thought would be a 'non-conformist institution', outside his control. Carpenter was a Liberal Modernist who loathed all forms of Catholicism. There were already two theological institutions in his diocese – the Leeds Clergy School (1876) of moderately high churchmanship, and Bishop's College, Ripon, founded by him on modernist lines in 1897. Carpenter tried to prevent Samuel Bickersteth, Vicar of Leeds, from presiding at Leeds meetings to be held the day after the one in London. Samuel was Cyril's second cousin, and Carpenter's former curate.

Frere happily agreed to a consultation. He also asked Davidson to mediate with the Bishop of Ripon. The Hostel had been simply a lodging house for second and third year ordinands, but now C R wished to start men at Leeds, which required a proper Community House with its own chapel, which needed the bishop's permission. Frere wrote to the bishop: 'we sincerely desire to show all possible allegiance everywhere to the Episcopate'. The bishop's reply of 11 May was brusque:

> I do not see my way to sanction the establishment of a branch of your Community in my diocese. Setting aside the fact that there is a very grave difference of views to be reckoned with, I have steadily set myself against sanctioning an establishment of any propagandist institution in my diocese, when the authority, government and direction of the same is wholly outside my control . . . I see no advantage in the establishment of an organization which could not fail to occasion constant difficulty and unhappy friction.

When Davidson saw Frere at the end of April he realized that Frere also was very anxious about some Mirfield publications and that he wanted the

Archbishop to strengthen his hand by deputing someone to examine them. Davidson's determination to voice his public disapproval was increased by cuttings of letters in the *Yorkshire Post* denouncing the Community forwarded by the bishops of Ripon and Wakefield. The Bishop of Chester wrote complaining bitterly about a mission conducted by Healy in one of his parishes. What is the good of having a Royal Commission if the Archbishop sets his seal on Mirfield teachings? he asked. In addition cuttings reached Lambeth from all over the country reporting protestant alarm about the meeting.

The meeting on 13 May 1907 at Church House, Westminster, presided over by the Archbishop, which was intended to be an impressive launch of an appeal for £7,000 for the work of the Hostel, turned into a mixture of nightmare and farce.[4] Protestant objectors, inflamed by orchestrated and virulently hostile publicity, were urged to attend to make a protest. As the audience entered, groups handed out pamphlets 'The Latest Act of Treachery! ROMANISING MONKS, Under the Patronage of the Archbishop of Canterbury.' Another pamphlet 'Englishmen to Arms! Refuse to subscribe One Penny to this Monkery', accused the Community of 'enticing young people into the hateful Confessional'. When the Archbishop rose, J. A. Kensit (who had succeeded his father in the Protestant Truth Society) stood up and shouted. H. H. Martin, organizer of the Society and the Wycliffe Preachers, jumped on to the press table, banged his umbrella on the Archbishop's table and shouted 'You ought to go to Rome! You are anti-Christian and anti-British'. Others shouted 'What do you get £15,000 a year for?' When he began 'You all know why we are here today' Martin retorted 'Yes, to promote Popery in the Church of England'. Kensit was promised an opportunity to speak later and quiet was restored.

The Archbishop began uncontroversially by commending CR's plan to balance theological education with a general education at Leeds University. But then astonishingly he publicly arraigned CR:

> There are publications by some members of the Community of which I distinctly and actively disapprove. If a man presented himself to me for Ordination, and I found he was the author of certain of these tracts, I should decline to ordain him until he had withdrawn or altered them . . . I have looked through about sixty of the smaller ones, and while some of them have the character I have described many others are excellent . . . The Community does not hold itself as in any way responsible for the publications of its individual members. My friends, I do not see how that repudiation of responsibility can effectively be maintained. Some of these are called 'Mirfield Manuals' . . . If, therefore, this plan is to go forward with public support, if I am to retain the somewhat undefined Visitorship, in which after some modification of the rules, I succeeded Archbishop Temple, that point about the books and tracts and the Community's responsibility for them must be reconsidered. I have already been in communication with Mr Frere upon the subject,

and I look forward to a revision of that whole question, and, I hope, to the withdrawal of some of the publications altogether.

He ended with a hope for successful negotiations with the Bishop of Ripon, so that the Hostel would be under 'his general supervision and control' and with an appeal to support CR's plans under their 'inspiring leader' (a tribute which must have sounded pretty hollow).

Frere in his speech explained the proposed Hostel and obsequiously welcomed 'with much enthusiasm the Archbishop's promise that he would help them to get into line, or keep in line, with the doctrine and discipline of the Church of England'. C. F. G Masterman praised CR for trying to break the class character of the ministry. The Dean of Westminster (Armitage Robinson) implicitly rebuked the Archbishop by commending CR's refusal to exercise censorship. He referred to difficulties which Von Hügel was experiencing with the Roman Curia. The Church of England, unlike the Church of Rome, rejoiced in the 'free utterance of personal convictions'. Indiscretions were preferable to censorship. The meeting was widely reported nationally and locally. Protestant societies gleefully reprinted Davidson's condemnation. 'Dr Davidson Repudiates "The Mirfield Manuals"' ran the headline in the *English Churchman*. There was 'little hope of the Mirfield product being of real value to the Church', commented the *Record*.

Davidson had written calmly to Bickersteth on 6 March: 'I well understand what you say about the varieties of men, and the impossibility, even if it were desirable, of securing one type of thought.' But since then Davidson had been under intense pressure from some of the bishops and protestant groups. He had also been specifically asked by Frere (he told Bickersteth) to exercise some supervision over Mirfield's publications. So when he blackmailed the Community in public by threatening to withdraw as Visitor unless it accepted his censorship, this was not only a sop to those who accused him of being soft on 'popery', it was also his response to Frere's request to bolster his authority as Superior. Afterwards Davidson learned that Frere had made a similar request to the Bishop of Wakefield who had replied that he might withdraw licences from brethren who transgressed doctrinal limits.

Two parallel meetings in Leeds on 14 May passed off quietly, though members of the Protestant Truth Society distributed leaflets and asked questions. Gore spoke. Some of his happiest memories were of his time with the Community. 'Can I forget the rock whence I was hewn?' He celebrated this alliance between the church and a modern university, which would provide the clergy with the essential foundation of a liberal education. Like the Dean of Westminster, Gore homed in on the issue of censorship. He wryly recalled Archbishop Temple's quip when they had discussed CR's tradition of literary freedom: 'You wouldn't have got any community to sanction *your* books'. The proposed censorship of CR publications would be 'theological tyranny'. He implored the laity to support resistance to censorship. If a clergyman wrote a book which was disloyal to the church, the bishop could withdraw his licence. The Community was loyal to the Church of England and deserved 'the least possible shackling upon the thoughts and freedom of the individual'. (Here spoke Gore the friend of oppressed poachers. Yet Gore the game-keeper the previous year had been one of the first bishops to prohibit the use of the *English Hymnal* – he objected to some hymns which invoked the saints.)[5] After the meetings Gore wrote to Frere to say how deeply he felt about censorship of writings by priests in communities, who being unbene-ficed were already totally under a bishop's control. He wrote to Davidson that he could not agree that community clergy should be under stricter controls than other clergy, and quoted Temple's quip. Frere told Gore that the Archbishop was not asking for general censorship but modifications to the 'Manuals' which he (and he hoped the brethren) would be ready to make. However, attention had been focussed on Healy's *Definite Church Teaching* which was published independently. He hoped that the Archbishop would not adopt censorship. Their enemies would be triumphant if the Archbishop resigned.

The right of brethren to publish without Community censorship had been established in 1896 though they were reminded that the Rule stated that community life involved some sacrifice of individual proclivities; it also asserted: 'Nothing shall be finally required of any of the brethren which violates his conscience.' In that year Chapter asked Sampson to publish his book of devotions anonymously, because they were too 'advanced'.

Three days after the Church House meeting Frere received a letter from some brethren addressed 'Dear Walter' but ominously headed 'Without prejudice to our future action'. They wrote to 'strengthen' his hands in his negotiations with the Archbishop. They were ready to welcome advice from the Visitor about their writings but 'we cannot give him any right to issue any order or demand any alteration'. They were quite prepared to submit writings at the Visitor's request to five theologians approved by Chapter. The Archbishop should be told 'in the *last resort* that some members of the Community will not allow him any such power as he may be tempted to claim'. They expressed their loyalty to Frere. 'But it would not be fair to allow you to yield in negotiations with the Archbishop any point which we might have to disown . . . ' Obviously they (like Gore) believed that Frere had yielded too much already. Davidson was a skilful persuader. Gore once said: 'When I go up the stairs at Lambeth, I say, "Charles you be very careful". When I come down the stairs, I say, "Charles, you know that you never meant to agree to that".'

Davidson had now got the bit between his teeth. On 17 May he wrote asking for a meeting about the 'Mirfield Manuals'. Before the Church House meeting Bickersteth had delivered 150 of them to the Archbishop which he had read 'with characteristic thoroughness'. How melancholy that Davidson, who in his correspondence constantly complained of over-work and in 1905 had caused widespread indignation by saying he was too busy to meet 450 unemployed men led by the Revd F. L. Donaldson of CSU, should spend his time censoring penny 'Manuals'. Frere in an internal memorandum argued that the Visitor and Community had the right to take cognizance of brethren's teachings. The title 'Mirfield Manuals' suggested that the Community was responsible for their content. Perhaps the title should be changed?

Meanwhile at Mirfield the Kensitites were busy placarding the area to announce a meeting to expose the 'Mirfield Monks' at the Town Hall on 6 June, admission threepence or sixpence.[6] CR announced a rival meeting at the same hour, but cunningly held it outside the Black Bull and made it free: 'Save your Brass and Come to the Open Air Meeting'. About five hundred packed into the Town Hall where Kensit was flanked by two Nonconformist ministers. No local chairman had been found, so a Cheshire mayor was imported who declared to Nonconformist cheers that he was a Protestant and a member of the Church of England, denounced the brethren for believing in transubstantiation, masses for the dead and the seven sacraments and suggested they should follow Benson to Rome. Kensit, a pile of 'Mirfield Manuals' to hand, attacked the writings of Healy and Sampson. For three hours a passionate debate raged in which Bickersteth and Healy participated. A large crowd also gathered at the Black Bull. A poster proclaimed: 'THE MIRFIELD MONKS HAVE NO WOMEN – THEY GET YOURS THROUGH THE CONFESSIONAL'. Frere, relaxed and genial, standing on a chair, retailed the history of the Community. They were brothers who wanted to create a family life – nothing very wicked about that. Their Rule had been approved by both the present and previous Archbishop of Canterbury. The Bishop of Wakefield had invited them to the diocese. Before any of them could preach they required his licence. When they first arrived people said that they did not know what they were up to at the 'House of Correction' but they hoped it was not on the rates. They based their life on Acts 2. They did not take vows, but made promises, though there was nothing wicked about vows – vows were made at baptism, marriage and ordination. They were asked why they did not marry. He had never heard that marriage was compulsory. Jesus had said that some should not marry for the sake of the kingdom. They did not take a vow of poverty but lived simply. A man had told him that because he wore a cassock he was Romish and ought to wear trousers. Roman Catholics wore trousers, Frere replied, so he would still be Romish.

As early as 1899 CR missioners had been attacked by Wycliffe preachers. The Kensitites established a special fund in 1907–8 to counter every CR mission with one by their preachers. Even Bull's purity missions suffered. In October 1908 at a mission in Bristol a huge mob threatened Healy's life and he had to be escorted to and from church by three hundred men. At Barry in

November he had to abandon what was intended to be a three or four weeks' mission after only a week.

On 6 July 1907 the Archbishop in a conciliatory letter largely exonerated the 'Mirfield Manuals' about which he made such a fuss at Church House. But he argued that with such a title the Community must accept responsibility for their contents, and he objected strongly to Healy's *Definite Church Teaching* and Sampson's *The Chaplet of our Lady*. He had no wish 'to hamper the Community unfairly', acknowledged Frere's willingness to listen to criticisms and hoped adjustments could be made so he could continue as Visitor. C R gave way on the major issues. The 'Mirfield Manuals' would be renamed 'Manuals for the Million'. In every copy a note would explain what responsibility belonged to the writer and what to the Editors. It would cost £40–50 to change the title immediately but the remaining stock would quickly run out and the new 'Manuals for the Million' would appear in the autumn. Healy was revising his book and Sampson would either withdraw his name from his book or withdraw the book altogether. Frere would withdraw his name from the edition of the Sarum *Order of Compline* (which he had edited with G. H. Palmer) or issue a new edition omitting the Appendix which contained material regarded as unsuitable for Anglicans. Frere also conveyed Chapter's opinion that 'a censorship in the sense of a corporate veto . . . was contrary to the traditions of the Community of the Resurrection, inconsistent with the spirit of liberty and respect for the individual, and likely to prove a source of weakness and practical difficulty if ever it came into operation'. It also proposed a more restricted definition of the role of the Visitor; disagreements about dogma should be referred to three theologians nominated by the Visitor, but Chapter could nominate two others in addition if not satisfied with the Visitor's choice.

Davidson deferred consideration of the redefinition of the Visitor's role, but was unmoved by the concessions. A public statement must be made about the publications which had been criticized. Authors, whose independence was now to be guaranteed, might decide no changes were necessary. 'Merely to strike out the author's name while a booklet well-known to be his continued to be published unaltered, would be almost to trifle with us.' Had not he and Frere publicly pledged action at the meeting? If the new 'Manuals' were simply re-issues of the old material under a new cover would not the public feel hoodwinked? Was it true present editions would soon run out? Had not Bull publicly announced after the meeting that he had ordered fresh copies to be printed? Should not the series be edited by someone outside the Community and be accompanied by a statement disconnecting C R from it? On 14 August Frere replied from holiday, adding pointedly that he wished it were possible for the Archbishop to be on holiday too. *Definite Church Teaching* was being revised. He presumed the old edition would be withdrawn. The new 'Manuals' would include a statement disavowing Community responsibility.

Then Healy wrote indignantly to Frere. The Archbishop now acknowledged that his condemnations at Church House were based on inadequate grounds. Healy rejected Frere's implication in his speech that the Community needed to be brought into line. He would resist the change of name for the 'Manuals'. The public would assume that the change had been made because of the Archbishop's condemnation. He refused to make any serious changes to his own book; the Archbishop had provided no detailed criticisms of it. Frere replied: 'My dear Samuel, I carefully abstained from saying what *sort* of changes you were likely to make to the Archbishop . . . May God guide us all in the difficulties and give us patience, humility and courage.'

Davidson continued the pressure. It was better to change the contents of *Compline* (he wrote to Frere) than to omit his name. The 'Manuals' should be edited by outsiders. Many loyal churchmen were anxiously awaiting the outcome of the Church House meeting. Frere responded in October. In spite of all that C R could do, the publisher of the 'Manuals' insisted on selling the existing series but agreed to insert a disclaimer confining responsibility to the author alone. Bull would alone edit the new series, without the Superior. Some ladies would write new booklets. C R had bought up the existing stock of Sampson's book. Healy was revising his. C R would have to subsidize it so that the new edition could replace it. A revised edition of *Compline* was in preparation. The Community 'is putting itself to considerable expense in order to meet criticisms with which it does not altogether sympathize'. By December Davidson was writing 'My dear Frere' but was as unyielding as ever. Publications being revised should immediately be withdrawn from sale. He could not accept the new definition of the Visitor's functions. The 'Mirfield Manuals' must include a statement disclaiming Community responsibility. The name of the Community should not appear on any of the brethren's booklets, nor should they be sold by the Community.

Frere made another visit to the Archbishop in December. Was it then that Davidson made the remark: 'It seems to me that you are trying to combine two incompatibles – individual liberty and corporate authority'? They discussed a letter dated 13 December to be made public which summarized all that the Archbishop felt had been achieved since the Church House meeting. At the end of the letter the Archbishop stated: 'The whole controversy, and the detailed labour which it has involved, have convinced me of the inconvenience and even disadvantage of the Visitorship of a Community such as yours being entrusted to one who holds so onerous an office as does the Archbishop of Canterbury.' Once again protestant pamphleteers made damaging accusations. 'Exposure of the Mirfield Monks' claimed: 'The Romanising character of the Mirfield Community is such that in December 1907, His Grace the Archbishop of Canterbury publicly withdrew his support from the Institution.' This should be 'a sufficient warning to all law-abiding Churchmen to have nothing whatever to do with the Mirfield Monks'. It went on to quote from a lecture by Hugh Benson given to a Roman Catholic meeting in October 1907 giving an account of his time at Mirfield ending 'it is this High Church teaching that is building the bridge over which Anglicans will come into the true fold'. A Church Association pamphlet claimed that the disclaimers in the new 'Manuals' 'jesuitically gained greater freedom from responsibility through the Archbishop's intervention than they had before, whereas the public are hoodwinked into the belief that the Archbishop has by this means mitigated the Roman virus of the manuals'.

The patched up peace between Davidson and CR was shattered by a brusque letter from Healy to Davidson dated 16 December. Healy said that since he had much other work to do, his revised edition of his book would take some months to appear. 'I think I ought to inform you that I am not prepared to lower the standard of teaching in the book, or to stop the sale of the present edition until the new edition is ready for sale.' The Archbishop was furious and reverted to the formal 'Dear Mr Frere':

> The whole tone of the letter and the attitude he assumes in regard to what I have said seem to me deplorable . . . I should on public grounds deplore it were I now to be obliged to make a public statement to the effect that I have withdrawn from the Visitorship on account of the refusal of a member of the Community to withdraw from circulation, pending its re-issue in an amended form, a booklet to which I have taken grave exception.

In January 1908 Chapter pressed Healy to make a conciliatory gesture. CR dreaded lest Davidson should resign in anger. Healy wrote to the Archbishop offering to withdraw the original edition of his book. CR made him a grant to buy up the remaining stock.

Divisions within CR went deep. There was much explicit or implicit support for Healy's defiance. Frere wrote to Rackham 'I cannot justify Samuel's attitude', but he admired what was for Healy a wonderful 'restraint and patience'. He told the vicar of Leeds: 'The Community of the Resurrection does not hold itself responsible for the strength of his language or the accuracy of his Theology but it has unbounded confidence in his zeal and devotion and his capacity for finance.' Unlike most of the brethren Healy had graduated at Durham not Oxford or Cambridge. After three curacies in the North-East, in 1891 Healy went to assist the famous Father Burn, forty-one years vicar of All Saints' Middlesbrough, 'the Dolling of the North', pioneer of the Parish Communion, ardent member of CSU, supporter of George Lansbury, defender of the poor and scathing about the rich and for some years 'under the ban' for Catholic practices.[7] Healy believed that a missioner needed an Evangelical's love of souls, a Catholic's religion and a sense of humour: he had all three. Gore said 'Samuel's at his best with the Catholic poor'. Like Dolling, Healy was an Irish raconteur with a short fuse. Like Dolling, Healy was angry with the Church of England for its betrayal of the poor, hence his inevitable suspicion of an establishment figure like Davidson. When he spoke for the controversial Socialist candidate, Victor Grayson, at the Colne Valley by-election in 1907, the response of the people moved him to tears: 'never have I seen crowds so swept by waves of the Holy Spirit'.

It was not only Healy who was giving Frere a difficult time. Bickersteth and Bull had also written direct to Davidson. Bickersteth wanted the maximum appeasement of the Archbishop and kept writing sneaky letters to him. In January 1908 he told the Archbishop that he had threatened to leave the Community if it took Healy's side against the Archbishop. On the opposite wing, Bull was trying to force the Chapter into greater belligerence by what Bertram Barnes called 'arrogant browbeating'. Chapter had done all it could to restrain the violent attitudes of Bull and Healy, but Healy 'almost of necessity thinks that a boat that tacks has lost its compass'. Barnes wanted Chapter to deprecate all private letters to the Archbishop. 'Chapter was pretty strongly determined to say nothing to the Archbishop for the sake of peace and settlement, so long as there was any danger of the words being interpreted in any quarter as a condemnation of Samuel's book.' The Archbishop had been trying to make Healy into a 'scapegoat' so that he might have 'at least one scalp to display to the Kensitites'.

In January 1908 Frere wrote to the Archbishop to relay the decisions of Chapter. After gratitude to him for making public the steps that the Community had taken to respond to his criticisms, Frere went on with feeling: 'It has we hope done something to remove the suspicion under which we have lain ever since the Church House Meeting and to give us and our friends a better defence against the organized hostility and persecution which has hampered our work since.' Chapter did not endorse Healy's letter, but did not believe that the errors in his book were serious enough to warrant its withdrawal. The revised edition would be ready in a few weeks. C R would pay for the removal of Frere's name from the *Order of Compline*. It withdrew the suggested redefinition of the Visitor's role, but proposed that each brother should be responsible for his teaching to the bishop who licensed him. Chapter could not forbid brethren to describe themselves as members of the Community in publications: 'we were taught by our founder to regard election as giving a brother the right to use our name'. Brethren deeply regretted the annoyance caused to the Archbishop, but they hoped that he would remember that his words of disapproval had been given greater weight than his expressions of approval.

There was now a lull in the correspondence, though the Chaplain in March sent copies of the continuing correspondence between Lambeth and Kensit. Davidson wrote of his perpetual perplexity about his relations with C R. 'The Community is, I know, subjected at present to keen criticism of an unfriendly sort, some of which is I think not unreasonable, while some is undeserved;

some again is probably due to political rather than religious opinions.' How could he justify his Visitorship to himself and others when he could not endorse some of CR's teaching? To be Visitor was inappropriate for one 'so over-burdened with duties, and so trammelled by his peculiar position in the Church'. He therefore suggested he should resign from the end of the year with the minimum of publicity. Frere replied that CR had no right to press him to continue. Frere wrote a final letter of fervent gratitude on 1 January 1909. He had often had to write tough letters to the Archbishop on behalf of Chapter, but in his private communications Frere acted as Davidson's admiring ally.

During the last two years of Davidson's Visitorship, CR's name had been dragged through the mud, the Kensitites had been boosted, CR had been financially crippled, the energies of the brethren had been diverted into wrangles and squabbles, Frere had suffered a breakdown. Davidson was not wholly to blame. Frere, Healy, Bickersteth and Bull had their share of responsibility. CR had made a colossal blunder by inviting Davidson in the first place. He came to the task basically unsympathetic to CR's ethos, in the context of his work on the Royal Commission and convinced that he must justify himself to those who were harrying him. A sympathetic diocesan bishop as Visitor would have kept himself and CR out of the limelight.

In March 1909 Gore became the Visitor. He gave authority for experimental Holy Week services which Davidson had refused. But he wished the collect for the Jews to be less harsh: 'the faithless Jews' put them among the 'lowest of the low'; this was unjust to the contemporary Jew. In July 1911 Gore held the first Visitation of CR, and interviewed individually all brethren and probationers. CR had been in existence for nineteen years before a Visitor actually made a Visitation. Davidson had conducted a draconian inquisition lasting five years without ever once setting foot in Mirfield.[8]

During 1908 CR had received further damaging publicity through a novel, *The Soul of Dominic Wildthorne* by the popular Methodist writer Joseph Hocking. First serialized in the Free Church *British Weekly* in thirty instalments between December 1907 and June 1908, then published in book form, it was enthusiastically commended in protestant pamphlets for giving an accurate picture of Mirfield. Though Hocking claimed that the novel was not about a particular institution, the 'Community of the Incarnation' was situated in a Yorkshire manufacturing town called 'Meremeadows' and had Oxford connections. The brothers trained poor lads like Dominic for the ministry. The Community aimed to strangle Dissent and to leaven the Church of England with Romish ways so that it could return to Mother Church. The Superior was sympathetic to the poor and honest in all but ecclesiastical questions. The gardener at the Community asserted that Yorkshire people would not have anything to do with popery, protestant monks or 'falderols' in worship. Dominic wanted to be a novice but admired Maggie, the pretty daughter of a dissenting landowner. She went to hear him preach. The service was a copy of pagan ceremonial. His sermon belonged to the middle ages and ignored biblical criticism and science. The Archbishop had given his blessing to the Community but only with reservations. Dominic attended a House of Commons debate in which an MP attacked Anglo-Catholics as traitors to the Reformation and the Romanism in thousands of parishes as revealed by the Royal Commission. He also instanced the Community founded by a celebrated bishop, one of whose members with a 'well-known name' had gone over to Rome. He quoted from a lecture given by this convert (in reality the remarks by Benson frequently quoted in protestant pamphlets). Dominic visited Rome and met not only Fr Tyrone [Tyrrell], whose writing had been condemned by the papal encyclical on modernism, but also Maggie. He returned to Yorkshire and married Maggie: 'the man who had come out of great darkness, and whose face was towards the Light'. Rackham thought the novel 'very revolting'.

CR *and Socialism*

The departure of Gore and Carter had weakened the links between CR and CSU. The second much more boisterous wave of Christian socialism which now developed in CR mostly identified itself with the emerging Labour party.[9] But the older, mild CSU tradition lingered in the general atmosphere. So Latimer Fuller described CR in South Africa as 'Socialism in its perfect, because its Christian form'. It seemed natural for CR at Mirfield to entertain members of the Huddersfield Co-operative Guild and to insist that builders on the site were paid trade union wages. In 1905 Philip Snowden was invited by Bull to address brethren and students. Snowden came from a West Riding, Methodist and working-class background, and was Labour MP for Blackburn from 1906.

The General Election of January 1906 was a decisive turning point for the Labour movement as well as a sweeping victory for the Liberals. At the 1900 General Election only two Labour candidates had been elected, but in 1906 twenty-nine became MPs and called themselves the Labour Party. In addition twenty-four miners and Lib-Labs were elected, making a total of fifty-three working-class MPs in the Commons. The main religious influence upon the Liberal and Labour parties came from Nonconformity. The Free Church Council at the 1906 General Election had openly campaigned for Liberal candidates. Of the 400 Liberal MPs 157 were Nonconformists. A considerable proportion of the working-class MPs had Nonconformist roots. Asquith, Prime Minister from 1908, spent part of his Congregationalist boyhood in Mirfield. But it was Lloyd George who best represented politicized Nonconformity. Several CR brethren were among those Anglicans who were determined to redress the religious balance by forging links between the Church of England and the Labour movement.

Labour's electoral success in 1906 produced a second wave of Christian socialism in CR in which the pivotal figures were Frere, Bull, Healy (and later) Figgis. When Frere was a curate in Stepney he had also served as area CSU secretary and was elected as a Labour candidate to the local Board of Guardians. In 1892, shortly after joining CR, he preached what he described as 'rank Socialism' in a series of Advent sermons on 'Social Duty' at St Philip and St James, Oxford: 'my first effort to a swell audience: shy and perhaps violent' (he noted in his diary). His contacts with John Carter in CR deepened his socialist convictions. In 1906 out of the 17 or so brethren and novices in England, 14 joined 165 clergy of the Church of England in signing an Address to the Labour Party to congratulate it on its achievement. In 1906 and 1907 Frere and Bull organized two conferences in the Quarry between clergy and Labour leaders. Six brethren joined the Church Socialist League founded in 1906.

The Quarry conferences had continuing controversial consequences for CR, so first we shall turn to Neville Figgis, a highly original political thinker who arrived at Mirfield in 1907 but whose activities did not cause public controversy.[10] His father, J. B. Figgis, had been a distinguished Nonconformist minister. Neville's readiness to stand against the tide, his high valuation of preaching, his contempt for establishment Anglicanism and his defiant gesture in joining CR: all owed much to his Nonconformist upbringing. He went up to St Catharine's College, Cambridge to read mathematics but turned to history in his fourth year. But uncertain mental health, inherited from his mother, compelled a period of withdrawal. His brilliant scholarship and celebrated dinner-parties brought distinction to his college and revived its fortunes. F. W. Maitland attracted him to mediaevalism, Lord Acton awakened an interest in Catholicism and Mandell Creighton drew him to Anglicanism. But what should he do with his life? Creighton wrote to him in 1891: 'a continuous career at Cambridge is not the best thing for a man . . . its temptations are towards easy indolence'. Instead he advised him to have the courage to make a great 'venture' (he suggested India): 'Go, without any attempt to forecast or adjust the future . . . if you go, go *at once* . . . Never dally . . . ' He went not to India but to Wells Theological College and was ordained in 1894. By 1901, after six years back in Cambridge, his aversion to any form of exercise and his love for good food combined with intense intellectual activity brought on another breakdown. Advised to give up intellectual work, he took a college living at Marnhull, Dorset where he remained for five years. It was while seeing one of Shaw's plays that he decided he must go to Mirfield. Like Shaw he had no time for sham religion. 'I am going to Mirfield' (he wrote) 'because I have more and more come to see that if we want people to think we are sincere in Christianity, it is desirable to live so that you . . . appear to *mean* it i.e. a life of poverty.' It was this call to poverty which he stressed to his parishioners. He believed he needed a disciplined life of thought and prayer, wanted to make a stand against worldliness, and that his uncertain mental health would be improved by the support of the communal life. In a later sermon he said that complacency was the worst of the defects of the Church of England – a quarter of which came from the clergy and a good half from their wives. 'I do not believe that we shall ever get out of it until the marriage of priests becomes the exception instead of the rule. That is what has made the Church so much of an upper middle-class sect.' In another sermon he echoed Creighton's advice: 'You must "give all for all". You can never win any kind of peace or self-possession unless you have risked all to get it.'[11]

Just when CR's reputation for socialism was hitting the headlines, Figgis arrived at the front door in frock coat and top hat. Already a well known historian and political theorist, he was too independent-minded to fit into a specific political allegiance and was too keen a critic of progressivism to proclaim socialism as part of a general human advance. 'Neither pure socialism nor absolute individualism finds warrant in the Gospel.' But human beings were naturally 'associative': 'Ethically considered, the most thoroughgoing Christian movement of the last century was the Trade Union movement, which expressed the principle of brotherhood.' As a pluralist he believed the state should be a 'community of communities' and therefore attacked collectivism and was attracted to Guild Socialism.[12] Figgis deeply influenced Maurice Reckitt, later the historian of the Christian social movement. Reckitt likened him to Chesterton's Father Brown, and remembered walking with him by the sea at St Leonard's, ceaselessly talking and continually dropping his umbrella. Reckitt listened enthralled, but had to keep picking up the umbrella.

On 23 June 1905 Keir Hardie MP, founder of the Independent Labour Party, published an 'Open Letter to the Clergy' in the *Labour Leader* asking for their help during the next Election. During the Election in January 1906 Frere and Bull spoke for ILP candidates in Leeds and Dewsbury. They then boldly organized a conference between clergy and Labour leaders in the Quarry on Saturday 5 May. The *Church Times* correspondent (11 May) reported:

> When I reached the House of the Resurrection about noon to-day there was a strangely unfamiliar look about the place. The entrance-hall and rooms were full of men in aggressively secular dress, many of them in knickers and cloth caps, with the 'Clarion' badge, and the few clergy one met wore the ordinary garb of the parish priest instead of the habit of the Community.

Though CR had given its 'full consent' to the meeting the invitations had been sent by Frere and Bull as individuals. Most of the 350–400 who attended came from Yorkshire and Lancashire, including nearly 100 clergy, some of them members of CSU and GSM. 'It was remarkable' (said the *Leeds and Yorkshire*

Mercury on 7 May) 'inasmuch that agnostic and Anglican were to be seen ascending the pulpit in turn, each advocating co-operation with the other for a common end – Socialism.' Frere welcomed the delegates and recalled his election as a Labour candidate fifteen years previously. Since then his interest in socialism had steadily increased. CR was 'communistic'. Its basis was 'From each according to his capacity and to each according to his needs'. For them socialism was not a mere theory, but 'the groundwork of their lives'. Bull proposed a resolution asking for more co-operation between Church and Labour to spread 'the principles of collectivism' through 'more aggressive propaganda'. The present competitive system was 'utterly contrary to Christianity' which taught brotherhood. The agnostic seconder praised the 'High church party' for doing more for socialism than any other group of Christians. A second resolution, from two local councillors, urged meals for children, old age pensions, work for the unemployed and taxation of land values. The highlight of the conference was the arrival of Keir Hardie, greeted by a standing ovation. He then sat beside Frere smoking his pipe, waiting his turn to speak. He appealed to Christ as the justification for socialism. Speaking in a quarry reminded him of fourteen years as a miner and four years as a stone quarryman. A few years ago Labour would have regarded such a conference as an attempt to 'nobble' the movement; now they felt confident enough to participate. At the end a collection to defray expenses was suggested, but Frere explained that hospitality was one of CR's principles. So instead a collection was given to the locked-out miners nearby. The conference had gone so well that everyone wanted another. The *CR Quarterly* (JB 1906) printed an anonymous account:

It was rather an anticipation of the coming millennium when the Labour lion shall lie down with the Clerical lamb and all shall be led by the Babe of the Manger . . . These strong earnest men are as a matter of fact on fire with love for our Master and for His teaching, though they know not that they love Him. They deny Him in words, and profess Him in act. So many claiming the high name of Christian, profess their Master in word and deny Him in act . . . I would rather be of the first class than of the second . . . But . . . it cannot be denied that there is in the Socialist movement a deep-rooted distrust, not only of the Church, but of the Churches, of religion altogether . . . The scene of the Conference added not a little to its success. It was out of doors, notwithstanding a chilly sting in the air, and this alone made the Labour men feel at home as they would never have done in any building that we could have found for them . . . The speech of Keir Hardie in particular revealed to the clerical side a depth of spiritual earnestness and a religious tone about the movement . . . Keir Hardie himself, notwithstanding his red tie, might have been a Bishop speaking in the loftiest vein in his Cathedral. Keir Hardie's Cathedral was our Quarry . . . Churchmen went away with a new sense that even the political side of the new Social agitation is really after all one of the manifold ways in which God is working out His purposes.

CR followed up the conference by devoting the five Quarry Sunday sermons in July to Christian socialism. Audiences steadily grew from 700 at the beginning to 2,300 for the final sermon by Bull. Fitzgerald, Healy, Bickersteth and Horner were the other preachers. All but Horner were publicly identified with some type of socialism.

> A noticeable feature of these congregations in the open air was the large percentage of men who attended, and in particular of that class of men who very often are conspicuous by their absence from the ordinary services in a building. There is something non-committal about attendance at an open air service even though you come miles to be present. Or is it that there is really some repulsive force about the swing-door, the verger and the stately churchwardens of the regular places of worship? (*CRQ* MD 1906)

The Quarry conference was one of the stepping stones which led to the founding of the Church Socialist League (CSL) by about sixty Anglican priests and a few laymen at Morecambe on 13 June 1906.[13] Among the signatories to the letter of invitation to Morecambe of 14 May were at least eight clergy who had attended the Quarry conference, including its convenors, Frere and Bull. The League was created partly because of dissatisfaction with the elitist and southern ethos of CSU and GSM. CSL like the ILP had northern origins. By 1906 Gore had concluded that efforts to give CSU new life had failed, and while it should continue as a research organization it should 'leave the Socialists to make a fresh start'. In 1908 CSU reached the peak of its influence and then rapidly declined. GSM was dissolved in 1909. So there was room for a new organization. CSL's outlook was summed up by F. L. Donaldson's slogan: 'Christianity is the religion of which Socialism is the practice.' CSL became committed to the 'establishment of a democratic commonwealth in which the community shall own the land and capital collectively'. Thus CSL, unlike its predecessors, had a specific political programme and had links (at this stage) with the Labour party. Bull and Healy spoke at Morecambe. Bull joined the committee. Though a southerner, Bull had developed a romantic attachment to the North. He wrote in 1906: 'When we Northerners want a little rest and sleep, we scamper off to London and the South, with its quaint old-world ways and its dreamy life. Then back again to the North with its strong, rich, vigorous life, where the destiny of England is being wrought out by strong, thoughtful men . . . .'[14] A 1907 list of CSL members included six brethren: Frere, Bull, Healy, Fitzgerald, Francis Hill and Bertram Barnes. Links between CSL and CR were maintained. In August 1914 CSL held a conference at the House and Figgis debated 'The Church's Duty Toward Social Reconstruction' in the Quarry with F. L. Donaldson, F. W. Jowett the Liberal MP, and George Lansbury, President of CSL.

On 27 April 1907 a second Quarry conference was held. Again Frere and Bull explained that though most of the brethren and students attended it was not an official Community occasion. Despite the cold, showery weather about 300 arrived. Only two or three women had attended the conference in 1906. This time there was a strong delegation including the suffragettes Mrs Emmeline Pankhurst and Miss Annie Kenney. The conference was conducted in an informal and friendly manner. Frere took out his pipe and others followed his example. He proposed that a telegram should be sent to Keir Hardie who had been unable to be present. Frere proposed reaffirmation of the first resolution of the previous year proposing co-operation between church socialists and Organized Labour. Pensions was the subject of the second resolution proposed by Healy. The third resolution calling for women's franchise was proposed by Bull who defended the militancy of the suffragettes. This was remarkable, for Anglo-Catholicism was known more for its misogyny than for its feminism, though Gore argued for the granting of the franchise to women in church and state. Mrs Pankhurst and Miss Kenney and other women supported him.[15] F. L. Donaldson proposing the fourth resolution demanded justice for the unemployed, seconded by J. R. Clynes M P, an Oldham man who worked in the mill from the age of ten and imbibed his socialism from Carlyle, Ruskin, Mill, Emerson and Renan. The *CR Quarterly* (JB 1907) wrote:

> The number of Socialists in the Community is not a large one, but there are many in the Community who think it disastrous that the Church should be so wholly associated as it is in the public mind with conservatism in politics . . . The effect of last year's conference was clearly visible. Those who came together were much less apologetic or self-conscious.

The resolutions of this conference had covered more ground than those of the previous year. This conference had attracted Mrs Pankhurst and her followers and tackled the role of women. Why then was it not repeated? No one could claim that centuries of alienation of working people from the church had been cured by two conferences. Did its organizers think that now C S L would take over the bridge building? Public controversy following this second conference of 27 April merged with controversies created by the Church House meeting on 13 May, which were reinforced by the Kensitite meeting in Mirfield on 6 June. Therefore probably C R concluded it had started more than enough hares for the time being. An article by Frere (*CRQ* CD 1907) provided an epilogue. It was often said that the church, especially the clergy, must stand aside from politics. But churchmen are also citizens. The church should be politically comprehensive, therefore we cannot 'acquiesce in the common view that the Church is tied hand and foot to Conservatism'. C R with its wide range of opinions was much more comprehensive than the church, Frere concluded.

Hostile letters and articles in the press combined political and religious criticisms. A letter in the *Pall Mall Gazette* for 10 May 1907 reacted to the forthcoming Church House meeting in the light of the recent Quarry conference. A community founded for missionary work was 'joining hands with the Church's inveterate foes'. On 4 May the *Yorkshire Post* began to print a series of highly critical letters about C R. The vicar of St Mary's Hunslet, Leeds, responded to the Leeds Hostel Appeal by a catena of forty-six quotations from Healy's *Definite Church Teaching*. A Mr Nixon was not a bit worried by Mirfield's doctrine, but had been alienated by the 'socialistic' Quarry conference. He had 'rejoiced' when the College began, but had now withdrawn his subscription. Frere replied to both correspondents in the issue of 7 May. The Community could not be held responsible for the views of its individual members. Uniformity could only be secured by 'narrowness of mind and suppression of individuality . . . a considerable number of us hold views very hostile to those of Socialism'. Mr Nixon responded that the Community had 'a collective responsibility' for its members, and 'it is not very brave on Mr Frere's part to disown it'. Whereas he and others took every opportunity of proclaiming socialism, the anti-socialist brethren were silent. The 'last straw' had been the conversion of the Quarry services into occasions for socialist propaganda. Another correspondent described C R's attempt to infiltrate the new University of Leeds as part of 'that silent, secret, unspoken, but splendidly engineered movement' to convert the younger generation from protestantism. In October Frere was in controversy with the evangelical *Record* and unwisely used language designed to appeal to its readers' prejudices. He accused it of giving 'a puff to Roman Catholic proselytizers' and 'playing into the hands of the enemy' by quoting extracts from the 'autobiographical effusions' of Benson, 'a deserter to the enemy'. C R had made many efforts to retain his loyalty and in the process 'put up with many things in his views and conduct of which it disapproved'.

In the *Yorkshire Post* for 17 June 1908 Mr Nixon returned to the attack. Since he had not seen anything to complain about for twelve months he had renewed his subscription to C R. He was astonished when his money was returned by the treasurer [Healy] who pointed out that since the Community had not repented of its socialism, it would be false to retain his subscription. Some correspondents warmly praised C R, but one of its many critics challenged Frere (who had claimed brethren held a wide variety of opinions) to name those who opposed socialism and those who would be willing 'to preach or lecture in defence of the Evangelical or Protestant character of the Church of England'. On 24 June, 'A Former Well-Wisher' quoted at length from a report in the *Brighouse Echo* of a speech by Healy at Elland. Millions were suffering poverty because of the capitalists. He favoured action by revolution rather than through Parliament: 'it would be all right to put twenty big landowners and twenty large capitalists to death, if by doing so the present system could be altered and put right . . .' On 26 June Healy denied this report.

On 27 June the public heard at last from one brother who was not a socialist – Horner, Warden of the College. Since C R had been accused of subjecting young men to socialist indoctrination, his statement that he did not expect social redemption from 'extreme Socialists' was opportune: 'their method of stating their case does not incline me to a more favourable view of their aims; and this applies to the propaganda of some of the brethren in the Community as well as to those outside'. He protested against those who harmed the College by attributing to him views which he repudiated. A further example of Healy's capacity to inflame appeared on 1 July. In a sermon in Bath, Healy said 'there is no parallel in the world's history to the ghastly failure of the Church of England'. The great masses of the people were outside it. Almost overcome with emotion he concluded: 'The Protestant religion had no claim on man's heart. It was inspired and founded by the devil . . . If the Catholic religion was a lie, a blasphemy, then to Hell with it!' Correspondence raged on daily in which both Frere and Healy intervened. Their letters on 11 July closed the correspondence. (Chapter was deeply concerned at the effect all the controversies were having upon the reputation and financial position of Community and College. Healy was now such a red rag that his treasurer's notices had to omit his name.) Frere wrote on behalf of Greater Chapter and explained: 'One of the root principles of our Rule, and one specially dear to our founder Bishop Gore, is the sacredness of individuality.' But each brother should exercise restraint and remember his duty to the common life. Healy expressed deep regret for the pain given to friends of the Community and some brethren, apologized for refusing the donation, explained that he did not advocate the assassination of landlords and capitalists, many of whom were kind and generous Christians, and regretted the exaggerated language he had used about the Church of England. (Protestant pamphleteers gleefully reprinted what Healy was alleged to have said at Elland and Bath.)

On 18 July CR held its annual At Home, attended by about 700 people. Frere tried once again to explain CR's understanding of corporate and individual responsibility. Bickersteth reported that work on the new Hostel building could not be resumed without more money. One lady had revoked a bequest of £1,000. The Rector of Elland, deputizing for Lord Halifax, proposed a vote of confidence in the Community, despite his disagreements with the utterances of both Bull and Healy. CR had helped scores of parishes and while others bemoaned the lack of ordinands CR had acted and established the College. The vote of confidence was passed unanimously.

That month Chapter resolved that if harm were done to the Community by one of the brethren, it should bring this before him. It could dissociate itself publicly from his action. Though the Community exercised no censorship, individual brethren should exercise the utmost possible self-restraint if they felt obliged to take a line which might grieve other brethren or compromise the Community. So a vital element in the Gore tradition had been vindicated.

After a couple of weeks at Mirfield, Keble Talbot described Frere as 'much the biggest man here'. By July Chapter 1908 Frere had had six and a half strenuous years as Superior, during which new ventures had been started at

Mirfield, Leeds and in South Africa. Since 1904 he had been in constant and contentious correspondence with the Archbishop. He had had to grapple with bitter public and internal controversies. Not surprisingly in October 1908 he had his second breakdown in four years (this time with neuritis) and was away for three months, staying mostly at St Paul's Deanery with Robert Gregory, still Dean at 89. When Frere returned to Mirfield he decided he must cut down his commitments. Longridge was recalled from South Africa to assist him as Assistant Superior. The South African brethren protested, but those at Mirfield explained that his recall was vital to prevent Frere's total breakdown.

Withdrawals

Between 1908 and 1913 four of the brethren withdrew from the Community in very different circumstances.

In 1907–8 an alarming crisis arose about Caleb Ritson, Warden of the College, when students revolted against his harsh regime and some said that if he were not replaced, they probably would not continue. Ritson was dismissed in January 1908 and replaced by Horner. Ritson was given leave of absence for six months. He seems not to have realized what had gone wrong, was sore at his dismissal and disillusioned with the Community. In July he remained in his stall at the renewal of pledges and left soon after. He was given £35 for his furniture and went to parochial work in Beckenham.

In 1909 Healy was the centre of another (and as it turned out, his last) drama. The *Church Times* published a long letter from him on 22 October about church endowments. These were given 'to support a celibate priesthood and the Catholic religion'. The church's title to these endowments was not clear nor was their origin pure. The church received extortionate rents. Its interest from industry was contrary to Luke 6.34. Endowments enabled 'many of the clergy to live idle and fruitless lives' and the laity became parasites. The church had been indifferent, with a few exceptions, to the sufferings of the poor. Disestablishment and disendowment would bring us to Christ who 'for our sakes became poor'.[16] Four long letters the following week refuted his historical assertions. A terse letter from Frere appeared on 5 November: 'I write at the request of our Chapter to dissociate the Community from the letter of our brother Samuel Healy, printed in your issue of October 22.' On 19 November Healy ate humble pie. His statements that the endowments were given for a celibate priesthood, and that Luke 6.34 forbade interest and profits from industry were incorrect. He added that he had received much support for church reform both from brethren and from the church at large.

Greater Chapter in January 1910 was fraught and painful. Healy asked for release. For Healy the final straw was CR's refusal to allow him to work for Lansbury in the General Election that month. After two days of anxious discussion it was resolved by a majority vote: that as he had long been uncertain of his position in the Community, and only renewed his pledge in July 1909 with some misgiving; that as throughout he had been absolutely loyal to the Community and now submitted himself to its judgment; without creating a precedent, release was granted. He was given a statement that his release was not for either doctrinal or moral reasons, the rights over his publications and £25. He could apply for further help. In chapel the Superior released him as he knelt before the altar: 'By the authority of the Chapter I release you from your promise so far as it was made to the Community.' Psalm 143 was then recited. Healy left Mirfield the same day and went to work as organizing secretary of the Church Socialist League. He was a curate in four parishes between 1911 and 1920 (enabling him to do socialist and mission work), then became rector of two small parishes in remotest Lincolnshire. In 1933, a couple of years before he died, CR gave him £20, redeeming its promise of further help given twenty-three years before. Rackham commented in the Chronicle:

> For a long time past Samuel had been growing more and more to identify the Gospel with socialism, and to lose patience with all church authorities as acquiescing in the rule of capitalism; convinced that it was his mission to preach socialism, he felt that he could not fulfil it in the Community and lost his hold on the principles of the Religious Life.

The same Chapter took an even more painful decision. One of the brethren had been uncertain about renewing in July 1909 partly because he thought he was in love. Hearing of Healy's decision he decided to withdraw, refusing an order to return. It was decided unanimously to expel him. Despite being expelled he was given £10. He became an incumbent and stayed in the same parish for thirty-five years.

The South African Chapter believed that the Rule provided no means of releasing a brother and that the expulsion should not have been voted upon before the votes from South African brethren had been received. Rackham wrote:

> The departure of these two brethren caused a good deal of heart-searchings and agitation among the Brethren. There was a discussion on the question of permanent vows and each brother testified as to his view of the binding character of the 'permanent intention' of our rule. A committee was formed to report on the power of the Superior, and another to make suggestions by which the form for the first making of the Promise might be made more emphatic and bring out the idea of permanence implied.

When they heard that both Healy and Ritson were getting married in June, an even deeper depression settled over the brethren. Healy's marriage was particularly galling since his final drama only eight months previously had been over his contention that endowments had been given to maintain a celibate priesthood. Talbot wrote to his brother Neville on 6 July 1910:

> I think that we are finding that what suited a small group of friends round Gore, can hardly carry the weight, or sustain the stability, of a growing Community whose scope is ever being widened. Our democracy, individual liberty, temporary pledges, and, generally, what may be regarded as our 'human' affinities, all are under trial, and I want to ask you to pray that we may be so shaken that the things which cannot be shaken may abide.

That month Greater Chapter decided on a stricter regime: there was to be more prayer; newspapers would not be available until 11 a.m.; cassocks were to be worn in the House and elsewhere; there were to be more Quiet Days, more theological study, and a more simple diet. Sampson wanted everyone to wear a scapular. Rees proposed a habit and life vows.

A less dramatic crisis broke in 1913. Latimer Fuller was one of the first three brethren to go to South Africa in 1902, and in 1912 accepted the bishopric of Lebombo, in Portuguese East Africa. He hoped some brethren might join him, but this was not feasible. CR released him in December, with the precedent of Gore in mind, though brethren were sad that he had accepted without waiting for a decision from Chapter. He was consecrated in January 1913. A few months later he announced his engagement. This led to a breach with the South African brethren. Fuller wrote in reply to a disapproving letter from Francis Hill that he disagreed with the brethren's approach. Marriage was as great an ideal as celibacy. He had refused to consider the possibility of marriage until released from CR. By December 1914 relations had improved sufficiently for him to be invited to lunch. Fuller's release raised questions which have featured in CR history. Is it right for brethren to become bishops? If so, what should be their relationship to the Community? It was not until Nash became co-adjutor Bishop of Cape Town in 1917 that the form of association known as 'Prelate Brother' was devised. But this has meant different things for different brethren. Fuller is the only brother in CR history to become a bishop who subsequently married. Anglo-Catholics have sometimes advocated clerical celibacy as a sacrificial act, sometimes (as did Bull, Figgis and Dolling) as a means of making priests classless. The attitudes of Anglo-Catholicism towards celibacy and clerical marriage have been complicated by the strand of homosexuality in that tradition.[17]

At General Chapter July 1913 Longridge was elected Superior, and Talbot became assistant Superior. A number had wanted Talbot as Superior. Frere favoured Bickersteth or Horner. After eleven years Frere needed a break and CR needed a change. He was keenly aware that other communities (including SSJE) had suffered when the same Superior had continued too long. In 1911 Frere had been suggested to the Prime Minister as Dean of St Paul's. But if the offer was ever made, Frere would have declined it as he was too much of a Community man. In 1916 he was re-elected Superior. In 1922 Talbot succeeded him. In 1916 Longridge became the first Prior of the Mother House, relieving the Superior from having to deal with its day-to-day domestic life. It was an important act of delegation in the light of Frere's breakdowns of 1904 and 1908–9.

From its beginning CR had wanted to do something to bridge the gulf between the church and the working class. Some of the controversies in this chapter arose from that desire. From August 1914, brethren were given a unique opportunity as chaplains to test out their theories and redeem their promises as they came face to face with working men in the trenches.

5

The First World War

'Economically an Anglo-German war is impossible': that is what just over half the students at Mirfield decided in a college debate early in 1914, obviously influenced by Norman Angell's immensely popular anti-war book *The Great Illusion* (1910). After 1912 international tension had declined. War between civilized nations seemed increasingly improbable. Canon W. L. Grane, like Gore and Frere a member of the Church of England Peace League, in his book *The Passing of War* (1913), concluded that war was becoming an anachronism. Neville Figgis was a lone voice among churchmen. 'Something is crumbling all around us' he wrote in 1912. Again he declared: 'We can almost hear the thunders of the avalanche of war – war on a scale unknown. Hardly does the world even look stable any longer.'[1] Theologically and temperamentally (he suffered depressions) he was out of sympathy with the evolutionary optimism which had informed much of *Lux Mundi* and the ethos of CR.

The widespread refusal to face the real tragedy of the First World War – hence such adjectives as 'futile' and 'unnecessary' – arises from the belief that there is always an underlying harmony in world affairs which diplomacy can actualize. In fact, at each stage, there were few choices of any substance available; the weight of past history and the self-propulsion of the war machine were too strong. Neither was there some simple military or diplomatic master-stroke which could have swiftly terminated the war. Consequently throughout, human beings often seemed more victims than prime movers.[2]

The churches of Britain and Germany were theologically and pastorally ill-prepared for the challenges of war. They were impelled by their traditions and self-interest to propagate a nationalistic Christianity.[3] In both countries church allegiance had been ebbing before the war. The churches believed (wrongly) that war would reverse this trend. German Protestants wanted to prove themselves the guardians of national culture. British and German Roman Catholics needed to show that they were not alien intruders. The Church of England hoped to demonstrate that it was the church of the nation and so justify its continued establishment. The Free Churches wished to live down their reputation as political and social dissenters. The moral appeal of

the cause of 'little Belgium' was extremely powerful: even one third of
Quakers of military age enlisted; the only British pilot to shoot down two
Zeppelins was a Cadbury. Of the three English religious traditions it was
Roman Catholicism which was the most uncritically patriotic. Within the
Church of England, those of the Catholic tradition were most likely to be
sensitive to the trans-national dimension of Christianity, whereas Evan-
gelicals and Modernists were mostly erastian and nationalistic. The Free
Churches, like the Church of England, had their hyper-patriots, but a much
higher proportion of conscientious objectors.

All the major institutions of Europe were sifted by the war. Ordinary people
wrestled with deep theological questions about the nature, purpose and
omnipotence of God. What spiritual resources were there for the multitudes
of the bereaved? Were those who died without faith saved by their courage in
battle? Were aerial bombing, poison gas and reprisals contrary to Just War
restraints? Was the war God's judgment on a rotten civilization? What had
happened to the dreams of an inevitable advance to international peace? If the
churches had not been divided, could they have prevented war? – ecumenical
contacts between the churches of Germany and Britain were still minimal in
1914. The Anglican and Free Churches had long bewailed their lack of
influence upon working men; now they were given a unique opportunity to be
in close contact through their chaplains, what would result? And how did CR
react to, and how was it affected by the most cataclysmic event of the twentieth
century in Europe?

The Home Front

At Mirfield on 31 July the deepening crisis was marked by a daily recitation of
the collect for Epiphany 2. On 7 August the rule against the reading of
newspapers before 11 a.m. was rescinded. From 21 August the Angelus was
recited daily at noon with special intention for the war. After a gap of twenty-
one years the prayers for the Royal Family (disliked by Anglo-Catholics as
erastian) were resumed at evensong. Prayers were said daily for victory, 'our
enemies' and for the dead. The war created financial problems. Building work
had to be paid by an overdraft. The library grant was reduced. Brethren were
to request financial help for preaching engagements from the parishes. They
had to manage on half the usual peculium and to be frugal about clothes,
stationery and food. A rudimentary blackout was enforced after April 1915.
The Superior through the *Church Times* (23 July 1915) offered hospitality to
convalescent servicemen: 'There is no hunting or shooting, but there is a large
house with a good library and a chapel'. CR also sheltered Belgian refugees.
By 1916 with so many brethren and probationers away as chaplains, to the
effervescent Bull the house was gloomy and dull, only relieved by the liveliness
of Frere and Figgis. The London Priory which had started its life in Kensington

in July 1914, moved to more suitable accommodation near Paddington station in December 1915. But its work was affected by air raids. People were reluctant to attend evening meetings.

The effect of the war on the College and Hostel was drastic. Students were allowed to volunteer (some had been members of the Leeds OTC). By Christmas 1914 thirty-one per cent had enlisted mostly as combatants, but some in the Royal Army Medical Corps, though those in their final year had been ordained. After Trinity 1915 the bishops did not accept as ordinands any who were fit to serve in the forces. Horner, the Warden, advised clergy not to become combatants; instead they should serve as chaplains, in the RAMC or Red Cross; the war created new pastoral needs, so clergy and ordinands should not be panicked into enlisting. In July 1915 the College was closed and all the students lived at the Leeds Hostel. In 1916 Kelham Hall, the House of the Society of the Sacred Mission, was requisitioned, so their brethren and remaining students migrated to the College at Mirfield, and stayed there until March 1919. By 1917 seven former Mirfield students were chaplains and sixty-three Mirfield ordinands were serving in the forces.

As the war went on, and clergy were in short supply (some had gone to be chaplains, ordinations had dwindled) the demands on the remaining brethren increased. Longridge and Sampson took charge of parishes; Murray became chaplain to a soldiers' convalescent hospital; Hart and Jeayes were chaplains at Gretna Green munition works; Bull and Seyzinger tended wounded soldiers in London; Horner became chaplain to Queen Ethelburga's school, Harrogate.

CR in the armed services

French Roman Catholic clergy were conscripted as combatants from the beginning of the war. Anglican bishops urged clergy not to become combatants, but a few did. In 1916 Charles Fitzgerald, a chaplain in France, encountered a combatant priest who had been a British officer in the Anglo-Boer War, and who said mass for his men in the trenches as well as leading them into battle. 'I wish I knew if he is right . . . it seems to me so incongruous' commented Fitzgerald. Keble and Neville Talbot, both chaplains in France, also debated the issue. Neville, who had fought in South Africa before ordination, now felt cut off from his men. Should he become a combatant? he asked. Keble understood his brother's dilemma – he was opposed to chaplains being officers – but he argued that the chaplain 'is set apart . . . to represent and make possible the peace which subsists beneath and survives the *débacle* of war . . . priests have to detach themselves from the more particular, temporary and sectional undertakings of warfare . . . to safeguard and dig channels for forces other than those of violence'.

Why did Hubert Northcott, professed in January 1918, enlist as a private in the Artillery that summer? Was it his response to the crisis on the western front which led the bishops to agree that clergy could now volunteer for combatant (and non-combatant) service? Did he want to bridge the gap between church and servicemen? Was it his personal kenosis? Was he following the example of the French priests? Northcott was the most private of men so we can only guess at his motives. He had grown up in a vicarage, and had been ordained to a curacy after Rossall and Oxford, so he had not lived with ordinary people before. He felt very much the new boy, learning to salute properly, learning not only the use but also the spirit of the bayonet; was it not good to feel a complete fool occasionally? He had not abandoned his priesthood when he donned khaki: 'Perhaps opportunities will come . . . Nor do I see how I'm to begin. However, I'm learning to love the lads here, and that is one essential for any effective work.' He knew that if he were regarded as a 'camouflaged chaplain' that would inhibit the men. When he was on cookhouse fatigues a chaplain called. Northcott, forgetting that he was coated in jam and grease, shook hands. 'Of course, after our own discipline, Army discipline is a comparatively easy thing.' But it meant being a Christian 'under almost impossible conditions'. When he could go to church it felt wrong not being at the altar. But 'my present position gives me the opportunity of a very valuable experience. It seems to me worthwhile that one of us . . . should be having it, if only the whole Community can in some way share it, though it means that one has to forgo his own functions for the time.'

He embarked for France in September and travelled to base camp in a cattle truck. How ironic it was – a priest sorting out the Salvation Army's swill tubs; he said Terce on the job. He asked himself repeatedly where were the churchmen – 'camouflaged under a mask of indifference'? The men were not moved by religion because they were like convalescents after an illness, with every faculty dormant except the physical. He took part in an attack and acted as a stretcher-bearer. He was glad to be in the thick of it. After the daily worship of Mirfield it was startling to have only attended mass once that month. He summed up war: 'Only the infinite pity is sufficient for the infinite pathos of human life.' When war ended the Colonel asked him to assist the chaplain, J. N. Bateman-Champain (later Bishop of Knaresborough). So he began to say mass again, held Sunday evening mission services and created a discussion group. The quartermaster had never come across a chaplain who was a private in thirty years' service. But that was what Northcott wanted. He was discharged early in 1919.

The pastoral and theological discoveries of the most perceptive of the chaplains focussed many issues of immense importance for both the church and CR.[4] 'Why are the men whose courage, good comradeship, gallantry and cheerfulness we are bound to admire indifferent to Christianity?' asked Studdert Kennedy in the Anglican chaplains' symposium *The Church in the Furnace* (1917). Why have four-fifths of young men little or no connection with the church? Why is there such widespread ignorance of its teaching? asked the interdenominational symposium *The Army and Religion* (1919) prepared by a group chaired by Bishop E. S. Talbot whose members included Walter Frere. The Roman Catholic and Free Church chaplains could concentrate on their own flocks. Only about half the total chaplains were Anglicans, but they were expected to look after the seventy per cent of the men who declared themselves 'C of E'. Some soldiers thought that Holy Communion was for officers only – a terrible indictment of the elitist image of the Church of England.

Keble Talbot and Frederick King were the first of the brethren to become chaplains.[5] By the end of the war sixteen were or had been chaplains – in France, South-West Africa, Jerusalem, Salonika, Egypt, India, Gallipoli and in the navy. Keble Talbot, Frederick King, Timothy Rees, Richard Barnes and Eustace Hill were awarded MCs. Some probationers went as chaplains. Two probationers (Humphrey Money and Ivan Tunnicliffe) were never professed; Guy Pearse who had been professed in 1907 withdrew after the war. Several already had military connections. Talbot's uncle was a General. Hill (who like Bull had been a chaplain in the Anglo-Boer War) was the son of a Major-General. King, who as a layman had often driven trains past Mirfield, had (like Bull) been deeply involved with the Church Lads' Brigade; openly militaristic, it fed recruits into the Territorials. Many brethren had been members of the OTC at public school and university. There were few pacifists in the Church of England during the First World War, and apparently none in CR. The Anglican pacifist movement dates from the 1930s and by then a small number of brethren were pacifists. However, vocal peace campaigning has never been part of the CR tradition.

For the first couple of years chaplains were thrown into the deep end without any training. Osmund Victor was sent to France a week after joining up. When Talbot reported to Woolwich in mid-August 1914 he found that the Chaplains' Department was in chaos. It had no clear idea about the role or disposition of chaplains, and had made no provision for either service books or horses. It was five days before he, his brother Neville, other chaplains and 750 men finally disembarked from an old stinking cargo boat at Rouen. For a fortnight he was left hanging about until he was attached to a hospital. The Chaplain-General, Bishop Taylor Smith ('really rather an old ass' Talbot told his mother) was a naively patriotic and pietistic Evangelical who while being shaved would ask the barber about his soul. The *Church Times*, the Church Union and Bull conducted a protracted campaign against Taylor Smith and his department for discriminating against Anglo-Catholics as chaplains. Yet none of the CR chaplains seemed to suffer from discrimination. Probably the Mirfield connections with the episcopate helped. It is said that when Taylor Smith interviewed Talbot and discovered that he was from Mirfield he stalled about his application: there were few vacancies, but he would be in touch. He asked for Talbot's address. He replied 'Farnham Castle'. The Chaplain-

General looked up sharply: 'Are you a visitor there?' 'Yes I am holidaying with my parents.' 'You mean your father is . . . Bishop of Winchester? . . . Well then, I think we can probably arrange a chaplaincy for you . . . ' Yet a Cowley novice was cashiered for hearing confessions. Another source of conflict was that some Anglo-Catholics wanted to turn Church Parade into a eucharist. Neville Talbot, however, argued that most of the men needed evangelistic services first.

The contentious and panic-stricken correspondence in the *Church Times* and elsewhere about widespread religious indifference and ignorance at the front, reflected a conviction that not only the parochial clergy, but also the Church of England over many centuries, were being weighed in the balance and found desperately wanting. How could it continue to claim to be the national church?

A number of important themes emerge from the letters of the CR chaplains.

The deep revulsion they felt about the war was often shared by the men. Hill described his experience of stretcher-bearing: 'What a real priest's stole a stretcher shoulder strap is! How ever did Christ stand the strain on back and arms so long . . . How long will Christianity countenance this way of settling disputes and continue to put painted ribbons on sepulchres full of wounded groans and dead men's bones? Self sacrifice can surely grow on less putrid soil than war!' He told the men on a Quiet Day that 'Love of Right was to be our incentive not Hate'. Over lunch the Colonel expressed his bafflement: 'Well, Padre, you think it is all right sticking Germans. You love 'em and stick 'em?' Talbot became more and more aware of 'an instinctive sense of incongruity in the minds of people out here between the occupation of fighting and their Christian profession.' He instanced an officer who declined to receive communion in France, but would do so happily at home. 'I think a good number of people are holding their religious convictions and habits in suspense during the war.' The CR chaplains were keenly aware of the paradoxes of war. King wrote from Gallipoli: 'War is Hell! And yet it is instrumental in drawing from men deeds of unparalleled heroism and self-sacrifice.' Talbot commented: 'I don't suppose that many men will ever be so much alive if they live for fifty years more. And the chaff and merriment makes it all the more poignant.'

In October 1914 Talbot, outraged by the destruction of Louvain and Rheims cathedral, wrote to his parents: 'I feel very much inclined to preach a Holy War. I don't suppose the prophets were deterred because there were some good people in Babylon and Assyria.' But he warned that atrocity stories should be treated with caution. By December 1915 he was reacting against Bishop Winnington Ingram's call for the church to 'mobilize the nation for a Holy War'. He thought that there was as much danger in the church adopting that line as in pacifism. 'Indeed, her deep failure lies not in what the press etc. thinks her incapacity to arouse the patriotism of the nation, but in her incapacity to bring the nation to penitence, humility and a vision of the City of God.'

Like many, outside and within the churches, CR chaplains found that only imagery derived from the Passion of Christ made any sense of the slaughter, though this could be used (as Wilfred Owen pointed out) as a glib justification for the war and the national cause. Bull (like many soldiers) remarked on the number of unscathed crucifixes standing in the devastated battlefield areas. In his missions he distributed crucifixes with ribbons attached by pious ladies. The soldiers received them 'in a state of mystic exaltation' he believed. In his *Peace and War* (1917) he told how saddened he was when he saw young soldiers and thought of their likely fate. Then God rebuked him 'Nay, they are lambs for the sacrifice'. Hill was a heroic chaplain to South African troops in the bitter fighting round Delville Wood in July 1916. After the war he wrote an article about the memorials there, 'Why Delville Wood had to have a Cross', with that mix of biblical imagery and Tennysonian chivalry so popular in the public school tradition (Hill was on the staff, later headmaster, of St John's Johannesburg): 'The road up to the Wood was in fact the Way of the Cross.' Holy Communion gave the men 'the strength of the Great Crusader'.[6]

When Timothy Rees died in 1939 after eight years as Bishop of Llandaff, one of the hymns by him which were sung at his funeral was 'God is love', now included in several hymn books. This and his hymn 'O crucified Redeemer' teach that God suffers in and with humanity, a belief which he hung on to when he served as a chaplain from 1914–19 in Gallipoli, Egypt, the Somme, Passchendaele and latterly at the VD hospital at Etaples. In the fierce fighting to capture Thiepval in 1916 (where now stands the massive, haunting memorial arch by Lutyens to over 73,000 men with no known graves) Rees saw so many he had prepared for confirmation and confession mown down. Night and day he was burying the dead, seeking the wounded in shell holes, strengthening the fearful. His hymns about the suffering God parallel the teaching of Studdert Kennedy and the theodicy of the popular novel by H. G. Wells *Mr Britling sees it Through* (1916). The belief in a suffering God is familiar now; then it was a new and creative shift in theology.[7] Fitzgerald spent Holy Week 1916 comforting the wounded and dying and supporting the surgeons in a hospital and felt closer to the crucified Christ than during his pre-war devotional Holy Weeks.

At first chaplains were forbidden to visit the front line, but later as a result of their protests they were allowed to move about freely, except in the first stages of a battle. Hill wrote forcefully from the trenches in stubby pencil: 'The men feel it if the CF always absents himself when they go up . . . Shell-fire we must ignore as others have to. We need not go over the top wiring or patrolling but we can't leave the dead unburied behind the front line because of shells landing there. I was laughed at for refusing a captured Hun dug-out and sleeping in a shell-hole under a stretcher.' A chaplain was expected to reinforce morale – an ambiguous role. When some men were wavering during a furious attack, Hill yelled 'Hold on, men – for God's sake hold on! You can only lose your bodies once; but your souls are going to last for ever.' And the line held.

During the war social deference still prevailed not least in the services. (But afterwards many disillusioned ordinary people blamed the social and religious establishment for the war.) A lieutenant in Gallipoli in 1915 was asked by a badly wounded soldier: 'Shall I go to heaven or hell, sir?' The officer replied with absolute confidence 'To heaven'. Anxiety about one's eternal destiny; the possibility of hell; the belief that an officer would know the religious answers: these familiar features of the First World War had almost disappeared by 1939. First war chaplains (like other officers) naturally assumed and were readily granted a parental role, as members of the ruling class.[8] Chaplains sometimes commented *de haut en bas* on the men's letters they were required to censor. Talbot described it as 'a task which brought me often to the verge of tears and laughter; their letters are such an odd mixture of conventional and wonderfully limited phraseology, and the most pathetic wistfulness for their homes'. He greatly admired the 'courage, humour, simplicity and tender-heartedness' of the British soldier, but added: 'He is like an irresponsible child.' (That such condescending comments could be reprinted in the *Quarterly* suggests that C R did not expect it to have many working-class readers.) When he spent the night rescuing the wounded, one asked 'Are you our clergy?' and he put his arms round Talbot and clung to him 'feeling, I suppose, he was not alone in a friendless world'.

Before the war, the C R chaplains were accustomed, like other Anglo-Catholic priests, to ministering largely to those of their own tradition. It was a painful shock to discover that the vast majority of those who registered themselves as 'C of E' were totally deficient in churchmanship. Hill lamented that the servicemen did not treat Anglican chaplains as 'Catholic priests'. Freestone reported that many loved the Church of England and admired Roman Catholicism, but that Anglo-Catholicism was almost unknown and that almost all distrusted its blending of the two. Neither of the two Talbot brothers were theologically attracted to Roman Catholicism, but they, like other chaplains in the Catholic tradition, were envious of Rome for producing soldiers familiar with sacramental shorthand, so vital for crisis ministry. So when Pearse produced a *Soldier's Book of Devotion* with definite sacramental teaching, it met a great need. Talbot handed out prayer cards; they were readily accepted; but he suspected that many kept them simply as souvenirs. However, when Talbot sometimes celebrated the eucharist instead of the usual Parade Service, many told him how much they appreciated it. Despite appeals in the church newspapers, King at Grantham received only six commendations for his 15,000 men. 'Most of the men belong to that class which, under normal conditions, are outside the reach of the influence of the average parish priest, and who regard him as a being of almost another race altogether.'

Talbot asked some searching questions about what kind of religion servicemen both wanted and needed. 'I am sure that the only way . . . is by not despising the prosaic business of serving the men's bodily needs . . . And the test which your old Tommy applies to religion and religious persons is not so far wrong. He really asks, "Will they take trouble for other people?"' So wherever possible he tried to create a welcoming club with a canteen, books and magazines and with a screened-off chapel for a daily mass. But he found the instinct for worship almost non-existent. The men revered Christ as teacher, but there was little 'Glory to God' in their religion. He asked whether the British would ever want to worship in large numbers through the 'trellis-work' of the church's seasons. A sergeant-major told him frankly that most of religion meant nothing to the men: 'we believe there is One above; we believe you have got to live as decent a life as you can; and that there will be a "kind of reckoning" some time.' A general had told his chaplains that they were to reinforce morale by preaching duty, honour and discipline. Talbot granted that probably this moralism was the main avenue to God for most of the men, but it seemed 'a shorn and pedestrian religion'.

In 1903 Bishop E. S. Talbot had warned his clergy not to dismiss the widespread 'diffusive Christianity', the 'penumbra' of embodied Christianity.[9] Keble Talbot, influenced by the *Lux Mundi* tradition and by his mentor von Hügel in particular, believed that fully mature religion had to be expressed institutionally, but disliked 'churchiness'; he combined a belief in the transcendent glory of God with a sense of his immanence in science, art and ordinary life and people. So he reacted against a widely publicized article by Walter Carey, then a naval chaplain (*Church Times*, 7 January 1916): 'ordinary Anglican religion won't do; it doesn't save souls in any volume . . . therefore it must be scrapped . . . the only forms of religion in the Anglican Communion which have any life in them are the Evangelical and the Sacramental . . . I raise the standard of revolt . . . Dignified Anglicanism has failed.' Keble Talbot commented:

> I am sure that we have got to recognize a greater variety in the life of the spirit than we are very ready to do. I am all for 'standards of revolt' against cold-mutton-fat religion: but I am fain to ask whence comes the generosity, humility and devoted obedience characteristic of many whom one meets here, except from the Spirit of our Lord? And is that to be despised or accounted irreligious which shows itself supremely in action, while little aware of the more mystical or devotional ways of religion? There is many a man who simply *must* not be cold-shouldered out of the Church; yet I doubt whether he will ever prove anything but restive in a 'Catholic' atmosphere.

Worship took many different forms. Talbot was conducting an open-air service when a puppy appeared and yapped at every man in turn; when it was tied up it howled. Then a goat, the company mascot, appeared and began to butt the sergeant-major round the square. Then the puppy broke loose and danced deliriously round both sergeant-major and goat. Then a gun began firing. Finally a gas alert sounded and everyone dived into their masks. Roman Catholic chaplains in France had the advantage of being able to use the churches, a facility normally denied to other chaplains who had to try and create a worshipful atmosphere in hut, canteen or school. Barnes, endeavouring to create a chapel, was delighted when an officer produced a rail for the altar. But he was then embarrassed to discover it had been plundered from a derelict hotel.

C R chaplains helped the many chaplains who were spiritually drained by conducting retreats. As experienced missioners they were also better equipped than most chaplains to respond creatively to the need for evangelistic, non-liturgical worship. At Grantham, on Sundays King celebrated an early eucharist, drummed up cornet-players and a mouth-organ band for the several Parade Services and held an evening mission service. He faced an appalling challenge when in August 1915 he prepared to land with the troops at Suvla Bay, Gallipoli. All waited in tense silence at the rails of the transport ship tied to a destroyer. He passed word among a 1,000 men on both ships so that at a fixed moment they all could say the Lord's Prayer together. 'Then a pause, followed by a short extempore prayer for pardon for the past and protection through all the dangers that awaited us, we commended our loved ones, our cause, and ourselves into God's hands.' He ended with the Aaronic blessing. Then ashore onto the beaches, running, crouched, with his men, trying to avoid the murderous fire, the air filled with the shrieks of the wounded.

> One feels so helpless . . . a clasp of the hand as the wounds are hastily bandaged, a muttered prayer, a drink of water, and that is about all. Oh, the agony of it, as one by one you see the lads you have learned to love shattered and broken and covered with blood, or cold and still with the glaze of death already on their eyes.

Later he took cigarettes, caramels and the reserved sacrament to the men in improvised trenches. Returning across the open plain in the darkness he said Compline from memory, including Psalm 91 'Thou shalt not be afraid of any terror by night'. On his first Sunday he spent six hours burying the dead.

On the lychgate at the entrance to the Community cemetery at Mirfield there is an inscription to W. H. Freestone, buried at Salonika. He had gone there as chaplain in 1916. The Anglo-French landing in October 1915 had aimed, but failed, to save Serbia from defeat. He shared his eucharistic equipment with a Serbian Orthodox priest. His altar was made by Serbian soldiers. He taught both Serbs and Nonconformists about the Church of England and translated the Communion service into Serbian. In December

1916 he was just about to say mass in a tent when a plane started bombing; he went to support a nervous soldier and was killed by bomb splinters. He was buried near the Roman road over which St Paul had journeyed. Though still a probationer, CR counted him as a professed member of the Community. Before going out he had completed his book *The Sacrament Reserved*, inspired by Frere, which was published posthumously. Stanley Spencer, the idiosyncratic painter who was also in the Macedonian campaign, later commemorated it in murals for the chapel at Burghclere, which culminate in the astonishing resurrection of the soldiers above the altar.

Ralph Bell, from the North Riding laconic gentry, served as a naval chaplain, utterly free from *angst*. Latterly he was in the eastern Mediterranean. He disliked the Turks and considered that Orthodox stained glass was suitable only for a coffee room in a second class hotel. He accompanied British forces which occupied Baku on the Caspian Sea, part of the anti-Soviet offensive. 'I am glad to say there are no Bolsheviks here' he reported from Batumi on the Black Sea. 'It's a funny little war' he said, adding with unashamed paternalism: 'Rights of self-determination may be all right for grown-ups; they do not do for children.' On days-off he enjoyed hunting wild sheep and shooting partridge and snipe.

Attitudes to war

Longridge, the Superior, in September 1914 accepted the general British line: we were at war not for glory or aggression, but to uphold solemn pledges. He continued to be optimistic that arbitration would replace war. Bickersteth assured readers at Christmas: 'In the German hosts arrayed against us there are not only the disciples of Nietzsche and Bernhardi . . . there are gentle Christian men who love their wives and children, and connect, as we do, all the sanctities of home with Bethlehem and Nazareth; there are, for instance, our old friends from Oberammergau . . . ' Frere, a passionate European, in a sermon for the Church of England Peace League of 1916 refuted the popular notion that advancing civilization would abolish war. In war-time the League should try to prevent the coarsening of attitudes.

The war-time apocalyptic mood in which people drew gleefully upon the *schadenfreude* of the cursing psalms, the denunciatory prophets and the book of Revelation, appealed to both the best and the worst of Figgis. His presentation of Christianity as a series of stark alternatives repelled the eirenic Talbot. After reading Figgis' *Civilisation at the Cross Roads* he concluded that his father's appreciation of 'diffusive' Christianity had 'a deeper and more human quality' than Figgis' 'holy-water-or-you-frizzle' approach. Figgis had been one of the few to prophesy a coming catastrophe. When it arrived, his initial reactions were hyper-patriotic. In 'The Sword and the Cross', an article in *Challenge* on 18 September 1914 (reprinted in *Some Defects*) he roundly declared that if we believe that our cause is just we should pray for victory and sing the *Te Deum* if this were granted. 'I believe that at this moment no man is more truly working for the cause of God in the world than the soldier in the trenches.' The belief that war is wrong was 'Tolstoyism' not Christianity. 'Suffering and death are the worst of calamities only on a voluptuary theory of the universe.' The rejection of the sanction of force was 'Manichean . . . logically destructive of the In- carnation and the Resurrection of the Body'. In his preface to *The Fellow- ship of the Mystery* (1914) he wrote: 'The new Teutonic Christianity . . . is conducting its first mission – with the bonfire of Louvain for its Bethlehem star . . . The conflict is . . . between light and darkness, God and His enemies, Christ and Satan.' It was common in England to blame German thinkers like Nietzsche for the war. Figgis told a London audience that Nietzsche had justly attacked Christianity because we had forgotten the strong Christ who chose not anaemic but assertive sinners for disciples. Elsewhere he described Nietzsche as both a foe and a friend to Christian- ity. Despite his caricature of Christianity, 'The passion of his flaming soul, his sincerity, his sense of beauty, his eloquence, the courage of his struggles with ill-health, the pathos of that lonely soul craving for sym- pathy, his deep psychological insight and sense of prophetic mission – all these give him a spell which it is hard to resist.' It reads like a portrait of Figgis himself. Figgis, the ex-Nonconformist, gleefully predicted that the war would bury 'the tepid weak tea of respectable choristers' Anglicanism'. The war had ended sentimental optimism about progress; we had learned the reality of evil. Implicitly attacking the *Lux Mundi* tradition, he argued for a shift back from incarnation to atonement; 'the Alexandrian age' of English religion dominated by Westcott was finished. We had been forced to realize 'our own distinctiveness, our unique quality as Christians'.[10] On 2 June 1918 Figgis preached what turned out to be his last sermon at the University Church, Cambridge, as the Germans were sweeping across France and it looked as if the Allies might lose the war. He walked to the pulpit, looking unhealthy and bloated, crippled with arthritis, leaning on a stick, and in his harsh voice announced his text: 'The Lord sitteth above the water-flood; the Lord remaineth a King for ever.' 'Does He?' Figgis asked. He compared the nation's plight with the sack of Rome which had caused Augustine to write *City of God*:

> Nobody now professes to believe that earthly blessings attend on the virtuous man, as a thing of course. All Christians accept the doctrine of the Cross, that strength may be made perfect in weakness – that apparent loss, even of power to work for God, may bring real gain. In words we believe that, but we find it hard in act – in our own case. Still harder is it in the national cause. Yet nations, like individuals, may be

the greatest when they have to tread the *via dolorosa*, like Belgium now. The age-long triumph of English freedom might conceivably come, not after a victory, but out of a disaster unparalleled.[11]

Here his faith in the transcendent God enabled him to set disaster into a distinctively Christian perspective without gloating.

Figgis' life was a combination of private disaster and public acclaim. The publication of *Civilisation at the Cross Roads* was delayed because the corrected proofs went down with the Titanic, a ship which came to symbolize the complacency of the age which the book had assailed. When he travelled to lecture on Nietzsche in Illinois in 1915 his boat was harried by German submarines. He told his audience of Nietzsche's serious accident from which he never recovered which led to 'that long agony which ended with his madness'. This happened to Figgis. In January 1918 he set out again to lecture in America. The liner was torpedoed off Northern Ireland. Figgis escaped in an open boat, but his manuscript on Bossuet, on whom he had been working for years, perished with other material. Only four weeks before he had been operated on for an arthritic knee. He never recovered from the shock of the shipwreck. In March 1919 his doctor brother and another doctor decided he should go to a mental home at Virginia Water where he died in April aged 53. He was the first to be buried in the Community cemetery which had been created in 1913.[12]

Bull, as an imperialistic socialist and romantic patriot, ardently supported the war. By contrast, Keir Hardie, shattered by the failure of international socialism to prevent the war, died a broken man in September 1915. The Church Socialist League was also divided about the war. In *Our Duty at Home in Time of War* (1914) Bull asserted that ultimately Christianity would make aggressive wars impossible. But war could be used by God to remove evil like a surgeon. We needed to confess our sins, to pray for victims on both sides, to plead the daily eucharistic sacrifice and to pray for the dead. To say the Angelus at noon would unite us with the French and Belgians. (Bull conveniently forgot German Roman Catholics.) All available men should enlist; those with scruples should join the Red Cross or RAMC. 'Women can exercise a wholesome pressure of contempt for those who are inclined to shirk this duty of offering themselves.' He ended: 'God, in calling us to this work, has absolved our nation of its sins.' His addresses *Peace and War* (1917) aimed 'to justify the honourable profession of our Royal Navy and Army as against the false teaching of Pacifism'. They owed more to the platform than the pulpit: 'And after a year of crucifixion our Nation answers with unflinching resolution "To the last drop of our blood"', he told the congregation of St Paul's Cathedral in July 1915. Elsewhere he argued that worship had been perverted by the substitution of mattins for mass, so obscuring the belief in sacrifice. Yet over every soldier's grave could be placed 'He saved others,

Himself he could not save' (Matthew 27.42). Pacifism, however, was a mixture of materialism and sentimentality. As long as society was atomistic and competitive, war was inevitable, so by the war God was teaching the necessity of brotherhood.

Gore had reluctantly become Bishop of Oxford in 1911. Birmingham had been urban and compact. Oxford was feudal, largely rural and with 670 parishes, unwieldy. After two years he was so despondent and felt so trapped that he contemplated resignation, but concluded it would look like running away. When war broke out, he wrote a fine Pastoral letter to be read to the congregations:

> A terrible war is being waged among the chief Christian nations of Europe. This in itself ought to move us to horror. Sixteen hundred years ago, when Europe was becoming Christian, it was advanced without any hesitation, as one of the proofs of our Lord's divinity, that even the most savage nations, on accepting His Name, must cease to wage war and use only the weapons of peace. How sadly has this boast been falsified. Truly war is not a Christian weapon . . . Nevertheless there are circumstances when the safety of our own country and our obligations to sister countries compel us to go to war . . . such was our lamentable duty in this crisis.

That autumn in his Primary Visitation he told the diocese:

> The Bible is full of patriotic emotion; but even more conspicuously the Bible is full of a great warning against the sufficiency of patriotism, against the sufficiency of the thoughts natural to flesh and blood. Some of the most conspicuous figures in the Bible, like Jeremiah, are called to the truly terrible vocation of appearing as unpatriotic . . .

But he said that it was Britain's duty to engage in this war. Self-sacrifice for the nation was not distinctively Christian, but by it we are reminded that the Christian is to be self-sacrificial.[13] It was easy to surrender to patriotic emotion, he confessed in an article. But when war ended everything would depend upon whether 'the true counterpoise to war, the spirit of universal human brotherhood' had been nourished in war-time: 'we need a great body of men and women who can cultivate even now a spirit of detachment . . . who can discern the meaning of the Kingdom of God'.[14]

To appreciate the courage of these utterances, and of his later protests against the treatment of conscientious objectors, one should remember, for example, that some congregations refused to sing German hymns like 'Now thank we all our God', that the *Church Times* (9 June 1916) was appalled that music by Handel was played at Kitchener's requiem and that Bishop Winnington Ingram declared in 1915: 'Christ died on Good Friday for Freedom, Honour and Chivalry, and our boys are dying for the same things.' Unlike Figgis and Bull, Gore was sensitive to those elements in the biblical and Christian traditions which questioned unequivocal patriotism, and to the fact that clergy, feeling marginal and scorned as non-combatants, were tempted to indulge in compensatory bellicosity. Gore's belief in a transnational church, his sceptical temperament, his inability to join enthusiastic groups and his distrust of majorities enabled him to maintain a salutary, but anguished, detachment.

The war gave a new urgency to the question of the fate of those who died without explicit faith. In 1914 prayer for the dead was uncommon in the Church of England. Because grief was so widespread, and the teachings of Anglicans and Free Churchmen so confused and meagre, spiritualism flourished. The widespread belief that the sacrifices of the soldiers were akin to that of Christ banished the already muted teaching about hell. However, Anglo-Catholics were able to offer to the bereaved prayers for the dead, requiems and purgatory. So Bickersteth (*CRQ* CD 1916) said that we could not believe that the many who were dying without faith and absolution were going to hell. Christ went to preach to the spirits in prison. 'I can think of none whose case is hopeless.' Rightly understood purgatory was a place of preparation and cleansing. (What a contrast with his forbear, Edward Bickersteth, who in 1846 denounced universalism and successfully moved an additional clause to the basis of the Evangelical Alliance which asserted 'the Eternal Punishment of the wicked').[15]

Yet there was no discussion in the *CR Quarterly* about the morality of reprisals, the use of poison gas, the bombing of civilians. The pressure on churchmen in war-time not to rock the boat is always intense. Even during the war (at least at the front), and more so when it was over, people felt betrayed by the nationalistic Christianity which most in the churches had so fervently preached.

Ecumenism

The spontaneous truce of Christmas 1914 when troops played football and sang carols in no man's land has haunted the European imagination ever since. There were also occasions during lulls at the front, when the sound of hymn singing could be heard across no man's land on Sunday evenings. Sometimes both sides would know the tune and they would sing together. Within the British forces, Anglican, Free Church and Roman Catholic chaplains faced the same dangers and many of the same pastoral problems. There was some contact and co-operation between Anglicans and Free Church chaplains; some contact but few joint ventures between them and their Roman Catholic colleagues. Yet particularly after the 'Kikuyu' controversy in 1913 (when Anglicans and Nonconformists in East Africa had proposed a federal union) Anglo-Catholics were terrified lest ecumenism meant 'pan-protestantism'. So the *Church Times* kept a beady eye open for any bishop who promoted war-time services of prayer with Nonconformists or for instances of inter-communion at the front. It loudly protested when a Congregationalist minister read a lesson at Salisbury cathedral. The Vatican door was firmly closed, but Orthodox doors were opening. Anglo-Catholics desperately wanted the Catholicity of the Church of England strengthened through official recognition from churches with indisputable Catholic pedigrees. The war provided opportunities for this. In July 1915 the clergy of Canterbury Convocation resolved: 'the alliance with Russia ... affords a unique opportunity for deepening and extending the friendly relations which already exist between ourselves and the Orthodox Eastern Church'. The great Russian novels which had been translated before the war were now read more widely. Several books appeared about Orthodoxy. Picture magazines showed Orthodox priests blessing troops before battle. Even Nonconformists who had always hated Tsardom became pro-Russian when the Tsar prohibited vodka.

Frere had paid four visits to Russia before the war. In June 1909 he represented Cambridge University at the centenary celebrations of Gogol's birth. In 1910 he spent a month's holiday in Russia and Finland. In 1912 he, with other clergy, joined the British parliamentary delegation to Russia and gave some lectures. Afterwards he sent a copy of the CR Rule to the Russian church. A Russian priest came to Mirfield for three months. From January to March 1914 Frere lectured in various centres in Russia. He told them that Anglicans needed to broaden their horizons; that the Church of England also repudiated papal supremacy, but it allowed more variety than any other branch of the Catholic church.[16] In the *Church Times* (19, 26 June) he wrote that there was no quarrel between the Russian and English churches, only lack of contact. He characterized the Russian church as 'timeless', was moved by its fellowship with the departed and by its music, but considered its liturgy lacked sequence and climax.

During the war Frere was in great demand as a lecturer on Orthodox theology and music. He also knew continental Roman Catholicism well from his pre-war visits. In a Quarry sermon (*CRQ* MD 1915) he pointed out that Europe could not worship together. Thus Christian witness was weakened. He proposed a new united spiritual effort with our Roman Catholic allies in France, Belgium and Italy and with our Orthodox allies in Russia and Serbia. This might then unite us with 'our foes, with the Roman Catholics and Lutherans of the Central Empires'. (The Free Churches, we note, did not figure in the ecumenical union.) In October 1916 Frere helped Wakefield Cathedral choir to sing the Russian Contakion for a special service for the fallen. First sung in England at St George's Windsor by command of Queen Victoria for the death of Tsar Alexander III in 1894, then included in the *English Hymnal* (1906), its use spread widely during the war – it was sung at St Paul's for memorial services for Edith Cavell (1915) and Lord Kitchener (1916) and at the burial of the Unknown Warrior at Westminster Abbey on 11

November 1920. Later when Frere was Bishop of Truro, he included Russian church music in his musical gatherings. After hard committee work at Lambeth he would sit down at the piano there and sing Russian songs.

Mirfield developed a ministry of ecumenical hospitality. In the autumn of 1915 the Central powers attacked and occupied Serbia driving the British and French back to Greece. Many, including the remnants of the Belgrade Theological Seminary, fled through Albania to the west. The plight of the Serbians was widely publicized in England. Four monks, a priest and other Serbian refugees lived at the Retreat House, Mirfield during 1916. Others stayed at the London Priory. The Bishop of Wakefield allowed them to receive communion and to celebrate their Liturgy in the chapel. In early 1917 twelve Serbian ordinands came to stay. In 1918–19 sixty Serbian ordinands were trained in Oxford. Those whom Gore welcomed to Cuddesdon arrived in tattered uniforms and sheepskins. Frere, assisted by Cuthbert Hallward, looked after others at St Stephen's House. In 1951 one of the students, now a bishop, came to Mirfield to pray at Frere's tomb.

In December 1915 King and some of the troops were evacuated from Gallipoli to a nearby island. There he joined in the Orthodox Christmas. He was impressed by the hold of the church on the people, the four collections at the Liturgy, the bells attached to the thuribles, the rigour of the Advent fast, the lack of reverence for the reserved sacrament, the antidoron. Fitzgerald kept Easter 1918 with the Greeks in Bethlehem. 'The Greeks are certainly looking forward in hope to reunion with the Church of England and I do pray that this may be one result of the war.' In 1919 he was grateful to the Patriarch of Damascus for lending a frontal, six candlesticks and a mat for a confirmation in a YMCA cinema marquee.

The French Roman Catholic church, however, was generally inhospitable, even hostile. 'It is a constant sadness that we are debarred from the many fine churches' wrote Talbot. (But at that date would many Anglican churches have been made available for Free Church worship in similar circumstances?) Humphrey Money said that the devotion of French worshippers made him long for reunion. There are very few references in CR chaplains' letters to Nonconformists. CR was then, and for a long time to come, hostile to this side of ecumenism.

The Russian dispersion following the revolution opened up new possibilities of Anglican-Orthodox contacts, particularly after the establishment of the Russian Theological Institute in Paris in 1925. Gore was a speaker at the first Anglo-Orthodox conference in St Albans in 1927. Frere attended the second meeting there in 1928 when the Fellowship of St Alban and St Sergius was founded and became its first Anglican President. Over the following years several brethren made notable contributions to its annual conferences including Gore, Frere, Talbot, Thornton and Curtis.

Evangelism in war-time

CR continued its Quarry services. In July 1914 the subjects included 'The Woman's Question' (Frere) and 'The Living Wage' (Talbot). In 1915 sermons were preached on 'Religious Revival', 'Social Reconstruction', 'Re-union of Christendom' and 'Brotherhood of Nations'. In 1919, like many other church organizations, CR concluded that former chaplains would draw the crowds, and Victor, Rees, Hill and King preached.

CR organized several conferences at Mirfield. Among speakers at a conference in 1915 on 'Problems arising out of the War' were the socialist Hewlett Johnson, then a vicar in Cheshire, and Talbot's uncle, Edward Lyttelton, Headmaster of Eton, who had just caused uproar by advocating the internationalizing of Gibraltar as a conciliatory gesture to Germany. A year later he had to resign from Eton, a broken man. A 1916 conference on retreats included Fr W. H. Longridge SSJE on the Ignatian method. A conference in 1919 for laity and clergy on 'Industry and Education' was addressed by E. Kitson Clark, Maurice Reckitt and Albert Mansbridge. CR organized several post-war 'Schools of Instruction' for the clergy, part retreat, part lectures. In 1919 Frere lectured on Mysticism, Asceticism, Modernism and Ritualism; F. G. Belton (a well-known confessor) on Moral Theology 'with a special study of the Modern Sex Problem'; Bull on Preaching, Intercession and Meditation; Windley (a former architect) on Art and Religion. In 1920 Studdert Kennedy was among the lecturers. In all these various ways CR proved a valuable educational resource for the church.

In the early weeks of the war anxious worshippers thronged the churches. It was widely believed that the religious revival for which the churches had been working for many years had at last arrived. But it did not last. In the early part of 1915 the Archbishop of Canterbury was under pressure to respond to the charge that the Church of England was not measuring up to its responsibility to the nation in war-time. 'Spiritual mobilization' became the slogan of the hour. Davidson called a group together (which included Frere). Out of this came the National Mission of Repentance and Hope held in the autumn of 1916.[17] Frere in October 1915 wrote of the failure of the church to respond to the needs of the nation:

> Prayer for the dead is one of our greatest levers and our neglect of it one of our worst faults. Our neglect of the H. Euch. comes in the same category: we are starved and dumb, particularly in face of death. While of preaching we have already too much and for lack of the prayer it runs to waste.[18]

Though the group emphasized corporate repentance as the aim of the mission, in practice there was a good deal of confusion, because apart from Christian socialist clergy everyone thought that evangelism meant winning individuals to personal commitment. The Church of England had never before attempted to run a mission in every parish – nor has it ever attempted to do so since. Conservative Anglo-Catholics and Evangelicals protested when it was suggested that women speakers should be used. Gore, like other bishops, employed some women as 'Messengers' to parishes, and when the Mission was over, in November 1917 licensed twenty-one women for pastoral and evangelistic work in his diocese.

During the lead-up to the Mission, many church people (including Gore at first) were extremely sceptical about it. In the course of a long-running and almost wholly critical correspondence in the *Church Times* Fr M. Conran SSJE, a chaplain, said (17 December 1915) that at one time people approached a mission with enthusiastic expectation, but missions were now 'worn out'. They might help the churchgoer but did not reach the outsider and certainly not the soldiers he met. Instead we should teach people to pray. He advocated the use of a modified form of the rosary, in groups, to which many soldiers, ignorant of the faith, readily responded. Longridge (3 March 1916) said it was easy to criticize the bishops, but as clergy we must acknowledge 'our miserable failure and worldliness'; by penitence, retreat and prayer we must recover spiritual power and urge the laity to do the same. The *Church Times* throughout was gloomy: 'Only one of the many letters that we have received on the subject of the Mission approves of the date ... or the scheme so vaguely outlined, or the limitation of the subject to repentance and hope ... our correspondents have said quite plainly that they regard the scheme with the greatest mistrust ... ' (25 February). 'The history of revivalism is a melancholy record of reaction and failure' (19 May). CR, however, threw itself into the Mission. Brethren conducted preparatory clergy retreats and acted as parish missioners. Clergy from Leeds and Mirfield deaneries held retreats at the Retreat House and for these CR conceded that celebrants might wear surplices and stoles not vestments. The Quarry sermons in July 1916 were devoted to the Mission. However when it was all over Bickersteth wrote that though CR had loyally taken part, he could not share the apparent satisfaction with its results; it was not really a mission as CR understood the term, the time had been ill-chosen and some missioners were unsuitable for evangelistic work (*CRQ* MD 1918).

The Mission was conducted not only in the parishes, but also among servicemen. Talbot ran a mission service for ten evenings in December 1916 at Talbot House, Poperinghe created by Tubby Clayton. (Originally it had been called after one of its founders, Neville Talbot; later it became associated with the memory of his brother Gilbert killed in 1915.) Talbot wrote: 'What one feels is that all the capacity for loyalty and sacrifice ... must be brought into the service of our Lord and of his Kingdom ... ' But his letter ends: 'Now we are back in mud and misery, and for a time our own plans for bringing the National Mission before men must largely be in abeyance. On each side the guns snarl away like chained dogs . . . and everybody slithers about in the desolate morass.'

By the end of 1916 the National Mission Council had to face the unpalatable truth that generally the Mission had been attended only by churchgoers. True, parochial barriers had been broken down, there had been more prayer, the case for church and liturgical reform had been strengthened, some missioners had urged the claims of social justice, the ministry of women had been encouraged. The five follow-up Committees in 1919 published their Reports on every aspect of the life of the Church of England and proposed an impressive package of reforms. But there was no indication that any more people wanted to repent and hope with the Church of England. Oswin Creighton (son of the former Bishop of London), one of the most remarkable chaplains, wrote about the men's attitudes to religion:

> . . . they simply have no apparent feeling for religion as I have learnt it. Have I learnt it wrong, or is the way I have learnt it one and theirs another? . . . The pious, narrow, self-satisfied, exclusive, moral world within – the weak, kindly, happy, loose-moralled, generous, spontaneous, tolerant world without. Which is better? Can the National Mission break down the barrier? . . . I sometimes feel inclined to wonder why God hides Himself so inscrutably from our experience. Or is it that the Church has taught us for so long to look for Him in the wrong places?[19]

The fortnight's Woolwich Crusade in September 1917, during which the Archbishop of Canterbury, nine bishops (including Gore) and 200 missioners (including Bull) tried to reach the munition workers, revealed the deep hostility of some working-class people towards the church. They judged the church by Christ and concluded it was 'a mere class institution useful for keeping Labour in its place and providing comfortable billets for clergymen', reported the *Church Times* (21 September), Two men, supported by part of the crowd, heckled the Archbishop and the Bishop of Dover at an open-air meeting: 'Look at 'em: never done a day's work in their lives'; 'Got soft jobs and we have to find the money'.[20] What message did Bull take back to the missioner brethren at Mirfield?

The post-war world

During the latter stages of the war politicians sustained morale by fostering expectations of radical social change. Some chaplains were also fostering expectations of considerable change in the church. All this was congenial to many in CR. The Report of the Fifth Committee on 'Christianity and Industrial Problems' chaired by E. S. Talbot (whose members included Gore) was a development of the CSU tradition. Frere was a member of the Second Committee whose Report on 'Worship' responded to the urgent pressure from chaplains for liturgical change arising out of their experiences in the forces. At General Chapter 1919 CR decided to divert money from the chapel fund to the starving children of Europe. Like many churches and chapels in the hopeful 1920s CR took out a corporate subscription to the League of Nations Union.

At the 1907 Quarry meeting with Labour leaders Bull had proposed a resolution in favour of women's suffrage. In 1912 Gore shared a platform with Maude Royden, the Anglican feminist, to celebrate what he called 'the freedom of women for self-realization'. But in his Primary Visitation of 1914 he warned that he might collide with the women's movement, because male headship was fundamental. In 1916 he addressed General Chapter on the feminist movement in relation to the Christian ministry. In 1919 he preached at a service to celebrate the first anniversary of the granting of women's franchise. But he made clear that while he supported the ministry of women as deaconesses and pastors, he was strongly opposed to their ordination.[21] When in 1921 Royden with Dearmer founded the Guildhouse, Eccleston Square to provide experimental evening worship not subject to the Prayer Book and a context in which Royden could minister, Bull was among its sponsors. Despite these efforts by Gore and Bull, the *Quarterly* went on ignoring the women's movement for many years.

In its early years, through Gore, Rackham, Figgis and Healy, CR was associated with efforts to gain more self-government for the Church of England. In 1918 Bull announced (*Church Times*, 7 June) that he had become convinced with 'the force of a divine inspiration' that the time had come for disestablishment and had formally offered to support the Labour Party, if it advocated this. (It was never adopted as Labour policy.) CR in Africa enjoyed the experience of serving in self-governing Anglican churches. But after the Enabling Act of 1919 gave a measure of self-government to the Church of England, CR lost interest in campaigning for more freedom, though individual brethren (Raymond Raynes, for example) supported disestablishment.

In 1919 Gore resigned as Bishop of Oxford at the age of sixty-six. He wanted (he told Archbishop Davidson) the leisure to write, preach and teach. The adoption of a baptismal rather than a confirmation franchise for the new Electoral Rolls was the occasion but not the cause of his resignation. Gore was delighted that it was to be announced on All Fools' Day. He had contemplated resignation before. When the 1908 Lambeth Conference had considered recognition of Presbyterian orders, Gore, recovering from appendicitis, was carried in on a litter and threatened resignation; the bishops immediately surrendered (Henson recorded). He had threatened to resign over Henson's appointment to Hereford in 1917. Now he longed for freedom and detachment. 'I am so happy' he told his sister. In January he had explained to William Temple: 'It is partly that Broad and High and Low and Conservative are all against me . . . Also I'd like to join the Labour Party.' After G

Bickersteth asserted that he had never liked being a bishop because it placed him in a position of privilege, uncongenial to one who was 'always at heart a Religious' (*CRQ* CD 1933). This was a romantic portrait of an enigmatic personality. Friends in the Church Reform League viewed his resignation as a tragic vindication of their campaign for smaller dioceses. But there is no evidence that if he had remained at Birmingham he would have decided otherwise. He looked forward to retirement with all the excitement he had always felt before his annual holiday. He would no longer feel a trapped victim.[22]

For CR the most fitting war memorial seemed the extension of the College at Mirfield. After demobilization there were fifty students and some had to be accommodated at the Retreat House. An appeal for £20,000 was launched in 1919. The foundation stone was laid in July, but only a small section was ever built. The Holy Cross chapel completed in 1924 at the east end of the Community church, became a memorial to Freestone and eighteen students killed during the war. Their names are recorded on a plaque set into its wall.

England emerged from the war a more plural and more secular society. Certain groups were convinced that they had the key to the post-war era. Roman Catholics, exulting in a flow of distinguished converts, contended that only an authoritative and trans-national religion focussed on the papacy would bring peace and order to a divided world. Anglo-Catholics argued that the experience of chaplains had shown that only a dogmatic and sacramentally based religion would convert England. Modernists believed that only a forward-looking faith, purged of obsolete doctrines, could speak to the new era. Agnostics claimed that the war had destroyed the credibility of religious belief and institutions. In a sense they were all both right and wrong. In the long run 'diffusive Christianity' became the dominant religious mode in England, modernist in doctrine but tinged with enough Catholicism to give it that nostalgic and historic flavour that the English require from both their churches and their public houses. God, like so many of the European monarchs, had been dethroned, and now exercised mainly ceremonial functions: the real power was exercised elsewhere by others. Christianity became more about the kind neighbour than the awesome God. The post-war world offered more leisure, more physical mobility and an increasing variety of attractive pursuits on Sundays.[23]

Anglo-Catholicism entered its most triumphant phase and was reshaping the ethos and outward appearance of the Church of England.[24] Many younger brethren were convinced that the future lay with the type of Anglo-Catholicism which steered its course with one eye on Rome, and brushed aside the English Catholicism of Gore and Frere. For had not Keble Talbot, Anglican to the core, discovered how pastorally successful Roman Catholicism was at the front and in the parishes of France?

All the hopeful talk during the first years after the war of a new world and church cleansed by precious blood rested on the belief that this war had ended war, and that there was a capacity and a will for radical change. The favourite text of the period was 'Behold I make all things new'. But former chaplains who had pledged that they would never return to the old grooves soon found themselves comfortably reassured to be back in them again. Few lessons of the war were taken to heart. So *A Study of Silent Minds* (1918) by Kenneth Kirk (later Bishop of Oxford), an outstanding meditation on his chaplaincy work, was highly praised and then forgotten, even by Kirk – he ceased to include it among his published works. Talbot and Northcott, who could have contributed significantly to a new approach to the theology and spirituality of both the church and CR, buried their war-time experiences. More than eighty years after the chaplains returned home, there is still no sign that the Church of England (or indeed any church) has begun to face the questions that were wrung out of them with such pain and anguish.

6

Community Relations

Keble Talbot

Keble Talbot succeeded Walter Frere as Superior in 1922. Soon C R began to be known in upper-class church circles as 'Ted Talbot's Community', a nickname which persisted after he ceased to be Superior in 1940. 'Ted' was his family name. He was 'Keble' in C R because there was already an 'Edward' (Symonds). C R has never been called by the name of any other of its Superiors. This nickname suggested not only Talbot's pre-eminence but that he was 'one of us', that C R was now tamed and gentlemanly, very different from pre-1914 when it had been pilloried as socialist and popish. Michael Ramsey in the 1930s visited Mirfield to discuss whether he should join C R. In conversation in 1983 he recalled it as radiating 'a liberal culture of a slightly aristocratic kind . . . a rather charming gentlemen's club'.

In 1920 more than half the bishops of the Church of England were connected with the peerage or aristocracy; they met the leading men of the nation in the London clubs; the effective control of the Church Assembly was in the hands of the Cecil family and their relatives. If William Temple's appointment as Bishop of Manchester in 1921 (Archbishop of York 1929) represented the post-war sympathy of some bishops with Labour aspirations, Cosmo Gordon Lang (Archbishop of Canterbury 1928–42) represented the continuing alliance between the Church of England and the upper classes.[1]

So when Matthew Trelawney-Ross visited Mirfield in 1923 to make enquiries about C R, he wrote to his parents: 'Yes: Father T[albot] *was* in Morshead's house, Dad, and he was very interested at hearing you were a Wykehamist.' Some bishops who mistrusted Anglo-Catholics accepted ordinands from Mirfield because 'Ted' was Superior; they knew him and revered his father. Temple at the College Festival in 1931 described Mirfield approvingly as 'the centre of a Liberal Catholicism'.

Some had wanted Keble as Superior in 1913. By 1922 his war-time experiences had matured him. In 1919 he became Prior and Novice Guardian. In 1919 he preached at Buckingham Palace and the next year was appointed Chaplain to the King. Some wanted Frere to continue because he had everything at his finger-tips. However, Frere said that he would be happy to step down. Keble seemed the only alternative to Frere. Bull trenchantly argued that though Frere was a great leader, his gifts had paralysed those of other brethren. If he were to continue, no one else would be trained in government and know the inner affairs of CR. Bull (with the approval of Frere and Talbot) wanted the Superior to hold office for not more than three continuous terms of three years. Frere could become Warden of the Hostel and take an academic post. They all knew Keble's 'power for leadership and for friendship'. Frere was a formidable Superior to follow. Keble felt a mere 'cart-horse' succeeding a 'race-horse'. Indeed Frere had been vexed by him the previous year when he had been away for six months, visiting the African houses and then comforting his brother whose wife had died; yet he was Prior, Novice Guardian and college lecturer; he was chairman of a crucial committee of enquiry into the college, but had gone off without even leaving an interim report.

Keble was born in 1877 at Keble College, Oxford where his father was Warden.[2] His mother, Lavinia, was a Lyttelton; her father was George, Lord Lyttelton; her mother was Mrs Gladstone's sister. Of Lavinia's brothers and sisters: Neville became a general; Arthur, Bishop of Southampton; Edward, Headmaster of Eton; Alfred, Colonial Secretary; Lucy married Lord Frederick Cavendish; Hester (a step-sister) married C. A. Alington, later Dean of Durham. Keble's sister, Mary, married Lionel Ford, Headmaster of Repton, then Harrow, finally Dean of York. When Keble's father became vicar of Leeds in 1888, Keble was repelled by its ugliness and grime. But he went off to Winchester College and then to Christ Church Oxford where began his lifelong friendship with the future Lord Halifax. Apart from his father, the greatest influences on Keble's life were Scott Holland (his godfather), Dolling and Baron von Hügel. As late as 1948 he wrote about Holland: 'I tingle as I read him, and am filled with a solemn awe, mingled with exaltation.' Dolling regularly travelled from the Winchester Mission in the Portsmouth slums to preach in the college chapel. Though Keble thought Dolling looked like an 'old pork-butcher', one of his sermons had such a profound effect on the sixteen year old boy, that he put £1 in the collection, his pocket money for a whole half term. Keble always remembered how Dolling wrote to him at his confirmation: 'Let it be never far from your mind that the Son of God was contented to be betrayed, spat on, and killed, in order that you, Ted Talbot, might come to the full measure of your manhood.' In 1895 Keble stayed at the Mission, admired his work among the poor and met Adderley, the Franciscan, who was visiting. Dolling, who was very un-Tractarian, took Keble to the theatre. Von Hügel was a close friend of Keble's father. Keble regularly quoted von Hügel in his retreat addresses.

Keble arrived at Mirfield at the end of 1906 and became a probationer in January 1907. The fact that he was not professed until three and a half years later (the normal probation lasted one or two years) shows how uncertain he felt about his vocation. He had first met Frere when he was one of his father's examining chaplains. Frere's influence drew him towards Mirfield, and Gore was one of his father's oldest friends. During his early years at Mirfield his vocation was severely tested when he was put under considerable pressure to accept various attractive posts outside the Community.[3] In 1908 he felt a 'tug' when H. M. Burge, Headmaster of Winchester, asked him to take on the College Mission. Bishop Palmer also offered work in India. But he refused both: he must serve his probation at Mirfield in the hope God would call him to remain. However, he was conscious of mixed motives: 'a mixture of indolence and "pride which apes humility" which prevents me from making large ventures'. In 1909 the Governors of Pusey House unanimously offered him the Principalship of Pusey House. He longed to be able to accept. Scott Holland wrote that it was a God-given opportunity and put him under added pressure by pointing out that he would be near his brother Neville, who had just become chaplain of Balliol. When Keble refused, Holland wrote that it was 'a dreadful blow'. Did Holland think Keble was unsuited to C R? In 1914 after four years' profession, he was asked to succeed his brother as chaplain to Balliol. Again Holland strongly urged acceptance. C R was divided about this. Longridge argued that his own brother's life had been ruined by S S J E's failure to give him work appropriate to his gifts. Some thought that Keble was so irregular in his habits that he would go to pieces outside the Community. Bull contended that there was a great danger of communities allowing corporate interest to crush individual vocations. Gore supported acceptance but said that C R had altered since he left. Keble stated that he felt called to minister to individuals of 'his own class'. He reported to his brother:

> Frere moved a direct rejection of the proposal: and I was left with departure from the Community as my only alternative. Five only voted against Frere's motion (including Bull and the Superior) but even if they had defeated it and left the ultimate decision to me, I could not, I feel sure, with a good conscience and loyalty have accepted Balliol . . . I did to-day move that the Community should not declare that it was *incompatible* with C R: but I only did so in order to prevent this being established as a precedent for future Community policy . . . But there is no doubt that the general mind of the Community *does* consider it incompatible . . . No doubt Frere's very penetrating and decisive views were the chief determining factor . . . what was urged about the necessities of community life and discipline does find a living echo in my mind. That does not mean that I should not have come if the Community had with anything like a real majority left it to me, nor that I do not still think that they ought to have run the risk in such a case . . . To me it is of course a very big disappointment, I had set my heart on it – perhaps wilfully . . . I can't pretend to take it gladly: at present I can only pray to be kept from any resentment or complaining. And no doubt it is good that I should learn that I am vowed to 'obedience' and that sometimes the yoke hurts.

Chapter formally voted on three resolutions proposed by Bull and seconded by Longridge. 'That since the corporate manifestation of a life is the essential purpose of our Community, and its chief work is to restore the Common Life to the Church the Community does not consider that the Balliol proposal will further these ends.' Fifteen voted in favour, none against; Talbot and Wicksteed abstained. 'That while such work is not absolutely incompatible with our ideals, it would strain our life to the utmost, and if allowed at all, could only be allowed as a rare exception.' Four voted in favour, including Longridge and Bull; seven voted against, including Frere; six abstained. The third resolution left the issue to Keble's conscience; if he still felt called, he would be allowed to go to Balliol for four years. Only five voted for, including Longridge and Bull; eleven voted against, including Frere; two abstained. It was a revealing and an important episode: it showed how even after seven years of living at Mirfield and a few months in charge of probationers, Keble was still uncertain about his commitment to community life; that the different understandings of CR between Gore and Frere persisted in CR itself; that though CR was committed to a corporate life, a minority considered detached service compatible with this. The issue of detached service has been a recurring theme in CR's history.

But temptations recurred. Just as he was settling back into community life after five years as a chaplain, in 1920 he was invited to be a candidate for the Wardenship of Keble. That would be incompatible with membership of CR Chapter decided. When he became Superior in 1922 he wrote to his mother: 'About Mirfield and me. Yes *au fond* I know that it is my life; I have no permanent doubt whatever.' But sometimes he longed to be married. Unlike some celibate Anglo-Catholic priests, Keble rejoiced when his friends married, even if they had hoped to come to CR. He told his brother in 1910 that marriage should not be deprecated – it was not good for man to be alone. But some were called to celibacy for the sake of the Kingdom. The real alternative to marriage was community life. If he had not come to Mirfield he would 'have tried eagerly to marry' because he could not live alone. Two further suggestions seem to have been rejected by Keble without difficulty. In 1923 Lang wanted him to be Bishop of Whitby. In 1929 there was a suggestion that he should become Dean of Christ Church, Oxford. Keble's father had once remarked to Frere that he had hoped Keble would become a bishop. Frere replied that being Superior was more widely influential.

When E. S. Talbot was Bishop of Winchester from 1911 to 1923, Keble oscillated between the blackened industrial West Riding and Farnham, a soft Surrey market town with graceful Georgian houses, crowned by the castle where bishops had lived since the twelfth century. E. S. Talbot, as a CSU supporter, believed in a more equitable distribution of wealth. But he loved Farnham Castle. 'To treat the tradition of 800 years as fit only for the scrap-heap does not commend itself to me as likely to promote among our people the finer feelings which link themselves with history.'[4] The Woolwich munition workers' historical and social perspective was, we recall, starkly different.

When in 1920 Peter Green, the saintly and astringent priest, refused the see of Lincoln because episcopal incomes and palaces were a stumbling block to the work of the church, both Archbishop Davidson and George V were incredulous. Keble and Neville questioned whether the castle was appropriate for a bishop, but they also loved it. Keble also holidayed regularly at Garrowby with Halifax (in 1931 he paid his twenty-sixth visit in twenty-one years) and with his cousin the Countess of Antrim in Northern Ireland, and sometimes shot grouse with Sir Walter Riddell in Northumberland. When in Rhodesia he had to travel second class with 'the less desirable kind of white settler', but enjoyed the 'spaciousness and dignity' of Government House in Salisbury. When he visited India in 1930 he naturally stayed with his old friend the Viceroy Lord Irwin (later Halifax). Temperamentally Keble was a southerner: 'country such as the Cotswolds puts one rather out of tune with Leeds and Mirfield' he wrote. Yet whenever he returned, he rediscovered Mirfield was 'home'.

'There was an ease of life under his regime', wrote Richard Barnes 'perhaps sometimes too easy, for one was inclined to leave too much to the Superior.' By temperament he was a synthesist, skilled at avoiding conflict, sensitive to the needs of individual brethren. Unlike Gore and Frere he was not an academic, though he read widely. Nor was he an original thinker. Frere was a superb organizer, Talbot was proverbially disorganized. Yet in 1928 he was writing twenty or thirty letters a day, on top of a number of letters of spiritual counsel.

When Keble was Superior it was always difficult to close Recreation for he was a superb raconteur. Trevor Huddleston in conversation recalled: 'In those days we used to meet in the community room after supper, even the novices, and when Keble wasn't in the house it was as dull as ditchwater, when Keble was there it was as though a light had come on.' Keble regarded as un-Christian the teaching of Thomas à Kempis that conversation with others resulted in spiritual deprivation: ascetics rarely stressed the love of God through his creatures. He was also a great encourager, marvellously generous in expressing gratitude to others. 'He had a wonderful way of lifting you up and making you feel a bigger and better person.' But some were embarrassed by his chintzy language ('Our darling Mother Julian', 'How darling if we find . . . '). One who said Keble had made his life worth living also tore up the seven-page letters Keble kept writing to him. At their worst, his letters were oppressively pietistic. When Neville's wife died in childbirth after three years of marriage, he wrote: 'I almost exult that you should be in agony . . . thus in the end only come love and life . . . '

Frere had never been part of the Gore and *Lux Mundi* tradition but Talbot restored CR's link with that through his veneration for his father and Scott Holland. The departure of Gore had weakened CR's connections with the aristocracy; under Talbot they were strengthened: an odd development for the years of the General Strike, the Great Depression, mass unemployment, the rise of the Nazis in Germany, when even in the Conservative Party, those like Baldwin and Chamberlain were rising at the expense of the old aristocracy. One of the brethren who idolized Talbot confessed: 'I think it would have been very difficult then for someone from a poor working-class family to feel at home.'

'Thank you, Father Talbot, for being so *sure*', said a young woman after one of his retreats. At one level he *was* sure – sure of God, sure of Anglicanism, however much he admired the Roman Catholicism represented by von Hügel. 'It is said: "There is no discipline in the Church of England." The answer is: "The Church of England *is* the discipline."' By the time he became Superior he was sure that his life lay within CR. Because of his background and family connections he was at ease with the highest in the land. Yet beneath the debonair exterior, self-doubt nagged away, not least about how he should exercise authority. In 1936, after only three years, CR decided to end its experimental work in Borneo. The South African brethren were dismayed that this was caused by lack of available personnel, and raised the whole issue of authority in Community life:

> We recognize that the peculiar ethos of our Community allows a greater weight than has been usual to a brother's own opinion of his suitability and availability for a particular work. We recognize further that our Community began its life in the heyday of nineteenth century democracy and was of set purpose designed to incorporate and apply those principles in the Religious Life. Our Superior's executive authority is constitutional and our obedience is tempered with a wide measure of personal freedom . . . We are very concerned that it should not come to err upon the side of excessive personal choice . . . Though normally it may be desirable that a brother should go 'with a glad heart' to any work, yet there may well be occasions when for him, and for the work itself, it may be necessary that he should go with a sad heart and in fear and trembling. We cannot think therefore that a Novice should offer himself for membership in the Community with any mental reservations whatever concerning spheres of work, or even family obligations.

When in 1928 Keble had failed to persuade either Osmund Victor to return from Africa to be Warden of the college, or Bernard Horner to go to Africa, he wrote: 'I am not of that Napoleonic cast which can try and hurl people about irrespective of their own strongly expressed convictions and inclinations.' So he now responded to the South African brethren that the Community ought not to be a juggernaut.

Everyone agreed that Keble was no businessman. Whereas Frere acted swiftly and precisely, Keble circled round and round a subject before coming to a decision. His lengthy letters to the South African Provincial were often hand-written with additions written vertically at the top and sides of the page. He ended one letter 'As is too often the case, I am afraid that this letter lacks the note of decisiveness.' In another he wrote 'I am afraid that this letter only adds to the list of letters which you must feel to be very useless and tentative and merely ruminative.' Barnes thought CR ought to have given Keble a break for three years and put in 'a businessman'. But no one 'ever wanted to dethrone Keble'. His personal letters also reveal much self-doubt. So, for example, he thought himself an incredibly bad college lecturer. When he was elected Superior he told his mother that he lacked *joie de vivre* and always had to struggle against lassitude. In 1920 he reacted to an invitation to contribute to the symposium *The Return of Christendom*: 'At present . . . I am smitten with the familiar palsy of brain and hand, which afflicts me directly I am called on to launch out.' (The 'palsy' evidently continued for he did not contribute to the book.) In 1932 he became distraught when Lang pressed him to write Gore's biography – he refused. Not surprisingly, someone who knew Keble well perceived a layer of depression beneath his high spirits.[5]

All these factors made his eighteen years as Superior a considerable strain, not least because brethren type-cast him as the one who could be relied upon as a perpetual fount of zest and laughter, when sometimes he felt grey inside and full of anxiety about a forthcoming engagement. In 1934, towards the end of Keble's fourth term, Cuthbert Hallward wondered whether he would be glad to give up the following year; hitherto such suggestions had seemed like treachery. Though Keble showed no sign of strain, Hallward asked whether in fact he was being crushed. One guesses that the brethren's adulation prevented Keble from bringing his wounds to them for healing. The result was his breakdown in 1940.

In 1907 he had joined Healy in speaking for the controversial Socialist candidate at the Colne Valley by-election, but his articles in the *CR Quarterly* (MD, CD 1911) suggest his real sympathies were with the CSU. 'The trouble is not that one man is rich and another poor. It is that the social body is not strong enough to hold together in coherent relationship its various members.' After the war his interest in party politics declined, though in 1919 he supported the railwaymen's strike, in 1926 he thought that the miners had a good case and he commended Tawney's *Religion and the Rise of Capitalism* (dedicated to Gore) to his parents. He became increasingly interested in the detached world of 'Christian sociology' promoted by Reckitt. His fine obituary of Gore in the *CR Quarterly* almost entirely neglected Gore's political activities and attitudes. His friendship with Halifax increased his sympathies with Conservatism.

Charles Gore

In 1917 James Nash was appointed coadjutor Bishop of Cape Town and became the first 'Prelate Brother'; that meant he was still associated with CR but kept a rule modified to take account of the nature of his work. When he retired in 1930 he returned to Mirfield and was re-elected as a full member.

However, in 1920 the South African brethren asked General Chapter to rule that in the future brethren were not to accept bishoprics. Though this request was refused, in 1933 Talbot wrote: 'I wish someone would be offered and refuse a bishopric.' (He had himself refused.) CR should witness to 'a life which is learning freedom from ambition (except for God) and the desire for "influence" and is detached from personal glory . . . '

On 25 March 1919 Gore wrote to Frere about his impending resignation:

> Should *you* wish me, would the *Community* wish me, to rejoin? The spiritual reasons *for* doing so are obvious. On the other hand is (a) a certain carnal disinclination (b) a certain desire to avoid responsibility to others, such as a community involves (c) a consciousness that very old men are rather a drag on a community, seeing that they want looking after etc . . . But I should like an answer from you . . . whether the Community would prefer that I should stand to it as James does or that I seek ordinary membership.

Frere replied by return: 'We want you back and here – there is not a doubt of it. We have said so whenever such a possibility has been talked of: and we had the hope in mind too when drawing up the Prelate Brotherhood.' He suggested Gore should begin by living at Mirfield as a Prelate Brother; he could stay at the London House when he needed to be 'in the stream'. Time would show whether he should come back into full membership. 'To some of us older ones it is a long cherished hope that we had hardly dared to cherish coming to realization.' He looked forward to welcoming Gore in October.

However, Gore recoiled from 'the intensely corporate life' of Mirfield.[6] He told Frere that the Professorship of Theology at King's London and the Mastership of the Temple were being mooted. He had also been offered a canonry at Westminster. This had a unique appeal for him, and would not prevent his being a Prelate Brother. But would it preclude full membership? Might CR open a House at Westminster again, he wondered. People might sneer at its 'worldliness', but it would provide both opportunities and freedom. A few days later Frere floated another possibility to the brethren. He had been urged by many people to stand for the Dixie Professorship at Cambridge. He hoped CR would allow him to refuse as he had done with the Divinity Professorship. But if he were elected, might CR accept the invitation to take over St Anselm's House there, which would be also more suitable for Gore if he returned as a member than either the London House or Mirfield? (St Anselm's had been founded in 1909 as a Cambridge equivalent to Pusey House.) But most brethren did not approve of Frere standing, and CR did not take on St Anselm's.

But in the end Gore's yearning for freedom prevailed. He turned down the Westminster canonry and professorships at London and Oxford, despite being in financial need, for though he had a small annuity, he had refused a pension.

He moved instead to central London and rented a four-bedroomed house ('my beloved hovel') in Margaret Street which belonged to the famous Anglo-Catholic church of All Saints' nearby. He assured the Archbishop 'I have already explained to several people, that there is no tradition or law suggesting the agreement of a tenant with the religious opinions of his landlord.'

Immediately Gore's resignation was announced, W. R. Matthews, Dean of King's London, invited him to become a lecturer. Ironically Matthews was not only a member of the Modern Churchmen's Union but also something of an admirer of the thought of Rashdall, Gore's old enemy. Gore accepted. Matthews recalled: 'I formed the opinion that he was, by temperament, pessimistic. I had expected that a man so notable as a pioneer of Christian Socialism would be all for adventure and reform, but this was not his attitude in practical affairs . . . In any situation where more than one event was possible, he expected the worst.' Matthews thought that the Mastership of the Temple would have been ideal for Gore and was sad that the opposition of protestant benchers had prevented it. When Matthews was appointed preacher by another Inn of Court, Gore responded 'Ah, yes, you are the kind of man they like' – which did not sound like a compliment. Matthews considered Gore's judgments of people sometimes 'almost cynical'. Returning from a visit to the East, Gore remarked: 'Well, perhaps the Eastern Church beats us by being certainly in the Apostolic Succession, but we beat them by having more Apostolic morals.'[7]

Gore's retirement was one of the happiest times of his life. He lectured all over the country, he continued to be active over a wide range of social, industrial and international issues, he relished many foreign trips, ministered regularly at Grosvenor Chapel, saw countless people in need but also immensely enjoyed going to concerts and plays. Two young friends, discovering Gore had never seen a Charlie Chaplin film, took him to the 'Gold Rush'. He told his sister that he had not laughed so much for years. His declared intention to study and write was amply fulfilled. His trilogy *Belief in God* (1921) *Belief in Christ* (1922), *The Holy Spirit and the Church* (1924), was followed by *Can We Then Believe?* (1926), *Christ and Society* (1928), *Jesus of Nazareth* (1929) and the Gifford Lectures *The Philosophy of the Good Life* (1930). During that period he also edited *A New Commentary on Holy Scripture* (1928).

In January 1920 Gore was elected as a Prelate Brother of CR. This gave him exactly the degree of both association and detachment which he wanted. He became known as 'Senior' again or 'The Founder'. It was right also for the Community. He had discovered at Radley that he could not live in close relationships (was there a hidden sexual fear here?). He had never been a monastic. 'I am unable to approve of pure enclosure without some such practical work, as Father Benson also was', he wrote.[8] But he told the CR London Festival in 1925 that the central object of the brethren, 'underneath all their activities was a certain kind of life . . . one of concentration in prayer and thought . . . what the French call *recueillement*, contemplation, meditation, recollection . . . '

It was not only Gore's aversion to community life and his desire for freedom which prevented his return to full membership of C R. He was also distressed by theological and liturgical developments within Anglo-Catholicism (some of which were represented within C R) as he made clear in *The Anglo-Catholic Movement To-day* (1925). He rejoiced in what the movement had accomplished: its abandonment of an infallible book; its stand for social justice; its belief that salvation was not just for the elect or for explicit believers. But he was scathing about 'the Romanizing tendency' of some contemporary Anglo-Catholics who accepted all Roman doctrine and practice apart from submission to Rome. They had no right to propagate the Immaculate Conception and Assumption, the invocation of saints as in the 'Hail Mary', the duty of every priest to say 'his Mass' daily ('individualism'), an absolute rule about fasting communion or to conduct Devotions to the Blessed Sacrament. He made his own position clear in 1919: 'I'm not likely to become either a Roman Catholic or a Mohammedan.' When Devotions were proposed at Grosvenor Chapel he threatened to resign from the staff. Anglo-Catholics should 'rejoice' at the Revised Prayer Book, he said in 1927. But some were hostile to it. Drawing on Habbakuk, some Anglo-Catholics vituperatively called Gore 'the evening wolf'. Why are some kinds of Anglo-Catholics so vituperative?[9]

So when C R began reservation at Mirfield in 1928 and informed the bishop, Gore was 'grieved', Bickersteth reported to the brethren. Gore wrote to reassure Talbot he had no desire to interfere, but that he would cease to be a Prelate Brother if the bishop refused permission and C R defied him. In November that year Keble wrote to his brother describing 'a curious and rather painful argument' with Gore during his summer visit:

> He raised the question of 'development', ecclesiastical and theological. He insisted that 'you younger men' are impatient with a 'Word of God' once delivered, and are relying upon something you call 'experience', which in the end lands you either at the feet of the Pope or of George Fox! In particular we were departing from the classical appeal of the Fathers (and of the C of E) to Scripture. He got very impatient when it was suggested that already, well within the confines of the NT, there is a movement and development of interpretation; and still more when it was suggested that the appeal of the Fathers to Scripture – so often verbalist or allegorical – was secondary and instrumental to their purpose of maintaining and carrying forward an attitude towards our Lord as Redeemer, which is the identical substance of the Church's experience, expressed in many different forms. He became very peevish and gloomy.[10]

Gore had taken to corresponding on postcards during the war as a gesture of economy. They also suited his terse wit. 'I am afraid it is one's duty to keep alive' he wrote to Mrs Illingworth who had been ill, advising her to obey her doctor. 'The pot is well, but how about the kettle?' he asked his sister Caroline in 1929. So in 1926 he told Mirfield on a postcard that he desired to continue in the fellowship of the Community and to be buried in its cemetery. In a letter to Talbot in 1931 he gave the copyright of his books to CR; he hoped for a requiem at Grosvenor chapel, then cremation (he was a vice-President of the Cremation Society); could his ashes be buried at Mirfield? Did the brethren approve of cremation? But he could not predict how soon he would need either requiem or cremation. (In 1913 when brethren had discussed cremation, some were opposed to it as un-Catholic; Fitzgerald was worried about its effects on the astral body; so in true CR tradition, cremation was left to the conscience of the individual.)

When Gore resigned from Oxford he ceased to be Visitor, who has to be either the Archbishop of Canterbury or a diocesan bishop. In 1920 J. A. Kempthorne, Bishop of Lichfield, Vice-Chairman of the Industrial Christian Fellowship (founded in 1920 out of the defunct CSU) succeeded Gore. There followed Curzon of Exeter and then Wynn of Ely, but it was not until Michael Ramsey was elected in 1956 that any Visitor made as much impression on CR as Gore.

When a stranger from Leeds asked Gore if he knew Yorkshire, he replied with a twinkle 'I once knew a little place called Mirfield'. In fact he kept up a regular annual visit of ten days or so for General Chapter and Commemoration Day. It became a custom for Gore to give his personal blessing to those newly professed, and to bless the crowds from the terrace on Commemoration Day, looking like a mediaeval picture with his cope and mitre and white beard. In 1924 he took the six-day annual Community retreat and expounded the teaching of Cassian, the fourth-century monastic founder. It was (wrote Talbot) 'as if the formative principles of our Community took flesh and a voice . . . He is extraordinarily impressive and searching and real.' He sat next to Talbot in choir and recited the Creed with 'a kind of defiant insistence . . . as though he were saying "Do you want to know the worst? Well, here it is: I believe . . . and I believe . . . and (that is not all) and I believe . . . in the life everlasting. There! you have got it. What about it?"'

Walter Frere

In August 1923 Frere was asked by both the Prime Minister and Archbishop Davidson to accept nomination to the see of Truro. Frere was now almost sixty. He was well known in scholarly circles as a historian, musicologist and liturgist, and in the church because of his leading role in the process of Prayer Book revision. But he had consistently refused major posts, academic and ecclesiastical, believing that he and the brethren were committed to a community not an association. He had opposed Gore's Westminster canonry in 1894 and his acceptance of a bishopric in 1901. Recently he had led the opposition to Talbot's desire for detached service. There was also now a strong opinion in CR against accepting bishoprics, or even honorary canonries. Gore, however, continued to hold a much looser concept of CR membership. When Bishop of Oxford he had invited Rees to become his diocesan missioner; to Frere this would have meant Rees leaving CR. Rees declined.

Davidson thought he had got it all neatly arranged. His letter would arrive first, expressing his long-felt desire to have Frere 'in the Episcopal College' and telling him that the vacancy at Truro provided the opportunity. In fact Frere received the Prime Minister's letter first and without consulting the brethren immediately refused. He explained to Davidson:

> The task set before me ever since I was up at Cambridge has been to take a hand in recovering Community life for our Church. It was set before me there graphically – I have never forgotten the road, the gate, the 'beyond' which framed the task . . . I have never felt that I could put that second to any other form of service . . . I can't but think that I can do my bit of *service* to the Church and to our Church better *as I am* . . . There lies the inwardness of my refusal and its promptness . . .

But, as Frere knew all too well, Davidson was not a man to accept defeat. He told Frere that the bench needed someone who could speak on behalf of Anglo-Catholicism in a sane and scholarly way: 'you are the man'. As a bishop he could do much to promote community life. Frere replied that he would consider all this but he was 'incurably a community man'. He had always believed that he could best help the bishops by devilling for them. Davidson responded that community and episcopal life could be combined, and that Truro could be a suitable diocese for this. This opened the way for Frere to change his mind. Truro's needs, we note, were secondary. Nor did Davidson ever say, as has been asserted, that he wanted Frere because the bench needed a liturgist. Funnily enough, Frere told Keble Talbot when discussing the Archbishop's letter, that he did *not* represent the Anglo-Catholics, who at best regarded him as a sympathetic moderate. At the Anglo-Catholic Congress that July, Frere had protested against the greeting sent to 'the Holy Father' (in Rome) because it would be misunderstood.[11]

The brethren at Mirfield, with one exception, eventually agreed that Frere should accept, though some like Talbot thought his present position provided him with more freedom to use his great gifts for the church than he would have as a bishop. Bull, however, who always enjoyed being a barrack-room lawyer, appealed to the Visitor contending that Frere's determination to continue as a full member was unconstitutional. The Visitor disagreed but recommended an amendment of the Constitution to include the possibility of a bishop as a full member. Bull argued also that being a bishop was not a Community work.

The diocese could not be under the control of CR. Frere should have become a Prelate Brother like Nash. How could CR ever grow if its best men were always being skimmed off? (Yet Bull had earlier supported Talbot's desire for the Balliol chaplaincy.) Talbot agreed there were risks; but it was extremely unlikely that Frere would act in such a way that CR might have to disassociate itself from him. To avoid breaching the confidentiality of the negotiations the South African brethren had not been informed until September. When it was proposed in the South African Chapter that CR should make Frere a gift, three abstained; Eustace Hill and Cyprian Rudolf voted against sending affectionate greetings. Obviously a few brethren thought Frere had betrayed his own principles. In January 1924 General Chapter decided that Frere should retain his vote, administer his own stipend, but report on his use of money each July, and that Truro should be a Community House. Bull registered his protest.

The announcement was made in October 1923. Henson told the Archbishop that the appointment was defensible 'only on the assumption that the Reformation Settlement was dead.'[12] Henson had in mind Frere's participation both in the 1923 Congress and in the meetings with Roman Catholic leaders at Malines. Protestant alarm at the appointment of a 'Mirfield Monk' was voiced in the Yorkshire and Cornish press. Though the Church Union gave him a gift, advanced Anglo-Catholics reacted like left-wingers in the Labour Party when one of them is selected to serve in the Cabinet: his selection proved he was not 'sound'.

From now on, Frere came annually to Mirfield for the July Chapter and stayed frequently at the London House. When he attended his first Commemoration as a bishop in 1924 he wore not only cope and mitre, but also episcopal gloves. Bishop E. S. Talbot, just resigning from Winchester, presented Frere with a pastoral staff given him in Leeds. 'I used to carry it about myself as a Tram Bishop like a banjo in its green baize' he explained. Frere, economical as ever, purchased only the minimum necessary for his office and used his Mirfield cassock for everyday wear. He and the brethren lived at 'Lis Escop' (the Cornish for 'Bishop's Court') – a vicarage until the first Bishop, E. W. Benson (1877), took it over and renamed it. (It is now the home of the Sisters of the Epiphany.) This entrancing house, extended in Queen Anne's time and later by Benson, looks down over wide lawns and gardens, lush in the mild climate, through the slender arches of the railway viaduct to the fine cathedral designed by Loughborough Pearson in a northern French style, rising assertively above the town clustered around it. George Longridge and William King came to live with Frere and did much to deepen the spiritual life of the diocese. Rupert Mounsey, former Bishop of Labuan and Sarawak, who arrived at Mirfield in 1924 at the age of fifty-seven, also resided for increasingly lengthy periods and became assistant bishop in 1930 after Frere had a stroke. Mounsey is remembered as a persuasive but peremptory missioner – 'Take my coat, boy' (to a server), 'Kneel, woman' (during prayers at a mission service).

'Walter Frere, Bishop of Truro! Well, I hope and believe he will make a very good, because a supernaturally-minded, one' commented von Hügel. At the end of 1934 after Frere announced his resignation, Hallward, who had come down to superintend the winding-up of the Truro House, summed it up as 'a great episcopate'. But he feared that many had not realized this because of Frere's self-abnegation and 'defence mechanisms'. He thought him 'morally greater' than Gore because he was 'more selfless'. At the outset Frere had challenged Davidson by his insistence upon the claims of the Religious Life. He had also challenged the church and diocese by a radically new style of episcopal life. At Lis Escop there was a small domestic staff, but the atmosphere was austere – the large drawing room was hardly furnished at all. Each bedroom had an iron bedstead with hair mattress, a chair, chest of drawers and a gas ring for hot water. It soon got about the diocese that the bishop actually cleaned his own boots, carried guests' bags to their rooms, and served and cleared at meals. When a dignified couple stayed, the wife was heard to remark 'What an extraordinary establishment'. One should re-member that this was the era when ordinands preparing for their retreat at Fulham Palace, London, had to be assured that evening dress was not required. Though Frere, who in 1906 and 1907 had presided at the Quarry meeting with Labour leaders, was now less overtly political, he defended Jack Bucknall, an old Mirfield student, when 2,000 signed a petition demanding this curate's removal because of his fiery socialist sermons.[13]

Through his work in the central councils of the church and through his ecumenical activities, Frere put Truro on the map, though there were complaints that he was away from the diocese too much. If to Methodists, who were predominant in his diocese, he appeared an unyielding Anglo-Catholic, in private he considered that the common Cornish pattern of attending the eucharist in the parish church in the morning and going to chapel in the evening quite commendable. His strong historical sense enabled him to harness the growing sense of Cornish identity by inaugurating pilgrimages to holy places in the diocese and by sanctioning a calendar of Cornish saints. At the cathedral, of which he was also Dean, he found an outlet for all his musical and liturgical gifts. A nave altar was soon in place. Reservation began in a hanging pyx. He contended that a pyx was not only in accordance with English usage, but by being above the heads of the people, it diffused rather than localized the presence.[14]

Frere enjoyed being a bishop more than Gore, partly because administra-tion was congenial to him, though he came to the episcopate too late in life. But no other CR bishop has ever followed Frere and taken his home with him. Perhaps those who become bishops have to 'leave home'? The Cornish people, who pride themselves on their warmth, found it difficult to get close to

Frere. It was not only that he seemed an unapproachable 'monk' but that he was surrounded by monks. Some remember him as showing warmth only to children and animals. The portrait presented to him in 1933 (a reproduction of which hangs at Mirfield) shows him in his simple CR cassock, not looking quizzically straight at the camera as in CR photographs, but far into the distance. Certainly his detachment was as formidable as his industry. When he went to speak for Timothy Rees, Bishop of Llandaff, he sat on the platform correcting proofs until his turn came. His episcopate was made more difficult because the Kensitites had had him in their gun-sights ever since the Church House meeting of 1907. 'The Mirfield Monks' in the Truro diocese now became a chief target for their demonstrations. In 1932 they used crowbars and hammers to smash the furnishings of the famous Anglo-Catholic church at St Hilary.

In February 1935 Frere resigned. In the Diocesan Gazette for once he let down his guard: 'The last note is of farewell, not so much sad in my ears, as thankful to God: and grateful to Cornwall. But it has stolen half my heart.' Others, like Gore, have found it almost impossible to return to Mirfield after their episcopates. Frere, like Nash, found it altogether natural.

From his earliest days as a priest there was a creative interaction between his liturgical theory and practice. As a curate in Stepney (1890–2) he introduced perhaps the first Parish Communion in the Church of England.[15] His *New History* (1901) became the standard work on the Prayer Book for the next fifty years. In *Some Principles of Liturgical Reform* (1911) Frere in effect outlined the Anglican liturgical agenda for the next twenty-five years. For most of his life he played a major role in liturgical revision both at home and overseas. He made the single most important contribution to the shaping of the 1927 revision of the Prayer Book. But after its rejection by the Commons and the attempts by the bishops to secure more support by amending it, Frere publicly repudiated the amended Book. Gore thought Frere 'needlessly pessimistic' and pleaded for Anglo-Catholics to accept the 1928 revision despite its defects. But Frere's change of mind (which Lang thought owed more to psychology than theology) finally destroyed his credibility on the bench. After the defeat of the 1928 Book in the Commons the bishops in 1929 in effect authorized its use. Frere now changed his mind again, authorized it in his diocese and used its eucharistic rite daily in his chapel. At Truro Cathedral the new Book, bound up with *Hymns Ancient and Modern* (the ultimate accolade?) replaced the 1662 liturgy.[16]

It will be remembered how equivocal a role Frere played in the negotiations between CR and the Archbishop over his role as Visitor in 1907–8. Hallward, though a great admirer of Frere, conceded: 'I am afraid that the world that hears him in the Assembly is often more impressed by that perversity in debate, which we know so well, and finds him tiresome and puzzling.' They think of him as 'flippant, unreliable, unstable, delighting overmuch in being unexpected, paradoxical', but miss his greatness. In 1941 Mervyn Haigh, formerly Davidson's chaplain, now Bishop of Coventry, made a similar assessment. Haigh loved and revered Frere, 'so humane and so sure of God'.

> But, *but*, *but*, in the main and increasingly towards the end, there was no doubt that he really staggered the Bishops by the increasingly paradoxical and seemingly 'clever', subtle and even insincere kind of way in which he commended his views, not for the reasons that everybody felt must be his reasons, but sometimes almost for diametrically opposed reasons which looked like the reasons that he thought would commend themselves to those out of sympathy with him. This weakened his influence more and more until he almost ceased to have any. This has always been a real problem to me.

When he returned to Mirfield in 1935 Frere described the C R eucharistic rite as 'liturgically deplorable' and, unlike that of 1928, as lacking 'full church authority'. The preface to Frere's last work *The Anaphora* (1938) reveals his bitter frustration with developments in Anglo-Catholicism (and also with some in C R?): the liturgical awakening in East and West was being met 'in a small but influential part of the Anglican world, by a determined, obscurantist and retrograde movement which poses noisily as catholic, but is really anarchist in method though mediaeval in outlook; for it aims at re-establishing, often in defiance of law, a position which is historically untenable'.

Visitors to Lis Escop remarked on a signed photograph of Cardinal Mercier (it now hangs at Mirfield) – Frere's memento of the conversations held between some Anglicans and Roman Catholics at Malines between 1921 and 1926.[17] Frere was a member from the beginning. In 1924 he told the brethren at Mirfield that they ought to be asking 'What sort of a Pope would we welcome?' Gore joined the third meeting in 1923, alarmed by the 'concessiveness' of Frere, Lord Halifax (the elder) and Armitage Robinson. Archbishop Benson once described Halifax as a solitary chess player who wanted to make all the moves on both sides of the board. So Halifax was annoyed when Gore introduced a note of frank realism. Gore's appeal to scripture and the early Fathers; his temperamental aversion to being dominated by anyone; his tendency detected by von Hügel to judge everything by whether it was English; all combined to make him a determined enemy of papal claims. After reading the biography of Margaret Hallahan, the founder of a Roman Catholic order, he exclaimed: 'There are few propositions to which I would less readily assent than that of the late Mother Margaret Hallahan, who observed that when she was fortunate enough to see the Pope celebrating Mass, it was as though she beheld the God of earth prostrate in adoration before the God of heaven.'[18]

After Cardinal Mercier and Abbé Portal died in 1926 the meetings also died. But they had been like a spring day in a prolonged winter. A completely new approach had been adumbrated in the paper 'The Anglican church united but not absorbed' by Dom Lambert Beauduin of Amay, which Frere said 'took our breath away'. In 1930 a monk from Amay stayed at Mirfield. CR through Gore and Frere had contributed to the thaw that was slowly beginning.

Timothy Rees

When Timothy Rees was offered the see of Llandaff in 1931 it produced none of the agonizing debate either within him or CR that had occurred when Frere had been asked to go to Truro. Unlike Frere, he had no wish to take brethren with him. Frere's arrangement would have 'confined and embarrassed' him as a bishop, he thought. In any case he would not have been elected if he had insisted on remaining a full member. So he became a Prelate Brother. CR gave him £400 with the promise of more if he needed it. But Talbot was sad: 'he is one whom one would least readily part with. His kindness, good temper, affectionate humour, shrewdness are rare and precious.' He had become Warden of the College at Mirfield in 1922 at a critical moment after an enquiry and his predecessor's resignation. Rees attracted a number of Welshmen to the College and on Sunday evenings he would read Welsh literature with them and sing Welsh hymns. 'Wales was dear to him beyond compare', wrote Talbot. 'Its history, its language, its music, its countryside were as fire in his blood.' The students presented him with his episcopal ring. As CR's finest mission preacher he had made a deep impression in New Zealand, Canada and Ceylon, and of course in his native Wales as well. He was grateful for his Nonconformist upbringing. In 1905 when he was chaplain of St Michael's Theological College, he told the Llandaff Diocesan Conference: 'It has taken us nearly half a century to discover that a man may be a Catholic and an Evangelical too.' Catholicism devoid of Evangelical fervour was dry, Evangelicalism divorced from Catholic order was narrow and shallow.[19]

Rees was elected on the first ballot. His Welsh birth and education (Lampeter not Oxbridge), his fluency in Welsh, his early ministry in the Llandaff diocese: all commended him. He arrived at a critical time for both the principality and the church. In some areas of his industrial diocese nearly half the workers were unemployed. The Church in Wales had been disestablished and disendowed in 1920 after a bitter and protracted campaign conducted by the Nonconformists and Liberals, fuelled by Welsh nationalism and class antagonism. Why (asked the campaigners) should a minority church be established and endowed? To them it was the 'English church': no Welsh speaking bishop had been appointed between 1714 and 1870. In 1913 Gore supported disestablishment in the Lords, but other Welsh and English bishops presented almost united opposition. After disestablishment the church became more Welsh, but it was insular, lacked theological resources and evangelical fervour. It was hoped that Rees would help to repair these deficiencies. He brought with him an experience of the world-wide church. His eloquence as a preacher (particularly in Welsh) and his gifts as an evangelist would demonstrate that Nonconformity had no monopoly of either. Perhaps Rees with his Nonconformist background could bring healing between church and chapel now disestablishment was an accomplished fact? In any case, Rees was fifty-six; his predecessor had retired at eighty-four.

In his enthronement sermon he said: 'My heart goes out in sympathy to the broken lives and the broken hearts that are the result of this depression . . . Would God I could make some contribution to the solution of this crushing problem.' God was as interested in the borough council as in the diocesan conference, as concerned for decent housing as decent churches. 'There is nothing secular but sin.' He offered friendship and co-operation to the other churches represented there. Afterwards the leading Nonconformist minister present commented: 'This man has not been in touch with the Free Churches in days gone by for nothing.' That evening in the cathedral Rees preached a rousing sermon entirely in Welsh.

Rees had come home. Half the clergy were old friends. Though his occupation of the large eighteenth-century Bishop's Palace (which he renamed 'Llys Escob') attracted some criticism, he lived simply and entertained the unemployed as generously as everyone else. He used so much of his income for diocesan purposes that when he died only part of his bequests could be paid. As a result of his work as an army chaplain and for both Toc H and the Industrial Christian Fellowship, he had developed a deep sympathy with working men. He formed a group of free-lance priests who, on a stipend of £100 a year with their base at Llys Escob, worked full-time caring for the physical and spiritual needs of the unemployed. He made friends with the leaders of industry, formed and chaired the Llandaff Industrial Committee, and in 1935 led a deputation to the Minister of Labour in Whitehall to plead the needs of the depressed areas.

In his enthronement sermon he had said: 'I realize with a vividness that almost makes me shudder that the degree of success or the degree of failure that will attend my leadership as bishop of this diocese will depend entirely upon the number of seconds during the twenty-four hours that I deliberately surrender myself to the leadership of the living Christ.' He tried to spend each Friday as a Quiet Day at St German's Roath. But apart from that he never stopped, preaching two or three times a Sunday, conducting missions and retreats, active in the promotion of Welsh culture and raising money for new churches, one of which, the Church of the Resurrection, Ely, was modelled on the Community church, Mirfield. But such a pace took its toll and he died in April 1939. He had hoped to do ten years and then return to Mirfield. Nonconformists had enjoyed his preaching; but though he had been co-operative on social questions, his refusal to participate in united services saddened them. A Jewish rabbi praised him as one of the first to denounce the persecution of Jews in Germany.

Stability

CR continued to expand. In 1912 there were twenty-eight professed brethren. By 1922 numbers had grown to forty-two plus two prelate brothers (Gore and Nash). From one angle CR looked like a group of gifted individualists and pioneers. Indeed as Bickersteth acknowledged in his 1905 'Restrospect', some were drawn by a call to the Religious Life independent of any particular external works, while others saw the Community as providing 'the ideal background' for their work. What then bound the brethren into a community? They had all been prepared to make the same act of self-oblation in order to foster a Christian community such as that (idealized) one described in the early chapters of Acts. For several brethren their desire to live in community was also a direct expression of their Christian socialism; this provided an additional motive for living in simplicity with a common purse. A few were more fired by a desire to prove the Catholicity of the Church of England by helping to recover the traditional Religious Life within it. Nearly all shared a similar social and educational background – public school and Oxbridge – of which the communal, worshipping life of CR was both a continuation and an intensification. But all, for various reasons, were looking for community life in an alternative family. They also shared a common calling to a disciplined life and to celibacy, though again motives were varied. All of them shared a broadly Catholic churchmanship, leavened in several cases by Evangelical influences, though some were much more concerned about Catholic externals than others. Most identified readily with the incarnationalism of the *Lux Mundi* tradition. They shared a common calling to evangelism. If the educational tradition from which most of them came emphasized the value of community, it also fostered a sturdy individualism, even eccentricity. Some of the stories about the eccentric behaviour of some of the older CR brethren are very similar to those told about some Oxbridge dons and some members of aristocratic families. So the brethren continued to share Gore's belief in the need for a good deal of liberty for the individual within the broad framework of the common Rule. They also shared a common concern for the church overseas. Indeed in 1914 it was agreed that every brother should, if possible, spend two or three years in an overseas house during his first ten years of profession.

But CR, like any other Religious Order, had also its strains and sources of instability. To these we now turn.

In 1920 Clement Thomson, Chad Windley and Guy Pearse withdrew from the Community. Thomson, first professed 1899, became a parish priest. Chad Windley, first professed 1914, withdrew because of family obligations. He was partially paralysed; unable to obtain pastoral work, he returned to his architectural profession, but died in 1925. Pearse, first professed 1907, stayed on in the services as a chaplain until 1920, and after two spells as a Diocesan

Missioner, returned to being Warden of a servicemen's residential club. There were other shocks. Humphrey Money and Ivan Tunnicliffe who had been chaplains while still probationers, decided not to return to Mirfield and spent most of their subsequent ministry in parish work. For a time it looked as though Gerard Sampson, first professed 1895, would also leave. In the latter part of the war he had looked after Ravensthorpe parish, near Mirfield. When war ended he wanted to stay on. CR refused permission. He decided not to renew his pledge. Some disapproved of the cordiality of Talbot's draft letter to him, and commented sharply that Sampson seemed to think he could use Mirfield as a boarding house at intervals and as an alms house at the end. After two months' reflection Sampson returned to CR. Obviously it was the experience of living outside the Community during the war which led Pearse, Money, Tunnicliffe and Sampson to question their vocations.

The withdrawal of three professed brethren, two seasoned probationers and Sampson's doubts all resulted in much heart-searching. How could stability be promoted? asked General Chapter in 1920. Longridge, the respectable traditionalist, electrified everyone by advocating life vows. That was thought too revolutionary. Frere, then Superior, argued that the general tendency in the western church was towards temporary vows. But did the wording of the promise encourage a brother experiencing difficulties to leave? Had CR got the balance right between individual work and communal life? At the same Chapter brethren discussed the secondment of Bertram Barnes to go back to work for UMCA for two years and the fact that Francis Hill in South Africa, as Director of Missions, was often unable to attend Chapter. When Kempthorne made his Visitation in 1923 he urged the brethren to spend more time at home.

General Chapter in January 1922 agreed to certain 'stability proposals'. The annual 'promise' with a life long intention became 'I . . . profess my intention to remain in the Community for life'. Anyone desiring release must give six months' notice. No one could be released except by a majority vote of the whole Community. If a release were refused a brother could appeal to the Visitor. Yet a brother still had his 'liberty of ultimately leaving the Community if his conscience bids him do so'. Only George Longridge, Bernard Horner and Henry Alston elected to remain under the original system of an annual promise.

But whatever the merits of the new system it did not halt withdrawals. Between 1922 and 1941 six more departed. At least three of these withdrawals were influenced by the new post-war awareness of psychological factors in human motivation. Interest in psychology had been greatly stimulated during the war by the successful use of psychotherapy with soldiers suffering shell shock, including the poets Wilfred Owen and Siegfried Sassoon. Thus whereas F. G. Belton's *A Manual for Confessors* (1916) ignored psychology, Kenneth Kirk's *Some Principles of Moral Theology* (1920), which had originated as lectures to chaplains, recognized the value of psychotherapy. *Psychology and the Christian Life* (1921) by another former chaplain, Tom Pym, sold 34,000 copies in sixteen years. It was now gradually becoming respectable to desire sexual fulfilment. Marie Stopes' *Married Love* (1918) became a standard sexual manual. In 1921 she established Britain's first contraceptive clinic. The vast correspondence she received from all kinds of people, including Anglican clergy and their wives, revealed widespread sexual ignorance and misery. All these changes were part of the new post-war climate in which CR lived and worked. Several of the many new books on psychology and religion were given favourable reviews in the *CR Quarterly*. In 1920 a doctor lectured at one of the CR clergy schools on Psychology and Religion: 'The Unconscious Motive'; 'Sex and Emotional Development'; 'Religion, Emotion and Reason'; 'The Evidence of the Unconscious'. In the post-war period an increasing number of clergy underwent psychotherapy, including Michael Ramsey, Joost de Blank and Henry de Candole. The older generation mostly remained sceptical. For Gore, 'instinct' meant the moral instinct – duty. He frequently quoted Wordsworth's description of it as 'Stern Daughter of the Voice of God'. During his 1928 visit (as we saw earlier) Gore had deplored the trend which located authority in experience rather than in doctrine and scripture. This trend was exemplified by William James' enormously influential book *The Varieties of Religious Experience* (1902), reprinted twenty-eight times in the next following fifteen years, and within Anglo-Catholicism by the symposium *Essays Catholic and Critical* (1926). Advanced Anglo-Catholics often argued for Tridentine styles of worship, not for doctrinal reasons, but because they gave a richer religious experience, as verified by the crowds thronging the churches in Catholic countries.[20]

Three who withdrew had undergone psychotherapy with Talbot's approval. He became sympathetic to its use if, for example, it resulted in freedom from compulsions. So one through therapy discovered the complexity of motives which had led him to CR. Psychosomatic ailments which began on arrival had intensified as he drew nearer profession. Another believed therapy had altered his sexual orientation – for the first time he was now free to marry. Another concluded that the easy choice would be to stay, but that he ought to have courage to face 'the world'. But the South African brethren criticized Talbot for regarding therapy as a first rather than a last resort. In any case the therapist must be 'a Catholic'. Osmund Victor commented on a particular case:

> There is nothing unique about the situation. Sooner or later all have to go through a period of doubt, disillusionment, intense loneliness spiritual and mental, and even of disgust with the Religious Life and with CR in particular . . . this is a normal happening in the middle ways of life . . . Sooner or later too, most if not all, experience some strong attraction from outside – whether through a desire for

marriage or as the result of an offer made as to work . . . This represents the first
occasion on which release has been sought since the old system of annual renewal of
vows was given up . . . a real attempt to secure greater stability . . .

Because of the changed system 'going out' was now a more serious matter.
Those who had withdrawn 'may have gained in peace . . . but they certainly
seem to have suffered a loss in power'. He distrusted the process of raking
over old motives. Psychology was still experimental.

But psychotherapy had inaugurated a more dynamic, more complex
understanding of personality which poses fundamental questions. What
degree of freedom do I need to make a binding choice? How do I know God's
will? Might God's purpose for me alter as the result of profound inner change?
It is said that adaptation to marriage requires a balance between a sense
of established, autonomous identity and a capacity for dependence. What
happens to a marriage or to a monastic vocation if that balance alters
drastically? In any case it is more difficult for Anglicans to remain faithful to
vows of religion than for Roman Catholics. A Roman Catholic Religious is
sustained by the teaching of the whole church. But only a section of
Anglicanism teaches the value of celibacy and the Religious Life. Moreover,
whereas a Roman priest under Religious vows who becomes a secular priest is
still bound to celibacy, an Anglican priest who ceases to be a Religious is free
to marry.

Crises in the Religious Life often occur at roughly the same intervals as in
marriage: in the first two or three years (hence the importance of the novitiate
followed by a period of temporary vows before final profession); or after
roughly ten or twenty years. Of the eleven who withdrew from CR between
1919 and 1941, ten fell into these three categories. Withdrawals from
communities like marriage breakdowns also tend to occur in clusters. One
withdrawal can unsettle others. External factors, like war, disrupt monastic
and marital vocations, alike. A community, like a marriage, can suffer from too
rapid or too unevenly distributed change. A community, like a marriage, can
deteriorate by fearfully hanging on to a pattern of life which has become
anachronistic.

Of the eleven, eight spent all or much of their subsequent ministry in
parishes. In one sense this was inevitable since all were priests. But most of
those coming to CR were looking for prayer, discipline, community rather
than an escape from parish work. Some brethren believed that CR should
include among its works the care of an English parish – as SSM has always
done. In 1917 and 1919 Chapter favoured parochial work, perhaps in the
South Yorkshire coalfields. In 1938 Bell reopened the question. But CR refused to take on a parish, not because it was incompatible with the Religious
Life (after all many brethren in Africa worked in parishes) but because of a
shortage of numbers.

In 1938 Eustace Hill aged sixty-five, after thirty-two years in CR, withdrew and became a Roman Catholic.[21] Hill had been particularly well-known in South Africa as a heroic chaplain during the war and as Headmaster of St John's, Johannesburg. Though he had always been highly critical of brethren who were what he called 'Romanizers', he decided that Anglicanism had sided with 'the world' when the Lambeth Conference of 1930 gave a qualified approval to contraception. Moral issues had always been of supreme importance to him. After a chaplaincy to a punitive expedition against Zulus who refused to pay the Poll Tax in 1906, he returned his medals because he thought the action unjust and cruel. He had promised his mother when she became a Roman Catholic in 1904: 'if ever the Pope stood *contra mundum* on a moral issue I would join him'.

In 1908 and 1920, Lambeth Conference committees and resolutions had condemned contraception because it defeated one of the purposes of marriage, discouraged self-control, treated sexual intercourse as an end in itself and led to a declining birth-rate especially among 'the superior stocks'. However, in 1930 the bishops affirmed that intercourse had a value of its own. Abstinence was the best form of birth control, but a majority agreed that for 'morally sound' reasons other methods could be used. Many Anglo-Catholics were horrified. Gore became a vehement foe of this concession. He had helped to found the League of National Life, which campaigned against contraception. CR joined it. This controversy revealed the deep repugnance of some Christians towards sexual pleasure, though *The Threshold of Marriage* (1932) – later published by the Church of England Moral Welfare Council – advised couples how to achieve sexual fulfilment. By 1950, 340,000 copies had been sold. Gore argued that once sexual intercourse was allowed as an end in itself, this could justify extra-marital and homosexual relations. It was of course difficult for Anglo-Catholic homosexuals to celebrate sexual pleasure in marriage when they had to struggle to be continent. Neville Talbot was an emotional opponent of the concessions at the 1930 Conference. But Keble thought they would do more good than harm. Keble agreed neither with total *laissez-faire*, nor with Gore who believed that penitents who continued to use contraceptives should be refused absolution.

After the 1930 Conference Hill became obsessed by this issue. For him contraception was 'essentially evil', an evasion of the cross. If the Empire fell it would be because of 'unnatural sins'. He was also terrified that Africans might learn about contraception from missionaries. In England he worked ardently for the League but clergy complained that his sermons emptied their churches. When he visited a public school, a pupil was surprised to be given a lecture on the evils of birth control in the confessional but afterwards proudly displayed the pamphlets which Hill sent him by post. Hill refused to be licensed by any bishop who had supported the Lambeth resolution. When after his conversion he became a lay oblate at Prinknash he had to be dissuaded from distributing anti-contraception literature in the streets. Instead he ferociously wielded a mattock in the garden against the weeds and sometimes the plants as well. When two brethren visited him in the early 1940s they discovered that he followed the Litany of our Lady with his private recitation of the Prayer Book Litany: 'We do things better liturgically' he explained, as though he was still an Anglican.

Contraception was still being condemned by the Superior, Raymond Raynes, in the 1950s. In 1957 one of the brethen publicly denounced it as 'licensed prostitution'. But in CR, as in Anglo-Catholicism generally, such condemnations were by then becoming infrequent. They virtually ceased after the Lambeth Conference of 1958 boldly declared that what people had been doing for more than a generation was right after all. Anglo-Catholics took remarkably little notice of the papal condemnation of contraception in *Humanae Vitae* (1968), thus showing their selective attitude to Roman authority.[22]

Hill was the first brother to become a Roman Catholic since Hugh Benson thirty-five years previously. Since then nine have followed. Gore's basis for Anglican authority was rejected by advanced Anglo-Catholics, who regarded Roman Catholicism as theologically, morally and liturgically the norm (but disregarded what was inconvenient). The stockade mentality of Anglo-Catholicism and its lack of an agreed understanding of authority has left it without any coherent criteria by which to evaluate the immense theological, moral, liturgical and social changes which have swirled in and around the church ever since the movement began. Hence groups of Anglo-Catholics have frequently threatened that if the Church of England were to do this or change that, they would secede. The precariousness of Anglo-Catholicism, exemplified by Hill's conversion, has been a source of instability in the Community throughout its history.[23]

7

Between the Wars

Mirfield

'Home is where one starts from' (T. S. Eliot). For the brethren this meant Mirfield. Those in Africa, Leeds, London, those at Mirfield itself, had all started here as novices. Annually you recalled your decisive walk along 'Tin Street' (as the temporary cloister was known) to be professed in the church – still only a quarter completed in 1920. From the station in the valley below you set out for Africa, or on yet another parish mission in Manchester or New Zealand. The Mother House was different from any other, larger in size and numbers, with young novices, professed brethren and by the mid-1930s old men like Nash and Frere. Here the power was concentrated, however democratic the constitution, here the Superior resided. When you were trekking by donkey in Rhodesia or working among miners on the Rand, Mirfield was incredibly remote. But you knew that eventually you would return there and discover how much you and the Mother House had changed, that what once had been familiar territory was now occupied by strangers. It is said that when Trevor Huddleston returned from Africa amid a blaze of publicity, one of the old brethren turned to him and enquired 'Been on a parish mission?'

A brother from Africa visiting Mirfield in May reported grimly that he was writing letters in a greatcoat and that the hills were covered in fog. Another enjoying the warmth of a Rhodesian Lent imagined Lent at Mirfield: bean-pie and gardening in the bitter wind. Another on his way to Africa, enduring the 'Emperor worship' of ship's Mattins, consoled himself with the thought that it was at least better than Mirfield with its soot and fog-coloured wallpaper. There was of course less sun in those days before the Clean Air Act. The smoke from trains and factories hung over the valley lifting only during holidays and strikes. When the sun shone there would be bowls on the lawn. When the evenings became chilly there was good talk round the fire in the parlour or a game of peggoty, sitting on Windsor chairs which some thought made it look like an old inn.

Contact with local people was diminishing by the 1930s. The Mirfield Civic

Society, in which Frere and Longridge had taken a leading role, had folded. Brethren stopped attending local parish churches for Sunday Evensong in 1921. However, those who worked for the Community and College as gardeners, handymen and cooks provided important local contacts. Many spent most of their working lives with CR – a significant tribute. The annual servers' festivals fostered relationships with northern parishes. J. B. Seaton, Bishop of Wakefield 1928–38 was a good friend to CR – three brethren had been at Cuddesdon when he was Principal. A. W. F Blunt, Bishop of Bradford 1931–55, conducted the Community retreat in 1935. As a socialist and Anglo-Catholic (he was the only bishop to have a tabernacle on the altar of his chapel) he was doubly acceptable. When Mounsey returned from Truro in 1935 he became assistant bishop and presided over the diocese when Blunt was ill or away. Blunt used the brethren a great deal, and Evangelicals who were predominant in the diocese were surprised to discover what effective evangelists they were. Local papers regularly reported the activities of the Community. The *Yorkshire Post* in 1932 wrote warmly about 'the hold which Mirfield has gained on the affections of the North'. But some local suspicion, even hostility, persisted. A car driver picked up Talbot on the road and told him CR represented his two chief hates – socialism and Roman Catholicism. But he took him to the station.

The Community continued to widen its contacts: through retreats at Mirfield and elsewhere; through individuals coming to stay – the office of Guestmaster was created in 1934 – including Dietrich Bonhoeffer who in 1935 was looking for a model for his seminary in Germany, T. S. Eliot, a friend of Geoffrey Curtis, who came to read his poetry to the College in 1938 and C. E. M. Joad who was helped to faith by Thornton, Talbot and Curtis; through those who used the brethren for spiritual direction; through former students of the College who spread the knowledge of CR in their parishes; through the many books and pamphlets written by the brethren; through Quarry Services, Commemoration Day, missions at home and overseas and the Fraternity.

It was not until the 1930s that the Quarry Services regained their popularity. Attendances had slumped badly in the 1920s despite advertisements in trams and on cinema screens. Some years they were not held at all. But in 1931 crowds turned up to hear three odd-sounding sermons on 'Sunday Cinemas', 'Hospital Sweepstakes' and 'The Next War' (the value of the League of Nations). When William Temple preached in 1936 3,000 people came. Most of the sermons were directly theological, as in 1939: 'Why We Believe in God'; 'Is God Almighty?'; 'Is Prayer Worthwhile?'; 'What is the Church For?'. It is remarkable that up to 3,000 would brave the uncertainties of the weather and listen to a sermon on hard, backless benches for an hour. Unless an outside preacher was well-known, sermons by brethren were preferred. They were one way of sharing the life of the Community; many of the brethren had an affectionate following. Sometimes particular groups were invited – Friendly Societies, sporting and cycling organizations, for example. In 1933 the architect of the Scarborough Open Air Theatre planned, and Ralph Bell organized, a reconstruction of the stage and an enlargement of the amphitheatre after the removal of stone for new buildings at the College and the House. After further improvements in 1936 using material excavated during the building of the west end of the Community church, 3,000 could be seated.

Commemoration Day, which resumed in 1919, drew steadily increasing attendances. Its purposes were to welcome, invigorate, inform and increase supporters and to dispel ignorance about the Religious Life. It began in the afternoon with an outdoor service and addresses on the work of CR; then there was classical music in church, then after tea the play performed by the students as a rule – perhaps Shakespeare, Shaw's 'St Joan' or 'HMS Pinafore' in the Quarry preceded by community singing of hymns and popular songs like 'Ilkla Moor'; then Solemn Evensong in church concluding with a procession and the haunting hymn 'O what their joy and their glory must be' (still sung at Commemoration Evensong). By the 1930s the plays were becoming more specifically religious, no doubt influenced by the revival of religious drama by George Bell as Dean of Canterbury in 1928. But the churches and chapels were ceasing to include among their functions the provision of general culture – this was now available through the BBC and extra-mural departments. In the 1920s the Kingdom of God had been in the forefront of the ecumenical movement. Now the watchword of the 1937 Oxford Conference, conscious of the pressures of totalitarianism, was 'Let the Church be the Church'. The church was becoming more self-conscious, more introverted.

Numbers at Commemoration Day rose from about 2,000 in the early 1920s to 5–6,000 by the 1930s. It required a lot of organization. A special train ran from Leeds to Battyeford station. The LMS issued half-price tickets over a sixty mile radius. In 1931 26,000 cakes and 31 gallons of ice cream were provided. Its transformation into a major occasion owed much to Elwin Millard. 'Bishops in full pontificals shrank into insignificance before that enormous figure in shirt-sleeves and shorts, crowned with a white solar topee, shouting directions through a megaphone and every now and again giving vent to that great crowing laugh which was known in church circles from one end of England to the other.' Up to 1929 it had been technically a College Festival. In that year a separate College Festival was created and Commemoration Day became a specifically Community occasion. In 1933, the centenary of the Oxford Movement, the early High Mass was moved to 11.30 a.m. and was incorporated into the public programme.

Beyond Mirfield

After the war CR conducted fewer Parish Missions. In 1923 Chapter considered this aspect of CR's work.

CR Mirfield: from top to bottom: Retreat House, Community House, Library and Cloister, Church, College. The Quarry is to the left beyond this picture.

2 High Mass in the Community Church before the liturgical changes of recent years.

3 The Community gathered at Mirfield in 1901: top row (left to right) – John Carter, Walter Frere, Clement Thomson; second row – Waldegrave Hart, Charles Gore (Senior), Charles Fitzgerald; third row – George Longridge, Richard Rackham, Gerard Sampson, Cyril Bickersteth; front row – Samuel Healy, James Nash. (Paul Bull was absent.)

4 Cosmo Lang, Archbishop of York, addressing 2,000 men from the Bible classes of the Wakefield diocese in the Quarry, June 1909.

5 Fr Keble Talbot CR (Superior 1922–40)

Fr Ralph Bell C R.

7   Fr Harold Ellis C R (Novice Guardian 1937–44) and
Fr Raymond Raynes C R (Superior 1943–58).

From left to right: two former students of the College – the Archbishop of
Central Africa (W. J. Hughes) and the Bishop of Johannesburg (Ambrose
Reeves) with Fr Trevor Huddleston C R and Fr Jonathan Graham C R
(Superior 1958–65) after the last Quarry Service, 1958.

9 St John's College Johannesburg

10 Oliver Tambo teaching physics at St Peter's School Rosettenville.

11 Sophiatown 1936. The CR Priory is in the foreground, the school in the centre, Ekutuleni on its right, the church of Christ the King behind.

12 Fr Aelred Stubbs CR, then Principal of St Peter's College Alice, Cape Province, with a group of ordinands in 1970.

13 St Augustine's Penhalonga: procession to bless the buildings of the first
    African secondary school, 1939.

14 Codrington College Barbados: Commemoration Day 1957.

15 Bishop Walter Frere CR after singing the Litany in the Russian Orthodox
Cathedral, Paris 1936, with Metropolitan Eulogius on the left.

16 Fr Hugh Bishop CR (Superior 1966–74) and Archbishop Michael Ramsey
(Visitor to CR) welcoming Cardinal Suenens to Mirfield in 1969.

17 Fr Eric Simmons CR (Superior 1974–86) meeting Pope Paul VI in 1977.

18 Fr Jeremy Platt CR, 1991, in a squatters' camp near Johannesburg, where he lives and works.

Frederick [King] introduced the subject . . . and a somewhat desultory discussion followed . . . Paul [Bull] expressed his fear lest Missions were becoming too mechanical – the machinery too perfect, and the main aim – the conversion of souls – being lost sight of. He also emphasized the need of having men and lad visitors in preparation for a Mission. There was some talk of the advisability of separating the sexes and Richard [Barnes] spoke of the experiment of having a children's week first – to get the children as it were out of the Missioners' way at the crisis, and also to act as an advertisement for the Mission itself. 'Renewals' were also discussed. Bernard [Horner] spoke against them and Edmund [Seyzinger] thought them dangerous, though they might come at the end after careful preparation. The main objection to them seemed to be that people should be brought to so solemn an act as the renewal of their baptismal vows without realizing at all what they were doing, while the Missioner on his side was using it mainly as a means of obtaining an interview afterwards.

It is striking that on work so central to CR's life discussion should be 'desultory'. Talbot believed that CR must explore new methods of evangelism – perhaps a mission on the Scarborough sands and a shop on the Huddersfield road which would provide tea and answers for doubters. Neither materialized. In 1942 he wrote:

The methods of evangelism . . . have become more tentative and less assured of their efficacy to reach the vast mass of people who have lost all touch with the organic tradition of the Church . . . To be sure, missions have continued right up to the outbreak of the present war; but our missioners would be the first to say that we have need of a fresh understanding from God the Holy Ghost of how to bring the Gospel alive again in the lives of this 'sub-Christian' generation.[1]

Perhaps the greatest disappointment in the ministry of Cyril Garbett (Archbishop of York 1942–55) was the Parish Mission (not conducted by CR) at St Mary's Portsea in 1913. By modern standards it was successful, starting with a procession of 1,200 and concluding with a eucharist at 5 a.m. with 1,000 communicants. Afterwards many of the 360 candidates for confirmation had been influenced by the Mission. But he concluded that systematic parochial visiting was now more effective. He wrote in 1953: 'It is comparatively easy to know the good news the Church should give; it is much harder to know how to get it across. Waste of effort and disappointment are caused by the frequent failure to see that evangelistic methods once successful are now too often ineffective.'[2] But there were other obstacles which Garbett did not mention. The Good News was usually verbal not embodied. The most powerful imperative – salvation from hell – had now disappeared. The message of the Christian social movement was directed not against the heathen but against social evils and the church for not doing more to remedy them. A hymn in *Hymns Ancient and Modern* (1889) entitled 'For Church Defence' began: 'Round the Sacred City gather/ Egypt, Edom, Babylon;/ All the warring hosts of error,/ Sworn against her, move as one.' But many Christians now believed that there were also errors in the church and truths in the world: had not the world caused church to change its attitudes to contraception and the role of women? And there were now many attractive alternatives to going to church.

A full CR mission team consisted of brethren, students, nuns, laypeople. Every house in the parish was visited. The mission aimed to produce candidates for baptism and/or confirmation and to persuade many to adopt a rule of life. The CR resolution card explained that 'The Catholic Rule of Life' was to pray and read the Bible daily; to fast and to give to God and the poor; to attend mass on Sundays and Holy Days; to receive Holy Communion and to use sacramental confession regularly; to be 'a missionary of Jesus Christ'. A mission also strengthened the bond between the parish and CR, particularly when parishioners became members of FR. A mission conducted by Seyzinger in Temple Balsall in 1913 resulted in the establishment of a Parish Eucharist and breakfast there, a pattern which was widely followed.[3] At Christ Church, Stepney, where St John Groser, an old student and a well-known socialist, was vicar, Alfred Drury conducted popular question and answer sessions each evening one week in Lent 1934. He endeared himself to the vicar and people alike by joining their march to Hyde Park against the Means Test. Brethren were particularly busy during Lent and Holy Week. In 1920 they conducted Lent courses in thirteen parishes and preached during Holy Week in twenty-one churches.

Brethren were also in great demand as missioners and retreat conductors overseas. In 1910 and 1913 Fitzgerald and Rees spent several months in New Zealand. Rees conducted missions in Canada in 1914, Ceylon and India in 1922 and again in Ceylon in 1929. Seyzinger made five visits to the United States and Canada. Bickersteth conducted missions in South Africa, India, Japan, Korea, Manchuria and Canada. These and other visits resulted in the creation of overseas branches of FR, a trickle of vocations from some of these countries and requests to CR to establish more overseas houses – which had to be regretfully declined.

CR entered into longer commitments in Australia and Borneo. During the 1920s CR helped to establish the Community of the Ascension at Goulburn, Australia. In 1919 the three founding members spent some time at Mirfield. In 1921 Hilary Jeayes spent a year at Goulburn and witnessed the first professions. Bell spent three years there, returning via New Zealand and Ceylon. But the Community did not prosper and in 1942 it was dissolved. Cecil Cohen, one time Superior, eventually returned to Britain, was professed in CR in 1951 and died at Mirfield aged ninety-three in 1982. CR had a link with Borneo through Mounsey. Three priests trying to start a community there asked for CR's help. In 1933 Wilfrid Shelley and Basil Thomas arrived in Kuching on a prospecting mission in association with SPG, living next door to the Bishop, Noel Hudson, an old friend of CR. Thomas wrote: 'It is a huge relief to find oneself once more back in a Catholic atmosphere'. The schoolgirls 'genuflect and kneel down ... no fuss, no self-consciousness, never having heard the word Protestant, never having dreamed, even in their worst nightmares, of Mr John Kensit!'. Shelley reported: 'Some disappointments over the confessions ... The people are dears but they haven't got much sense of sin yet.' Oswald Philipps, Andrew Blair and Lawrence Wrathall came to join them in training ordinands and general pastoral work. Talbot went out in 1936 and concluded that CR was unable to sustain long term work in Borneo. So CR withdrew in 1937 from this ill-conceived experiment.

At one time brethren acted as wardens and confessors to eighteen religious communities in Britain and to others overseas. Figgis was the first Warden of the Oratory of the Good Shepherd (created 1913) – Frere followed him. From 1918 to 1955 Seyzinger was Warden of the Society of the Most Holy Trinity, Ascot. Its Reverend Mother, Alice of the Holy Sepulchre, signed her letters to him, 'your most loving and grateful child'. Biggart became Warden of the Society of the Precious Blood, Burnham Abbey in 1934. CR's much valued relationship with these enclosed nuns continued until 1988. There were also particularly close connections with the Order of the Holy Paraclete, Whitby (Frere drew up the Rule) and with St Peter's Community at Horbury.

The Lambeth Conference of 1920 and 1930 expressed generous appreciation of the work of Religious Communities, and recommended a closer relationship with the episcopate. This was unwelcome to those Anglo-Catholics who vehemently believed that episcopacy was of the *esse* of the church but distrusted actual bishops. That Frere represented the bishops at a meeting with representatives of the communities in 1930 was a reassurance to some but a red rag to others. However the creation of the Advisory Council on Religious Communities in 1935, and the choice of Kenneth Kirk, Bishop of Oxford (one bishop whom most Anglo-Catholics did trust) as a member, then from 1938 as chairman, did much to integrate communities into the general life of the church.[4]

The Fraternity of the Resurrection by 1945 had about 230 local groups and a membership of around 6,000. The *CR Quarterly* sold 8–9,000 copies. In a church with little corporate discipline, whose members' loyalties often were limited to the local church, it was enormously valuable to have disciplined groups of priests and laypeople whose horizons were widened by contact with CR. However, Talbot complained privately that some FR members seemed to regard the Elder Brother (of the Prodigal Son) as their patron saint. FR gained extra members when the Society of the Resurrection, out of which CR had grown, ceased to exist in 1924. The first annual FR Summer School for women was held in 1922 at Wantage where Frere taught them descants as well as theology. Annual Festivals, held in London and elsewhere, were another means of communication between CR and its supporters. Generally letters to FR in the *Quarterly* were devotional in content. But when Kenneth

MacLachlan was FR Warden in the late 1930s and 1940s he told companions that they must not treat prayer as a stockade. He had no time for 'spurious pietism' and recommended books by Temple, the (radical) *Christian News-letter* and the Report of the Malvern Conference (on church and society). In 1941 he told them that the alliance with Russia should make us more sympathetic to the aims of Soviet society.

What did FR branches do? One had sixteen members including five companions who met quarterly after Sunday Evensong. Usually one of the brethren would speak – perhaps on FR or South Africa or prayer. The branch organized Quiet Afternoons, study groups, a library and an Open Meeting every two years addressed by a CR Father, attended by perhaps 180 people. FR included some remarkable personalities. Ruth Kenyon who died in 1943 had been a JP and a member of the Labour Party, the Christendom Group and the Hastings Education Committee and a leading light at the annual Anglo-Catholic Summer School of Sociology. Hannah Harvey, secretary of the London FR (who died the same year) had been a skilled vestment maker. When Queen Victoria died she was summoned to Osborne and transported across the Solent by destroyer. There she worked two days and nights on the funeral pall, closely watched by the Kaiser. She had helped with CR Parish Missions since 1903 and had organized the CR stall at the annual Missionary Sale of Work at the Royal Agricultural Hall, a remarkable occasion whose patrons included three princesses, two duchesses, two marchionesses and six countesses. The Countess of Antrim (Talbot's cousin) presided over the CR stall. Other valuable support came from the Mirfield Needlework Association which in 1924 presented 20 pairs of sheets, 79 pillow cases, 125 towels and 204 cloths and dusters for CR's use.

In 1929 CR drew up a rule for oblates, but it was not until 1931 that the first two were elected. Oblates may be priests or laymen (though most laymen have been ordinands). They make an annual commitment to celibacy, simplicity of life and the spirit of obedience, and undertake specific obligations about prayer, the eucharist, fasting, almsgiving, confession, study, retreats and periodic residence at a CR house. They, like members of FR, report regularly about their observance of their rule. The numbers grew slowly, but thanks particularly to careful fostering by the present Warden, Gabriel Sandford, they have now expanded to well over thirty. Since 1991 an oblate, David Lane, not one of the brethren, has been Principal of the College.

Politics

Before the war CR was identified in the public mind with socialism. The few brethren who were unsympathetic to socialism remained silent. As we saw in Chapter 4, CR's socialist reputation, reinforced by the Quarry conferences with Labour leaders and Healy's vociferous pronouncements, caused a serious withdrawal of financial support. Healy left, Frere became politically more cautious.[5] After the war CR continued to have a socialist reputation, partly because socialist brethren got the publicity, partly because Gore's political views and interventions were regarded as representative of the CR ethos. But in fact the proportion of brethren who were willing to identify themselves publicly as socialists had declined. In 1906, 165 clergy signed an Address to the Labour Party congratulating it on its recent electoral success and urging it to press forward to 'ownership by the people and for the people'. Out of the total of about 17 brethren and novices in England, 14 signed it. Drury (not yet a member) and Scott Holland also signed. In 1923, 510 clergy signed a Memorial to the Labour Party congratulating it on becoming the official Opposition and offering their support. Only 8 brethren signed – together with some old students of the College, including Jack Bucknall and St John Groser and three former brethren, Carter, Healy and Money.[6] Though CR continued to have a social conscience, by the 1930s this was largely focussed upon the problems of South Africa rather than upon those at home.

In 1919 Frere began a letter by advocating the retention of the Gloria at the end of the eucharist, then went on to say that the recent successful railway strike demonstrated that Labour must be offered a partnership in national affairs. CR had decided it should develop closer relationships with local workers, so during that winter some workers regularly met with some brethren at the House to discuss social questions. However, one or two of the men were more interested in evangelism than socialism. In the summers of 1919, 1920 and 1922 the local Labour Party held its Garden Parties in the grounds. From 1926 onwards CR gave various anonymous donations to funds for the families of strikers and other workers in distress. Drury and Dieterlé took a keen interest in the Mirfield centre for the unemployed created in 1933. In 1938 the centre made kneeling desks and a cross for the lower church and a group of unemployed were invited to tea and bowls. Between the wars three brethren publicly identified themselves with the Labour Party. In the 1920s Bull and Drury spoke for Labour candidates at elections. In the 1924 General Election Bull was assisted by Ambrose Reeves, then a student, later Bishop of Johannesburg. When in 1922 a Leeds Labour candidate publicly stated he was supported by the Mirfield Fathers (some had written to him privately) the Community feared a controversy. In 1929 a group of students signed the nomination papers of a local Labour candidate but they made it clear they were not members of CR. In the late 1930s Drury and Langdon-Davies spoke at meetings of the Socialist Christian League in Huddersfield.

After 1918 Christian socialism became increasingly factious and dominated by theorizing intellectuals. The Church Socialist League, in the founding of which Frere, Healy and Bull had played an important part, in 1916 decided that it was 'a religious not a political body'. It was dissolved in 1923 having split three ways. The main residue was dominated by Guild Socialism, a strand in

CSL which had been much influenced by Figgis and which was fatally attractive to the nostalgic element in Anglo-Catholicism. This strand was expressed in a symposium organized by Maurice Reckitt, *The Return of Christendom* (1922) to which Bull and Thornton contributed and for which Gore wrote an uneasy introduction. The Anglo-Catholic Summer Schools of Sociology were created in 1925 as a response to Bishop Frank Weston's rousing call to the 1923 Anglo-Catholic Congress to find Jesus in the slum as well as in the tabernacle. Unlike their Roman Catholic counterparts which had a large working-class membership, the Anglo-Catholic summer schools were dominated by middle-class theorists. Those who threw in their lot with the Labour Party risked confusing a specific programme with the Kingdom of God, but at least they were participating in real politics with working people, as in the original Quarry meetings. But Reckitt epitomized the inauthenticity of much Anglo-Catholic social thought. Since he lived off the profits of Reckitt's Blue, he never had to work for his living and could devote his life to prolific writing and endless meetings about reorganizing society while ironically steering clear of actual contact with politics, business and working people. Hence (as Pickering observes) 'Anglo-Catholics failed to make any lasting impression on the non-Christianized working-class masses . . . They showed minimal interest or ability in entering into party politics . . . Thus Anglo-Catholic thinking never penetrated the Labour Party.'[7] Anglo-Catholic and other Christian socialists share responsibility for the failure of the Labour Party during most of this century to attain office.

When Roland Langdon-Davies (professed 1937) was asked what attracted him to CR he replied: 'What it stood for: Anglo-Catholicism mixed with socialism'. (Staunch Tory brethren never in public raised their heads above the parapet.) Trevor Huddleston, Martin Jarrett-Kerr and Dominic Whitnall were all influenced by Basil Jellicoe, the Somers Town priest and housing reformer. Huddleston and Jarrett-Kerr were also appreciative participants in the Summer Schools of Sociology. Talbot, who had become a disciple of the Christendom Group, remarked blandly in his survey of CR 1892–1942: 'the early impetus towards identification with the ranks of politicial Socialism has been greatly qualified. The need we now acknowledge is, not to endorse some programme of secular politics, but to learn to proclaim a doctrine of society, informed by an authentically Christian understanding of man's nature and call, and controlled by Catholic theology.'[8]

One would not gather from reading the *CR Quarterly* for the inter-war period, that these were the years of women's franchise, the first Labour Government, the General Strike, the Great Depression and the collapse of the League of Nations. There was occasional social comment buried in the book reviews, though it is highly significant that the seminal works of the crucially important American social thinker Reinhold Niebuhr were not reviewed. Niebuhr's ethical thinking was rooted in what he learned from ministering in Detroit during bitter disputes in the car industry. He learned that it was fatally easy for the minister to proclaim abstract ideals, but that it was only when he agonized about their applicability to specific issues that his ministry gained 'reality and potency'.[9] What increasingly gave 'reality and potency' to C R's work in South Africa was that from 1934 some brethren were living in the African townships and experiencing at first hand the needs of the people. That C R had no such comparable commitment in England explains the sparseness of its comment on the issues which were shaping, and in some cases destroying, the lives of ordinary people in this country.

Anglo-Catholicism

By the 1920s Anglo-Catholicism was the most dynamic force in the Church of England. Theologically, politically and liturgically it had moved a long way since Pusey and Liddon. Now it was Gore's turn to feel stranded. At its best it delivered Anglicanism from provincialism, nationalism, puritanism, moralism and drabness, and fostered heroic sanctity and social action. 'The devout soul who was taught to look up when the bell rang for the elevation of the host, and the boy from the poorer household who served conscientiously Sunday by Sunday at the eleven o'clock High Mass, learnt what it means to adore a transcendent and glorious God . . .'[10] Returning chaplains, fed up with the ineffectiveness of ordinary Anglicanism, gave the movement an extra boost.[11] Yet Anglo-Catholicism was sapped by negative features. Pickering has drawn attention to its wide range of unacknowledged and unresolved ambiguities. Its societies proliferated and quarrelled. There were even two different societies promoting devotion to King Charles the Martyr. Anglo-Catholicism expressed itself in two distinct styles of worship. Some followed Frere and Dearmer and promoted English Use, 'Prayer Book Catholicism'. Others followed Rome. At Chichester there was English Use at the Cathedral, while the Theological College, feeling very superior, followed Fortescue's *Ceremonies of the Roman Rite*. A third option was emerging in the 1930s. Derived from the continental Roman Catholic Liturgical Movement, it resembled a modern version of Prayer Book Catholicism. In 1933, the centenary of the Oxford Movement, *The English Missal* appeared in which a thin rivulet of Prayer Book text ran apologetically between dominating embankments of the Roman liturgy. Yet that year Gabriel Hebert S S M (*Church Times* 6 January) described how some continental Roman Catholics were abandoning practices which advanced Anglo-Catholics were fighting to introduce. It was this Liturgical Movement which eventually succeeded in persuading the *whole* Church of England to model the content and style of its new liturgies on Rome, whereas only a section of Anglo-Catholics ever followed the old Roman Use.

Yet there was something more seriously flawed about Anglo-Catholicism than disputes about liturgical usage. At its heart was a canker, a defective morality born of equivocation and self-deception about authority, and an unwillingness (understandable at that time) to acknowledge that homosexual attitudes dominated certain key areas of the movement creating misogyny and a coterie mentality. Some Anglo-Catholics were obsessed with liturgical minutiae, like the devout woman who complained to the priest who had worn his maniple on the wrong arm: 'You quite spoiled my mass.' To some, religion was an entrancing 'play-time' (Betjeman's description in 'Anglo-Catholic Congresses') indulged with eclectic congregations while the parish went hang; hence too the retreat into mediaeval fantasy at Thaxted and Walsingham.[12] CR manifested the strengths and the defects of Anglo-Catholicism, but Gore's teaching that religion was about moral righteousness and CR's West Riding milieu mostly saved it from preciosity.

In 1920 the first Anglo-Catholic Congress attracted 13,000; 70,000 enrolled for the last of that series in 1933, and a congregation of 50,000 attended High Mass at the White City Stadium.[13] 'The Elevation at Mass will be marked by the sounding of trumpets' announced the programme. Six men from a local parish communicated. So the letter of the Prayer Book was obeyed, though not its spirit. There was some covert controversy in the *CR Quarterly* about the 1920 Congress. (LD, MD 1921) Jeayes was scornful of it, but warmly commended the SCM, which he described as the most important movement in the Christian world. Symonds (whose novitiate was prolonged because his father, an advanced priest, regarded CR as unsound) dismissed Jeayes' arguments without mentioning his name. One brother withdrew from CR in 1925 partly because he could no longer remain 'in a body predominantly and increasingly Anglo-Catholic'.

Brethren made notable contributions to the Congresses. At the 1920 Congress Gore asserted: 'divine justice requires a certain equality of distribution' in society; he asked his hearers to stand to show their opposition to contraception and their support for the indissolubility of marriage. Thornton drew out the political implications of the Kingdom. Frere said that while the western church suffered from regimentation, Orthodoxy suffered from never having experienced 'the thrill' of reform. In 1923 Gore focussed on the teaching of the Hebrew prophets about the moral character of God. Frere argued that the church should have room for both corporate authority and private judgment. In 1927 Thornton pleaded for private and corporate devotions to the sacrament. In 1930 he asserted that Catholicism was 'something much larger than Roman Catholicism'. Biggart commended the pursuit of holiness. In 1933 Frere paid a warm tribute to Evangelicalism. Talbot (described simply as 'A Religious') proclaimed: 'It is no part of true Catholicism to divorce free inquiry and rational criticism from personal devotion'. Thus the brethren contributed some of CR's distinctive emphases to the Congresses. (CR also took a leading part in organizing and giving papers to the local Congress held in Leeds in 1922.

The *Church Times* (30 June) believed its serious and eirenic atmosphere owed much to CR's influence.)

The tensions within Anglo-Catholicism were more evident in the contributions from other sources at the national Congresses. In 1920 Leighton Pullan appealed for 'patent fidelity to the Prayer Book' and N. P. Williams was scathing about those who treated the papacy 'as an infallible authority on all points, *except* the crucial one of the necessity of communion with itself'. But C. J. Smith argued that a non-communicating mass taught worshippers to move from a religion of self-centred receiving to one of sacrificial giving and there were several rousing calls to battle. The Centenary Hymn likened Anglo-Catholics to the Israelites carrying the Ark across the wilderness and turning 'the alien foe to flight'. Bishop Weston unconsciously exposed the Anglo-Catholic dilemma about authority in his remark in 1923: 'I ask for obedience to the Bishops in so far as they themselves obey the Catholic Church'. Yet the Church Union was able to point to the many scholarly works it had promoted ranging from Gore's *New Commentary* (1928) to F. P. Harton's *Elements of the Spiritual Life* (1932).

Attitudes of the brethren towards the burgeoning movement are evident in the writings of Northcott, Thornton and Symonds, in passing remarks in the *CR Quarterly*, in changes in Talbot's theological outlook and in liturgical developments.

Geoffrey Curtis believed that Hubert Northcott should rank after Gore and Frere as the third creative force in CR, because as Novice Guardian 1922–37 he created the first proper novitiate. Northcott's appointment was a recognition that novices needed more than a topping upon their previous formation through university, theological college and parish work. One odd feature of CR's history is that before and after Northcott some appointments, short in duration and unsatisfactory in character, suggest that the office of Novice Guardian has not been regarded (as it should be) as the most important after that of Superior. Some Guardians have been idiosyncratic, preparing novices for what the Guardian wanted CR to be rather than what it was. Some have been kindly amateurs. CR, like other communities, has suffered from the lack of an extensive Anglican monastic tradition, and fearful of insularity has sometimes drawn uncritically upon Roman models. In 1933 Northcott contributed 'The Development and Deepening of the Spiritual Life' to *Northern Catholicism* edited by N. P. Williams and Charles Harris. Northcott turned his back on the Prayer Book and the Tractarians and relied heavily upon contemporary Roman spirituality: the eucharist primarily as sacrifice (reinforced by non-communicating attendance which teaches 'self-oblation rather than consolation'), reservation for prayer and devotions, reparation, the cultus of the saints, contemplation, mortification. 'Moderation is not a characteristic of the Catholic religion.'

Northcott thought R. M. Benson had an almost oppressive sense of the eye of God upon us. Yet there was something of Benson's rigour in Northcott himself.

Two newly professed brethren were advised by Northcott to go to Huddersfield and sell all their 'secular clothes'. They did so. In retrospect one commented: 'It was a very non- CR thing to do.' Another recalled his novitiate under Northcott: 'it was a bit too negative, all the prohibitions . . . Forsaking the joys of this world to find joy and fulfilment in God.' But another recalled his excellent novice talks and how he always stood up for the novices if they were criticized. Yet he was distant, impersonal. His letters to brethren overseas were like treatises on spirituality, giving no news either of himself or others. A former student said that just when he needed someone to open him up, Northcott battened him down even more tightly. Others however found him a tender and down-to-earth confessor. His *Commentary on the Rule* (1955) was more monastic than Frere's, more astringent. If the novice 'has dreamed of hours of absorbing prayer or spiritual converse with holy seniors, he finds instead cups to be washed, corridors to be swept, and brethren after all not so holy.' He told the College that when an enthusiastic nun exclaimed 'I want to be a rapier in the hand of God', he had replied 'God may want you to be a potato peeler'. (His humour could be savage.) He was scathing about traditions of spirituality he thought dangerous like the Jesus Prayer – it could induce mere self-hypnosis.

His teaching was fully expressed in *A Venture of Prayer* (1950). He did not allow what he still called 'the new psychology' to deflect him. So he acknowledged the dangers of masochism but told for qualified approval of Fr Doyle SJ flinging himself into a bed of nettles and scourging himself with razor blades, of a nun who wrote to a former pupil living in sin that she was daily scourging herself until the blood ran for her sake. He was critical of Bunyan's picture of the solitary pilgrim but he taught an individual not a liturgical spirituality. There are thirty references to St John of the Cross, but no mention of Jeremy Taylor, George Herbert, John Donne, Thomas Ken, Thomas Traherne, William Law, John Keble or of Prayer Book spirituality. References to ordinary life are sparse. It represents the strengths and weaknesses of pre-war Anglo-Catholicism – it breaks out of insularity, but ignores the English tradition. Yet there are touches of greatness. Sooner or later (he wrote) our methods of prayer fail, 'we are left once more face to face with God, helpless "and with no language but a cry"'.

Stories about Northcott depict him as always struggling to save CR from laxity. He did not approve of taking holidays but he broke down and had to be sent abroad. Just as CR burdened Talbot by expecting him to be always bubbling with *joie de vivre*, so perhaps Northcott was burdened by being cast (or casting himself) in the role of guardian of CR spirituality. Roger Castle, the vivacious lay-brother, by mistake put cake on the table when it was a fast-day. Northcott came in and looked at it scornfully. 'There is no need to ice the cake with your look' responded Roger. When he was dying in 1967 he is said to have remarked to Roger 'I wonder sometimes whether I got it right?'. CR asked the same question.

The entry for 8 December 1917 in *Diary of a Dean* (1949) by W. R. Inge of St Paul's reads: 'A Mirfield monk came to stay and preach for me. He ate up all the food in the house.' Surprisingly this was Lionel Thornton, the unworldly theologian.[14] He moved into the front-rank of theologians with his contribution to *Essays Catholic and Critical* (1926) and his pioneering work of process theology *The Incarnate Lord* (1928) – both much admired by Michael Ramsey. He gained much from his membership of the Commission on Christian Doctrine, appointed by the Archbishops in 1922, which published its Report in 1938. Thornton had to defend it against the criticisms of some brethren that it was too liberal. Talbot joined a delegation of Catholics and Evangelicals which met the Archbishops in 1939 on behalf of 8,200 disquieted clergy. When the Commission ended, Thornton became increasingly isolated – he was not a member of a university faculty. His *The Common Life in the Body of Christ* (1942) was written on the principle that only scripture can expound scripture. It also reflected the political and liturgical collectivism of the period and Thornton's early connections with the Church Socialist League. But, like other biblical theologians he refused to consider whether what was scriptural was also true. His trilogy *The Form of a Servant* (1950–6) showed that he was now deeply committed to recondite typology, though the first volume included an exciting exposition of divine condescension and recapitulation.

His total lack of humour (jokes had to be meticulously explained) resulted in a lack of proportion. 'His fidelity to the Rule which he knew to the last comma, was unwavering and inflexible' commented his obituarist. Lecturing to the College on Moral Theology he asked what a priest should do on a sinking liner for Anglicans wishing to make their confessions. The answer was that they should all recite together the Prayer Book General Confession. The comic aspect of the situation completely escaped him. He was also, except in theological controversy, notoriously silent. Once a guest, seeing him sitting at tea isolated from the others, asked his name. Keith Davie replied 'That is Fr Thornton. He is writing a book on the Common Life.' Yet he was a great success when he paid a termly visit to a convent school. 'I'm good with young ladies' he remarked innocently.

Thornton, brought up an Evangelical, sought to solve the Anglo-Catholic dilemma about authority by locating it in the Bible. Symonds tackled it historically in *The Council of Trent and Anglican Formularies* (1933), a Mirfield version of Newman's Tract XC (1841). But unlike Newman, Symonds did not submit to Rome, though he provocatively dated his Preface 'Feast of the Assumption of our Lady'. He granted that Protestant views had often been tolerated, and even been dominant in the Church of England, but contended that 'the Catholic interpretation is the one which fits the formularies best in most cases, and in others is at least compatible with them'. Symonds' lack of commitment to Prayer Book teaching was demonstrated by his chapter on 'Communion in one Kind'; Anglicans should accept that reception in both kinds was not essential. He ended: 'Is it then too much to hope that a basis of reconciliation may be found in a general acceptance of the doctrinal decrees of the Council of Trent by those who are still ready to give loyal adherence to the present formularies of the English Church?' No wonder Anglo-Catholics were thought to be masters of equivocation. In *The Church Universal and the See of Rome* (1939) Symonds argued that to be cut off from Rome was not to be cut off from the church: but the papacy, which had become through autocracy a source of division, could with reform become the source of unity again.

Talbot, like his friend William Temple, was becoming theologically more conservative.[15] But like Temple, Talbot never lost his liberal instincts and his desire for synthesis. His father's Liberal Catholicism and von Hügel, who combined Catholic Modernism with a daily adoration of the sacrament, continued to be powerful influences. Talbot recoiled both from Thornton's biblicism and Symonds' certainty. But he had neither the scholarship nor the decisive temperament to frame criteria by which CR could sift the true from the false in Anglo-Catholicism and neo-orthodoxy. In 1942 he summarized some of the changes in CR:

> A generation comes for whom the old 'liberal' ideals hold only a faint attraction: there arise desires for a more rigorous authority, a more personal system of obedience . . . all the more because in this third period there is no parallel to the dominating influence of the first two great Superiors as centres of authority and unity . . . The theological climate of the last twenty years has changed . . . There is a readier hospitality of mind in the younger men towards other forms of piety and methods of prayer than were indigenous in the Anglican Communion fifty years ago . . . we are more sensible of the treasures of the great Roman and Orthodox Communions, and are, perhaps excessively, conscious of Anglican provincialism.[16]

Remarks in the *CR Quarterly* convey the triumphalism of Anglo-Catholicism. Shelley in an obituary described 'a life fragrant with those special virtues of humility and charity which are so seldom found outside the range of the Catholic Sacramental system'. Northcott described a visit to CR's mission in Rhodesia in 1933: 'it is a society of communicants, practising Catholics' who have 'a fine nose, perhaps too fine a nose, for heresy'. He told how when Christian pupils used to wash separately from catechumens, a boy caused a commotion by washing with the Christians though he was a member of the Salvation Army. 'But I am a Christian' he protested. But the boys told him he wasn't because he had not been baptized. Henceforth he washed elsewhere. For brethren one great attraction of working in Africa was that the church there provided a vision of what they hoped the Church of England would become. They did not have the frustration of teaching Catholicism only to have it denounced by other Anglicans, or even by the bishop.

Two breakwaters against the advancing tide were removed when Gore ceased to be Visitor in 1919 and Frere went to Truro in 1923. Mirfield was now without a liturgist. In 1929 CR asked the bishop's permission for a package of liturgical changes at Mirfield which included: the use of the interim or 1928 eucharistic rites as well as that of 1662; the omission of the Creed and Gloria on ferias and at requiems; the use of Benedictus and Agnus Dei; the kiss of peace as far as the subdeacon; ablutions after communion at most masses. The bishop agreed to these changes except for the altered place for the ablutions. ('TARPing' – Taking the Ablutions in the Right Place, i.e. the Roman, not the Prayer Book position – had become a badge of Catholicity.) In 1935 the South African rite was used at the High Mass for the first time, then replaced by the interim rite three years later. Hardly any brethren except Frere used the 1928 eucharist, which he thought greatly superior to the interim rite. Many Anglo-Catholics had an irrational hatred of the 1928 Book. From 1927 a gong was sounded and the church bell rung after the words of institution, contrary to Frere's teaching that the whole prayer was consecratory. But the High Mass still looked 'English' – albs not cottas, and no birettas.[17] Some brethren were always pushing at the limits and the multiplication of private masses encouraged liturgical individualism. Sitting for the psalms at the offices came in, and for a time the cursing verses (as in 1928) went out.

When Seyzinger was chaplain to an Anglo-Catholic Holy Land pilgrimage in the spring of 1929, Patriarch Damianos of Jerusalem presented CR with a relic of the Cross. 'This relic is of equal authority with the relics of the Cross possessed and prized by some of the great churches of Europe' the *CR Quarterly* asserted. Placed in an ancient silver reliquary given by Sir Alfred Jodrell ('the Lord Halifax of East Anglia') it was solemnly inserted into the altar of the Holy Cross chapel.

It was probably J. M. Neale who first revived reservation in 1855. Reservation and devotions gradually spread, despite episcopal censure and Articles xxv and xxviii. Pusey believed that reservation in the early church was for the sick only. R. M. Benson opposed reservation 'after the Roman manner' because 'it implies a denial of the Real Presence in the baptized'. Though Gore as a young man was emotionally attracted to devotions, he became convinced they were theologically wrong. 'The presence is controlled by the purpose' which is communion. Reservation for the sick or absent was legitimate and primitive. But non-communicating attendance and the cultus were distortions. Christ dwells in his members and God is present in the world; the substitution of an external shrine of his presence obscures both.[18] In 1917 Scott Holland wrote bitterly that while sometimes Anglo-Catholic sacramentalism could result in a Stanton or Dolling, it often encouraged worshippers 'to take of the food, to feed on the glory, to yield their souls to the Hush and Holy', to become 'entranced' before the reserved sacrament rather than to work for social justice.[19] Frere believed that reservation had three dangers: 'of substituting sentiment for devotion'; 'of materialism'; 'of losing the sense of God's Presence apart from the Blessed Sacrament'. Hence he favoured reservation in a pyx: 'it does not locate the Sacramental Presence . . . There is much less of the instinct to genuflect . . . it minimizes the tendency to bring Christ down and to look at the prisoner of the tabernacle on the worshipper's own level.' Reservation was permissable only for communion.[20] The 1928 Book allowed reservation, but forbade devotions.

By 1920 the church was deeply divided about reservation. Evangelicals opposed it fiercely. Moderate Catholics wanted it for communion only. For other Anglo-Catholics reservation and devotions were the next steps in the recovery of a supernatural faith and a religion of adoration; they said that the moderates were too cerebral and did not understand the needs of ordinary people. CR, SSJE and SSM were divided. In SSM, Herbert Kelly and his protégé Gabriel Hebert, like Gore and Frere, regarded the cultus as a distortion of the eucharist.

In 1917 CR's General Chapter unanimously agreed in principle to reservation for communion. Talbot had no great personal conviction about, or desire for, reservation; indeed he had theological qualms. However, he would not stand in the way of those who wanted it: 'in the present state of religion we cannot afford to lose any element which has approved itself on any large scale'. He doubted whether Anglicans had sufficient grasp on the primacy of God to keep devotion to the reserved sacrament in proportion. But the Real Presence had become more important to him and he was moved by the power of reservation to promote prayer. A visit to Rome in 1925 made him realize how strongly Roman Catholicism appealed to ordinary people as well as to the 'heroically aspiring'. In 1928 reservation in a pyx, for communion and private (but not public) devotion, was inaugurated at Mirfield. Three or four brethren disapproved but did not oppose it. Talbot thought the bishop had given permission; he had not, but his successor did. A lamp burned before the veiled pyx and brethren were recommended to make a reverence as they passed. The choice of a pyx not a tabernacle indicated that Frere still had some influence.

The Prayer Books of 1549, 1552, 1662 and 1928 were categorical that the eucharist was a corporate act of which the communion of the people was an essential part. The CR Rule stated that brethren should be present at the eucharist daily. In the early years there was only one daily eucharist. In 1901 Gore wrote that the separation of sacrifice from communion represented a 'seriously defective theology'. The eucharist was 'the sacrament of fraternity'.[21] Frere's *Commentary* (1907) declared: 'In offering the Eucharist, our ideal is primitive rather than mediaeval; for we regard ourselves as one body uniting in a common act of eucharistic worship, rather than as a number of priests each of whom will aim at saying his mass daily.' Throughout his life he regarded non-communicating attendance and the multiplication of masses as deformations. It is not clear when extra celebrations began at Mirfield, but private masses were frequent long before the First World War.

By 1920 General Chapter felt it was time to make a declaration of principle:

'The [daily] Chapter Mass represents the offering of the Community to God for His service and any masses said in addition to this . . . should not be so numerous as unduly to weaken the corporate aspect of our worship.' So no masses were to be said during mattins; on Tuesdays there was to be only one corporate celebration; as far as possible each priest should be able to say mass at least twice a week, but should not expect to be able to say mass daily. By 1939, in the new church with its many altars, there were so many masses being celebrated simultaneously that servers were asked to ring the bells very quietly. A few brethren were unhappy about private masses, but on the whole they kept quiet. They felt cowed by the supreme confidence of the advanced brethren. A would-be novice arrived in the mid-1930s but the number of private masses put him off. He returned after the war and for a time was converted to the practice. Mark Tweedy arrived in 1938, deeply attracted by the family life; he was worried by the private masses and the ceremonial, but stayed. Harold Ellis, the dominating Novice Guardian 1937–44, insisted that novices should serve mass daily and put them under pressure to say private masses as well. By the 1930s even priest-guests would say private masses too.

C R greatly developed relationships with Orthodox and continental Roman Catholics. These strengthened its sense of belonging to Catholic Christendom but did not discernably affect its theological outlook or liturgical practices. During the 1936 conference of the Fellowship of St Alban and St Sergius, Frere sang the Litany in the Russian cathedral in Paris standing in the traditional place of an Orthodox bishop – the first occasion an Anglican bishop had so presided. In April 1936 Anglican and Orthodox theologians met at Mirfield, under Frere's chairmanship.[22] There were several exchange visits between Mirfield and Orthodox ordinands. In 1936 Shearburn, the Vice-Principal, the son of an architect who had supervised the modernization of the Tsar's palaces, visited Yugoslavia (renewing contacts with former students who had trained at St Stephen's House under Frere) and forty-seven Romanian monasteries (*CRQ* CD 1936). A few brethren and students were becoming aware of the continental Liturgical Movement. Gabriel Herbert's *Liturgy and Society* (1935) set it within a wide historical and theological framework, and related the recovery of liturgical fellowship to a commitment to social justice; the 'great blunder' of Anglo-Catholicism had been its combination of an early individualistic Communion with a later non-communicating Sung Mass. Mounsey (*CRQ* CD 1934) described a visit to Maria Laach, a monastery in the vanguard of the movement; 'one felt *some* Anglicans are hopelessly out of date, in the way they imitate things Roman, which the best Romans deplore, and which they are trying hard to get rid of'. Shearburn (*CRQ* CD 1935, LD 1936) described the great value of continental Liturgical Missions. The mass is 'a community task to be carried out in a community spirit, in which all individual tendencies are lost'. A student reported in the *Mirfield Gazette* (Christmas 1934) that a Roman priest on the continent said he hoped that private masses would soon be a thing of the past and that the church would follow the Orthodox practice of concelebration. Yet none of CR nor any priest trained at Mirfield contributed to the influential symposia *The Parish Communion* (1937) edited by Hebert and *Sunday Morning: The New Way* (1938) edited by Brother Edward. The new emphasis upon the communal eucharist with its implications for social action ought to have appealed particularly to those in the CR tradition. But CR was moving in the opposite direction.

Geoffrey Curtis, who arrived at Mirfield in 1935, uniquely combined subtlety and naivety, rigour and liberality, a deep devotion to tradition with an inquisitive openness to all kinds of experience outside as well as in the church.[23] Reading Dostoyevsky's *Brothers Karamazov* as an undergraduate changed his life. He once listed what he had learnt from Orthodoxy: Dostoyevsky (that the world will be converted by beauty not by morals but by glory); visits to the Academy of St Sergius (poverty, glory, rats); Bulgakov, Zander, Bloom, Zernov; pilgrimages with the Orthodox; Mount Athos; apophatic theology; hesychasts; the Jesus prayer; transfiguration; cosmic theology; divinization. He stayed two summers at Chevetogne worshipping largely in the Byzantine church. As Sir John Lawrence said he 'played a notable part in that great spiritual movement which I call the western reception of Eastern Orthodoxy'. For Curtis, a romantic platonist, ill-at-ease with technological society, Orthodoxy was immensely attractive: 'indescribably beautiful is the worship of the Eastern Orthodox church, a continuous revelation in the conditions of time and space of the worshipful life of heaven'. Though Frere, Thornton, Shearburn and Tweedy deeply admired the Orthodox, it was only Curtis who took Orthodoxy into his system. Yet he reached out with ardour to Protestants and Roman Catholics as well, and was famous for his capacity for seeing the most unexpected (and sometimes improbable) connections between the different traditions. During three months in France in 1939 he was deeply impressed by the Liturgical Movement. It represented a blending of Catholicism with Evangelicalism – for him the goal of ecumenism. 'Mass said facing the faithful, with commentary both verbal and hymnal and intercession from two others besides the celebrant. It made almost anything Anglican seem very stuffy and sacerdotal, but I rather think that St Agatha's Portsmouth, under Dolling, may have been something like it . . . ' (*CRQ* LD, JB 1939).

Curtis' stay in France was the result of a visit to Mirfield in July 1938 by Abbé Couturier, the founder of the Week of Prayer for Christian Unity, the most notable Roman Catholic visitor since Abbé Portal in 1912. English Roman Catholics were aloof and often hostile towards Anglicans, but Couturier's visit reawakened hopes raised at Malines and afterwards quenched. Couturier proclaimed himself Mercier's disciple, expounded unity not by absorption but by convergence, expressed his dislike of the term

'Sovereign Pontiff' (the papacy should be organic to, not dominant over, the church), attended all the services, genuflected to the reserved sacrament, gave his blessing to the Community, received one from Bishop Mounsey and went away describing C R as 'one of the most vital centres of Anglicanism'. The visit led to the promotion by C R of the Week of Prayer (whose motto was 'the walls of division do not reach to heaven') and its adoption of ecumenism as one of its chief works.[24]

Anglo-Catholicism in reaction against Evangelical emotionalism, stood for impersonality in worship and reticence about the inner self. Northcott typified this spirituality. It was challenged from a surprising quarter – by the Oxford Group Movement, founded in the 1920s by Frank Buchman, an American evangelist who taught entire sanctification. In England the movement mostly affected Evangelicals, then at a low ebb. Bishops, guilt-stricken after the defection of the Methodists and Newman, though disliking its emotionalism, its naive concept of guidance and its group confessions, were ready to bless any new movement which brought people to church. Church newspapers regularly printed enthusiastic articles on such themes as 'I saw a New Heaven and a New Earth at Castle Bromwich'. (The parallels between Buchmanism and the Charismatic Movement are clear, though so are the differences.) In 1929 Osmund Victor reported that it was sweeping South Africa like a veld fire. At St John's College the boys met three times daily for prayer in chapel. Victor, with two brethren, attended a House Party: 'one of the most crowded and wonderful weeks I have ever known' – the sharing of sin and religious experience, people discovering that Christ was real, almost daily miracles, though discrimination was necessary (*CRQ* CD 1929). In England also, some brethren attended House Parties, and in 1934 met with leaders of the movement. Longridge told F R to be thankful for this revival, while being conscious of its dangers – its want of reticence in sharing, its tendency to regard only Groupers as true Christians, its readiness to claim private guidance of the Spirit, the subjectivity of its fellowship separated from church and sacraments. Aidan Cotton circulated a thoughtful memorandum on C R; the Groups had given him a deeper and more uninhibited experience of fellowship than he had ever known in the Community. Victor, commending the memorandum, said that two features of the movement – team-work and fellowship – ought also to characterize C R. The movement did not have any lasting effect on C R. But certain deficiencies in C R had been revealed. The challenge to more openness in relationships was forgotten and did not reappear until the 1960s.

The Gore Memorial Church

In August 1932 work began on a new wing of three storeys at right angles to the House at Mirfield, which pleasingly broke the monotony of its long frontage. The downstairs rooms were designed for the elderly – the Community had long ceased to be just a group of young contemporaries. The stone for this and for the College refectory and kitchens, also blessed in 1933, came from the Quarry. Hubert Worthington, who did distinguished work for Oxford and Manchester universities, was the architect. He and Gore had often holidayed together; Gore baptized and confirmed him in 1917 and later presided at his wedding. His buildings at Mirfield show the influence of Lutyens under whom he had once worked. They are the most satisfying and harmonious of all the buildings there.

But it was the Community Church which was the problem. The Chapel of the Resurrection had been completed in 1912, the flanking chapels of the Ascension and the Holy Cross in 1914 and 1924. The latter was largely financed out of a legacy donated by Fitzgerald. Its Turkish carpet had been sent by Bell from the Black Sea. But only one bay of the great nave had been completed. With its temporary walls and roof it looked like an outsize garden shed inexplicably stranded on the hill-side. All over the country there were unfinished churches begun in the days of Edwardian opulence; building costs had more than doubled between 1914 and 1920. Yet a CR brochure of 1921 still confidently asserted that if churchpeople really believed in the Religious Life, CR could have an abbey church rivalling those of the middle ages. In 1930 Victor, who had designed and superintended the erection of many of CR's buildings in Africa, told the brethren that Tapper's plan was hopelessly grandiose and expensive. The vault would be higher than that of Durham Cathedral; the nave would be longer than Gloucester and wider than Westminster Abbey; the total length would exceed that of Ripon; the total area would be almost that of Rochester. The whole scheme would cost something like £200,000. The upkeep would be phenomenal. (Victor had always preferred Temple Moore's rejected design.) So it was decided to shorten the nave by one bay, to use brick not stone and to omit the upper ambulatories. Instead of the nave being thirty feet higher than the Chapel of the Resurrection, it was to be virtually the same height. But how was even this more modest scheme to be paid for?

Then on Sunday 17 January 1932 Charles Gore died, a few days before his seventy-ninth birthday. Frere sang a Solemn Requiem in London. A few brethren (including Bickersteth) disapproved of the subsequent cremation. To Halifax the cremation was yet another of Gore's betrayals of Catholicism. 'I could shake the life out of him with my own hands', he exclaimed inappropriately. Fitzgerald, who had once worried about the effect of cremation on the astral body, lovingly brought the ashes to Mirfield. So at the last Gore returned not to his aristocratic relations, nor to Westminster Abbey (which offered him interment), nor to Oxford where he had spent thirty years, nor to Birmingham where he had come into his own as a bishop, but to a West Riding mill-town in which he had never spent more than a few days at a time.

At Radley, after much pain he had discovered he was unable to relate to the ordinary people he longed for the church to include. Despite his passionate commitment to fellowship, international, national and eucharistic, he was unable to live in the Community he had founded. Nevertheless, his choice of Mirfield as his resting place was a clear, if poignant sign of his commitment to the kenosis of Christ – poignant because he had been unable to express self-emptying in the form he had once hoped. The Whig aristocrat made his final, and characteristically defiant, gesture.

He was buried on his birthday, 22 January. The unfinished church stood out starkly above the valley shrouded in mist. Fitful shafts of winter sunshine pierced the gloom. A watch had been kept overnight at the catafalque on which lay his mitre and purple stole. Archbishop Temple and the Bishop of Wakefield in black copes and linen mitres processed through the crowded church for the Solemn Requiem. The singing of 'Dies Irae' and the Russian Contakion represented the western and eastern traditions of Christianity. Gore had been emphatic about divine judgment: 'The awfulness of death is that it does not change us, but only sets us naked and bare in the presence of the holiness of God.' The casket was lowered into the floor of the Chapel of the Resurrection by Roger Castle and Raymond Raynes, professed a few days previously. (Ironically it was Raynes who later as Superior seemed determined to extirpate Gore's influence from CR.) Over the grave a stone was laid 'CAROLUS GORE, EPISCOPUS, FUNDATOR'. The service ended with Gore's favourite hymn 'Jesus lives!'. As the procession left, the organist, at Gore's request, played the Allegretto from Beethoven's Seventh Symphony. Gore had once described the effect of Beethoven on a man in desolation and despair: 'It conveyed to him reassurance which nothing else could convey.'[25]

'No religious leader since Spurgeon and Newman has so distinctly impressed the English mind as Bishop Gore', commented the *Observer*. An old friend recalled his love for two passages of poetry:

> Yea, as my swift days near their goal,
>   'Tis all that I implore:
> In life and death a chainless soul,
>   With courage to endure. (Emily Bronte: 'The Old Stoic')

> Deep in the general heart of men
>   His power survives. (Wordsworth: 'Memorials of a Tour in Scotland',
>   1803 – III)

Both passages say much about Gore's moral strenuousness, his longing for freedom, his stoicism, his natural theology. But one must also record his last visit to the London House a month before he died when he read to the brethren from *1066 and All That* and laughed so much he had to keep stopping to recover.

Six months after Gore's death, with no sign of any proposal for a memorial to him, CR appealed for £50,000 to complete the Community church as the Gore memorial. To those who complained it was too grandiose, CR replied that Gore was of equal stature with Keble and Pusey who were commemorated by sizeable buildings at Oxford. But the Appeal was an embarrassing flop. Why did an appeal for £50,000 raise only £4,690 in four years? One reason was that it was launched in the middle of an economic crisis which hit the North (which contained many CR supporters) particularly hard. Did it also seem outrageous to commemorate an exponent of social justice with a huge monastic church at a time when even unemployment pay had been cut? Moreover Gore's memory had faded. He had alienated the advanced Anglo-Catholics. Talbot himself had grave misgivings because CR seemed to be exploiting Gore's memory for its own advantage. South African brethren feared that money which they needed was instead being spent on the church.

Because of the failure of the Appeal, further modifications of the design were mooted. Ben Roderick of Aberdare who had designed the striking Church of the Resurrection, Ely, Cardiff (1934) in Byzantine style influenced by Tapper's designs for Mirfield, was asked to produce a cheaper version of Tapper's plans for Mirfield itself. But Tapper's death in September 1935 put everything back into the melting pot. In 1936 his son, Michael Tapper, offered to take over though he felt awed by the task. Despite doubts about his abilities, CR accepted his offer. Victor was a tower of strength as clerk of works. When he returned to Africa in 1938 Shearburn took over his role. Tapper's new plans, exhibited in 1936, envisaged a massive Byzantine dome above the high altar. They showed a west front much as it is today, modern, yet not modernistic, powerful without being threatening, yet lacking an organic connection with the nave which (as built) is banal within and without. The clerestory windows which were to have been Byzantine were unfortunately replaced by portholes punched monotonously in the walls. Today as one sits in Michael Tapper's work one faces the earlier work of his father; the one is building; the other is architecture. In July 1936 the new venture was blessed. Times had changed and there were no daily prayers with the workmen as in 1911, nor were they offered 'temperance drinks'. But in 1937 thirty-six workmen were entertained to dinner. Crises delayed completion. It took six months to shift 6,000 tons of rock and soil to hollow out the crypt. Brethren and students turned out in the afternoons to wield sledge-hammers and load the horse-drawn carts. Then in July 1936 Tapper discovered that the rock under the western piers would not carry a dome. Why it was asked, had there been no preliminary survey? It took two months to reinforce the foundations with concrete and steel rods. A dome was now out of the question. Perhaps a modest lantern might be added at a later date? Victor looked on the bright side – a dome would have been very expensive to maintain in the West Riding climate. The various altars were dedicated to a judicious mixture of almost entirely male saints. Frere proposed that one altar should be dedicated to Holy Matrons and Virgins. He also raised the hackles of Biggart, Shearburn, Symonds and others by proposing that ashes should be interred in one of the chapels. Both proposals failed. Walter Tapper, who erected fine screens at York Minster and elsewhere, had proposed screens at Mirfield. His son designed one for behind the high altar, but it was never erected. Furnishings were given in memory of Bickersteth and Longridge who died in 1936.

Frere completed drafting the consecration service for the new church a few days before he died on 2 April 1938. His natural self might have retired to the warmth of South Africa or the rich musical life of a South German city, but as he once said 'I regard sitting on the least comfortable chair as *very* important'. However, he was allowed to bring his gramophone and wireless from Truro. CR did not possess a wireless so when Edward VIII abdicated, brethren crowded into Frere's room to hear the King's speech emerging from a large horn on which hung a photograph of Cardinal Mercier. Apart from listening to records, his only other concession to retirement was to grow a beard. Among those who enjoyed his liturgy lectures at the College was Ronald Jasper, later the chief architect of the *Alternative Service Book*. Frere, like Gore, was cremated. Hunkin, Frere's Modernist successor at Truro, generously came for the funeral. 'Thank you so much for coming', Talbot wrote, 'I hope our mediaevalism did not vex your righteous soul.'

Archbishop Temple presided at the consecration of the church on 6 July 1938. The large congregation included Gore's relatives. The tombs of Gore and Frere flank the high altar. Behind Gore's tomb, St Benedict's altar represents western monasticism. On it stand candlesticks given to E. S. Talbot by his fellow contributors to *Lux Mundi* when he became Bishop of Rochester in 1895. Behind Frere's tomb, St Basil's altar represents eastern monasticism. Sister Joanna, a Russian nun from Paris, came to paint a triptych of icons for the altar given by the Fellowship of St Alban and St Sergius. On either side are St Basil and St Seraphim. In the centre is Christ in majesty; before she painted his face she made a day's retreat. The triptych was blessed by a priest of the Romanian church in April 1939.

When the church was completed, Talbot felt both relief and unease. He tried to reassure those at the London Festival in 1938 that CR was still 'lightly perched on the branch' and was able 'at any moment to cut loose and to take flight'. This was an illusion. The erection of this huge church was more like dropping anchor. Buildings and institutions begin by expressing life, but end up determining it. The completion of the church pushed CR, at any rate at Mirfield, towards the Benedictine end of the monastic spectrum. Nor was Talbot in private altogether sanguine about CR itself. He was concerned that so many came to CR at an age when, for example, the acquisition of languages was difficult. Perhaps an amalgamation of CR and SSM was necessary to create a really strong Order? 'They get the youth.' The Community had grown from 40 in 1920 to 62 in 1938, but it still had to refuse the vast majority of invitations to new work.

Talbot held office for eighteen consecutive years – too long. In 1939 he wondered whether to step down, but he was counselled otherwise. He wanted Carl Runge to succeed him, but Runge was not widely favoured. The result was the worst of all possible worlds. In 1940 in two ballots Horner received almost twice as many votes as Talbot. Talbot withdrew and Horner was elected. Aged sixty-seven he could only be a benign caretaker. Shortly after Talbot broke down and had to have a prolonged rest. In 1943 CR made a decisive break with the past and elected Raymond Raynes. Unlike all previous Superiors he had spent nearly all his professed life in South Africa. So in the next two chapters we turn to the history of CR in Africa.

8

Pioneering in South Africa

In March 1903 Nash, Fuller and Thomson arrived in Johannesburg to pioneer CR work in South Africa.[1]

Modern South Africa has developed out of the interaction, often bloody, between blacks and whites, British and Dutch. After the British took over Cape Colony in 1795 tensions grew between Dutch residents and British rulers. During the Great Trek (1834–40) 15,000 Dutch farmers went north to escape anglicization and British racial policies, and established their own states in the interior. The Dutch Reformed Church severed its links with Holland and established its own seminary at Stellenbosch, and so protected itself from liberal theology. Though all the various churches reflected racial divisions, it alone created totally distinct churches for the various races and a theological justification for racial separation. The Afrikaners (as the Dutch became known) formulated a potent, populist theology of their own history based on the Old Testament, in which the Great Trek became the Exodus; the blacks, the Philistines; the Battle of Blood River, the sealing of the covenant; Transvaal and Orange Free State, the Promised Land. But the attitudes of all whites to missionaries was ambivalent. They wanted missionaries to 'civilize' the blacks to make them a more tractable labour force, but fiercely resisted any attempts to educate them 'above their station'.

The conflicts between British and Afrikaner, exacerbated by the discoveries of diamonds and gold, came to a tragic climax in the Anglo-Boer War (1899–1902). Fundamentally the war was caused by Britain's attempt to establish supremacy over the gold producing areas ruled by the Boers whose outlook was more agrarian than capitalist. The bitterness of defeat for the Boers was deepened by the sufferings caused by the concentration camps and the burning of their farms.

The brethren arrived less than a year after the signing of the peace treaty in May 1902. In 1902–3 the British government and Lord Milner, the High Commissioner, helped by his 'kindergarten' of young British administrators, concentrated on the reconstruction of industry and agriculture and the reconciliation of the two white communities. The need for reconciliation with the other seventy-eight per cent of the population, which supplied all the cheap labour, was ignored. The British, intent on securing the goodwill of the Boers, granted self-government to the conquered republics in 1907, paving the way for the inauguration of the self-governing Union of South Africa of 1910. The Mines and Works Act (1911) restricted skilled work to whites. The Natives Land Act (1913) prohibited blacks from purchasing land in 'white areas'. The movements of blacks were controlled by pass laws. The creation of what was known later as the African National Congress in 1912 and of the National Party in 1914 expressed the growing polarization between black and white. After 1918 (as in 1902) blacks vainly hoped their war service would be rewarded, but post-war governments imposed further harsh restrictions. Many British continued to live in imperialist enclaves. Alan Paton, born to British parents in Pietermaritzburg in 1903, did not hear Afrikaans until he was twenty-one. Britain was still 'home'. In his school hall plaques commemorated those killed in wars against Zulus *and* Boers.

The Anglican church in South Africa remained inchoate until Robert Gray arrived as Bishop of Cape Town in 1848. The judgment in the Colenso case in 1865 in effect secured the independence of the South African church from Crown and State. Colenso, remembered for his liberal attitudes to the Bible, also fought courageously for the rights of the Zulus. Ironically for Anglo-Catholics it was Colenso, the erastian and liberal, who was the first Anglican leader in South Africa to stand with the blacks. Colenso, influenced by F. D. Maurice, took a benign view of African religion, and wanted to include as much as possible of it in Christianity.[2] By contrast, Zonnebloem College in Cape Town, founded by Gray for the sons of African chiefs, took them out of their culture to anglicize them. Much missionary work, including that of CR, followed Gray and took Africans out of their culture into new Christian communities.

No African clergy were present at the first Provincial Synod (1870) at which the Church of the Province was constituted. Nor after three quarters of a century of work was anyone there who had actually been born in South Africa. The Anglican church continued to look like an imperial importation, not least during the Anglo-Boer War. W. W. Jones, the Archbishop, tried to maintain a degree of impartiality, but under pressure from Kitchener agreed to preach to 6,000 troops and a crowd of several thousand at a special service in Pretoria when war ended. Before the service Kitchener distributed VCS and other decorations. Part of Cape Town Cathedral was built as a memorial to the British dead. Lieutenant-General Lord Methuen, fresh from the war, told a London meeting of the Cape Town Diocesan Association in 1903 that the church and army had worked 'hand in hand . . . let the Dutch realize that . . . no Empire that this world had ever produced, could compare with that of Great Britain. (Hear, hear).'

'England without an empire! Can you conceive it? England in that case would not be the England we love', exclaimed Joseph Chamberlain, former Colonial

Secretary, in 1906. The British churches celebrated the Empire as a means of spreading the Gospel, civilization and education. Many Christian socialists shared this vision; they justified the war as a defence of black rights. One of the early 'Manuals for the Million' edited by Bull was entitled 'The Church and the Child Races'. But the 1908 Lambeth Conference condemned separate churches for racial groups. In 1930 the Lambeth bishops criticized the Anglo-Saxon races for racial superiority. Colonies could only be defended if they aimed to share government with 'the subject race'.

In order to evangelize, missionaries had to learn the language, culture and religion of each country. Because Africans were much easier to convert than Buddhists, Muslims, Hindus or Jews, this confirmed missionary opinion that African religion was 'primitive' and therefore not worth much study. Among the minority of Christians who followed Maurice or *Lux Mundi*, there was potentially a new sensitivity to other faiths. But such sensitivity seemed incompatible with evangelism. Much more characteristic were the popular hymns used to express and excite missionary fervour, like 'From Greenland's icy mountains', 'Thy Kingdom come, O God' and 'Fling out the banner!' all of which portrayed other faiths and cultures as darkness and ignorance. Queen Victoria after the Indian mutiny in 1857 issued a proclamation disclaiming any right to impose Christianity upon Indians. No such proclamation was issued for Africa.

Though the Anglican church was independent of the state, at the turn of the century the leadership of both was intimately linked. Frere's relative, Sir Bartle Frere, neighbour to the Gore and Holland families in Wimbledon, had been High Commissioner. Milner had overlapped with Gore at Balliol. Lord Selborne, who succeeded Milner in 1905, was a keen supporter, with his wife, of CR's work. He had been associated with Gore as Vice-President of the Church Reform League and when he returned to England, he became a key figure in the central councils of the church. Alfred Lyttelton, Colonial Secretary 1903–5, was Keble Talbot's uncle and had been a member with Gore of the Synthetic Society. Herbert Gladstone, the first Governor-General, was a cousin of Keble's mother and had given a donation to the Leeds Hostel. General Sir Neville Lyttelton, Kitchener's successor, was Keble's uncle and had been at Eton with Scott Holland. It was Sir Neville who laid the foundation stone of the church at Ladysmith, built as a memorial to the 3,000 British servicemen who had died in the siege. Neville Talbot, who had served in the army during the war and had defended the concentration camps, became Bishop of Pretoria in 1920. When Michael Furse (Bishop of Pretoria 1909–20) became Archdeacon of Johannesburg in 1903, he discovered that the Governor of the Transvaal was the brother of his friend Algernon Lawley, an old Etonian like Furse. Lawley had been Nash's vicar at Bethnal Green. The first Dean of Johannesburg was married to the daughter of a former Governor-General. Johannesburg Cathedral seemed the right place to commemorate the British dead of the Anglo-Boer War, Lord Milner, George V, George VI and Elizabeth II. (Recent additions are more indigenous.) Consider that the Mission of Help (1904) originated from a remark made by Cecil Rhodes to the wife of the British High Commissioner.[3] The forty clergy who came from England to rouse the parishes after the devastation of war, were entertained by various governors, and travelled by special railway coach with Joseph Chamberlain's ex-chef to cook for them. Bickersteth and Fitzgerald from Mirfield and Scott Holland were among the missioners. Holland was a bit defensive about all the red carpets – 'we were pretty well rolled-up inside the administration' – but had not St Paul accepted the hospitality of the Governor of Malta and preached successfully to a proconsul? Bickersteth explained to Africans that though the mission was not for them, they would benefit as it would make their masters more kind and lead them to conduct family prayers.

So it was not surprising that when bishops from the 1920s began to criticize South African racial policies, Afrikaners were dismissive of what they called the 'English church'. It seemed like a continuing agency of British imperialism, always interfering. Its Anglo-Catholicism offended their protestantism. They accused it of being hypocritical, for few white Anglicans followed the lead of their bishops. When Keble Talbot visited his brother the Bishop of Pretoria in 1921, he was horrifed to hear about the violent storm created by whites when a white priest in Pietersburg allowed an African to receive communion in a white church, even though he had knelt at the back and received last. But church leaders knew that the work of the church depended financially upon white congregations and shared many of the assumptions of white paternalism. So they were unlikely to take radical action in such cases. There was justice in the Afrikaners' accusation that too many bishops came from condescending Oxbridge, seldom bothered to learn Afrikaans, denounced South African racial policies and then after a few years returned 'home' to another job or to retire. It was not until 1974 that the first South African-born Archbishop (Burnett) was elected.

CR in Johannesburg

What drew CR to South Africa? Gore believed passionately in a multiracial and multicultural Catholic church. From the beginning CR had hoped to make some contribution to the church overseas. In 1900 Gore, anguished by the war, urged the clamant needs of South Africa. The Rev. J. T. Darragh, who had been in charge of the Rand area since 1887, suggested a house in Johannesburg. In 1902 the closure of the Westminster House and the end of the war cleared the way. In March 1902 William Carter,[4] Bishop of Zululand, a member of SR and of the original group at Pusey, who was about to become Bishop of Pretoria, asked Frere whether CR might work in Johannesburg, then in the Pretoria diocese. When Carter moved to Pretoria he inherited a divided and demoralized diocese almost the size of Great Britain, with only 25 clergy, many of whom were elderly. In some areas its work had been suspended by the war. In eighteen months the number of clergy increased to 63, twelve new districts were opened and seven new churches built. Carter, a former slum priest, tartly pointed out that the Transvaal spent more on Pretoria zoo than on African education. Carter hoped CR might work among managers and miners on the Rand. He had discussed the needs of the area with both Milner and the Director of Native Affairs; the church had done almost nothing in the mines; there was only one 'native church' in Johannesburg; yet work among whites was of even greater importance because their character so affected the Africans; a CR House would be a spiritual and intellectual centre. Frere responded warmly but stressed that CR could only undertake work compatible with community life.

During the summer CR received advice and collected information. 'Johannesburg is a gorgeous place' wrote one priest 'I don't think that there would be much roughing it . . . it is full of electric lights, etc. But it is dry and you occasionally can only get a bottle of soda-water to have your bath in.' Others suggested that cool drinks could be ensured on the journey by hanging water bottles outside the railway carriage, that everything was expensive apart from wine and tobacco and that money and pleasure were the two gods. The principal army chaplain (a member of SR) wrote that with the diocese in low water there could be no greater boon than to have a CR House which would 'set a standard of work and life that is almost unknown in this very commercially-minded population'.

There were already several Anglican communities in South Africa: the Cowley Fathers and All Saints sisters were in Cape Town, the East Grinstead sisters in Johannesburg. In 1902 the Society of the Sacred Mission took over the remnants of the Society of St Augustine at Modderport, which in 1867 had been the first Anglican overseas community. Three women's communities had been founded in South Africa between 1874 and 1887. In 1903 the Wantage sisters (CSMV) began work in Pretoria. Carter used to say that the best thing he had ever done for the Transvaal was to invite CR and CSMV to come to the Pretoria diocese.

The three brethren landed at Cape Town in January 1903, and spent a few days with the Cowley Fathers before going to Pretoria to stay with the bishop until their house was secured by Darragh, an Irish priest of exceptional energy and organizing ability. Less than a fortnight after arriving in Johannesburg in 1887, he had laid the foundation stone of St Mary's church. Johannesburg was then still a collection of tents with a few corrugated iron buildings. It had only been founded in December 1886 when the first building plots were sold.

By March the brethren had settled into a four bedroom corrugated iron house at 10 Sherwell Street. Originally a farm house, it had latterly been an orphanage. Central for the city and the Rand, the railway station was only ten minutes' walk away, and there was a good tram service. But an iron building, an oven in summer and an ice-box in winter in an unhealthy part of the city, was not ideal. Other brethren kept arriving, so by 1922 about twenty (nearly half of the Community) were based in South Africa or Southern Rhodesia, an indication of the depth of CR's commitment to Africa.

William Plomer, the writer, described the city where he spent part of his boyhood:

> Standing more than five thousand feet above sea-level in a limpid, sun-baked, rarefied atmosphere, the city . . . had been conjured out of the waving grass by greed for gold. Seen from a distance it differed from others by the prevalence of whitish mounds . . . the excreta of gold-grubbing . . . Beneath them man-made shafts extended for three or four miles vertically into the earth, and in these mines, a single one of which might employ ten thousand men, a large population, mainly black, toiled hard and sometimes dangerously for gold. The black men had come to the Rand not because they wanted to but because they had to earn money to pay their taxes and could not earn it at home . . . Arriving from all parts of southern Africa to seek work, the unskilled black migrants of many tribes came as strangers, uneducated and bewildered, to the white man's new, urban, industrial world . . . On arrival they were obliged by law to report to a 'pass office' . . .

Plomer's father worked in the Johannesburg pass office. The family lived near CR.

> The older residential parts of the town, such as Doornfontein near which we lived, already had atmosphere. Quick-growing cypress, mimosa and eucalyptus groves were already tall and shady; they lent an air of age and mystery to villas and small mansions built in the Nineties by newly rich German Jews, Scotch engineers, speculators in real estate, successful doctors or tarts.[5]

Nash too enjoyed the cosmopolitan city with its fine shops and buildings, and the policemen in London uniforms directing the traffic.

The most vexed question for CR, as for the church, was how to relate the work among the two races.[6] Nash believed that it was essential to keep both types of work together, for the prejudice against black Christians was very strong. Brethren invited whites to share evensong and supper with black catechists under training, but the whites did not want blacks in their churches. In practice parish churches were for whites; mission churches for blacks. In 1906 Carter opposed the creation of assistant bishops for black work: bishops wanted to be fathers-in-God to black and white alike. But some of the black as well as white clergy advocated a specialization of ministry according to race. Henry Alston wrote in December 1904:

To me it is very sad the native and the white work being separated. I have not been here long enough to pass an opinion upon it, but it does seem to be against the spirit of Christianity. Of course it is quite obvious that the natives just emerging from savagery cannot be treated in the same way as whites, there must be restrictions. There must be in many ways separations. But when they have become Christians it does seem to me that the altar is one place where they certainly can meet, but it is not so.

In 1962 the church's policy of separate development was stoutly defended by Alban Winter in his survey of sixty years of CR African work to which he had made an outstanding contribution for thirty-nine years.[7] The still mostly heathen Africans needed priests who knew how to convert them and build up their faith. Africans wanted more colourful worship in their own languages. They needed their own organization within the church so that they could develop their own leaders. The policy was vindicated (Winter believed) by the emergence of black catechists, then deacons, then priests and now bishops. The tragedy was that Winter's arguments were used by others as a cover for virulent racialism. Yet liberals who recoil from any talk of separation do not reflect that some blacks (and feminists) have used similar arguments themselves. An old black priest said in conversation that he owed everything to CR. He had been baptized by Latimer Fuller, encouraged to go to school by Aidan Cotton, trained as a teacher at Grace Dieu (started by Fuller), trained as a catechist by CR and later ordained, and deeply influenced in his ministry by Raymond Raynes. CR did not make us dependent, he said, we were weak and needed assistance.

Yet it was easy to fall into condescending ways. Nash wrote (*CRQ* CD 1903): 'The Catechists' names are Matthew, Titus, Stephen, Michael and Apollos. Their surnames I must leave to an expert like Latimer. I can only say they generally seem to begin with "M".' The unwillingness of whites to pronounce surnames gave Africans a truncated and subordinate identity. For many years brethren called African servants 'boys'. Francis Hill, who devoted thirty-five years to black Christians, referred to a young black man who had been 'spoiled' by coming to England as a military servant: 'I must try to keep my eye on this boy [sic] and judiciously sit upon him occasionally.' (*CRQ* JB 1911)

CR from early days made stands for black rights. Fuller wrote (*CRQ* JB 1912) of the Africans' desire for self-government and freedom from interference by whites. But he believed the church must be under strong white control. Biggart (*CRQ* LD 1914) described the current strikes. South Africa needed a society like CSU. Blacks had to live under great restrictions, were not allowed on trams, needed permits to travel by train or ride bicycles in town, and had to be indoors after 9 p.m. In 1921 twelve brethren sent a letter to the *Rand Daily Mail* protesting against the injustice of the 'Native Poll Tax'. Francis Hill explained (*CRQ* JB 1924) why brethren often attended court when Africans they knew were on trial: 'there is so much injustice to natives in the courts.' A CR pamphlet lamented that promises that land would be made available to Africans remained unfulfilled. 'They have no right to buy, hire or acquire interest in Land, except in areas which are not yet defined, and except, of course, in the Native Reserves which are already overcrowded.' Yet whites were free to buy land in black areas. The repeal of the Natives Land Act would 'remove a great source of native unrest'. (By this grossly unjust Act, whites who were twenty-one per cent of the population had received ninety-two per cent of the land.) When Francis Hill relinquished his role as Archdeacon of Native Missions in 1938, African clergy paid tribute to his work for those made homeless by the Act. After his death in 1942 an African teacher wrote how grateful she and others were for Hill's annual resolution at synod against the Act, which he never gave up though to some the gesture seemed futile. The number and gravity of protests by C R brethren grew over the years. Yet the daily life of C R was a continual protest, for brethren treated members of otherwise despised races as fellow human beings. When a white C R Father in his cassock raised his hat to a black domestic servant in the street, her little son was incredulous. The C R Father was Trevor Huddleston, the little boy Desmond Tutu.

During its first fifty years in South Africa C R's work was astonishingly varied. It is amazing that so much was accomplished by such a comparatively small group. But it contained some very remarkable individuals. Through them many, of all races, experienced the power of the resurrection to bring new life and hope.

Transvaal

Fuller was given charge of African work in the Pretoria diocese (the size of Italy) for nine years until he became Bishop of Lebombo. He made his first trek in April 1903, much of it on foot. Many of the villages had not been visited since before the war. He prepared people for baptism, heard confessions, dealt with disciplinary cases and gave communion. Each year he spent about one hundred and fifty nights in African huts. In 1906 he arranged the purchase of a farm at Pietersburg, and with his own hands sank a well, built a dam and put up the first buildings of a training college for African teachers, Grace Dieu. One of his great achievements was to make Africans realize that if they were to become self-reliant with their own ministry, they must pay for their own churches and clergy and gradually take over administrative responsibility. In 1909 he was appointed Archdeacon of Native Missions. He could be tough with other religious groups. In his *Romance of a South African Mission* (1908) he told how he came across a group of former Lutherans. 'So I began to explain what the Church is, when it began; showed how long it had been the holy Church before Luther was even born; how by its standard, Lutherans are far from the truth . . .' In the early days C R was responsible for taking services in some eighty places in the Transvaal. At first churches were looked after by catechists, many trained at the college in Sherwell Street. Some were ordained as permanent deacons but they became dissatisfied when others were priested, so the idea of permanent deacons was abandoned.

Rand

In 1922 the diocese of Johannesburg was carved out of the southern part of the Pretoria diocese, so removing the northern Transvaal from CR's care. CR now concentrated on the area which it had been given in 1903 – 60 miles across, and 40 miles from north to south, with Johannesburg as the centre: an area of 2,500 square miles with a black population of some 80,000.

By the autumn of 1903 CR had made contact with twenty-three settled congregations, had started ministering to Africans in twelve mines and to train catechists. By 1923 the Rand Mission was working among 200,000 Africans in 80 church centres with 6 CR priests, 8 black priests, 10 black deacons, 48 catechists and 70 teachers. Francis Hill's business training prior to Oxford was invaluable in administering this huge complex venture. By the 1920s half the world's gold came from the Transvaal, and most of this from the Rand. Digging out this gold were 200,000 Africans, coming and going at the rate of 40,000 a month, recruited not only from South Africa but also from bordering territories, separated for a year at a time from their families, plunged into the complex life of a community feverishly pursuing wealth. At first it was difficult for brethren to obtain access to the mine compounds. Managers feared outside influences. But gradually brethren won their trust and many assisted with materials to build churches, schools or meeting rooms.

Herbert Bennett gave himself to the work of the Mission for thirty years. Originally a Church Army officer he kept relics of his former ministry in a series of lantern slides each labelled e.g. 'Father come, Mother's drunk'. He was famous for his ability to scrounge materials, so when he approached, mine managers beat a hasty retreat. On one occasion a manager, finding a shed missing, chased him. 'What are you doing pinching my shed?' Bennett with innocent wide-open eyes replied in his high pitched voice: 'You said that I could take all the loose corrugated iron that was lying about.' He arrived at a particular place one Saturday expecting to see the church finished. But he had to put on the roof, make the altar, fit the door and put six windows in ready for the next day. On holiday he thought nothing of doing a 2,300 mile round trip to meet those who had been touched by missioners at the mines, hoping they had become missionaries to their own people. During Lent he would go round the compounds, showing lantern slides, so some 40–50,000 saw something of the gospel each year.

In February 1924 Bennett was sent by the bishop to look after the 10,000 people who had converged on an area near Lichtenburg in the greatest diamond rush in South African history. He cycled over ground which looked as if it had undergone an artillery barrage and found conditions appalling. Drunks staggered about in the rain and mud, enteric fever was rife and 400 children were running wild. He appealed for tents, books, footballs, cooking utensils, primus stoves and an organ. What he managed to achieve single handed in five weeks of such unremitting work that sometimes he had no time to eat, was 'phenomenal' commented the press. Through the press he also conducted campaigns against the ill-treatment of Africans in the mines and against the courts for dealing leniently with whites convicted of serious assaults. He was impelled to speak on behalf of 'the voiceless'. 'The sun has long set on the day when natives were "kept in their place" by fear.'

Finance was a constant headache. By the 1920s Hill wanted to improve priests' houses and to replace old iron and wooden churches with brick buildings. One African mine congregation gave £150 out of wages of £4 a month for a new church. The mine company, told what the congregation had given, donated £100; C R gave £50, diocese £25, the Africans another £80. Blacks were only just getting used to a money economy and believed that since C R was white it had unlimited funds. By the mid 1920s it became clear that the pioneering days were drawing to a close for the Rand Mission. Between 1926 and 1930 the work was gradually passed over into the hands of black clergy under the diocese, but Hill continued as 'Director of Native Missions'.

By the turn of the century African Christians could choose between three types of church: one of the black churches controlled by white missionaries such as those provided by the Dutch Reformed Church; a black section of a multi-racial church in which there was a distant hope of eventual equality and responsibility; an independent black church in which Africans could exercise responsibility, develop their own style of worship and belief and which often synthesized elements from both Christian and African religions. In 1904 there were three independent black churches with 25,000 members; by 1970 there were over 3,000 with some 3.5 million members. The independent churches became a focus of black identity among urbanized and detribalized Africans in revolt against the white-dominated mainstream churches.

In its early years in South Africa C R made contact with the black 'Order of Ethiopia'. The name recalled the claim of the ancient church of Ethiopia to be the original indigenous African church. In 1892 Mangena Mokone had left Methodism and created the 'Ethiopian Church'. Another Methodist minister, James Dwane, joined in 1894 and soon became leader. Dwane applied to the Anglican church for ordination and recognition of his group within it. In 1900 this group was recognized by the Archbishop as the Order of Ethiopia. Dwane was appointed Provincial, made deacon and later priested. In 1907 C R was asked to look after the Order in the diocese. C R, which had some degree of independence from the structures, and was committed to a black ministry, felt a natural sympathy with the Order. In 1983, after over eighty years of waiting, the Order received its first bishop, Sigqibo Dwane, grandson of the founder and trained for the ministry by CR. In 1976 he had become the first Principal of St Peter's Theological College who was not white or a member of CR. The history of the Order shows that the pressure for separate development came from blacks as well as whites. Likewise many Africans have found it easier to join black religious communities rather than those (like CR) with an English ethos.

Training for Ministry

Between 1903 and 1977 CR trained the majority of black Anglican clergy in South Africa, including Desmond Tutu. This has been one of its most remarkable and enduring achievements.

Hitherto there had been no systematic training for an African ministry, though there had been various small-scale ventures. In 1905 when the first catechists were made deacon after training by CR, there were still only seven African deacons in the Pretoria diocese, and no African priests. At Sherwell Street there was the closest possible connection between the worship of the Community and College. In 1904 the diocese agreed to buy the house next door. On this site CR built a bookshop, and behind the house a schoolroom and dining room for students and a two-storied dormitory. There fifteen to twenty students could be accommodated, and there was room for a night school. Each student cost 7s.6d a week of which the student found 2s.6d. By 1906 forty-five students had passed through the college; seven of them had been ordained as deacons, the others had become catechists.

Students were expected to attend Prime at 6.55 a.m., Mass, mid-day meditation, Evensong and Compline. No smoking was permitted before 10.30 a.m. Only English was spoken in the mornings. Basic education in reading, writing, arithmetic and drill preceded what sounds to have been a highly academic ordination syllabus: Bible, early church history, Prayer Book, pastoral theology, the Constitution and Canons of the Church of the Province, doctrine, the three creeds and Thirty-Nine Articles. Some services were conducted by students in their own languages. On Sundays students shared in the evangelistic work in the mine compounds. They paid for part of their keep by housework, printing and work in the bookshop. The first African priest to be trained by CR was ordained in 1910.

By 1920 there were thirty-two black clergy in the diocese, of whom fifteen were priests. Apart from a few permanent deacons the others would return after a few years to train for priesthood. All but one had been trained by CR at St Peter's College. CR had also trained 150 catechists and in 1920 half the students were being trained for that ministry. They continued to be trained at the college until 1937 when separate provision was made for them as educational standards in the college had risen. During vacations the college was used for retreats and refresher courses. The staff sent out Bible study and sermon notes to its former students.

As general educational standards among Africans had risen, in 1922 entrance levels for ordinands were raised, even though for a time this reduced numbers. Some brethren thought too much emphasis was being placed upon academic standards. The best opportunity for blacks to gain higher education was through training as teachers, and most of the better educated ordinands were ex-teachers. Since most of these were married, funds had to be provided for their families during training. In 1934 it was decided that the Junior or Teacher's Certificate should become the minimum entrance requirement. The deacons' course was lengthened to three years. In 1938 the first graduates from Fort Hare African College began to arrive. One was Alphaeus Zulu who became the first black bishop – Assistant Bishop of St John's in 1961 and Bishop of Zululand in 1966. In 1941 an anonymous gift of £4,000 was added to existing funds and the size of the college was doubled.

Rosettenville

African women were drawn into Johannesburg to work as domestic servants but white employers often simply provided them with a hut at the bottom of the garden and left them to their own devices. Lady Selborne, wife of the High Commissioner, interested herself in their welfare and in 1907 raised money to provide a deaconess and two women workers to look after both those in the city and those on the farms. Fuller now proposed a further development: the creation of a residential school for the training of black servants. A site was found at Rosettenville, then on the southern edge of the city. When Nash first visited the African church there in 1905, his bicycle was broken into two by the rocky road. The proposed school was greeted with alarmed protests. The lady secretary of the Committee acknowledged in the press that it was 'a most unpopular subject'; but asserted that 'on the correct treatment of the native does our existence as a white nation in South Africa depend'. The 'black peril' was becoming more serious every month, and house-boys were a danger to white women. The girls would not become like those in England who, when educated, thought themselves above housework, for this was to be an 'industrial' school. But even this statement with its many concessions to white prejudice, failed to satisfy critics. A Miss Boyle argued that the employment of black female servants on low wages would force white domestics into destitution or prostitution. Mr Fuller had no understanding of 'the powerful animal instincts of the adolescent Kafir girl'; increasingly whites were opposed to having their children looked after by black servants. But a leading article defended the scheme. It was so much safer for white women to have a black female servant than a male 'whom, to put it bluntly, she can only at her peril have between her and a closed door'. In these exchanges the sexual origin of much white racialism was clear. Lady Selborne's support helped to quell opposition and to raise money, and in

March 1909 she opened the buildings of St Agnes' Industrial Boarding School and the Archbishop blessed them.

Meanwhile at Sherwell Street there were growing numbers of students, more of whom stayed for ordination training, and there was no room for further building. The city centre with its distractions and temptations was not the best place for quiet study. So it was decided to move the whole operation to Rosettenville where there was plenty of space for building. Since it was still sparsely populated, regulations restricting black residence did not apply. From the kopje sixty miles of the Reef were visible. Osmund Victor, College Principal from 1910–16, a short fiery priest with boundless energy, had great architectural skills. In consultation with F. L. H. Fleming (with whom he had been at Denstone College) he planned the new site. The first new buildings were blessed on St Peter's Day 1911. The large campus with its mostly single-storey brick buildings with their pink corrugated iron roofs supported by white colonnades, was arranged in a series of quadrangles, and enhanced by lawns, gardens, flowering bushes, playing fields and a great variety of trees. It remained the headquarters of C R in South Africa until 1986.

An anonymous writer (*CRQ* C D 1924) set the work at Rosettenville within the context of Johannesburg:

> It almost seems as though man had gone out of his way to produce sordidness, misery and materialism, if not for his whole species then certainly for the 'coloured' portion of it. The dull grey monotony of their lives is inexpressible in words, though it may be only the greyness that precedes the dawn, for there are glimmerings of light . . . One of the brightest of these is the school and colony of Rosettenville.

Yet tragically the white population was 'on the whole antagonistic'. Apart from missionaries there were only six or seven members of F R in South Africa. White fears resulted in 'blind cruelty and repression'.

In November 1925 St Peter's church on the campus was dedicated by Bishop Nash. Much of the building work had been done by students. It was another fruit of the architectural co-operation between Fleming and Victor. It served the students and a local black congregation, most of whom were domestics. It was built in a basilican style – this was easier to construct and seemed to Victor the most appropriate style for Africa. A stone from Livingstone's house of the 1840s in Mabotsa, western Transvaal, set in an aisle wall, was a surprising reminder of a great Protestant in a church designed for transcendent worship focussed on the sacrifice of the mass. When Talbot visited it in 1926 he was immensely impressed:

> The church is a real joy. A native woman from the country district on being asked if she liked the church, said 'It isn't a church: it is the gate of heaven.' Wasn't that delightful? And truly it is one of the most worshipful buildings I know. All is nobly

focussed upon the sanctuary, which is approached by six or seven broad steps . . . The baldachino, of a very beautiful blue touched at the base and capitals with gold, and ceiled in passion-red, is of the shape which I have always wished for at Mirfield . . . the services, with all the students, the hostel boys and the St Agnes girls forming the main nucleus of the worshippers, are most devout and reverent . . . The tone of their singing is what that of black velvet would be, could it sing . . . The rich, blurry effect is increased by the fact that . . . they sing to English, Dutch, Sechuana and Sekosa words all at once . . . The fire and emphasis imparted to one's halting words by the interpreter is something wonderful. (*CRQ* JB 1926)

African Schools

CR also made a crucial contribution to the primary and secondary education of Africans. In 1903 there were forty-five state schools for whites in Johannesburg but none for blacks. Whites were either indifferent or actively hostile to African education. The authorities' grudging and parsimonious financial aid reflected this. Until 1903 Transvaal provided no money for African education, and even in 1909 was only giving aid up to Standard III. In 1913 a member of the Provincial Council actually proposed the deletion of all grants from the Transvaal budget. Yet Africans' demands for education were steadily growing. Gradually the Union took over education finance. By the 1920s the government was paying the teachers' salaries, leaving missionaries and parents to pay for buildings and equipment. But there was much overcrowding. Stephen Carter, CR superintendent of schools, instanced one school with 200 children, with 4 teachers in one room 40 by 15 feet. A CR Appeal stated: 'The Government does everything to provide free education for the white children. The natives have largely to fend for themselves. The Missions are their only friends.'

By 1906 CR had established 13 primary schools with 430 children on the Reef and in rural areas. By 1947 there were 44 schools with 10,000 children. From 1921–47 Stephen Carter was superintendent of the whole operation, visiting each one each term, some more frequently. Travelling 500 miles a month by motorcycle and side car (later by car) laden with apparatus he would arrive, examine the children in religious education and discuss school affairs with the staff. Teachers could feel very isolated as they were often the only educated Africans around. Carter had a vast amount of administration – returns of school attendance, requests for grants, innumerable letters about money and buildings. In this for several years he was ably assisted by Nimrod Tubane, an old boy of St Peter's school. Talbot with his customary sensitivity and felicity in July 1946 wrote to Carter:

The other night in Chapter we passed with strong accord a motion of high appreciation and gratitude for the noble, patient and self-effacing work you have done through all these years . . . Much of the work may often have seemed very thankless, and weariness of spirit as well as of body may well have beset you at times. And it has had not the glamour that attaches to some works of the Community . . . For myself I can honestly say that, especially when I was Superior and tried to have in my thoughts and prayers the care of all the Community's works, I found myself continually thanking God that old Stephen was in his place, patiently and unself-regardingly shouldering his heavy responsibilities, without parade or complaint, year in, year out.

In 1947 CR handed over all the schools to the diocese apart from the ones in Rosettenville, Sophiatown and Orlando. It has often seemed right for CR, like other communities, to pioneer a particularly arduous piece of work, then having established it to hand it over to others.

When Alban Winter arrived in 1920, one of the first discussions he heard was about the low educational standards of the ordinands. He therefore proposed the creation of a school at Rosettenville offering primary and secondary education for boys. In 1922 a start was made with six boarders. Three years later secondary education was begun and by the end of 1927 the first two students had been entered for the Junior Certificate, which gave entrance to Fort Hare, the only university for blacks in the Union. At that time St Peter's was the only secondary school for blacks in the Transvaal, but pupils came from all over South Africa and from Southern Rhodesia and Portuguese East Africa. In 1924 a hostel was built with accommodation for 40. In 1931 St Agnes' combined with St Peter's under Winter as headmaster. St Agnes had outlived its usefulness as an industrial school. Girls also now wanted secondary education. CR would have liked to have admitted white children but this would have created such an outcry that the whole venture would have been imperilled. By 1939 there was boarding accommodation for 120 boys and 70 girls. By becoming a boarding school pupils had opportunities for both study and recreation impossible to find in their homes in the townships and rural areas. In 1940 the primary school was moved to Orlando.

Winter was the driving force. The son of an impoverished priest, he left school early and after a tough working life came to ordination through the beneficent Mirfield system which gave him a fresh start in life. Thus he had a personal motive for promoting African education. From his profession in 1920 he devoted the next thirty-nine years to this, first at Rosettenville, then at Penhalonga. His drive was inseparable from an irascible temper. 'He would beard any lion in its den . . . His tactic was usually to make himself so objectionable to the bullied officials concerned, that, in sheer desperation, they would finally agree to his requests' (*CRQ* MD 1971). In 1933 he travelled to America on a grant to investigate black education there. He objected to segregation partly because the 'easy-going' African needed to be roused by 'the dynamic of the west'. In 1935 Winter was succeeded by H. W. Shearsmith, the first lay headmaster. In 1938 nearly half the teachers were Africans. From 1940 D. H. Darling and then Michael Stern presided over this great institution until its tragic closure in 1956 under the Bantu Education Act.

The school was not wholly academic. Daily church attendance and the presence of the brethren and ordinands created a powerful religious atmosphere. Games, dancing and scouting flourished, though for crazy racial reasons African scouts had to be called 'Pathfinders'. The singing was of such a high standard that Columbia's first record of African music included the school choir. Plays and concerts were announced on exuberant posters like this one for May 1939: 'A GRAND CONCERT. Students of St Peter's School, Rosettenville on point of filling you with joy again. THE GREATEST EVENT OF THE YEAR FOR ALL . . . If you miss this, know that you have missed the very cream of life. MAKE HAY WHILE THE SUN SHINES . . .' The Poster ended with a Latin motto.

Osmund Victor in his widely circulated diagram 'The Upward Path of Native Education' explained in 1931 what was being attempted: pupils starting in farms or townships proceeded upwards through mission schools to teacher training or industrial colleges or to Fort Hare. Beyond the hill on which Fort Hare stood, stretched high peaks of 'the mount of Knowledge' behind which the sun rose. This progressivist diagram echoes those on British trade union banners.[8] A CR Appeal brochure of that period asked 'What does the Native Need?' and answered: 'Protection from Exploitation. Christian Education. A place in the Civilization of Christendom'.

Roger Castle, a lay brother, who arrived in 1932 and became Warden of the hostel achieved an extraordinary hold over the boys with his artistic personality, un-English spontaneity, authentic spirituality and total unconventionality. He was amused by the combination of a crucifix, holy picture and an English railway poster in each room, but was intensely moved by the boys' piety:

> There are very few white boys that I know of, who would get out of a warm bed on a freezing morning and go and kneel on his bare knees on a concrete floor for twenty minutes as the minimum in a church whose temperature strongly resembles that of the Union Cold Storage (. . . Of course it's perfectly all right in summer.) But there is a boy who has done that, with very few breaks, for a whole year. There is another small one, who was a waif and was picked up in town by one of the other boys, who, because his name is Stephen, knelt in front of the Blessed Sacrament on the eve of his birthday, in the position he imagined St Stephen was in when he was stoned. And this in a dark church, after Compline, quite alone . . . After Compline every evening more than a quarter of the whole population stays behind to do its own private praying. (*CRQ* MD 1934)

He added: 'I hear that ours is the only institution in the land where a European eats with his pupils.' He developed an art department and persuaded artist friends to give lessons. Rumour suggested the department was partly financed by a friend's night-club takings.

Castle came of a part-Jewish family engaged in ship breaking and timber. Educated by governesses and tutors, his knowledge of literature and art was prodigious. He spoke French, Dutch and German. After running away from home he sold lemonade on a Rhine steamer, then moved to bohemian Paris where Modigliani, the painter, lived in the flat above. For a time Castle made a living as part of a music hall act. After the war (in which he won the MC) he taught at Leominster Grammar School, living in a gypsy caravan in the station yard, which, drawn by a horse called Virgin, took him round Wales in the holidays. He went on to teach in Jersey and then South Africa where he met CR. His arrival at Mirfield in 1929 forced CR to think again about lay brothers. He was, like Sydenham Hoare, clearly an educated gentleman, but despite pressure he refused to be ordained. In this clerical society he had the stamina and character to stand up for his own distinct vocation (in which he had Talbot's support). He was the only lay brother until a second was professed in 1940. Winter and Castle were so very different that the eirenic Talbot wrote to Victor the Provincial in 1932: 'do your best to oil the bearings so that they don't get hot'. Though Castle could be extremely tough on miscreants, he had an immediate sympathy for the oppressed. Returning from Africa, with CR's permission he stopped in Spain for a time to help the refugees from Franco and was appalled by the poverty of the people in contrast with the riches of the church. In 1947 he wrote about South Africa:

> I went to the squatters' townships – Moroka where they shot the policeman. I can't begin to tell you how frightful it was. Acres and acres of sacking hovels with no water and no sanitation, and no amenities of any sort. Pits dug right outside the doors (or rather gaps in the sacking) for latrines . . . Dust blowing, flies everywhere, litter and hatred.

His obituarist wrote: 'I know no one of whom it could be more truly said that where he went, life and hope began to spring afresh, and lives were actually and visibly changed.' (*CRQ* MD 1971)

Students went on from St Peter's to become doctors, nurses, politicians, teachers, academics, administrators, priests. The 'Black Eton' (as it was known) deeply influenced Es'kia (Ezekiel) Mphahlele who was at St Peter's 1935–7. Senior to him were Joseph Mokoena, later Professor at Fort Hare, and Oliver Tambo, later President of the ANC. Lucas Mangope, also at St Peter's, by contrast became President of the puppet state of Bophuthatswana. Mphahlele is now one of South Africa's leading academics and a distinguished novelist. 'It was very much a high class institution' he said in conversation, with 'a climate of real scholarship'. Black and white teachers, lay and CR were all devoted. Though pupils had to be especially well behaved living in a white suburb, the discipline was not rigorist. 'We tended to think of the CR Fathers as something special . . . You wouldn't normally think of going to have a chat with any of the Priory people . . . except for Brother Roger . . . Our worlds were quite apart and yet they weren't aloof, but just too busy.' There was 'a laissez-faire attitude towards students discussing politics' unlike other mission schools. But in the 1950s when he was in close touch with Trevor Huddleston and Martin Jarrett-Kerr, he felt their political activities did not get much backing from other brethren. The drawbacks of St Peter's were typical of mission schools (he said): you came to get through the syllabus with flying colours and then were supposed to go out and serve your own people.

> [Missionaries] come to a situation where they think that they can do some good. They think of uplifting people and not interacting with them . . . The idea that they came to receive did not exist. That could have developed much later. They came to uplift, they were doing you a favour and that's why you were not allowed to talk back and say how certain things hurt . . . I often felt cheated myself in later years.

But in *Down Second Avenue* (1959), which includes an affectionate portrait of Roger Castle, he wrote about St Peter's: 'For the first time in my life I felt a sense of release.' Mphahlele's point that CR was better at giving than receiving is illustrated by the fact it took thirty-six years for an article by an African to appear in *CR Quarterly* (MD 1939): a schoolboy wrote about prayer but, we note, not about politics or social conditions.

A CR booklet stated in 1944: 'Whereas twenty years ago [the Priory] existed as a somewhat forlorn and lonely group of buildings on the veld with nothing but a few gum trees to keep it company, it is now enveloped by thousands of houses and numberless streets, with their constant stream of traffic.' Now it was surrounded by a white suburb, with racial prejudice ever increasing, the whole operation was under threat. In 1937 a Ratepayers Association demanded that since it was 'a Native Priory' it should move. In 1938 the Minister of Native Affairs proposed removal to Orlando. In 1947 a Johannesburg city councillor presented a petition from 2,500 residents of his Rosettenville ward urging expropriation. Ordinands who for years had paid pastoral visits to black servants had to stop because both white residents and police objected. In 1947 CR offered seven acres of land for a recreation area for black workers in accordance with the expressed wish of the municipality for such facilities. After vehement opposition by white residents CR withdrew the offer. Instead CR offered a piece of land at a cheap price for a new hospital on condition that a section would be reserved for blacks. The hospital was built but until recently only treated whites. The whites' opposition to the presence of black students was totally hypocritical, for they were happy to have 16,000 black servants living in the gardens of their houses.

CR's work for African education was urgently needed. In 1905 only 2.1% of African children between the ages of seven and sixteen attended school. Though by 1953 the proportion had increased to 41%, the average school life of attenders was only four years, and only 2.6% were in post-primary classes. Though CR education had no explicit political aim, its work, like that of other missionaries, played a crucial role in developing an educated, articulate and responsible black leadership in the state as well as in the church.

St John's College

The dynamic Darragh, founder of various institutions in Johannesburg, in 1898 also created St John's College for white boys.[9] When it reopened after the war in 1902 it soon ran into debt, not least because it had to face stiff opposition from the recently created Johannesburg College (later King Edward VII school) backed by state money. Milner believed that state schools would help to reconcile the two white communities, but that British and Dutch church schools would be divisive. In 1905 the bishop asked CR to take on St John's. In January 1906 Nash became headmaster assisted by Thomson, and a little later by Henry Alston and Eustace Hill. They were all public schoolmen so they had a model to work to. Nash had already been teaching part-time at St John's. A church school seemed all the more vital because the government had recently forbidden clergy to take religious instruction in state schools. To Nash, the government's opposition to church schools reflected the desire of human beings to keep God out of the crucial areas of life, whether politics or education. Firmly convinced of the superiority of English culture and Anglican religion, he was not prepared to soft-pedal in the interests of 'reconciliation'. CR's commitment to work among blacks was now balanced by an equally definite commitment to whites.

Visiting all the parents in a borrowed trap, Nash announced a reduction of fees, a broadening of the curriculum and a new emphasis on games. But new buildings were urgently needed, and T. H. Cullinan, a diamond magnate, was persuaded to give £5,000. A magnificent site was purchased on an escarpment in the Houghton estate, where the rich were building their houses. Herbert Baker, the leading architect in South Africa, was asked to prepare plans. Nash, continuing the CR policy of enlisting the support of the powers-that-be, invited Lord Selborne, the High Commissioner, to attend the stone-laying by Mrs Cullinan in January 1907. In retaliation Johannesburg College was moved next door. St John's College Council was strengthened by the appointment of Bishop Carter as Visitor, Archdeacon Furse as chairman and governors representing powerful local interests including Cullinan, Geoffrey Robinson, a friend of Furse from Eton days, (later as Geoffrey Dawson editor of the *Times*) and C. F. Stallard, later founder of the white supremacist Dominion Party, a friend of Nash and CR. Selborne opened the first buildings in August 1907 and voiced his strong support of church schools. Nash, Alston, Thomson and Hill now lived at St John's. Thus CR's work was firmly divided on racial lines.

CR made a major financial contribution to the College, both directly through loans and gifts, and indirectly through receiving a small annual grant but not salaries. By 1910 there were 140 pupils including 28 boarders. In 1912 William Plomer joined the boarders:

> The fathers were mostly excellent creatures, late-Victorian Englishmen from Oxford and Cambridge, dedicated to a somewhat austere Anglo-Catholicism. Neither cranks nor fanatics – though one had a fierce, ascetic look like a half-starved bird of prey – they were mostly more like large good boys than schoolmasters. Their cassocks and birettas lent them an air of distinction. As soon as we were dressed of a morning we assembled in the chapel and sang, as plainsong, the simple hymn:
>
> > Now that the daylight fills the sky
> > We lift our hearts to God on high
>
> . . . After the brief early service we ran like stags, headed by an athletic long-legged Resurrection father in a flapping cassock, across the main playing-field and back to our breakfast, which always began with maize-meal porridge.[10]

St John's continued to be supported by the top people. Lord Gladstone, the Governor-General, supported the 1913 extension Appeal, which in England was commended by Lords Selborne, Milner and Methuen, Sir Neville Lyttelton and Geoffrey Dawson. The next Governor-General, Lord Buxton, laid the foundation stone in December 1914 and Patrick Duncan, later Governor-General, chose the Latin inscription for it. The annual Shakespeare play at St John's was a great social occasion for Johannesburg, like a Gala Night at Covent Garden.

Though in 1912 Eustace Hill lamented that St John's lacked both prefects and fags – he had been at Lancing – the staff worked hard at creating public school traditions for what Victor called this 'half-baked' country. There were gowns and mortar-boards, an Old Boys' Dinner, Cadet Corps, and a School Song (composed by Nash) sung to 'Down Among the Dead Men':

> Then Ho! for the Sports, and the Gym Display,
> Old Boys' Gaudy, and Shakespeare Day . . .

In 1925 four halberds and two helmets arrived from Britain to give what Cyprian Rudolf called 'a touch of the Old Tudor Banqueting Hall' to the new refectory. Hill created an annual ritual in which a boar's head was carried up accompanied by banner-bearers in mediaeval dress while a carol was sung in English and Latin. When the buildings were completed in 1932 the tower was obviously English Gothic, the quadrangles recalled monastic cloisters, the chapel interior was classical. But the general impression seen from the playing fields below is of distinctively South African architecture.

A former headmaster in conversation remarked that CR taught the boys 'self-giving and patriotism'. The second of these might be surprising, but Nash was as highly patriotic at St John's as he had been at Radley:

> King, Country, and Master call –
> Come on, St John's – and St John's for all.

Eustace Hill's two passions were said to be the Army and St John's – his father had been a Major-General. Alston's great uncle was General Sir Ian Hamilton, commander of the Gallipoli invasion. Carl Runge, headmaster 1931–4, had been in the army during the whole of the First World War. David Downton once went to the theatre to see Noel Coward's 'Cavalcade' and was so stirred he got up and cheered half way through.

Nash was proud when by December 1914 some eighty boys were on active service: 'We . . . are doing our part for the British Empire'. The British hoped that the participation of South Africa would unify the British and Afrikaner in what Bishop Furse called 'Race Comradeship' – once again the blacks who served were ignored. Hill went to be a chaplain to the South African forces in September 1914 – he had previously been a chaplain in the Anglo-Boer War. He loathed war but believed that it was redeemed by the spirit of self-sacrifice:

> Giving a cup of cold water, or washing a man's feet, or sharing a cloak, or going an extra mile with him, has a new significance for me now . . . I was a bit surprised at a Quartermaster saying: 'My conviction is that the battlefield is no place for a clergyman, as he lessens the killing-spirit.' I have always felt that the Church has been, if anything, too generous in support of war . . . I told him duty was the driving power in a fight, and not blood-lust . . .

His courage during the six day battle of Delville Wood, after which only 800 of the 3,000 South African troops survived, became legendary. In a later battle he asked for volunteers to follow him into no-man's land to collect the wounded, 'Do you believe in God? If you do, follow me!' He was badly wounded in foot and arm. His foot healed, but his right arm had to be amputated. He refused to wear his MC but had it set in a crucifix and placed in the chapel. He returned to St John's in 1919 after some tough months in a POW camp, his memory and hearing impaired, but a national hero. Nash's School Song already included Delville Wood and two battles in Africa. Hill became a strong supporter of the League of Nations and paid tribute to conscientious objectors who had stood for peace. One of the four regimental crosses from Delville Wood was formally received at St John's in 1924 and placed in the Upper Chapel in 1931.

In 1917, after eleven years as headmaster, Nash was appointed as coadjutor Bishop of Cape Town, to assist his old friend William Carter who had been Archbishop since 1909. As headmaster he had rescued the school from almost certain oblivion and built it up to a famous institution of 300 boys. Longridge wrote to him in January 1917: 'We shall all miss you much for you are one of the links with the old days of Pusey House and Radley – dear old days of which one often thinks and somewhat sighs after.' He lived in a pleasant house at the foot of Table Mountain. In close consultation with Frere he made a notable contribution to Prayer Book Revision in South Africa. At the age of sixty-eight he returned to the Pennine starkness of Mirfield.

Nash proposed that Thomson, who had twice looked after the school when Nash had been on furlough, should succeed him. Thomson did not want the job. He was a natural second-in-command, not a leader. He did his best for almost three years, but the school did not prosper. In photographs he had often looked strained and unhappy. In July 1920 he did not renew his pledge. He resigned as head from the end of the year. In 1921 he married the former headmistress of the preparatory school. He spent the rest of his ministry in Welsh parishes.

Edward Symonds replaced him. Talbot wrote that he would in time make 'a very efficient Head' but he 'would have been a greater man if he had a year or two of complete scepticism – or even of modernism. As it is you rather wonder why he should be so interested in and confident of answers to questions which he has never really asked. But he is as good as gold.' A brilliant scholar, an inspiring teacher, but no administrator, his appointment was another mistake. After ten months he broke down, resigned and returned to England. Confidence in CR's judgment was now badly shaken. Nash came back to be headmaster for a term in January 1922 and restored morale. During that term a strike by white miners ended in violence and deaths. Hill officiated at the burial of thirty-two of the dead. He refused to allow the dead to be divided into loyalists and rebels. 'Let them lie together' he said. His conscience was also troubled by the treatment of black miners. He wrote to the press: 'they are wounded that we may have comfort, they die that we may live ... As Christians we tolerate unfair taxation which drives the boys to the mines, a colour bar which prevents them from ever improving their position on the mines, we allow stores to exploit their wants. What good have we done them?'

In March 1922 Hill became headmaster. He owed his appointment to his war-time fame and the two rapid resignations. He got away with eccentric behaviour which would have been tolerated in no one else. If a caller on the phone said something with which he disagreed, he would shout 'I can't hear you, I'm deaf' and abruptly put the phone down. At a Sports Day seeing someone vaguely familiar, he asked her how her boy was doing. She turned out to be a spinster on the prep school staff. He was also a great beater. He inadvertently beat a luckless boy from King Edward's who arrived with a message and an innocent Confirmation group in mistake for some miscreants. Though his war-time experiences had aged him and he was not an academic nor a gifted teacher, his courage, simplicity and determination shone out. During his eight years 'Mad Jack', as he was known affectionately, put the school back on its feet and completed the main building work. There was an emotional farewell in December 1930. When H. M. Muller, who taught Dutch and Afrikaans, made the presentation, Hill pointed out that thirty years ago Muller was being shot at by the British. Now Dutch and British 'must be the very best of friends'. The white workmen put on a cricket match. A week later there was a separate occasion for blacks when the 'building boys' played the domestics.

Carl Runge, of Anglo-German stock, came from Mirfield to succeed Hill. After Charterhouse he had followed his father into banking. After war service, Oxford and Cuddesdon, he was ordained at the age of thirty-two for Pretoria diocese. Though an unwilling candidate (he did not like teaching), Runge brought to St John's a cosmopolitan sophistication and a first hand knowledge of finance and administration. He was equally at home entertaining the Governor-General or singing songs with Greeks at a nearby cafe. He worried more openly about the privileged nature of the school than some C R staff. By 1933 there were 477 boys in the school.

For over a decade C R had debated whether it should withdraw. The school was essentially Nash's creation. Neither C R's hopes for more brethren with teaching abilities nor Nash's hopes for a lay teaching order had materialized. The demands of school life made regular communal life and worship difficult to achieve. Yet, some brethren argued, if C R withdrew, fees would rise and it would become a school for only the rich. School religion would lose its edge and warmth and the Council, which was by no means wholly Anglican, would have control. C R would lose white goodwill, essential for its work among Africans. Victor, defending the £80,000 spent on St John's at the 1930 C R London Festival claimed: 'I do believe that our white population does in some way provide the steel framework which holds and stabilizes Africa.' Raynes, who latterly was a housemaster, loved the school: through it he believed white South Africans could be challenged to serve their country by healing its wounds and injustices. He once cancelled an entertainment because the boys refused to carry in their chairs arguing it was a job for black servants. Runge was C R's last card, but after eleven months he argued for withdrawal. If C R continued, the money saved by employing brethren should be allocated to bursaries for pupils from poor families. Chapter in January 1934 was deeply divided, but a majority voted for withdrawal at the end of the year.

The College's gratitude to C R was later expressed by the erection of a fountain in the College quadrangle, renamed Pelican Quad after the pelican feeding its young which surmounts it. Appropriately in view of the English ethos which C R brought, the design echoes similar fountains in Oxford and

Cambridge. A panel in the chapel records the fifteen names of brethren who had taught there. The names of four houses – Nash, Thomson, Alston and Hill – and the portraits of brethren which hang in the hall are other reminders. The text from Wisdom over the entrance to the laboratory block (1919) recalls the Christian humanism of the *Lux Mundi* tradition: 'By measure and number and weight thou didst order all things.' Once hopelessly in debt and housed in corrugated iron huts in central Johannesburg, under CR's leadership, St John's had grown into one of the most famous white public schools in Africa housed in probably the finest school buildings in the southern hemisphere.

A favourable assessment of CR's contribution to St John's would claim that by simply being around as members of staff with no salary, brethren witnessed to a different set of values. Under Hill's influence, the College adopted the township of Sophiatown as its mission and regularly raised money for it and visited it. White boys from the lush conditions at St John's were astonished to find sixty children to a class. When Raynes went to Sophiatown he took groups of black children to Gilbert and Sullivan performances at the College. Boys also visited the black Reformatory at Diepkloof of which Alan Paton was Principal. Despite misgivings Paton sent his sons to St John's; the equally radical Ambrose Reeves sent his son too. If only one ex-pupil (Gordon Arkell) joined CR, there was a steady stream of ordinands. The character of CR's contribution to St John's is a reminder that despite its radical reputation, the Community has also included a strain of Christian Toryism summed up in Nash, once a member of the Guild of St Matthew, devoted to King and Country, institutional tradition and *noblesse oblige*. Others would criticize CR for giving a tacit endorsement to racial and class segregation symbolized by the two separate cricket matches for whites and blacks at Hill's farewell. There was a huge gulf not only between St John's and the townships but also within the school itself between the facilities and accommodation for whites and those for the black servants. The whites had more than enough privileges without the kudos of CR's endorsement. When bishops attacked the country's racial policies, government ministers would retort by pointing to the exclusive white church schools. It was not until 1980 that the first black pupils were admitted to St John's.

CR had now no full-time commitment to any white institution in South Africa. Moreover brethren's parochial contacts were almost entirely with whites of British origin, yet they realized from the 1920s that the Afrikaners were now in the ascendent. Victor in 1927 pointed out the significance of the unveiling of Kruger's statue in Pretoria with its total absence of Union Jacks: how very different from the early days when there were British magistrates and troops everywhere. CR made contact with the Dutch Reformed Church through the regular missionary conferences and over social issues. Nash could administer confirmation in Dutch and Bertram Barnes was capable of celebrating in six languages, but some brethren could speak neither Afrikaans nor African languages with any fluency. In CR's first fifty years in South Africa, only two white South Africans joined: Jerome Dieterlé of Anglo-French ancestry who spoke Afrikaans, Dutch, German and various African languages fluently, and Gordon Arkell whose father came to fight in the Anglo-Boer War and stayed to farm and married a South African. Arkell always believed that CR never tried to understand the Afrikaner. How could CR ever become indigenous when brethren thought of England as home? From time to time they discussed whether furloughs should be given up. Some did forego them. When Talbot visited South Africa in 1926 he was impressed by a German missionary and his wife who had been there for sixteen years and never expected to see their own country again.

Sophiatown and Orlando

CR work in South Africa took a momentous new turn when Geoffrey Clayton, the new Bishop of Johannesburg, inducted Raynes to be priest-in-charge of Sophiatown on 13 December 1934.[11] Living in Sophiatown radicalized CR. Sharing the total life of an African township was quite different from living with Africans at Rosettenville where they were abstracted from their homes and placed in an environment created by whites. Talbot had wondered whether Raynes should return to Mirfield to be Vice-Principal of the College or go out to Borneo. Fortunately he decided on Sophiatown, for it was there that Raynes did the greatest work of his life. In December 1933 Clayton had written from England to Rosettenville confessing his colossal ignorance of South Africa, but rejoicing that he was to have CR in his diocese. He owed much to the Community. As an undergraduate he had been deeply affected by a CR mission, and had been lastingly influenced by the teaching and friendship of Figgis. Talbot thought Clayton 'able and efficient' but 'rather uncouth and graceless'. Alan Paton in his fine biography of Clayton was frank about his 'irritability, his damns and his blasts' but summed him up as 'a great, strange, extraordinary man, who had chosen the task of holding up the weak and binding up the broken'.

Sophiatown stood on a hill about five miles north-west from the city centre, with white areas on two sides. It had been deliberately neglected because the municipality wanted blacks to live instead in its regimented and characterless locations. Sophiatown was a great mixture of people ranging from the old established and respectable, to the lawless who moved there to get away from surveillance in the locations. Whites regularly campaigned for the removal of Sophiatown. Early in the century a Pole had bought the area and as the city spread, sold plots to Africans, Indians and Chinese who were not allowed to buy freeholds in the city. He called it after his wife Sophia. Sophiatown, with nearby Martindale and Newclare, were unique because only there could urban Africans be freeholders. Sophiatown was grossly overcrowded but in

Trevor Huddleston's opinion, it had more 'vitality and exuberance' than any other suburb in South Africa. When Raymond Raynes, David Downton and Matthew Trelawney-Ross moved to Sophiatown it had a population of at least 50,000. There were already Anglican churches for Africans and Coloureds, Anglican schools and a hospital. In 1927 African infant mortality on the Reef was appalling: 700 in 1,000.

In the middle of 1927 Dorothy Maud started work in Sophiatown, sent by SPG. She was Michael Furse's niece and the daughter of J. P. Maud, Bishop of Kensington, a member of the embryonic community at Pusey House in 1889. In 1913 he became Vice-President of the Church's League for Women's Suffrage. When the church in the First World War was worried about the welfare of women munition workers Dorothy took a job on the production line. Her passion for social justice had been quickened by the writings of Studdert Kennedy.

In 1929 Dorothy Maud opened Ekutuleni ('House of Peace-Making') and helped by other women, made it a centre for social and religious work among women and children. The foundation stone had been laid by three children, one white, one black, one coloured. She joined the battle for improvements: standpipes for fresh water, street lighting and proper roads. Well-connected and self-assured, she enlisted the support of successive Governor-Generals and their wives. She established contacts with the white parishes and schools, so whereas Ekutuleni had been largely financed from Britain, four-fifths of the money for Leseding in Orlando came from within South Africa. Simply by living in Sophiatown Dorothy refuted the white belief that Africans were automatically a menace to white women. At the centre of her life were the daily eucharist and a deep faith that God would provide. She hung quotations from Joan of Arc in her office: 'For a work begun God sendeth thread'. She, like Raynes, was pierced by the extraordinary faith which Africans can offer. So Granny Julia, asked by one of the women about prayer, replied: 'Sister, you go to a fountain when you want water and just bring the pot to it.' When Raynes told an old lady who came to church daily that she need not come when it rained, she replied: 'My Lord comes to the church each day, why should I not be there to lay myself at his feet?'

Talbot thought Maud had probably done more to commend the missionary cause to whites than anyone else. But now he was apprehensive that CR might not have brethren who could match 'her greyhound pace'. In the event she and Raynes made a perfect complementary pair. She was forty, he was thirty-one. She had the self-confidence of her class and was an accomplished public speaker. He was awkward with women. But the first time they met he opened up to her about the recent death of his father, probably the first woman to whom he had ever revealed himself. It was a liberation. Mosley commented in his *Life* of Raynes: 'This unique partnership in the Church seemed to happen at a unique place at a unique time. There was a sudden release of growth and flowering. The seeds of this, now scattered, are going back into the earth; but their life is ineradicable.' Raynes found at Ekutuleni, opposite the Priory, a companionship which he often did not find within the Community, a pattern which was repeated when he became Superior. He called in several times a day. Plans were often discussed with Maud before they were put to the brethren. People had said it would be impossible for three monks to work with five women. But it worked marvellously and they shared not only worship and work, but picnics, outings and meals together. Like other brethren in Africa, Raynes' affections were unfrozen by the warm spontaneity of Africans, especially the children. Some Africans nicknamed him 'Kalofo' – golfstick, because he was tall and bent at the top; he loved that. There was fun amidst the squalor and violence. One day a female witchdoctor fled naked into the Priory and hid under the table. When Raynes preached against pilfering by some of the washerwomen and said that stolen clothes must be handed in, that evening the Priory was full of women's underclothes. When troubles and disappointments seemed overwhelming he would say: 'It doesn't matter if your heart is broken, you must never give up, and never stop minding.' The appalling injustices gave him a righteous outlet for his anger and aggression. He was never to find such human warmth or such a just cause again. By 1938 when he went to Mirfield on leave brethren were beginning to talk of him as a future Superior.

In six years the mission built three churches, seven schools and three nursery schools catering for over 6,000 children, and expanded the hospital. At the highest point, with money from Mr Smith, a rich white baker, they built the great church of Christ the King. Raynes told the architect that he wanted a church to seat 1,000. He replied that he could only build what looked like a garage for the money available. Raynes liked the idea of a holy garage. When Smith discovered it could not be seen from a distance he gave money for a tower with a four-sided clock – no mere ornament when few of the people could afford clocks or watches. A nun came to paint frescoes on the chancel arch. The Virgin had a look of Maud and St Francis had Raynes' head. Smith also gave money for a swimming pool, only the second for blacks in the whole of South Africa.

The church was there to promote the Kingdom, and that meant agitating for better amenities, encouraging Building Societies to give more reasonable mortgages, defending blacks who were constantly being arrested for pass and other minor offences – 600 every weekend in Johannesburg. Children regularly ran up the hill to the Priory shouting 'Arrested' and one of the Fathers would dash down to the courtroom to help. In 1938 Raynes told the London CR Festival that every white child received free education but the government provided no schools for Africans and only made grants for teachers' salaries if parents paid fees. There were 90,000 children on the Reef, but only 18,000 were in school. Hardly a weekend went by without at least one murder. 'It is pathetic and damnably unjust that these lovely people upon whom the prosperity of South Africa depends, are going to rack and ruin because those in authority, those who have the money, will do nothing.'

The work was undergirded by the daily mass and offices, though under the pressures it was difficult to say all the offices together. CR life had to be strong enough for mutual support, yet flexible enough so that the many urgent pastoral demands could be met. The Sunday High Mass at Christ the King with 700–800 present was particularly impressive and some white supporters came; hymns were sung in four different languages and the sermon was interpreted into two of them. Raynes told the mission workers on their annual retreat:

> In Jesus I see the gentle compassionate love of Mary, the passionate love of St Paul, the impulsive love of St Peter, the sweet reasonable love of St John, the agonizing love of St Francis, the persevering love of St Theresa, the fierce love of . . . Ignatius, the reflective love of an Aquinas, the innocent love of the child saints . . . pouring themselves out in love – because it is the essence of love to share and give.

In 1935 CR was asked to look after Orlando as well. It was a new location, five miles from Sophiatown, and ten miles from Johannesburg. The first 3,000 houses had only two or three rooms, no floors or ceilings. With tin roofs they were unbearably hot in summer and freezing in winter. They were built in rows with no street names, and with total impersonality numbered from 1 to 8,000 (by 1944). The roads were unmade so after a few days of rain they were seas of mud with holes two or three feet deep. For several years there was no waterborne sewage, gas or electricity, and only one water tap in the road for every ten houses. The mission built a church and schools. Maud's women workers were forbidden to live in Orlando, so they built Leseding ('House of Light') on unappropriated farmland. By 1940 there were four primary schools, which with the nursery schools, catered for some 3,000 children. Three white businessmen provided most of the money. Raynes and his supporters battled with the municipal authorities for better physical amenities and medical facilities. When Raynes declared publicly 'We are in the happy position of the only available recreation being fornication, and that is not provided by the City Council' the Town Clerk issued a summons for slander, but on reflection withdrew it.

By 1944 there was a population of some 55,000 in Orlando. On Lady Day as the congregation came out they saw hundreds of people driven desperate by overcrowding, trekking across the river to squat on municipal land. Claude Lunniss and other brethren lent a hand as they created make-shift dwellings with poles and sacking. The municipal response was to build single-room breeze-block dwellings without doors, chimneys or windows as temporary accommodation. That year the government decided to provide 2d a day per child for a school meal. Soon 6,500 children were being fed daily in Sophiatown and Orlando by the mission. By 1954 there were four Anglican churches in Orlando. A house next to Leseding became the CR Priory of St Mary at the Cross in 1948. It was an important moment when in 1945 a black priest conducted a mission to Sophiatown, because over the years some of the African leaders and clergy resented what they regarded as the white domination of the mission.

CR's work in the townships showed that it was possible to develop an unselfconscious and genuinely working-class Anglo-Catholicism which urban Anglo-Catholic priests in England always hoped to create but rarely achieved. Anglo-Catholicism in South Africa, removed from the peculiarities of the English scene which often kept it fixated in adolescent naughtiness, came of age, and instead of fighting the bishops fought against racial injustice.

Meanwhile two huge changes had taken place in CR's work in the townships. In January 1943 Raynes was elected as Superior. Maud and her workers, anticipating this, decided to give up Ekutuleni. Maud returned to England to test her vocation and was professed at Wantage in 1949. Four Wantage sisters set out in 1943 to take over but their boat was torpedoed and when they landed at Lagos covered in oil some Roman Catholic sisters kindly reclothed them. They did not reach Sophiatown until the beginning of 1944.

Raynes' departure was delayed by illness (his relentless way of life was destroying his health) and problems of obtaining a passage in war-time. But in April 1943 he was promised a place as chaplain to a troopship. He had an emotional send-off: a watch inscribed 'from your African children', a rug of sixteen jackal skins, a shield decorated with feathers (the sign of a victorious chief) and a set of warm underclothes from a local garage-owner. Maud wrote: 'It was awful letting him go, for all the people minded so dreadfully – they kept coming with their heart-breaking presents of a few cigarettes or one or two very cheap hankies, or a shilling for the journey.' It was a huge wrench for him. He had asked Clayton to tell Mirfield that he was unsuitable to be Superior. Clayton refused. 'Do not be sad' Raynes told the people 'I will send a new father to you'.

When he arrived at Mirfield, a brother unknown to him opened the door and looked after him in his illness. It was Trevor Huddleston. Raynes told him about Sophiatown. After a fortnight he decided Huddleston should succeed him. Huddleston, aged twenty-nine and only professed for two years, thought himself too young and inexperienced. But he went. Clayton at his licensing preached on 'Let no man despise thy youth'. When in 1988 Huddleston was asked on television what he had learned from Africans he replied:

> I learned everything. When I went to South Africa I was totally immature. I had had the usual upper middle-class education, school, then university, then theological college. I learned everything from Sophiatown. It was one of the most vital places

upon earth. I think that the main characteristic of the African people is this extraordinary zest for life at all kinds of levels. I loved every moment of my life there.

But his story belongs to a later chapter.

Sekhukhuniland

Those who pause to read the inscriptions on the lychgate at the entrance to the cemetery at Mirfield may notice how many brethren are buried overseas, from Borneo to Stellenbosch, from Penhalonga to Johannesburg. By 1991 thirteen were buried in Sekhukhuniland at the remote Jane Furse mission about a hundred and sixty miles north-east of Johannesburg. Three of them were transferred there in 1956 from the all-white cemetery in Johannesburg.

The first major contacts between blacks and whites in the area were tragically bloody. An Afrikaner army invaded in 1876. In 1879 a British army captured Chief Sekhukhuni and imprisoned him in Pretoria. In 1897 Canon Farmer, head of mission work in Pretoria diocese, visited the area and discovered some Anglicans and four catechists. But despite regular pleas for help, no Anglican missionary visited Sekhukhuniland until 1908 when Fuller set out in a cart with four unruly mules and two African evangelists. The journey took three and a half days on boulder-strewn tracks through rivers and thick bush. Reaching the kraals he had to wait until everyone returned from work and then preached to groups by moonlight. Fuller reported that there was much to be done. A few years later a deacon trained by CR built three churches and two schools. After his death Fr Augustine Moeka, also CR trained, took over.

In 1918 Jane Furse, the only child of the Bishop of Pretoria, died of scarlet fever. She had hoped to become a doctor for the Africans. In her memory a hospital was built and began work in 1921. Talbot visited it in 1930. Though he admired Penhalonga he wished that Francis Hill's plea for work in the northern Transvaal had been heeded instead.

Thus when the Bishop of Pretoria approached CR in 1938 to take over the mission, it had long been interested in the area. Sekhukhuniland was a native reserve of 80,000 square miles with an almost wholly heathen population of about 200,000. Francis Hill, Henry Alston and Gregory Evans comprised the initial party. Housekeeping was difficult; the nearest decent shops were sixty-seven miles away in Lydenburg. The postman who also brought the butter and meat only arrived twice a week; cooking was on a primus stove; rivers could be forty yards wide; the rains washed away the roads. 'The well-educated, even practising, Christian native, is sometimes a most objectionable person, but there are many exceptions' reported Alston after years of looking after white pupils and parishioners in Johannesburg, but he was sad to see those Africans who were more able than some whites, suffering so many disabilities. The children were 'full of the joy of earthly life . . . but they are dark within'. It was as different as could be from Johannesburg, with its detribalized and urbanized Africans. There and at Penhalonga blacks were eager for education and responsive to evangelism; here tribal and racial solidarity resisted penetration. Who could understand its mysterious depths? The language was difficult to learn, many children did not want to attend school, qualified teachers never stayed long, the area was ridden with superstition and drink. The temperature could reach 113 degrees and in 1941 there were only ten confirmation candidates.

Perhaps a contemplative could provide more spiritual power? So in 1946 Hubert Northcott arrived and stayed for ten years. By then the hospital had an operating theatre (given in 1939 by the Frere family), and over a hundred beds. It also trained nurses. The primary school had 300 children and adults. Brethren and the local black priest looked after the hospital church and a number of outlying and mostly struggling congregations. Arkell, a former farmer, created an irrigation system and grew vegetables and sisal. Christianity had been preached for eighty years there by different denominations. 'Some fruit still abides. But very much of it seems blighted . . .' lamented *Mirfield in Africa* (1944). A 1947 brochure about CR's work in Africa included a photograph of a bare-breasted girl with the caption: 'The Sleeping Beauty . . . one of the thousands in Sekhukhuniland waiting for the light of the Gospel and the Kiss of the Prince of Peace'. Francis Blake (*CRQ* MD 1949) eschewed such mawkishness: Africans had been given second-rate land, agricultural methods were primitive, the soil was being eroded, there was much disease, the men worked away in towns or mines and the initiation schools were powerfully influential. There were only 300 Anglicans and only 39 catechumens and hearers. At Marishane there was a small African group of Anglican nuns, and the grave of Manche Masemola, a young girl beaten to death in 1928 because she wanted to become a Christian.[12] We need so many things in Sekhukhuniland, Blake wrote, not only material things but also 'patience, charity and understanding amongst the European workers on the Mission: cheerfulness and perseverance in the face of all the difficulties'. CR developed an annual pilgrimage to Manche's grave on the scrub covered kopje.

By the end of the 1950s Sekhukhuniland was regarded by some brethren as a rather hopeless mission. The work was hard and unrewarding. It was very remote and difficult to staff. But the government had given £50,000 to re-equip the hospital out of war memorial funds. When Derek Williams arrived in 1957 there was still no Pedi dictionary or grammar. He wrote a striking article (*CRQ* JB 1961) about evangelism contending that the early missionaries failed because they travelled around too much and the people did not know them. So the Gospel became a worn out story and baptism 'a corny joke'. Instead, the evangelist must be a familiar figure always turning up. The white missionary could no longer pose as the fount of all wisdom; 'he has continually to ask for forgiveness of his sins and (in South Africa) the sins of his own race. He has constantly to desire to listen and to learn. That, perhaps is the most urgent reason why he learns the language of his people . . . learning one of the many languages of the Africans is an excellent method of humiliating one's self before them, of offering one's self to be taught . . .' Having prepared the ground the evangelist was now ready to preach the gospel which included bringing people into the Christian community (Africans think communally) but also into an individual relationship to Christ. 'Hence the necessity frequently to preach in the church about judgment and hell-fire and each man's need of the salvation which is to be found in Jesus only.' (Had anyone else in the Community spoken of hell, let alone hell-fire, since the days of Hugh Benson and Paul Bull?)

Why did CR withdraw in 1961? Was it simply that CR was over-extended and that the pioneering work was done? Was it because CR was divided about the purpose of the mission? Some had hoped for another Penhalonga. But in any case that was impossible after the Bantu Education Act. Or was it enough simply to be there, a quietly persistent presence? 'It would have been by far our most worthwhile job if we'd stayed there' one brother said in conversation. Another who had also worked there rejected the line that CR ought to be in places like Johannesburg where its influence could be felt. That was an unworthy love of the limelight, a wordly idea of success. He echoed the conviction of others in Africa that crucial decisions about Africa were taken far away in Mirfield by brethren some of whom had no experience of Africa and who judged everything by Mirfield itself. 'But Mirfield is completely different from anything else that Mirfield ever produced.'

In 1991 the former Priory was dilapidated and its grounds overgrown like some seedy setting for a novel by Graham Greene. But nearby, the bell for the fine new church secondary school was designed (the inscription said): 'to call God's people to the coming of his Kingdom'.

Francis Blake, a former Prior, described his many memories of his nine years, the hospital, the village congregations, the overnight vigil at Manche's grave before Mass at the altar there, the children, the chiefs, the courteous hospitality of the people, the under-nourishment, the lack of water and the poor crops that the boulder and thorn covered land yielded:

> It was a thrilling experience to be out in the early mornings on the veld: to watch the sun come up with a rush over the Loulou Mountains in the east; to see the storm clouds gather on the summer afternoons, only for them to be swept away and the much needed rain to fall elsewhere; to notice the lovely changing colours of the kopjes and the distant hills with the prevailing blues and purples of the Transvaal on the winter evenings after cloudless days . . . At night there was the brilliant expanse of the stars, the names of so many of which I learnt but have now forgotten. There I

would know all the phases of the moon, but now when living in Johannesburg I hardly know what the moon is doing on any particular night . . . Those of CR who will be called to die in this part of the world may be glad that their bodies will be laid to rest in the graveyard at Jane Furse under the wide open skies . . . (*CRQ* LD 1962)

9

Pioneering in Rhodesia

A visit in 1983 to the Anglican cathedral in Harare seemed to say it all.[1] Significantly it was next to the Parliament building and close to other centres of power. In the oldest part, in and around St George's chapel (whose name immediately established the English connection) the whites' version of the country's history was evoked by memorials to those killed by 'rebel natives' in 'uprisings', campaigns and patrols. 'Pioneer Corps 1890' was inscribed over the chapel screen, and inside was the list of names of those 'who occupied Mashonaland' and a cross made out of cigar boxes by a trooper for the first wattle and daub church of 1890. The stone for the completion was laid by Sir Humphrey Gibbs as Governor, a devout Anglican, in 1963. When he laid the stone in 1977 for the hall and offices, he had become a private citizen – Ian Smith had declared independence in 1965. Two memorials list those killed (all whites) when guerrillas shot down two passenger planes during the civil war, yet no one erected a memorial to the many African Christians killed by government troops. They were written off as 'rebels'. But at the entrance to the cathedral is a plaque which belongs to a new world – set in the floor and inscribed in two African languages as well as in English it is dedicated simply 'To all who died in the war. 1982'. The change symbolized by this plaque was as sudden as it was belated. It was not until 1981, a year after independence, that the Anglican church appointed its first black diocesan bishop. By 1983 the Dean and most of the staff were African and part of the parish magazine was in Shona. Unlike the Roman Catholic cathedral in Harare which does not contain a single colonialist plaque, the Anglican cathedral makes visible the close connection between the Anglican church and the rulers of Rhodesia. Whereas by the 1920s in South Africa the bishops had to deal with what they regarded as an alien government, until 1980 the Rhodesian rulers were 'kith and kin'. So over the years Rhodesian bishops' criticisms of government policies were more muted than those of the South African bishops.

The story of the Anglican church in Southern Rhodesia[2] began with an extraordinary trek of 3,000 miles, mostly on foot, from Kimberley to the Zambesi in 1888 by George Knight-Bruce, Bishop of Bloemfontein, a man of great courage and stamina. He had been appointed when a mere curate at St

Andrew's Bethnal Green at the age of thirty-three in 1885. (Nash succeeded him at St Andrew's.) Knight-Bruce was critical of white treatment of blacks but believed that white rule was essential to bring peace between the Mashona and Matabele people. On his trek he took eight African Christians but no whites. He dealt with attacks of malaria and dysentery with mustard plasters and massive doses of quinine and Warburg's Fever Tincture.

Meanwhile the Pioneer Column was assembling. Knight-Bruce, convinced that the new area would need a bishop, provisionally accepted the post. Canon Balfour, one of the three chaplains to the Pioneers, arrived at Fort Salisbury in September 1890. 'The flag was run up. I addressed the force in two or three words; said, "Prevent us, O Lord"; 21 guns were fired, all saluted the flag and shouted three cheers for the Queen . . . The colonel gave up his tent to me at 7.30 a.m. for a Celebration. I was so glad to thank God for His great mercies . . . and plead the great Sacrifice for this hitherto untaught country.' The prayer desk in the church he built was made out of a whisky case and 'Milkmaid Brand' was clearly visible on the lectern. Gradually life in this frontier town became a little more genteel and Lord Grey at Government House soon had a scarlet bicycle with a coronet stamped on the mudguard. But in the countryside settlers were given a free hand to seize land and cattle from the Africans who were slaughtered by punitive expeditions when they resisted.

The founding of St Augustine's Penhalonga

Knight-Bruce arrived by sea at Beira in May 1891 to become Bishop of Mashonaland with two carpenters and five African catechists, including Bernard Mizeki who in 1896 became Mashonaland's first martyr. They reached Fort Umtali (now Penhalonga) on 1 June after a tortuous journey partly by steamer which kept grounding on the sandbanks, followed by a long trek through forests, and grass sometimes above their heads, accompanied by five carriers. Fort Umtali was a collection of little log huts situated on a steep hillside, 4,000 feet above sea level, standing at the junction of half a dozen converging valleys. Knight-Bruce's 'palace' was an unlined tin shanty of one room. After holding a service for the troopers, he set off to Salisbury, walking most of the way, to obtain permission for a site for the mission headquarters and farm. He was convinced that African Christians would revert to heathenism and be harmed by white settlers unless they were brought into mission farms and villages. On 2 July he started work clearing the site for what was to become St Augustine's mission. Building and brick-making began on 4 July. Ten days later the doctor and three nurses arrived having walked the last one hundred and forty miles. A china tea-service was the one luxury the nurses brought. Their daily afternoon tea reminded them of England. John Wilkins, a carpenter who had worked with Livingstone and had been a pall bearer at his funeral in Westminster Abbey, arrived in August only to die a few months later. Fever and dysentery were rife. The doctor lasted only a month. The bishop's illnesses were severe and frequent. When he went to England at the end of 1891 to raise money and recruit staff, illness delayed his return. In June 1892 Douglas Pelly, then a layman, arrived and built a church in Umtali which had now moved a couple of miles from the mission. The bishop eventually returned to the mission in May 1893. But in January 1894 he again developed blackwater fever and had to resign. He died, aged forty-four, two years later. His successor, William Gaul, a tough, peppery bishop barely five feet tall, went about in a khaki drill apron, khaki clerical coat and helmet. He was more acceptable to the whites than Knight-Bruce who was thought to be pro-African.

During the next eighty years the rights of Africans were trampled on by the state and all too slowly recognized by the church. In 1901 Arthur Shearly Cripps, a memorable priest who had been influenced by Gore, arrived and became a champion of Africans. In 1912 he proposed their inclusion in the synod, but this was not effected until 1921. The first African deacon was ordained in 1919. When he was priested in 1923 three other Africans were made deacon. All had been trained by CR. Edward, son of Francis Paget, member of the Holy Party, contributor to *Lux Mundi*, became the fifth bishop in 1925. When he discovered that no Africans had been invited to his enthronement he had to threaten to hold it in the African church in Salisbury before he got his way. When Paget stayed at an African priest's house he received abusive letters. The social and educational policies of the government enforced white supremacy, reinforced by the demands of the white settlers who increased from 33,620 in 1921 to 223,000 in 1961. The Land Apportionment Act (1930) resulted in the eviction of 50,000 Africans from their land between 1931 and 1941 to make room for whites. By 1924 the various churches had established 1,216 African schools. Yet even by 1940 there were only two government schools for Africans. Education for whites was free. Africans had to pay for theirs. It is in this context that the establishment of St Augustine's and what it achieved for Africans must be judged. It 'probably contributed more skilled manpower from all walks of life – the church, teaching, public service, politics, business and the professions – than any other [mission] in the whole country'.[3]

In 1895 Bishop Gaul visited Penhalonga. Finding the brick foundations which Knight-Bruce had laid practically with his own life-blood, he knelt down and resolved that with God's help he would complete the work. In 1897 for the third time Umtali moved and occupied its present site to be near the railway, leaving the mission isolated twelve miles away. But life was tough even in new Umtali; sometimes lions raided outbuildings and the rats were almost as fierce. In 1897 it was resolved to refound the mission at Penhalonga with an industrial college as a memorial to Knight-Bruce. Helped by funds from SPG and SPCK a start was made in August 1898 with two African catechists and five members of the Evangelist Brotherhood, a short-lived group founded in Lichfield by a former Salvation Army officer. Douglas Pelly who had been ordained in 1895, went to England in 1897 to recruit staff. He had intended to join the Brotherhood, but got engaged. The Archdeacon of Mashonaland, having breakfast on holiday in Milan, was handed a letter: 'My dear Archdeacon, I'm so happy . . .' So Pelly returned a married Principal in August 1898. At first the staff were housed in temporary huts which leaked so badly that they had to sleep under umbrellas. By early December however, before the rains began in earnest, the permanent brick accommodation was ready, much of which still stands today. By January 1899 there were nine pupils. The mornings were devoted to basic education. In the afternoons there was bricklaying, book-binding and gardening. Each boy had his own plot of land. Mattins and Evensong were said daily in Shona with Holy Communion, Sext and Compline in English. After Compline the boys conducted prayer meetings in their tents. Visitors remarked on the school's excellent discipline. 'Natives, as a rule, are naturally so lazy and unpunctual' Pelly explained. In January 1899 Bishop Gaul visited Penhalonga, ordained one lay brother, professed him and others, dedicated the new buildings and baptized a whole Mashona family in the river.

But during the next six months the whole operation nearly fell apart. Pelly and his wife had to leave after repeated attacks of fever. Others also left. Only two brothers remained. With great courage they continued to run the school, made evangelistic expeditions and provided medical care. The white priest at Umtali gave support. Hezekiah Mtobi, a black priest from South Africa in charge of an outstation, spent most of the festivals at the mission and gave help with the language and mission strategy. He had arrived in 1896 having lost all his possessions when his ship was wrecked on the Mozambique coast. He then struggled up country, regularly insulted by all the whites he met, and started work at Mtasa.

It was the appointment of E. H. Etheridge (Bishop of St John's 1923–43) as Principal which really set the mission on its feet. He arrived in December 1900 in time for a great baptism in a rocky basin near the house followed by confirmation. Afterwards the bishop addressed a largely heathen congregation who 'listened with wrapt attention to his description of the Creation, the Fall, the Restoration of Man by Jesus Christ in Baptism, and the grace of the Christian life'. By 1903 there were 90 pupils. In January 1904 'Mother Annie' (Miss Annie Dalby, a tiny but formidable nurse and teacher) with two other women arrived to start St Monica's school for girls. It was hoped that St Monica's would not only provide education but also Christian wives for the ex-pupils of the school who might otherwise lapse from their faith. From 1903 the first teachers trained by St Augustine's began work in various parts of the country.

Bishop Gaul greatly admired the missionary work of the Roman Catholic orders. He was convinced that community life was essential for pioneering mission work. In February 1902 he wrote to Frere at Mirfield about the need for Religious in his diocese. 'Look around at the married clergy in a Colony. Here and there the life of the Missionary and his wife are magnificent: but is it *war*?' Domestic anxieties dull fervour and quench 'the spirit of martyrdom'. Great work could be done if men and women would forsake all and follow their Master. Etheridge was a member and two other staff were associates of SR. Were any brethren coming out with the advance party of the Mission of Help to South Africa? If so, could they help us to develop the Religious Life? Perhaps Frere or another brother could come and conduct a retreat and consider establishing a branch House at St Augustine's. Anglicans were in a minority in the United States because they 'were not shepherded by their own mother – be-wigged and be-ruffled and be-starched and bewitched with her Establishment'. No reply survives to this passionate plea. But in 1906 Frere landed at Beira, reached Umtali and cycled the rough twelve mile track to see Penhalonga before travelling to Johannesburg.

In July 1912 James Nash and Bertram Barnes inspected the mission because the bishop (now F. H. Beaven) and Etheridge were pleading with CR to take it over. That month Etheridge sent a detailed report to Frere: the farm with £400 worth of stock had some 4,400 acres; 113 boys and 79 girls boarded; the mission looked after white and black churches in Penhalonga and four kraal church schools; there were 800 communicants, 1,000–1,200 catechumens and hearers and about 20,000 Africans in the district. The staff was six, of whom three were priests: Etheridge, Harry Buck and John Hallward. Etheridge had always thought that St Augustine's would be ideal for a religious community. Priests came for a time then left to get married. The whole diocese would benefit from the presence of a Religious Order. The bishop had asked him to leave to superintend all diocesan mission work. Hallward and Buck might become members of CR; both had considered Cowley. Hallward was already a member of SR. But Frere replied that CR could not take on the mission for a year or so. In 1913 Etheridge became Archdeacon and Hallward and Buck took charge. Hallward, co-founder of Plumtree school was appointed head, but Buck was the power behind the throne. Buck was an accomplished Shona scholar and the mission published Shona literature including a reader for schools and a hymnbook. (Later Hallward, taking the name Cuthbert, was professed in CR in 1917 and Buck in 1919.) Neither were decisive leaders and things were very difficult; Buck got across Mother Annie; school discipline deteriorated.

CR at Penhalonga

By 1914 CR was able to take on St Augustine's. Longridge, now Superior, argued that if CR now refused, the mission would probably collapse. Longridge told the bishop that CR could not take on further financial responsibility in addition to the College at Mirfield, work in South Africa and the new London House. He proposed that as in South Africa the diocese should support the first brethren and that CR would pay for any beyond that number. CR wanted the diocese to own the mission; it owned only what was absolutely necessary, for example, the Mother House.

Longridge appointed Bertram Barnes as head of the mission. Barnes always retained something of the independent-minded liberalism of his Unitarian upbringing. A photograph of 1936 shows Raynes in cassock and biretta with Barnes in a light grey suit with prominent pocket handkerchief and a huge white beard looking like a visiting professor. He enjoyed reading and re-reading Dickens' novels in sequence to trace the development of his mind. He was known as 'Fr Gadget' for his many inventions: for example, by pulling a string the occupant of an outside privy could hoist a flag indicating that it was engaged. Before profession in 1906 he had worked with the Universities Mission to Central Africa in Nyasaland and was heartbroken when he had to return to England because of blackwater fever. He had developed a remarkable aptitude for languages and translation, and made a notable contribution to a project to reduce the Shona dialects into a unified language. At Penhalonga he wrote much of his *Johnson of Nyasaland*, the biography of a great UMCA missionary.

Longridge stressed to Barnes the importance of keeping up community life. He should not start too many projects which would take him away from Penhalonga. The bishop told Barnes that he was to be 'the *real* Head' of the mission; '*I insist on this.*' Etheridge offered advice – quinine, mosquito nets and forbearance with the staff were vital. The prestige of the mission had suffered through unwise spending and lack of supervision. Buck was going to other work. Hallward left for Mirfield in 1915.

Barnes arrived at Umtali from Johannesburg after a three day train journey on 6 January 1915. Robert Baker, professed for only a month, arrived from Mirfield in February. He was to spend the next thirty-two years at Penhalonga. Before university he had been a railway engineer. He became a great pioneer priest who kept the accounts, dispensed medicines, extracted teeth, circumcised, trained ordinands and whose architectural skills were admired by Walter Tapper. Once while conducting a Three Hours at Penhalonga he told the congregation to sing a very long litany and that if he wasn't back by the end, to sing it again. When eventually he returned he explained that he had been delivering a baby. 'By instinct and upbringing a stiff Tory High Churchman' (*CRQ* LD 1954) he was brusque with Nonconformist missionaries. Though he could speak Shona quite well he did so with a defiantly English accent. There were also a newly-ordained white priest, two laymen, three African teachers, Mother Annie and four white women teachers. Mother Annie, dressed like a nun, continued her independent ways. She kept a herd of cows which provided milk, butter and cheese. She expected the mission to maintain her cowsheds but bought and sold cattle without reference to anyone. She wanted the cows milked at 11 a.m. but the brethren said milking should take place after mass. In 1919 sisters of the Community of the Resurrection from Grahamstown (no connection with CR) took over from her at St Monica's. A government inspector in 1915 reported that at St Monica's 'industrial work' was paramount. Domestic skills and learning to milk cows were more important than spelling or multiplication.

A visitor to St Augustine's in 1915 wrote:

> Umtali lies in a valley surrounded by a tumbled pile of mountains, green and well-wooded, with huge granite rocks standing out against the skyline. I sallied forth in the motor which plies between Umtali and Penhalonga, and for the first few miles the road climbs steeply up to the summit of Christmas Pass from which a glorious view is obtained of the two valleys in which Umtali and Penhalonga lie. From there we run down to the hamlet Bartissol. From here a boy carried my bag up the track which rose quickly to a spur of the hills and then began to wind round the side of a kopje, next came an avenue of blue gums, and the goal was reached. Is there a more romantically situated mission than this? Perched on the side of a hill the view is superb across the valley to the mountains, the crest of which is the boundary of the farm . . . On Good Friday the service of the Stations of the Cross was held out of doors for the benefit of the catechumens and heathen. The pictures were hung on the trees of the avenue . . . On Holy Saturday the most impressive event was the Solemn Baptism of 70 adults by immersion in the open air font outside the church. The first Easter Day Eucharist began at 6 a.m., two more followed and were not over till 10 a.m. Large numbers came in from outstations, some having walked over 20 miles.[4]

In 1916 CR strengthened the work by sending two brethren who had considerable parochial experience before coming to Mirfield. Alfred Drury arrived in March. Baker, he reported, looked thin and worn but Barnes presided over the mission like a genial judge in Israel. An ardent socialist, Drury proposed that the litany of the Church Socialist League should be used in chapel. Barnes after two years travelling by motor-cycle on the Rand found it a huge change to ride on a mule. 'We do our own ploughing, sowing and reaping. We undertake the daily care of the cattle kraal and the gardens and orchards . . . We grind in our own mills, by hand or by water power.' The boys helped to pay for their own education by farm work. Later that year Wilfrid Shelley arrived and undertook the arduous trekking round the outstations. Some children had never seen a white face and were terrified. After a worrying first year, with four brethren the mission now forged ahead. Teacher training began in earnest in 1917. Some returned to be trained as deacons and priests. Many were middle-aged men who had already taught at outstations.

Spanish flu (which killed millions throughout the world 1918–19) reached Penhalonga. There were many sick at the mission and in the village. One died at the mission; there were seventy deaths in Penhalonga. Baker made up sixteen whisky bottles of pneumonia medicine and ten gallons of cough medicine and he with another brother moved to the edge of the gold compound, two and a half miles away, to minister to the sick there and in the surrounding area. This work gave the brethren an entrance into the mining community (the mine employed 3,000 Africans).

Africa provided an outlet for many brethren who felt most fulfilled in parochial and practical work. One such was Ralph Bell who wanted C R to run an English parish. He arrived in 1924 for four years with (it is said) thirteen pieces of luggage including golf clubs and a gun. Straight as a ramrod, with the brusque speech and wry humour of the North Riding squirearchy, he enjoyed being in charge of the upkeep of the mission roads and 150 cows, oxen, pigs and chickens. Later at Mirfield when he was in charge of the grounds he was known as 'Pharaoh'. He looked after the white congregation at St Michael's in the village, for whom he produced a parish new-sheet beginning 'My dear People'. He wrote in one: 'If you come then don't expect any fireworks; we do nothing in the sensational stunt line, you will find just an ordinary simple service with a dull sermon towards the end.' When the village heard that Aidan Cotton had written a book allegedly favouring mixed marriages, white mineworkers set off to the mission threatening to burn it down. A mine manager telephoned a warning. Bell met the irate miners on the road, told them that no one in the Community took any notice of what Fr Cotton thought and they dispersed peacefully.

Whites were suspicious of St Augustine's because it promoted African advancement. C R seems to have made surprisingly little effort to get alongside the whites in Penhalonga and Umtali, though the mission had an annual Agricultural Show and competed in a similar show in Umtali. But for most of the time the mission lived as an isolated and self-contained unit. When in 1937 the school was moving towards secondary education it did not contribute to the Umtali show because it did not want to draw the attention of whites to this controversial development. In 1930 Talbot wrote after a visit that Africans were pressing forward and no barriers could hold them: 'I don't think the white people as a whole here even dream of what is happening under their eyes – they protect themselves in an armour of ignorant cynicism, welded by fear.' In an article (*CRQ* C D 1932) Baker argued that the church had to take a lead against repression not by agitation but by 'developing' the Africans. Africans were now deeply affected by European life. He heard an African whistling the Marseillaise and discovered he had served in the Labour Corps in France during the war. Another disappeared for some time and when he turned up he had been to Durban, Singapore and Calcutta. More and more Africans were familiar with the world of cars, planes, gramophones and machinery. By 1929 nine African clergy had been trained at St Augustine's. When the altar for the shrine to Bernard Mizeki, the Mashonaland martyr, was dedicated at

Marondera in 1936, the senior African priest of the diocese presided at the mass. Two years later the shrine, designed by Baker, was consecrated, and is now the focus of an annual pilgrimage. A window to Mizeki was placed in the cathedral. At St Augustine's by 1921 there was a consultative mission council with black participation. But there was no doubt who ran things and procured the finance.

Shearly Cripps admired Penhalonga but some brethren were critical of his attitudes. He tried to live an African style of life and walked everywhere. He lived simply – he patched his boots with beef tins. He insisted that Africans built churches in their own style. Because he disagreed with the church's acceptance of government money for education, he later refused to be licensed by the bishop. He rejoiced in a daily mass, but was quite ready to worship with anyone from Dutch Reformed to Roman Catholics and Methodists – then a rare attitude. Brethren considered Cripps aloof from the diocese, unfair to the government and that it was the duty of whites to give Africans the best of European culture. Yet Cripps came from a similar background to many of CR – Charterhouse and Trinity, Oxford. Like Gore, his mentor, he resisted regimentation. Perhaps Cripps, 'God's Irregular', represented something free and Spirit-blown which CR lost because it was devoted to institutions. His Franciscan poverty was only possible because he was a free-lance individualist. Cripps wanted to preserve African culture by keeping Africans in rural areas. Was this a version of William Morris' Merrie England, another form of white paternalism?

To gain white support, missionaries had to show that Africans could be 'civilized', which meant inculcating them with white culture and Christianity. At this stage many Africans, wanting to be honorary whites, were easily persuaded to despise their own culture and religion. So when in 1936 new school buildings were opened by the Governor at St Augustine's, the Litany was sung to Byrd and the Mass to plainsong. (A few years later African music began to be used in the church. As early as 1929 Trelawney-Ross had pleaded for a genuinely African liturgy.) Pupils put on a performance of the 'Mikado', and there was a grand march past of the whole school with flags flying, sports trophies held aloft while the Governor took the salute beneath the flagstaff. Pupils were also taught Morris dancing and English rounds. A CR flag committee decided on which days the flag should be flown: Church Feasts, Empire Day, King's Birthday and Rhodes Day. There were close relationships between CR and successive Governors. When Talbot preached in 1938 at the consecration of Salisbury Cathedral (architect Sir Herbert Baker) he was entertained at Government House by Sir Herbert and Lady Stanley.

The appeal literature from Penhalonga up to the late 1930s was often histrionic. A leaflet of 1915 was entitled 'Waking Up!':

For 2,000 years or more the Natives of Rhodesia have been asleep. Witchcraft and

Worship of the spirits of the dead have kept them back from progress . . . At last, contact with European civilization and with the Christian Religion is waking them from their age-long sleep. Their eyes are opening to their long tale of backwardness and stagnation . . . The new day has its dangers for this child race. They are apt to pick up the evil things of civilization . . . For them it is now Christianity or nothing.

Here as in most other missionary literature Christianity has been identified with an evolutionary understanding of history regarded as progressing from the primitive to the civilized, from darkness to light. A 1944 brochure *Mirfield in Africa* was subtitled 'Another Twenty Years Onward and Upward'. The achievements were massive and measurable, but in view of what has happened to African countries since independence the nature of both colonial and missionary enterprise needs drastic re-examination. An article by one of the staff in 1927 asserted: 'The Mashona is still a child and his mind is as a blank slate; you can write what you will.' Yet three years later Trelawney-Ross described some of the searching theological questions posed by pupils during a school mission:

Our Lord cured the disease of sin by His death. Why does sin still exist? . . . Why should the whole world suffer for the fault done by two persons? . . . Why cannot women read the gospel in church? . . . Were Adam and Eve really there, or is it only a fable? . . . Worshipping mashawe (departed spirits) is not bad . . . Our mashawe is just like the customs of the Church. (*CRQ* J B 1931)

Treks (by donkeys at this stage) took some brethren away for five or so weeks at a time. By the late 1930s there were forty outlying communities to visit. Such communities could be broken up by forced removals. Reginald Smith was angry in 1936 that a whole village with a congregation of forty and a flourishing school had been moved because a white farmer had bought the land for forestry and Africans had no security of tenure. Baker also feared they would fall prey to dissenters in their new surroundings.

Trekking was an arduous adventure which could be hazardous. Occasionally there were lions and leopards, regularly there were snakes and scorpions. Reginald Smith recorded 103 degrees in the shade on one trek. Maurice Bradshaw came to one river which was waist-high, so he and his 'trekking boy' had to carry above their heads all that they had unloaded from the donkeys – bedding, clothes, food and medicines. African Anglicans were subject to church discipline about moral questions and were expected to make their confessions. Europeans escaped such systematic discipline, a distinction which Cripps criticized in synod. Denys Shropshire heard 5,000 confessions a year on trek. The simple outdoor life had its attractions for the English brought up in the scouting ethos. Bradshaw, who arrived in 1938, was thrilled to be eating the same old tinned food as in Borneo, boiling water on open fires, making rough meals by light of a smoking paraffin lamp. When brethren noted that Cotton had put on weight, they remembered that he had been trekking for a total of twenty-six weeks by donkey.

In 1929 one of the brethren realized that the chalice at a particular outstation was an unusual shape. Looking at it more carefully he saw inscribed on it 'G. S. Hoare, Winner of the House Fives Cup, Eton 1895'. He also observed that the leather case for the vessels had belonged to Timothy Rees and listed the places where it had been used: '1915 Hospital Ship Mediterranean', '1916 Somme', '1917 Passchendaele', '1918–19 51st General Hospital Etaples'. He remembered that all the portable Communion Sets from former CR chaplains had been brought to Africa.

For many brethren Africa was an immense emotional liberation. Smith contrasted the repressed, decorous services for whites with the lively African masses where the women suckled their babies, the music was sung with deep feeling and everyone made their confessions beforehand. One brother taking communion to a sick woman was moved when schoolchildren knelt as he passed. Brethren could develop a free Catholicism in the tradition of Dolling, teach the rosary and conduct Stations of the Cross and there was no fear of protestant or episcopal displeasure. The people deferred to their priestly and paternal authority in a way that was rare in England, but the deference had as much to do with race as with religion. Above all there was the spontaneous warmth of the children who would run, arms outstretched, give a hug, then hold hands. Smith in conversation described how drastically Penhalonga changed him:

> I knew that I had got to be nice to the African people and love them, but I was all stiff inside and I'd sort of smile and shake hands and I wouldn't really want to have anything to do with them. The change came one day when I was standing on the open space in front of the church at Penhalonga, and there were two small black toddlers and an ox broke away and charged across the open space. The children screamed and rushed to me and held me round the legs. I suddenly realized that they were not black but just children, so I picked them up and kissed and comforted them and that changed my attitude. From then on I was human with African people.

He stayed at Penhalonga twenty-eight years.

Baptism could appear to the African to be as much about gaining the favour of the white Father as finding favour with God. With some anguish Roland Langdon-Davies wrote about 'coping with candidates for the catechumenate and for baptism in the villages in their thousands, ready to do almost anything to be baptized, and submit to almost any degree of irritation and brusqueness on the part of the harassed "father" . . . the candidates beating their heads against walls, moaning half through the night outside one's hut, because they have been "failed" for baptism.'

'I wish you could see the new church' Hubert Northcott wrote on his first visit in 1933, 'there is something a little reminiscent of some of those Italian churches in Florence, with their wide piazza in front, giving distance, almost aloofness . . .' Its twin west towers, sixty feet high, at the end of a 150 foot nave, face inwards to the piazza, but stand out against the sky and mountains behind. The basilican church makes a powerful statement: that European Catholic Christianity has been permanently planted in Africa – it is southern Europe which it evokes not England. The interior is cool and spare, designed to focus awed eyes on the Elevation of the Host. The church needed to be large to accommodate the hundreds who flock to St Augustine's from far and near for the festivals. It was built close to the remains of Bishop Knight-Bruce's kitchen where Victor had created an outdoor altar. The huge church designed by Baker, helped by Victor and guided by designs prepared by Fleming, cost a mere £4,000. The half million bricks were baked and laid and the woodwork made by Africans at the mission. It had taken four years to complete and Baker's ingenuity enabled it to be built round the old church which was then knocked down and removed when the new was ready. It was very different from the thatched church Cripps built at Maronda Mashanu in 1912 which evoked the ancient ruins at Zimbabwe with openings for birds to fly in and out.

A touching connection between the church and England was created in 1958 when a fourteenth-century Angelus bell inscribed 'Ave Maria Gratia Plena' was hung in one of the towers. Removed from a Bedfordshire parish church at the Reformation, for centuries it struck the hours for a courtyard clock at a nearby manor house. At Penhalonga in 1983 when it rang, everyone whether walking or working paused and prayed.

The great church was consecrated by Bishop Paget on 23 July 1932. Sir Herbert Stanley, then South African High Commissioner, entered to the singing of 'God save the King'. Afterwards Stanley wrote to Baker: 'May the Divine Grace rest on the work of the Mission and bring, through that work ever more of those who walk in ignorance and darkness into the way of the light and the knowledge of the truth.' For those staff who were keenly aware of the power of evil in the area, the church building was a triumphant proclamation of that confident faith. A teacher from England said in conversation that there was a frontier within the African which Christianity rarely crossed. 'You would not get them to walk past the graveyard at night because they believed evil spirits wandered in there at night.' A boy who believed that he had been bewitched went home and died even though the doctor said there was nothing wrong with him. 'You can feel the power of spirits at Penhalonga – there is the stone where we were told human sacrifice had taken place.'

Baker bore so many responsibilities at the mission that the Africans nicknamed him 'the back of the crocodile'. Another of his achievements was the creation in 1935 at Penhalonga of the czr (Chita che Zita Rinoyera) the African Sisters of the Holy Name, the first such Anglican community in

Rhodesia, under the guidance of a CR warden and the white sisters. The Grahamstown sisters worked at Penhalonga until 1953. Both they and the Whitby sisters who followed them provided much needed mothering for African pupils, as well as strengthening the teaching staff.

Crowds of people came from outstations for Christmas communion, but Easter was the great feast. Groups came and camped at the mission for their final three weeks preparation for baptism and confirmation and did manual work in return for their food. During Holy Week a great Passion Play was performed in the church and on the piazza. Then came the baptisms and confirmations on Easter Eve and after the early Easter mass with perhaps 1,000 communicants, oxen were roasted and in the afternoon some 3,000 sang and danced on the piazza. Total immersion in the river stopped in the 1950s, because of the risk of bilharzia. Some Africans also had asked why they should be immersed when whites in their churches were not. So the baptismal gowns were cut up for theatricals.

'The education is very largely industrial and agricultural' Talbot reported after a visit in 1926, though of course everyone learned the three Rs. So there was bootmaking, brickmaking, carpentry, tailoring, printing, agriculture for the boys; the girls learned housewifery, weaving and sewing; both did dairying. Inspectors and white supporters were happy with such a programme. 'We do not encourage lazy people. All natives at the central station must work as part payment for their schooling' a 1920 leaflet reassured subscribers. Some in CR in the 1920s believed that the 'book-fed native' tended to become 'conceited'. However Harry Buck contended that pupils should learn not only manual skills but also psychology, politics, economics and sociology to fit them for future leadership. Nevertheless brethren saw themselves as parents. 'My dear son' (or daughter) Buck wrote, ending his letters 'your loving Father'. Such language sometimes created confusion, as when an ex-pupil married and was described in a newspaper as 'the son of Fr Barnes'.

By the mid-1930s St Augustine's was moving towards a more academic education. In 1934, Winter, who had done marvels creating secondary education in Rosettenville, arrived at Penhalonga to be head of the Primary school and Teacher Training department. The educational standards for African clergy, teachers and nurses needed to be raised. It was both undesirable and impractical for Africans to have to go to South Africa for secondary education. Secondary education was essential if Rhodesia was ever to have its own university. But the attitude of the government was lukewarm, even hostile. It was uncertain whether it would provide any funds. Winter had to face criticism inside as well as outside CR: 'it would produce conceited Africans, and separate them from their backgrounds', to which he replied that those were dangers in all education; 'they would be over-educated for the available jobs', to which he responded that Africans must be allowed to do a greater variety of jobs and that the number of secondary pupils would be small.

By 1938 the government was beginning to soften after much pressure from Baker and Winter.

In January 1939 St Augustine's became the first secondary school for Africans in Rhodesia. Between 1941 and 1957, 266 candidates successfully passed the Certificate. But it was some time before the government gave grants. Fortunately the Beit Trustees, s p g and s p c k helped with bursaries and money for buildings and equipment. Pupils benefited greatly from the teaching of Benjamin Baynham. After a curacy he arrived at Penhalonga in 1938 to teach for half a crown a week plus his keep and saw through the first crucial years of secondary education before going to Rosettenville to train as a novice in 1942. Unlike most brethren he had had to struggle for his own education, so he readily identified with the Africans' own struggles. His first pupil was Herbert Chitepo and Baynham discussed with him his own conviction that Africans would come to power. But pupils still did industrial work for six hours a week and twice a week worked in the garden – the brethren, sisters and ordinands did manual work in the afternoons too: seeing whites and blacks working together astonished visitors. The academic side of education became increasingly dominant, and critics charge that its needs took over the mission and that the less able pupils suffered.

Trelawney-Ross wrote in 1929 that Penhalonga ought to be the most monastic c r house because it was isolated and self-supporting. But those two characteristics created many of its problems. There was little contact with local missions; Nonconformists were looked down upon, Roman Catholics distrusted. The mission was run as a self-contained diocese, but with its headquarters in the West Riding. Trekking brethren worked for weeks isolated from the other brethren; when they returned the others were often preoccupied with the many needs of the institution. At St Augustine's brethren worked in compartments and found a lot of their community life in their work areas rather than with other brethren. As early as 1923 Talbot was concerned about the cost to community life at St Augustine's and asked whether c r should withdraw. One brother on his way to Mirfield in 1924 stayed at Rosettenville, and commented that there he experienced 'brotherhood after three years negation of it at Penhalonga'. The Provincial Chapter in 1931 suggested St Augustine's would benefit from a more meditative recital of the offices and more private prayer. In addition, though the setting was idyllic, brothers suffered a good deal of disease in the earlier years, particularly malaria. Overwork was a temptation on an isolated mission with so much to be done. At one mission retreat someone read from J. H. Oldham's *Life* of Florence Allshorn, a missionary who concluded that the greatest problem on her mission was relationships with colleagues: 'it was identical with our experience' one teacher commented. Yet a layman who taught at Penhalonga in the 1950s and 1960s described it as 'the happiest time of my working life because of the close personal relations'. St Augustine's also felt isolated because many of the whites in nearby Umtali continued to be deeply suspicious of it. A lay teacher recalled how in the early 1950s she and another white teacher met by chance Herbert Chitepo, a former member of staff, then Rhodesia's first black barrister, in a shop in Umtali. The shop assistant immediately reported to the police that two white women had been speaking to a black man. When the two women arrived back at the mission the police were already there waiting to question them.

The need for regular consultation with Mirfield created problems. Those in Africa felt that those in England did not always understand their work, that they were not always consulted and that there was insufficient devolution of authority over minor issues. Even though major CR decisions were taken at General Chapter on which overseas houses were represented, those resident at Mirfield set the general tone and policy. The appointment of a Provincial in 1921 helped a little to devolve authority but there was a limit to devolution so long as CR planned its work and deployed its manpower centrally.

CR and racial questions

From the survey of CR's first fifty years or so of work in Africa in this and the previous chapter, it.is clear that the forthright approach to racial questions of Raynes and Huddleston had not always characterized CR's work in Africa. Baker, for example, deplored the Rhodesian Land Apportionment Act (1930) but concluded 'the matter is largely out of our hands'. CR's attitudes to racial injustice in South Africa became much more polemical when brethren began to live in the townships from 1934. By contrast, brethren at Penhalonga were largely isolated from the racial oppression in Rhodesia. The range of brethren's attitudes can be gauged by looking at the writings of Cotton, Victor and Shropshire.

Aidan Cotton was born and ordained in Canada and came to Mirfield in 1909. From 1911, for thirty-four years, he served in Africa as Principal of St Peter's College, Prior of Penhalonga, Prior of Rosettenville and finally in Sekhukhuniland. In *The Race Problem in South Africa* (1926) he proposed complete territorial segregation but advocated very occasional mixed marriages which would serve as bridges between the races. In *Racial Segregation in South Africa* (1931) he reiterated these proposals while rejecting what he described as the Calvinist belief that no change of status was possible for Africans. In an astonishing passage he extended his proposals to Southern Rhodesia, which he explained to Africans as follows:

We have come into your country as immigrants: first because we are strong and you are weak; and secondly because neither for yourselves nor for the world at large are you making the best use of this portion of the earth's surface. Your tribes have no peace one with another . . . You lack national spirit and unity; you are without individual freedom and security and dignity. You are ignorant of very many of the discoveries whereby, in the world's long history, human life has been enriched. You have no literature. Your religion is not only defective; it is marred, as is indeed, your whole outlook on life, by your mistaken magical conceptions . . . We come, then, we take possession of your country for our Sovereign – not as blatant conquerors, but as preceptors and as rulers. We do not despise your ancient polity, and so we set aside areas which in your old way of living would suffice for your present needs . . .

But Africans (he continued) would be free to work in the white areas 'under our leadership, under our system, and at present for the most part under our mastership'. It is surprising that Talbot felt able to write even a guarded Preface to Cotton's book. He explained in a letter that if Bull had liberty to proclaim his socialism, Eustace Hill his opposition to contraception, then Cotton must have freedom to express his views. Cripps in his *Africa for Africans* (1927) had adopted a similar line, though mercifully without Cotton's arrogant bombast, but in 1950 inserted a rejection of segregation into the remaining copies of his book.

Cotton also had strong views about CR's work in Africa. In a memorandum of 1932 he asserted that its African Houses lacked 'peace and happiness' and brethren in CR as a whole worked individualistically. He proposed an 'abjuring of excitement'. In the Benedictine system excitement and pugnacity (Cotton himself had both) were quelled through routine work done under obedience. He contrasted the fellowship of the Oxford Groups with CR: 'How is it that with all our Communions, all our Confessions, all our striving after common ideals, our experience of fellowship is as disappointing as in fact it is?' In another memorandum of 1937 he proposed an amalgamation of all Third Orders (including FR) in South Africa to combat racialism, divorce, contraception and masturbation and to promote celibacy, continence and prayer. There was clearly a dotty side to Cotton, but some of the questions he posed about CR here and elsewhere were extremely pertinent. We should also remember 'Baba Cottoni' as Africans called him affectionately, riding his donkey around the outstations reading the works of Shakespeare.

Osmund Victor's popular book *The Salient of Africa* (1931) was much more representative of CR's missionary attitudes than Cotton's writings, though he included them in his bibliography. For Victor it was 'The Dark Continent' (frontispiece) to be conquered and enlightened – hence the title which evokes the bloody battles of the First World War to extend the Ypres Salient against enemy attacks. (Victor was a former chaplain.) Though it was natural for two diverse peoples to want to live separately it was 'madness' to enforce segregation by legislation. The church must manifest the abolition of barriers proclaimed by St Paul. Yet Africans needed 'a measure of separation' to develop their own form of Christianity though, alas, this easily became segregation, as when black servants were prevented from attending white churches. The Victorian progressivism of Victor's outlook is summed up by the diagram 'The Upward Path of Native Education' in which the African climbs 'the mount of Knowledge'. Though Victor enthused over plays devised by Africans on biblical themes, he showed no real interest in African religion or culture. Africans were there to be converted, educated, helped, defended. An older black priest in conversation implicitly supported Victor's approach: without CR (he said) we would all be still common labourers. But younger Africans became disillusioned and bitter when having been 'educated' and 'civilized' they were still denied votes and job opportunities, and for these and other reasons questioned the basic assumptions of missionary work.

Denys Shropshire's approach was quite different from that of either Cotton or Victor. Shropshire worked in Africa for twenty-seven years and became a distinguished anthropologist. Winter, who saw everything in simple antitheses, remarked snidely in Shropshire's obituary (*CRQ* MD 1962) that he became so fascinated by local religion 'that some among us began to think that he was more interested in their heathen and primitive background than in the preaching of the Gospel'. His *The Church and Primitive Peoples* (1938) pleaded for 'careful discrimination, preservation, transmutation and transformation of the religious and cultural institutions and beliefs of the Southern Bantu, by and within a full-orbed presentation of the Christian religion'. When in 1940 he studied the social life, laws and customs of Sekhukhuniland, in preparation for his *Primitive Marriage and European Law* (1946), chiefs and headmen were delighted that a missionary should interest himself in their culture. Shropshire's approach was a development from *Lux Mundi* in which Illingworth had offered an account of God's seamless revelation in creation and incarnation and celebrated God's indwelling presence in science, philosophy, art, and other faiths. 'The pre-Christian religions were the age-long prayer. The incarnation was the answer.' So for Shropshire ancestor worship was fulfilled in the Communion of Saints, African sacrifices were fulfilled in the eucharist. Africans had their shrines, sacred places and libations. So did Catholic Christianity. Catholic Christianity is not Christo-centric or individualistic but offers a corporate, objective, hierarchical, and sacramental order 'lest the precious, communal values of the Bantu race be destroyed'. One practical consequence of this was that those with more than one wife should not on baptism be required 'to send away the women whom they have honourably married and who are the mothers of their children'. Shropshire's 'inclusivist' approach was developed within CR by L. S. Thornton in his monumental book *Revelation and the Modern World* (1950). Later it was expressed in the 'Christian Presence' series edited by Max Warren, to which Martin Jarrett-Kerr contributed *The Secular Promise* (1964). It was an approach totally at variance with that of Karl Barth and Hendrik Kraemer. More recently the 'inclusivist' approach of writers like Shropshire has been attacked as a form of Christian imperialism by writers like John Hick.[5]

In the 1940s and 1950s CR was embarrassed by the segregationalist views of

Basil Peacey, the first old student to become a bishop. He had spent his youth in South Africa and from 1917 served the rest of his ministry in South Africa. In 1929 he was consecrated Bishop of Lebombo at Rosettenville. But for the bishopric he might have joined CR. After going to Lebombo he married the formidable daughter of Senator Willie Hofmeyr, a fervent Nationalist. She converted him to Afrikaner racial policies. In 1935 he resigned and became Rector of Krugersdorp, near Johannesburg. When war broke out many Afrikaners were either neutral or pro-Nazi. Peacey caused a public sensation by refusing to allow the singing of 'God save the King' in his church. He was forced to compromise and allowed it to be sung as a prayer, kneeling, which satisfied no one. The congregation and funds began to melt away. Clayton was furious, and was relieved when he moved to a parish in Cape Province. In 1954 Peacey retired because as a supporter of apartheid he was at variance with the bishops. He refused to attend the 1958 synod because of the outspoken views of Joost de Blank, Clayton's successor. On the final pages of CR's copy of Peacey's booklet *When He Separated the Children of Men* (1954) Osmund Victor wrote a stinging critique concluding 'The whole thesis is in direct contradiction of Ephesians 2 and Colossians 3.' But Peacey claimed that Cotton's writings supported his proposals.

By this time traditional missionary work was beginning to be challenged by black Christians. The first Assembly of the All Africa Conference of Churches declared in 1963:

> We submit that missionary activity on this continent has not followed the New Testament pattern where the Apostle, whose weakness in lack of support from some foreign conquering power was really his strength, planted the seed of the Evangel, trained a few indigenous leaders, and left the Church to develop according to local genius, initiative and intuition.

Canon Burgess Carr, a Liberian Anglican, at the Third Assembly in 1974 (which supported a moratorium on foreign missionary work), denounced the 'naive hypothesis of cultural progress which places the western man at the top of an imaginary scale of evolutionary development'.[6]

The Christian tradition of *noblesse oblige* out of which CR grew was immensely self-sacrificial in its giving, but not in its receiving.

Confident Catholicism

The Second World War

The Second World War produced no national trauma like that created by its predecessor. Its military character, social and religious impact were very different. By 1939 both the nation and the churches had matured and were more prepared. Whereas the Great War is looked back upon with horror, many look back nostalgically to 1939–45 as Britain's 'finest hour'. The letters of chaplains and men in the first war were full of theological reflection, quotations from the Bible, Shakespeare and Bunyan. This time their letters were like the poetry of the period, laconic and free from *angst*.[1]

At the beginning of the war Curtis wrote a challenging article (*CRQ* CD 1939) which reflected the achievements of the ecumenical movement between the wars (in which he had played a part) in promoting the trans-national character of Christianity. Echoing William Temple and George Bell, Curtis wrote: 'There is always the danger that in time of war the Church will be so busy fulfilling its secondary duty of "stimulating sound patriotism", that she will neglect her primary duty of giving witness to the supernatural loyalty to Christ . . .' This must be expressed in the church's worship: the soldiers and the dead of *both* sides must be prayed for; the translation and publication of banned German theological works must be encouraged; atrocity-mongering and the spirit of hatred opposed.

The effect of the war on the daily life of CR in England was immediate. It was impossible to black out the upper church, so the crypt was used for some services in winter, though Compline was said in darkness upstairs – familiar phrases had a new meaning 'Thou shalt not be afraid for any terror by night'. The House cellars became an air-raid shelter for brethren and the nearby school. Regular ARP practices were held. One night Nash, now nearly eighty, caused great amusement by appearing in the cellar in his pyjamas wearing, not carrying, his gas mask. ARP and firewatching had to be organized. The mowing shed became an ARP post. The sick room was made ready to receive casualties. The Home Guard used the Quarry for practices. The participation of brethren and students in ARP and the Home Guard created more contact with local people than for twenty years or more. Richard Barnes, as captain of the local fire officers, regularly patrolled Battyeford streets in his white tin hat. Two brethren volunteered to be ambulance drivers. The cricket field was let to a local farmer. In 1942 the front lawn was ploughed up and yielded three tons of potatoes. CR won prizes at a local 'Dig for Victory' show. An aged couple and a few disabled helpers were the only domestic staff left, so brethren had to do much more domestic work. It was rumoured that CR was the centre of the black market, because the chapel bell was heard ringing many times a day. Each time it rang it was thought to be summoning brethren to yet another meal.

The novitiate emptied; aspirants cancelled – bishops required them to remain in their parishes. As Giles Ormerod and Benjamin Baynham could not travel from Africa, a temporary novitiate was created at Rosettenville. The Retreat House at St Leonard's was requisitioned and did not function again until 1945. Some German Jewish refugees came to stay at Mirfield. One whom CR had got out of Germany in 1938 became the Superior's secretary. Bell, who had long contended that CR should include the care of a parish among its works, to his delight was asked to look after Eton College Mission, Hackney during the war. When the sirens sounded he cycled round the streets reassuring and visiting the people, oblivious of danger. The London Priory in Pont Street was rendered uninhabitable in 1940 by bombing and brethren had to disperse. Instead a house in Holland Park was acquired and opened in 1944.

Commemoration Day was cancelled for the duration, but Quarry sermons continued. In 1942 four sermons by outsiders on 'The Freedom Worth Fighting For' attracted over 1,000 people, including mill-workers and servicemen, though the three by Christian socialists (Bishop Blunt, Fr Groser and Ivor Thomas MP) were dismissed by the Chronicler as 'humanistic'. The success of war-time policies of planning and fair shares boosted socialist self-confidence in CR as in the country generally. William Temple's *Christianity and Social Order* (1942), a Penguin best-seller, advocated a socialist pattern for post-war reconstruction. A sympathetic view of the communist system was purveyed by Government sponsored Anglo-Soviet friendship weeks. In the CR *Quarterly* Drury and MacLachlan attacked the individualistic pietism of many Christians, called for church people to work for a new form of society and appealed for a sympathetic understanding of the Soviet system (CD 1941, LD 1942). The war-time revival of Christian socialism in CR was also reflected in *Mirfield in Africa* (1944): 'While Polygamy and other things of Heathenism make their last bid for survival, Capitalism awaits the mortal stroke . . . Africans are both naturally and traditionally collectivists.' The British General Election of 1945 did not (the Chronicler recorded) produce the usual fierce political disagreements in CR. Labour brethren regretted having to vote against Churchill and some of his colleagues; Conservatives warmly admired the Labour leaders who had helped to win the war.

Before the war theological liberalism had been under a cloud. During the war

many leading Christian thinkers celebrated its demise. But Talbot, writing in
the dark days of 1940, with invasion imminent, refused to join the requiem:

> I do believe that the British world does carry a treasure at the heart of which is
> Christ. But we are earthen vessels. Must they be broken that the treasure may
> somehow be released? I find nothing to gloat over in the bankruptcy of 'liberalism'
> now so much derided. After all, the liberal ideas are the precipitations of the
> Christian *veritas* in the human order. But equally, no doubt, they have no final
> foundation except in the Catholic dogma – or rather in the reality which the dogma
> declares. Oh! that there may be a great and realistic awakening, a breaking of
> idealistic dreams, a facing of the terror and mercy of the Cross.

Note here that, like Temple, Talbot asserted that faith is in the reality to which
the dogma bears witness, not in the dogma itself. So during the war he went on
questioning, and refused to be intimidated by the dogmatists. Yet he knew that
the world of his parents, for which he longed sometimes, was past. Talbot
represented the older Liberal Catholicism now being superseded in CR by a
new dogmatism represented by Raymond Raynes. The new dogmatists in the
English churches argued that only a forceful doctrinal faith could stand up to
secularism. They tried to strengthen their cause by claiming that all Hitler's
Christian opponents were dogmatists, all his Christian allies were liberals.
Andrew Blair, one of those closest to Raynes in CR, used this argument not
only to discredit theological liberalism but also Lutheranism, the Enlighten-
ment and the Church of South India (*CRQ* MD 1945). Over against Blair and
the dogmatists it can be argued that it was precisely the lack of a deeply rooted
liberal tradition in theology and politics in Germany which encouraged
irrationalism, of which Nazism and Barthianism were different expressions,
that some of Hitler's strongest supporters were theologically extremely
orthodox and that Bonhoeffer in his *Letters and Papers from Prison* showed how
far he had moved from dogmatic orthodoxy.[2]

In CR, three deaths were other reminders of an era which was passing. Bull
died in 1942. His funeral was attended by representatives of the Labour Party.
Nash, the last of the founding members, and Sampson (professed in 1896)
both died in 1943. A resplendent hanging rood over the sanctuary, designed
by Michael Tapper, marred by the insipidness of the figure, commemorates
Nash and his South African episcopate.

Only seven brethren served as chaplains, a much smaller proportion than in
the First World War. Both Horner and Raynes were opposed in principle to
brethren going on detached service. Some like Shearburn thrived – having
survived Dunkirk, he became Deputy Assistant Chaplain-General in India
and entered Burma with the liberating army. He returned as Bishop of
Rangoon in 1955 and during the next eleven years prepared the church to
stand on its own feet. He saw that the time would come (as it did) when

missionaries would be forbidden. He sent two Burmese ordinands to Mirfield for training. One of them, George Kyaw Mya, has been a bishop since 1979. C R was glad to see Shearburn made a bishop, because this gave him the scope for his gifts which it could not provide. Justin Pearce managed to continue his expert work as an entomologist in spare moments during an R A F chaplaincy. (In 1954 a species of beetle was named after him as a tribute to his work.) But some brethren felt lost without the support of the fellowship and worship of C R. Chaplains, like their first war predecessors, discovered how alienated most of the men were from institutional religion. But they did not agonize about it to the same extent as their predecessors. In C R only Hugh Bishop produced the kind of memorable letters so characteristic of the first war. That was partly because of his eloquence and perception, partly because he spent three years in P O W camps, the only places in the second war where there was a comradeship comparable in closeness to that of the trenches.

Bishop, at Talbot's suggestion, became a chaplain at the end of 1940 barely a year after profession. He was then a triumphalist Anglo-Catholic. In a review (*CRQ* L D 1940) he remarked: '. . . not even the most sanguine and presumptuous humanist would dare lay claim to so thorough-going and far-reaching an optimism as that which is the unassailable possession of the humblest Catholic.' On his first Sunday as a chaplain he had prepared for the eucharist, but no one came, and he felt very isolated. He joined an exercise and spent one night in a shed with cows and rats, but it was so freezingly cold that he spent most of the night walking and running to keep warm. He flew the flag by substituting a simple non-communicating eucharist for the usual Parade service of hymns, lesson, canticle, address, which could give the impression that God was an adjunct to the national cause. The Chaplain-General forbade him to continue this practice and ensured he was posted overseas. Hugh, passing through Cairo, reported to Mirfield the sad news that there were probably no vestments anywhere in that diocese. Captured at Tobruk in June 1942, he was housed in a former Cistercian monastery, rat-infested, unheated, dilapidated, disused but beautiful, high up in the Apennines. But community and religion flourished. Of the 470 officers and 60 other ranks, 210 communicated at the Christmas eucharist and there were up to a dozen at daily mass. As well as an early celebration on Sundays, he instituted a non-communicating mass sung to Merbecke. His Sunday evening lectures were packed out. 'He was the finest and noblest speaker that I have ever heard' reported a subaltern. Several were ordained as a result of Hugh's ministry to them in the camp. In 1944 he reported from a camp in Germany:

I've learnt a good deal about what and how 'the educated young Englishman' thinks in these last two years and I am convinced that the only religion which will win him is the Catholic Religion. And it must be presented to his mind and conscience honestly, reasonably and fearlessly. Compromise and 'moderation' (as distinct from discretion) doesn't pay and doesn't work. I do really believe we shall have the ball at our feet after the war; pray God for good priests. (*CRQ* MD 1944)

The attractions of Rome were sometimes very great. He longed for certainty and authority; he had seen the results of division in Jerusalem; he had been shaken by his disputes with the Chaplains' Department. In 1942 he was horrified when Carl Runge (a chaplain with the South African forces) communicated non-Anglicans and celebrated in the evening. CR censured Runge for both actions. (Brethren were also appalled that year when Osmund Victor as Dean of Salisbury, Rhodesia, invited a Free Church minister to preach.) Runge was doing impressive work, but his uncertainties about his vocation increased when as a chaplain he was away from CR. He eventually became a Roman Catholic in 1952. Hugh arrived back in England on Ascension Day 1945, pale and thin. When he visited the sisters at Burnham, one remarked 'That young man won't live long'. He became Warden of the Hostel in 1946. He looks a haunted man in the annual photographs.

Talbot had been deeply disturbed by Hugh's treatment by the Chaplains' Department. Surely chaplains must be free (he wrote to his brother in 1941) to present the faith in the way they think best. He defended Hugh's use of a non-communicating mass:

> ... the right end at which to approach and present worship is not directly the Communion end but first of all Offering . . . To be sure Communion is integral . . . [but] it seems to me that men whose lives are already, on the natural level, being caught up into an action of self-offering willy-nilly, may find contact with the supreme Christian mystery just at that point . . .

CR sent a memorandum, drawn up by Talbot, to the Archbishops. The Chaplains' Department should allow a non-communicating eucharist, after suitable instruction, as a Parade service. No service now was familiar to the majority of men. Therefore it was right for them to start with the central act of the church's worship. (CR also pleaded for officially recognized chaplains' retreats and for Anglican chaplains to be responsible to a bishop, not to senior chaplains who might not be Anglicans.)[3]

Raymond Raynes

Raymond Raynes (1903–58), Superior from 1943 to 1958, was brought up in an earnest evangelical and somewhat spartan home. At Oxford Raymond proved intelligent, but no academic – he got a Fourth. Politics and the arts did not interest him. He became engrossed by the church. He felt increasingly called to an ascetic life. In Africa he found a cause. People responded to his uncomplicated dogmatic faith. First at Sophiatown, then as Provincial, he proved a decisive leader. He was at home in a self-governing and synodical church whose bishops were of the Catholic tradition. When he returned as Superior he found the establishment, complexity and variety of the Church of England intolerable. In Africa, as a parish priest, the personal and social needs of the Africans had daily determined his ministry and informed his prayers. As Superior he put all his energies into CR, into ecclesiastical politics, into the conversion of individuals. He remained committed to social justice in South Africa. He kept clear of the social problems of England.

For years he had been driving himself relentlessly. To some this was heroic self-sacrifice; to others he seemed intent on self-destruction. After an intestinal operation in 1941 he was never really well. He looked gaunt and hawklike, with his stoop and cropped hair. He ate and slept even less. Michael Ramsey was a Durham Professor when he first met Raynes in 1943. 'I found him frightening, austere, fanatical. I was conscious of the clash between what he stood for and the rather liberalized and comfortable sort of Catholic churchmanship in which I had lived.' Later he became aware of Raynes' humility, gentleness and wisdom and a friendship developed. Ramsey judged that his faith was Jesus-centred rather than Trinitarian; Raynes reminded him of an early Jesuit or early Methodist, or 'half-Salvation Army'. Nicholas Mosley wrote: 'He was unlike any other person I had met in that his great authority did not seem to come from his own personality, but from a transparency to something beyond him.' Brethren with whom he talked into the early hours experienced his understanding and sympathy. Others found him forbidding or flippant and kept their distance. As in Africa, he found most of his nourishing relationships outside the Community. To Rowan Williams the importance of those like Raynes 'is not their rightness or their balance, but in the depth at which they disturb you' (*CRQ* MD 1983).

Raynes was a startling change from the debonair, demonstrative, well-connected Talbot. Talbot expounded Christianity from within the riches of European culture. It was natural for him to liken Christ to Orpheus in the story of Odysseus and the Sirens. He was aware (like the Bible) of the ambiguity of religion. 'God is not half so religious as the curate' he would quote. Talbot ruminated round a question. Raynes was dogmatic, decisive. Talbot was sympathetic to those who could not identify with the institutional church, yet who cared for the things which matter to God. To Raynes belief in the church was on the same level as belief in God. His mission addresses were blunt and earthy:

> I'll tell you why lots of people have committed suicide – either because they haven't been taught, or because they were too proud, to make their confession. It's a damnable device of the devil to keep people away from our Lord to raise all this nonsense and fallacy about the simple, straightforward gift of our Lord to the Church, the sacramental means of forgiveness. People say 'Ought I to go to

confession?' Well, what do you mean by ought? What do you want? When you kneel
and say 'the burden of my sins is intolerable', do you mean it? There is only one thing
to do with that intolerable burden – 'Cast thy burden on the Lord'. And how do you
propose to do it? 'Must I go to confession?' Do you want to learn more and more of
the depth of the love of Christ, or don't you? I can't make any one go to confession; I
can't make them clean their teeth, but I know it is a good thing to clean your teeth
and I know it is a good thing to go to confession.[4]

He was equally dogmatic about moral questions. He once spoke about
marriage and divorce to the College. He was asked what he would say to a
remarried couple, with a family, who wanted to be confirmed. He replied that
because of the children they should not be required to separate, but that they
should give up all sexual relations. A novice, Norwood Coaker, a former South
African Advocate, had the courage to denounce Raynes' advice as a recipe for
disaster.

Talbot was always the gracious host to guests. Raynes often ignored them.
The genteel recreation in the parlour over which Talbot had presided
withered. Raynes wanted to get rid of ease and gentility. He wanted to end the
identification of Anglicanism with middle-class moralism, niceness and
appeasement. In his early years as Superior he made a virtue out of being rude
to bishops. It was said at Mirfield that Raynes had three topics – Bishops,
British Rail and Blacks, and that only Blacks could do no wrong. A chairman
of a conference on temperance enquired earnestly: 'And how would *you*
approach the drink problem, Father Raynes?' He replied 'With a corkscrew'.
It was not the kind of humour to appeal to Evangelicals or Nonconformists.
He wanted the Church of England to be of the people, like the Anglicanism of
the Johannesburg townships. In his *Thoughts of a Religious* (1959) there is a
section 'In praise of the Vulgar' – he argued that churches could be so
artistically correct, and services so dignified that they cease to be homely.
Talbot never praised the vulgar. But Raynes followed Stanton and Dolling,
not Dearmer and Frere. Talbot was the perfect ex-Superior. He paid
generous tributes to the new life and decisive leadership Raynes was bringing
to CR. But Talbot feared that he was getting too involved in church politics.
'He has a pugnacious impulse which makes him want to charge whenever he
sees error raising its head.'

There were a few who resented the new regime, including Horner. But
most were longing for change and leadership. Ellis, Blair, Huddleston and
Bishop were particularly enthusiastic. Ellis rejoiced: 'Now we shall have a
Superior who goes to the altar every day.' Raynes appointed Blair as Prior.
Blair's humour and commonsense oiled the wheels – not Raynes' *forte*. But as
a devoted disciple he did not always stand up to Raynes when necessary or
understand those who questioned the new policies. Bishop wholeheartedly
welcomed moves towards a stricter form of the Religious Life. As a novice he

had read Cuthbert Butler's *Benedictine Monachism* and both as an individual and as Novice Guardian (1949–52) interpreted the CR Rule in as Benedictine a spirit as possible.

In July 1943, a couple of months after his return, Raynes presented a formidable package of proposals to his first General Chapter. There were several minor but revealing proposals such as the restoration of the cursing Psalms, and regulations about where women could be entertained (only in the waiting room) and where their confessions could be heard (only in parish churches). The major proposal was a new form of profession and a clarification of the method of release. There would now be a first profession for three years (but with a life-long intention) followed (unless CR or the individual decided otherwise) by final profession. For the first time the word 'vow' was used. The change was considered sufficiently important for brethren who wished to renew their profession under the new form to be able to do so.

Raynes believed that CR suffered from individualism. He told Chapter in 1944 that the church was not a democracy but a hierarchy. Obedience should be thought of not simply as a means towards efficiency, nor even as a cure for self-will. Obedience to the Superior should be regarded as obedience to Christ – Raynes here echoed the Benedictine understanding of obedience to the Abbot. Some were alarmed by what they regarded as authoritarianism. But it fitted in with the current climate of social and theological collectivism, in which individual needs were subordinated to those of the community.[5] True, Raynes continued to accept the CR tradition of safeguarding the liberty of the individual, partly out of conviction, more because he was bound by the Constitution. However, the new regime exerted a powerful if subtle pressure towards conformity. This was increased by Raynes' readiness, most unwisely, to hear the confessions of brethren. More now shaved their heads or closely cropped their hair like Raynes, more wore scapulars regularly, as he did. (Talbot never wore one.) Scapulars looked more monastic. Raynes tried to secure more uniformity of dress – standard cassocks; regulation belts; no trousers showing; sober socks; no slippers in public places. Cassocks should almost invariably be worn as a witness to simplicity and community allegiance. There was more fasting – not many now ate lunch on Fridays. Raynes wrote a standard preface for a series of 'Mirfield Books': each author had 'complete freedom of expression' but the editors ensured 'the essential orthodoxy' of each book. Raynes prefaced his *Darkness no Darkness* (1958): 'I have no desire to teach any new thing, and my intention is that all that is written is to be interpreted in accordance with the dogmas and doctrine of the Catholic and Apostolic Church.' That sounded impressive – just what a dutiful Roman Catholic would write. But what did it mean when written by an Anglican? In 1946 the Bishop of Bloemfontein said he would resign as South African Visitor if an article in the *CR Quarterly* (CD 1945) which included the (Roman

Catholic) 'Divine Praises' represented CR teaching. (The author was Jonathan Graham.) Raynes replied that articles were not officially endorsed by CR. He assumed that the bishop objected particularly to 'Blessed be her holy and immaculate conception', so Raynes treated him to a general defence of the clause adding (speciously) that the Church of England had never condemned the doctrine.

Martin Jarrett-Kerr's book *D. H. Lawrence and Human Existence* (1951) had to be published under a pseudonym ('Father Tiverton'). Raynes thought that CR supporters might be shocked by a book on Lawrence from Mirfield. The publishers were cross, for Jarrett-Kerr's name was widely known. Could he therefore ask someone well-known to write a preface? T. S. Eliot agreed to do so. As a result it achieved a much wider circulation. Ten years later Raynes' successor Jonathan Graham agreed rather reluctantly to its republication under Jarrett-Kerr's own name.

Yet it is important not to oversimplify or to make Raynes too dominant. So one should also remember Bell, a great Community man yet also a memorable individualist, for many years in charge of the grounds, with his red neckerchief and battered hat. After the war he ran a small farm at the back of the House. His hens produced 850 eggs a month. His pigs won a cup in 1956. His right to keep them had been discussed in Parliament. Mucking out was part of the novitiate. He also grew tobacco. His room, Dickensian with its open fire and dusty bric à brac, was festooned with tobacco leaves being cured to make 'Mirfield Mixture'. (The brethren were then great pipe smokers. Certain missioners were dreaded by clergy wives – it took a fortnight to air the room after each visit.) Through Bell's honorary membership of the local Nab Working Men's Club and through his weekly column in the *Dewsbury Reporter* ('Father Bell speaks') he became a much-loved local figure. Further afield he was valued for his rural Lent missions, cycling from parish to parish. When a Colonel visited Mirfield, Bell took him to see the pigs. The Colonel later reported: 'Father Bell says that no Gentleman would refuse to make his confession'.

Defining Catholicism

In 1943 the Allies invaded Italy; Germany was bleeding to death on the Russian front; the Burma-Thailand railway was completed at the cost of 16,000 POWs dead through starvation and disease; and Churchill seeing film of obliteration bombing raids on Germany asked 'Are we beasts?' In 1943 Raynes was also engaged in a life or death campaign – against the proposed united Church of South India (CSI). Ellis was put in charge of propaganda. Gore had worried about the scheme in the 1920s. In January 1943 Talbot joined a deputation which met Temple (now at Canterbury) to deplore the scheme. A few months later Raynes led a deputation to Garbett of York –

Ramsey refused to join because he thought Raynes was taking 'an impossibly rigid line'. Raynes signed an Open Letter to Temple in November from five out of six Superiors of the men's communities (SSM was the absentee); they threatened secession if the scheme were adopted.

In 1919 a group of Indian Christians issued a statement drafted by V. S. Azariah (first Indian Anglican bishop): missionary work in India was ineffective because Christian divisions had been 'imposed upon us from without'. From this flowed prolonged negotiations to unite episcopal and non-episcopal traditions in one church for the first time. At the outset the church would be inaugurated and new bishops consecrated from all the previous churches. From then all ordinations would be episcopal. There would be no re-ordination of existing ministers who had not been episcopally ordained. The scheme's supporters argued that once essentials were agreed, there could be a union in the trust that common worship and mission would produce further convergence. But Anglo-Catholic opponents wanted everything guaranteed in advance. They charged that CSI would be doctrinally vague and its ministries of uncertain validity. They were terrified that a similar scheme would be adopted in England. But CSI was inaugurated in 1947. In 1953 Huddleston wrote to Archbishop Fisher 'I am one of those who found it extremely hard to remain within the Anglican fold at the time of the South Indian Scheme settlement. I can only regard the Church of South India as a schismatic body, and I can see no possible benefit to the ecumenical movement through its creation.' (Alan Paton teased Huddleston about the mismatch between his racial inclusiveness and his ecclesiastical exclusiveness.) Yet that year Fr Dalby, Superior of SSJE, after a visit to CSI reported that its practice of episcopacy was 'wonderful'. In 1965 Tweedy described its new *Prayer Book* as 'one of the best liturgical productions of recent years'. In 1955 the Convocations agreed to recommendations from a Joint Committee (of which Raynes was a member): the bishops and episcopally ordained ministers of CSI were recognized; members of CSI could receive communion in the Church of England.[6] So ended the biggest and bitterest ecclesiastical controversy since the 1927/8 Prayer Book. The turn around of opinion represented the greatest débâcle in the history of Anglo-Catholicism. Some denounced Raynes and his friends as traitors. A few went to Rome. For a time bravely defiant notices at All Souls' Leeds (and elsewhere) warned CSI communicants that they were not welcome. The controversy, which had preoccupied some of the best minds in the movement for a dozen years, was too quickly forgotten, for important lessons could have been learned from it. It illustrates how distraught Anglo-Catholics become if the delicate balance of centripetal and centrifugal forces in Anglicanism is disturbed.[7]

However, CR was also at work on other ecumenical fronts. From 1940 CR held occasional theological conferences with Roman Catholic, Free Church and Anglican Evangelical theologians. In 1948 Raynes spent a month lecturing and preaching in Sweden. CR established contacts with the communities of Taizé and Grandchamp which had grown out of the continental Reformed tradition. Members of these and Swedish communities visited Mirfield. Curtis was the pivotal figure in these and many other of CR's ecumenical ventures.

Supported by most brethren, Raynes made CR's worship more orderly and more Anglo-Catholic. The many pages in the minutes books devoted to detailed liturgical changes, together with the new CR Office Book prepared by a team under Wrathall, show how tightly organized CR worship was becoming. (Karl Popper said that people are mobile like clouds, not precise and predictable like clocks. The Anglo-Catholic approach to worship was clock-like, leaving no room for spontaneity.) Liturgical individualism was curbed by allowing only the interim or South African rites. The most major change was made in 1944. The corporate communion was transferred from Sundays to Tuesdays; on Sundays and feasts there was to be a High Mass; Sunday Mattins was transferred to Saturday evening creating more time for private masses on Sunday morning. The adoption by CR of a non-communicating High Mass brought it into line with most Anglo-Catholic parishes and communities (though SSM never adopted it). But it had been repudiated by Gore and Frere and was anathema to Liturgical Reformers both Anglican and Roman Catholic. Curtis sorrowfully called the new weekend pattern 'our liturgical slum'. Private masses had now become the norm. Few attended the daily corporate mass. The priest's duty was to offer mass and he could not do this in the congregation, it was said. A few brethren were deeply unhappy with these changes. For nine years beginning in 1935 Aidan Cotton made a series of protests. He invoked the letter and spirit of the Prayer Book, quoted Gore and Frere and appealed to the South African Visitor. The CR memorandum to the Archbishops about non-communicating eucharists for worship in the Forces particularly disturbed him: for the first time CR was advocating this for the church at large, thus setting aside 'one of the major decisions of the Reformation'. He wondered how he could continue in CR. Horner as Superior assured him that by having a daily corporate communion as well as private masses CR did justice to both sides. But in 1944 Cotton wrote to Raynes: 'As long as I live I shall be most deeply grieved and ashamed if Religious priests are the ones to lead our Anglican clergy back to such a perversion of their priesthood.' Raynes and Chapter did not debate general theological principles (as Cotton wished) but replied that Prayer Book rubrics were created without reference to religious communities, that Frere's *Commentary* was not binding, that a community could not be bound by the views of its early members, that private masses were not contrary to the Rule, that bishops had given permission.[8]

Cotton, having battled to no avail for nine years, now gave up formal protests. But a much more serious challenger emerged in Joseph Barker, Principal of the College, widely admired in CR and by students, a potential Superior. By the time he completed his *Sacrificial Priesthood* (1941) he had doubted its traditionalist conclusions. Very unusually for an Anglican he became obsessed by Luther. In February 1948 he wrote to Raynes. The new church had encouraged an increase in private masses; the Sunday corporate communion had been abolished; 'the tendency to look towards Roman authority' was growing ever stronger and resulted in a loss of integrity. So-called 'enrichments' in worship 'blunt spontaneity and encourage self-consciousness, arouse suspicion, deflect attention from the essential simplicity of the faith, and tend to sever from the main stream of Anglican traditions and ways'. It was impossible to teach students one way while C R was pointing another. He had resigned as Principal and was now asking for release from C R, a process which took over a year. This could hardly have come at a worse time for Raynes. One of the younger brethren, doing important work, particularly close to Raynes, left C R in painful circumstances that summer. Raynes' response to Barker was both defensive and accusatory. He denied any following of Rome and any fundamental theological change. Everyone was allowed to follow his conscience about private masses. Attendance at the Sunday High Mass was voluntary; communion could always be given to any who asked. The maintenance of Prayer Book Mattins and Evensong and the use of the South African rite were evidences of solid Anglican piety. He accused Barker of looking upon C R as a mere 'background' for his work, of never having identified himself with the Community, of trying to escape from 'the path of renunciation put before you by God'. Raynes was being disingenuous. Private and non-communicating masses were not Anglican – nor were they Orthodox, but they were Roman. If Raynes and other Anglo-Catholics had been less emotionally fixated on Rome, they would have been freed to consider the Eastern Orthodox tradition of concelebration. Raynes had no interest in Orthodoxy. A brother who knew him well commented: 'Raymond's ideas were apparent in such comparatively minor matter as dress (never remove your habit), haircut (cropped), demeanour in choir (eyes always on the book) and similar outward observances, all taken from standard Roman Catholic instructions and commentaries on the Religious Life.' In 1949 Barker left C R for parish work. Tweedy, who saw both sides as Barker's Vice-Principal and Raynes' Chapter Clerk, described it as 'one of the most tragic episodes in C R history . . . He was the nearest thing to Keble Talbot'.

At the end of January 1949 Raynes insisted on allowing himself to be considered for the vacant see of Johannesburg, despite having been re-elected as Superior less than a month before, and despite overwhelming opposition from the brethren. Two of his closest friends, Blair and Ellis, thought it would be intolerable for the Johannesburg brethren to have their former Superior as bishop. At the end of February Ambrose Reeves was elected. The incident reveals how wretched and restless Raynes had become.

During this difficult and unhappy period (probably between mid-1948 and mid-1949) Raynes caused some of Gore's papers to be destroyed, though precisely what was destroyed and what were the circumstances of the destruction can only be inferred. In the controversies about the eucharist, Raynes had been irritated by the constant appeal to the views of Gore and Frere. The preparation of the memoir of Frere (published in 1947) had drawn attention to Frere's views and the ethos of the early days of CR. Talbot was devoted to Gore and enjoyed telling stories about him. Fr St John OP, with other Roman Catholics, visiting Mirfield in 1939 remarked that it was steeped in the spirit of the incarnation; the Chronicler commented that this implied 'the still abiding influence of our Founder'. Raynes believed that SSJE and SSM had been hampered in their development because of the continuing influences of their powerful founders. The story is that Symonds, then Librarian, was asked by Raynes to destroy a collection of Gore's papers. He did so reluctantly, despite being theologically and politically antipathetic to the Gore tradition. But he accepted a view of obedience, foreign to the CR tradition, but held by himself and Raynes. When Symonds told Blair (the Prior) what he had done, Blair was horrified and remonstrated with Raynes both about the destruction of the papers and for acting without reference to Chapter.[9] The story reveals how fanatical and autocratic Raynes could be when (as in this case) he was free from all restraint.

Raynes' attitude to CR's past became an issue again in the mid 1950s. Some of Talbot's essays and retreat addresses were collected and both published in 1954. His relations and friends now wanted Godfrey Pawson of CR who had edited his essays to prepare a volume of his letters. They felt that Liberal Catholicism was at a discount and that authoritarianism was in the ascendent; the church needed the spirit of Talbot. But two publishers declined the letters. They thought two books were sufficient. Raynes agreed. A supporter of the project complained to Lord Halifax:

> I sometimes wonder whether Fr Raynes' policy in many things is not a deliberate, although perhaps not fully conscious, attempt to wipe out the whole of the tradition of the Founders of Mirfield and to establish his own, and that possibly the suppression of these letters is only part of that endeavour.

Talbot continued to refuse attractive invitations. In 1942 Halifax, the former Foreign Secretary, now Ambassador in Washington, wanted him to come as a private chaplain. He decided against it. CR needed concentration not dispersion, he believed. He should live more deeply as a Religious and help to sustain the central life of the Community. In 1944 he declined to go as a chaplain at Allied Headquarters in France. In 1948 he was fascinated, when staying with the Halifaxes in London, to dine with the Duke and Duchess of Devonshire, the American Ambassador and Winston Churchill. During the war, Churchill had approached Talbot through Halifax to offer him a bishopric (probably Bath and Wells). It is said that if he had accepted he would have been Churchill's choice for Canterbury in 1944 when Temple died. But Talbot felt his first duty was to CR and that in any case he was too old. 'The Church of England might have been shaken to its foundations by the arrival of a Saint at Canterbury' wrote Brendan Bracken.[10]

Talbot died in October 1949. A priest said of him:

> He seemed by natural right to belong to a time when the Christian was at home in the world because, in spite of all its waywardness, it was still at heart a Christian world. That assurance has almost disappeared and we think of the time when this was possible, with an immense nostalgia. It was a period when what we call Anglicanism seemed paradoxically both mature and youthful: it offered an established and achieved position from which lively and stimulating forays could be made . . . Perhaps it was a fragile moment, but it was a very glorious one: the prophets, for all their high seriousness, had not forgotten how to laugh; if there are any successors to them, one has not remarked a capacity for religious mirth. And in that period – let us call it the period of Liberal Catholicism – Fr Talbot was an indispensable *animator*.[11]

Halifax collected gifts from Talbot's friends for a memorial at Mirfield. At first CR thought of erecting a screen behind the high altar. But it decided instead to replace the heavy but appropriately Byzantine baldachino, designed by Walter Tapper, in the Chapel of the Resurrection with one designed by his son intended to convey Keble's lightness of touch. Perhaps it does, but its Arts and Crafts ornamentation (now greatly simplified) and its Festival of Britain structure make it an incongruous visitor.

Stretching the Community

Raynes made great demands not only on himself but also on the brethren. They complained that he did not allow missioners time to recharge between engagements, nor authors time to produce mature work. At one stage the brethren at Mirfield were fulfilling fifty to seventy engagements a month. There were new demands on their time. Hitherto they had cleaned their rooms and the church and done some of the gardening. Now under the influence of Bishop's Benedictinism they were required to do a lot of the domestic work as well. Chores were to be seen not as interruptions, but as an essential part of the life. Another pressure came from the large number of guests. A further pressure was created by the unparalleled numbers coming into the novitiate. One year there were 24 novices. By 1958 there were 85 professed brethren. By then CR had three theological colleges, the Leeds Hostel, Penhalonga, four retreat houses and five South African houses to staff, and the care of FR, 18 religious communities in Britain, 3 in Africa and 15 other societies.

Raynes widened the range of CR immensely by opening the novitiate to all-comers, lay as well as clerical. In this, Bishop was an influential supporter.

Wrathall, though one of CR's best Novice Guardians, had to be persuaded that there were Christians among the laity. CR still exerted subtle pressure on lay novices to be ordained, especially as it was then possible to be ordained in the novitiate. By 1958 there were eleven lay brethren, whereas twenty years previously there had been only one. Some came from different social and educational backgrounds than CR had been used to, and of course, unlike priest novices, none had been clericalized in theological colleges and parishes. At least three had been conscientious objectors including Nicolas Graham, Jonathan's brother, who had been imprisoned for six months. Of the ex-combatants nearly all had been privates or NCOs, whereas CR had usually drawn from those who had been (or would have been) officers. Huddleston was Novice Guardian for a couple of unhappy years after his return from Africa, but found time between his many speaking engagements to raise some important questions about the novitiate. All lay novices should have a trade or profession or be trained for one, but was such training (or indeed ordination training) compatible with the novitiate? He reorganized the novitiate so that novices now had their own separate corporate life.

Raynes made evangelism one of his main priorities. Never before (or since) has a Superior undertaken so many missions. Mosley records the powerful impact and relentless demands of his addresses in parishes, at house parties and CR Summer Schools. A chaplain described his address at London University: 'How vividly I can still recall that gaunt figure, like some dead general of the Jesuits, leaning over the pulpit splitting open souls like filleted herrings!'

The decline of allegiance to the Church of England (and even more to the Free Churches) among both insiders and fringers has been very marked during this century. Since Roman Catholicism emerged from its fortress it has suffered from the same eroding forces as the other churches – attendance at mass has dropped by a quarter since the 1950s. So in the Church of England the numbers of Easter communicants per 1,000 of the adult population were: 93 in 1900, 70 in 1960, 42 in 1987. The number of baptisms per 1,000 live births (a good index of its relation to the wider population) were: 650 in 1900, 554 in 1960, 289 in 1987.[12]

Edward Wynn in his Visitor's Charge of 1946 said that like the rest of the church he was baffled about evangelism: 'I can remember when a course of sermons by a mission preacher would fill a church; very rarely does that happen now. We do not seem to be able to reach them that are without.' He asked CR, which had always been in the forefront of evangelism, to explore new methods. CR after the war revitalized old methods and experimented with new ones, but it never tackled the deeper issues implied in Wynn's challenge. CR knew perfectly well what the faith was, and thought that all that was necessary was to discover new and more modern methods of conveying it.

Augustine Hoey had done a lot of acting at Oxford, then served in Hackney for eight years before being professed in 1950. He pioneered a new style of mission using live tableaux in the streets and in the churches. In articles in the *CR Quarterly* and in *Go Quickly and Tell* (1959) he said that missions used to aim to bring in the lost sheep. Nowadays people did not regard themselves as lost. It was pastorally and educationally wise to start with what was real to people – issues of right and wrong, marriage, death, before going on to the Bible, the sacraments, the church, prayer, the saints and heaven. At the beginning of a session about death the congregation would be startled to see a coffin carried in, from which Hoey arose dramatically to give his address. He advocated first a teaching week to make the congregation more evangelistic, followed two years later by an evangelistic mission, after eighteen months a school of prayer, after another two years a family mission. In 1952 his Quarry sermons were illustrated by tableaux on episcopacy, priesthood and the marital and monastic vocations. In his sermon about 'The Shining Glory of Episcopacy' he asked Nonconformists how they could minister without episcopal authority. A Free Churchman reacted angrily to this in the local paper.

In the 1950s the London House organized 'Shoe' and 'Slipper' parties which offered systematic expositions of Christianity. (The idea and the names were borrowed from the CR Retreat House in Johannesburg where Mrs Kermack, the Warden, found such gatherings so successful that she compared herself with the old woman who lived in a shoe.) About 80 came to the parties held in the summer house at the bottom of the Priory Garden. Access was by the tradesmen's entrance so women were able to attend. 'No woman darkened the door of the Priory if we could help it' recalled one of the brethren. Women's confessions were heard at Bickersteth House, Kensington, originally created to provide residential and non-residential facilities for young ladies from 'good families' and later renamed after Cyril Bickersteth. One of the brethren was chaplain.

In 1954 brethren gave forty-eight Lent courses and preached in forty different churches in Holy Week. But customs were changing. Lent groups began to replace devotional addresses after the success of 'The People Next Door' groups organized by the British Council of Churches in 1967. The revised Roman Catholic Holy Week rites of 1955, soon adopted by Anglo-Catholic churches, stressed liturgical participation more than preaching. The Good Friday Three Hours' service with its seven addresses was now often truncated and subordinated to the Good Friday Liturgy; in some churches it disappeared. So invitations for Lent and Holy Week preachments declined. There were a few invitations to house groups and house eucharists, but these provided little contact with fringers. By the early 1960s Stewardship Missions were preferred by many priests because they tackled the increasingly urgent financial problems of the parishes and appealed more than evangelistic missions.

In the post-war period CR also organized, and in some cases published, a steady stream of pamphlets and books about the Catholic faith. Its illustrated guides to the eucharist were particularly popular and useful. Its form of self-examination for confession *Seven Times Seven* broke away from pietism. *The Priest's Book of Private Devotion* (a favourite ordination present) asked: 'Do I endanger my faith by lightly reading infidel books?', 'Have I given scandal . . . by crossing my legs when in choir?', 'Have I bravely borne witness against what is evil? e.g. birth-control?' *Seven Times Seven* asked: 'Am I a pleasure to serve when shopping, or anything but?', 'Do I care about people underfed or homeless or persecuted or despised?', 'What reform (or revolution) do I work for?' *Mirfield Essays in Christian Belief* (1962) is the only symposium ever produced by CR. Its most memorable passage was by Curtis:

> How large, how enthusiastic would be the multitude that attended a first Anglican *Catholic-Evangelical Congress* in the Albert Hall! How clear and thankful will be the witness given there by both Catholics and Evangelicals that their concord has been made possible largely through the labours of great Christian minds which we think of as belonging rather to the Critical and Liberal movements. Through these the Church of England has been able to do for the whole Church that which Rome was not yet free to do and the need for which the East was too far from the centre of modern thinking to comprehend.

Despite Curtis' characteristic hyperbole, this breathes a large generosity of spirit which had informed Gore, Frere and Talbot at their best, but which had been latterly eclipsed in CR. The most memorable review came from C. S. Mann, lately of Nashdom, who wrote in the *Church Quarterly*: 'Whatever may have been the temptations of members of the Community of the Resurrection, a savage Jansenism has never been among them.' One of the contributors, Jarrett-Kerr, was also employing his wide knowledge of many areas of thought in lively apologetics, both on the radio and in print. Bishop, who began to establish himself as a notable broadcaster on radio in 1946, appeared in a television programme about CR in 1956. One reviewer called him the 'most arresting personality I have seen on a television programme for years'.[13]

In 1944 CR created a lay apostolate, 'The Legion of the Resurrection'. It had its own quarterly magazine. Its members kept four simple rules: Sunday mass, confession, intercession, evangelism. A leaflet explained:

> The Church is God's army on earth. You who are legionaries are in the advance guard: shock troops of the army. On you lies the task of attacking the enemy and freeing his captives by winning them for Christ and His church. Fix on *one* person who is doing nothing or little about his religion. Make him your target . . .

When its Warden left CR in 1948, it lost its original impetus. However, it continued until 1956; its magazine lasted until 1961. This attempt to create a kind of Anglo-Catholic Salvation Army was another example of Raynes' determination to break CR's upper-class and academic image. Its creation implied a vote of no confidence in FR. The militarism of its language (it was launched just after D-Day) is a reminder of the arrogance with which some brethren proclaimed their faith in the days when (as Hugh Bishop put it) Anglo-Catholicism thought it had the ball at its feet.

Two new Houses

In 1945, at the invitation of the Archbishop of Wales, CR took over St Teilo's residential hostel, founded by Timothy Rees in 1935, for about 30 (male) students at Cardiff University. Philip Speight, its first Warden, hoped that it would provide something of the common life of the older universities, centred upon the daily worship of the chapel. He and four other brethren were also occupied in the Province conducting missions, conventions and retreats. Simon Herdson, a blunt Tynesider who looked like a boxer, spent eight years at St Teilo's. He was once conducting a mission at a prison. After the hymn the prisoners sat down. There was a pause. Herdson remarked 'I know what you are thinking – "What an ugly beggar"'. One of the brethren was also chaplain to Anglican students in the university. CR hoped that St Teilo's would also stimulate the creation of an indigenous Welsh community – a hope never realized. Its buildings were, however, ramshackle and required constant attention. After the hostel had to close for rebuilding in 1955, it reopened in 1958 as a much valued retreat house. But by ceasing to be a university hostel, it had ceased to be 'the nerve centre' (as it had been called) of Anglican activity in the university and a frontier post in the crucially important world of higher education. In 1968 CR withdrew from St Teilo's after twenty-three years work in the Province.

In 1954 CR declined invitations to open houses in New Zealand and the United States and instead accepted charge of Codrington College, Barbados. When Christopher Codrington, Fellow of All Souls, Oxford and Commander-in-Chief of the Leeward Islands died in 1710, he left estates in Barbados to SPG to found a college staffed by scholars living under the three vows. The College began life as a grammar school in 1745, then in 1830 became a theological college and was affiliated to Durham University in 1875. When CR arrived, Codrington's wish for monastic scholars was fulfilled for the first time. CR felt a special obligation to choose the poorest of the three countries to which it had been invited. Cecil Sayer, the Principal, an old Mirfield student, had worked for this for ten years. It is likely that if CR had not come to the rescue the College would have closed, for the buildings were dilapidated, there were few staff, morale was low. But it was also a difficult moment for CR to take over for the Classical Faculty of the College had just been closed by Durham (because the University of the West Indies had opened) and the last classical scholar left as CR arrived in 1955. CR was (irrationally) blamed for this closure.

The initial CR party led by Jonathan Graham had just arrived when Janet, a hurricane, tore in: 'always giving one the impression that it could not get any worse, then getting it' (as he wrote). Hundreds of refugees flooded into the College, the focal point for the whole area. Up the hill at the estate church of Holy Cross, a huge crowd of refugees sang hymns under the enthusiastic direction of Humphrey Whistler. Anselm Genders was meanwhile collecting old ladies by car in a 90 mph gale. Miraculously Barnabas Dugdale kept appearing with al *fresco* meals. The hurricane blew a huge palm-tree into the lake in front of the College. It also blew away many of the local suspicions about the foreign monks who had come to take over their College.

'Not every theological college rejoices in its own lake and its own swimming pool, standing in the midst of its own plantations', wrote Genders (Graham's successor as Principal). 'Codrington College must rival, equal, or excel her theological sisters elsewhere – in beauty as well as in age!' Genders, Wheeldon and Rhymer had served in the Navy; Sanford had been a naval chaplain. So the College was run like a naval establishment. One student found this hard to take, but later discovering how isolated a priest can be in the West Indies, and how easy it was to get slack, he realized how vital it was for priests to be disciplined. Academic standards were very high. At various times the staff included Norman Blamires (former Warden of St Paul's Grahamstown), Godfrey Pawson and Christopher Millington (former Principals of Rosettenville) and David Lane (an oblate, now Principal of the College at Mirfield). Three different courses had to be run for the thirty or so students of widely differing ages. For virtually all of them this was to be their only experience of higher education, so while ordination training rightly included an element of withdrawal, they also had to be prepared for the challenges that independence was bringing. In addition there were some prospective ordinands in the College to be prepared for 'O' and 'A' levels. Brethren also did a little teaching in schools and staff and students ran a dispensary for the area. Looking after Holy Cross were Whistler and Sanford, called respectively 'disordered holiness' and 'ordered holiness' by a local headmistress. They were (a former student said) 'a real example to the students of what a parish priest should be'. Then there were retreats and missions to conduct and isolated clergy on neighbouring islands to be visited. Some mistakenly thought that they could live at a West Riding tempo despite a temperature of 90 degrees and a humidity of 90 per cent. This misjudgment took its toll.

To local people, anyone living at the College was automatically in the top social bracket. Graham wrote: 'our position here is sometimes unpleasantly reminiscent of Dives and Lazarus; for the country population to whom we minister is poor, undernourished and largely unemployed'. The planters regarded the brethren as people of class. But Barnabas was clearly not upper crust, and people were deeply impressed by his very simple life style. He, like other brethren, found the people refreshingly religious. When he preached at mid-day Holy Week services at Trinidad Cathedral never less than 500 people came. When he took a mission in Grenada he started each day at a 6.30 a.m. mass and then sat talking to people all morning, visited all afternoon, and preached to crowds in the evening.

In 1969 C R came to the conclusion that it could not staff three theological colleges. Millington had died. In 1963 Nicolas Graham, who was just about to go out as Principal, suddenly died. A few brethren considered that the needs of the West Indies were greater than those of England and argued that Mirfield should close so that C R could continue at Codrington. But Barbados had become independent in 1966 and it seemed inappropriate for expatriates to be running Codrington. Sehon Goodridge, whom C R had trained at Codrington, became Principal in 1971. The West Indian vocations which C R had hoped for never materialized. When C R went to Codrington it set aside £10,000 and used the income to subsidize the College. In 1972 it generously donated this sum as an endowment. Until 1976 four brethren continued in a small Priory at St David's, looking after some parishes and doing retreat and mission work round the islands. In 1977 Genders returned to that part of the world as Bishop of Bermuda.

Changes and chances

Raynes was re-elected again in 1952 and 1955. But at both elections a significant minority wanted another Superior. (Once again, if the Superior's term of office had been limited to, say, three terms of three years, much pain and frustration on both sides could have been avoided.) He was frequently unwell. He was often away. At first he had wanted brethren to share Christmas at Mirfield. Now he himself usually spent Christmas away with friends. Yet when he told Chapter he was going to America for another series of missions, no one had the courage to demur. By 1957 he knew that his time as Superior was coming to an end. He could not bear the thought of being on the back benches again, so extraordinarily, in view of his health, he allowed himself to be considered for the bishopric of Mashonaland. The General who had so confidently begun the Long March to full Catholicism was now weary, and his campaign against C S I had resulted in a semi-rout; in C R some troops were dropping out. Blair later was to say wistfully 'We had hoped to go further'. But what did he have in mind? Raymond giving Benediction with a monstrance from the west balcony of the church to kneeling crowds on Commemoration Day, some said. In 1957 House and church were connected by a permanent cloister (with library above). Raynes insisted that it should include the first two storeys of a colossal campanile some one hundred and twenty feet or so high. The triumphalism of that plan and its abandonment after Raynes' death reveal much about what Raynes wanted C R to be and about C R's ultimate refusal to fulfil his hopes.

In 1958 Jonathan Graham was elected Superior. For the next six months until he died at the age of 55, Raymond was desolate and ill. His friend the Abbot of Nashdom wrote of him: 'He was a stove in which God kindled the fire of his love, but . . . there was no means of shutting off the draught. The fire must roar fiercely on and consume the fuel to the last cinder . . . There is an element of tragedy in Raymond's story, inherent in his temperament' (*CRQ* MD 1961). To the end he could steer his course with the maps and compasses of the Oxford Anglo-Catholicism of the 1920s. The Roman lightships would always be in place to guide him past the shoals. But how could he have navigated a course, if he had lived longer, with the lightships breaking from their moorings, the compasses going crazy and the maps withdrawn for revision? Already in his later years Catholicism had started to change. Pius XII in *Mediator Dei* (1947) endorsed the Liturgical Movement. In the Church of England the Parish and People Movement, which aimed to reform both church and liturgy, was inaugurated in 1949 and was largely led by those in the Catholic tradition.[14] Four former students, Robert Nelson, Ernest Southcott (both of whom had once been novices) Ronald Jasper and Basil Minchin were emerging as leaders of liturgical reform. The *Quarterly* carried articles about French priests who said mass on the kitchen table before going to work in factories. Tweedy commended Minchin's book about new eucharistic patterns with the priest facing the people. In 1954 Chapter discussed Southcott's pioneer work in Halton, Leeds, based on the house church and house eucharist. Two years later the church at large learnt about it in his book *The Parish Comes Alive*. Roman Catholics began to relax the eucharistic fast. The new Holy Week rites prescribed an evening mass for Maundy Thursday. The new Holy Week pattern was adopted at Mirfield in 1957.

The pace of change quickened in Graham's period of office. In 1962 Sunday Mattins was restored; in 1964 the Sunday High Mass became a communion again. A student from the College who in 1959 had refused to go to a parish because its vicar declared that cremation was contrary to the teaching of the church, was amused to hear in 1966 that Roman Catholics were now allowed to be cremated. In 1965 Rome sanctioned concelebration. Inevitably some Anglo-Catholics were totally bewildered, like the priest in Cambridge who after the Friday fast was relaxed put up a notice 'We no longer pray for the Pope'. In CR some were jubilant; the Prayer Book had been in some measure vindicated. Others were bitter that all they had fought for was being betrayed. Some Roman Catholics like Cardinal Heenan felt the same.[15]

But these changes were just part of a more general shift of perspectives outside as well as inside the church. When the Labour Party won power in 1945 it was widely hailed or feared as a revolutionary break with the past. In retrospect one is struck rather by a sense of continuity, symbolized by the fact that the governess who taught Attlee had previously taught Churchill. Leaders of the new government had mostly been nourished either by *noblesse oblige* Anglicanism or by Victorian Nonconformity. The real break came not in 1945 but in the late 1950s and 1960s with the end of rationing and conscription (both inculcated deference to authority), the Suez crisis, the inauguration of commercial television (and consumerism), the acquittal of Penguin Books for publishing *Lady Chatterley*,[16] the retirement of Archbishop Fisher (1961), the opening of the Second Vatican Council (1962). Suddenly only those statements of faith which took doubt seriously gained a hearing – *Soundings* (1962), *Honest to God* (1963), *Objections to Christian Belief* (1963) – and its companion *Objections* by Roman Catholics and Humanists. Nicholas Mosley, whose grateful biography of Raynes appeared in 1961, wrote of *Honest to God* in the radical Anglican weekly *Prism* in May 1963: 'Should we not now just be glad that we are at last giving reverence to the God that we have enshrined for so long but have ignored – the God of movement, of change, of the world's liveliness?' That month Dr Ronald Fletcher in *New Society* (2 May) declared: 'Never accept authority; whether that of a jealous god, priest, prime minister, president, dictator, school teacher, social worker, parent, or of anyone else whatsoever, unless, in your own seriously considered view, there are good reasons for it.' In these and other remarks of the time we catch a cry of relief that forms of faith and authority which had become oppressive were being lifted. By 1970 the laws about homosexual conduct, abortion and divorce had been liberalized, protection had been given to ethnic minorities, women had been granted equal pay and the age of majority had been lowered to eighteen, so effectively ending the parental role of colleges and universities. In this new world some clergy felt deeply unsure of their role and turned with enthusiasm to seek a new professionalism through training in pastoral psychology with 'clinical theology' created by Frank Lake in 1962. The goal of individuation and self-fulfilment was replacing the call to self-sacrifice. Confession was being replaced by counselling.[17]

The C R *Quarterly* reflected many of these changes. In 1960 its cover changed from an ecclesiastical to a secular design. Much more attention was now given to the world beyond the church. There were film reviews; Mosley described how reading *Lady Chatterley* as a young man taught him that sex could be beautiful; Monica Furlong wrote: 'whether people go to church or not may not matter as much as we think'; in another article she introduced the new theme of 'Christian Openness'; Arthur Longworth and Mark Tweedy passed on the new teaching that it was the community not the priest which was the celebrant of the eucharist. Wheeldon, now Principal of the College, expressed his gladness that Anglicans did *not* have a final authoritative court of appeal: 'We may have to walk in darkness and perplexity for longer then we should wish . . . Above all, the Church must not be fearful . . . Neither should she be a face-saving liar and pretend that she has never had to learn or change her mind' (C D 1966).

Jonathan Graham's uncomplicated faith and natural acceptance of hierarchical authority was at odds with the spirit of the age. In the novitiate his only worry had been that he had none of the doubts he had been told to expect. The first old student to be Superior, he was more at home in institutional life than any Superior since Frere. If Raynes had seemed a downmarket general, part Jesuit, part Salvation Army, Graham came over as the upmarket urbane headmaster – indeed his father had been an Uppingham housemaster. He exercised a stringent discipline. When Bishop was passing through London and wanted to stay the night to attend a charity premiere of the African musical 'King Kong' – he had met the cast in Johannesburg – Graham said firmly 'No': it was Lent. Graham's refusal was all the more extraordinary because the musical had been launched by the Arts Federation of South Africa founded by Huddleston, the chairman of which was now Jarrett-Kerr. Graham's humour was by turns entertaining, self-protecting, savage. When he returned from Barbados he remarked 'It's good to be back in the West Riding. I like my evenings to begin at half past two.' When Robert Mercer arrived as a novice, Graham ignored him for a fortnight, then asked 'When are you leaving?' From some of his sermons people crept away stunned. His transcendent faith lifted people on to another plane (though they sometimes wondered whether this was an evasion of what was on the lower plane). His consolation could be bracing: 'All I beg of you is not to think that the world has fallen in if your hopes are smashed to little bits.' Unlike Raynes he was a wholehearted Community man. At Christmas he stayed at Mirfield and read Dickens to the brethren. 'Read Dickens' was his prescription for almost all ailments.[18]

All his instincts were naturally conservative. He used to joke that he never read a book less than fifty years old. But he had the grace to admit when he was wrong. So his first reaction to the proposal for CR participation in the new ecumenical Federal Seminary in South Africa was wholly negative. But he allowed himself to be won round and was soon defending it against hard-line brethren who asked when disputes arose: 'Is it in the book or isn't it?' Graham responded: 'unity with other Christians demands taking risks which are not in the book, because there ain't no book which has faced the subject'. But he also wrote with genuine anguish about 'responsible people apparently pulling to bits all that we have been taught to consider sacred or beyond question' (*CRQ* LD 1964).

Graham approached the new era crab-wise, his humour mixed with horror. In 1965 he died just as suddenly as his brother two years earlier. Eager spirits in CR now looked for a Superior who would approach the new ways with unfeigned (but not uncritical) enthusiasm. Hugh Bishop, who had done an excellent job revitalizing the College, and who through the media was in touch with this new world, seemed to them the only choice, despite doubts about his tendency to self-dramatization and a *penchant* for intense relationships. Bishop had for years suppressed his instinctive liberalism under a severe and dogmatic religion. His supporters among the brethren had come to believe that CR had done the same. They looked forward eagerly to venturing with him into the world that the 1960s and Vatican II had opened up. At first it all went marvellously well.

College and Hostel

The best ministers of the church are gentlemen by breeding and education, declared Samuel Wilberforce, Bishop of Oxford, in 1864; not only are they on equal terms with the leaders of thought; the poor also prefer them.[1] However, during the nineteenth century the gentleman amateur in all professions was being replaced by the specialist. The Tractarian teaching about the priestly nature of the ministerial calling recovered a specialist identity for the clergy. Wilberforce himself in 1854 founded Cuddesdon Theological College, the first to have a common life with echoes of seminary tradition. But to Hensley Henson in 1900 the Anglican clergy were still 'declericalized':

> The normal training of the English clergy, at school and university, is entirely non-professional, hence they are the most theologically ignorant and the best educated ministry in existence, and the worst informed on all matters of ecclesiastical technique; but hence also they are the most vigorous and healthy in moral tone, and the sanest in political action. They think, and speak, and act in ways which are essentially similar to those of their Christian neighbours . . .[2]

Non-graduate ordinands (about a quarter of the total in 1900) trained at theological colleges. But before the First World War many graduates were ordained without any specifically ministerial training. It was not until after the war that graduates were required to spend at least a year at theological college. So neither Gore (ordained 1876) nor Henson (ordained 1887) went to theological college, but were ordained straight to Oxford fellowships. Randall Davidson (ordained 1874) had a mere three months informal preparation before being ordained to a parish. For Anglo-Catholics the possession of an Oxbridge degree (perhaps not even in theology) and a gentleman's upbringing were wholly inadequate for priestly formation; ordinands needed a period of communal life and disciplined worship before ordination. So Frere spent a year at Wells. Cosmo Gordon Lang (later Archbishop of Canterbury) went to Cuddesdon for a term, stayed a year and returned annually for Holy Week to what he called 'my Holy Place – my Mecca'.

The pattern which Henson described had its merits. Ordinands were educated with their contemporaries (and not separated from them as in the Roman seminary tradition). This encouraged them to set their ministry within a broad context, discouraged sacerdotal separatism and led them to seek support and friendship from laity, not just from fellow priests. They did not suffer from always looking back nostalgically to the corporate life and worship of theological college, nor had they learnt a clerical spirituality which separated them from the laity. Contrast the attitudes of traditional Roman Catholicism:

> Apart from his own family the priest should seek his recreation in the main with his fellow-clergy. They are safe company. He can relax more easily among them without the danger of giving scandal . . . If it should ever happen that the company of clerics is no longer attractive we should seriously examine the manner of our lives . . . It is, therefore, the more regrettable that certain priests should spend so much of their time with the laity. When we are among the faithful we are bound to be, in a sense, on duty. When we seek relaxation our place is not among them. For our relaxations are not theirs. Theirs should not be ours.[3]

But the pattern Henson praised had serious drawbacks. University theology was almost entirely academic. Graduates in other disciplines who had not attended theological college lacked adequate theological training. A curate's first vicar might be an inadequate mentor. In any case, some theological colleges were small, badly-staffed, short-lived and lacked a proper corporate life and discipline. In England more and more people lived urban lives but many colleges were situated in cathedral closes, thus encouraging nostalgia for the pre-industrial world. Moreover, would-be ordinands from poor backgrounds discovered that financial help was sporadic and sparse. Those lacking education had few opportunities for improving their education to qualify themselves for ordination training. Some colleges were decidedly upper-class. Only Oxbridge graduates were admitted to Farnham by B. K. Cunningham (Warden 1899–1914, Principal of Westcott House 1919–34). There were only two rules for the eight or nine students – they had to attend Mattins daily; they had to dine in evening dress. All the colleges were independent foundations – none had been created by the Church of England itself. It was not until 1912 with the creation of the Central Advisory Council of Training for the Ministry that they began to be more regulated.[4]

Founding the College and Hostel

That CR should in 1903 begin ordination training at Mirfield (and Johannesburg) and create a Hostel in Leeds in 1904 was entirely congruent with its aims. The Preface to the Rule describes its works as 'pastoral, evangelistic, literary, educational'. Gore as a young don created a weekly group to study the Greek New Testament. As Vice-Principal of Cuddesdon and as Principal of Pusey House he exercised a remarkable influence upon ordinands. At Radley, CR provided a year's spiritual and theological training for graduates. In 1897 it created a fund to help poverty-stricken ordinands.

In May 1901 Bull went to see the radical new scheme of ordination training devised by H. H. Kelly, founder of the Society of the Sacred Mission.[5] Kelly had left Oxford with a third in mathematics and a fourth in history. Reading Kingsley and Maurice had delivered him from 'narrow religionism', from 'protestantism' but not (he wrote gratefully) from 'evangelicalism'. He did not attend a theological college. As a curate he realized that there was no scheme which would train poor boys from the parish for ordination. Encouraged by Scott Holland ('the only man I knew among the big people') in 1891 he founded a missionary college in Kennington whose members had to agree three conditions: no guarantee of ordination, no pay and no marriage. Out of this developed SSM (1892–4). In 1897 SSM moved to Mildenhall and in 1903 to Kelham. From 1902 students were specifically trained for ordination and it was no longer a missionary college. But students were asked to remain unmarried until they had repaid the cost of their training.

Kelly did not fit into any ecclesiastical category. He thought *Lux Mundi* an uneasy compromise between theology and philosophy. He shocked conventional Anglo-Catholics by his enthusiasm for SCM and by such remarks as: 'The clergy are so absorbed in getting people to "come to church" that the church services have become a substitute for God.' Separation from the world had no place in his understanding of the Religious Life: 'No form of life may ever be taken as an end in itself – that belongs to God only . . . of all the snares which beset religion, the habit of confusing love for God, which is self-forgetfulness, with the pursuit of lovingness, which is a virtue of the self, is the easiest and the most disastrous.'[6] He was proud to be isolated from the establishment. Of course (Kelly remarked) everyone in the 1890s knew who Gore was. But they asked him: 'Who the dickens are you?' Gore 'was a scholar; not a "fourth in history". He belonged to a very important group . . . I do notice that the "important people" form a world of their own. They all seem to know one another. I never belonged to it.'[7] (At Mirfield on Commemoration Day 1988 the Director of SSM told how a Franciscan, a Benedictine and a Mirfield Father were discussing which community God loved best. They went to pray, leaving a pencil and paper for God to indicate his verdict. They returned and read his message: 'I love all my religious communities equally, signed God CR.')

Kelly offered not the preferred pattern of degree followed by theological college, but an integrated course presenting theological perspectives on the world. 'We were studying . . . what God was doing on the Somme, and at Westminster, and at Tilbury Docks.' Kelly's vision was magnificent. In practice it was defective. The course separated students from their contemporaries – especially if they came (as some did) in their mid-teens. They absorbed one system of thought and education with no chance to test it against any other. The College was so integrated into s s m that it lacked a proper degree of autonomy. By setting itself against the norms it never gained wholehearted episcopal acceptance. The course also depended crucially upon the theological genius of one man – Kelly himself.

So Bull brought his experience of Kelly's scheme to the brethren in July 1901. He knew boys who were prevented from being trained by lack of money. Yet if they were Free Churchmen, their training would be free. 'We have invented a class priesthood with a money qualification.' Gore agreed: 'We seem . . . to have patented a new form of simony.' The fact that the number of ordinations had fallen from 745 in 1891 to 569 in 1901 gave c r an added impetus. c r proposed a scheme which combined theological training at Mirfield with a degree at Leeds.[8] c r lacked anyone of the craggy originality of Kelly. But because the c r scheme included an element of university education and had the backing of Gore, Frere and Talbot it was eminently respectable. Bickersteth's father, the Bishop of Ripon, said in 1876 that a university education had advantages which a theological college training by itself could not provide. In 1902 Archbishop Frederick Temple wrote to Hugh Benson about c r's new venture:

> There is a huge peril, as I think, in men taking to the technical study of theology with a view to ordination, without its being based upon adequate education of a general sort, and I therefore rejoice to see that you contemplate preparing all your men for a degree in Arts before they become theologians.[9]

When Davidson and Gore supported the Hostel appeal in 1907 they echoed Temple's argument (see above pp. 106, 109). Cyril Bickersteth (*CRQ* LD 1903) explained that no student would be rejected because of poverty or class, but all must be capable of mental, moral and spiritual improvement. The common life would purge selfishness and the worship of a Religious House would promote devotion. The College would not inculcate ready-made opinions. Faith without reason became superstition. Echoing *Lux Mundi* he said that students would learn that 'Greek Philosophy was in its way a part of the preparation of the world for Christ'.

In July 1902 it was resolved that the College would open in January 1903. The conversion of the stable block was begun under the direction of the Warden, Caleb Ritson, who had trained as an architect. An appeal was launched; the training would be free but students would be expected to provide their own clothes and pocket money. After ordination and before any engagement to marry, they would be asked to repay half the cost of training (i.e. usually £125) over five or six years. The conditions of entry included a sound elementary knowledge of Latin and Greek. Only those in their late teens could be admitted.

Ritson eventually proved a disastrous Warden. *Crockford's* records his attendance at London University, but no degree and no theological college. Ten years later in 1894 he was made deacon but was not priested for five years. After curacies he arrived at Mirfield in 1901, was professed after only a year's probation and immediately appointed Warden. The foundation stone of the College was laid on the Feast of St Simon and St Jude (28 October) 1902 by Mrs Walker Brooke, the local grand lady, a generous supporter of CR and the College. When the first nine students arrived in January 1903 the buildings were not quite finished. On St Mark's Day the Bishop of Wakefield came to bless the College. Before Hugh Benson left CR that summer he composed a Latin epigram, in which he characteristically celebrated flight from the world. It was inscribed on a plaque placed in the entrance hall on which was hung a stirrup found during the reconstruction. It reads (in translation): 'Look! The College drives out the horses. So finally the noise of the world gives way to the peace of heaven, and this remains. Let it advise you, servant of God, to abandon the noise and the trifles of the world and to reach for the heavenly peace.'¹⁰ By July 1905 the third side of the open quadrangle and the tower were completed. Gore blessed the extension. The Scottish baronial tower with its heavily studded door and its Gothic windows added a naive dash of romance to what was otherwise an unpretentious, vernacular building. The tower flagpole on which fluttered St George's banner was given by the workmen.

In 1903 it was decided that students should not take a London degree but should graduate through the Yorkshire College (which in 1904 became Leeds University). In 1904 the College was affiliated to the university after a visit from the Vice-Chancellor and two professors. CR decided to open a Hostel, so that students could participate fully in the life of the university, which would be impossible if they travelled daily from Mirfield. So CR purchased two large semi-detached houses in Springfield Mount, near the university. These became the Hostel of the Resurrection. The brother-in-charge was known as 'Custos' (the title 'Warden' dates from 1928). The terms 'Hostel', 'Custos' and 'Warden' showed how determined Frere was that the new establishment should be rooted in ancient precedents (*CRQ* LD 1907). By affiliating to a university which had originated in the needs of local industry for technical education, CR deepened its commitment to the North. Kelly in *Training for Ordination* (1901) wrote that 'the newer universities' were more suitable for the men he had in mind than 'the intensely free and somewhat self-indulgent atmosphere of the older universities (however good for men brought up in public schools)'. The trustees of Pusey House donated £1,000 from a bequest from a Leeds man. It was hoped that the Hostel would be to Leeds what Pusey House was to Oxford. The Hostel, one of the earliest residential halls at Leeds, opened in October 1904 with six students. As they were on the spot, unlike the vast majority of students, and deeply committed to the idea of community, they made a particularly valuable contribution to university life.

Their first year was spent at Mirfield studying for the Intermediate before coming to Leeds for the other two years of the degree course. They then returned to Mirfield for their two years' ordination training. Teaching for Matriculation and Intermediate at Mirfield was partly provided by tutors, lay and ordained, who were not members of CR. One was Edward Symonds who arrived in 1903 with firsts in Mods, Greats and theology. Professed in 1911 he was still a much loved teacher at the Hostel in the 1970s. Prospective students lacking basic qualifications could have preliminary tuition in Latin, Greek and Mathematics in Westcote rectory in the Cotswolds or at Ellesmere College, a Woodard school. Many of these early students came from that segment of society – the aspiring working class and the lower middle class – which had been the backbone of Nonconformity. Their fathers were for example carpenters, grocers, chemists' assistants, labourers, railway workers, teachers, clerks.

At Mirfield the pressure was intense because students did a lot of manual and domestic work. Ritson's eleven pages of 'Standing Orders' covered every likely (and unlikely) eventuality. Theological students rose at 6.15 a.m., except those on kitchen duties, who rose at 5.30 a.m., lit the kitchen fire and prepared breakfast, tea and supper and cleaned kitchen, scullery and pantry. The mid-day meal was eaten at the House, at a separate table. At first the theological students at Mirfield wore gowns in chapel; from 1907 they wore cassocks, but girdles not belts, to distinguish them from the brethren. Those who did not remain for communion had to report after breakfast to the Warden what they had read. Between breakfast and meditation there was housework – blankets and sheets were to be placed on a chair not the floor when making beds. 'When a room is dusted, all the moulds and architraves of doors and windows are to be gone over.' 'The cleaning of teeth must be done only in private rooms, for important hygienic reasons.' Greater and Lesser Silence were observed. 'All unseemly noises (such as whistling)' were forbidden. Students gardened two afternoons a week; other afternoons were spent in sports or walking. But there was to be 'no loitering about the College or grounds between 2.30 and 4 p.m. except with the sanction of the Warden'. All study was in public rooms. Students' rooms were not for sitting in, nor were any lights allowed in them. 'When using a bath care must be taken not to plunge suddenly into a full bath nor to splash the floor unduly.' Each evening students recorded breaches of the rules and presented a weekly list of them to the Warden. 'Individual eccentricities require pruning' the Standing Orders explained.

Of course until the early 1960s student life in all institutions was strictly regulated. Yet even within the exceptionally tight framework at Mirfield there was a lot of fun and stimulus. Sport was encouraged: football, rugby, fives (in a court in the Quarry) and regular cricket matches between brethren and students – Talbot was a fine bowler. The Debating and Literary Society heard papers on Cromwell, Matthew Arnold and the Jesuits, and debated the municipal ownership of the drink trade and the abolition of the armed forces. Motions for the abolition of the monarchy and the nationalization of the railways were defeated, the *CR Quarterly* announced, to the relief of those who imagined the College was a hot-bed of revolutionaries. Under Frere's influence musical life flourished. Students acted in the plays for Commemoration Day. In 1908, when CR's alleged socialism was causing public uproar, they put on 'A Socialistic Adventure'; the student authors intended it as a defence of socialism; others thought it a refutation.

Students bore Ritson's harsh regime for a long time before they complained. They had genuine reasons for gratitude to CR. They did not want to wreck their chances of ordination. But rumblings began in July 1907 about the Standing Orders. In December Ritson refused to summon the doctor to a sick student. Another student called him. He came and diagnosed a bad heart. Students complained to the tutor (Horner). Some said they would not return after Christmas if Ritson continued. At a College Council meeting students accused the Warden (who was present) of a 'reign of terror' and demanded his resignation. This was extraordinarily courageous at a time when authorities usually dismissed complaints and complainants – there were so many applicants that the protesting students could have easily been replaced. Students also complained that they did not have enough time to study because of navvying in the garden (then being constructed) and all the cooking; that the food was inadequate; that to reside for eleven months with only a month's break was a great strain; that some teaching was poor. It was a formidable indictment for which not only Ritson but CR too must be blamed. Ritson resigned in January (he left CR in July). Horner, gentle, wise and courteous who, unlike Ritson, had experienced corporate student life (at Hatfield College, Durham) replaced him. He withdrew the Standing Orders. He replaced the incompetent tutors. He appointed a couple to cook to relieve students of kitchen duties. He submitted the diet to two doctors. As a result the Council was gratified to hear in June that 'no more than eight of the students now suffer from chronic constipation' and extra fruit was provided for them. There were now to be three terms a year with holidays between. (The eleven months' residence with but one holiday had been designed to save parents the cost of travel and maintenance.) Two other brothers now resided in the College in addition to the Warden. Horner participated fully in student life and played half back in the football team.

Although CR insisted on high academic standards it was prepared to be flexible in cases of students of calibre. Thus St John Groser, one of the greatest priests ever produced by Mirfield, after six years on the course was ordained in 1914 without a degree. Though he had attended Ellesmere College from the age of fifteen (his parents were in Australia) he found Greek and Latin a great trial; he had to sit Matriculation three times and spent only a year at Leeds. Unlike some, he was not converted to socialism by the Mirfield ethos – Philip Speight, a fellow-student (CR from 1924), for example, remembered how he had served Mrs Pankhurst with tea when she attended the 1907 Quarry meeting with Labour leaders. Though Groser became the most famous Christian socialist in the East End, at Mirfield he refused to go to hear George Lansbury because he was an 'agitator'. However, when in 1914 he went to a slum parish in Newcastle he was outraged by the contrast between its poverty and the wealth of the landowners with whom he had spent vacations; without realizing it, Mirfield must have quickened his social conscience. Later Lansbury became one of his closest friends. It was to Gore that he turned for support when his socialism brought him into conflict with London diocesan authorities.[11]

In 1907 Frere presented some fascinating evidence about the course to the Archbishops' Committee on 'The Supply and Training of Candidates for Holy Orders'. By then there were fifty students at Mirfield and twelve at Leeds. Each year some two hundred applicants were rejected mainly because they were aged over twenty. The annual intake of about twelve was selected from about one hundred other applicants. Some had matriculated before entry. Some studied for Matriculation at Mirfield. A large number arrived with only elementary education, having worked for some years. They sat an internal examination to test knowledge and aptitude. Some needed two years to prepare for Matriculation so their course lasted seven years.

> The men come from very different homes, in each case a poor home, but the men must be capable of polish . . . We have a good number of sons of clergy, others from middle class, shopkeeper class, artisan and working class . . . very few from agricultural homes and only one domestic servant. We find no difficulty about manners though they have to be learnt . . . I do not suppose our average man would know what to do at a dinner party. He would probably be [more] at home at a middle class high tea than most of our clergy are, and it must be remembered there are many more high teas to attend than dinner parties in most parishes . . . They probably will not suit an exclusively rich congregation. Possibly they will not be as acceptable in some ways among the very poor as the right sort of well-bred man is . . . but they will do in my judgment far better in middle class parishes than the public school and university man does . . . As regards the accent we find the cockney dialect to be the most prohibitive . . . Some of our best men come from elementary school teachers . . . they represent the cream of the working class . . .

Students were instructed in teaching, helped in Bible classes and missions (visiting and open-air preaching), and were particularly interested in social questions. A variety of views was encouraged among students as in the Community. The question in the ordination service about belief in the scriptures was not a stumbling-block. They were taught what the Bible was 'and in what sense the question is a reasonable one'. The disciplined life of meditation and prayer put all questions into their right context.

By Christmas 1906, £7,500 had been raised for the College. C R now wanted £7,000 to build the first half of the permanent Hostel. As we saw in Chapter 4 an appeal was launched by the Archbishop of Canterbury in 1907 amid great controversy and in the teeth of the wishes of Bishop Boyd Carpenter of Ripon. Temple Moore, one of the finest of Edwardian Gothic architects, was chosen to design it. Devoted to the Yorkshire abbeys (he restored Rievaulx in 1906) his work emphasized the continuity of the Church of England with its mediaeval past, and so was attractive to C R and the historically minded Frere.[12] Work began in December 1907, but because of a financial crisis stopped in May 1908 with only the basement completed. The cost had been gravely underestimated. The first students were not ordained until 1908 so no fees were being repaid. The maintenance fund was £1,500 in deficit. Bickersteth (*CRQ* JB 1908) assured those who had withheld contributions for political reasons that C R was not corporately committed to socialism. Frere (*CRQ* CD 1908) issued a stark warning: it would be impossible to take new students in 1909 without more money. As a result contributions picked up sufficiently for work to begin again in January 1909.

On 21 April 1910 the Hostel (costing £17–18,000) was blessed by Gore and officially opened by Lady Frederick Cavendish. The Vice-Chancellors of Leeds, Cambridge, Durham and Manchester attended. Their presence indicated C R's ability to pull in the establishment, and that like the building itself, this new venture had carefully cultivated historical roots. Indeed the Vice-Chancellor of Leeds paid tribute to the Hostel for reviving the common life in a non-residential university. He congratulated C R in deciding 'to throw their students into the free and liberal atmosphere of the open University . . . in which every shade of opinion on religion, politics and social matters was represented'. The Bishop of Ripon at last agreed to license the chapel for the eucharist (previously students had attended All Souls') but restricted its ritual. However, his successor (T. W. Drury) in 1915 agreed to license the brethren and that the Hostel could now be an official branch House of C R.

After ten years C R had much to celebrate. By Christmas 1912, forty had been ordained, and sixty-five were in training. But £4,000 a year was required for maintenance of students. In 1913 extensions to the College enabled students to eat all their meals there. Brethren at the House missed their daily presence at the mid-day meal.

Talbot, in a letter to his brother (July 1910), assured him that C R was giving much thought to theological education:

> Of course we are committed, without redress I think, to methods very different from Fr Kelly's; in some respects the complete opposite. Deliberately the arts course, degree, etc were assumed as a normal part of the training . . . we do not challenge

the ordinary axioms of education, but assume them, perhaps without sufficient scrutiny. Kelly's very interesting theory about the place of theology in his educational order, whether right or wrong, strikes sparks; and we have got nothing correspondingly original . . . What we profess is to secure (i) for men of all sorts, and (ii) under the continuous condition of a religious house, the training which is given elsewhere only to a limited class . . . [with] the simplicity, discipline and fellowship of a common life . . . [At] Kelham the Community and College are fused; here the College is only one offshoot of the Community, whose life is largely independent of it. And from this has arisen our weakness. The College has been too much a by-work . . . Hence we have been amateurish and happy-go-lucky . . . Of course we have no architectonic mind like Fr Kelly's . . . E.g. I have been chucked at the dogmatic theology . . . Is theology the science of the whole, or of a part? Is it the intellectual envisagement of a Gospel of Creation, or of a Gospel of Salvation? the geography of a straight road and a narrow gate, or of the whole countryside? Correspondingly, is religion the way through and out of a naughty world? or the benedictory illumination of all human activities? . . . I question whether Theology, not only can, but ought, to try to overcome that 'ever-not-quite' element . . . which bids us remember that the world has something dark and fearful in it through which we must win our way to God.

But as this passage indicates, Talbot taught and thought better than he knew.

Between the wars

'My own opinion is that the pre-war theological college system, as judged by the padres it produced, did not come well out of the experience of war; the devotional training had been along too narrow lines and depended too much on favourable environment, and when that was no longer given the padre was apt to lose his bearings.' So reflected B. K. Cunningham, Principal of Westcott House, Cambridge, in 1919 after a period of ministry to chaplains in France.[13] Others were also highly critical. For a time the Church of England seemed prepared to tackle the problems with which SSM and CR had been grappling for nearly twenty years. In February 1918 Archbishop Davidson promised that the church would finance the training of all suitable service ordinands in need of assistance. After the Armistice Keble Talbot ran one of the preparatory courses for service ordinands in France. A 'Test School' to provide general preliminary education for them was created in a disused prison in Knutsford in 1919. A working party under Frere drew up its curriculum. But once the ex-service ordinands had passed through, to Frere's dismay Knutsford ceased to receive church funding. A number of its students had come to Mirfield. Knutsford continued as a private institution; for a time Frere was chairman of its Council.[14]

For fifteen years CR sponsored and partly financed a splendid venture which began in 1925 at Tatterford, a tiny Norfolk village. Its rector, W. T. Hand, was one of the first two ordained from Mirfield in 1908. Frere and Rees asked him to create a school for those with only elementary education to qualify for courses at Leeds and elsewhere in the context of a spiritual discipline based on Mirfield. Life was spartan (though Mrs Hand's meals were not). The earliest students lived in army huts. There was only cold water for ablutions. A critic remarked that it was sad that the students had to study in a stable. Hand reminded him that Christianity began in a stable. Tatterford made it possible for 150 priests to be ordained. CR also helped individual ordinands – for example in 1926 it financed a student at Knutsford for two years and also sent money to his mother for his clothes, fares and holidays.

In 1920 CR ceased to ask for repayment of fees. To make repayments from a curate's salary was a heavy burden. It was generous of CR to waive repayments because between the wars College and Hostel accounts were often deeply in the red. So when Rees became Warden in 1922 he immediately had to appeal for funds through the *Church Times* to keep the College open: this raised £2,000. But by 1931 CR needed £10,000 annually for one hundred students at Leeds, Mirfield and Tatterford. In 1934 there were five hundred applications for twenty places at Mirfield, a clear sign of the continuing need for CR's system.

When the College was planned in 1903 the present quadrangle was only a third of the total scheme. In 1919 CR appealed for £20,000 to complete the College as a war memorial, so it could take one hundred students. CR gratefully acknowledged that already £25,365 had been given to build the College and Hostel and £36,500 for fees and maintenance (of which those now ordained had repaid £8,686). John Bilson, a leading architectural historian, prepared plans in association with Chad Windley. Windley's drawings show a grandiose quadrangle to the north of the existing College, linked to the church by a cloister, with a squat castellated Tudor entrance from the drive. The College was also to extend across the drive with a five storey castellated tower gateway like that of Trinity College, Cambridge, with wings on either side fronting the road. The foundation stone of the first small instalment was laid in July near the tower (which was to be removed under the scheme) providing a few extra rooms. But the money for further building was not forthcoming and the completion of the Hostel (for which an appeal was launched in 1926) took priority. So the Bilson scheme was abandoned. Its one completed section looks slightly forlorn and oddly juxtaposed against the tower entrance, particularly as the new admirable refectory, accommodating one hundred, built with a large legacy in 1933, continued the line of the tower northwards. The refectory was enhanced by a roundel over the high table carved by Eric Gill and given by Hubert Worthington, its architect, in memory of his friend Charles Gore. (The Stations placed in the Church in 1956 were carved by Joseph Cribb, Gill's best pupil.)

In 1926 Rees set about raising £20,000 to complete the Hostel; Shelley, its

Custos, supervised the work. Temple Moore, its architect, had died in 1920, but his partner, Leslie Moore, completed the building. An anonymous donation of £13,000 made this possible. The completed Hostel had now over double the accommodation and a fine chapel – the rood was generously given by the architect. The Hostel was blessed on St Luke's Day 1920 by Frere. The Vice-Chancellor of Leeds congratulated the Community for so skilfully adapting a mediaeval precedent for a modern university. But Bishop Burroughs of Ripon, a former Oxford don, with extraordinary maladroitness, spoke of the older universities as 'the real thing' and modern universities as 'counterfeit presentations'. The Vice-Chancellor of Manchester was heartily cheered when he refuted the bishop's gibe. Burroughs also criticized the Hostel for not including Evangelicals and Modernists. The *Church Times*, which dismissed Burroughs' remarks as 'the thinking aloud of a tired and inexperienced man', commented that those who kept their faith in 'the rough-and-tumble of a secular University' lacking the Christian framework of Oxford and Cambridge, would be better able to minister to the masses. Talbot's hope for a second hostel in another university to feed into Mirfield was never realized.

The completion of the Hostel changed the pattern. The first three years were now spent at Leeds. The College no longer uneasily mixed first with fourth and fifth year students, but was now wholly a theological college. The Custos of the Hostel now became 'Warden'; the Warden of the College became 'Principal'. By 1933 there were fifty-seven students at the Hostel. The Sunday morning Sung Mass, open to men of the univeristy, guest nights and the annual Carol Service provided opportunities for sharing its social and religious life with other students, particularly those from overseas. Until the first Anglican chaplain to the university was appointed in 1957, brethren exercised a general ministry to students and the Hostel functioned like a chaplaincy centre. Sir Michael Sadler (Vice-Chancellor 1911–23) was a great supporter. In 1920 he presented the Hostel with a crucifix by the controversial Serbian sculptor Mestrovic on permanent loan. (It is now at Mirfield.) Most, but not all, students, went on to Mirfield. The friendly rivalry between College and Hostel was expressed, for example, in riotous rugby matches on Collop Monday (before Lent) and Foundation Day (28 October). Before Com-memoration Day Hostel students resided at the College for three weeks tidying the grounds under Ralph Bell's strenuous direction and rehearsing for the Quarry play.

But it was not a closed system. A number of students began to come to Mirfield from other universities, particularly after the Hostel was completed. Ambrose Reeves, one of the first externals, arrived from Cambridge in 1924. Mirfield shaped his spirituality and deepened his social convictions. He went on to study at General Seminary New York for a year. Orthodox students came to stay. An Armenian visitor writing in the *Mirfield Gazette* was puzzled why Anglo-Catholics massed all their troops on the Evangelical and Modernist fronts but left 'the Roman front defenceless'. In 1937 four Mirfield students postponed their ordinations for a year to study in Romania. Participation in conferences organized by the Fellowship of St Alban and St Sergius and SCM also widened horizons. The annual conference with the local Congregationalist, Baptist and Methodist theological colleges sometimes produced condescending comments in the *Gazette*: 'Our nonconformist friends have so little to offer men and women to-day apart from the emotional side of religion and they tend to see our point of view more and more.'

Students led disciplined lives. No student was allowed to become engaged. Temporary or permanent clerical celibacy was pressed on them by some brethren. At the College in the 1920s students still submitted a weekly report to the Principal on their observance of the rule. However, in 1922 Chapter made one concession: 'We do not refuse to allow Hostel students to play tennis on the university courts on Sunday afternoons.' 'Deacons' Fortnight' for those about to be deacons and for those who returned to prepare for their priesting was particularly valued. It included a silent retreat, opportunity to share experiences, hopes and fears and lectures on pastoralia, including the confessional.

'Most of the students, if they had any politics, seemed to be socialistic', according to a student of the 1920s. But socialist students had to be prepared for strenuous arguments with Edward Symonds, a staunch Tory. Socialists at the Hostel severely criticized anyone who joined the OTC. During the 1926 General Strike about half the students supported the strikers. Voting figures in debates indicate the strength of radical sentiment. In 1931 the National Government with 554 seats had the confidence of only 19 out of 35 students. In 1935 the voting was 22–8 in favour of disestablishment. Between the wars a tiny minority of Anglo-Catholics supported Fascism. In 1934 the *Gazette* carried an article signed 'Blackshirt': Fascism opposed Marxism, upheld 'Unselfishness' and stood for 'complete religious toleration'. This was very mild compared with two vicious anti-semitic and pro-Nazi articles in the magazine of Chichester Theological College of that period.[15] The normal political debates in the *Gazette* were about socialism. In 1926 St John Groser argued that to confine the church's ministry to individuals contradicted the sacramental system and the corporate nature of the church. There were vigorous responses the following year. During the 1924 General Election Reeves campaigned for local Labour candidates. In 1929 four students spoke on Labour Party platforms. It was mostly the socialist students who attended the Anglo-Catholic Summer Schools of Sociology. The fact that by 1930 nearly one fifth of former students worked overseas reflected CR's tradition of commitment to the needy.

From 1929 regular College Festivals reinforced loyalty to College and Community. When Frere preached at the 1935 Festival shortly after retiring, he outlined three main defects in the Church of England: ecclesiasticism – in clergy houses there was more talk about the externals of religion than saving souls; reliance was placed on ecclesiastical machinery rather than on visiting and pastoral work; priestly individualism had run riot. When Frere died in 1938 a student recalled his address to two College servants he confirmed in the Chapel of the Ascension: 'There was a breath-taking simplicity, so that one listened charmed, fascinated, spell-bound, helpless with joy.' Hand remembered how in January 1903 Frere had appeared at Wakefield station with his special smile to welcome the first three students including himself. Staff changed at Hostel and College as they did at other theological colleges. But only Mirfield and Kelham students enjoyed the inestimable benefit of being affectionately associated with the life and worship of a Community which was always there, however much the College might change, and which included memorable characters with flashes of sanctity. The two outstanding Principals of these years were Timothy Rees (1922–8), the fervent Welsh missioner who had rescued the College out of a post-war crisis, and the shy, courteous and austere Thomas Hannay (1933–40) who became Bishop of Argyll and the Isles in 1942 and Primus in 1952. Unable to drive a car, he became a much loved figure in the buses, trains and ferries of western Scotland and then retired (unlike some Prelate Brothers) with perfect ease to Mirfield. By 1938, impressed by the experience of CR which the Hostel and College provided, nine old students had joined the Community.

Fifty years of change

Since the end of the Second World War both the form and context of ministerial training in the Church of England have changed radically. (Some of the changes in the social context of ministry were sketched in the last chapter.) The number of residential theological colleges has been reduced from twenty-six in 1953 to sixteen. But there are now fifteen non-residential courses, some of which also train lay ministers, and diocesan schemes for local ordained and lay ministry. In the late 1950s, when I was a student at Mirfield, traditional Anglican guideposts were still firmly in place: *The Thirty-Nine Articles* by E. J. Bicknell; Proctor and Frere's *History of the Book of Common Prayer*. SPCK grants provided me with *Liturgy and Worship* (1932) and *Essays Catholic and Critical* (1926). The Revised Version of the Bible was still the standard text. Those students who believed in the priesthood of all ordinands ensured the validity of the (more-or-less) Prayer Book eucharist by saying silently in their pews the Roman Canon from the ubiquitous *English Missal*. Today Prayer Book, Articles and *English Missal* all gather dust, and Anglo-Catholics look instead for guidance to the decrees of Vatican II and the documents of the Anglican-Roman Catholic International Commission. The ecumenical scene has altered beyond recognition. Relations with the

Orthodox seemed very important to Anglo-Catholics until the Vatican turned hospitable. The sudden Roman and Anglican lust for modernity, relevance and activist worship, which stripped liturgy and buildings of mystery and antiquities, also created a chasm between western and eastern styles of piety. One by one, schemes and covenants with the Free Churches failed. The bright hopes of Anglican-Roman convergence opened up by Vatican II were dimmed by the election of a Pope better at locking stable doors than understanding why so many horses prefer to gallop on the hills. At an unofficial level, Christians now shop around and communicate where they please. Outwardly all the churches look more Catholic – Methodist Presidents now wear pectoral crosses and an Evangelical priest commends the rosary; but in reality individualism runs riot.

The broadly-based Anglo-Catholicism typified by *Catholicity* (1947) – whose authors included Michael Ramsey and T. S. Eliot – began to be fragmented by the radicalism of the 1960s. Since then, first the Anglican-Methodist scheme and more recently the issue of women priests have produced divisions among Anglo-Catholics as bitter as those about *Lux Mundi* and csi. Uncertain about whether women will become priests and disturbed by recent conservative episcopal pronouncements about homosexuality, Anglo-Catholics hesitate to offer for ordination. The 'coming out' of homosexual ordinands in the 1970s nearly wrecked two theological colleges, but the proportion of them at Anglo-Catholic colleges remains high. Meanwhile Anglican Evangelicalism burgeons, but as it spreads and its leaders become bishops, the Anglican and English knack for neutering the extremist is already at work – Anglo-Catholics, like other Nonconformists, can tell Evangelicals all about that.

As recently as 1975 there were only ninety-two full-time and twenty-five part-time deaconesses in the Church of England. By 1988 there were five hundred and three full-time women deacons, and more part-time; a quarter of ordinands in training were women. For over twenty years cr brethren have ministered alongside sisters at St Katharine's Stepney. At the time of writing the novices at Mirfield are all lay. Laymen play an increasingly important role in cr – conduct the offices, preach, take missions and preside at meals on occasion. But these developments in cr have not been reflected in the College.

Thus certain basic questions have to be asked about any ministerial training. Is it preparing people for the ministry of the whole Church of England and not just for a section of it? Is it preparing them for collaborative ministry – male with female, clergy with laity? (When students from the College visited the German Roman Catholic seminary at Trier in 1990 they discovered it also trained women pastoral assistants.) Is it teaching theology not as a static deposit but as a relationship with the dynamic God fertilized by prayer and meditation, by church and world, by togetherness and aloneness, by study and manual work, by a ministry to social structures as well as to individuals: a theology which has deep roots in the great variety of the Christian tradition yet open to the God of Good Friday outside the gate of church and society? Is it creating a flexible style of leadership?: 'He can take the lead when occasion demands without self-consciousness or follow the leadership of others without any servility because he accepts himself; and his peace of mind does not depend either on dominating or being ruled by others.'[16] In some local ministry schemes the parish priest must share the training with laity under an outside tutor. True, the priest is to be a walking sacrament. Hensley Henson described him as a 'publicly certified' Christian. Yet however richly symbolic the priestly role, the Christian priest is not a separate cultic figure, but one who presides over a community, like a midwife enabling the body to bring forth new life, who focusses with particular clarity and representativeness what should be true of the church as a whole.[17]

Joseph Barker resigned as Principal of the College in 1947 because of his disagreement with Raynes. Raynes, always suspicious of the College and academics for their liability to develop liberal measles, typified by Barker, was determined to bring the College back into line. So, to the dismay of some brethren, he appointed Douglas Edwards, a combative guardian of orthodoxy, but unsuitable for this major role.[18] Two years later he was replaced by Andrew Blair, a Scottish Friar Tuck and no academic – he called his Church History course 'From Nell Gwyn to Wally Simpson' – but shrewd and warm, with nine years' parochial experience. The church authorities were concerned that the College lacked corporate worship. Having rejected Michael Tapper's plan for a separate building, the lower Church was converted into a Chapel, with a daily mass (except on Tuesdays when students joined with CR) for those not serving private masses. Academically students were rather left to their own devices. Some resorted to correspondence courses with Wolsey Hall.

However, the 1944 Education Act had provided grants for access to higher education precisely for those for whom the CR system had been designed, so its original purpose had in fact disappeared. The number of students coming to the Hostel dropped and places were filled with Paying Guests (PGS). In 1953 those at the College with degrees from other universities started to outnumber those from Leeds.[19] In 1952 the Hostel began to take Qualifying Candidates (QCS), usually from working-class backgrounds, who worked for GCE qualifications under CR and lay tutors. As always Symonds rose to the challenge and learnt enough chemistry to conduct a laboratory in the basement. 'Come on wretched fellow', he would say like a teacher from a public school novel, 'it's time to make our stinks.' Tweedy recalled: 'It was a miracle that the old man didn't blow us all up' – Symonds was then in his seventies. Some went on to the university and Mirfield, others to non-graduate courses elsewhere. But the new colleges of further education eventually were providing better facilities than the Hostel. By the end of the

1960s it had become virtually an ordinary hall of residence. Silvanus Berry as Warden needed all his eirenic skills to preside over a heterogeneous community of PGs, a few QCs and twenty or so ordinands including some post-graduates from College. But CR was having to find a considerable subsidy each year, and the Hostel no longer was fulfilling its original purpose. In 1976 CR sold it at a fairly nominal sum to the university which now uses it for Adult Education. Some chapel furnishings went to Mirfield, others to parish churches. Thus another frontier post in the student world from which vocations to ministry and CR might be expected was surrendered. The university had lost a unique institution and a Religious Order from the heart of its campus. Some Evangelical institutions were already running correspondence courses in the Christian faith coupled with residential weekends. Shortly after the Hostel closed the diocese of Ripon began to expand lay training and to devise local ministry courses and needed facilities. But CR was still too shattered after the crisis of 1974–5 (to be described in chapter 13) to make creative adventures.

In 1955 Raynes appointed Hugh Bishop to be another 'sound' Principal. Though Bishop had caused disquiet as Novice Guardian (1949–52) by an intense friendship with one of the novices, in fact he was still one of the most rigorist of brethren. For some years he had tried to go the extra mile by not normally drawing his peculium. By this time he was in great demand as a preacher at public schools, famous London churches and as college missioner for Oxbridge university missions. His mixture of charm, austerity, culture and Delphic authority compelled many; a few, however, actively disliked him. He was determined to bring the College into the Anglican mainstream. Hitherto CR had continued to finance students to preserve an independence from church authorities which he was keen to surrender. So now students were funded by grants as in other colleges. CR, however, continued to pay for a number of overseas students to come to Mirfield. Physically the College was drab and uninviting, but under Laurence King's direction it was smartened up. As numbers increased an extra floor was added to the Bilson building. By 1959 there were fifty-three students.

The framework was strict and traditional. Daily Mattins, Meditation, Evensong and Compline were compulsory, though Sunday Evensong could be attended elsewhere. On Saturdays only the period between lunch and Evensong was free; in the morning students cleaned the College and studied. A quick dash to a Leeds cinema was possible, though there was not always time to see the whole film. In the late 1950s women guests were allowed to come to coffee after Sunday High Mass but they were separated in another room. Yet within this framework there were stirrings. Bishop's growing impatience with aspects of religion was evident in his College and public addresses. He warned the 1958 Anglo-Catholic Eucharistic Congress against a petty, trivializing religion. He quoted Nietzsche on Christians, 'All very alike, very small, very smooth, very wearisome'. He quoted Emmanuel Mounier's *Spoil of the Violent:*

> The bourgeois would like to turn the catholic, apostolic Church into the back parlour of a shop, a confidential salon where anaemic virtues stagnated in a curtained half-light, ignorant of everything unconnected with ecclesiastical gossip, the troubles of a pious clique and the sterile confidences of lonely lives.

The College also heard this quotation, but Figgis' call to 'give all for all' as well. Politically Bishop moved leftwards as a result of a visit to Africa in 1960. A study of four theological colleges in the 1960s revealed that while many students arrived at Mirfield as a-political pietists, when they left their political consciousness had been raised to a much higher level than students at the other colleges; at Mirfield this meant a move leftwards. Again, while *Honest to God* was disliked at Evangelical colleges, it was received warmly at Mirfield. Radicalism was effortlessly overrunning the Maginot line of Anglo-Catholic orthodoxy, taking the complacent old guards with their obsolete weapons by surprise.[20] Paul Ferris visited the College in the early 1960s:

> At Mirfield, they have the knack, rarer among Anglicans than Roman Catholics, of combining the secular with the religious. Their worship is highly organized, there is much academic distinction, they are good at publicity . . . Whereas at an extreme Evangelical college, the agnostic is soon on edge, half afraid some ebullient student may start to accuse him of something in a loud voice, at Mirfield co-existence is easy; the note of accusation is absent.[21]

Bishop abhorred ecclesiastical or ritualistic chat. But the Holy Week and Easter Liturgy moved him to the core. All but the old brethren were away; the College occupied the stalls, said the offices and enacted the great rituals culminating in the marvellous Easter Vigil which begins before dawn and reaches the creation stories when the light is breaking. Often there were forty guests, mostly students. In his time the College also sang the Beaumont Folk Mass to skiffles and washboards (disturbing the private masses being murmured upstairs), paid a memorable visit to Halton, produced 'Waiting for Godot', exchanged visits with the Methodist college in Leeds and with seminarians at Roe Head where Charlotte Bronte once taught. The *Mirfield Gazette* in 1958 (the year of *Anglican Essays in Self-Criticism*) broke with tradition, and omitting news of old students, concentrated on the failure of the church to communicate. The *Gazette* continued to print substantial articles. Sadly some years ago it was replaced by an annual Principal's letter.

Bishop courageously removed those brethren whose lectures were played out, and replaced them by lecturers from Durham and Leeds universities. From time to time there had been lay tutors – Nicolas Graham who had rocked Uppingham by asking to be excused cricket so he could read more poetry, came as a lay tutor in 1946 to teach backward students, and was professed and ordained in 1951, becoming a Warden at the Hostel of singular charm and understanding. But the appointment of outside lecturers in major subjects was quite different – a sign that CR could not adequately staff three theological colleges itself. Bishop's wide contacts also brought in a galaxy of outside speakers.

For some time students had been allowed to be engaged. In 1959 they were allowed to marry before their last term. So for the first time women attended chapel. But they had to sit in the back row. Bishop's ten years as Principal were his happiest years in CR. Yet except in the hottest weather he would clutch his cloak around him as though he was always cold within.

William Wheeldon (1966–75) and Benedict Green (1975–84) developed what Bishop had begun. Bishop was Superior for virtually the whole time Wheeldon was Principal (unlike previous Superiors he gave the College a good deal of autonomy). Green had been tutor and Vice-Principal under Bishop and Wheeldon and had held the interregnum between them. So the Liberal Catholic ethos continued. Wheeldon, who arrived from being Acting-Principal at Codrington, was the first Principal to have been trained at both Hostel and College. His first priority was to improve the teaching. With John Tinsley as Professor of Theology at Leeds (later Bishop of Bristol) CR had gained confidence in the department. All non-theological graduates now read for the Leeds Diploma or the degree. Some brethren became associate lecturers in the department. The decision in 1966 not to move the College to Leeds was prompted by the realization that students would not wish to lose the ethos and worship at Mirfield. In 1972 the first married member of staff was appointed, the first of a succession of priests with parochial experience to oversee Pastoral Training. The decision not to allow students to serve private masses made possible a truly corporate College eucharist – it also reduced the number of private masses. Another major change occurred in 1969 when the College began to take up to a quarter of married students. The common life was preserved by housing them locally, by adjustments to the timetable and by providing free meals for families in the refectory. Married students and their families made a lot more contacts with local people. The abolition of the ban on drinking in local pubs also broke down barriers. It was a significant moment when two College babies were baptized at the Easter Vigil in 1972.

In the 1970s a number of colleges amalgamated or (like Kelham) closed because of a drop in ordinands. Mirfield stayed open on its intrinsic merits, but also because with a largely unpaid staff and its (now) considerable reserves its fees were low. Wheeldon wrote about the drop in vocations: 'If you want clergy ask more from them. What they are terrified of is the prospect of being useless or being involved in a round of irrelevancies.'

Green was the first academic to be Principal. The publication of his widely praised commentary on St Matthew in 1975 and the arrival on the staff of Rowan Williams, then a layman (now Lady Margaret Professor of Divinity, Oxford) put Mirfield on the academic map. Because of a huge increase in university fees, the link with Leeds had now to be confined to the few who were doing a degree. Green wrote in his 1979-80 Report:

> Now that we no longer have the Leeds Hostel, and all men under thirty who have not read theology already do three years with us, students face a longer period of withdrawal from the workaday world than they ever did previously in our system, and I have from time to time been aware over the past year or two of an increased tendency to churchiness . . . I certainly see the need for slanting the programme of outside speakers towards secular matters rather than ecclesiastical ones.

The request from local dioceses to run an annual month of in-service training for one priest from each (beginning in 1982) also opened up the College.

Under Denys Lloyd (1984–90), the first Principal to lead a College pilgrimage to Walsingham, the College stood for 'definite Catholicism'. A priest who came for in-service training, knowing the College's leftish reputation, discovered that though some students attended meetings of the local Labour Party, many believed that the Church of England needed deliverance from 'woolly liberalism' by the type of uncompromising leadership represented by Mrs Thatcher. Another priest after preaching to the College about collaborative ministry noted that the Principal the next week preached on the importance of hierarchy. One of the great achievements of this period was the creation of the 'Mirfield Certificate', an imaginative integration of the academic, the pastoral and the spiritual. The aims of the College were redefined as: growth in holiness, wisdom and pastoral effectiveness. Students learn to share responsibility through group work and corporate decision making.

Theological colleges like Mirfield with a particular emphasis on the common life are the last remaining bastions of the old Oxbridge Benedictine tradition. Even in the 1950s Oxbridge colleges still commonly insisted that undergraduates dined five nights a week. Today's undergraduates prefer cafeteria service to formal Hall, so the candles on High Table shimmer on the silver and the portraits (the college iconostasis) but the nave (as it were) is often empty. Former Mirfield students from various eras, asked why they chose that college, all emphasized the immense value of its common life and the common prayer between students and brethren. Some had wanted to explore a possible vocation to the Religious Life. 'It is clear that God has priority at Mirfield' one commented. When Lloyd became a Roman Catholic in 1990 he was succeeded by David Lane, a former professor in Toronto, who played a pivotal role in the creation of the 'Mirfield Certificate'. He writes of the College:

First, we here do start with an enormous advantage: as a college under the direction and aegis of the Community of the Resurrection, we are provided with a large number of role models of priesthood and laity . . . So we do not start with a complete blank to fill in: what is a priest? who is a priest? what or who is a layman? Over the years, for staff and student, living or departed brethren provide a multitude of unselfconscious embodiments of ministerial response to the divine call. Those who know the Community will not regard this cluster of exemplars as monochrome, even if cassocks are black and scapulars grey. (*CRQ* LD 1991)

Africa: Triumphs and Tragedies

Believing in South Africa

'The relations between Europeans and Africans in this great land are still far from being equitably adjusted', blandly wrote the Archbishop of Cape Town (J. R. Darbyshire) in 1944. 'But surely, if slowly, a more sympathetic and liberal attitude on the part of Europeans to the African people is growing up.' The confident tone of this Foreword to *Mirfield in Africa* was echoed in the sub-title – 'Another Twenty Years Onward and Upward'. But the text by one of the brethren was less sanguine:

> The political future of the Union of South Africa is one large question mark. Few but the blind can imagine that her 'Native Problem' is solved . . . Great subterranean forces drive men and nations forward to their destiny . . . Will the forces of Christian liberation be strong enough to guide the future development of the South African state into paths of peace and racial co-operation? Or will repression of one race by another lead to some horrible catastrophe?

Are there signs here that the old evolutionary optimism was beginning to crack under the impact of war and the influence of Reinhold Niebuhr?

Yet there seemed reasons for cautious hope. The Smuts' government of 1939–1948 was perhaps the most liberal regime since the Union of 1910. By taking South Africa into the war against fierce Afrikaner opposition, the British connection was strengthened. Blacks served overseas and returned more than ever dissatisfied with their lot. During the war-time economic boom, Africans flocked to the towns – the black population of Johannesburg increased from 244,000 in 1939 to 400,000 in 1945. During and after the war they felt economically strong enough to run strikes and bus boycotts. Some whites returned with a new social vision for South Africa. The Torch Commando movement was one expression of this. In the 1940s and early 1950s Africans and white liberals struggled together for racial justice with a real hope that the frontiers of prejudice were being pushed back.

During the war the South African brethren were under pressure. Runge had gone off to be a chaplain. Victor had become Dean of Salisbury, Rhodesia.

It was impossible to go on leave to England or for Chapter, and almost impossible for new recruits to get passages. Christopher Millington had to travel via Brazil to Rosettenville. Huddleston threw his gas-mask overboard as he left Liverpool but the convoy was bombed on the way. When in 1946 the first snapshots to be exchanged for seven years arrived at Mirfield and Rosettenville, some brethren were hardly recognizable. After the war CR expanded in confident hope. In 1947, the year before the Nationalists came to power, CR issued an appeal for £25,000 for its African work – science laboratory, dormitories and swimming pool for St Peter's school; the completion of St Benedict's Retreat House opposite; a hostel, a club and churches for the townships; hospital, school and church building in Sekhukhuniland; dormitories, dining hall and a new teachers' training college at Penhalonga – and more.

St Peter's Theological College made an outstanding contribution to the episcopate as well as to the parish ministry: Alphaeus Zulu (1939) the first black Anglican bishop in South Africa; Desmond Tutu (1958) now Archbishop of Cape Town; Peter Hatendi (1955) the first black diocesan bishop in Zimbabwe; Lawrence Zulu (1958) Bishop of Zululand from 1975; Philip Mokuku (1957) Bishop of Lesotho from 1978; Khotso Makhulu (1955) Archbishop of Central Africa from 1980. Godfrey Pawson (Principal 1956–60) brought all the resources of his very English scholarship. Martin Jarrett-Kerr, also on the staff, skilled in synthesizing disparate fields of knowledge, became enthralled by African culture. His article on this theme (*CRQ* LD 1960) began characteristically: 'I had occasion to quote, for a little book I was writing, a passage on African Witch Doctors in an essay by a Social Anthropologist whom I know and respect.' African culture was rich in music, poetry, prose and the visual arts (thereby refuting the dismissive attitudes of whites like Aidan Cotton to African culture). He quoted with delight from the African poet Léopold Senghor: 'New York let black blood flow into your blood/That it may rub the rust from your steel joints, like an oil of life,/That it may give to your bridges the bend of buttocks and the suppleness of creepers.'

Consider CR's contribution to the formation of Desmond Tutu; brought up in locations near Johannesburg, the son of a headmaster and a domestic servant, going at first to secondary school barefoot over the dirt streets, seeing black children scavenging for food in the dustbins outside white schools. From the age of thirteen he stayed at a CR hostel in Sophiatown. He developed tuberculosis and during those twenty months in hospital Trevor Huddleston visited him every week. Tutu writes about Huddleston:

> He was so un-English in many ways, being very fond of hugging people, embracing them, and in the way in which he laughed. He did not laugh like many white people, only with their teeth, he laughed with his whole body . . . His office in Sophiatown would have very many street urchins playing marbles on the floor and the next

moment when he had shooed them out he would be meeting ambassadors and high-placed officials and leading businessmen.[1]

Tutu considered joining CR but trained as a teacher instead. He refused to continue as a teacher under the Bantu Education Act, and so went to Rosettenville to train for the priesthood:

> It is from these remarkable men that I have learned that it is impossible for religion to be sealed off in a watertight compartment that has no connection with the hurly burly business of ordinary daily living, that our encounter with God in prayer, meditation, the sacraments and bible study is authenticated and expressed in our dealings with our neighbour, whose keeper we must be willy nilly.[2]

He was amazed when Timothy Stanton, not only the Vice-Principal but also white, actually joined in doing menial chores with students. In 1962, Aelred Stubbs, then Principal, arranged for Tutu to go to England to read for a theological degree so he could return as the first black member of staff. CR was among groups which found money for Tutu and his family to go. When later he was Dean of Johannesburg it was Stubbs who deepened his political awareness by introducing him to friends of Steve Biko, then in detention.

CR helped to create African leadership in arts and politics as well as in the church. *Drum*, an exuberant magazine found, in 1951 and based in Johannesburg expressed the vitality of the new urban black. Seven out of its twenty African staff had been educated at St Peter's school, including its literary editor Es'kia Mphahlele. *Drum* also represented the new political aspirations focussed in such figures as Walter Sisulu, Nelson Mandela and Oliver Tambo, all of whom (like many of its readers) had migrated from country to city. Tambo was depicted in the 1947 Appeal brochure teaching a physics class at St Peter's. Born in the Transkei, he went to board at an Anglican mission at Holy Cross. 'It was a new world', he said. At sixteen he came to St Peter's school. After graduating at Fort Hare he was expelled from the subsequent teaching course for voicing students' grievances to the staff. Teaching now seemed impossible, but St Peter's offered him a job, during which he studied law part-time. In 1952 he and Mandela put up their brass plate MANDELA & TAMBO and crowds flocked to seek their help. In 1954 Tambo, an ANC leader, was 'banned' for two years, restricting his movements (so hampering his work) and forbidding him to attend any gatherings, even of a social nature. In fury at the church's failure to defend one of its most faithful members, Huddleston penned one of his most controversial articles, 'The Church Sleeps On', for the London *Observer*.[3] In 1956 Tambo was accepted as an ordinand by Ambrose Reeves, Bishop of Johannesburg, with Huddleston's encouragement, but in December he, with Mandela and Sisulu, were among the 156 arrested and charged with High Treason. Later when

Huddleston became Bishop of Masasi and said a weekday mass at Dar-es-Salaam he would often find Tambo, by then ANC President and in exile, in the congregation – just like the old days in Rosettenville and Sophiatown.

Alan Paton's novel *Cry, the Beloved Country* was published in 1948.[4] It seems dated now, but it is still a haunting book, though black radicals dislike it because the Zulu priest seems an 'Uncle Tom'. The huge sales of the book (still 100,000 a year) made the Sophiatown mission famous throughout the world. Though CR is not mentioned, the connection was soon spotted. In correspondence with me in 1983 Paton confirmed that it was based on the CR mission, that 'Father Vincent' was based on Huddleston, and that the name derived from that of Vincent Wall, a much loved member of CR, who was shot at Rosettenville during the night in April 1942 by an intruder. One of the vast numbers of people who were deeply affected by the novel was a young white South African woman, Mary Benson, who had never given her country's racial problems any serious thought, and who now gave the rest of her life to the struggle for racial justice.[5] The novel was made into a film partly shot in Sophiatown and its Priory. When it was shown in Leeds in December 1952, Roger Castle spoke for five minutes each evening before the final performance about CR's African work. At a Leeds meeting linked to the film one of the speakers was Herbert Chitepo, educated at Penhalonga, then a lecturer at the London School of Oriental Studies.

Anthony Sampson, editor of *Drum* in the 1950s (who encouraged Huddleston to write *Naught for your Comfort*) assessed Sophiatown as 'the most lively, important and sophisticated' township on the Reef. 'In its crowded and narrow streets walked philosophers and gangsters, musicians and pickpockets, short-story writers and businessmen.'[6] Paul Singleton of CR described a day at the mission:

Haul on the rope, boom, boom, boom, goes the old bell . . . Tap-tap-tap; here comes old blind Miriam to her daily Mass (never misses a service in fact) led by her small niece, Yvonne, aged eight and a charmer. Paddle, paddle, paddle – the bare feet of my server . . . Twenty people there by the end of the Preparation and thirty-five to forty by the end of the Epistle . . . We are just sitting down to breakfast when an African houseboy comes in and says 'John has been arrested, Father', so it's saucers on top of cups and out we go to see the very usual sight of upwards of two dozen African men handcuffed together in a dismal crocodile . . . All are Pass offenders . . . 8.20 Prime and Terce sung in Chapel. Greater Silence ends. There's no such thing as Lesser Silence in Sophiatown, for by 8.30 the place is buzzing with life and problems. Already there is a queue of folk on our front stoep . . . Meanwhile the phone rings, 'Please Father, I am a reporter for a German newspaper' . . . Better look in on old Ben on the way home (had his leg amputated just below the knee – pushed under a bus by tsotsies) [gangsters] . . . His message when he knew his leg had to come off was 'God is good, I've got to have my leg off, Father.' Lives in a corrugated iron (tenth hand) shack with his dear old wife. The inside walls are corrugated cardboard from old 'Surf' cartons.

So the day went on: confessions to be heard; couples to be prepared for marriage; people in distress 'My daughter has been raped, Father'; 'I have nowhere to sleep, Father'; Evensong sung by a congregation of thirty, then clubs and organizations to visit; just before Compline a man turns up 'Wounded, Father' – first aid in the bathroom; the wound was not bad, he was very ticklish and everyone got the giggles – such a relief to laugh. Sometimes there are as many as fifteen wounds to be dressed. After Compline, bed – and the night noises of Sophiatown – maybe the man who smokes *dagga* and gets DTS, or the dogs howling, or the door bell and a request to ring the maternity hospital (the Priory had one of the few phones in the area) (*CRQ* MD 1957).

CR in Africa bridged many racial gulfs, but never managed to become a genuinely multi-racial community itself. Its ethos was too English and too many of the brethren were formed by the middle and upper class social and educational system for it to develop in a more corybantic direction. It was not the simple life that discouraged Africans – that seemed comfortable and wealthy by African standards. Some brethren, realizing the gulf, discouraged Africans from joining. Though four or five started as novices only two ever stayed. During the war a temporary novitiate was created at Rosettenville, but some time had to be spent at Mirfield either as a novice or soon after profession. And Mirfield was a long way away for an African in every sense. Leo Rakale, son of one of the earliest black priests trained by CR, was professed in 1946. Fortunately Raynes told the brethren to get him a warm overcoat (unavailable in England because of clothes rationing), as Rakale arrived during the coldest, longest winter for seventy years. Rakale lived for twenty years with the constant threat of arrest, prosecution, imprisonment and banishment because he refused to apply for a permit to live in Rosettenville. He was constantly humiliated by white officials who referred to him as 'the boy-priest' – African men of any age were called 'boys' by whites in South Africa. One of his great achievements was the uniting of St Cyprian's African congregation with that of the cathedral. No other African remained in CR until Simeon Nkoane was professed in 1959. Coming to Mirfield for part of his novitiate was an extraordinary experience, the only black face in choir. At first he was not able to believe in the friendship and love he was offered by all those whites. Later he became Dean of Johannesburg cathedral and then a suffragan bishop. 'Three cameos come to mind at the thought of Simeon – Simeon laughing, Simeon praying and Simeon surrounded by his people . . . Even in the darkest times, the months when he was attending funeral after funeral of youngsters killed on the East Rand his joy kept climbing back out of the pit . . .' (*CRQ* CD 1989). In 1964 a novitiate was again established at Rosettenville, but only two professions resulted (in 1980) – but no blacks. It was too busy a House for a novitiate. When Rakale came there as a novice he was disappointed; he had expected more prayer and less individualism. But in any case, the racial restrictions then prevailing prevented Rosettenville from being multi-racial. The Society of the Sacred Mission, though different from CR in social composition, was equally English; no African was professed in it until 1979. For CR to have established a separate but associated African community (CZR at Penhalonga was created by African initiative) would have looked like an endorsement of apartheid. During his time in Masasi Huddleston came to the conclusion that none of the established orders (including Mirfield) would appeal to African men. He longed for Africans to develop their own form of the Religious Life.[7] But a black priest said that it was not in the African tradition to look for 'an alternative family'. However, CR at its new House in Johannesburg hopes that black and white will come to test their vocations there so that a more indigenous community can develop.

Apartheid

'Today South Africa belongs to us once more' exulted Dr D. F. Malan (a former Dutch Reformed minister) after the victory of his Nationalist Party in May 1948. For the Afrikaners it was as though they had finally defeated the British in the Anglo-Boer War and that British imperialist interference in South Africa (of which the British bishops of the Anglican church seemed an instrument) was at last routed. The Nationalists' fundamental goal was permanent white supremacy, and apartheid was the means to achieve this. Apartheid was not totally new but a systematic and ruthless application of widespread white attitudes and practices. Smuts after all was a segregationalist. Elderly Africans remember the days when no African was allowed to walk on the pavement, but only in the gutter. Legislation began to roll. Marriages and sexual relations between the races were forbidden. Every individual was classed by race and the blacks divided into tribal groups. The Group Areas Act (1950) divided the country by race. Since 1960 three and a half million blacks have been forcibly removed to other areas. Colour bars were enforced in all public amenities and transport. The Native Representative Council was abolished, depriving blacks of even a minimum say in government policies. The Coloureds of Cape Province were removed from the common electoral roll. Pass Laws compelled blacks to carry identification papers at all times. The Bantu Education Act (1953) introduced state controlled education for blacks designed to fit them for a permanently subservient role. The Suppression of Communism Act penalized anyone who could be accused of 'communism' for opposing apartheid.

During a visit in 1991 it was evident that apartheid was being gradually dismantled. But something of what apartheid meant was evident in 1983. A black bishop staying (illegally) at Rosettenville could not travel on the same bus with us into the city. Coming out from the Sunday mass at the cathedral which had united all races together, we were then compelled to stand at racially separated bus stops. An old sick African whose home had been demolished in Sophiatown could only legally live with white friends if they registered him as their servant. As a Christian he resented being forced to tell lies: to get a pass he had to pretend to be living in Soweto. Yet apartheid was never allowed to interfere with the whites' demand for resident black servants. 'I just couldn't accept the cup from a black hand' explained a white Anglican as he was served a cup of coffee by a black servant. A black member of C R was arrested and brought to the Priory in handcuffs because he had forgotten to carry his pass. 'I'll arrest every bloody kaffir in this place if they break the law' the policeman declared. Annually 2–300,000 were arrested for Pass Law offences. Since many were too poor to pay the fine a large proportion were imprisoned or deported to the artificially created homelands.

Faced with such evils, with protests ignored or banned, it was inevitable that African activists and white liberals should divide the country into 'oppressors' and 'oppressed'. But, just as legitimate criticism of Jews and Israel since the holocaust is often rejected as anti-semitism, so legitimate criticism of liberation movements is often rejected as racialism. Just as British liberals having rightly agitated for Indian self-rule lost interest once that was achieved, so anti-apartheid campaigners have been culpably silent about the problems of post-liberation Africa; problems, if acknowledged, are blamed on colonialism or multinationals. The failure of C R itself to become multi-racial illustrates in miniature the difficulty of creating a unitary state out of people from different backgrounds and cultures as in South Africa or Northern Ireland. The two worst legacies of racialism have been the division of the world into heroes and villains and the immense difficulty of creating satisfactory political structures after years of the intoxicating rhetoric which was required to convince the powerless that white domination could be overthrown.

Ten months after the Nationalists came to power, Geoffrey Clayton was enthroned as Archbishop of Cape Town in February 1949. Ambrose Reeves came out to be his successor at Johannesburg, and was consecrated in June – ironically one of his consecrators was Basil Peacey, like Reeves trained at Mirfield. Clayton, a wary ecclesiastical statesman, spoke up forcefully for racial justice, but distrusted Trevor Huddleston, Michael Scott and Ambrose Reeves as fanatics who put politics above the church. Scott, whom Huddleston got to know in Sophiatown, was imprisoned for three months in 1946 for joining the Indians in passive resistance, then went to live in a shanty town where he was also arrested. He was declared a prohibited immigrant in 1950 and spent the rest of his life as a tireless publicist for the rights of African peoples. Huddleston paid tribute to Scott for opening his eyes. Reeves and Clayton never got on. Reeves was a devoted family man, Clayton a misogynist.

Reeves was a small man with big ears who looked always tense and worried, earnestly committed to social righteousness, influenced by Gore, Temple and Studdert Kennedy; Clayton was rotund with a back-slapping merriment which softened enemies. Reeves, a grammar school boy, was brought up in poverty; Clayton the son of a comfortably-off bishop, went to Rugby. Adrian Hastings judged that Reeves 'took on a more precise political role than any other bishop of any communion before or since . . . only Bishop Reeves was willing to get down to the hard grind of endless committee work in co-operation with black politicians, Marxist lawyers and progressive businessmen over such practically vital but complex secular issues as the bus boycott, mass evictions, the provision of financial aid to the accused in the Treason Trial, the publication of the facts about Sharpeville.'[8] As a diocesan bishop he was autocratic. He soon clashed with CR over what he regarded as its liturgical excesses.

Over the following years nearly all CR's works were one by one destroyed under apartheid legislation.

Rosettenville itself, which had been under sporadic threats since the 1930s as a multi-racial campus in a white area, was now in jeopardy. The property was attacked and a night watchman had to be employed. But life went on. Racially mixed audiences came to hear distinguished speakers on social and religious issues including Robert Sobukwe, President of the Pan Africanist Congress (later imprisoned on Robben Island) and Dr A. B. Xuma, then President of the ANC. But by the 1960s attendances fell because of the general tension and legislation forbidding 'mixed entertainments'. For a time CR could exercise an important ministry of hospitality to people of other races. African and Asian travellers coming to or through Johannesburg from other countries were not now allowed to stay in hotels. After incidents when high ranking visitors were told to sleep on the floor in black hostels, some airlines arranged for such passengers to stay at the Priory. Even government departments would phone asking CR to put up officials from newly independent African states. So the world learned more about CR. Distinguished black South Africans also stayed. Tutu, then a student at the college, remembers how Chief Albert Luthuli and Professor Z. K. Matthews came to speak to the students in 1958 after charges against them in the Treason Trial were dropped. Matthews had resigned as Acting-Principal of Fort Hare because of the Bantu Education Act thereby forfeiting all his pension rights (he had been on the staff since 1936). He and Luthuli came to stay again in March 1960 to consult their lawyers. At the end of that month, they, together with Hannah Stanton, a mission worker (whose brother was a member of CR) were among the 230 arrested after Sharpeville. Tambo was another regular visitor. CR contributed to the Treason Trial Defence Fund and Raynes appealed for donations in the *CR Quarterly*. As regulations tightened, this ministry of hospitality became more hazardous. The multi-racial Liberal

Party, of which Paton was a founder, and in which he found inter-racial friendships rare in the church, met at Rosettenville for its summer school in 1963. The police arrived and ordered them to leave as they had no permit. Special Branch made raids from time to time. Usually they were foiled by skilful deception, but sometimes guests were discovered and arrested.

On 10 February 1955 Trevor Huddleston said mass before sunrise, for, despite all the protests, the demolition of Sophiatown was to begin that morning. Huddleston had publicly supported schemes to deal with its slums and overcrowding. But the demolition was not to improve Sophiatown but to abolish it, and to remove the people (many of them freeholders) elsewhere. The township was already known world-wide because of Paton's novel. Huddleston had also discovered that sometimes individual and communal injustices could be righted by publicity. Representatives of the world press were already outside the Priory.

On the broad belt of grass between the European suburb of Westdene and Sophiatown . . . a whole fleet of Army lorries was drawn up: a grim sight against the grey, watery sky. Lining the whole street were thousands of police, both white and black: the former armed with rifles and revolvers, the latter with the usual assegai. A few Sten guns were in position at various points . . . In the yard, military lorries were already drawn up. Already they were piled high with the pathetic possessions which had come from the row of rooms in the background. A rusty kitchen stove: a few blackened pots and pans: a wicker chair: mattresses belching out their coir-stuffing: bundles of heaven-knows-what, and people, soaked, all soaked to the skin by the drenching rain . . . The first lorries began to move off for Meadowlands eight miles away to the west.[9]

'Meadowlands' sounded charming – in fact it was a location on the edge of Soweto, further from the city. Fares would be more expensive. People would need permits to visit it. It was totally impersonal. (At one time the Mandelas' address was '8115 Orlando'.) Over the next few years Sophiatown was flattened.

Until 1955 ninety per cent of African education from primary to teacher training was in the hands of missions. The government was determined to destroy their influence. Dr Verwoerd, then Minister of Native Affairs, explained: 'Until now [the African] has been subject to a school system which drew him away from his own community and misled him by showing him the green pastures of European society in which he is not allowed to graze.' The Bantu Education Act created agonizing dilemmas for the churches.[10] Reeves and CR so abhorred the concept of Bantu education that they refused to lease the buildings to the government. But Clayton and the other bishops believed that leasing was the lesser of two evils. Ever since, Africans have supported the stand by Reeves and CR because their predictions about the dire consequences of the Act have been lamentably fulfilled. So in March 1955 with a heavy heart CR closed St Cyprian's in Sophiatown, the largest black primary school in South Africa. CR reopened it ten days later with government permission as a private school: five hundred and fifty children immediately enrolled; soon there was a waiting list for another six hundred. Parents paid what they could afford. But in February 1956 the government ordered it to close. Leseding and Ekutuleni, created by Dorothy Maud, were also forced to close. CR stayed in Sophiatown until June 1962, by which time most of the residents had gone. The new white suburb built on the site was gloatingly named 'Triomf' (Triumph). Christ the King is now a 'Protestante Kerk'.

At Meadowlands CR built the appropriately named 'Church of the Resurrection', dedicated in 1961. For a couple of years brethren looked after the people, many from Sophiatown, but it was unsatisfactory because as whites they were forbidden to sleep overnight, though occasionally they bedded down in the church. CR withdrew from Orlando in 1959 because the bishop believed that the plant would be expropriated if CR remained. CR's move from Orlando was so abrupt that the whole church council resigned. Orlando, like Meadowlands, was now looked after by black clergy. James Khuele, a former churchwarden, remarked in his history of the Orlando churches how difficult it was for the new priest: the people had become dependent on CR for 'spoon feeding' financially and in many other ways. (Clergy and Religious find it hard to resist playing the collusive parent-child role. When the idealized parental figure acts badly or toughly, the dependent get angry.)

In August 1955 St Peter's school, anticipating its closure, put on a jauntily defiant concert and dance advertised as 'The Last Kick of a Dying School'. The Huddleston Jazz Band played. The closure in December 1956 was marked by a High Mass with the bishop preaching and a supper and dance for staff and students. Huddleston had explained: 'There is only one path open to the African: it is the path back to tribal culture and tradition: to ethnic groups; to the reserves; to anywhere other than the privileged places habited by the master race. It is because we cannot accept such principles that we are closing St Peter's'. Peter Abrahams, the author and former pupil, wrote: 'In weeping for St Peter's I weep for a new generation of slum kids for whom there will be no escape, as there was for me, through St Peter's.'[11]

Next came the closure of St Peter's Theological College (though unlike the school, it was able to move elsewhere). Individual permits for students to be resident were now required. Institutions under 'European supervision' had to move to sites adjoining 'Native Reserves'. No permits for new students were issued after January 1961. Dr Ulrich Simon, the English theologian, of Jewish parentage, who had fled from Nazi racialism, was staying and lecturing at Rosettenville. He attended the wake in June 1962:

For the last time the college doors were thrown open to former students and friends.

They came for hundreds of miles . . . The Fathers welcomed everyone and no one was without bed or food. The nuns served the community. The climax came with a Solemn Eucharist, followed by an open air banquet. All Christian denominations were present. I talked also to a man who turned out to be a spy of the police. No matter: everyone talked openly. The people sang and danced, then rested on the grass. Many children and babies were held in mothers' arms. Were there five thousand, or more? The proceedings began, and I was overtaken by that ecstasy which I had first experienced so many decades ago. Here was the light reflecting the *Beatissima Lux:* men serving and being served, spontaneously and in good order. Here all the cultures met, for Indians and Chinese could also be seen on the grass. The theme of the final farewell evoked tears and laughter. We were transfigured: it was good to be there.[12]

In the midst of all these removals and endings came another removal, another ending. In July 1955 Raymond Raynes decided to recall Trevor Huddleston to Mirfield to become Novice Guardian.

Huddleston describes himself as 'a child of the Raj'.[13] His father at one time commanded the Indian Navy. He remembers moments in his early life which revealed and stimulated his social conscience: a poor Indian being turned from the door at Christmas; barefoot, undernourished children seen on visits to Lancing College Mission in Camberwell; hunger marchers passing through Oxford; missions to the hop-pickers; Basil Jellicoe preaching about his housing trust at St Pancras, derived from his belief in the incarnation; the influence of Studdert Kennedy; attendance at two Anglo-Catholic Summer Schools of Sociology; his curacy in a working-class parish in Swindon. He visited Mirfield: 'I was much impressed by the feeling of the community: the way the brethren were very aware of the world. It was not a reclusive community, it was an active missionary order.' And it was influenced by Christian socialism. He was beginning to embody the ringing speech by Frank Weston, Bishop of Zanzibar, to the 1923 Anglo-Catholic Congress; 'You cannot claim to worship Jesus in the Tabernacle, if you do not pity Jesus in the slum.'

It was South Africa which gradually (to use his own revealing term) 'politicized' Huddleston. He was haunted by the failure of the German churches to stand against the Nazi persecution of the Jews. Huddleston's fundamental concern was that Africans should enjoy fullness of life. So he did much to promote African culture, theatre and music. International musicians came to play in Sophiatown. After a concert by the Amsterdam String Quartet, six blind Africans came up to feel the shape of the instruments which they had heard for the first time. Yet he was always the priest. When he was staying up half the night to write *Naught for your Comfort*, he also made time for visits to the dying mother of Norman Montjane to whom he dedicated that book.

By the 1950s Huddleston was hated by the government and its supporters. He was subjecting South Africa to damning publicity through the world's press. Unlike Raynes he was at ease with well-to-do whites. Some thought him debonair – not an adjective ever applied to Raynes. To Anthony Sampson, Huddleston seemed everywhere – African functions, ANC meetings, cocktail parties, funerals. 'Most distinguished visitors to South Africa seemed to find their way, somehow or other, to Huddleston's cell.' In June 1955 when he spoke to 3,000 people at the Congress of the People (which passed the Freedom Charter) the ANC presented him with its highest award. By contrast Paton and other white liberals stayed away because Communists were among its organizers. When the 156 were arrested in December 1956 for treason one of the charges against them was their involvement with this Congress. But a tragic gulf was opening up between him and Clayton, who was also CR's Visitor. Clayton, Scott and Huddleston all hated racial prejudice. Huddleston, like Scott, was an absolutist. Clayton advocated 'the gradual removal of the colour bar'. Huddleston loathed gradualism. Scott had felt unsupported by the church in his campaigns. So did Huddleston and he angered Clayton by sending him what he later termed 'impertinent' letters: 'At the time I really was so deeply involved emotionally that I have no doubt that I wrote too strongly.'[14] But Huddleston knew what it was like to live in a township. Clayton did not. Huddleston's motto was 'Always act on impulse'. Clayton hated emotionalism. Huddleston was prepared to rebel against authority. Clayton reacted harshly against anyone who questioned his authority.

The clash of temperaments and tactics came to a head after Huddleston's article 'The Church Sleeps On' in the London *Observer* (10 October 1954):

> . . . there is no future for the missionary work of the Church in South Africa unless it recognizes at once that it is caught up into a tragic situation which needs immediate and desperate remedies. And I can see no sign either that the Church does recognize this fact, or that it has any real desire to apply swift and remedial action . . . I am now more convinced than ever that the State in South Africa has already become a tyranny – and that in consequence Christians with a conscience should be prepared to resist its laws and take the consequences.

The church slept while Africans were forcibly removed, while the Bantu Education Act was being implemented, while a 'dictatorship' was being created. 'The Church sleeps on – though it occasionally talks in its sleep and expects (or does it?) the Government to listen.' He proposed a cultural boycott of South Africa. Afrikaners were infuriated by such calls for international interference. Clayton feared that they would induce South Africa to leave the Commonwealth. The article seemed a personal attack. Were Clayton's frequent denunciations of apartheid really the church talking 'in its sleep'? Clayton's faith in the church transcended that empirical, sinful reality which so scandalized Huddleston.[15] Some were alarmed by Huddleston's call to resist unjust laws. Yet in 1957 when a Bill threatened to enforce racial segregation in churches, Clayton, on behalf of the bishops, drafted a letter to the Prime Minister: if it became law, they would not obey it. After the draft was agreed, Clayton with unwonted warmth took Reeves by the arm; 'I don't want to go to prison. I'm an old man . . . But I'll go if I have to'. Clayton died the next day. On 14 July a pastoral letter was read in all Anglican churches: the clause should be ignored. Was it only when the church itself was threatened that the bishops offered more than words? The bishops' stand was an unconscious recognition that Reeves and Huddleston were right: the opposition to a totalitarian regime required more than dignified verbal protests. Yet if the churches were divided about tactics, so were the opposition groups.[16]

In June 1954 Raynes made a special visit to Johannesburg to see Trevor Huddleston believing that Trevor would not be allowed back if he came to Mirfield for his regular consultation as Provincial. In December Clayton decided to resign as South African Visitor because (he wrote to Raynes) Huddleston, the Provincial, showed by private letters and public articles he had no confidence in his leadership. Huddleston immediately went to see Clayton who reacted with unprecedented affection and amazingly withdrew his resignation on the spot. (Clayton's moods could change suddenly.) Huddleston reporting this to Raynes added: 'I think it was my fault in writing too strongly: I have been pretty "wore-out" by this endless crisis and said too much.' Clayton had also complained to the Archbishop of Canterbury (Fisher). In 1955 Fisher came to inaugurate the Anglican Province of Central Africa at Salisbury Cathedral. He had heard that there were two experiences he must not miss: the Copper Belt and Huddleston. When they met at Penhalonga in May, Fisher told him that his methods were 'entirely wrong'. After the argument Fisher proclaimed sunnily 'the score is about deuce' and insisted on being photographed arm in arm with his adversary.

In February 1955 Raynes despatched Jonathan Graham on a tour of African Houses. He reached Rosettenville on 23 March. Raynes seems to have already decided in principle to recall Huddleston. One of Graham's tasks was to test possible reactions. So he spoke with two brethren (Sidebotham and Rakale), with Oliver Tambo (who wept at the idea) and finally in June with Clayton who reacted: 'He has so much to give; and what is best for him must be best for the Church.' Graham arrived back for July Chapter and spoke about Huddleston with deep admiration (such a display of unqualified emotion was very unusual for him). Though Graham was reserved and conformist, he understood perfectly how Huddleston's prayer and pastoral love had led him to make a stand and to seek world-wide publicity. 'TH incomparable' he noted in his diary, but recommended his recall. Huddleston was under enormous strain. Police followed him everywhere. They ransacked the Priory and took away papers. There was the constant threat of imprisonment or deportation. The authorities were waging a personal war against him. It was said that the destruction of Sophiatown was speeded up to spite him. Meanwhile there were seventeen novices at Mirfield; the Novice Guardian was a dear but ineffective. So after a night of prayer Raynes took the most difficult decision of his life.

When the news broke in October 1955, supporters in England and Africa were dumbfounded. Some were outraged. They put great pressure on Raynes (who had also once returned from Africa against his will) to change his mind. Trelawney-Ross wrote to Mirfield that the South African brethren felt devastated, as if Montgomery had been withdrawn just after El Alamein. What answer could they give to the bewildered multitudes who were asking 'why?' and 'why just at this time?' Though some brethren thought Trevor too impulsive and that all the publicity was giving the government an excuse to take drastic action against CR, they all loved him. The official statement said that the recall was 'a perfectly natural and normal occurrence', that a new Novice Guardian was needed (which was true) and Trevor was the best man for the job (which turned out not to be the case). Raynes flew to Johannesburg in November. He told brethren that he would have been even more extreme than Trevor; the more brethren and bishops arrested, the better. To Deane Yates (the headmaster of St John's) and his wife he described his awesome sense of responsibility for Trevor. He might be attacked or killed at any time; he could be arrested and being a diabetic, imprisonment might cause illness or death.

No one who knew Raynes thought he was acting at the behest of the Archbishop of Canterbury or the South African government. How influential was Clayton's letter? Clayton had been determined to resign without publicity. But in the circumstances would another bishop have agreed to be Visitor?[17] Yet any public controversy would have damaged Clayton, not CR, in the eyes of Africans and white liberals. Clayton's letter certainly did not cause Trevor's recall, but Raynes may have concluded from that dispute that Trevor was at the end of his tether. Nor was he recalled because he was getting in the way of African political leadership. African leaders were regularly arrested and silenced. Trevor had the attention of the world's press to an extent that they did not, so he helped them by publicizing their cause.

But Africa had started a process of change in Trevor. His experiences were propelling him towards theological and political attitudes quite different from those of Raynes. Perhaps Raynes sensed this intuitively and that is why he seemed to have difficulty in articulating his reasons for the recall. In October 1955 Raynes dedicated a lecture at Leeds University to Huddleston. It was a passionate repudiation of apartheid. Yet he also warned against easy political slogans like 'The Brotherhood of Man'. Christians were not to be 'influenced unduly by ideas and ideals of Western humanism'.[18] Elsewhere he had declared: 'Can anyone be of the Truth who is not of the Church? Can we separate Christ from His Body?'[19] However Huddleston, passionately committed to the overthrow of apartheid, happily co-operated with anyone who shared this aim – Christians of other traditions. Communists, Jews, atheists. Although outwardly he was still theologically at one with Raynes (they were both fiercely opposed to the South India ecumenical scheme) in actual practice he was finding both Christ and Truth outside the church. So after three episcopates, at the age of seventy, Huddleston said that if he were younger he would now devote his life to the inter-faith dialogue.[20] The seeds of this immense theological change were sown in Sophiatown.

When Trevor became Bishop of Masasi in 1960, CR gave him Gore's pectoral cross through which he senses the support of CR's Founder, for he is deeply indebted to Gore and the *Lux Mundi* tradition: the incarnation leads to politics; the church and eucharist should be paradigms for society in demonstrating the life of interdependence and mutual sharing. Like Gore, Huddleston believes that the Religious Life should be incarnate in the world not a withdrawal from it. He wrote in a CR memorandum in 1955: 'I believe that South Africa does in fact offer a very special and precious opportunity to brethren – the opportunity to be a bit venturesome, a bit strong in initiative, a bit of a nuisance, maybe, to established ideas of conventional Christianity . . . It seems to me it is better to risk a bit of worldliness – for the world's sake – than to become a community of men "living the life", or trying to, in a vacuum.'[21] Like Gore, Huddleston preaches the church should be in solidarity with the poor. Yet though Gore was always political, he was never politicized. Ultimately he agreed with Tennyson: 'Our little systems have their day . . . And thou, O Lord, art more than they'. Raynes stoutly fought racialism but basically as parish priest, not as politician. If he had stayed, would he ever have joined the ANC? For Trevor it became customary to go from Sunday mass to a demonstration. For Raynes the church always had absolute precedence. Huddleston was moving towards the view that the needs of the world were prior to those of the church and that the church was significant only when it served humanity.

Did Raynes think that Huddleston had become devoured and politicized by one issue, that there was a danger that instead of his work being that of 'the Community done through him' (Rule) it was becoming his own work? If so, his recall to be Novice Guardian would be the most immediately available way of bringing him back to the centre of the Community's ethos by entrusting him with the task of passing that on to novices. Perhaps Raynes thought it would also prepare him to be a future Superior? Huddleston returned to Mirfield in June 1956 after an American lecture tour. Yet he was Novice Guardian for only two years. In 1958 Graham, Raynes' successor, seeing that his heart was really in his campaigns to arouse world opinion against apartheid, moved him to the London Priory. Did Raynes, who died that year, believe he had succeeded or failed to achieve his aims?

Naught for your Comfort (1956) has dated less than *Cry, the Beloved Country*;

it is more immediate, less self-consciously literary. At the beginning Huddleston wrote that he knew when he made his vows that one day it would mean 'the taking-up or the laying-down of a task entrusted to me by the Community'. At the end, after lovingly recalling the people of Sophiatown, he asked: 'Do you think that I can give up fighting or rest contentedly in my priestly life, when this is what I am trying to protect from plunder . . .?' The tension between these two statements was resolved when in 1960 he became Bishop of Masasi; as a prelate brother his work ceased to be subject to CR's direction.[22]

Huddleston's replacement as Provincial was a huge contrast – his old friend Sidebotham, a reserved, methodical Mancunian. Clayton wrote to Sidebotham in March 1956 'To be quite frank, your predecessor's letters to me were all about himself, and his personal grievances against me. That was really why I wanted to resign from being Visitor. But the Superior has asked me to carry on.' Sidebotham had to hold things steady in the wake of both Huddleston's recall and the Treason Trial, which involved some of CR's closest friends. Then on 21 March 1960 came the massacre by police of a demonstration at Sharpeville. The injured were brought to Baragwanath, the largest 'non-European' hospital in South Africa, on the edge of Soweto. For some years brethren, OHP sisters and theological students from Rosettenville had acted as its Anglican pastors.[23] As the casualties started to arrive, the Superintendent made a distraught phone call to Keith Davie at Rosettenville asking him to come immediately and also to inform the church authorities of what had happened. Davie left a message for Reeves and set off to Baragwanath. Reeves arrived later that day, informed the press (the news went round the world) and came on the following days with lawyers who took affidavits from the wounded despite attempts to prevent them. Later at a Judicial Enquiry the judge commented that but for the bishop and his lawyers, only the police case would ever have been heard. Britain now for the first time joined other nations at the UN in condemning apartheid. On 30 March a State of Emergency was announced and 230 were arrested, including some connected with Reeves' investigations. On 1 April Reeves was visited by three African friends who told him that he was also about to be arrested. He consulted with his advisers, including Sidebotham, Vicar-General of the diocese, who counselled him to leave South Africa so that the vital information he possessed both on paper and in his head, could reach the outside world. That night he left for Swaziland. When he returned on Saturday 10 September he stayed at the Retreat House at Rosettenville. On Monday the police arrived and served him with a deportation order and took him straight to the airport. At the end of the year the Archbishop (Joost de Blank) and the other bishops advised him to resign as he would never be allowed back.[24]

The closure of CR's major works, many of which had been built up over half a century, created a mood of deep depression among the South African brethren. Jonathan Graham spoke to this in a characteristically robust and transcendent sermon at St Peter's Rosettenville in October 1958. His text was 'She named the child Ichabod, saying, The glory is departed from Israel':

> Of course it was nothing of the sort! And when people shake their heads gloomily and talk of Ichabod and use the phrase 'departed glory', they are practically always talking nonsense . . . But we should know better than to talk about departed glories when what we believe to be valuable Christian works are closing down; when loss and removal and persecution and deprivation are the daily lot of Christians . . . It is one of the most astoundingly original parts of Christianity that its founder announces every kind of hardship and persecution as the *normal* condition of life for his followers and bids them rejoice . . . When all these things – troubles, anxieties and persecutions – begin to come to pass, 'look *up* for your redemption draweth nigh' . . . the guarantee and pledge of this optimism is the Resurrection of Jesus Christ from the dead. (*CRQ* LD 1960)

In 1961 the laconic Sidebotham was replaced as Provincial by the effervescent Claude Lunniss. Africans called him 'Areng' (Let's go) or 'Serurubele' (Butterfly). Over a glass of sherry to welcome him he proposed a toast 'No further retreats' and announced that CR was 'determined not to be pushed around any more'. Lunniss was a tonic, but CR was trapped, like Balaam with the way getting narrower and the walls higher, and there was no escape.

Transmutation

> Because I cannot hope to turn again
> Consequently I rejoice, having to construct something
> Upon which to rejoice.
> (T. S. Eliot: *Ash Wednesday*)

Something creative had to be done with the large and now empty buildings at Rosettenville. In 1956 the school was sold on extremely generous terms and became St Martin's church secondary school for white boys. That was the year when the government closed the newly created private school for blacks in Sophiatown. The government had of course no objection to the creation of this new private school for whites. CR used the money to promote African education. Some Africans were bitter at the sale, but from 1980 it began to include boys (and girls) from other races. CR created a bursary fund to help poorer parents with the fees. Until 1985 CR supplied the chaplain. The college was skilfully transformed by Ronald Haynes into a retreat and conference centre and later given to the diocese. Local African servants asked for somewhere to study in the evenings, as this was difficult in their garden huts. Out of this grew 'St Peter's Night School' where large numbers, ranging from the illiterate to those studying Junior Certificate, are taught in St Martin's classrooms.

The ministry of protest continued alongside the usual round of chaplaincy, retreat and mission work. So, for example, in May 1980 fifty-three clergy from all the churches except the DRC, led by Timothy Bavin, Bishop of Johannesburg (now Bishop of Portsmouth) marched to John Vorster Square to protest against the detention of John Thorne, a Congregationalist minister. (The common cause was creating close ecumenical relationships as had happened in Europe during the war.) All were arrested, among them Kingston Erson and Simeon Nkoane of CR and the Tutus. Blacks and whites were held in separate cells. Next day a crowd turned up in court (including the Archbishop of Cape Town, Burnett) who dumbfounded the authorities by praying and singing hymns and Freedom songs. Those arrested were released and fined. In June Leo Rakale and Norwood Coaker died. Coaker, a white South African lay brother, after a distinguished legal career had been professed at the age of sixty-six. A joint requiem and funeral was held at Rosettenville, but since Leo's undertaker did not have a permit to bury whites, Norwood had to have a different firm.

In May 1980 Nkoane, then Dean of Johannesburg, was charged under the Group Areas Act for living in a flat next to the cathedral. The charge was later dropped on condition he applied for a permit. Rakale ministered to the banned, including Helen Joseph and Winnie Mandela. (When Archbishop Ramsey visited Helen in 1970 she had been banned for eight years; Mrs Ramsey had to wait outside as three people would have constituted an illegal meeting.) Rakale had been on the cathedral staff when Dean Gonville ffrench-Beytagh was arrested on political charges in 1971. As a result Rakale's passport was withdrawn for several years. (When the police searched the Dean's flat they took away J. A. Baker's *The Foolishness of God*, a theological classic which they mistook for an atheist diatribe.) Timothy Stanton was summoned to appear in court in 1983. He refused to make a statement about a devout white DRC student whom he knew and who was detained under the Internal Security Act (later sentenced to fifteen years). In vain the magistrate quoted Romans 13. Stanton said: 'I have no idea what he has done or is supposed to have done . . . to give evidence for the State in their case against this young man would be a thing of which I would be deeply ashamed for the rest of my life.' Stanton was sent to prison for six months (*CRQ* LD, JB 1984).

Two lay brothers exercised a remarkable ministry. Charles Coles, an ex-VD orderly and ex-librarian, though he had no academic qualifications, became an erudite seminary librarian and later an editor of Theological Education by Extension. In his latter days (he died in 1987) he was both a permanent deacon and a perpetual walker:

When he wasn't actually working or praying Charles was walking round the streets, talking to anyone who would talk. The more disreputable they looked the more Charles was likely to talk with them. He walked and talked early in the mornings before mattins. He wandered round the streets of Johannesburg during lunch breaks . . . making friends with waiters, street cleaners, unemployed, way out musicians and even some 'quite nice' people as well. As soon as he got home he was off round the streets again, just getting back for Evensong (or often later). Supper ended he was out again, often in pouring rain, and even after Compline, Charles would be seen disappearing up to the school workers' compound, a most notorious place of drink, fighting and the rest, for a last chat with some of his friends. Of course it led to tensions in the priory. Charles would bring his disreputable friends in, wanting money, or a bed, or a job for them . . . Charles gave away his own clothes and blankets to any who needed them . . . He had strange guests turning up in the middle of the night; often more than one of them slept on his floor. Or on one occasion he himself slept on the floor because his bed was already full! (*CRQ* CD 1987)

When Barnabas Dugdale was in the Signals, he read Dostoyevsky's *Brothers Karamazov* which revolutionized his life. In Ceylon he picked up two volumes by Gore which also deeply affected him. Apart from keeping the accounts and catering at Rosettenville, and (arthritic though he was) dancing with visiting Africans, he ministered to meths drinkers and down-and-outs. Like Charles he was often stopped in the street by whites and told he was a Communist and threatened with dire consequences because he had so many black friends. 'The days of being significant have gone' he said in conversation in 1982, with relief, little realizing he was part of CR's new humbler significance.

Gradually the rules forbidding the presence of ladies at the Priory relaxed. In the 1930s the wife of the African cook had to sit on the pavement outside to wait for her husband. In 1966 women were allowed to attend evensong provided they were silent; a year later they could join in. Soon women were allowed to come to meals and brethren began to share meals and worship with the OHP sisters opposite. 'We've married OHP and we should stay together' happily commented one of the brethren. In the bleak years when so much of CR's work had been destroyed and life was tense, these wider relationships were a source of new strength. In society racial segregation was intensifying; but in Rosettenville sexual as well as racial segregation had been broken down.

Alice

One of the most exciting transmutations was the participation of St Peter's Theological College in the interdenominational Federal Seminary, at Alice, Cape Province, inaugurated in September 1963.[25] By 1960 the Anglican, Congregational, Methodist and Presbyterian churches were being forced by apartheid to find new sites for training of African ordinands, and had agreed in principle to a Federal Seminary. This would not only concentrate resources, so providing better training, but also being large and interdenominational would, it was hoped, be able to withstand government pressures more effectively. But where could an inter-racial seminary be sited? Eventually Alice was chosen, near the historic Lovedale Presbyterian mission with its liberal tradition and Fort Hare University. Some, particularly the Anglicans and Congregationalists, were worried by the proximity of Fort Hare. But there was no other site available and perhaps in the long run Fort Hare, now for Xhosas only, would change? The government allowed the creation of the seminary because it wanted from the Church of Scotland a black corridor to join Fort Hare to the black mainland so it was no longer a black island in a white area.

The bishops now invited CR to run the Anglican constituent college. But how would CR react to an interdenominational venture after years of bitter campaigns under Raynes against union schemes with the Free Churches? The paper circulated by Jonathan Graham, the Superior, before Chapter in January 1961 was a bombshell. To join with the Free Churches would be contrary to 'the Catholic and Apostolic Rule of Faith' to which CR was bound by its constitution. 'We should, in fact, be there on false pretences, because we are not training men in the same faith as they or with the same end in view.' He also believed that the majority of brethren would take his line. Aelred Stubbs, the Principal of St Peter's College, in his circulated reply reminded CR that the invitation had come from the bishops, that St Peter's would have a proper degree of independence, that the ecumenical influences would not be all in one direction, that when Pan-Africanism was in the air the churches must draw together. The Chapter vote was so decisively in favour that Graham offered to resign. But when he came out to Africa in January 1962, travelling by car from Johannesburg to Alice calmly reading *War and Peace* in the back seat, he was converted to the project.

The scheme had immense strengths. First, it was inter-racial. The seminary cunningly persuaded the government that it was essential for discipline for white and black to live on the same campus. The government insisted that Coloured and African students should live separately but this was ignored. The staff was multi-racial. The mixing of all the various racial groups (who had previously had little close contact with each other) and the proximity of Fort Hare with its strikes and protests heightened the political consciousness of seminary students who with the staff became keenly aware of the political implications of theology. Desmond Tutu, who came on to the staff, was also chaplain to Anglicans at Fort Hare. The Tutus were amazed that such an oasis as the seminary could exist in South Africa. It was, however, legally impossible to take white students as well as black. Keith Davie became parish priest and made the Alice church multi-racial. Secondly, it was the first time that either CR or the Anglican church with their Catholic ethos had participated in anything so ecumenical. At first intercommunion was out of the question but eventually it became acceptable to virtually everyone. Thirdly, the new exciting chapel of Christ the King at St Peter's, designed like three African rondavels joined by a nave, facilitated a deep liturgical renewal directed with infectious enthusiasm by Mark Tweedy. If the Free Church staff brought higher academic standards, the Anglican contribution was liturgically and spiritually richer. Fourthly, because the seminary was the largest and most professional theological institute in southern Africa, intellectually it was a far more challenging and stimulating environment for ordinands than Rosettenville. Finally, for sixty years CR had worked only in the Transvaal. For the first time it was experiencing a different aspect of South Africa.

Brethren discovered that the Eastern Cape, not Johannesburg, was the heartland of African resistance. Soon after the arrival of the CR advance party in February 1963, some students from Lovedale were arrested and charged with belonging to an illegal organization. Keith Davie and Noel Williams looked after the Anglican prisoners. Among them was Kaya Biko for whom Aelred Stubbs appealed in court. Stubbs formed a pastoral relationship with the Biko family and a close friendship with Steve (Kaya's brother). Steve Biko became leader of the Black Consciousness Movement and died after police assaults in 1977. That friendship drastically altered Stubbs' attitudes and perspectives. For five years he exercised a particular ministry to the banned, beginning with one of his own students. His activities were closely watched by the police. A fortnight after Biko's funeral when he was visiting Mirfield, a young man called from the South African Embassy. His permit to live in South Africa had been withdrawn.

One member of the Biko circle was Mamphela Ramphele, a young woman doctor. Revolted by the segregated DRC in which she had been brought up, her first experience of Anglican ministry came from Stubbs' visits to Biko. When she was banished from the Eastern Cape to the Northern Transvaal (eight hundred miles away) she was shunned by white Anglicans there as both black and banned. Yet she discovered that 'there are qualitively different ministries within the Anglican community' through her friendship with Aelred Stubbs and visits from Timothy Stanton ('the visiting Christ' her mother called him). The relationship of Biko and Ramphele to CR brethren indicate that the religious sceptic and political dissenter can feel a kinship to Religious who by their calling are also standing against the norms of both society and church.[26] Because the Religious (unlike the parish priest) does not have a family to protect or an institution to recruit for on which his livelihood depends, he is capable of offering a more unconditional and more risky ministry.

But the initial anxieties about the proximity of the seminary to Fort Hare were tragically fulfilled. In November 1974 the government informed the seminary that it would be expropriated in one month's time because Fort Hare needed more room to expand. In reality, other land was available nearby. The fact was that the government did not want Fort Hare to have an inter-racial community on its doorstep which encouraged its students to think independently and politically. Disaffected students from Fort Hare had found counsel at the seminary. The seminary was also paying the price of its refusal in 1972 to allow Fort Hare to purchase its land and buildings. All former assurances of security proved groundless. As usual all protests proved futile. Stubbs (who had been succeeded as Principal by Theodore Simpson in 1972) called at the Priory in the vacation after visiting Biko, the day the catastrophic news had been received. After Compline he leaned against the stone wall outside the chapel and looked at the College empty and silent in the moonlight and wept.

In March 1975 the Federal Seminary moved to Umtata in the Transkei, to St Bede's Theological College. Its arrival in thirty-eight pantechnicons was greeted with drums and dancing. For a couple of months everyone lived in tents until mobile homes arrived, sharing an experience of 'forced removals' like so many in South Africa, and meditating on the theme of the pilgrim church. Then a few seminary students held a service to commemorate Sharpeville. Transkei, about to become a homeland, fearing trouble from the Pretoria government, threatened that all Anglican property would be confiscated unless the bishop told the seminary to move. So after only nine months, once more the seminary took to the road. It settled temporarily near Petermaritzburg. By 1977, when plans for new buildings at Imbali were well advanced, the time was ripe for CR to hand over to indigenous leaders. In any case CR could no longer staff two theological colleges. So its seventy-four years of training ordinands in South Africa ended. CR could rejoice that one of its black ordinands, Sigqibo Dwane, succeeded Crispin Harrison as Principal, but also that it had made an immensely valuable contribution to the ordained ministry of southern Africa, not only through those trained at St Peter's, but also through many trained at Mirfield who had come out to Africa. Former students speak gratefully of having received from CR an example of discipline and dedication and a conviction that the church must have a particular care for the poor and dispossessed.

Stellenbosch

Clayton characterized the Calvinism of the DRC as 'a false interpretation of the Christian faith'. Joost de Blank, of Dutch ancestry, who succeeded him in 1957 was convinced that apartheid must be tackled theologically as well as politically. After Sharpeville, de Blank called for the expulsion of the DRC from the World Council of Churches (WCC). In December 1960 a WCC delegation met representatives of eight South African churches including the DRC in Cottesloe. The DRC gave some ground on racial issues and de Blank apologized for some of his more heated utterances. But under pressure from the Prime Minister the DRC synods rejected the Cottesloe declaration and withdrew from the wcc.[27] One of the severest of the DRC critics of Cottesloe was Dr Andries Treurnicht, later a government minister, who was to play a role in the story of the CR house at Stellenbosch.

CR's contacts with the DRC during nearly seventy years of work had been minimal. Cottesloe had focussed attention upon relationships with the DRC. In 1968 at the height of Afrikaner power, CR accepted the Archbishop's invitation to go to Stellenbosch, in the heartland of Afrikanerdom, the second oldest town in South Africa. CR sent an excellent group. Robert Mercer (later Bishop of Matabeleland) a born parish priest became rector. A white Zimbabwean of South African parentage and schooling, he knew some Afrikaans. Bernard Chamberlain, a priest of singular determination who had once fought Communist terrorists in Malaya, with a flair for students, became Anglican chaplain to the university and learned Afrikaans. He threw down what could have appeared as either a bridge or a gauntlet by enrolling as a part-time student at the DRC seminary, founded in 1859. The others were Michael Twine, a white South African lay brother and Afrikaans speaker who had farmed in the Cape, and Gerard (formerly Geoffrey) Beaumont. Beaumont had become well known in the 1950s as a composer of church music in a 'Family Favourites' style. He had been professed in 1962 at the age of fifty-eight. The fact that CR had not turned him into a grey saint so impressed his friend Harry Williams that he thought that CR might be right for him too.[28] The house was run more like a family than a priory. The people of the parish ranged from those living in shanties to the wealthy in Cape Dutch houses. Brethren kept open house – one day fifty-seven people came of whom thirty were fed. But apartheid was strict. After multi-racial worship a multi-racial cup of tea was permissible, but not a multi-racial bazaar or sitting together on a park bench. There were probably informers in the congregation and in the confirmation classes.

After a couple of happy years disasters struck. Beaumont died in August 1970 after a characteristically rollicking time in hospital, drinking whisky with the doctors, composing comic verse and teaching the nurses songs. The notice for the local paper announced: 'he died merrily. Olé'. Then Dr J. S. Gericke, Vice-Chancellor of Stellenbosch University and Moderator of the DRC Cape Synod twice summoned Chamberlain and accused him of proselytizing. Andries Treurnicht's daughter had been attending his confirmation classes.

In 1970 the wcc announced grants for humanitarian purposes to certain liberation movements including some in South Africa. This was widely represented as 'wcc funds for guerillas'. Mercer discussed the grants in a pew leaflet, expressed his doubts about them, but asked whether 'demented racialism' had not provoked them. A violinist, who was also a fervent Nationalist, after a concert in church picked up a leaflet. He was horrified and took it to Gericke, who rushed to Cape Town to show it to the Prime Minister,

.

who then produced it in Parliament saying it supported terrorists. In September Mercer and Chamberlain were served with deportation orders.[29]

Hugh Bishop, the Superior, did not want CR to accept defeat and restaffed Stellenbosch, but the specially suitable gifts of the original team were unique. One of the new staff, Aidan Mayoss, who did lively work at the University, wrote after four months in 1973 that before he arrived he had been tempted to agree with those who argued that CR should retreat from South Africa because of England's many needs. He now realized how vital it was for CR to be in South Africa. CR continued at Stellenbosch until early in 1976. By then, with the removal from Alice the previous year, it had become isolated from the rest of CR.

Now that all CR's works on the Rosettenville campus were closed except the Priory, it would have been destructive to have continued to camp out there, haunted by the memories of the past. Some brethren were glad that CR had given up institutions. However, at Mirfield there were powerful voices urging total withdrawal from Africa. Some said that what CR had been doing there had no particular connection with the Religious Life, and that in any case, even without government action, CR would have voluntarily handed over its works to Africans by the 1970s.

Fortunately CR decided to maintain a presence in Africa (it had withdrawn from Penhalonga in 1983), and in 1986 Kingston Erson masterminded the move to two (now three) bungalows in Turffontein, three miles to the west of Rosettenville. The Houses are small enough to allow an informal family atmosphere, large enough for conferences and retreats and for an important ministry of hospitality. CR and OHP continue to share some worship and meals together. Francis Blake continues as Anglican chaplain to Baragwanath hospital. Jeremy Platt has been living over a year in a shack on a squatters' camp with a makeshift chapel next door. Crispin Harrison, the Provincial, is Canon Theologian of the new diocese of Christ the King. As CR's temporal power was removed, so brethren became more convinced of the importance of prayer for South Africa. When Stubbs could no longer live in South Africa he spent four years in Masite, Lesotho, at a multi-racial house of contemplative nuns. He continues to pray for: 1. Hope, making possible 2. Repentance, making possible 3. Internal Settlement, and *then* 4. Reconciliation and Reconstruction (*CRQ* LD 1985). Stanton writes: 'It was David Rabkin [a fellow political prisoner] who taught me, as we walked round and round the exercise yard in Pretoria Central Prison that there are many different ways of playing a part in the liberation struggle ... As a priest and a monk I consider prayer is the most important work I have to do' (*CRQ* Epiphany 1991).

CR's contribution to South Africa has been quite out of proportion to its numbers. Again and again during the past ninety years it has had the courage and foresight to discern and to man the crucial frontier posts: providing education for blacks and whites; training Africans for ministry; sharing life in the townships; offering a ministry of solidarity and hope to the persecuted. It was CR which in large measure created the ethos of the diocese of Johannesburg. By its training of most of the black priests of the Province, it has deeply affected the life of the whole Anglican church. CR has been the keeper of the church's Christian conscience – salt as well as leaven – because it has lived for values which have been harshly derided, particularly since the Nationalist victory of 1948.

Zimbabwe

The work of CR in Zimbabwe was not confined to Penhalonga. Osmund Victor was a notable Dean of Salisbury (Harare).[30] A year after his profession in 1909 he began to hold major posts in CR: the first full-time Principal of St Peter's Theological College; Novice Guardian at Mirfield; an army chaplaincy; CR Provincial 1920–36 in South Africa and also a leading missionary strategist in the Anglican church. His architectural skills were employed at Rosettenville, Penhalonga and Mirfield. Because his heart was in Africa he declined to become Principal at Mirfield. However, at the beginning of the war, with no major post in CR in prospect, he was invited to become acting Dean of Salisbury for six months – it was impossible to get anyone from England in war-time. By 1940 he was so popular that from the Governor downwards, everyone said he must stay for good. He gripped congregations with his oratory. Occasions such as the Battle of Britain and D-Day evoked all his romantic patriotism.

But CR was divided about his being Dean. Runge said that it was good for him to settle to a major job, more responsible than anything that CR could offer; that he had worked for so long on his own that he was no longer a team-man. Horner the Superior, and Raynes the Provincial, were both opposed to any form of detached service, even military chaplaincies. It was not enough that Victor stayed regularly at Penhalonga and kept the Rule. In 1943 Raynes, now Superior, decided that he should return after the war to Mirfield for at least six months. But the churchwardens wanted him to stay to complete his many projects both at the cathedral and in the whole area. Raynes was adamant. It had been a mistake from the beginning, he wrote to the Provincial, Eric Goodall in 1944:

> I do not believe myself that the seconding of people to do particular work on their own for protracted periods is ever a good thing, and to my mind quite contrary both to the letter and the spirit of the Rule and of Community life . . . the work concerned becomes very much an individual concern and consequently has not got the sense of being a work of the Community . . . he is likely to become more and more detached from the Community and find it more and more difficult to readjust himself to living in a Community House and sharing in the Community life and work.

But what would CR have done with him if he had returned? When Goodall suggested that he might take charge of St Mary's parish Rosettenville, Victor was appalled: 'it would be rather a case of living one's life backwards'. When peace arrived Victor was busy with plans to add a war memorial cloister to the cathedral. In 1948 Talbot, an old friend, appealed to him to return. 'We must help one another in the later stages of our lives, though I should understand if you were reluctant to leave South Africa . . . But don't delay too long, or I shall be away. I struck seventy, eight days ago.' By the time Victor returned in 1954 Talbot had been dead for five years. Victor had gone to be Dean for six months and stayed fifteen years.

The story illustrates a theme in CR's history. Frere wrote in his *Commentary* that each brother's gifts were to be developed and taken into account, but that brethren, particularly those with strong personalities, should leave their personal development in the hands of the Community. In practice it has proved difficult to know what to do with a brother with a marked capacity for responsibility: there is a limited number of major posts in CR, and he may not be offered a bishopric. For the frenetic Victor to have taken on a small parish after Salisbury would have been a mortification: but would that mortification have been fruitful or destructive? Would he simply have gone pop? For even in retirement in his mid-seventies he was still travelling incessantly and writing a thousand letters a year.

From 1972–7 Robert Mercer exercised a memorably idiosyncratic ministry as rector of Borrowdale, Harare and then for ten years as Bishop of Matabeleland. His diocesan letters were enlivened by affectionate vignettes of the brethren: Jonathan Graham used Psalm 102 to show that the recitation of the psalter was independent of personal mood: 'One can't *feel* like a pelican in the wilderness every twentieth morning of the month.' It had been Mercer's sympathy for the under-dog which had led him to explain the WCC grants when at Stellenbosch. Now he got across the Zimbabwe government for criticizing its treatment of dissidents. In 1986, with a frankness rare in the episcopate, he announced that he was resigning because the 'diocese would benefit from a change . . . I have run out of ideas.'

But CR made its most substantial contribution to Zimbabwe through St Augustine's Penhalonga. In 1948 Arthur Wells, then Principal, put forward a development programme costing £25,000: new accommodation for 100 teacher training students to equip them to teach higher forms, which meant additional lecturers and new classrooms for their teaching practice; improved medical facilities; the rebuilding of the girls' dormitories; better accommodation for the domestics; improvements on the farm; more adequate electricity and water systems. (Yet brethren continued to sleep in the same bare rooms built in 1898.) The Beit Trustees, firms and individuals generously financed several of these projects. CR gave two-thirds of the royalties from *Naught for your Comfort*. When Benjamin Baynham arrived as Principal in 1951 his brisk and decisive personality was needed to resolve serious financial and personal problems at the mission. He remained seventeen years. He believed that one of its great strengths was that, unlike Rosettenville, it had a living connection with the district through the work of the trekking brethren. He was concerned in 1962 that only two of the staff of thirty-one teachers (half white, half black) were members of CR: since education was 'a special form of evangelization', there should be at least four CR teachers, and always a brother preparing to come out by being trained as a teacher. New brethren should learn Shona before arrival. 'None of us speaks Shona at all well.' The truth of this was confirmed by a piece written later by a fourth form boy:

> I have bitter feelings towards the whole idea of having our Mass on Sundays said in Shona. In fact I believe that it is wrong and should be stopped . . . First, our priests are pretty poor in Shona. They are trying hard to improve their standard but not so successfully. One or two of them admitted – on being asked – that they did not know some of the things they say when they are conducting High Mass. This is pretty poor in itself because it means you say prayers to the Almighty without the slightest idea what you mean.

The priest (he added) hesitates between words so that the congregation cannot understand what is being said. Worse still the priest pronounces a word in such a way that it means something absurd. 'The priest, instead of saying "archangels" . . . begins to talk about kidneys.' The Principal (Daniel Pearce) believed that this opinion was widely shared. (Such amateurishness represented a devastating failure to take African identity and culture seriously.)

After the Second World War, the growth of academic excellence depended upon the recruitment of a highly skilled staff of whom Lorna Kendall (later head of Religious Studies at Christ Church College Canterbury) was the first to arrive. When in 1945 this twenty-four year old got off the train at Umtali she was amazed to be welcomed by Brother Roger with a big hug. She was, however, invited to the Priory only twice a year and had to get special permission to use the Library as this meant passing the bedrooms of the brethren. When teacher training ceased the secondary school expanded in the buildings of the former college and in 1968 'A' level work began. Academic standards were high. In 1971 all fifty nine 'O' level students were placed in the first division, the first time this had happened in Rhodesia.

'Knowledge is power' proclaimed a large notice outside one of CR's neighbouring schools. Pearce wrote two award-winning plays about the Africans' desperate desire for academic success. In 1976, 2,400 applications were received for 180 places at Penhalonga. Some brethren worried that Matric was becoming more important than Christianity. Yet on a visit in 1983, though the school prayers were as formal as those of a 1950s public school, twelve to forty pupils would be present at a weekday voluntary mass. On

Sunday lines of people from all over the mission converged on the great church, pink in the early morning sunlight, standing out against the wooded hills the other side of the valley: brethren, sisters, staff, students, mothers with children on their backs, domestics and manual workers. The High Mass with 600 communicants was almost entirely in Shona with English and African music, some of it accompanied with drums, maracas and tambourines. In the afternoon a sixth former led a lively unofficial charismatic service with much singing, clapping and drumming. The schools have continued to expand since CR left in 1983. There were 1,600 pupils in 1989 of whom 900 were in the secondary school. A system of bursaries has always enabled poor parents to send their children. The financial advantages of having a mission run by Religious were considerable: cheap staff kept fees lower; CR and OHP provided a network of generous supporters. But CR also created dependence and a false sense of security.

The mission was not solely a place for academic study. The clinic served a wide area and in 1983 was treating an average of 760 patients a month. At the school there was a happy social life with film shows, debates, dances and a variety of plays – Shakespeare, dramatizations of local history, and in 1954 'Cry, the Beloved Country' in which Edgar Tekere, now a controversial politician, played the delinquent son Absalom. Under James Woodrow church music reached a very high standard. On Sundays after conducting the choir at Evensong, Woodrow would doff his cassock and putting on a white suit with brilliant scarlet bow-tie he would preside at the school dance at which the pupils would show off their skills. They had learned these in the dancing class which he had taken over from Betty Gawthorpe. A pupil described what fun it was: 'The gentlemen press their trousers and beautiful shirts and wash their tennis shoes, while the ladies press their long frocks . . . Everything is wonderful and colourful. The air is filled with aromatic smells, obviously caused by all sorts of cosmetics . . . there are usually two records of Jive and one of Rock and Roll. Some of the best dances are the Fox Trot, Moonlight Saunter, Quickstep, Gay Gordons, Lancers and Valeta.' (How very un-Tractarian; but how like the parish dances enthusiastically promoted by Dolling at St Agatha's Portsmouth, so enjoyed by Gore.) Next morning Woodrow would be in church as usual at 5 a.m. for his hour of prayer before Mattins and Mass.

CR did an immense variety of other things: chaplaincy to OHP and CZR, care of local churches, supervision of the farm, hospitality to visitors and retreatants, spiritual direction. Maurice Bradshaw chaired the Diocesan Translation Committee which was revising the versions of Bible, hymns and Prayer Book. There was also the care of some forty-two outstation churches and schools. By the early 1960s Land Rovers had replaced the donkeys, and there was now an African priest in each district. Jacob Wardle was a trekking brother for twenty-seven years, and latterly looked after the southern area.

Before he went back to Mirfield in 1983 an ox was roasted in his honour. By the end of the 1960s the northern areas were beginning to be handed over to resident black priests. Lucina Culver, a parish worker from Umtali, once accompanied Noel Williams on a four day trek:

> Each morning we had Mass at a different church made of mud plastered walls or home made bricks, with cow dung floors smoothly polished and in some cases stained green by rubbing with leaves. They had holes in the walls for windows but no glass or window frames, roofs made of thatch or corrugated iron with masses of holes in them. When it rains the churches must get flooded, but no need to worry, it will soon dry and there is nothing there that can hurt . . . All the way through the service people kept coming in, but no one minded. If there was no bench they sat on the floor. Lots of children, boys and men on one side, women and girls on the other. One morning the church having collapsed due to white ants, we had a lovely service out under the trees . . . Feeding time for the breast fed babies goes on all through the service, and when fed, back the mothers sling them on their backs . . . By the end of the service we were always packed close and the church very full . . . On the last morning they had a band, home made rattles and drums . . . And when the band struck up again for the last hymn, and one very old grannie started dancing, all in the church danced too . . . One morning one woman was to be given her Mothers' Union uniform. One of the other members put it on her in church while the others all clapped and sang and danced around her. All this was quite unofficial, just something that they had worked out for themselves. They will sing for hours. (USPG *Network* June 1970)

St Augustine's attracted a high proportion of individualists, excellent as pioneers, but not good at team-work. Kenneth Skelton, Bishop of Matabeleland, when Visitor in the 1960s strongly urged the brethren to deepen their community life, especially as they worked among Africans who had a rich tradition of communal living.

It was possible for a white liberal like Edward Paget (a bishop in Rhodesia 1925–57) to go on working for racial understanding in the belief that this could be peacefully achieved. After all several of the Governors were devout Anglicans – Sir Herbert Stanley in 1936 attended the first pilgrimage mass to the Mizeki shrine with an African as chief celebrant; Lord Llewellin, like Stanley an appreciative visitor to St Augustine's, received communion at an inter-racial ordination in 1954; Sir Humphrey Gibbs was a weekly communicant at Salisbury Cathedral. Yet Kenneth Skelton recalls how routinely abusive many whites were to Africans in the 1960s: one of the Bulawayo Cathedral congregation called them 'our black animals'; when Canon Leonard Sagonda, a saintly and venerable African priest dropped in, a member of the office staff called out 'Do these boys have tea?' When Sir Godfrey Huggins, the Prime Minister, grudgingly allowed a few Africans to attend the 1951 Victoria Falls constitutional conference, he ordered them to live in huts and to eat separately.

The story of Herbert Chitepo, a former pupil and teacher at Penhalonga, illustrates the ultimate powerlessness of white liberals to achieve radical change in Rhodesia. When he returned from England as Rhodesia's first black barrister in 1954, legislation was necessary to allow him to practice in the centre of Salisbury. At one trial the Native Commissioner insisted that Chitepo conducted his defence of the accused sitting cross-legged on the floor. He was regularly insulted in shops and restaurants. Paget took up his cause and baptized his child at Bishop's Mount. But Gonville ffrench-Beytagh, Dean of Salisbury, who also befriended him, recalled: 'I saw him gradually change from being a person of good-will, who wanted to make partnership work, to a bitter, anti-white extremist. I don't blame him. It was no use his being accepted by the more liberal European individuals if he was rejected by the whole social system.'[31] Having lost hope of a peaceful solution, Chitepo left Rhodesia in 1962 and began to organize guerilla activity from Lusaka. However Rhodesia never suffered from an equivalent to the Bantu Education Act – St Augustine's remained free to provide a high-class education for Africans. But brethren did very little to try to change the attitudes of the nation as a whole in order that African talents fostered at Penhalonga and elsewhere could be utilized. The mission was isolated and largely self-contained. Unlike their South African colleagues the brethren never lived in the Rhodesian townships. Though Tekere remembers St Augustine's as a school which encouraged political discussion, brethren (until the civil war) stayed out of national politics.

After the failure of the Central African Federation (1953) to live up to its slogan of 'partnership' for the races, and after Britain failed to intervene with force when Ian Smith declared independence in 1965 (who then in 1970 turned Rhodesia into a republic with racial discrimination and repression on South African lines), African leaders in Rhodesia eventually concluded that nothing would change unless they took up arms. The response of the Rhodesian churches to the events following UDI was, with certain exceptions, confused and ambivalent. There were only two Anglican leaders who showed they understood why the patience of African leaders had run out: Kenneth Skelton and Patrick Murindagomo (suffragan Bishop of Mashonaland, who had trained as a teacher at St Augustine's). Government propaganda persuaded many white church people that the civil war was a conflict between Christianity and godless Marxism.[32]

Victor de Waal contends that it was the fear of engaging in conflict about fundamental issues which made war inevitable. When war came most white Christian leaders, believing that they were neutral, advocated 'reconciliation'.

This adoption of a 'neutral' stance by the Christian churches [was] . . . based on a double fallacy. In the first place, not only does neutrality itself almost inevitably work towards the maintenance of the *status quo*, but it is virtually impossible for the consciousness of individuals or institutions not to be conditioned by their environment . . . Secondly . . . Christians individually, and the churches as human institutions, are not exempt from the temptation to play safe and to invite others to do the changing. The example of Jesus Christ, however, should make it clear to them that a mediator cannot remain neutral, and that the work of reconciliation is bound to be supremely costly.[33]

Hugh Bishop, newly elected Superior, preached in Salisbury Cathedral on 27 February 1966 on 'Father forgive them, for they know not what they do'. He claimed the right and the duty to speak about Rhodesia since CR had been working there for fifty years. The most frightening characteristic of British people in Africa was their 'insensitivity' to what Africans felt and thought. '"We have struck a blow," said Mr Smith on November 11th last year, "for the preservation of Christianity". How insensitive do you have to be to believe that?' asked Bishop. He went on to quote Zambian churchmen's statements about 'the illegal regime' and its 'tyranny', its use of beatings, torture and even killings (*CRQ* LD 1966).

During the sermon fifty people walked out in protest. Dean Wood, an old Mirfield student, defended Bishop against the bitter criticisms which ensued: people ought to know what many Christians outside Rhodesia were saying. Cecil Alderson, Bishop of Mashonaland, however, joined the critics: he should have consulted with the Dean before preaching to an unknown congregation; it was wrong to quote from unconfirmed reports from Zambia; it was contrary to charity to refer to 'the illegal regime' (yet Alderson preaching in Salisbury Cathedral after UDI had said 'I repudiate this illegal act'). The sermon also angered two of the brethren at Penhalonga: it dragged CR's name through the mud; instead of leaving Rhodesia the next day the Superior should have stayed to face his critics; CR was left to pick up the pieces. But Hugh Bishop knew that it was difficult for critics to be heard. Later that year Dean Wood's reasons for refusing to allow a celebration of the anniversary of UDI in the cathedral were censored out of the *Rhodesia Herald*.

After Mozambique achieved independence in 1975 the guerrilla war intensified. The Mozambique border is only a mile from Penhalonga. St Augustine's was now in the front line.[34] Students had already shown themselves to be politically aware. In 1962 when Nkomo's ZAPU was banned by the government, students broke windows and refused to receive Sunday communion. In 1966 CR gave a donation to the churches' fund for restrictees' families. Two Africans asked in the *CR Quarterly* (MD 1967) why missionaries sought to convert Africans but not white imperialists? In 1975 the war began to have a dramatic effect on the school when eighty-seven of the brightest students (mostly boys) absconded and went over the border to join the guerrillas. Before they went they burned their Cambridge 'O' level certificates as a gesture of self-sacrifice and renunciation. When Keble

Prosser, the Principal, announced the exodus publicly, pointing out the character of those who had gone and the evident magnetism of the cause, he was villified. Life at the mission was tense. In July 1975 a dusk to dawn curfew was enforced in the border area, including St Augustine's. Prosser received death-threats. The police raided the school and made arrests. The Provincial Education Officer lectured the school on the wickedness of the 'terrorists'. But in 1976 another forty-four students went over the border. In August guerrillas mortar-bombed Umtali damaging property (but killing no one) in retaliation for a raid by government forces who, crossing at Penhalonga, had killed some 1,200 – women and children as well as guerrillas.

The brethren were divided in their attitudes to the guerrillas. Some, including Prosser, openly supported their cause. Two were hostile. Jacob Wardle, driving the ancient Land Rover, regularly risked his life (for many roads were mined) determined to visit frightened villagers and the barbed wire encampments into which government forces had herded others. Many suffered violence and intimidation from both sides. The guerrillas guaranteed his safety and warned him if they had mined roads. The love that Africans felt for him helped to safeguard the mission from attacks. Stephen Faussett, who had become a novice at the age of sixty-two, had grown up in Dublin where he and his mother had thrown stones at the British. So he had a natural affinity with the insurgents. His only concession to the war was to sleep with his teeth in when things were tense, in case he was killed during the night. 'His courage gave courage to the rest of us, so that without him we might not have survived' commented Prosser. Though Noel Williams had no sympathy for the guerrillas they also protected him in the remote area of Marange where he founded and ran a technical school.[35] African teachers at Penhalonga gave one tenth of their salaries to the guerrillas; their supporters among the brethren gave what they could.

In June 1978 helicopters and troops attacked huts on the mission and killed twenty-seven: ten guerrillas, ten of their girl friends (including three from the school) and seven villagers. On 23 June missionaries and their families were massacred at the Elim mission near Umtali. This was given worldwide publicity. (Atrocities by government forces were hushed up.) On 26 June African teachers advised the brethren and OHP sisters to leave. The next day they moved to Umtali and for about a month some of the brethren commuted to the mission from there, returning to residence by stages. The OHP sisters did not return.

Since St Augustine's was regarded by the guerrillas as the most supportive mission in the country, they turned up regularly. In August 1979 the guerrillas had just assembled the students for a lecture, when security forces arrived and surrounded the hall. Fortunately they acted calmly and a massacre was avoided, though one guerrilla was killed as he tried to escape. Students fled and hid – one pretended to be a statue in the church. The next day the dead guerrilla was exhibited for identification, but no one gave him away. Prosser was interrogated about his dealings with guerrillas – a capital offence. He and the mission were under enormous pressures from both sides and forced into moral compromises, like Dietrich Bonhoeffer, the anti-Nazi German pastor who wrote from prison:

> The great masquerade of evil has played havoc with all our ethical concepts . . . We have been silent witnesses of evil deeds; we have been drenched by many storms; we have learnt the arts of equivocation and pretence . . . Will our inward power of resistance be strong enough, and our honesty with ourselves remorseless enough, for us to find our way back to simplicity and straightforwardness?[36]

Just before and after the cease-fire (December 1979) four local whites were killed by guerrillas. In February 1980, when Prosser allowed Mugabe's ZANU-PF to hold a rally on the football field, whites were enraged. In March, two hours before the election of Mugabe was announced, police and soldiers raided the mission and tore down ZANU-PF posters and rifled the dormitories.

The school celebrated the victory with a dance. Thirty former guerrillas returned. Several re-joined the ballroom dancing class. In 1982 a school war memorial of a guerrilla (the idea of students) was unveiled by Mugabe, now Prime Minister of Zimbabwe, to the horror of local whites. Noticeably it includes no Christian symbolism or text. No Anglican was among the sixty-seven or so missionaries killed during the war. This and the witness of St Augustine's has to be taken into account when assessing the role of the Anglican church. Bishop Hatendi (now Bishop of Mashonaland, educated at Penhalonga) was selected to preach at an inter-denominational service to celebrate independence on 20 April 1980. The next year he, together with Jonathan Siyachitema (now Bishop of The Lundi), the Ministers of Youth, Industry, Mines and Information in the new government, all from St Augustine's, signed an appeal for its work: an indication of the great contribution it had made to the leadership of church and state in Zimbabwe.

The war delayed the long debated departure of CR from Penhalonga. It did not want to be accused of running away during the war. After independence CR decided that it was time for St Augustine's to be run by Africans. In September 1983, to widespread regret, CR withdrew after sixty-eight years' work. However, Keble Prosser decided to remain as Principal and eventually withdrew from the Community.

Conclusion

During the last ninety years CR has given richly and generously to Africa. Africa has also given richly and generously to CR. Charles Hooper writes:

African people, generally, exert a demand on their priests, a demand which has become muted among many Europeans. To them he is not a cheerer up of idle hours, a convenor of bazaars, a scoutmaster, a chairman of parish councils, or a genial jolly good sort. He is, primarily, a priest, from whom they require the Sacraments, teaching, the understanding of perplexities, solace in the time of illness, the drying of tears, and the sharing of joys. It is the response to this demand, the demand for a priest's office and his heart, which, as much as the calibre of the men themselves, has gone to the making of the eminent missionaries of Africa.[37]

But that experience of priesthood led Hooper (born in South Africa, trained at Mirfield) into political confrontation. (He is now a member of CR.) Yet was Africa, whose people responded readily to evangelism and whose problems seemed to have clear solutions (churches, hospitals, schools), sometimes an escape from the intractable religious indifference of England? CR began its work in Africa in close alliance with the imperial power, but because it was open to the radical demands of the gospel, it was led into conflict with the powers-that-be. CR played a part in the process of persuading the English to accept the transmutation of Empire into Commonwealth, and when Britain turned in upon itself and became bored with the Commonwealth, it continued to be a reminder that God is not a white Englishman.

For many brethren, until recently, CR meant not Mirfield, but Penhalonga or Sophiatown, Orlando or Rosettenville. Over against Mirfield with its greater size, complexity and formality, the various small priories have, at their best, been more like homes than institutions, with the fun and challenges of face-to-face relationships. Nicolas Stebbing remarked in his obituary of Charles Coles: 'Like so many in CR, it was sending him out to Africa in 1962 which was the real making of him.' What could replace that decisive experience?

13

Loss and Gain

Renewal

When Hugh Bishop was installed as Superior on 3 January 1966 Michael Ramsey, Archbishop of Canterbury and Visitor, preached:

> The sickness in our Church is a sort of malaise of the soul, seen in a weakness in faith and a scepticism in prayer and a priesthood which sometimes tends to lose heart. So come the tendencies to clutch at remedies which are themselves part of the sickness, such as substituting psychological harmony for holiness or trying to justify the Gospel and the Church in terms other than the terrible loving-kindness of God . . . Here I believe the Religious Orders can greatly help in the healing of our sickness, by being themselves, by living by the mystery of Christ and by loving us patiently . . . the Community is today more than ever involved upon the frontier . . . Today the concern of the Christian for the frontier and for those beyond the frontier is often expressed in phrases like 'the caring Church' and 'the serving Church' . . . No service of the world is greater than every act of the contemplation of God, for every such act helps the world to recover the soul which it has lost. (*CRQ* L D 1966)

After Ramsey's initial fumbling when *Honest to God* was first published in 1963, he quickly recovered his touch and Anglican radicals (most of whom came from a Catholic background) came to feel he was in critical solidarity with them. He criticized them for spiritual shallowness and obsession with the contemporary, but because of his Nonconformist upbringing, he shared their dislike of establishment Anglicanism; having absorbed F. D. Maurice and Karl Barth he understood the radicals' (and Bonhoeffer's) impatience with 'religion'.[1]

Nearly a thousand letters and telegrams congratulated Hugh on his election. Some brethren were sceptical, but in the first year or so many (but not all) were won round. The tide of change and renewal was running strongly. Jonathan Graham had dipped his toes in, but he preferred to sit at the water's edge and comment caustically on those who had plunged in. Hugh, by contrast, in his years at the College had already begun to identify the movement of the tide with the Spirit of God. The distaste of radicalism for religiosity found a powerful echo in his own experience; its talk of a 'New Reformation' appealed to his dramatic temperament. So in his first message in the *Quarterly* he wrote: 'we look forward to the future with trust and hope, and a certain sense of exhilaration'. One brother recalled: 'I felt that Hugh was prepared to face some fairly radical questions about the shape of the Community's future.' To another 'Hugh meant liberation'. 'Hugh is providing the leadership we need' commented the Chronicler, and there are a number of subsequent tributes in the Chronicle to Bishop's skilful chairmanship of Chapter and to the way in which he quickly established a common mind among its members. Ironically the tributes Bishop received from brethren were extraordinarily similar to those in the first years of Raynes as Superior when he too had caught an equally strongly flowing, but very different, tide.

The renewal of the church and its religious communities was a burning topic as the result of Vatican II and the radical movement in the Church of England. In the summer of 1965 Bishop spoke to a meeting in Oxford attended by representatives of all the Anglican communities (with Roman Catholic observers). From this flowed not only similar regular consultations, but also a good deal of change within the communities. In the *Times* (4 February 1967) Bishop characterized them as 'Communities of Protest': 'a protest against a merely nominal and conventional Christianity in the Church on the one hand and against a thoughtless secularism in the world on the other . . . God knows there is need for more loyal rebels in the Church today and it is the function of the religious communities to provide homes for them where their insights and efforts can be sanctified and used constructively to the glory of God and in the service of man.' At the Oxford conference that July he began with the teachings of Vatican II. The Religious Life was not something separate from or higher than the baptismal vocation but a special expression of it, an eschatological sign. The vows were extreme and aggressive expressions of the three-fold renunciations at baptism, for as John the Baptist said of the kingdom: 'men of violence take it by force'. A Religious House should be a place where 'transcendence may be more perceptible'. There were three dangers for religious communities: exclusivism – Religious may become preoccupied with themselves, expect special treatment and isolate themselves from the life and worship of the parish churches; pharisaism – they may become obsessed with minutiae of rule and liturgy; conservatism: 'it is only by going forward that we can be saved even though it means leaving the security of the past and risking everything' (*CRQ* MD 1967).

When Eric Simmons, then Novice Guardian, spoke to a meeting of northern communities in 1971, he was critical of current trends in spirituality. The contemporary mood of empiricism, open to whatever confronted us, led to the rejection of authority and tradition and to the claim for total individual freedom. A God totally immersed in the world lacked transcendence. Current teaching about prayer stressing the discovery of God in others rejected the tradition of withdrawal and detachment. But over against this 'extrovert and optimistic, aggressive and masculine and pragmatic' spirituality, Simmons set the concept of prayer as presence: 'Just as a man is present in different ways to a stranger or a friend or a lover, so prayer develops beyond the stage of *saying* prayers to an abiding sense of being present with God in all our manifold daily activities.' At the same conference Benedict Green tackled another crucial issue, poverty. He said that it lay close to the heart of the gospel but already by St Paul it had changed to mean simple subsistence. The history of religious communities showed the dangers of corporate wealth. Franciscan history demonstrated that it was difficult to institutionalize poverty. The Little Brothers and Sisters who earned their own livings sharing the uncertainties of the labour market had given a new meaning to poverty. The majority of Religious who practised a community of goods had to find ways of practising poverty (for example by tithing) if they were to protest against the fashion of the world (*CRQ* JB 1971). Harry Williams in *Poverty, Chastity and Obedience* (1975) interpreted it psychologically: 'Poverty takes pleasure in a thing because it is, and not because it can be possessed . . . Poverty is faith in myself as my own bank . . . Because the resources within me are always only latent, I must be content to have nothing until the moment of need arrives.'[2]

The CR Rule does not speak of 'poverty' but rather of seeking 'to have the fewest and simplest wants that are consistent with health and the needs of his work'. But it has always been difficult to know what this means. Simplicity of life for brethren in Africa seemed wealth to many Africans. Does the monastic author need a word processor, or should he be content with a manual typewriter or even a pen? Is it appropriate for Religious to use cars when public transport is available? Or should they choose to hitch-hike rather than use either? Casual conversations with local people in Mirfield about CR usually include appreciative comments, but often end with something like: 'Of course the Fathers have a cushy life, no worry about unemployment or how to pay the bills.' Influenced by the Little Brothers and Sisters and convinced that in the future more clergy would have to earn their own living, Bishop encouraged five brethren, clerical and lay, to do the same while continuing to live in a CR House. Most had to be trained first. One became a psychiatric social worker, another a child care officer, another an assistant hospital chaplain, another a youth leader, another worked in a Family Service Unit. But it was not wholly successful. Three of the five eventually left CR – indeed some seemed attracted to the idea precisely because they did not find it easy to live in community. For their part many brethren did not support or understand the idea. (Many parish clergy are likewise suspicious of non-stipendiary priests.)

Discussion of liturgical change soon bored Bishop, and he felt a considerable attraction to the older forms of worship – he greatly enjoyed reciting the sonorous Latin grace at College. But he accepted, indeed promoted, liturgical reform. In what was to some a very painful process CR was fortunate to have the direction of its two liturgists, Green and Tweedy. In common with other communities the seven offices were replaced by a four-fold pattern of Mattins, Mid-Day Office (which could include non-scriptural readings), Evensong and Compline. Lay brothers could now hold any post in CR except those of Superior, Prior and Novice Guardian and could lead its daily offices. Gradually concelebration came in and private masses decreased, though Bishop was one of those who could not see what difference it made whether a priest was assisting standing at the altar or in his stall. He favoured the adoption of the Series II eucharistic rite partly because it brought CR worship more into line with that of the parishes. At funerals *Dies Irae* with its theme of judgment was replaced by hymns about the resurrection. The Athanasian Creed went on being faithfully recited until 1976 – the Prayer Book rubric requiring it had been sacrosanct to Anglo-Catholics. In the 1870s Liddon threatened to cease ministry if the rubric were altered. A nave altar-table appeared in 1973 but fortunately disappeared two years later. The eucharistic fast was now treated as a matter of courtesy rather than law. From 1966 those attending Commemoration Day were invited to receive commun-ion at the High Mass. FR Companions instead of reporting quarterly on a complicated form about how many times they had broken the rules, were now asked to write an annual letter to their Wardens about their discipleship based on a rule of life worked out personally with a spiritual director.

For most of his time as Superior, Bishop was a member of the Church Assembly and its successor the General Synod. He quickly became one of those whose words commanded attention. He represented those in the Catholic tradition who wanted it to flow into the mainstream of the church. So, though at first he attended meetings of the Anglo-Catholic group (of which Raynes had been a leading member) his now deep distrust of party labels and his support for the Anglican-Methodist unity scheme caused him to leave it. In 1970 he became one of the sponsors of the New Synod Group, those of different traditions who wanted to press forward with reform and renewal. Whereas under Raynes, CR was officially committed to the prolonged campaign against the CSI scheme, brethren were now openly and not too polemically divided about the Anglican-Methodist scheme. When on 13 July 1968 the *Times* published a letter from Bishop, Curtis, Hoey, Jarrett-Kerr, Green, Simpson and Wheeldon supporting the scheme, they received rebuking letters from Geoffrey Fisher, the former Archbishop, who was vigorously campaigning against it. When after twenty years of negotiations, in 1969 and 1972 it failed to gain sufficient votes, Curtis was particularly sick at heart at what he regarded as the humiliation of the Church of England (*CRQ* JB 1973). Michael Ramsey wrote to Curtis, an old friend, on 20 June 1972:

Our church has 'made an ass of itself' . . . I am left with no particular belief or enthusiasm for *the Church of England as a thing*. None at all! The significance of the C of E had been that, in contrast with Rome, it stood for *intellectual integrity*. But it doesn't. Its particular raison d'être in history is undermined.

The debacle revealed how incapable some Anglo-Catholics were of creative adventure even when the most Catholic-minded Archbishop since the Reformation validated it. Hugh Bishop's standing in the Assembly was enhanced in 1970 when in a debate about the need to reduce the number of theological colleges, he asked for an objective assessment of whether Mirfield should continue. In 1970 he became one of the three representatives of the Church of England to the newly created Anglican Consultative Council, an inner cabinet for the whole Anglican Communion. He was also well-known in Synod for his concern about racial questions and in 1971 became chairman of the Board of the Community and Race Relations Unit of the British Council of Churches.

CR was now fostering ecumenical relationships on all fronts. Since its foundation CR had little contact with Free Church people who had often been referred to in derisive terms. But in 1971 Neville Ward, the remarkable Methodist minister and spiritual writer, conducted the Community retreat. He astonished brethren by basing his addresses on the Sorrowful Mysteries of the Rosary – which were to form part of his *Five for Sorrow, Ten for Joy* published that year. In 1972, Dr Haddon Willmer, a Baptist theologian from Leeds University gave the Holy Week lectures. In 1970 and 1983 the Community retreat was conducted by a Roman Catholic priest and nun respectively.

In June 1958, after four years' negotiation, five Anglican Religious, including Mark Tweedy, spent a fascinating fortnight's visit to Russian monasteries.[3] No Anglican Religious had been there since Frere in 1914. As an ordinand Tweedy had visited Estonia and Russia in 1936 in a party led by Ambrose Reeves, then working for the World Student Christian Federation. That year Tweedy became a member of the Fellowship of St Alban and St Sergius, came under the spell of Nicolas Zernov, was captivated by Orthodox worship, but was too much of a western progressivist ever to be deeply influenced by Orthodoxy. In June 1960 three Russian monks paid a return visit. The tour was organized by Tweedy who thought they were coming for three weeks, but when they arrived he discovered that they had only come for ten days, later extended to fourteen, so the whole programme had to be re-arranged. They travelled in a large Rover belonging to Nicholas Mosley and a pre-war baby Austin belonging to a Mirfield student, 'a small machine of the thirteenth century', one monk described it. The monks sang Vespers on the way. The English replied with 'For all the saints' during a traffic jam at Baldock. At Windsor the interpreter fell ill so Tweedy had to explain in halting Russian what was meant by the Order of the Garter. They visited a wide range of religious houses including Mirfield, but thought Nashdom and West Malling were closest in ethos to Orthodox monasticism. It is notable that apart from one visit to a Low Church Evensong in Oxford no attempt seems to have been made to introduce them to anything like the full range of Anglicanism. From then until recently there were few references to the Orthodox in the *Quarterly*. But in 1984 Aelred Stubbs visited Mount Athos with his friend James Ramsden. In the last few years, partly under the influence of George Guiver (professed 1985) a polyglot and polymath, CR interest in Orthodoxy has revived and was expressed by a visit to Romania by him, Peter Allan, Paul Holland and Nicolas Stebbing in 1990.

In 1963 Eberhard Bethge (Bonhoeffer's biographer and friend) and other pastors from the Rhineland visited Mirfield for a retreat. In return Roger Castle (fearfully) and Zachary Brammer (boldly) hitchhiked all the way from the Pear Tree pub in Mirfield to the Rhineland to visit these pastors and other Christian groups. In 1965 Bernard Chamberlain, who is half Austrian, with Roger and Zachary conducted a pastors' retreat in the Rhineland. Christopher Lowe, another brother with fluent German, regularly visits Christians of different traditions in Germany and eastern Europe. Protestants particularly warm to his biblically based retreats.

In 1969 Cardinal Suenens of Malines came to Mirfield to pray at the tombs of Gore and Frere and to speak about the Malines Conversations. In 1976 Anglicans and Roman Catholics gathered at Mirfield to commemorate the fiftieth anniversary of Cardinal Mercier's death. The readings at the Mid-Day Office were from Mercier and Frere. In 1981 when Suenens' successor visited Mirfield he celebrated mass at the high altar (the first Roman Catholic bishop to do so) and preached. In 1982 a united service was arranged by Chamberlain and the local fraternal to pray for the Pope's visit. Held in the Community church, it was packed out, to the surprise of those brethren who dislike disturbances to the routine which special occasions create. Contacts between CR and the German Roman Catholic Benedictines at Trier which began over twenty years ago, have deepened greatly during the last decade. In 1983 the two communities made a compact to support one another in prayer and work: 'We ... have in our contacts with one another experienced the richness and the unifying power of God's Spirit.' Guiver before coming to Mirfield had spent a sabbatical year at Trier and commented: 'part of our British poverty is our ignorance of the riches of the Church in Europe'. In 1985 Crispin Harrison spent six months' study leave at Trier. The two communities are in some ways quite different – unlike CR very few of the monks at Trier are priests, and they look after two demanding parishes. But both have an academic tradition and train ordinands, both share in the Benedictine tradition, Trier by its foundation, CR through the Benedictinism diffused into its life by the Prayer Book and Oxbridge.[4]

During the late 1960s and early 1970s CR launched three new ventures:

at Stellenbosch (described in the last chapter) in London and Manchester. It withdrew from Cardiff in 1968 and Codrington in 1969.

In 1968 C R moved its London work from Holland Park to the Royal Foundation of St Katharine in Stepney. Created by Queen Matilda in 1148 near the Tower of London for work among the poor, in the early nineteenth century it became a kind of royal almshouse in Regent's Park. When under the patronage of Queen Mary it moved back to East London in 1948, with Fr Groser as its Master, it rediscovered its original function. To the Georgian vicarage was added a conference wing and a chapel built as part of the 1951 Festival of Britain. Groser's conception of the Foundation showed the influence of Mirfield which had trained him and Conrad Noel's Thaxted tradition which he had supported. Groser had known Gore in his retirement. Frere had befriended Groser's brother-in-law Jack Bucknall when his socialism had outraged his Cornish parishioners. The male and female staff at St Katharine's lived and worshipped as a community and served the social and educational needs of the area. In the chapel a free-standing altar with a hanging pyx above and a Christ in Majesty behind (carved by Groser's son) was set in the context of the mediaeval stalls and panelling from the original foundation. Groser combined the intellectual activity of regular conferences with weaving his own vestments and creating beautiful gardens out of the discouraging soil. The large mediaeval-style crucifix in the chapel porch from the set of the film of T. S. Eliot's 'Murder in the Cathedral' (in which Groser had played Becket) symbolized his conviction that the church must be prepared to stand against the state.[5]

To continue the Foundation's ancient tradition of a mixed community, C R invited the Deaconess Sisters of St Andrew to join them. (In 1984 some from the Community of the Sisters of the Church replaced them.) C R continued and expanded the retreat and conference work of the Foundation with a particular emphasis on the arts (music, painting, dance, poetry) on Christian-Jewish weekends (very appropriate for that area) and on frontier issues like race relations. It continued the work in schools and among the needy and elderly and provided a context in which a variety of people could meet – dockers, Rotarians, social workers, a homosexual support group. For some years it provided a series of outstanding chaplains for London University including Brother Dunstan Jones, one of the most original and talented brethren in C R's history. Brought up in straightened circumstances by his widowed mother (his father had been a Methodist minister) he studied physics, mathematics, psychology and philosophy for his degree, then as a conscientious objector worked for much of the war as a Shelter Warden in Coventry. After joining C R he went on to postgraduate work in philosophy at Leeds for an M A then a PhD. He kept brethren in touch with the scientific world with which many were entirely unfamiliar.

When Trevor Verryn of South Africa did an analysis of C R's work in

England in 1978 (following his similar report on its South African work in 1976) he praised its great variety, which he urged it to maintain. When many were alienated from the parish structures, St Katharine's provided a particularly valuable alternative way of relating to the church. Verryn, like others, also commended CR for demonstrating there the complementarity of men and women in the life of the church. The Foundation was an appropriate setting for a conference of Religious from France, Germany and England in 1987 about their role in the city. Peter Allan of CR commented: 'if we are to live with our finger on the pulse of the world, then we must live in intimate dialogue with the city' (*CRQ* LD 1988). When CR withdraws from St Katharine's shortly it will no doubt remember that and the criticism of some brethren that it attracted too many well-heeled outsiders and not enough local people.

If St Katharine's was one form of faith in the city, the creation in 1973 of Emmaus, a House of Prayer, in a high-rise block of flats in Hulme, inner-city Manchester, was another. The slender contemplative strand within CR probably goes back to Gerard Sampson. It was expressed in differing forms by Hubert Northcott, Cedma Mack and Geoffrey Curtis. In 1948 Trevor Huddleston and Keith Davie proposed the creation of a contemplative CR House as a counterbalance to its activism. Davie used to say that every community needed its desert. Northcott disagreed with this proposal: it would remove the most prayerful brethren; it would cause friction if one House had a quite different regime from all the rest. Instead CR should start an enclosed community separate from CR but associated with it. Nothing came of either proposal at that time. The general opinion was that the enclosed life was incompatible with the CR tradition.[6]

However, by the end of the 1950s, Augustine Hoey, after many years of mission preaching, influenced by the enclosed nuns of the Society of the Precious Blood (SPB) Burnham Abbey, sensed a vocation to their life of intercession. Eventually in 1972 he was allowed to test this by living a partially withdrawn life at Mirfield. But he really felt called to pray in the inner city and to live in an ordinary house. Inner city life was familiar to him from his eight years as a curate in Hackney. So in 1973 he moved to a council flat in Hulme. Nearby were a couple of professional thieves who lived on the Robin Hood principle, stealing from the affluent city shops to sell things cheaply to the many poor people around. Sometimes they would donate stolen food to Augustine. But when they offered to 'fix' his electricity meter, he totally baffled them by politely refusing. Brethren came to stay at weekends. Eventually he was joined by Alexander Cox. But when Maurice Bradshaw also wanted to come permanently, the flat was too small. So they moved Emmaus in 1977 to a redundant Victorian vicarage in the partially derelict dock area of Sunderland; even in the town centre seagulls fly down the streets and perch on the traffic lights. Near Emmaus are down-at-heel shops with their windows covered permanently with rusty iron grills. A rag and bone man on a rickety horse-drawn cart, like something from England of the 1930s, shouts his wares as he rattles along. Opposite Emmaus is a vast quadrangular block of flats like those in East Berlin. Some think that Emmaus would be a more total incarnation and kenosis if it were in those flats. But that would make it impossible to receive the large number of visitors who come to share the silence. When illness forced Hoey to give up, Aelred Stubbs took over. After theological teaching and ministry to the banned in South Africa, he had lived for four years with the enclosed s p b nuns at Masite, Lesotho. Later Simon Holden, a former Warden of Burnham Abbey, joined him at Emmaus. On Sundays they worship with the local congregation at their Parish Eucharist and keep open house at tea-time. The silence in the House is as luminous as the reproduction of Rembrandt's painting of the Emmaus scene in the dining-room. The heart of Emmaus is being with God for the sake of people. It recovers the natural priesthood of human beings, obscured by the association of priesthood with the life of a clergyman, and is expressed not only in prayer but also by cooking, shopping, cleaning, gardening. In an area of poverty and dereliction Emmaus affirms the people and the area simply by being there. This affirmation is particularly important because St John's church (of which Emmaus used to be the vicarage) has been demolished and Holy Trinity nearby, which used to be the symbol of Sunderland's mercantile achievement and civic pride, is now closed and redundant.

Crisis

By 1970 when Hugh Bishop was into his second three-year term as Superior he was, through television and radio, by far the most widely known Anglican Religious (apart from Trevor Huddleston) and a greatly respected figure in the central councils of the church. Externally he seemed supremely imperturbable. Internally he was in increasing turmoil.[7]

He had been born in 1907 near Shifnal in what was then feudal Shropshire. His father was a prosperous farmer who enjoyed hunting. Hugh was shipped off to prep school at the age of ten; there and at public school he hated institutional life with its lack of privacy, its demands for conformity to the group, the harshness of the regime. Yet in 1937 he arrived at Mirfield to test his vocation, determined to make a decisive act of self-sacrifice (which in later years he regarded as including an element of self-punishment), to make a defiant gesture for the primacy of God and against the primacy of money. His social conscience had been quickened by a curacy in Workington, a working-class town with high unemployment, and he had supported his rector's campaign against the Means Test. His life in c r followed an unusual pattern. Less than a year after profession he became a chaplain for five years, three of them in p o w camps. After the war, except for three years, he occupied a series of posts (Warden of the Hostel, Novice Guardian, Principal of the College) which gave him a good deal of independence.

As we noted earlier, his years at the College were marked by a growing frustration, sometimes anger, with certain aspects of religion. In 1966 – his first year as Superior – he expressed his deep theological uncertainties to Trevor Huddleston. These uncertainties developed into a crisis about orthodoxy, but *not* a crisis of faith – his faith in God never wavered. He increasingly questioned many of the church's doctrinal formulations (particularly the incarnation) and found it difficult to believe in the finality of the Christian revelation the more aware he became of other religions. Yet he felt keenly the paradox that as Superior of CR he was automatically expected by the church to be a spokesman for orthodoxy.

In 1969 Harry Williams resigned as Dean of Chapel, Trinity College, Cambridge and arrived at Mirfield finding (he recalls) the House deserted like the *Marie Celeste*. He had first become a controversial figure because of his highly original reformulations of Christian faith and practice in terms of psychological experience in his contributions to *Soundings* (1962), and *Objections to Christian Belief* (1963) and in his collection of sermons *The True Wilderness* (1965). His writings at Mirfield have included: *True Resurrection* (1972), *Poverty, Chastity and Obedience* (1975) and *Tensions* (1976). In the concluding sections of *Some Day I'll Find You* (1982) he describes how Mirfield provided the context in which he realized that the more deeply a gospel incident spoke to him, the less interested he was in whether the incident had actually happened; in which he realized that what he termed 'the Christ Reality' was to 'a unique degree', but not by any means exclusively, embodied in Jesus. It was deeply reassuring to Hugh that Harry, who had found a way of communicating the Christian faith to many inside and outside the churches for whom the traditional formulations had gone dead or had never been alive, wanted to join CR. If there was room in CR for Harry's views, could there be room for his also? So, as Harry acknowledges, Hugh's support for his election to profession was crucial.

Secondly, Hugh had this life-long aversion to institutional life. But the public saw him as the quintessential monk. So again there was a painful tension between the public role and the inner reality. By 1973, when he was in the middle of his second term as Superior, he was sixty-six. The thought of spending the rest of his life in a CR House filled him with deep dismay. Shifnal had always been 'home', never Mirfield.

Thirdly, he had always longed for one close relationship, and this had been a source of inner conflict throughout his time at CR. The choice seemed to be summed up in words by Ferdinand Mount which he came across later: 'To proclaim community is to condemn particularity. To seek fraternity is to flee from intimacy' (*Encounter* October 1976). In the 1960s he increasingly found this anchorage with Robert Towler, a former student of Hostel and College, who had not been ordained but become a lecturer in sociology at Leeds.

In March 1971, towards the end of his second term, Hugh circulated a memorandum to a group of senior brethren about his difficulties with both institutional life and orthodoxy. They urged him nevertheless to stand again for a third term, partly because there was no obvious successor. After his re-election in January 1972 he made it clear that this was his final term. In memoranda of May and October 1973 he repeated his difficulties in stronger terms to the group, which on the latter occasion included Harry Williams. In October he sent all three memoranda to Archbishop Ramsey, the Visitor, and offered to resign then so a successor could be appointed in January 1974, who would be in place when the Archbishop made his Visitation arranged for July. But after consulting some senior brethren Ramsey counselled him not to resign but to complete his term of office until December 1974. He wrote to Hugh: 'I do indeed understand that your "faith" is sure – your "structuring" of it in terms of orthodoxy and institutions unsure; and I feel very much for those who so find themselves.' Trevor Huddleston, Bishop of Stepney, wrote to Hugh on 27 November after receiving the memoranda:

Indeed the memoranda are really only an amplification and development of what you were thinking, and of what you told me you were thinking, when we walked together during the Community retreat in 1966 ... I recognize so clearly in everything you wrote the ring of truth and the integrity which would make it impossible for me to be critical in any way ... I know in myself so many of the factors present to you ... I share with you, at a very deep level I think, a great distrust of the institutions presently claiming to express the truth of the Gospel. Also a great suspicion of all the elaborately structured answers to the mystery of life ... I suppose that my passionate belief in the Incarnation – which has been for me the force behind *all* my thinking and doing in social concern – is where, at that level, we differ most.

However, Hugh's inner turmoil had for some time been undermining his effectiveness and authority as Superior. Just before Christmas Trevor wrote to the Archbishop about the unhappy state of the Community as conveyed to him by some brethren. As a result on 2 January 1974, during Chapter, the Archbishop phoned Hugh to say that he had reconsidered his offer to resign and had concluded that this would now be the wisest course. Hugh asked the Prior (Donald Patey) to phone Lambeth and the Archbishop confirmed what he had said. On 3 January Hugh announced his resignation to a stunned Chapter and asked for a year's leave of absence. He left Mirfield the next day to stay with Robert Towler in Leeds. Patey, now temporarily in charge, spoke with heartfelt gratitude about Hugh's relationship with him as Prior. Patey hoped he might return to the Community and that he would visit Mirfield regularly. A few days later he did come over to attend Peter Hewitt's funeral but in June he asked for release from CR.

Brethren and friends of both Hugh and CR were still reeling from the shock of his resignation, and the new Superior had been in office for only a few months, when Hugh made a tragic misjudgment and agreed to appear on BBC television with Robert Towler to explain his difficulties with orthodoxy, his resignation and his withdrawal from CR. Almost immediately the programme began on 1 December he realized he had blundered. For the rest of his life he bitterly regretted its making and transmission. In 1982 he asked for (and received) forgiveness from the brethren for the hurt he had given them and particularly through this programme.[8]

Recovery

In May 1974 Eric Simmons, the Novice Guardian and former Warden of the Hostel, was elected Superior, the first to be educated at both Hostel and College. When the Archbishop installed him in July he expounded St Mark's account of the resurrection. 'The women come to the tomb. Who will move away the stone because the stone is very heavy? They look – the stone is gone! Something has happened beyond human hope, beyond human asking, beyond human resource!' (*CRQ* MD 1974). In fact CR took some years to recover. Hugh Bishop's resignation revealed as well as precipitated a crisis. The loss of a famous Superior was for CR one among many experiences of loss. The gravity of CR's crisis was brought home by the closure of the novitiate for three years, mainly because the Community was in such turmoil that it was not in a fit state to receive any novices. At July Chapter the new Superior told brethren that CR was facing a crisis, possibly even a catastrophe; it was ageing – how could it staff all its houses?; its past successes had gone to its head; the common life had deteriorated; perhaps CR needed to become a different type of community?

The church at large was also in crisis. After Vatican II there was an exodus from Roman Catholic Religious Orders. World-wide the number of Bene-dictines dropped by nearly fifteen per cent between 1960 and 1975; in 1969 alone, some 6,500 nuns left their communities. Some communities changed so rapidly that older members felt bitter and alienated; some changed so slowly that younger members left and novitiates dried up. Some of the brightest Roman Catholic priests in England left the ministry, including Charles Davis, a prominent theologian who in 1966 left the church as well. It made him feel he had 'rejoined the human race', he recalled in *A Question of Conscience* (1967). Many Anglican religious communities were also in turmoil. Between 1963 and 1988 the number of female Religious in the Church of England fell by over half – from 2,013 to 976. (By contrast the number of male Religious dropped only slightly in that period.) After the College at Kelham was included in the theological college closure programme of 1971, SSM had to rethink its life from top to bottom. The huge plant at Kelham with its remarkable chapel was put up for sale in 1973 and the brethren dispersed to smaller establishments. All theological colleges were in difficult straits. The number of those in training fell from 1,357 in 1963 to 728 in 1973. Morale in the colleges sank as they faced more closures for the second time in three years. Michael Ramsey retired to Cuddesdon in 1974 expecting to participate in the traditional life of the College he had known as an ordinand. But the Principal was a theological radical, the College amalgamated with Ripon Hall (a Modernist foundation) and students were uncertain about sexual morality. These various crises in the church were set within and affected by a grave national crisis. Inflation rose from nine per cent in 1972–3 to twenty-four per cent in 1974–5. Britain's oil import bill quadrupled after the Arab-Israeli war of 1973. An influential article in the *Times* (3 February 1975) argued that inflation was having such a dire effect on the Church of England that clergy would soon have to earn part of their living in secular jobs. At the CR Chapter in January 1974 the Bursar announced that the value of CR's investments had fallen by forty per cent in the previous six months. The General Election of February 1974 was held in the extraordinary context of a State of Emergency and a three-day working week. People asked: 'Has Britain become ungovernable?'

The catastrophe in CR which Simmons had feared did not happen, but CR experienced a gradual resurrection. This was largely due to his leadership over the next twelve exhausting years. He concluded his Commemoration Day sermon in 1981: 'The most defeating experience is always the place where God is waiting for us, waiting to begin again with us . . . This is how we are born again, as the Messiah himself was – in the grave' (*CRQ* MD 1981). Simon Holden, the new Novice Guardian, pointed out that our second birth, like the first, was often bloody and disorientating, (*CRQ* LD 1984). When the present Superior, Silvanus Berry, was elected in 1987 the Chronicler looked back at Eric Simmons' period of office:

> The Community would hardly exist but for Eric and his patient pulling it out of the Slough of Despond into which it had sunk in the 1970s. He brought order back into Community life, he re-affirmed the importance of its spiritual dimension and the priority of worship as well as of the common life . . . During Chapter Eric was conspicuously concerned that all should take due part and responsibility in decision making . . . Brethren who had remained silent for years in Chapter were enabled to speak.

He knew that he was not a powerful personality like Raynes or Bishop. He had no ambition to be (like them) a national figure in the affairs of the church. This was beneficial, for CR had been too dependent on magnetic Superiors. The pressure exerted on Bishop to stand for a third term and the refusal of brethren to allow him to resign in October 1973 had its earlier parallels when Talbot and Raynes also went on three years too long. So Eric constantly emphasized that work must be done by and with the Community. He quoted Mao Tse-Tung: 'When the job is done, the people will say we did it.' It was not easy to change from a paternal to a fraternal pattern, and a few felt lost without a dominant Superior. It was not the only loss (or gain).

CR had to face the painful fact that the spectacular glories of the work in Africa were now past – CR withdrew from its last two sizeable African institutions, Penhalonga and Rosettenville, in 1983 and 1986. The loss was particularly felt by those brethren who had been most fulfilled in African work and by those who had wanted to work in community as parish priests. The fact that CR now provides no similar outlet anywhere seriously diminishes the variety of its work and discourages this kind of priest (who at one time formed the bulk of the brethren) from joining.

Brethren were also affected by the decline of confident Anglo-Catholicism. When in 1978 and 1983, conferences at Loughborough tried to renew the Anglo-Catholic movement, many brethren were doubtful whether this could or should be attempted – a huge change from CR's earlier enthusiastic support for the Anglo-Catholic movement.[9] The English Church Census of 1990 revealed that the greatest decline was in those parishes which described themselves as 'Anglo-Catholic' or 'Broad'. The decay of Anglo-Catholicism, and particularly its lack of appeal for the young or for ordinands compared with Evangelicalism, has obviously affected vocations to the Religious Life. Contemporary Anglo-Catholic priests do not press for vocations to the Religious Life with the fervour of their predecessors. Older brethren lament how rarely now brethren are asked to speak about their life in Anglo-Catholic (or any other) parishes. In the Catholic tradition the celibate was once looked up to. Now the celibate is more often than not suspect or pitied. Yet as Archbishop Habgood writes:

> ... in the long-term the future lies with Catholicism. It must because only Catholic tradition is rich enough and stable enough to be able to offer something distinctive to the world without being captured by the world. But it must be a Catholicism which is true to its highest vision, and hence broad enough, hospitable enough, rooted sufficiently in sacramental reality, confident enough in its inheritance to be able to do new things, diverse enough, and yet passionately enough concerned about unity, to be genuinely universal ... A parish in my own diocese has, as I write this, advertised a Mass for 'the maintenance of Catholic Faith and Order in the Church of England' complete with a 'procession to the crowned statue of our Lady Queen of Heaven' and 'veneration of the relic of Saint Pius V'. I do not wish to carp ... but it is plain that the Catholic future cannot possibly lie in that direction.[10]

CR arose out of Gore's Liberal Catholicism. Though the meaning of that term changed over the years, and though the liberal tradition in CR was for a time eclipsed (though never extinguished), CR's basic instincts have remained liberal. In the 1980s liberals of all kinds were dismissed as 'woolly' and 'wet' by the prevailing ideology. It is probably significant that the 'Affirming Catholicism' movement, which seeks to recover a Liberal Catholicism, was launched in the same year that Mrs Thatcher was dethroned.

The creation of CR was inspired by Christian socialism. Though this rather declined in the Talbot years, it revived during and immediately after the second war. But in recent years Christian socialism has suffered from the same bewilderment as secular socialism. So Groser, who had been quite clear about socialist aims in the inter-war years when he was fighting for social justice in the East End, was bewildered in the 1950s when so many of those aims had been attained and the Christian commonwealth had still not arrived. The political consensus established during the war had become so tired and complacent that the startling shift in ideology in 1979 took place with remarkable ease. Though the CR Chronicler reported in 1979 that brethren continued to be 'largely right-wing socialist', they no longer proclaimed their convictions on public platforms. The fact that no Chronicler since then has commented on the political outlook of the brethren is another indication that Christian socialism has ceased to be a dynamic force in CR.

In the early and middle years of CR a number of brethren were Evangelical Catholics – Frere, Bickersteth, Bull, Figgis and Rees, for example. Probably Curtis was the last of this line. Evangelical Catholicism re-entered CR through four brethren who in the 1960s were affected by the Charismatic Movement. However the two youngest and most dynamic Charismatics left CR in the 1980s. CR's cerebral nut was too hard to crack. Humphrey Whistler played an important part in the Yorkshire Charismatic Revival. Latterly he spent periods at Lee Abbey, the Evangelical community, where he died in 1980. When he despaired of changing CR, one brother consoled him: 'Every fifth brick you drop, Humphrey, becomes in time a foundation stone!' He was greatly loved in Battyeford parish where he was honorary curate. Dominic Whitnall continues this vital link. Giles Ormerod's long and memorable ministry as a lay reader at the mission church (known as 'St Giles' Cathedral') resulted in several ordinands and a deepening of the whole life of the congregation.

From the first CR was committed to evangelism. But since the 1960s, like other Christians who are not Evangelicals, many brethren have seemed uncertain about the nature and purpose of evangelism. From 1903 CR had prayed for grace for its ordinands 'to prepare in all earnestness and zeal, that with entire consecration of heart and life they may labour hereafter in thy holy priesthood, and convert many sinners and save many souls'. Since 1979 the last phrase ('convert many sinners and save many souls') has been omitted. But no other definition of the priest's evangelistic work was substituted. Or again, the evangelistic side of Commemoration Day has been greatly curtailed. The tradition begun in the 1930s of putting on mainly religious plays continued until the end of the 1960s – the professionalism of post-war plays owed much to Pamela Keily, Drama Advisor to the Northern Province. Since 1972 plays have ceased and been replaced by a brass band and a Punch-and-Judy show. Numbers have remained high – 4–5,000 on average. Again, there have been no Quarry sermons since 1958. To the deep distress of evangelistically-minded brethren like Whistler, part of the amphitheatre was allowed to relapse into a bosky dell. The cessation of the sermons reflected not only changes in CR but a quite startling alteration in English religion. Quite suddenly in the late 1950s English Christians, even Nonconformists, would no longer flock to sermons.[11]

However, CR developed new forms of evangelism as well as continuing to conduct a (decreasing) number of parish missions. Sometimes evangelism, influenced by Charles de Foucauld and the French worker-priests, was expressed in terms of reparation and presence. So Barnabas Dugdale joined half a million at an Isle of Wight pop festival simply (he wrote) to be present, not to evangelize. A group of brethren and sisters conducted a mission in a mental hospital using methods derived from group therapy. A mission to Wormwood Scrubs used not only chapel services but also low-key conversations which might start with comparisons between the respective cells and disciplines of inmates and brethren. Gerard Beaumont and Jeremy Platt lived in Hemel Hempstead for some months to deepen the spirituality of parishioners. Jeremy made contact with local people by working as a floor-sweeper in a factory. When Bernard Chamberlain was a member of CR and the Bishop of Wakefield's Advisor on Community Relations he explored new frontiers. He and Whistler ran seaside multi-racial and multi-faith house parties. In 1979 he and Crispin Harrison ran a Jewish-Christian weekend at Mirfield which started with biblical charades to break the ice and went on to a sharing of the Sabbath and then the Sunday worship of the Community. In 1979 Chamberlain participated in the International Muslim Convention at Dewsbury with 8,000 resident and nearly twice that number as daily attenders. In 1978, 1980 and 1983 he and other brethren organized Anglo-Caribbean Festivals at Mirfield which also included local Vietnamese and Pakistani Christians. The decline of recent years in the members of FR and in the readership of the *CR Quarterly* reflected CR's withdrawal from frontier work. Aidan Mayoss, who pioneered the renewal of FR in 1967, is now engaged on a second rejuvenation and Nicolas Stebbing is seeking a wider readership for the *CR Quarterly*.

Until the 1940s CR drew a high proportion of novices from the top drawers of society who went on to provide the self-confident leadership of their class. When Harry Williams arrived in 1969 from Trinity College Cambridge, where the undergraduates under his care had included Prince Charles, he was twitted by some brethren (he records) because of his supposed taste for the grand life. But when C R was 'Ted Talbot's Community' the fact that a novice knew the Prince of Wales would have been treated as fairly unremarkable. The incident illustrates the changed social composition of C R. Other important feeders into C R have changed character or dried up. Until a generation ago many arrived after a long period of institutional life in preparatory and public school, Oxbridge (or Leeds/Mirfield), theological college and sometimes clergy house. But since the 1960s all educational institutions, even public schools and Oxbridge colleges, have modified many aspects of the common life, and some institutions have abandoned it altogether. The young enthusiastic Christian of today is more attracted to a Franciscan than a Benedictine spirituality. In the late 1950s the bishops were still exhorting ordinands to remain unmarried for the first few years. The practice of remaining unmarried for a few years after training was also common in other professions. Today many ordinands are older men with families. So clergy houses have almost disappeared. The attenuation or disappearance of the common life in educational institutions and the decline of celibacy undertaken for vocational or economic reasons affects the supply and character of novices, particularly to a community like C R which is more Benedictine than Franciscan. When novices now come from more diverse backgrounds and are as likely to be laymen as priests, the formation provided by the novitiate becomes crucially important. Once again radical change has brought gain as well as loss.

C R has also had to face the loss of some of its most promising and prominent brethren. Since 1960 some twenty-four professed brethren have withdrawn. In 1972 there were seventy-seven brethren in C R, two prelate brothers and eight Houses. In 1991 there were forty-four brethren, three prelate brothers and four Houses.

Since the crisis broke in 1974 C R has engaged in much self-scrutiny. Brethren looked back at the Visitation Charges of Michael Ramsey. He had exhorted them not to be so obsessed with liturgical change that they forgot that worship was 'a window into the life of God himself'; to remember that silence 'changelessly represents eternity'; to practise the art of genuinely collective discussion and decision-taking; to be less activist and to pay more attention to the quality of the common life. But he was not the one who could help C R to rediscover its partly lost sense of mission. The commissioning of the two reports by Trevor Verryn showed that C R was now ready to admit that it needed outside help. He defined C R's character as 'permanently experiment-al'. Brethren needed to accept their painful sense of powerlessness and humiliation and to meditate on these as experiences of Christ. In 1978 C R courageously invited twenty-one men and women, some still in their teens, some in their sixties, from eighteen experimental communities – Anglican, Roman Catholic and non-denominational, some Charismatic and Evangelical – to share life at Mirfield for ten days. Reactions varied greatly from deep admiration to sharp criticism. They all thought that CR had not yet discovered its full potential (*CRQ* LD 1978). As a result of these and other exercises brethren asked many questions. Do we expect the Superior to carry too heavy a load? Should vows be permanent or for a term of years? Is the Mother House too institutional? What is our understanding of obedience, chastity, sexuality, simplicity of life? How much openness and privacy do we need in the common life? How wide a plurality of belief and practice is compatible with membership of CR?

'Monastic witness is an ecumenical witness', wrote Aelred Stubbs. 'Since Vatican II we have a quite new sense of sharing a common vocation with our Roman Catholic brothers and sisters in religion.'[12] The CR committee which has been revising the Rule and Constitution since 1985 has benefited from this new ecumenical perspective, but as CR does not belong to one of the historic families like the Anglican Benedictines and Franciscans, it needs to have confidence in its own call and character. CR now defines this as living 'the baptismal vocation through a commitment to community life, sustained by common worship, and issuing in works that are primarily of a public character', and 'called specially to public, prophetic witness to the Christian hope of the Kingdom'. It remains to be seen how this – the most major constitutional revision in the history of CR – affects the life of the Community. During our century, ecumenists, liturgists and constitutional reformers in the Church of England have worked patiently to construct water-courses only to discover that they had sometimes miscalculated where the rain was going to fall. CR's future will be largely determined by the character of those who join it and by the extent to which it is prepared to take risks in exercising that 'public, prophetic witness to the Christian hope of the Kingdom'.

The reopening of the novitiate in 1977 was one sign that CR's sadness and depression were beginning to lift. The first professions for six years took place in 1979. Holden, then Novice Guardian, wrote of the novitiate as 'a space in a person's life, where the conditions are so structured, and so experienced, as to enable that person to make an authentic decision and commitment, whatever that decision and commitment may be'. We 'need to discern how far a Novice has the human equipment to journey and explore beyond the normal boundaries of everyday life . . . it is in the experience of being alone with God that a person works out the growth that is being called from him or her' (*CRQ* CD 1984). He was also keenly aware that there was a danger that Religious evaded risks and like other Christians used religion as a protection from the vastness of experience so the ark of salvation became a 'comfortable slave ship' (*CRQ* JB 1977, LD 1985).

Princess Margaret became the first woman to dine in the refectory when she attended CR's seventy-fifth birthday in 1967. From 1976 other women guests were able to eat there too. Nuns began to be invited to minister to the brethren as Community retreat-conductors and as guides for individual

Ignatian retreats. A few brethren also trained to be able to give Ignatian retreats.

There were other hopeful signs. The Church (which had been completed with an entrance porch in 1973) was redecorated in 1977 for the first time for fifteen years. New movable stalls were placed in the Chapel of the Resurrection and are arranged in a horse-shoe for the daily corporate eucharist. Under Peter Allan the music of worship has attained the highest standard within living memory. Frere had pioneered a plainsong revival. In 1991 Allan and other editors published *An English Kyriale*, a pioneering collection of congregational chants for the eucharist. Guiver, also professed in recent years, shows a remarkable capacity to combine liturgical scholarship with pungency of language in *Company of Voices* (1988) and in *Faith in Momentum* (1990). He produces an exhilarating variety of examples ranging from eighteenth-century Transylvania to Fred Astaire, and includes lessons learned from visits to both Milan and the Battyeford Co-op.

It would be foolish to try to calculate the gains and losses in CR since 1974. The brethren are more united and more tolerant – if some now work happily with Protestants there is also a monthly voluntary service of prayer before the Blessed Sacrament. CR is now less self-conscious – gone are the days when a Novice Guardian could suggest that novices should wear cassocks even to dig the garden. One of the most obvious gains is that CR no longer acts as if it knew all the answers – it now asks to be ministered to by a great variety of men and women. The new style Visitations now conducted by the Bishop of Salisbury (John Austin Baker) with a nun and an administrator are more searching than any previous ones, and the Visitation Charges are probably the most trenchant that CR has ever heard. Yet the losses, some of which were discussed earlier, are real and painful; some are beneficial; some suggest an agenda which is yet to be tackled.

Midwinter spring

'Midwinter spring is its own season' – so begins Eliot's 'Little Gidding'. The phrase refers in part to those twenty years when in the mid-seventeenth century the only Anglican religious community between the dissolution and the nineteenth-century revival lived and prayed in a hamlet in Huntingdonshire. But Eliot is also describing a stage in the spiritual journey when the winter sunlight, the 'transitory blossom of snow' on the hedgerow and the quivering of the 'soul's sap' promise a spring which is still in the future. So it seems with the Community of the Resurrection. Resurrection is given only when the cup of suffering is drained – it is *given* not engineered. To use psychological language, a neurosis only abates when it has completed its purgatorial work.

One can quantify the members of a religious community but not their faithfulness or their prayer.[13] In any community it is often those who do not attract great attention (and who may not appear in a history like this) who provide many of the bonds which bind it together. Fr Jean Leclercq OSB told the nuns at Fairacres: 'Just to be there, like a beast, as the Psalm says, without an answer, but simply keeping on, persevering. Patience, stability, *patientia*, *stabilitas*, not to leave . . .' Among the interlocking variety of vocations within creation (see Hopkins' poem 'As kingfishers catch fire') there must be room for those who, like the Old Testament prophets, act out disturbing question marks against the conventionalities. The cultivation of silence is one such prophetic act. Kierkegaard wrote: 'the first thing to be done is, procure silence, introduce silence; God's Word cannot be heard, and if, served by noisy expedients, it is to be shouted out so clamorously so as to be heard in the midst of the din, it is no longer God's Word.'[14] Perhaps the Religious has a particular vocation to use this silence to confront the terrifying dark side of God of whom R. S. Thomas writes in his bleak poems. Religious also need to deliver us from the tyranny of both secular hope and secular despair by being an eschatological sign, like the eucharist itself, of the final community which St Augustine described at the end of his *City of God*. Cuthbert Hallward of CR wrote in 1934: 'What seems to me to emerge out of the jumble of one's experience is that to live in charity is the hardest, the most surprisingly hard and most worthwhile of all ideals.'

Thomas Merton, after a long painful journey in which he had to shed the romantic monasticism with which he began, spoke of the monk as a 'marginal person'. CR has been most true to itself when it has taken risks and freed itself to live on the margins, on the frontiers and internalized that experience in prayer. One type of pioneering is clearly over. But there are other frontiers in a Decade of Evangelism in response to *Faith in the City* – perhaps a risky, embodied, combined response to both? Some frontiers are unexpected, hidden. Hilary Beasley, once a keen athlete, has spent long periods in hospital. Of this frontier he wrote:

> . . . much of the meaning of all this lies hidden in Gethsemane. Blind, cruel, pointless, total blackness, an agony beyond words. An agony which has been repeated in so many people . . . Agony which has been accepted, not passively, but has been faced and lived through. And from which sprang incredible victory and joy. And when the night goes on or the darkness comes and goes, when faith and hope lie shattered, there comes the faint knowledge that God knows what it costs, that he has been along the path and he still walks with us.[15]

Northcott used to say that religious communities manage to survive more or less satisfactorily for their first eighty years then lose touch with the original ideals of their foundation. Gore believed passionately that the Community should be a paradigm for church and society. God's character was righteous, hence Gore's commitment to social justice whether through CSU or his efforts to bring peace to the coal industry in the 1920s. Jeremiah asked the king: 'Did not your father eat and drink and do justice and righteousness . . . He judged the cause of the poor and needy . . . Is not this to know me? says the Lord' (22.15–16). At first Gore lived theologically on the frontier and though he later became defensive, his sense of the absurd witnessed to another more supple and apophatic theology. His commitment to the kenosis of Christ expressed itself in CR, CSU and his rejection of establishment Christianity. He was grateful for the English tradition, yet longed for a multi-racial Catholicism – his final collapse was caused by his six months' fascinated tour of India undertaken in his late seventies.[16]

Words which Norman Goodacre, a noted spiritual director, wrote in 1977 after forty years of annual retreats at Mirfield will be echoed by many people as CR celebrates its centenary:

A Community of the Resurrection you are, and that is what I have experienced when staying with you. (*CRQ* LD 1978)

Notes

1. Seek the Beginnings

1. Michael Ramsey in Paul Avis, *Gore: Construction and Conflict*, Churchman 1988, p. 4; E. F. Braley (ed.), *Letters of Herbert Hensley Henson*, SPCK 1950, pp. 68–9; cf. Ronald Jasper, *Arthur Cayley Headlam*, Faith Press 1960, p. 358; Adrian Hastings, *A History of English Christianity 1920–1985*, Collins 1986, pp. 82–4; third enlarged edition, *A History of English Christianity 1920–1990*, SCM Press and Trinity Press International 1991. See also James Carpenter, *Gore: A Study in Liberal Catholic Thought*, Faith Press 1960 – full bibliography; Gordon Crosse, *Charles Gore*, Mowbray 1932; John Gore, *Charles Gore, Father and Son*, John Murray 1932, 'Reminiscences 1971' (tape in Wimbledon Reference Library); G. L. Prestige, *The Life of Charles Gore*, Heinemann 1935; E. K. Talbot 'Charles Gore' in G. P. Pawson CR, (ed.) *Edward Keble Talbot*, SPCK 1954. Only a small amount of the manuscript material on which Prestige based his *Life* survives in the Mirfield archives and at the Borthwick Institute at York. There is, however, an extensive collection of newspaper cuttings about Gore at Mirfield. The material collected by Albert Mansbridge for a biographical study of Gore (and upon which Prestige drew) is in the Mansbridge Papers (65352–65362) in the British Library. Apart from a typescript of Nash's reminiscences (also in the Mirfield archives) there is virtually nothing about the early days of CR. The Liddon Papers (Keble College, Oxford) include a few letters from Gore to Liddon about his move to and life at Pusey House.

2. Stephen Paget (ed.), *Henry Scott Holland*, John Murray 1921; J. Heidt, *The Social Theology of Henry Scott Holland* (unpublished Oxford DPhil thesis 1975).

3. B. F. Westcott, *Disciplined Life: Three Addresses*, Macmillan 1886, pp. 3–15; in the Second Address (1870) Westcott suggested an association of families living under a common rule. Arthur Westcott, *Life and Letters of Brooke Foss Westcott*, Macmillan 1903, vol. I, p. 194.

4. See David Newsome, *Two Classes of Men*, John Murray 1974, Appendix F and 'The Assault on Mammon: Charles Gore and John Neville Figgis', *Journal of Ecclesiastical History*, October 1966; A. R. Vidler, *F. D. Maurice and Company*, SCM Press 1966, ch. 13. Cf influence of Westcott on C. F. Andrews: *What I owe to Christ*, Hodder 1933, pp. 81, 131.

5. Melvin Richter, *The Politics of Conscience: T. H. Green and his Age*, Weidenfeld and Nicolson, 1964.

6. Preface to *The Life and Work of John Richard Illingworth* edited by his wife, John

Murray 1917; includes accounts of the Holy Party, *Lux Mundi* and Longworth meetings.

7. Paget, op. cit., pp. 94–5; Henry Scott Holland, *A Bundle of Memories*, Wells Gardner, Darton 1915, pp. 63–4; Newsome, *Two Classes*, p. 88.

8. George Longridge, *A History of the Oxford Mission to Calcutta*, John Murray 1900.

9. Georgina Battiscombe, *John Keble*, Constable 1963; Perry Butler (ed.), *Pusey Rediscovered*, SPCK 1983; David Forrester, *Young Dr Pusey*, (Mowbray 1989), which tells the full story of Pusey's marriage for the first time; H. P. Liddon, *Life of Edward Bouverie Pusey*, Longmans, Green & Co., four volumes 1893–7.

10. Bernard Holland (ed.), *Baron Friedrich von Hügel: Selected Letters*, J. M. Dent & Son 1927, p. 254.

11. Holland, *Bundle*, pp. 99, 101.

12. J. O. Johnston, *Life and Letters of Henry Parry Liddon*, Longmans Green & Co. 1904; R. F. Wilson, H. P. Liddon, *The Memorial to Dr Pusey*, Rivingtons 1883.

13. J. F. Briscoe (ed.), *V. S. S. Coles*, Mowbray 1930.

14. Charles Gore, *The Incarnation of the Son of God*, John Murray 1891, p. 36.

15. See Carpenter, op. cit., ch. 7.

16. R. D. Middleton, 'Charles Gore', *Theology*, January 1953.

17. See A. M. Allchin, *The Silent Rebellion*, SCM Press 1958; P. F. Anson, *The Call of the Cloister*, SPCK 1956; Michael Hill, *The Religious Order*, Heinemann 1973. Histories of individual communities include: Valerie Bonham, *A Joyous Service: The Clewer Sisters and their Work*, Convent of St John the Baptist, Windsor 1989; Peter Mayhew, *All Saints*, Society of All Saints Oxford 1987; Sisters of the Church, *A Valiant Victorian*, Mowbray 1964; Barrie Williams, *The Franciscan Revival in the Anglican Communion*, Darton, Longman and Todd 1982; Thomas Jay Williams, *Priscilla Lydia Sellon*, SPCK 1950.

18. See Graham Davies, 'Squires in the East End?', *Theology*, July 1983; J. Embry, *The Catholic Movement and the Society of the Holy Cross*, Faith Press 1931; John Kent, *Holding the Fort: Studies in Victorian Revivalism*, Epworth 1978; J. E. B. Munson, 'The Oxford Movement by the End of the Nineteenth Century', *Church History*, Sept. 1975.

19. See Lionel James, *A Forgotten Genius: Sewell of St Columba's and Radley*, Faber 1945; Brian Heeney, *Mission to the Middle Classes: The Woodard Schools 1848–1891*, SPCK 1969.

20. *Report of Church Congress*, Bemrose & Sons 1888, pp. 728–30.

21. Placid Murray, *Newman the Oratorian*, Gill and Macmillan, Dublin 1969, pp. 191–2, 209–10 et passim.

22. See e.g. John Gott, *The Parish Priest of the Town*, SPCK 1887; Rosemary O'Day, 'The Clerical Renaissance' in Gerald Parsons (ed.), *Religion in Victorian Britain* (*RVB*), MUP 1988, vol. I; Anthony Russell, *The Clerical Profession*, SPCK 1980.

23. G. Rowell (ed.), *Tradition Renewed*, Darton, Longman and Todd 1986, pp. 64–7, 218.

24. Albert Mansbridge, *Edward Stuart Talbot and Charles Gore*, J. M. Dent 1935, p. 90; Gore, *Incarnation*, p. 110.

25. On Christian socialism and CSU see Percy Dearmer, 'The Beginnings of the CSU', *Commonwealth*, May 1912; Donald Gray, *Earth and Altar*, Canterbury Press 1986; K. S. Inglis, *Churches and the Working Classes in Victorian England*, Routledge 1963; Peter d'A. Jones, *The Christian Socialist Revival 1877–1914*, Princeton 1968;

Edward Norman, *Church and Society in England 1770–1970*, OUP 1976, *The Victorian Christian Socialists*, CUP 1987; Maurice B. Reckitt, *Faith and Society*, Longmans Green & Co. 1932, *Maurice to Temple*, Faber 1947, *For Christ and the People*, SPCK 1968; Gwendolen Stephenson, *Edward Stuart Talbot*, SPCK 1936, pp. 332–343. There is a collection of CSU pamphlets at Mirfield. For Hancock's sermon on Mary see *RVB* III, pp. 98–101.

26. Arthur Ponsonby, *Henry Ponsonby*, Macmillan 1942, p. 379.

27. Beatrice Webb, *My Apprenticeship*, Penguin 1938, vol. 1, pp. 203–9.

28. See Standish Meacham, *Toynbee Hall and Social Reform 1880–1914*, (Yale 1987); Inglis, op. cit. ch. 4.

29. Gore, *Incarnation*, pp. 38–9, 110, 211.

30. Forrester, op. cit., pp. 153–60; J. H. L. Rowlands, *Church, State and Society*, Churchman 1989.

31. On *Lux Mundi*, see Avis, op. cit.; Newsome, *Two Classes*; A. M. Ramsey, *From Gore to Temple*, Longmans 1960; two centenary symposia: R. Morgan (ed.), *The Religion of the Incarnation*, Bristol Classical Press 1989; G. Wainwright (ed.), *Keeping the Faith*, SPCK 1989.

32. Peter Hinchliff, *John William Colenso*, Nelson 1964, pp. 44, 95, 113. For attitudes of Liddon and Pusey to assertions that Christ's knowledge was limited, see Hinchliff, p. 178; *CRQ* CD 1933, p. 11.

33. See Peter Hinchliff, *Benjamin Jowett and the Christian Religion*, OUP 1987, 'Jowett and Gore', *Theology*, July 1984.

34. Paget, op. cit., p. 112.

35. Johnston, op. cit., ch. XIII. In 1885 Bishop King tried to persuade Liddon to hand over the task of writing Pusey's biography to two other authors because this prolonged work was making Liddon ill. It is probable that King, like other friends of Liddon, was also concerned that Liddon's immersion in Pusey's writings was making him gloomy and rigid. See Barry Orford CR 'A Letter to Liddon', *CRQ* JB 1989.

36. J. G. Lockhart, *Charles Lindley Viscount Halifax*, Geoffrey Bles 1935–6, vol. II, chs III, XIII.

37. S. C. Carpenter, review of Prestige's *Life*, *Theology*, December 1935; J. Conway Davies, 'Charles Gore', *Theology*, November 1932.

38. See F. L. Cross, *Darwell Stone*, Dacre Press 1943.

39. On SSJE see Anson, op. cit., Allchin, op. cit.; Martin L. Smith (ed.), *Benson of Cowley*, OUP 1980; M. V. Woodgate, *Father Benson*, Geoffrey Bles 1953.

40. M. Gibbard SSJE, 'R. M. Benson', *Theology*, May 1966, p. 197; W. H. Longridge SSJE (ed.), *Spiritual Letters of Richard Meux Benson*, Mowbray 1924, p. 10.

41. On SDC, see J. Adderley, *In Slums and Society*, Fisher Unwin 1916; Kathleen E. Burne, *The Life and Letters of Father Andrew*, Mowbray 1948; Geoffrey Curtis CR, *William of Glasshampton*, SPCK 1947; T. P. Stevens, *Fr Adderley*, Werner Laurie 1943.

42. W. H. Longridge, op. cit., pp. vii–xvii.

2. *The First Decade*

1. C. S. Phillips et al., *Walter Howard Frere*, Faber 1947. The Frere papers are in the Mirfield archives and the Borthwick Institute. On Frere's Diary see *CRQ* JB 1984.

The two letters of 1931 and 1934 by Frere to Mansbridge and Prestige about Gore quoted on pp. 51, 52 are in the Mansbridge Papers (65352) and the Frere papers (Deposit 5, Borthwick) respectively.

2. M. C. Bickersteth, *A Sketch of the Life and Episcopate of the Right Reverend Robert Bickersteth*, Rivingtons 1887; D. N. Hempton, 'Bickerstetch, Bishop of Ripon', *RVB*, vol. IV.

3. Owen Chadwick, *Hensley Henson*, OUP 1983, p. 41.

4. See Robert Holland, 'An American View of the Pusey House', *Church Times* 3, 10 July 1893, describing a visit of 1890–1, in which he emphasized the social mission of the embryonic community. In 1891 Holland was charged by John Carter with the creation of the CSU in the United States: see Jones, op. cit., pp. 189ff.

5. For Victorian rural parochial life see e.g.: Owen Chadwick, *The Victorian Church*, A. & C. Black 1970, vol. II (IV); James Obelkevich, *Religion and Rural Society*, OUP 1976; Gerald Parsons, 'A Question of Meaning: Religion and Working Class Life', *RVB*, vol. II.

6. See article on Gore by Canon Peter Green ('Artifex'), *Manchester Guardian*, 27 January 1932.

7. For male attitudes to church and eucharist, see Alan Wilkinson, *The Church of England and the First World War*, SPCK 1978, chs 5–7 (hereafter *CEFWW*).

8. Farrar (who had been Gore's form master) had proposed the creation of brotherhoods under dispensable vows to work in urban areas. He was not advocating a revival of monasticism. See *Chronicle* Convocation of Canterbury 5 July 1889, 12 February 1890; *Report of Church Congress*, Bemrose & Sons 1890.

9. Frederick Douglas How, *Bishop Walsham How*, Isbister 1898, pp. 362–3.

10. *Church Times*, 28 July–11 August 1893.

11. *Report of Church Congress*, Bemrose & Sons 1896, p. 563.

12. See Sheila Fletcher, *Maude Royden*, Blackwell 1989; Brian Heeney, *The Women's Movement in the Church of England 1850–1930*, OUP 1988; Alan Wilkinson, 'Three Sexual Issues', *Theology*, March 1988.

13. See G. K. A. Bell, *Randall Davidson*, OUP 1952 edition, pp. 127–31; James Bentley, *Ritualism and Politics in Victorian Britain*, OUP 1978. On the organizational response of the Church of England to social change, see Kenneth Thompson, *Bureaucracy and Church Reform*, OUP 1970.

14. *Report of Church Congress*, Bemrose & Sons 1896, pp. 342–6.

15. Norman, *Christian Socialists*. On churches' attitudes to the Anglo-Boer War see D. W. Bebbington, *The Nonconformist Conscience*, Allen & Unwin 1982; Margaret Blunden, 'The Anglican Church during the War' in Peter Warwick (ed.), *The South African War*, Longman 1980; Wilkinson, *CEFWW*.

16. See Mark Girouard, *The Return to Camelot, Chivalry and the English Gentleman*, Yale 1981; David Newsome, *Godliness and Good Learning*, John Murray 1961; Peter Parker, *The Old Lie: The Great War and the Public School Ethos*, Constable 1987.

17. On Dolling, see J. Clayton, *Father Dolling*, preface by Henry Scott Holland, Wells Gardner, Darton 1902; R. Dolling, *Ten Years in a Portsmouth Slum*, Swan Sonnenschein 1897; C. E. Osborne, *The Life of Father Dolling*, Edward Arnold 1903; Alan Wilkinson, 'Victorian Priest's Faith in the City', *Church Times*, 27 May 1988.

3. *Mirfield*

1. David Foss, 'A Little Local Counter-Reformation', *CRQ* MD 1988. For a general history of the area, see H. N. Pobjoy, *A History of Mirfield*, The Ridings Publishing Company 1969.

2. I am grateful to the staff of Dewsbury Public Library for drawing my attention to Frederick Glover, *Dewsbury Mills* (Leeds PhD thesis 1959), a copy of which is in the library; also to the staff there and at Mirfield, Heckmondwike and Huddersfield Libraries for supplying information about the area and the Heckmondwike Lecture.

3. Joseph H. Hird, *Mirfield, Life in a West Riding Village 1900–1914*, Kirklees Metropolitan Council 1984. Hird's critique of the church was in a long tradition of working-class protest; see e.g. T. Wright, 'The Working Classes and the Church' (1868), in *RVB* vol. III, pp. 321–6; Chadwick, *Victorian Church*, vol. II, pp. 262–9.

4. Tom Steele: *Alfred Orage and the Leeds Arts Club 1893–1923*, Scolar Press 1990. (I am indebted to the Revd Graham Kent for drawing my attention to this book.)

5. Paul B. Bull, *The Revival of the Religious Life*, Edward Arnold 1914. Dolling in a CSU sermon of 1895 (Osborne, op. cit., ch. XVIII), also criticized clerical marriage: wives and families encouraged upper-class pretensions, so removing priests from the world of the workers. He contended that clergy educated in public schools and universities would never understand working men. But Dolling himself was educated at Harrow and Cambridge. See also Francis G. Belton (ed.), *Ommanney of Sheffield*, Centenary Press 1936, p. 31.

6. Betty Askwith, *Two Victorian Families*, Chatto & Windus 1971; A. C. Benson, *Hugh*, Smith, Elder & Co. 1915; R. H. Benson, *Confessions of a Convert*, Longmans Green & Co. 1913; C. C. Martindale, *Life of Monsignor Robert Hugh Benson*, Longmans Green & Co. 1916; C. C. Martindale (ed.), *Sermon Notes by the late Monsignor Robert Hugh Benson – First Series: Anglican*, Longmans Green & Co. 1917; David Williams, *Genesis and Exodus*, Hamish Hamilton 1979.

7. Penelope Fitzgerald, *The Knox Brothers*, Macmillan 1977; Evelyn Waugh, *Ronald Knox*, Chapman and Hall 1959.

8. Quoted Peter F. Anson, *Abbot Extraordinary*, Faith Press 1958, p. 124.

9. Quoted Jones, op. cit., p. 75.

10. *Report of Church Congress*, Bemrose & Son 1906, pp. 19–27.

11. Kent, op. cit., pp. 242–57, 289–94; see also Gerald Parsons 'Emotion and Piety: Revivalism and Ritualism in Victorian Christianity', *RVB*, Vol. I.

12. W. H. Frere, *English Church Ways*, John Murray 1914, pp. 81–2.

13. See Geoffrey Rowell, *Hell and the Victorians*, OUP 1974; Wilkinson, *CEFWW* ch. 8.

14. On Skipworth see *The Builder*, 18 May 1895; 24 Oct. 1903; 16 June 1906; 20, 27 April 1907; A. Stuart Gray, *Edwardian Architecture*, Duckworth 1985.

15. On Tapper see Gray, op.cit.; typed memoir by Michael Tapper in RIBA Library, London; *Builder*, 30 May, 13 June 1903; 1 Oct. 1904; 2 Oct. 1909. Some of Tapper's various designs for the Church at Mirfield are preserved at Mirfield and in the RIBA Drawings Collection. The RIBA Collection also includes Tapper's plans for Liverpool Cathedral. St Cuthbert's Copnor, Portsmouth (by E. Stanley Hall, 1914–15) is the only Anglican parish church known to me which was *deeply* influenced in its design by Westminster Cathedral.

16. Some of the original All Saints' Lay Sisters came from humble backgrounds, some were illiterate. The first was professed in 1863. They were told not to 'carry their heads high' and to accept reproofs in silence. Despite pressure from the Chaplain General (a Cowley Father) and Bishop Furse of St Albans in the 1920s, the Choir Sisters resisted amalgamation until discontent among Lay Sisters forced matters to a head and Furse persuaded the Community to remove this division in 1932. (Mayhew, op. cit., pp. 37, 49, 203–4).

17. John Lambert Rees, *Timothy Rees of Mirfield and Llandaff*, Mowbray 1945, pp. 27–8.

4. *Crises and Controversies*

1. The Gore-Temple correspondence is in vol. 6 of the Frederick Temple Papers at Lambeth Palace Library.

2. The Frere-Davidson correspondence is in the Mirfield archives. Vols 423–4 of the Davidson Papers at Lambeth Palace Library includes also the wider correspondence about CR during Davidson's Visitorship. There are 850 items in the two volumes. Why did G. K. A. Bell entirely omit the controversy from his huge *Life* of Davidson (1935)? Because Frere was still Bishop of Truro? Because it showed Davidson in an unfavourable light?

3. For Davidson's Charge of 1899 and the Dolling controversy see Bell, op. cit., pp. 257–80.

4. There is a collection of press cuttings about the Church House meeting and a number of protestant pamphlets about CR in the Mirfield archives.

5. See R. W. F. Beaken, *Percy Dearmer* (Lambeth Diploma Thesis 1989), pp. 63–75.

6. An earlier meeting (probably in late 1903) had been held at the Town Hall, Mirfield by the Church Association and the National Protestant League at which Frere had responded to violent attacks on CR. It seems to have been prompted by the creation of the College and Benson's secession.

7. T. G. Fullerton, *Father Burn of Middlesborough*, G. F. Sewell, Bradford 1927.

8. For the roles of Davidson and Gore in relation to the Caldey community, see Rene M. Kollar, 'Archbishop Davidson, Bishop Gore and Abbot Carlyle' in W. J. Sheils (ed.), *Studies in Church History*, vol. XXII, Blackwell 1985.

9. There is a valuable Leeds University essay 'The Community of the Resurrection and Socialism 1893–1914' by Phil Knights, to which I am indebted, in the Mirfield archives.

10. On Figgis see D. G. Nicholls, *Authority in Church and State: Aspects of the thought of J. N. Figgis and his Contemporaries* (unpublished Cambridge PhD Thesis 1962); Maurice G. Tucker, *John Neville Figgis*, SPCK 1950; J. M. Turner, 'J. N. Figgis: Anglican Prophet', *Theology*, Oct. 1975. The Figgis papers are at Mirfield and the Borthwick Institute.

11. J. N. Figgis, *Some Defects in English Religion*, Robert Scott 1917, p. 47; *Anti-Christ and other Sermons*, Longmans, Green & Co. 1913, pp. 77–8.

12. J. N. Figgis, *Civilization at the Cross Roads*, Longmans, Green & Co. 1912, pp. 125–6; *Hopes for English Religion*, Longmans, Green & Co. 1919, p. 53; *Churches in the Modern State*, Longmans, Green & Co. 1913, pp. 47, 49, 80. Figgis' concept of the

neutral state, which took for granted that the various groups within it would cohere round certain minimum moral beliefs, rested upon the unconscious assumption that somehow the diffused Christianity (which he despised) would continue to provide the necessary social glue. See Raymond Plant in George Moyser (ed.) *Church and Politics Today*, T. & T. Clark 1985, pp. 323–30.

13. On the Church Socialist League, see I. Goodfellow, *The Church Socialist League*, (unpublished Durham PhD Thesis 1983); Jones, op. cit.; John Peart-Binns, *Maurice B. Reckitt*, Bowerdean Press 1988. The minutes of the inaugural conference of CSL and the first list of CSL members are preserved in the Library at Mirfield.

14. Quoted Jones, op. cit., p. 236. For an analysis of the nature of Bull's socialism see ibid., pp. 229–37.

15. Talbot in Phillips, op. cit., p. 59 gives the impression that Mrs Pankhurst gatecrashed the conference and created a disturbance. Such an action by such a notorious figure would have been reported by the press. In fact her eirenic intervention saved Bull's resolution, under attack from members of the Social Democratic Federation.

16. Figgis in *Some Defects*, p. 36 made a passionate plea for the poor and disinherited.

17. See David Hilliard, 'Unenglish and Unmanly: Anglo-Catholicism and Homosexuality', *Victorian Studies*, Winter 1982; W. S. F. Pickering, *Anglo-Catholicism: A Study in Religious Ambiguity*, Routledge 1989, ch. 8; Francis Penhale, *Catholics in Crisis*, Mowbray 1986, pp. 74–6, 147–8.

5. *The First World War*

1. Figgis, *Civilization*, p. ix; *Anti-Christ*, p. 31.

2. Frederic Manning, *Her Privates We*, Hogarth Press 1986, pp. 39, 108–9, 181–2; Trevor Wilson, *The Myriad Faces of War*, Polity Press 1986, pp. 2–3.

3. See A. J. Hoover, *God, Germany and Britain in the Great War*, Praeger, New York 1989; Alan Wilkinson, *CEFWW; Dissent or Conform? War, Peace and the English Churches 1900–1945*, SCM Press 1986 – hereafter *DC*.

4. On chaplains, see Wilkinson, *CEFWW; DC*; 'The Paradox of the Military Chaplain', *Theology*, July 1981.

5. CR chaplains' letters appeared in *CRQ* 1914–19; some of Talbot's war-letters were also reprinted in Pawson, op. cit., others are in the Borthwick Institute.

6. See e.g. 'Milites Christi', *CRQ* LD 1915.

7. See Francis House, 'The Barrier of Impassibility', *Theology*, November 1980; A. M. G. Stephenson, *The Rise and Decline of English Modernism*, SPCK 1984, p. 92; Alan Wilkinson, 'Searching for Meaning in Time of War', *Modern Churchman*, XXVII No. 2 (1985).

8. See e.g. Joseph Williamson, *Father Joe*, Mowbray 1973, pp. 80–1.

9. See the similar and influential analysis of soldiers' religion by Donald Hankey: Wilkinson, *CEFWW*, pp. 119–21; Wilkinson, 'Are we really the Body of Christ?', *Theology*, March 1983.

10. *Church Times*, 7 April 1916; Figgis, *The Will to Freedom*, Longmans, Green & Co. 1917, pp. 8, 312; *Hopes*, pp. 16–24, 105–6.

11. Figgis, *Hopes*, pp. 136, 145.

12. G. R. Elton in his introduction to Figgis' *The Divine Right of Kings*, Harper Row, New York 1965, wrote: 'The stringent regime of Mirfield helped to undermine his health and . . . forced him to devote his intellect to the ephemera of ecclesiastical and theological argument at the low level suitable to the aspirant cleric.' Elton also severely criticized Frere's treatment of Figgis. See letters in *Times Literary Supplement*, 16, 23 Sept., 7 Oct. 1965. Yet Figgis continued as a Cambridge examiner; was Hulsean Lecturer 1908–9; Noble Lecturer, Harvard 1911; Bishop Paddock Lecturer, General Seminary, New York 1913; Bross Lecturer, Illinois 1915; all four series of lectures were published. In 1912 he became honorary lecturer in the History of Political Theory, Leeds University. CR encouiraged him to apply for the Dixie Professorship, Cambridge 1917, and considered opening a House there if he were appointed. St Catharine's College, Cambridge, made him an honorary Fellow in 1909, and in 1948 created an annual Figgis History Prize. For Figgis at Mirfield see Pawson, op. cit.

13. Charles Gore: *The War and the Church*, Mowbray 1914.

14. *Oxford Diocesan Magazine*, November 1914.

15. See also Figgis, *Hopes*, pp. 178–83.

16. W. H. Frere, *English Church Ways*, John Murray 1914. See also Frere, *Russian Observations upon the American Prayer Book*, Mowbray 1917; *Some Links in the Chain of Russian Church History*, Faith Press 1918. Gore in *The Religion of the Church*, Mowbray 1917 edition, pp. 166–7 seemed chiefly interested to use Orthodoxy to refute papal claims and to legitimize non-papal Catholicism.

17. On National Mission, see D. M. Thompson 'War, the Nation and the Kingdom of God' in W. J. Sheils (ed.), *Studies in Church History*, vol. XX, Blackwell 1983; Wilkinson, *CEFWW*, pp. 70–90.

18. Thompson, art. cit., p. 343.

19. Louise Creighton (ed.), *Letters of Oswin Creighton*, Longmans, Green & Co. 1920, pp. 158, 159, 202.

20. See Wilkinson, *CEFWW*, p. 317; articles and correspondence *Church Times*, 31 Aug–21 Sept., 16 Nov. 1917.

21. See Wilkinson, 'Three Sexual Issues', *Theology*, March 1988.

22. F. A. Iremonger, *William Temple*, OUP 1948, p. 263; cf. J. G. Lockhart, *Cosmo Gordon Lang*, Hodder 1949, pp. 241, 342; Pawson, op. cit., p. 66; Prestige, op. cit., pp. 422–6.

23. See Wilkinson, *DC*, pp. 58–66.

24. See Hastings, op. cit., pp. 195ff.

6. *Community Relations*

1. Hastings, op. cit., 55–8, 252–3; Wilkinson, *DC*, pp. 137–9, 261–3.

2. On Keble Talbot see Betty Askwith, *The Lytteltons*, Chatto & Windus 1975; obituaries by Richard Barnes CR (*CRQ* CD 1949) and Martin Jarrett-Kerr CR *Christendom* March 1950; Lucy Menzies (ed.), *Retreat Addresses of Edward Keble Talbot*, SPCK 1954; Pawson, op. cit.

3. Cf. Menzies, p. 118.

4. Gwendolen Stephenson, op. cit., p. 264.

5. Cf. Menzies, pp. 113–4.

6. F. L. Cross, *Darwell Stone*, Dacre Press 1943, pp. 294–5.

7. W. R. Matthews, *Memories and Meanings*, Hodder 1969, pp. 105–7.

8. See Felicity Mary SPB, *Mother Millicent*, Webberley, Stoke-on-Trent 1968, pp. 55–6; cf. H. H. Kelly SSM, *An Idea in the Working*, Mowbray 1908, pp. 29–30; George Every SSM (ed.), *Herbert Kelly SSM: No Pious Person*, Faith Press 1960, pp. 94–5.

9. See Pickering, op. cit., chs 6–8.

10. See Avis, op. cit., p. 110; Carpenter, op. cit., ch. 4; *Theology*, Nov. 1932, p. 264.

11. The correspondence between Davidson and Frere is at Lambeth in the Davidson Papers XI:66–81; see also memorandum XIV:228–30. In 1946, Professor Claude Jenkins, one-time Chaplain and Librarian at Lambeth, wrote to C. S. Phillips, then preparing his memoir of Frere: 'the idea that any one wanted (among those in authority) Frere on the Bench as a liturgist is to me frankly incongruous'. Frere was one of the three people Jenkins remembered 'who had practically to be compelled' to agree to become a bishop. (Letters in Frere papers, Mirfield). For acerbic comments by some Anglo-Catholics about Frere, see Dom Anselm Hughes, *The Rivers of the Flood*, Faith Press 1961, pp. 69–72; Colin Stephenson, *Merrily on High*, Darton, Longman and Todd 1972, p. 55.

12. H. H. Henson, *Retrospect*, OUP 1943, vol. II, pp. 139–40. But Henson warmed to him – see pp. 262, 355–6. On Frere's episcopate see H. Miles Brown, *A Century for Cornwall*, Oscar Blackford, Truro 1976; Alan Dunstan and John Peart-Binns, *Cornish Bishop*, Epworth 1977; Phillips, op. cit.

13. See Gray, op. cit., pp. 156–7; Reg Groves, *Conrad Noel and the Thaxted Movement*, Merlin Press 1967; A. L. Rowse, *A Cornish Childhood*, (Jonathan Cape 1942), pp. 136, 160–5.

14. R. C. D. Jasper, (ed.), *Walter Howard Frere*, SPCK 1954, pp. 99–101, 262–4. The pyx, designed by Ninian Comper, had been originally given by Athelstan Riley to Caldey. When Frere's successor, Hunkin, stopped reservation at Truro Cathedral in 1945 it was loaned to CR and hung in the chapel of the Leeds Hostel until its closure; it was then returned to Truro Cathedral; it now hangs in St Mary's Penzance. (Lecture by Canon R. O. Osborne, Truro Cathedral Friends, 19 May 1990.)

15. Gray, pp. 155, 159. On Frere as liturgist see J. H. Arnold and E. G. P. Wyatt (eds), *Walter Howard Frere*, OUP 1940; Dom Gregory Dix in Phillips; Jasper, op. cit.; Jasper, *The Development of the Anglican Liturgy*, SPCK 1989.

16. Frere in *Guardian*, 23 March 1928, Gore in *Church Times*, 23 March 1928.

17. On Malines Conversations see Bell, *Davidson*; W. H. Frere CR, *Recollections of Malines*, Centenary Press 1935; Lockhart, *Halifax*; B. and M. Pawley, *Rome and Canterbury*, Mowbray 1974. The Frere papers about Malines are in the Borthwick Institute, York.

18. See F. R. Drane, *The Life of Mother Margaret Hallahan*, Longmans, Green & Co. 1934 edition, p. 430.

19. Rees, op. cit., p. 25; see also J. L. Rees, *Sermons and Hymns by Timothy Rees*, Mowbray 1946; Timothy Rees CR, 'The Church in Wales', *CRQ* MD 1911.

20. See Horton Davies, *Worship and Theology in England*, OUP 1965, vol. 5, ch. IV; Ruth Hall (ed.), *Dear Dr Stopes*, Penguin 1981; A. M. Ramsey, *Gore to Temple*, pp. 101–110; H. G. Wood, *Belief and Unbelief since 1850*, CUP 1955, ch. V.

21. See Dom Michael Hanbury OSB, *Br. James, oblate OSB (Eustace St Clair Hill)* *Pax*, Summer 1953.

22. See Wilkinson, 'Three Sexual Issues', *Theology*, March 1988; Bickersteth, *CRQ* MD 1934; Bull, *CRQ* CD 1934, *Lectures on Preaching*, SPCK 1922, pp. 291–304; Hill, *CRQ* JB, MD 1931; Raynes, *CRQ* JB 1950. Cf. letter from J. K. Hardman, *Church Times*, 25 May 1990.

23. See Pickering, chs 9–10.

7. *Between the Wars*

1. Pawson, op. cit., pp. 45–6.
2. Charles Smyth, *Cyril Forster Garbett*, Hodder 1959, pp. 127–9.
3. Gray, op. cit., pp. 163, 209.
4. See Anson, *Call of the Cloister*, pp. 480–8; Hill, op. cit., pp. 160, 236; E. W. Kemp, *The Life and Letters of Kenneth Escott Kirk*, Hodder 1959, ch. IX. cf. Resn. 5 of 1968 Lambeth Conference.
5. Frere ceased to be prominent in the CSL after 1912 – he considered its 1912 'Remonstrance' to the bishops too belligerent. (Goodfellow, op. cit., pp. 116, 221, 274ff.)
6. Barnes, Bennett, Bickersteth, Bull, Fitzgerald, Frere, Healy, F. Hill, Horner, Murray, Rees, Ritson, Symonds and Talbot signed the 1906 Address (Conrad Noel Papers DNO/5/3; Hull University Library). Bull, Fitzgerald, Frere, Hart, Jeayes, Talbot, Thornton and Wager signed the 1923 Memorial (National Museum of Labour History, Manchester).
7. Pickering, op. cit., p. 117, cf. pp. 132–4. For the Christendom Group see John Oliver, *The Church and Social Order*, Mowbray 1968, ch. 6; John Peart-Binns, *Maurice B. Reckitt*, Bowerdean 1988.
8. Pawson, op. cit., p. 46.
9. See Wilkinson, *DC*, pp. 206–14.
10. John Gunstone in John Wilkinson (ed.), *Catholic Anglicans Today*, Darton, Longman and Todd 1968, p. 186.
11. See e.g. 'On a Hospital Ship' [J. W. C. Wand], *Church Times*, 12 Nov. 1915.
12. See John Kent, *The Unacceptable Face*, SCM Press 1987, pp. 88–107; K. Leech and R. Williams (eds), *Essays Catholic and Radical*, Bowerdean 1983, pp. 110–3 (Judith Pinnington), 222–3 (Valerie Pitt); Francis Penhale, *Catholics in Crisis*, Mowbray 1986; Colin Stephenson, *Merrily on High*, Darton, Longman and Todd 1972, pp. 29–30.
13. The Report of each Congress was published the year it was held. Pickering provides useful analyses of these and later Congresses.
14. See Austin Farrer, *CRQ* LD 1953; Michael Ramsey, *Canterbury Essays and Addresses*, SPCK 1964, pp. 127–32. The Thornton papers are in the Borthwick Institute.
15. See F. H. Brabant, *Neville Stuart Talbot*, SCM Press 1949, pp. 127–8; Wilkinson, *DC*, ch. 7, 'The Retreat from Liberal Optimism'.
16. Pawson, op. cit., pp. 44–5.
17. See W. H. Frere CR, *The Principles of Religious Ceremonial*, Mowbray 1928 edition.
18. G. Congreve and W. H. Longridge (eds), *Letters of Richard Meux Benson*, Mowbray 1916, p. 10; C. Gore, *The Body of Christ*, John Murray 1901, pp. 131–41, 276 and 'Extra-Liturgical Uses of the Sacrament', *English Church Review*, Feb.

1917; see also W. H. Freestone C R, *The Sacrament Reserved*, Mowbray 1917.

19. Gray, op. cit., pp. 126–7.

20. Jasper, *Frere*, pp. 263, 99–101.

21. Gore, op. cit., pp. 274–6, 316, 325 and *The Anglo-Catholic Movement Today*, Mowbray 1925, p. 56.

22. See *Sobornost*, Sept., Dec. 1936; chapter 11 of Phillips, op. cit., by Nicolas Zernov. In 1930 Zernov, Secretary of the Russian Student Movement in Exile and enthusiastic promoter of the Fellowship, stayed several months at Mirfield (see *CRQ* MD 1935, 1936).

23. The Curtis papers are in the Borthwick Institute.

24. See Geoffrey Curtis C R, *Paul Couturier*, S CM Press 1964.

25. *The Religion of the Church*, ch. V; *Belief in God*, ch. II.

8. *Pioneering in South Africa*

1. For the context of the first fifty years of C R's work in South Africa, see F. H. Brabant, *Neville Stuart Talbot*, S CM Press 1949; Walter Carey, *Good-bye to my Generation*, Mowbray 1951; J. R. Cochrane, *Servants of Power, The Role of English-Speaking Churches 1903–30*, Ravan Press, Johannesburg 1987; Frank England and Torquil Paterson (eds), *Bounty in Bondage, The Anglican Church in Southern Africa*, Ravan Press, Johannesburg 1989; Michael Furse, *Stand Therefore!*, S P C K 1953; John de Gruchy, *The Church Struggle in South Africa*, s p c k 1979; Peter Hinchliff, *The Anglican Church in South Africa*, Darton, Longman and Todd 1963, *The Church in South Africa*, S P C K 1968; Cecil Lewis and G. E. Edwards, *Historical Records of the Church of the Province of South Africa*, S P C K 1934; Terence O'Brien, *Milner*, Constable 1979; Alan Paton, *Towards the Mountain*, Penguin 1986. Regular reports about C R work in South Africa appeared in the *CR Quarterly*.

I have followed modern usage and avoided 'non-white', 'native', 'Bantu' unless the historical context requires them, preferring the terms 'black' or 'African' to avoid the tedious repetition of 'African, Coloured and Indian'. By the end of the eighteenth century many Dutch thought of themselves as rooted in Africa, hence the term 'Afrikaner'. 'Boer' is the Dutch word for 'farmer'.

2. Hinchliff, *Colenso*; Martin Jarrett-Kerr C R, 'Victorian Certainty and Zulu Doubt' in D. Jasper (ed.), *The Critical Spirit and the Will to Believe*, Macmillan 1989.

3. See Arthur W. Robinson, *The Mission of Help to the Church in South Africa*, Longmans Green & Co. 1906.

4. O. J. Hogarth and R. L. White, *The Life of William Marlborough Carter*, Horshams, Paignton 1952.

5. *The Autobiography of William Plomer*, Jonathan Cape 1975, pp. 94–5, 99.

6. See e.g. Lewis and Edwards, op. cit., pp. 213, 597.

7. Alban Winter C R, *Till Darkness Fell* (1962), unpublished typescript in Mirfield archives.

8. Osmund Victor C R, *The Salient of Africa*, S P G 1931.

9. This section owes much to K. C. Lawson, *Venture of Faith: The Story of St John's College Johannesburg 1898–1968*, St John's College, Johannesburg 1968. See also Peter Randall, *Little England on the Veld: The English Private School System in South Africa*, Ravan Press, Johannesburg 1982.

10. Plomer, op. cit. p. 101.

11. For this section see Audrey Ashley, *Peace-making in South Africa: the Life and Work of Dorothy Maud*, New Horizon, Bognor Regis 1980; Nicholas Mosley, *The Life of Raymond Raynes*, Faith Press 1961; Alan Paton, *Apartheid and the Archbishop: The Life and Times of Geoffrey Clayton*, Jonathan Cape 1974.

12. See 'Manche Masemola', *CRQ* CD 1983.

9. *Pioneering in Rhodesia*

1. In this chapter the older names are retained as appropriate for that period: Southern Rhodesia (now Zimbabwe), Salisbury (now Harare), Umtali (now Mutare).

2. For the history of the Anglican church in Southern Rhodesia/Zimbabwe, see W. E. Arnold, *Here To Stay: The Story of the Anglican Church in Zimbabwe*, Book Guild, Lewes 1985; H. St John T. Evans, *The Church in Southern Rhodesia*, SPCK 1945; Geoffrey Gibbon, *Paget of Rhodesia*, Africana Book Society, Johannesburg 1973; G. W. H. Knight-Bruce, *Memories of Mashonaland*, Edward Arnold 1895; R. R. Langham-Carter, *Knight-Bruce*, Salisbury, Rhodesia 1975; Douglas V. Steere: *God's Irregular: Arthur Shearly Cripps*, SPCK 1973. There is much unpublished material both about the Anglican Church in Zimbabwe and about St Augustine's Penhalonga in the National Archives, Harare. Regular reports about St Augustine's appeared in the *CR Quarterly*.

3. Arnold, op. cit., p. 18.

4. Lewis and Edwards, op. cit., p. 724.

5. See e.g. John Hick and Paul F. Knitter (eds), *The Myth of Christian Uniqueness*, SCM Press and Orbis Books 1988; cf. 'Declaration on the Relationship of the Church to Non-Christian Religions' (1965) in Walter M. Abbott (ed.), *The Documents of Vatican II*, Geoffrey Chapman 1967; Lesslie Newbigin, 'The Christian Faith and the World Religions' in Geoffrey Wainwright (ed.), *Keeping the Faith: Essays to mark the Centenary of Lux Mundi*, SPCK 1989.

6. Elliott Kendall, *The End of an Era*, SPCK 1978, pp. 8, 94; cf. D. M. Paton (ed.), *Reform of the Ministry: A Study in the Work of Roland Allen*, Lutterworth Press 1968; Nicolas Stebbing CR, 'Moratorium in Mission', *CRQ* CD 1983. In 1775 there was not a single missionary at work among the African people. The great missionary movement from Britain and other European countries in the nineteenth century was in part an act of reparation for the terrible evils of the slave trade. *Patterns of Christian Acceptance: Individual Response to the Missionary Impact 1550–1950* (OUP 1972) by Martin Jarrett-Kerr CR (who worked in South Africa for seven years) includes this arresting and poignant dedication: 'In Memoriam: an unknown number of Jamaican slaves "owned" by my West Indian forbears. The voice of my brothers' blood crieth unto me from the ground.' (For obituaries of Martin Jarrett-Kerr, see Adrian Hastings, *Guardian*, 27 November 1991, Alan Wilkinson, *Independent*, 3 December 1991.)

10. *Confident Catholicism*

1. For comparisons between the two world wars, and for English Christianity in the Second World War, see Wilkinson, *DC*, chs 8–10.

2. See ibid., pp. 151–7, 219–30, 302–3; Robert P. Ericksen, *Theologians under Hitler*, Yale 1985; Klaus Scholder, *Requiem for Hitler*, SCM Press and Trinity Press International 1989, ch. 3. Talbot was a member of the Archbishops' Commission which produced *Towards the Conversion of England* (1945); he regretted that the Report used the term 'humanism' as a term of abuse as in the sub-heading 'Humanism – The Age-long Lie'.

3. See Hugh Bishop CR, 'Leaves from the Notebook of a POW', *CRQ* JB, CD 1945. On chaplains in the Second World War, see Wilkinson, op. cit., pp. 292–7.

4. Raymond Raynes CR, *The Faith*, Faith Press 1961, pp. 47, 48.

5. See Gregory Dix, *The Shape of the Liturgy* (1945); Gabriel Hebert, *Liturgy and Society* (1935); A. M. Ramsey, *The Gospel and the Catholic Church* (1936); L. S. Thornton CR, *The Common Life in the Body of Christ* (1942).

6. See *Faith and Unity*, Nov. 1965: Mark Gibbard SSJE, 'Growing Together'; Mark Tweedy CR, 'The South India Book of Common Worship'; Alan Wilkinson: 'The Convocations and the Church of South India'. (*Faith and Unity* was published by the Church Union.) Mosley, op. cit., ch. 20.

7. For trenchant comments on Anglo-Catholicism and CSI, see Donald MacKinnon, *The Stripping of the Altars*, Fontana 1969, pp. 20–2.

8. A. M. Ramsey in *Durham Essays and Addresses*, SPCK 1956, p. 20 defended the division between an early service for communion and 'worship, thanksgiving and the pleading of the Passion' as the keynotes of a later service. For a defence of private masses, see E. L. Mascall: *Corpus Christi*, Longmans Green & Co. 1953, ch. 8 – originally published in *CRQ* JB 1951.

9. The story was first made public in H. A. Williams CR, *Some Day I'll Find You*, Mitchell Beazley 1982, p. 330. Prestige in the Preface to his Life of Gore referred to documents, diaries and press cuttings which he had used. He wrote to Gore's sister in 1935 that he had returned some letters to correspondents, including herself, suggesting that eventually they should be deposited at Mirfield, but that he had returned other papers to Mirfield. There is an extensive collection of press cuttings about Gore at Mirfield, and a few of his letters there and at the Borthwick Institute, but neither possess much extant manuscript material about the genesis and early days of CR or about his personal life thereafter. Rackham's Diary (Prestige, p. 233) has also disappeared. In correspondence with Mansbridge in 1932 and 1933 Talbot listed some of the Gore papers then at Mirfield, some of which no longer exist. (Mansbridge Papers 65356) Some of the material used by Prestige is in the Mansbridge papers.

10. See letters from Brendan Bracken to G. Pawson in Talbot Papers 7/9–15 in the Borthwick. Bath and Wells became vacant in January 1943. Talbot was then 65. J. W. C. Wand accepted the bishopric. For Bracken's role in episcopal appointments, see J. Peart-Binns, *Wand of London*, Mowbray 1987, pp. 104, 118–20. After the war Talbot gave invaluable support to the establishment of St Catharine's, Cumberland Lodge, Windsor, and to its subsequent work as a centre for students, particularly from modern universities, where they could study Christian philosophy in the context of the common life.

11. Quoted Menzies, op. cit., pp. 13–14.

12. *Facts and Figures about the Church of England* (CBF 1962); *Church Statistics* (CBF 1989) (the figures for Easter communicants in 1960 and 1987 also include

those in Easter week); Michael Hornsby-Smith, *The Changing Parish*, Routledge 1989; Wilkinson, *DC*, pp. 56, 315–21.

13. *Church Quarterly Review*, CLXIV (1963); cf. *Theology*, Sept. 1963. See Martin Jarrett-Kerr CR, *Our Trespasses*, SCM Press 1948; *The Hope of Glory*, SCM Press 1952; *The Secular Promise*, SCM Press 1964; several of his broadcast talks were reproduced in *CRQ*. Hugh Bishop CR, *The Passion Drama, The Easter Drama*, Hodder 1955, 1958 – broadcast talks.

14. See Peter Jagger, *A History of the Parish and People Movement*, Faith Press 1978.

15. A Archer, *The Two Catholic Churches*, SCM Press 1986; Hastings, *English Christianity*, p. 579; Pickering, op. cit., p. 263, cf. p. 30, ch. 11; Wilkinson, 'Are We Really the Body of Christ?', *Theology*, March 1983; 'Requiem for Anglican Catholicism?', *Theology*, January 1978.

16. Martin Jarrett-Kerr consented to appear for the defence in the *Lady Chatterley* case. He was not called, but Bishop John Robinson, with whom he had corresponded about the book, did speak for the defence at the trial in 1960 and suddenly became a notorious national figure. Eric James, *A Life of Bishop John A. T. Robinson*, Collins 1987, pp. 85–95.

17. See Yvonne Craig: 'Not So Much a Network', *Theology*, March 1983; John Peters, *Frank Lake*, Darton, Longman and Todd 1989.

18. Graham's lively, popular book on the Old Testament (to which he was particularly devoted) *He Came Unto His Own*, Church Union 1957 begins with *A Tale of Two Cities*; see also *With My Whole Heart*, Darton, Longman and Todd 1962, *The Office of a Wall*, Faith Press 1966.

11. *College and Hostel*

1. R. G. Wilberforce, *Life of Samuel Wilberforce*, John Murray 1882, vol. III, pp. 155–6.

2. H. H. Henson (ed.), *Church Problems*, John Murray 1900, p. 21.

3. John C. Heenan, *The People's Priest*, Sheed and Ward 1951, pp. 194–5.

4. See F. W. Bullock, *A History of Training for the Ministry of the Church of England 1875–1974*, Home Words 1976. For examples of bad theological colleges see John Peart-Binns, *Eric Treacy*, Ian Allan 1980, pp. 35–6; J. W. C. Wand, *Changeful Page*, Hodder 1965, pp. 43–5. For financial, social and educational problems of ordinands see Peart-Binns, *Treacy*, pp. 21–3; Joseph Williamson, *Father Joe*, Mowbray 1963. Dates of ordination: Treacy 1932, Wand 1908, Williamson 1925.

5. See George Every SSM (ed.), *Herbert Kelly SSM: No Pious Person*, Faith Press 1960; H. H. Kelly SSM, *An Idea in the Making*, Mowbray 1908; *Training for Ordination*, privately printed 1901; *SSM An Idea Still Working*, SSM 1980. On episcopal attitudes to the SSM course see e.g. *Church Times*, 26 May 1933, p. 621.

6. Every, p. 90, Kelly, *Idea*, pp. 30–1.

7. Quoted Allchin, op. cit., pp. 247–8. Gore and CR were given entries in *Oxford Dictionary of the Christian Church* (1957), Kelly and SSM were not.

8. Paul Bull CR, 'Free Access to Holy Orders', *Church Times*, 29 August 1902, letter *Pilot* 2 November 1901; Prestige, op. cit., p. 218. Materials for the history of College and Hostel will be found in *CRQ* and *Mirfield Gazette*: see particularly *CRQ*: MD 1967, MD 1976, *Mirfield Gazette*, Christmas 1930, 1961–2.

9. Bickersteth, op. cit., pp. 169–70; Martindale, op. cit., vol. I, p. 194.

10. See Martindale, vol. I, p. 174n.

11. See Kenneth Brill (ed.), *John Groser*, Mowbray 1971; St John Groser, *Politics and Persons*, SCM Press 1949; College Festival sermon *CRQ* MD 1958.

12. See articles on Temple Moore, *Builder*, 9 July 1920, 27 April 1928.

13. J. R. H. Moorman, *B. K. Cunningham*, SCM Press 1947, p. 103.

14. See Pawson, op. cit., pp. 158–9, Wilkinson, *CEFWW*, pp. 80–8, 166, 277–80. I am indebted to Mr E. P. M. Wollaston for information about experiments in ordination training in this period.

15. See Wilkinson, *DC*, pp. 141–3.

16. Christopher Bryant SSJE, *Depth Psychology and Religious Belief*, Mirfield Publications 1972, p. 56.

17. H. H. Henson, *Ad Clerum*, SPCK 1958, p. 131; Edward Schillebeeckx, *Ministry*, SCM Press 1981, p. 41. On collaborative ministry see Robin Greenwood, *Reclaiming the Church*, Fount 1988.

18. See review of Edwards' *The Virgin Birth in History and Faith* (1943), *Church Times*, 12 March 1943.

19. See Robert Towler and A. P. M. Coxon, *The Fate of the Anglican Clergy*, Methuen 1979, pp. 138–42. 'This book is dedicated with love and respect to the memory of Nicolas Graham CR and with affection and gratitude to the Community of the Resurrection to whom the authors, between them, owe eleven happy years of student life.' Table of Entry 1908–1961 in *Mirfield Gazette*, 1960–1.

20. Ibid., pp. 156–8, 221; Hastings, op. cit., p. 555.

21. Paul Ferris, *The Church of England*, Gollancz 1962, p. 35.

12. *Africa: Triumphs and Tragedies*

1. Deborah Duncan Honoré (ed.), *Trevor Huddleston*, OUP 1988, p. 2.

2. Shirley du Boulay, *Tutu: Voice of the Voiceless*, Penguin 1989, p. 48.

3. Trevor Huddleston CR, *Naught for your Comfort*, Collins 1956, pp. 139–44.

4. See Alan Paton, *Towards the Mountain*, Penguin 1986; *Journey Continued*, OUP 1988.

5. Mary Benson, *A Far Cry*, Penguin 1990.

6. Anthony Sampson, *Drum*, Hodder 1983, p. 179.

7. Timothy Wilson (ed.), *All One Body*, Darton, Longman and Todd 1969, p. 162.

8. Adrian Hastings, *A History of African Christianity 1950–1975*, CUP 1979, p. 144. On Clayton, see Paton, *Clayton*; on Reeves, see John Peart-Binns, *Ambrose Reeves*, Gollancz 1973; D. M. Paton (ed.), *Church and Race in South Africa*, SCM Press 1958; on Scott, see Benson, op. cit., Michael Scott, *A Time to Speak*, Faber 1958.

9. Huddleston, op. cit., pp. 181–2. cf. Elaine Unterhalter, *Forced Removals*, IDAF Publications 1987.

10. See Muriel Horrell, *A Decade of Bantu Education*, South African Institute of Race Relations, Johannesburg 1964; Huddleston, op. cit., ch. 9; Paton, *Clayton*, ch. 27; Peart-Binns, *Reeves*, ch. 7.

11. Sampson, op. cit., p. 137.

12. Ulrich Simon, *Sitting in Judgment*, SPCK 1978, p. 162.

13. See *Father Huddleston's Picture Book*, Kliptown Books 1990. For the next section on Huddleston's recall see Mosley, op. cit., ch. 30.

14. Paton, *Clayton*, p. 257; cf. p. 261.

15. Ibid., pp. 240–2, cf. p. 121.

16. Ibid., pp. 277–80; see also Mandy Goedhals 'From Paternalism to Partnership?' and Bob Clarke 'Confronting the Crisis: Church-State Relations' in England and Paterson, op. cit. After this chapter was completed Trevor Huddleston drew my attention to Michael Worsnip, *Between the Two Fires: The Anglican Church and Apartheid 1948–1957*, University of Natal Press 1991, a most valuable study of Archbishop Clayton's views on church-state relations which analyses his sharp differences with Scott, Huddleston, Reeves and others.

17. See Charles Hooper CR in *CRQ* CD 1988, p. 12. Huddleston met Clayton on 7 Dec. 1954, not on 13 April 1955 as in Paton, p. 247.

18. *CRQ* CD 1955; cf. Raynes' sermon, Johannesburg Cathedral, Dec. 1955, *CRQ* LD 1956.

19. *CRQ* JB 1948. For a tribute to Raynes by Huddleston see *CRQ* MD 1983.

20. See Pauline Webb, 'The New Ecumenism' in Honoré, op. cit.· 'Huddleston: Inter–Faith Excitement', USPG *Network*, Autumn 1983.

21. Cf. Wilson, op. cit., pp. 157, 162.

22. In 1967 Huddleston described how Sophiatown had shaped his understanding of both religion and sociology, adding 'there is always a honeymoon period in life, when you fall in love, not only with someone else, but with something else, with the job that is really worth your life. Nothing can take the place of that period. This is *the* moment, and ought to be, and is. When you become old and grey, and full of years, like I am now, you do not expect that kind of excitement. Unfortunately, I wish you could, but there it is, that is the way life goes.' Lord Caradon, Charles Coulson, Trevor Huddleston, *Three Views on Commitment*, Longmans 1967, pp. 58–9. For two contrasting assessments of Huddleston see: Paton, *Journey*, pp. 140–1; D. M. MacKinnon, 'Christology and Protest' in Honoré, op. cit.

23. M. Jarrett-Kerr CR in *CRQ* JB 1987; Peart-Binns, *Reeves* chs, 14, 15; Ambrose Reeves, *Shooting at Sharpeville*, Gollancz 1960. For CR's work at Baragwanath Hospital see M. Jarrett-Kerr CR, *African Pulse*, Faith Press 1960.

24. For the subsequent story with its tragic consequences for Reeves, see: Owen Chadwick, *Michael Ramsey*, OUP 1990, pp. 135–6; Paton, *Journey*, pp. 197–200, 203–6; Peart-Binns, *Reeves*; John Peart-Binns, *Archbishop Joost de Blank*, Muller, Blond & White 1987, pp. 175–84.

25. In this section I am indebted to an unpublished history of Alice 1960–4 by Aelred Stubbs CR, to Crispin Harrison CR and to Theodore Simpson.

26. Mamphela Ramphele 'On being Anglican' in England and Paterson, op. cit.; Aelred Stubbs CR (ed.) *Steve Biko*, Penguin 1988, 'Steve Biko', *CRQ* CD 1977. Dr Ramphele is now Deputy Vice-Chancellor of Cape Town University.

27. On Cottesloe, see de Gruchy, op. cit., pp. 62–9; G. Sidebotham CR in *CRQ* JB 1961; Peart-Binns, *de Blank*, pp. 184–90.

28. H. A. Williams, CR, *Some Day I'll Find You*, Mitchell Beazley 1982, pp. 258–65.

29. During an interview with B. J. Vorster, the Prime Minister, in November 1970 Archbishop Michael Ramsey raised the deporations of Mercer and Chamberlain. 'If

other priests are subversive I will see that they are expelled too' responded Vorster. The interview revealed the powerlessness of courteous liberalism to make any impression on this type of dour and ruthless Afrikaner. For *Die Burger*, the Nationalist organ, the visit demonstrated the close connection between Anglicanism and 'British imperialism'. Chadwick, op. cit., pp. 262–3.

30. See Doris Thompson, *Priest and Pioneer: A Memoir of Fr Osmund Victor* CR, Faith Press 1958.

31. Gonville ffrench-Beytagh, *Encountering Darkness*, Collins 1973, p. 71.

32. For the recent history of Zimbabwe, see David Martin and Phyllis Johnson, *The Struggle for Zimbabwe*, Faber 1981; Martin Meredith, *The Past is Another Country*, André Deutsch 1979; Anthony Verrier, *The Road to Zimbabwe*, Jonathan Cape 1986. For recent church history, see Arnold, op. cit.; Norman Atkinson, *Teaching Rhodesians*, Longmans 1972; Paul Burrough, *Angels Unawares*, Churchman 1988; Paul Gifford, *The Religious Right in Southern Africa*, Baobab Books, Harare 1988; Michael Lapsley SSM, *Neutrality or Co-option?*, Mambo Press, Gweru 1986 – includes sermons and statements by Anglican leaders; Terence Ranger, 'Holy Men and Rural Communities in Zimbabwe 1970–1980' in W. J. Sheils (ed.), *Studies in Church History*, vol. XX, Blackwell 1983, and 'Religion in the Zimbabwe guerrilla war' in J. Obelkevich et al. (ed.), *Disciplines of Faith*, Routledge 1987; Kenneth Skelton, *Bishop in Smith's Rhodesia*, Mambo Press 1985.

33. Victor de Waal, *The Politics of Reconciliation: Zimbabwe's First Decade*, Hurst & Co. 1990, pp. 65–7.

34. The following section draws upon David Caute, *Under the Skin*, Allen Lane 1983.

35. For a racy account of Noel Williams' work see *CRQ* CD 1974, also CD 1986.

36. Dietrich Bonhoeffer, *Letters and Papers from Prison*, revised and enlarged edition, SCM Press 1971 pp. 4, 16; cf. Wilkinson, *DC*, pp. 300–4.

37. Charles Hooper, *Brief Authority*, Collins 1960, p. 126.

13. *Loss and Gain*

1. See Michael Ramsey, *Image Old and New*, SPCK 1963; *Beyond Religion*, SPCK 1964; *Canterbury Pilgrim*, SPCK 1974. For examples of the spirituality of this period (some of which influenced Hugh Bishop) see Monica Furlong, *The End of our Exploring*, Hodder 1973; Eric James (ed.), *Spirituality for Today*, SCM Press 1968; John A. T. Robinson and David L. Edwards (eds), *The Honest to God Debate*, SCM Press 1963; John Rowe, *Priests and Workers*, Darton, Longman and Todd 1965; A. R. Vidler, 'Holy Worldliness', in *Essays in Liberality*, SCM Press 1957; R. Voillaume, *Seeds of the Desert*, Burns & Oates 1955; Bernard Wall (trans.), *Priest and Worker*, Macmillan 1965.

2. On monastic finance, see also Paul Brett, 'The Ethical Use of Investment Funds', *CRQ* MD 1981; Christopher Cowton, 'Where Their Treasure Is: Anglican Religious Communities and Ethical Investment', *Crucible*, April–June 1990.

3. See Mark Tweedy CR, 'Russia's Vigorous and Expanding Church', *Observer*, 15 June 1958.

4. See Peter Allan CR, 'Anglican Monastic Spirituality', *CRQ* LD, JB 1991;

Robert Hale, 'Discovering Consanguinity: The Monastic-Benedictine Spirit of Anglicanism' in *Canterbury and Rome*, Darton, Longman and Todd 1982; Esther de Waal, *Seeking God*, Fount 1984.

5. Brill, op. cit., ch. 12.

6. For Raynes' high valuation of the contemplative life see his Epilogue to Curtis, *William of Glasshampton*.

7. The following section about Hugh Bishop's resignation as Superior and release from CR supplements (and at certain points corrects inaccuracies in) Harry Williams' account in *Some Day I'll Find You*, pp. 325–9.

8. See also Peart-Binns, *Treacy*, pp. 230, 242–3. For an account of the television programme see *Church Times*, 6 Dec. 1974. For Hugh Bishop's subsequent life and ministry see obituaries in the *Guardian*, 3 October 1989; *Independent*, 11 October 1989, letters in *Church Times*, 13 October 1989. In particular he continued his happy and fruitful association with the nuns of the Society of the Precious Blood, Burnham Abbey, which had begun when he was Warden (1952–73). He succeeded Frank Biggart, the first CR Warden, who had been mainly responsible for creating a sound financial basis for SPB.

9. See Richard Oakley CR 'Catholic Renewal', *CRQ* JB 1983, Godfrey Pawson CR, 'A Critical Approach to Anglo-Catholicism', *CRQ* MD 1983.

10. John Habgood, *Confessions of a Conservative Liberal*, SPCK 1988, p. 90.

11. After the First World War rhetoric was distrusted by the disillusioned who were angry with leaders of church and state for using it to promote the war effort. Rhetoric was even more discredited in the popular mind by newsreels of Hitler's Nuremberg rallies. By the 1960s the spread of cheap radios and of television enabled people to treat the human voice as verbal wallpaper. Cf. Rupert Davies (ed.), *The Testing of the Churches 1932–1982*, Epworth 1982, ch. 9; Hastings, *English Christianity*, p. 465; J. Neville Ward, *Enquiring Within*, Epworth 1988, pp. 66–7.

12. 'Monastic Witness' in Leech and Williams, op. cit., p. 197.

13. On the Religious Life today see e.g. A. M. Allchin, *Religious Communities in the World of Today*, SPCK 1970; Edna Mary Dss, CSA, *The Religious Life*, Penguin 1968; Monica Furlong, *Merton*, Collins 1980; Alan Harrison, *Bound for Life*, Mowbray 1983; Geoffrey Moorhouse, *Against All Reason*, Weidenfeld and Nicolson 1969; Daniel Rees *et al.*, *Consider Your Call*, SPCK 1978.

14. Quoted Alan Ecclestone, *A Staircase for Silence*, Darton, Longman and Todd 1977, p. 39.

15. Hilary Beasley CR, *The Best is Yet to Be*, Mirfield Publications nd.

16. See Rowan Williams, 'Watch Therefore', *CRQ* MD 1982.

General Index

Index of CR Names

This index includes the names of novices and professed brethren mentioned in this book. Not all these novices were professed; not all these professed remained in CR. The first names are those by which they were (or are) known in CR.